ELECTRICAL, ELECTRONICS AND COMPUTER ENGINEERING

for Scientists and Engineers

(As per latest VTU Syllabus)

THIRD EDITION

K.A. Krishnamurthy
Vice-Chancellor
Sri Siddhartha University
Tumkur, Karnataka
Ex-Principal, Malnad College of Engineering

M.R. Raghuveer
Professor of Electrical Engineering
University of Manitoba
Winnipeg, Manitoba
Canada

PUBLISHING FOR ONE WORLD

NEW AGE INTERNATIONAL (P) LIMITED, PUBLISHERS
New Delhi • Bangalore • Chennai • Cochin • Guwahati • Hyderabad
Jalandhar • Kolkata • Lucknow • Mumbai • Ranchi
Visit us at www.newagepublishers.com

Published by New Age International (P) Ltd., Publishers
First Edition: 1999
Third Edition: 2011

Branches:

- 37/10, 8th Cross (Near Hanuman Temple), Azad Nagar, Chamrajpet, **Bangalore**-560 018. Tel.: (080) 2675 6823, Telefax: 2675 6820, E-mail: bangalore@newagepublishers.com
- 26, Damodaran Street, T. Nagar, **Chennai**-600 017. Tel.: (044) 24353401, Telefax: 24351463 E-mail: chennai@newagepublishers.com
- CC-39/1016, Carrier Station Road, Ernakulam South, **Cochin**-682 016. Tel.: (0484) 2377004, Telefax: 4051303 E-mail: cochin@newagepublishers.com
- Hemsen Complex, Mohd. Shah Road, Paltan Bazar, Near Starline Hotel, **Guwahati**-781 008. Tel.: (0361) 2513881 Telefax: 2543669, E-mail: guwahati@newagepublishers.com
- 105, 1st Floor, Madhiray Kaveri Tower, 3-2-19, Azam Jahi Road, Nimboliadda, **Hyderabad**-500 027. Tel.: (040) 24652456, Telefax: 24652457, E-mail: hyderabad@newagepublishers.com
- RDB Chambers (Formerly Lotus Cinema)106A, 1st Floor, S.N. Banerjee Road, **Kolkata**-700 014. Tel.: (033) 22273773, Telefax: 22275247, E-mail: kolkata@newagepublishers.com
- 16-A, Jopling Road, **Lucknow**-226 001. Tel.: (0522) 2209578, 4045297, Telefax: 2204098 E-mail: lucknow@newagepublishers.com
- 142C, Victor House, Ground Floor, N.M. Joshi Marg, Lower Parel, **Mumbai**-400 013. Tel.: (022) 24927869 Telefax: 24915415, E-mail: mumbai@newagepublishers.com
- 22, Golden House, Daryaganj, **New Delhi**-110 002. Tel.: (011) 23262370, 23262368, Telefax: 43551305 E-mail: sales@newagepublishers.com

ISBN : 978-81-224-3161-2

C-10-09-5042

Printed in India at Mohanlal Printers, Delhi.
Typeset at Goswami Associates, Delhi

PUBLISHING FOR ONE WORLD
NEW AGE INTERNATIONAL (P) LIMITED, PUBLISHERS
4835/24, Ansari Road, Daryaganj, New Delhi-110002
Visit us at **www.newagepublishers.com**

Preface to the Third Edition

The authors are immensely pleased to release the third edition of the book. The chapters on DC machines, AC machines, electrical measuring instruments and a review of communication systems and oscillators which did not find a slot in the first edition were incorporated in the second edition. The fundamental concepts in the book are presented in an easily understandable manner. The textbook is presented in a simple, progressive and lucid manner.

To recapitulate, this book comprises of sixteen chapters covering fundamentals of electrical, electronics and computer engineering, network analysis, DC/AC machines, measuring instruments, Analog electronics, Digital electronics, Microprocessors and computer concepts.

In this edition, some of the topics which were not covered in the second edition and more worked numerical examples in each topic wherever needed have been included. The following gives the additions made in some of the chapters.

Chapter 3: In this chapter, more examples on Kirchoff's current law and Kirchoff's voltage law have been added.

Chapter 4: Introduces the concepts of inductance and capacitance from the view point of field theory. The circuit response is also explained. Electromagnetic induction, concept of mutual inductance, coefficient of coupling and good number of numerical problems have been added.

Chapter 5: Details the need for generation, transmission and distribution of AC voltage. The resonance circuits, as also the maximum power transfer theorem are also considered. In addition, to this detailed discussion on the performance of the circuit elements when connected to AC source and some more problems on single phase AC circuits are added. The three-phase circuits and measurement of three-phase power using wattmeter for balanced and unbalanced loads have been discussed. Three phase circuit problems are also included.

Chapter 6: Gives an insight into the DC machines. Their working principles and performance characteristics are discussed. Along with these theoretical aspects, some more problems on DC generator and motor are included.

Chapter 7: Detailed discussion on AC machines, problems on transformers, Induction motors and Alternators are covered with a brief discussion on their working principles and performance characteristics.

Chapter 10: Continues with the material physics, transistor model, SCRs and UJTs along with applications. In addition, transistor and FET amplifiers are also covered. Additional triggering circuits for SCRs, feedback amplifiers, distortion amplifiers with some worked examples on design are included.

Chapter 11: Covers the aspects about operational amplifiers, their necessity and applications.

Chapter 12: Is devoted to sinusoidal oscillators which are capable of producing sinusoidal oscillations from audio frequency range to several GHz. In addition to this, classification of oscillators, crystal oscillator, Wein-bridge oscillator is discussed in detail along with worked examples.

During the preparation of the Third edition, my colleague Prof. K.L. Ratnakar, of the Electrical and Electronics Engineering department chipped-in worthwhile contributions. He has provided a great deal of assistance in the preparation of the manuscript, as also improved readability and scope of the book. We are immensely pleased to express our sincere thanks and gratitude to him for his altruistic and untiring efforts, without which, this edition would not have seen the light of the day. The assistance of Instructor Mr. C.S. Mohan is gratefully acknowledged. We are extremely thankful to New Age International (P) Limited, Publishers, for bringing out this edition of the book in a record time. The first author of the book is highly indebted to the Management of Sri Siddhartha Institute of Technology, Maralur, Tumkur, Karnataka, (Presently Vice-Chancellor of Sri Siddhartha University, Tumkur and Principal of Sri Siddhartha Institute of Technology) for their encouragement and assistance.

Finally, we would like to thank our family members for the infinite patience and understanding they have demonstrated in allowing us to allocate family time to the writing of this book.

We wish you a happy and easy reading.

K.A. Krishnamurthy

M.R. Raghuveer

Preface to the First Edition

This book is written for everyone—students, scientists and engineers having an urge to understand the basic principles and applications of Electrical and Electronics Engineering. No prerequisite is required to understand the subject matter of this book. The fundamental concepts are presented in an easily understandable way. The text matter is presented in a simple, progressive and lucid manner.

This text may be separated into two parts, the Electrical Engineering and the Electronics Engineering. Chapters 1–5 deal exclusively with the basic theory involved in Electrical Engineering and to understand Electronics Engineering which is covered in chapters 6–10. A good understanding of the digital electronics is required to understand the microprocessor and its applications as microprocessor is a digital Machine. For this reason, therefore, digital electronics have been dealt with, fairly exhaustively.

Chapter 1: Covers the history of electrical and electronics engineering, concepts of charge, potential etc., as also the types of resistors and their ratings. Concepts of non-linear and incremental resistance is also introduced.

Chapter 2: Explains the current and voltage sources with practical examples. Concepts of open circuit and short circuit, ratings of dc machines and batteries are introduced.

Chapter 3: Presents the network theorems with a brief introduction of bridges for the measurement of non-electrical quantities.

Chapter 4: Introduces the concepts of inductance and capacitance in terms of field theory. Circuit response is also explained.

Chapter 5: Details the need for generation, transmission and distribution of ac voltage. The phases are introduced. Resonance circuits as also the maximum power transfer theorem is also considered.

Chapter 6: Continues with the material physics, transistor model, SCRs and UJTs along with applications.

Chapter 7: Covers the aspects about operational amplifiers, their necessity and applications.

Chapter 8: Details the number system, Boolean Algebra, concepts of Fan-in and Fan-out, various types of Flip-Flops, application of these for counters and realization of logical functions using commercially available ICs.

Chapter 9: Gives an overview of computer concepts wherein the basics of architecture, Hex notation, I/O devices, VDUs, Printers, RAMs, ROMs and mode of connecting them for various purposes is explained.

Chapter 10: Introduces to student to the wonder world of microprocessors. A typical microprocessor 8085 is introduced. Architecture, Addressing modes are explained. Instruction set is discussed. Minimal system is presented. Several examples are solved using the method of flow-charting. Use and interfacing of 8155, 8156, 8355 is explained in detail. Concepts of use of stacks, subroutines and interrupts are also introduced.

During the preparation of the textbook, many people have helped to produce this book. Mr. M.K. Venkatesha, Assistant Professor, Department of Electronics and Communication Engineering, Malnad College of Engineering, Hassan, provided a great deal of assistance in the preparation of the manuscript and proof reading of the typeset version; and we are pleased to express him our most sincere thanks to Mr. H.T. Kumar's skillful typing of the manuscript is highly appreciated.

K.A. Krishnamurthy
M.R. Raghuveer

REVISED Syllabus of VTU w.e.f. 2010 Session
BASIC ELECTRICAL ENGINEERING

Sub Code: 10ELE 15/10ELE 25 **Hrs/ Week:04**
IA Marks: 25 **Total Hrs: 52**
Exam Hours: 03
Exam Marks: 100

PART–A

Unit-I: 1 (a) D.C. Circuits

Ohm's Law and Kirchhoff's Laws, analysis of series, parallel and series- parallel circuits excited by independent voltage sources. Power and Energy. Illustrative examples. **04 Hours**

Unit-I: 1 (b) Electromagnetism

Faraday's Laws, Lenz's Law, Fleming's Rules, Statically and dynamically induced emf's. Concept of self inductance, mutual inductance and coefficient of coupling. Energy stored in magnetic field. Illustrative examples. **03 Hours**

Unit-II: 2. Single-phase A.C. Circuits

Generation of sinusoidal voltage, definition of average value, root mean square value, form factor and peak factor of sinusoidally varying voltage and current, phasor representation of alternating quantities. Analysis, with phasor diagrams, of R, L, C, R-L, R-C and R-L-C circuits, real power, reactive power, apparent power and power factor. Illustrative examples involving series, parallel and series-parallel circuits. **07 Hours**

Unit-III: 3. Three-Phase Circuits

Necessity and advantages of three-phase systems, generation of three phase power, definition of phase sequence, balanced supply and balanced load. Relationship between line and phase values of balanced star and delta connections. Power in balanced three-phase circuits, measurement of power by two-wattmeter method. Illustrative examples. **06 Hours**

Unit-IV: 4 (a) Measuring Instruments

Construction and Principle of operation of dynamometer type wattmeter and single-phase induction type energy meter (problems excluded). **03 Hours**

Unit-IV: 4 (b) Domestic Wiring

Service mains, meter board and distribution board. Brief discussion on Cleat, Casing & Capping and conduit (concealed) wiring. Two-way and three-way control of a lamp. Elementary discussion on fuse and Miniature Circuit Breaker (MCB's). Electric shock, precautions against shock –Earthing: Pipe and Plate. **03 Hours**

PART – B

Unit-V: 5. DC Machines

Working principle of DC machine as a generator and a motor. Types and constructional features. emf equation of generator, relation between emf induced and terminal voltage enumerating the brush drop and drop due to armature reaction. Illustrative examples.
DC motor working principle, Back emf and its significance, torque equation. Types of D.C. motors, characteristics and applications. Necessity of a starter for DC motor. Illustrative examples on back emf and torque. **07 Hours**

Unit-VI: 6. Transformers

Principle of operation and construction of single-phase transformers (core and shell types). emf equation, losses, efficiency and voltage regulation (Open circuit and Short circuit tests, equivalent circuit and phasor diagrams are excluded). Illustrative problems on emf equation and efficiency only. **07 Hours**

Unit-VII: 7. Synchronous Generators

Principle of operation. Types and constructional features. emf equation. Concept of winding factor (excluding derivation of distribution and pitch factors). Illustrative examples on emf. equation. **06 Hours**

Unit-VIII: 8. Three Phase Induction Motors

Concept of rotating magnetic field. Principle of operation. Types and Constructional features. Slip and its significance. Applications of squirrel-cage and slip-ring motors. Necessity of a starter, star-delta starter. Illustrative examples on slip calculations. **06 Hours**

REVISED Syllabus of VTU w.e.f. 2010 Session
FIRST SEMESTER B.E
(Common to all branches)

BASIC ELECTRONICS

Sub Code: 10ELN15/10ELN25
IA Marks: 25
Exam Hours: 03 — Hrs/ Week:04
Exam Marks: 100 — **Total Hrs: 52**

PART–A

Unit-I: Semiconductor Diodes and Applications

p-n junction diode, Characteristics and Parameters, Diode approximations, DC load line, Temperature dependence of p-n characteristics, AC equivalent circuits, Zener diodes Half-wave diode rectifier, Ripple factor, Full-wave diode rectifier, Other full-wave circuits, Shunt capacitor – Approximate analysis of capacitor filters, Power supply performance, Zener diode voltage regulators, Numerical examples as applicable.

Unit-II: Transistors

Bipolar Junction transistor, Transistor Voltages and currents, amplification, Common Base, Common Emitter and Common Collector Characteristics, DC Load line and Bias Point.

Unit-III: Biasing Methods

Base Bias, Collector to Base Bias, Voltage divider Bias, Comparison of basic bias circuits, Bias circuit design, Thermal Stability of Bias Circuits (Qualitative discussions only).

Unit-IV: Other Devices

Silicon Controlled Rectifier (S.C.R), SCR Control Circuits, More S.C.R. applications; Unijunction transistor, UJT applications, Junction Field effect Transistors (Exclude Fabrication and Packaging), JFET Characteristics, FET Amplifications, Numerical examples as applicable.

PART–B

Unit-V: Amplifiers & Oscillators

Decibels and Half power points, Single Stage CE Amplifier and Capacitor coupled two stage CE amplifier (Qualitative discussions only), Series voltage negative feedback and Additional effects of Negative feedback (Qualitative discussions only), The Barkhausen Criterion for Oscillations, BJT RC phase shift oscillator, Hartley, Colpitts and crystal oscillator (Qualitative discussions only) Numerical problems as applicable.

Unit-VI: Introduction to Operational Amplifiers

Ideal OPAMP, Saturable property of an OPAMP inverting and noninverting OPAMP circuits, need for OPAMP, Characteristics and applications – voltage follower, addition, subtraction, integration, differentiation; Numerical examples as applicable Cathode Ray Oscilloscope (CRO).

Unit-VII: Communication Systems

Block diagram, Modulation, Radio systems, Superhetrodyne receivers, Numerical examples as applicable.

Number Systems

Introduction, Decimal system, Binary, Octal and Hexadecimal number systems, Addition and subtraction, Fractional number, Binary Coded Decimal numbers.

Unit-VIII: Digital Logic

Boolean algebra, Logic gates, Half-adder, Full-adder, Parallel Binary adder.

Contents

Fundamental Concepts

1

CHAPTER

1.1 A BRIEF HISTORY OF ELECTRICAL ENGINEERING

Although scientific progress and the birth of electrical engineering can be traced back to events occurring in the sixteenth century, one of man's earliest engineering achievements probably occurred around 2600 BC. At about this time lodestone was discovered; devices constructed using this natural ore exploited its magnetic properties. Many investigators were fascinated with lodestone and over the years numerous experiments were conducted with it. However, it was only in 1269 that the first device of practical value viz. the magnetic compass, was constructed.

The discovery of the compass stimulated interest in magnetism and Gilbert who did considerable research in electricity and magnetism published his findings in 1600. Gilbert regarded the earth as a huge magnet and explained the behaviour of the compass on this basis. From his experiments concerning static electrification, Gilbert compiled a long list of materials that could be electrified by friction. He was the first person to use the term electricity but was not the first person to observe frictional electrification. That credit goes to the ancient Greeks and was observed by Thales in 600 BC.

There followed a considerable lapse of time until Otto Von Guericke, in 1660, discovered the first machine to produce electricity derived from friction. With this machine Von Guericke observed many electrostatic phenomenon and also succeeded in transmitting the charge developed by the machine, over a small distance, by using packing thread. In 1729, Gray discovered that some substances were conductors while others were insulators. He may have been the first one to use metallic wires as conductors. In 1745, the Leyden jar was discovered. In its refined version it consisted of a bottle partly filled with water; a metal rod was suspended above water level and held in place at the neck by a cork. The outer sides of the bottle were covered with silver leaf. The jar was capable of storing large quantities of electricity generated by the electrostatic machines of the day and very soon the Leyden jar became a popular research tool.

In 1745, Benjamin Franklin demonstrated the electrical origin of lightning by charging a Leyden jar from the string attached to a kite which was flown during a thunderstorm. From his research experiments he concluded that there is one kind of electricity and that all bodies contain it; when two dissimilar substances are rubbed together one receives an excess of electricity while the other loses an equivalent amount. He even spoke of positive and negative electricity and conducted innovative experiments in which positive and negative electricity neutralized each other. Franklin also designed a rotating device which operated on electrostatic principles.

At about this time, the first inventions took place in the field of measurement. The gold leaf electroscope and the torsion balance were discovered. The latter was used by Coulomb in 1784 to arrive at his law of electric force.

Up to this point all electricity was produced by friction or induction; the observed currents were therefore transient and resulted from the expenditure of stored energy. The discovery of Volta's pile in 1792, however, changed this concept. Soon powerful batteries were invented. It was then thought that there were two kinds of electricity. One was called voltaic and with it were associated heating and chemical effects. The other was called common, *i.e.*, the one derived from electrostatic machines, and with it were associated electrostatic effects such as sparks, etc.

In 1806, Davy proved the chemical nature of the voltaic cell. The great discoveries of Orsted, Ampere and Biot and Savart followed in 1820. The former two researchers discovered forces exerted on current carrying conductors by magnetic fields. Biot and Savart announced the law of force exerted on a straight current carrying conductor by a magnetic field.

Their work was followed by that of Faraday who demonstrated the principle of electromagnetism, electromagnetic induction and energy conversion. His findings were presented by him in the form of a paper to the Royal Society in 1831. Joseph Henry, Faraday's contemporary, discovered self-induction and the principle of the transformer. He also designed and built an electromagnet.

The discoveries of Faraday, Oerstd, and Henry are of great significance because they made possible the design and construction of dc machines.

In the following years many significant developments took place. Measuring and calculating instruments such as the galvanometer, planimeter and the slide rule were invented. The new measuring instruments made possible the verification of old laws and the establishment of new ones. In 1833, the first mechanical computer was designed by Charles Babbage. It had four basic parts which Babbage named as the store, the mill (where calculations were performed), a part which transferred information from the store to the mill and an output. Although Babbage devoted considerable time towards the construction of the device, it was never completed. Babbage also introduced the idea of punched cards for storing information. However he did not follow up on his idea. Meanwhile, the fundamental work of Ampere, Faraday and Henry led to other important inventions. Samuel Morse invented the electric telegraph and demonstrated it in 1837. In 1858, the first direct current generator was constructed and when the incandescent lamp was discovered by Edison in 1880, electric lighting was made possible. In 1875, Alexander Graham Bell invented the telephone.

Considerable progress was also achieved regarding theoretical aspects during this period. In 1839, Gauss and Weber proposed a system of electric and magnetic units. Their fundamental work was followed by those of Heaviside (1882), Lorentz (1894) and Giorgi (1901). In 1845, Kirchhoff stated his circuit theory laws and in 1873 Maxwell formulated his equations which introduced the concept of electric and magnetic fields.

The engineers and researchers at this time knew of alternating current and its method of generation. However, they were in favour of direct current as they felt that direct current had many advantages to offer. Besides, the alternating current motor had not been invented yet. The construction of transformers enabled the introduction of alternating current as it was realized that voltages could be stepped up or down easily. The transformer was not a new invention; both Faraday and Henry had used it earlier in their experiments. The first commercial transformer was built in 1886 and was followed by the first large scale ac installation in Buffalo in the same year. Alternating current generators evolved from direct current generators and operated at a frequency of 133 Hz. With the discovery of the induction motor by Tesla in 1888, such high frequencies were found unsuitable and discarded in favour of frequencies of 25, 50 and 60 Hz. In 1895 the first ac installation which converted the energy associated with a head of water into electrical energy in the form of 25 Hz ac was completed in Niagara falls. Soon transmission lines followed. At this time there were no standards. Single, two and three phase systems were in operation at frequencies ranging from 25 to 60 Hz. With the passage of time the use of direct current disappeared, and voltage and frequency standards were adopted.

During the year 1860–1900, other important developments took place. In 1878, Crooke revealed the results of experiments conducted with what is now known as the Crooke's tube. Crooke's fundamental work led to the discovery of the oscilloscope, radio tubes, X-rays etc. In 1880, Hollerith conceived of the idea of using punched cards to expedite and facilitate handling of information. His system was subsequently put into use in the 1890 census. Computer development was aided by the invention of tabulating machines which used punched cards. In 1887, Hertz demonstrated the existence of electromagnetic waves and in 1895, Marconi developed the first wireless telegraph. The origin of television can be traced to some experiments conducted with selenium cells in 1891. In 1898, steel wire was used as a memory device. Telephone messages were recorded along a length of steel wire in the form of magnetization whose variation corresponded to variations in telephone current.

Edison's experiments led to the discovery of the Fleming valve in 1904 and the triode in 1906. These discoveries revolutionized the field of electronics and during the first world war great developments were made but kept secret. After the war the communication industry developed at a fast pace. In 1924, the Western Union Telegraph Company introduced wireless picture services. Modern T.V. had its beginnings during this time with invention of the electronic scanner. Various improvements followed and standards pertaining to television were formulated in 1941.

Meanwhile, on the theoretical side Thomson and Millikan in 1906, found the mass of an electron and the charge associated with it. The period 1900–1940 witnessed tremendous progress in atomic physics. It was in this era that Einstein stated his theory of relativity and the hypothesis governing the interchangeability of matter and energy.

During the World War II, the research effort led to the invention of radar. This spurred the development of electronic equipment suitable for use at the higher frequencies. In 1947, microwave communication found its peace time use.

In 1945, the first electronic computer was built at the Massachusetts Institute of Technology. This was the first machine to use the binary system. The magnetic tape recording was first introduced in the thirties and was followed by magnetic cores as memory device for use in computers in 1950.

The evolution of the Transistor, in the fifties, to a reliable form enabled their use in a host of electronic devices including computers. The transistor in turn led to the development, in the sixties, of integrated circuits in which entire circuits are etched on tiny chips. The development of integrated circuits must be considered as being as revolutionary in its impact on electrical engineering and society as the invention of the Fleming valve in 1904. The design of integrated circuits has given birth to a whole new field of electronics called micro electronics. Integrated circuits have made it possible to reduce the size and cost of electrical systems and devices and at the same time increase their reliability and sophistication. Computer development is progressing rapidly due to advances made in integrated circuit design. In 1971, the microprocessor was introduced which has revolutionized the fields of measurement, data handling and control. Microprocessors are also finding applications in a host of devices ranging from scientific instruments to consumer oriented devices.

1.2 PLAN OF THE BOOK

From the brief historical review we see that Electrical Engineering had its beginning in the discovery of static electrification and electric charge. We will begin the book by considering the electrical nature of matter and the concept of electric charge. In what follows, the student will be introduced to the fundamental laws of electrical engineering and the basic tools necessary for the solution of electric circuits. The concept of alternating current will be introduced next and solution techniques applicable to alternating current circuits will be explained. While the first four chapters deal essentially with circuit theory the next two deal with modern semiconductor devices and their applications. The book ends, like the historical perspective with a consideration of microprocessors and their applications.

1.3 THE CONCEPT OF ELECTRIC CHARGE

Most of us are familiar with the classification of materials under two categories, conductors and insulators. For example, copper and aluminium are good conductors of electricity and are used in the manufacture of electric wires and cables which are insulated with rubber, polyethylene and other good insulators. What is it that is responsible for some materials being good conductors or insulators? The answer may be found by examining the atomic structure of matter. A detailed analysis and explanation is not intended here and is beyond the scope of this text. Rather, a cursory explanation will be afforded.

All matter is known to be composed of atoms whose mass, concentrated at its centre, is called the nucleus and is composed of protons and neutrons. The protons and the neutrons are of nearly equal mass, *i.e.*, about 1.67×10^{-27} kg each. The nucleus of diameter $\approx 10^{-14}$ m is surrounded by electrons which may be imagined to be moving around the nucleus in elliptic orbits. The electrons orbits determine the size of the atom and have diameters which are roughly ten thousand times that of the nucleus. In contrast with the mass of the nucleus, that of the electron is much smaller and is $\approx 9.1 \times 10^{-31}$ kg.

The student is no doubt familiar with the laws of mechanics and in particular Newtons law of gravitation. According to this law the force of attraction between two masses is directly proportional to the product of their masses and inversely proportional to the square of the distance separating them. Thus,

$$F = K\frac{m_1 m_2}{r^2} \qquad ...(1.1)$$

where K is known as the gravitational constant. Equation 1.1 may be used to calculate the forces between the three particles, the neutron, proton and the electron. If the results of this calculation are compared with experimental findings, it is found that the measured forces are much larger; in some cases the forces are one of repulsion instead of attraction.

Scientists therefore concluded that there was another property associated with the particles. This property is called electric charge. The proton is associated with a positive charge and is equal in magnitude to the negative charge possessed by an electron. The neutrons bear no electric charge. As matter, on the whole, is electrically neutral, the total charge of all the electrons must be equal to that of all protons. The charges exert forces on one another, but unlike the forces of gravitation, the electric forces may be either of repulsion or attraction. Like charges repel whereas unlike charges exert force of attraction on one another.

The electrons, imagined to be in orbital motion around the nucleus are therefore subject to an attractive electric force towards the nucleus in analogous fashion to the forces on the planets directed towards the sun in our solar system. However, rigorous wave mechanical considerations dictate that the electron orbits are not clearly defined. An atomic model of matter, consisting of a nucleus and electrons with well defined orbits is only a rough approximation.

1.4 ENERGY BAND STRUCTURE OF SOLIDS: METALS, SEMICONDUCTORS AND INSULATORS

Let us consider an isolated atom and accept, for simplicity, that the electrons are in motion around the nucleus in well defined orbits. This is in fact the Bohr model. The electrons closer to the nucleus possess lower energies than those farther from it (very much like a mass *m* possesses greater energy the higher it is above the earth's surface). Thus, each electron is associated with an energy level; between energy levels, gaps exist which electrons are not allowed to occupy. The outermost electrons of each atoms are able to interact with neighbouring atoms and participate in chemical bonds.

What happens when many atoms are brought close together as in a solid? The electrons of an atom are now subject to electric forces of other atoms. This effect is most pronounced in the case of the outermost electrons. Due to these electric forces, the energy levels of all electrons are changed. Some electrons gain energy while others suffer a loss. The energies of the outermost electrons undergo the greatest change. Thus, the energy levels, which were sharply defined in an isolated atom, are now broadened into energy bands. Each band consists of large number of closely packed energy levels. It so happens that, in general, two bands result. One is known as the conduction band and the other the valence band with the former band being associated with higher energy level. These two bands are separated by a region known as the forbidden energy gap. Each material has its own band structure. Differences in the band structure may be used to explain the behaviour or metals, semiconductors and insulators.

Metals: In metals the valence and conduction bands are very close together or may even overlap, *i.e.*, there is no forbidden gap. By receiving a small amount of energy from external thermal or electric sources the electrons readily ascend to higher levels in the conduction band and are available to move through the metal. This movement of electrons is really one of negative electrical charge and constitutes the flow of electric current. In metals the density of electrons in the conduction band is quite high. Consequently metals are good conductors of electricity.

Semiconductors: The two bands are separated by a forbidden gap of sufficient width; at low temperatures no electrons possess sufficient energy to occupy the conduction band and therefore, no movement of charge is possible, *i.e.*, no currents can flow. At modest temperatures, however, it is possible for some electrons to gain sufficient energy and make the transition into the conduction band. At room temperatures the electron density is not as high as in metals and as such, semiconductors cannot conduct electric current as readily as metals.

There is another class of semiconductors, containing impurities which are deliberately introduced, known as impurity semiconductors. The impurity atoms account for additional energy levels lying in between the valence and conduction bands and are able to supply electrons into the conduction band by temperature induced motion.

Insulators: In such materials the forbidden gap is very large. As a result, the energies required by the electron to crossover into the conduction band are impractically large. Thus under normal circumstances, such substances cannot conduct electric current.

Fig. 1.1 shows schematically the energy band structure associated with metals, semiconductors and insulators.

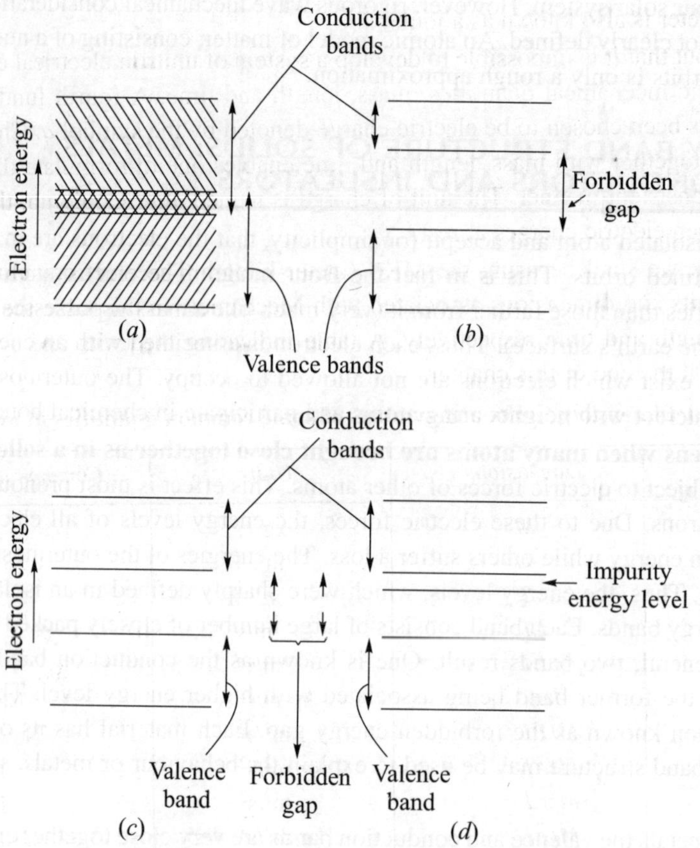

Fig. 1.1 *Energy band structures in (a) Metals (b) Insulators (c) Semiconductors and (d) Impure semiconductors*

We have seen that the flow of electric current is associated with the movement of electric charge; in metals it is due to that of electrons. Electrons are not the only carriers of electric current. In chemical cells such as the lead acid cell, current is carried by ions* provided by the solution in the cell.

1.5 UNITS

In mechanics, three basic quantities, length *L*, mass *M* and time *T* are sufficient to develop the units of measurement of other quantities such as force, energy, etc. For example, force is equal to mass times

---

*Consider an atom of a gas from which an electron has been removed by some process which imparts sufficient energy necessary for such an event to occur. The atom is left with a positive charge and is said to be ionized and is known as a positive ion. The removed electron is known as a free electron.

It is possible that, under certain circumstances, a free electron can attach itself to a neutral atom and form a negatively charged particle known as a negative ion.

Likewise, in solutions which, on the whole, are electrically neutral, +ve and –ve ions exist in equal numbers.

acceleration and has the dimensions MLT^{-2}. A force of 1 kg m/s^2 is required to accelerate a mass of 1 kg at the rate of 1 m/s^2. For convenience this force is called a Newton, so named in honour of Sir Issac Newton. Likewise, energy has the dimensions ML^2T^{-2}. Its units are Force × distance or Newton meter, N.m. A Newton meter is also known as a joule, *J*.

It so turns out that it is impossible to develop a system of units in electrical engineering with the aid of the tree basic mechanical quantities, mass, length and time. A fourth fundamental quantity is needed and this has been chosen to be electric charge denoted by the symbol *q*. Charge is measured in coulombs, *C*, and together with mass, length and time enables one to formulate the laws of electrical engineering in a consistent manner. The unit of charge is named after Coulomb, the discoverer of the law of force between electric charges at rest.

In this book we shall be using the MKS (meter-kilogram-second) system of units. Table 1.1 summarizes the units and dimensions associated with Mechanics. In this table the letters *M*, *L*, and *T* stand for mass, length and time respectively. A table indicating the units and symbols of electrical quantities appears at the end of this chapter.

Table 1.1 Dimensions, units and symbols of some common quantities in mechanics

Quantity	*Dimensions*	*Units*	*Common units and Symbols*
Mass	M	kg	kg
Length	L	m	m
Time	T	s	s
Velocity	LT^{-1}	m/s	m/s
Acceleration	LT^{-2}	m/s^2	m/s^2
Force	MLT^{-2}	kg m/s^2	Newton, N
Work	ML^2T^{-2}	kg m^2/s^2	Newton Meter
Energy	ML^2T^{-2}	kg m^2/s^2	N.m or
Torque	ML^2T^{-2}	kg m^2/s^2	Joule, J
Power	ML^2T^{-3}	kg m^2/s^3	J/s, Watt, W
Momentum	MLT^{-1}	kg m/s	

Although work, energy and torque have the same units, torque is usually expressed in N.m while energy and work are expressed in joules.

Some of the more common prefixes used with units are indicated in Table 1.2.

Table 1.2 Some commonly used prefixes

Prefix	*Symbol*	*Unit is multiplied by*
pico	p	10^{-12}
nano	n	10^{-9}
micro	μ	10^{-6}
milli	m	10^{-3}
centi	c	10^{-2}
deci	d	10^{-1}
kilo	k	10^{3}
Mega	M	10^{6}

1.6 COULOMB'S LAW

Coulomb's law states that the electric force between two charged particles at rest, carrying charges of magnitude q_1 and q_2 coulombs and separated by a distance of r meters in free space is given by

$$F = \frac{1}{4\pi\varepsilon_0}\frac{q_1 q_2}{r^2} \qquad ...(1.2)$$

F is the force in Newtons and ε_0, a constant, $\dfrac{10^{-9}}{36\pi}$ which has the units c^2/Nm^2, is the permittivity of free space. Whether the force is that of attraction or repulsion depends on the polarity of the charges q_1 and q_2. If q_1 and q_2 are of the same sign (*i.e.* both +ve or –ve charges) the force is one of repulsion. Should q_1 and q_2 carry unlike signs, the force is one of attraction.

The negative charge on an electron has a magnitude of $1.6.10^{-19}$ C. Two electrons separated by a distance of 1 mm in free space experience a repulsive electric force of 2.30×10^{-22} N. In comparison, the gravitational force is quite small; the ratio between the two forces, in the above example, is $\approx 4.10^{42}$. In view of this it may be puzzling why gravitational forces are important at all. The answer should become clear once it is understood that matter, on the whole, is electrically neutral. Electric forces can be observed or made use of only if positive and negative charges are separated. The force of gravitation given by Eqn. 1.1 is always one of attraction whereas the electric 'coulomb force' may be one of attraction or repulsion.

1.7 ELECTRIC CURRENT

In Section 1.4, we associated the flow of electric charge with that of electric current. Electric current, in fact, is defined as the rate of flow of electric charge. Mathematically,

$$\text{Current, } i = \frac{dq}{dt} \qquad ...(1.3)$$

and has the units of Coulomb/sec which is also known as an Ampere or Amp for short, and is denoted by *A*. This unit of current is named after Andre Marie Ampere who did pioneering work in electromagnetism. Thus, 1 Amp is the current due to the flow of charge at the rate of 1 Coulomb per second. The conventional direction of current flow is opposite to that of negative charges and therefore to the flow of electrons. Thus, if current is flowing from point *A* to *B*, it may be due to the flow of electrons or negative ions from *B* to *A* or positive ions from *A* to *B* or due to any combination of the above.

Example 1.1. *In a metallic wire, 10^{19} electrons drift across a cross-section per second. What is the resulting current flow?*

Solution. Charge on one electron = 1.6×10^{-19} C

Total charge movement per sec. = $1.6 \times 10^{-19} \times 10^{19} = 1.6$ C

$$\text{Current, } i = \frac{dq}{dt}$$

$$= \frac{q}{t} \text{ as the flow is uniform}$$

$$= 1.6 \text{ A.}$$

Example 1.2. *In a certain circuit the current decays according to the law $i = 10e^{-4t}$. Find the total charge that passes through the circuit.*

Solution.
$$i = \frac{dq}{dt}$$

$$\therefore \quad dq = i\,dt$$

and
$$q = \int_0^\infty i\,dt$$

$$= 10\int_0^\infty e^{-4t}\,dt$$

$$= 10\left[\frac{e^{-4t}}{-4}\right]_0^\infty = 2.5 \text{ coulombs.}$$

The current flowing through the filament of an ordinary incandescent 100 watt lamp is slightly less than an Ampere. On the other hand, thousands of amperes may flow in the conductors of a high voltage power transmission line.

What causes the flow of charges to constitute the flow of electric current? This question will be addressed in the following section.

1.8 FLOW OF CURRENT, POTENTIAL AND POTENTIAL DIFFERENCE

In an isolated metallic conductor, such as a length of copper wire, numerous electrons exist in the conduction band; yet there is no current flow. Although the electrons are in motion, due to interactive forces between them and the positive ions, it is essentially random in nature and at any cross-section the net movement of electrons across the cross-section is zero. Thus according to Eqn. 1.3, the current flow is zero. To enable an orderly movement of electrons, *i.e.*, current flow, one needs to establish across the ends of the wire an electric pressure. Such a pressure is provided by an energy source such as a battery.

Due to chemical actions in the battery, a separation of electric charges takes place. Negative charges accumulate at one terminal and positive charges accumulate at the other terminal. This separation of charges is not possible unless work is done on them. This should be evident from Coulomb's law. The charges of unlike polarity exert an attractive force on one another. In order to separate them, work has to be done by an external agency against the attractive force. In this case the work is done chemically. The greater the number of charges that suffer separation, the greater the work has to be done to accomplish this separation and the greater the potential energy of the separated charges.

The above situation finds an analogy in mechanics where work has to be done in raising a mass against the gravitational force to some height h above sea level. The greater the mass, the greater the potential energy that is established.

A special significance is attached to the work done per unit charge in the transportation of a small ±ve test charge from the ±ve terminal where ±ve charges have accumulated to the ±ve terminal. This is a measure of the amount of accumulated charge or a measure of the potential energy that has been established. The greater the accumulated charge the more the work that has to be done in the movement of the test charge because the coulomb forces of repulsion and attraction are larger. The work done per unit charge is known as potential and has units of Joule/Coulomb. This is known as a volt, named in honour of Volta who did pioneering work with batteries over a century ago.

In mechanics the work done in raising a mass from height h_1 to a greater height h_2 is equal to difference in potential energies at these two heights. Likewise, in the example under consideration the work done per unit charge is indeed the potential difference or voltage difference between the terminals of the battery.

When a length of copper wire is connected across the terminals of the battery (this situation is purely academic: such an experiment will have disastrous consequences as will be realized later) the electrons in the conduction band are set in motion by the electric force due to the accumulated charges at the terminals of the battery. But these electrons do not experience steadily inereasing velocities. This is because their motion is periodically interrupted by collisions with fixed atoms and ions. The motion is orderly, however, and across a cross-section there exists a flow of charge thus constituting an electric current. It must be noted that charges do not accumulate in the conductor, as many charges enter a cross-section as are leaving it. At any time, should the copper wire be disconnected from the battery terminals, its electrical neutrality is preserved.

But for chemical reactions in the battery, which maintains a potential or voltage difference across the terminals, the flow of current would cease as charges flow from one terminal to the other and neutralize each other. Also, the greater the potential difference or voltage across the battery terminals, the greater the accumulated charge and the greater the rate of flow of charge and therefore of current.

In summary, it is not possible to obtain current flow in a metallic wire from point *A* to point *B* unless there exists a potential or voltage differences between these two points. This is usually provided by an energy source such as a battery.

1.9 RESISTANCE—OHM'S LAW

From the explanations given in the previous section one realizes that the magnitude of current flow between two points is dependent on the potential difference or voltage between these points. What is the relationship between voltage and current? This is expressed by Ohm's law which states that in any conductor the potential difference *V* across it, in the direction of current flow, bears a constant ratio to the current flow *I* through it. This constant is called the resistance *R* of the conductor. Mathematically,

$$V = IR \qquad \text{...(1.4)}$$

From Eqn. 1.4 the units of *R* are Volt/Amp. This is known as an Ohm, identified by the symbol Ω and named in honour of George Simon Ohm who studied the flow of electric current in conductors. It is clear from Eqn. 1.4 that given an energy source, such as a battery, the current flow through a conductor connected across the battery terminals, can be controlled by varying the resistance of the conductor. If the resistance is small, the current will be large and vice versa. Such a control is readily provided by the use of a device known as a resistor which exhibits the property of resistance. Resistors with different values of resistance are available. If we want current to flow through a resistor then we must establish a voltage difference across it by using, for example, a battery. Fig. 1.2 shows a 6 ohm resistor identified by the symbol —ᴧᴧᴧ— connected across the terminals of a 12 volt battery. The positive and negative terminals of the battery are marked accordingly. The battery is identified by the symbol —|⊢; the shorter line always represents the negative terminal. Referring to Fig. 1.2, which is the simplest electric circuit, the potential of point *A* minus that of *B* is equal to 12 volts or alternatively the potential of *A* measured with respect to *B* is 12 volts. Since this voltage difference exists across the 6 ohm resistor, current flows. The value of the current is given by Eq. 1.4 to be 12/6 = 2 A and varies linearly with the voltage difference across the resistor. If this is increased to 24 volts then the current increases to 4 A. This linear relationship dictated by Eqn. 1.4 is shown in Fig. 1.3. In Fig. 1.2, according to the convention established in section 1.7, the direction of current flow is from *A* through the resistor to B and through the battery back to *A*. As charges move from *B* to *A* in the battery they experience a voltage rise. As the charges move from *A* to *B* via the resistor, work is done by them and they experience a voltage drop. Ohm's law may therefore be restated that the voltage drop *V* across a resistor is related to the current flow *I* through it by the relation $V = IR$. When current flows through a resistor, a voltage drop occurs in the direction of current flow. This is shown in Fig. 1.3. Note the polarity marking associated with the voltage drop which is written as V_{AB}. In this example, $I = 1$ A and $V_{AB} = 6$ volts. Also $V_{BA} = -6$ volts thus denoting a rise in potential from *B* to *A*.

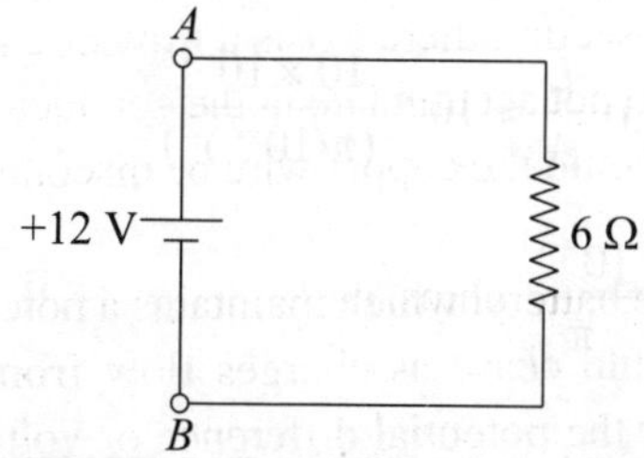

Fig. 1.2 *A simple electric circuit*

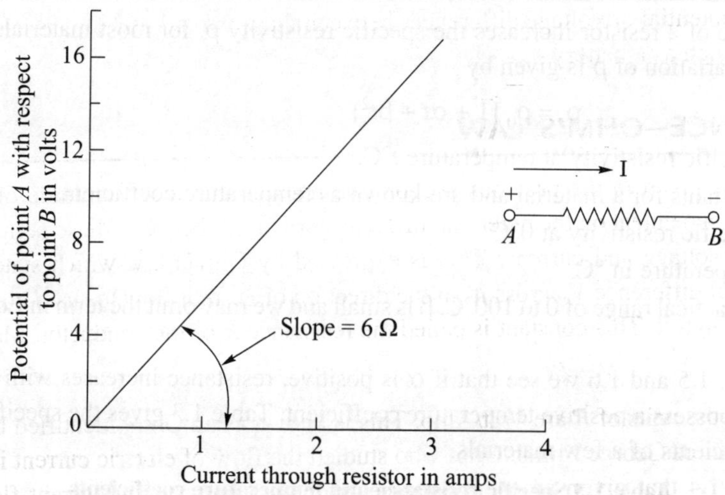

Fig. 1.3 *The linear relationship between voltage across and current through a resistor*

1.10 CALCULATION OF RESISTANCE AND RESISTIVITY

Resistance in electric circuits is analogous to mechanical friction and creates an impediment to current flow. This is due to collisions among electrons and between electrons and atoms of the material which in the production of heat.

It is possible to calculate the value of resistance if the material of which the resistor is made and the geometrical shape of the resistor are known.

The experimentally derived law

$$R = \rho \frac{L}{A} \qquad ...(1.5)$$

may be used to calculate the resistance R in ohms of a conductor of length L meters, of cross-sectional area A square meters and of specific resistivity ρ, a constant for a material, may be found by dimensional analysis to be ohm-meter. Eqn. 1.5 is valid if and only if the current flow is uniformly distributed throughout the cross-section of the conductor; this is usually assumed.

Example 1.3. *Calculate the resistance of a block of material of specific resistivity 10^{-6} ohm. m, circular in cross-section of radius 1 cm, and 10 cm long.*

Solution.

$$R = \rho \frac{L}{A} = 10^{-6} \frac{10 \times 10^{-2}}{(\pi(10^{-2})^2)}$$

$$= \frac{10^{-3}}{\pi} \text{ ohms.}$$

1.11 TEMPERATURE DEPENDENCE OF RESISTIVITY AND CONDUCTIVITY

As the temperature of a resistor increases the specific resistivity ρ, for most materials, also increases. The temperature variation of ρ is given by

$$\rho_t = \rho_0 \, [1 + \alpha t + \beta t^2] \qquad ...(1.6)$$

where ρ_t = specific resistivity at temperature t°C.

α, β = constants for a material and are known as temperature coefficients

ρ_0 = specific resistivity at 0°C

t = temperature in °C

Over the practical range of 0 to 100°C, β is small and we may omit the term in Eqn. 1.6 associated with it.

From Eqns. 1.5 and 1.6 we see that if α is positive, resistance increases with temperature; the resistor is said to possess a positive temperature coefficient. Table 1.3 gives the specific resistance and temperature coefficients of a few materials.

Table 1.3 Specific resistance and temperature coefficients

Material	ρ *ohm-cm*	α
Copper	1.67×10^{-6}	0.004
Iron	9.8×10^{-6}	0.006
Lead	20×10^{-6}	0.0034
Silver	1.59×10^{-6}	0.0041
Constantan	44×10^{-6}	—

The inverse of ρ, identified by the symbol σ, is known as conductivity. It has the units of ohm^{-1} m^{-1} or Siemens/m which is abbreviated as S/m. Materials with low conductivity have a high resistance and vice versa.

1.12 TYPES OF RESISTORS

There are many types of resistors available such as carbon composition, wire wound, carbon film and metal film. The carbon composition resistor is the most common and the resistance element is made up of carbon. In the film type of resistor a very thin film of either metal or carbon is deposited on an insulating base between two metallic electrodes; the thickness of the film determines the resistance. Since extremely thin films can be provided, high resistance values can be attained. The wirewound resistor, as its name implies, consists of a length of wire, of suitable resistance per unit length, wound on an insulating core.

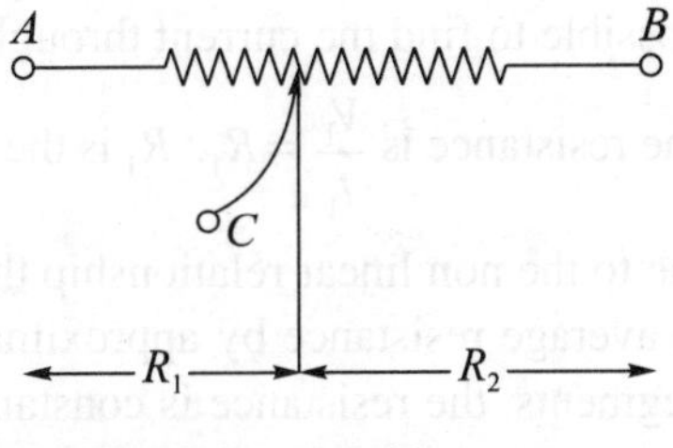

Fig. 1.4 *A variable resistor*

Variable resistors allow for the adjustment of the resistance value between zero and some value. Such resistors are known as potentiometers or simply 'pots'. Fig. 1.4 explains the operation of such resistors. The temperature dependence of a resistor depends on the type; carbon composition types are most affected by temperature changes. In these resistance increases by as much as 2% due to a rise in temperature of 20°C.

1.13 THE THERMISTOR

In some applications a resistor may be desired which exhibits a large dependence on temperature. Such a resistor is known as a *thermistor*. The resistance of a thermistor as a function of temperature is given by

$$R_t = R_0 \exp\left[\beta\left\{\frac{1}{t} - \frac{1}{T_0}\right\}\right] \quad ...(1.7)$$

where R_t = resistance in ohms at temperature t in °K

t = temperature in °K

R_0 = resistance at temperature T_0, 300°K (27°C)

β = a constant which is material dependent

Differentiating eqn. 1.7, we obtain

$$\frac{dR_t}{dt} = R_0\left(\exp\left[\beta\left\{\frac{1}{t} - \frac{1}{T_0}\right\}\right]\right)\left(\frac{-\beta}{t^2}\right) \quad ...(1.8)$$

For a change in temperature of 1°C the resistance decreases to a value $\left\{R_t - \frac{R_0\beta}{t^2}\exp\left[\beta\left(\frac{1}{t}-\frac{1}{T_0}\right)\right]\right\}$. The per cent change per °C is given by $\frac{1}{R_t}\frac{dR_t}{dt}$ and is equal to $-\frac{100\beta}{t^2}$.

By definition, this is the temperature coefficient and it is seen to be negative, i.e., the resistance decreases with increasing temperature.* If the temperature coefficient is –4% per °C the resistance is halved for a 25°C rise in temperature. A thermistor may be used to detect temperature changes by measuring the resistance changes which accompany it.

1.14 NONLINEAR RESISTORS AND INCREMENTAL RESISTANCE

When the relation between voltage drop and current flow is nonlinear, the resistor is said to be non linear and possesses a characteristic similar to curve OABC shown in Fig. 1.5. How shall we define R in such a case? From the graph it is possible to find the current through the resistor for any given voltage across it. At point A, for example, the resistance is $\frac{V_1}{I_1} = R_1$. R_1 is the resistance exhibited by the resistor when the voltage across it is V_1. Due to the non linear relationship the resistance changes from point to point. We may choose to define an average resistance by approximating the curve by linear segments OA, AB and BC. In each of these segments, the resistance is constant. For example in segment OA the resistance is $\frac{V_1}{I_1}$, in segment AB it is $\frac{V_2 - V_1}{I_2 - I_1}$. The more pronounced the nonlinearity the greater is the number of segments required in order to maintain an accuracy of representation.

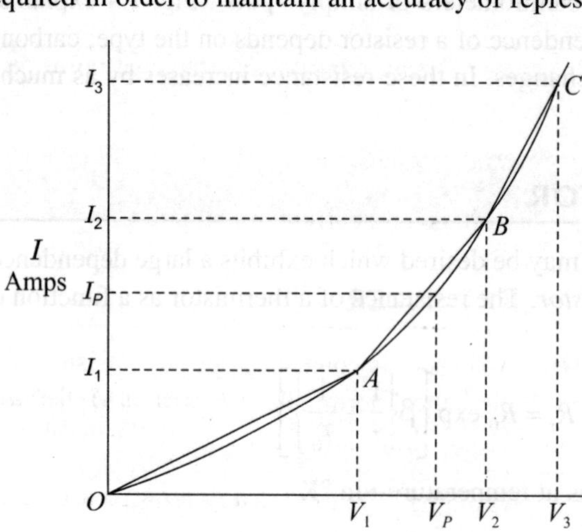

Fig. 1.5 *Nonlinear resistor characteristics*

*Thermistors are also available which exhibit a positive temperature coefficient. However, they do not find practical application as the resistance variation is much smaller.

Let us now consider the case when the operating point is at P on the nonlinear graph. The voltage across the resistor is V_P and the current is I_P; the resistance is therefore $\frac{V_P}{I_P} = R_P$. Suppose small changes in voltage take place about V_P. This may be due to small voltage changes at the terminals of a source connected across the resistor. What is the resistance as it appears to the fluctuating voltage source?

When the voltage changes to $V_P \pm \Delta V_P$ the total voltage swing is $2\Delta V_P$. The current change that follows is given by

$$(I)_{V_P + \Delta V_P} - (I)_{V_P - \Delta V_P}$$

$$= \left\{ I_P + \left(\frac{dI}{dV}\right)_P \Delta V_P \right\} - \left\{ I_P - \left(\frac{dI}{dV}\right)_P \Delta V_P \right\}$$

$$= 2\Delta V_P \left(\frac{dI}{dV}\right)_P \quad \text{...(1.9)}$$

The subscript P indicates that the $\frac{dI}{dV}$ is evaluated at point P.

The resistance change due to the voltage swing is

$$= \frac{\text{Total voltage swing}}{\text{Total current swing}}$$

$$= \frac{2\Delta V_P}{2\Delta V_P \left(\frac{dI}{dV}\right)_P} \quad \text{...(1.10)}$$

$\frac{dV}{dI}$ is known as incremental resistance. The incremental resistance at point P is found by evaluating $\frac{dV}{dI}$ at point P. Note that the incremental resistance at a point on the VI characteristics depends on its slope and not on the actual values of voltage and current at that point.

1.15 WORK, ENERGY AND POWER

Suppose a battery which develops a voltage V is connected across a resistor of R ohms as in Fig. 1.2. The existence of the voltage across the battery terminals is evidence of the fact that we now possess some energy to do work electrically. From Ohm's law a current I flows through the resistor. From Eqn. 1.3, $I = \frac{Q}{t}$ provided I does not vary with time. The total charge transported through the resistor in time t is equal to It coulombs. Since this charge moves downhill in potential, work is done by the charge. From the definition of potential, (section 1.7) the work is = VIt joules. By virtue of the work done, an energy of VIt joules is dissipated in the resistor and manifests itself in the form of heat; the temperature of the resistor increases. Although work and energy have the same units, conceptually they are different. In the battery, work of QV joules (= VIt joules) is done on the charges to establish the potential V corresponding to an energy of QV joules. When current flows this energy is transformed into heat energy or some other form of energy by virtue of the work done by the charges as they move down in potential. In the example under consideration the energy dissipated is equal to the energy stored.

Power is defined as the rate of expenditure of energy. The power dissipated in the resistor R is

$$P = \frac{d}{dt}[\text{Energy}]$$

$$= \frac{d}{dt}[VIt]$$

$= VI$ joule/s. A joule per second is known as a watt, W.

$$\therefore \quad \left.\begin{aligned} P &= VI \text{ watts} \\ &= I^2R \text{ watts} \\ &= \frac{V^2}{R} \text{ watts} \end{aligned}\right\} \qquad \text{...(1.11)}$$

In Eqn. 1.11, V is the voltage drop, in volts, across the resistor due to a current flow of magnitude I amperes through it. From Eqn. 1.11, it is seen that power varies in quadratic fashion with voltage or current for constant R. In such a case the voltage and current are related linearly. The horse power and the watt are related.

$$1 \text{ hp} = 746 \text{ W}.$$

The watt is a rather small unit of power. For example a clock radio consumes about 4 watts, the average electric iron 1000 watts or a kW. The total power consumption of a modern city with a population of about half a million is of the order of 1000 MW. The unit of electric energy is the watt-hour, Wh, or the kilowatt hour, kWh. The latter units is more practical as the watt-hour represents a small amount of energy.

Example 1.4. *A device is rated at 500 W and operates by connection across a 100 volt source. How much energy is spent by its continuous operation for 2 years? If energy costs are 5 per kWh, what is the cost of using this device? What current does the device draw?*

Solution. Energy expended in 2 years = 500 watts × (# of hours in 2 years)

$$= 500 \times 2 \times 365 \times 24 \text{ watt hour}$$

$$= 365 \times 24 \text{ kWh} = 8760 \text{ kWh}$$

$$\text{Cost of energy} = \frac{8760 \times 5}{100} \text{ dollars } \$ \, 438$$

$$\text{Current drawn by device} = \frac{500 \text{ watts}}{100 \text{ volts}} = 5 \text{ A}$$

$$\text{Resistance of device} = \frac{500}{(5)^2} \text{ or } \frac{100}{5} = 20\ \Omega.$$

1.16 RESISTOR RATING

The dissipation of power in a resistor results in its heating and an increase in its temperature. This increase should be kept within certain limits so that the resistance value does not suffer much change.

This is the reason why resistors are rated in watts. A 4 watt 1 ohm, resistor can dissipate more power than a 1watt, 1 ohm resistor and has a larger surface area. It is important to choose the power rating of a resistor so that it will not be exceeded in operation.

1.17 EFFICIENCY

Electrical energy can be converted to other forms such as thermal, mechanical, etc. During this process of energy conversion, losses occur and invariably the efficiency is never 100 percent. Therefore the electrical energy supplied to a motor, for example, to do some mechanical work, is greater than that actually required by the amount of losses in the system.

Example 1.5. *It is required to raise a mass of 10 kg through a vertical distance of 5 m at a constant velocity of 10 m/s. Find the input current to a dc motor which operates at a voltage of 100 volts. Assume the system efficiency to be 80%.*

Solution. Since the mass is not undergoing any acceleration, the force on it is that due to gravity alone and is equal to 10 × 981 = 98.1 Newtons where the acceleration due to gravity is = 9.81 m/s^2. The total work done in raising the weight or energy spent = 98.1 × 5 J. This is energy is spent in 0.5 sec, the time taken to raise the mass through this height.

$$\therefore \quad \text{The constant power expenditure} = \frac{98.1 \times 5}{0.5} = 981 \text{ watts}$$

Since the efficiency of the system = 0.8, the power needed from the electrical source is

$$= \frac{981}{0.8} \text{ watts.}$$

Since the motor operates at a voltage of 100 volts the input current from Eqn. 1.11 is

$$= \frac{981}{0.8 \times 100} \text{ amps.}$$

Note the motor must be rated at $\frac{981}{0.8}$ or 1226.25 watts at the very least.

Table 1.4 Units and symbols associated with electrical quantities

Quantity	*Unit*	*Abbreviated unit*	*Usual symbol*
Electric charge	coulomb	C	Q, *q*
Electric current	ampere, amp	A	I, *i*
Voltage	volt	V	V, *v*
Resistance	ohm	Ω	R, *r*
Resistivity	ohm-m	Ω-m	ρ
Conductivity	mho/m, Siemens/m	S/m	σ
Energy	joule	J	E
Power	watt	W	P

2 CHAPTER

Basic Circuit Concepts

2.1 INTRODUCTION

Our first example of an electric circuit was encountered in section 1.9. An electric circuit comprises of energy sources such as batteries, circuit elements such as resistors so that there exists at least one closed path through which electric current may flow. For example, Fig. 2.1 shows an electric circuit comprising of 7 resistors and 3 batteries. It is clear that there is at least one closed path available for current flow.

In this chapter we will state the laws of circuit theory which together with Ohm's law enable the solution of electric circuits. Techniques useful in the simplification and solution of electric circuits will be discussed. The student will be introduced to two different types of electric energy sources.

2.2 LUMPED PARAMETERS—BRANCH, NODE, LOOP

In Fig. 2.1 we notice that the resistances in the circuit are indicated at the locations identified by the symbol —ᴡᴡ—. The wires used to make up the circuit are either assumed to have zero resistance or their small resistance is included in the values of the seven resistors. This is known as the lumped parameter approach.

Portions of the circuit (Fig. 2.1) which contain elements of the circuit such as resistors or batteries are known as *branches*; *i.e., AH, GE, CG, EF*, etc. are *branches*. In this figure there are a total of ten branches. The point of intersection of two or more branches is termed a *node*. Points *C, E, G, F*, etc. are

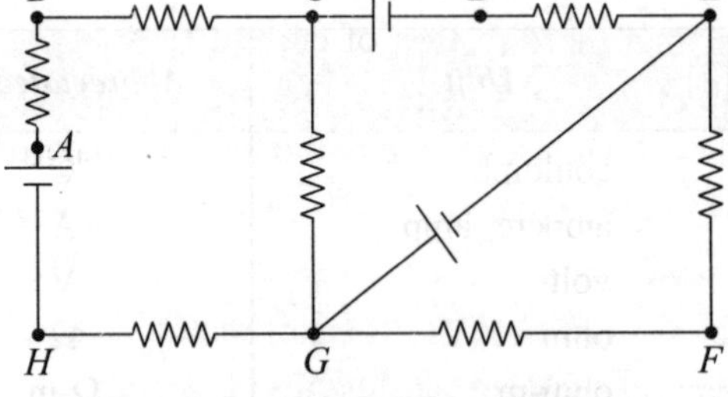

Fig. 2.1 *A simple resistance network*

nodes. Consider a closed path such as *ABCGHA*; this is known as a *loop* of the circuit. In Fig. 2.1 there are, in total, 6 loops. It is possible for one loop to include another within it. For example loop *CDEFGC* includes loops *CDEGC* and *GEFG*. In this circuit the batteries are the source for the resulting current flow through the branches.

2.3 KIRCHHOFF'S LAWS

In the electric circuit of Fig. 2.1 there are a total of 8 nodes and 10 branches. A little thought will make it clear that Ohm's law alone is not sufficient for finding the unknowns, *i.e.*, voltage across each branch and the current flowing through each branch. Additional criteria are necessary and are provided by Kirchhoff's laws.

Kirchhoff's First Law

This law states that at any point in the electric circuit, including nodes, the sum of the currents flowing towards the point is equal to the sum flowing away from it.

$$\sum_{\text{any point}} I = 0 \qquad ...(2.1)$$

This law is known as Kirchhoff's first law or the current law and is referred to as KCL.

Example 2.1. *Consider the four resistors meeting at one node as shown below in Fig. 2.2. These resistors form part of a circuit which is not shown. The currents flowing in 3 of the resistors are identified. Find the current I flowing in the 2 Ω resistor.*

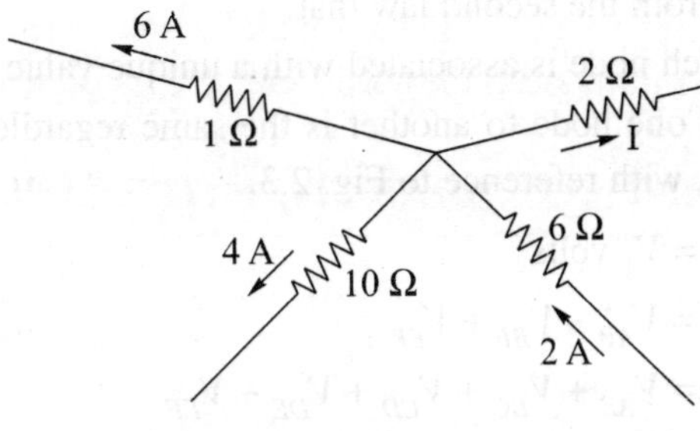

Fig. 2.2 *Demonstration of KCL*

Solution. We apply KCL at node *A*

$$I + 4 + 6 = 2$$

$$I = -8$$

The answer indicates that the direction of current flow in the 2 Ω resistor is opposite to that indicated in the figure.

Kirchhoff's current law is a consequence of the fact that charges can not accumulate at any point in a conductor.

Kirchhoff's Second Law

This law is known as the voltage law or KVL. It states that in an electric circuit the sum of the voltage drops in any closed loop taken in a consistent direction is zero.

$$\sum_{\text{Closed loop}} (\text{voltage drops}) = 0 \qquad ...(2.2)$$

Consider the circuit of Fig. 2.3. In loop *FABEF* the application of KVL in the clockwise sense yields

$$V_{AB} + V_{BE} + V_{EF} + V_{FA} = 0 \qquad ...(2.3)$$

In Eqn. 2.3, we note that $V_{EF} = 0$ as the resistance between E and F is 0. Also V_{FA} is negative.

Turning to loop *BCDEB* we note that there are no energy sources in this loop. Application of the second law yields.

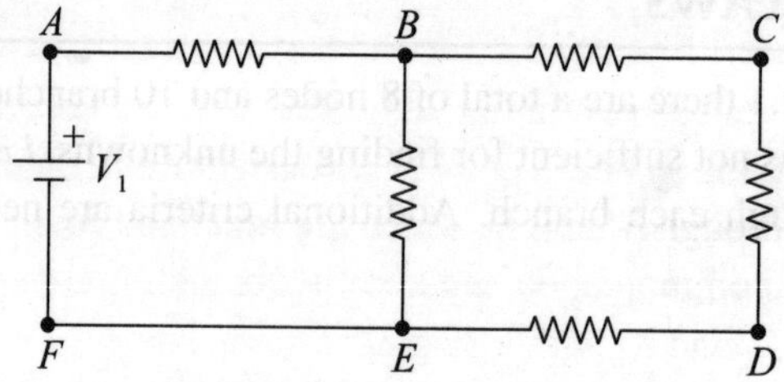

Fig. 2.3 *Verification of KVL*

$$V_{BC} + B_{CD} + V_{DE} + V_{EB} = 0 \qquad \text{...(2.4)}$$

Clearly all drops can not be positive. At least one term should be negative. If this is V_{BE} then it means current in branch *BE* flows from *E* to *B*. Therefore V_{EB} is positive and V_{BE} is negative.

The second law is a consequence of the principle of conservation of energy. In any closed loop the work done per unit charge (voltage drop) is equal to the available energy per unit charge (voltage rises or potential sources).

It can readily be deduced from the second law that

(1) In an electric circuit each node is associated with a unique value of voltage or potential.

(2) The voltage drop from one node to another is the same regardless of the path followed to calculate this drop, *i.e.*, with reference to Fig. 2.3.

$$\begin{aligned} V_{FA} &= V_1 \text{ volts} \\ &= V_{AB} + V_{BE} + V_{EF} \\ &= V_{AB} + V_{BC} + V_{CD} + V_{DE} + V_{EF} \qquad \text{...(2.5)} \end{aligned}$$

Example 2.2. *A part of a circuit is shown in Fig. 2.4. Given that $V_{bc} = -6$ and $V_{dc} = +4$ volts find V_{ab} and V_{ca}.*

Solution. From KVL we write that $V_{ab} + V_{bc} + V_{cd} + V_{da} = 0$

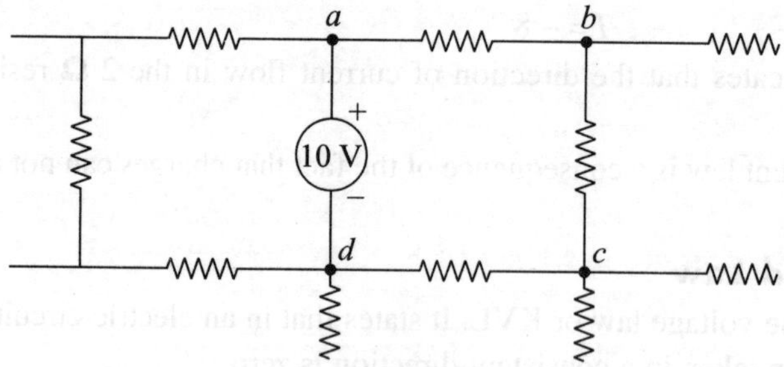

Fig. 2.4

Therefore,

$$\begin{aligned} V_{ab} &= -V_{bc} - V_{cd} - V_{da} \\ &= -V_{bc} + V_{dc} + V_{ad} \\ &= 6 + 4 + 10 = 20 \text{ volts} \end{aligned}$$

To find V_{ca}, we note that

$$V_{ca} = V_{cd} + V_{da} = -4 - 10 = -14 \text{ volts}$$

2.4 SERIES CIRCUITS

Consider a part of an electric circuit shown in Fig. 2.5. Here, two resistors of values R_1 and R_2 ohms are connected together to share a common node. By KCL, a current I entering at point A must exit at point C, *i.e.*, the same current flows through R_1 and R_2 which are said to be connected in series. Two branches are in series when they share a common node and no other branch is connected to this node.

Is it possible to replace R_1 and R_2 with a single resistor? The answer is yes. Consider the voltage drop from A to B due to current flow; it is equal to IR_1. Similarly the voltage drop from B to C is equal to IR_2. From KVL, the total voltage drop from A to C is their algebraic sum and is equal to $I(R_1 + R_2)$. If a single resistor is to replace the series combination; we must have

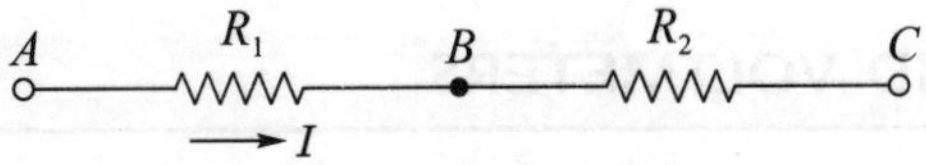

Fig. 2.5 *A series circuit*

$$I R_{eq} = I(R_1 + R_2)$$

or $$R_{eq} = R_1 + R_2 \qquad ...(2.6)$$

The extension to n resistors in series is covered by

$$R_{eq} = R_1 + R_2 + ... + R_n \qquad ...(2.7)$$

2.5 PARALLEL CIRCUITS

Consider the arrangement shown in Fig. 2.6. Here, each of two resistors R_3 and R_4 join two nodes A and B. Once again we assume that only a part of an electric circuit is shown. We wish to replace the two resistors by an equivalent resistor. Suppose current I enters at A. By successive application of KCL we conclude that the same magnitude must exit at B. The currents through R_3 and R_4 are different and are assumed to be I_3 and I_4 respectively. The voltage drop from A to B is given by I_3R_3 or I_4R_4 or IR_{eq} where R_{eq} is the single equivalent resistor joining nodes A and B. Clearly,

$$I_3R_3 = I_4R_4 = IR_{eq} \qquad ...(2.8)$$

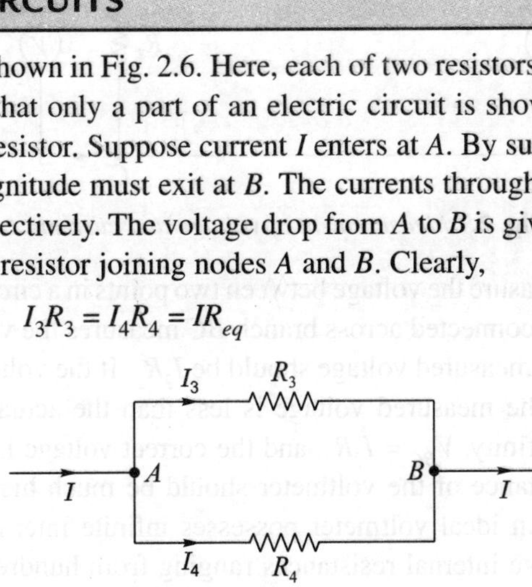

Fig. 2.6 *A parallel circuit*

From KCL, $$I = I_3 + I_4 \qquad ...(2.9)$$

Using Eqns. 2.8 and 2.9, one obtains

$$I = \frac{IR_{eq}}{R_3} + \frac{IR_{eq}}{R_4}$$

or

$$\frac{1}{R_{eq}} = \frac{1}{R_3} + \frac{1}{R_4} \qquad ...(2.10)$$

Equation 2.10 expresses the relation between R_{eq}, R_3 and R_4. The extension to n resistors R_1, R_2, R_3, R_4, ... R_n connected between A and B is handled by the equation

$$\frac{1}{R_{eq}} = \frac{1}{R_1} + \frac{1}{R_2} + \frac{1}{R_3} + \frac{1}{R_4} + ... + \frac{1}{R_n} \qquad ...(2.11)$$

The resistors R_3 and R_4 of Fig. 2.6 are said to be connected in parallel. Two or more branches are said to be connected in parallel if each one of them joins the same two nodes. The voltage drops across branches in parallel are identical.

2.6 AMMETERS AND VOLTMETERS

In order to measure the current flowing in a branch, ammeters are inserted in series with that branch. Ammeters are denoted by the symbol A. In Fig. 2.7, the ammeter reads the current in branch AB and therefore the current delivered by the source. Since the insertion of ammeter should not upset the circuit current, ammeters should have low resistance; an ideal ammeter has zero resistance. A practical ammeter is equivalent to an ideal ammeter in series with an equivalent resistance which is equal to the resistance of the ammeter.

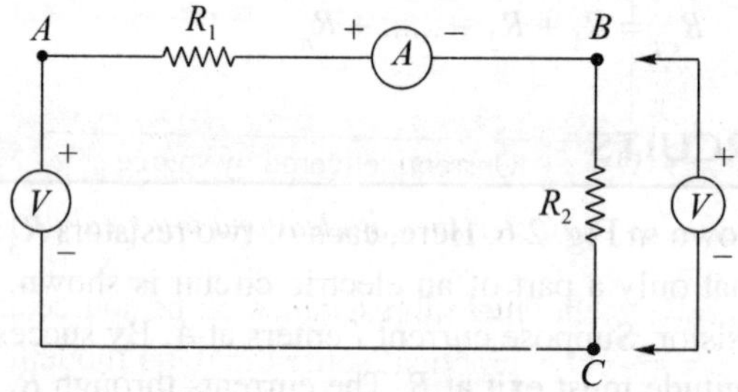

Fig. 2.7 *Measurement of voltage and current*

Voltmeters are used to measure the voltage between two points in a circuit. In Fig. 2.7 the voltmeter, denoted by the symbol V, when connected across branch BC measures the voltage across that branch. If the current through BC is I_2, the measured voltage should be I_2R_2. If the voltmeter draws current I_2', $V_{BC} = (I_2 - I_2')\,R_2$ and is $< I_2R_2$. The measured voltage is less than the actual. On the other hand if the resistance of the voltmeter is infinity, $V_{BC} = I_2R_2$, and the correct voltage is measured. For an accurate measurement, the internal resistance of the voltmeter should be much higher than that of the branch across which it is connected. An ideal voltmeter possesses infinite internal resistance and draws no current. Practical voltmeters have internal resistances ranging from hundreds of ohms to 10^6 ohms or greater.

2.7 VOLTAGE SOURCES

The batteries in Fig. 2.1 are sources of potential or energy. Introduction of these sources in a circuit causes current flow in the branches of the circuit. In this chapter and the next, we will be dealing with direct voltage sources only. A direct voltage source is one whose terminal voltage (voltage between terminals) is constant with time. A battery is an example of a practical direct voltage source. The volt-ampere characteristics of an ideal direct voltage source (*i.e.*, a plot of the voltage across the terminals of the source versus the current delivered by it) is shown in Fig. 2.8. It is seen that the ideal source maintains its potential at a constant value irrespective of the current (charge) drain from it. Practical sources have far from ideal characteristics as shown by the broken line in Fig. 2.8. The voltage at the terminals of a practical voltage source is seen to decrease with increasing current drawn from it. This variation may or may not be linear. In any event the relationship between terminal voltage and current may be expressed as

$$V_t = V_{\text{ideal}} - I_{\text{load}}(R) \qquad \text{...(2.12)}$$

where V_t = Terminal voltage of practical source.

V_{ideal} = Terminal voltage of practical source when current delivered by it is 0.

and I_{load} = Current delivered by the source.

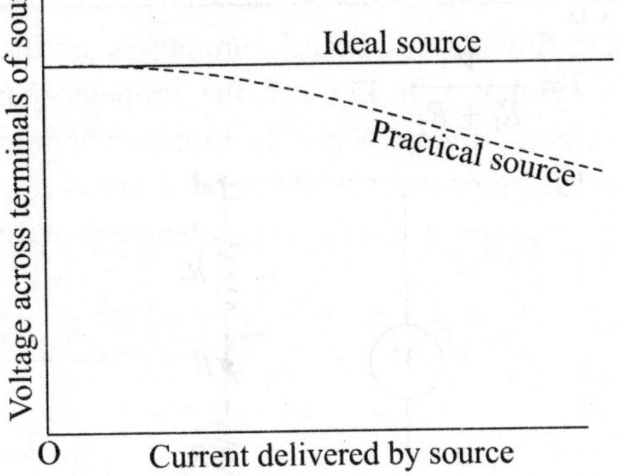

Fig. 2.8 *Volt-amp characteristics of ideal and practical dc voltage sources*

In Eqn. 2.12, *R* is known as the internal resistance of the source and is a constant if the volt-amp characteristic of the source is linear. A practical source may be modelled by the addition of a suitable series resistor to an ideal voltage source as shown in Fig. 2.9 which also shows the symbol commonly used to represent an ideal voltage source. This symbol should be not confused with that used to represent a voltmeter. Owing to the presence of internal resistance, same of the power delivered by a source is dissipated within itself.

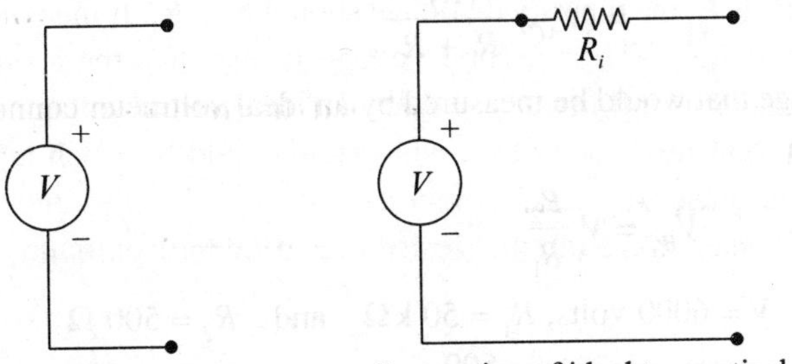

Fig. 2.9 *Representation of ideal and practical voltage sources*

If a resistor is connected across a voltage source, the direction of current flow is out of the positive terminal which is in accordance with the convention stated earlier. Under these conditions, the voltage source delivers power which is equal to the product of the current delivered by it and the voltage across it. For some reason, if current enters a voltage source at its positive terminal, the voltage source receives power.

Insertion of a direct voltage source in a circuit causes the flow of direct current in the branches of the circuit, *i.e.*, current whose magnitude does not vary with time. Since direct current results from the use of direct voltage sources the latter are commonly referred to as 'direct current' voltage sources or dc voltage sources. Machines designed to be operated when energized by a dc voltage source are referred to as dc machines.

2.8 THE VOLTAGE DIVIDER

Consider the circuit of Fig. 2.10. Resistors R_1 and R_2 are in series and are connected across a voltage source. The internal resistance of the source may be assumed to have been lumped with R_1, *i.e.*, contained in R_1. The current in the circuit is

$$I = \frac{V}{R_1 + R_2} \qquad \text{...(2.13)}$$

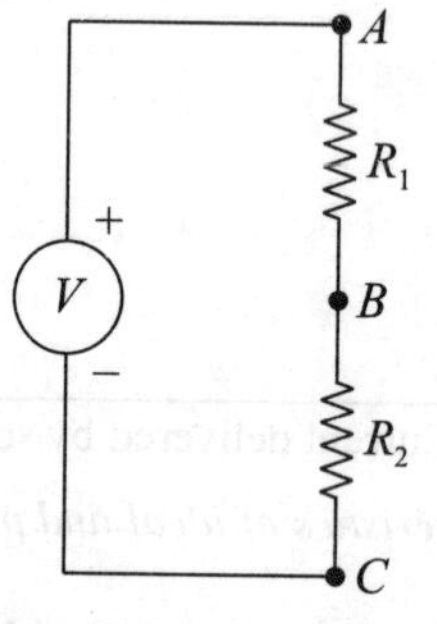

Fig. 2.10 *A simple voltage divider*

The voltage drop from B to C is

$$V_{BC} = \left(\frac{V}{R_1 + R_2}\right) R_2$$

$$= (V_{AC}) \frac{(R_2)}{R_1 + R_2} \qquad \text{...(2.14)}$$

This is the voltage that would be measured by an ideal voltmeter connected between the points B and C. If $R_2 << R_1$ then

$$V_{BC} = V \frac{R_2}{R_1}$$

For example, if $V = 6000$ volts, $R_1 = 50\ \text{k}\Omega$ and $R_2 = 500\ \Omega$

$$V_{BC} = V \frac{500}{50{,}000 + 500}$$

$$\cong \frac{V}{100} = 60 \text{ volts}$$

The voltage divider circuit is used to reduce the voltage to a lower and measurable value thus extending the range of a voltmeter.

There are many values of R_1 and R_2 which satisfy the requirement of a specified ratio of $\frac{R_2}{R_1 + R_2}$ which is known as the *voltage divider ratio*. If the voltage divider is introduced in a circuit to measure voltage, as is usually the case, two conditions must be satisfied.

1. The power consumption of the voltage divider must be small. This implies that the current through the divider should be small and that R_1, therefore, has a high value. If so, it ensures that introduction of the divider circuit (R_1 and R_2) does not have an upsetting influence on the circuit at a node of which the voltage is to be measured.
2. The resistance R_L of any device, such as a voltmeter, connected across the bottom end of the divider, R_2, should be >> R_2. This ensures that the parallel combination of R_2 and R_L is $\approx R_2$ and hence the divider ratio is not upset.

2.9 THE CURRENT DIVIDER

Fig. 2.11 shows an arrangement of two resistors in a circuit which constitutes a current divider. Current I flows into the combination of R_1 and R_2 in parallel. If the current through R_1 is I_1 and that through R_2 is I_2, and the voltage drop from A to B is V_{AB},

$$I_1 = \frac{V_{AB}}{R_1} \qquad ...(2.15)$$

$$I_2 = \frac{V_{AB}}{R_2} \qquad ...(2.16)$$

Also
$$I = \frac{V_{AB}}{R_{eq}}$$

$$= V_{AB}\frac{R_1 + R_2}{R_1 R_2} \qquad ...(2.17)$$

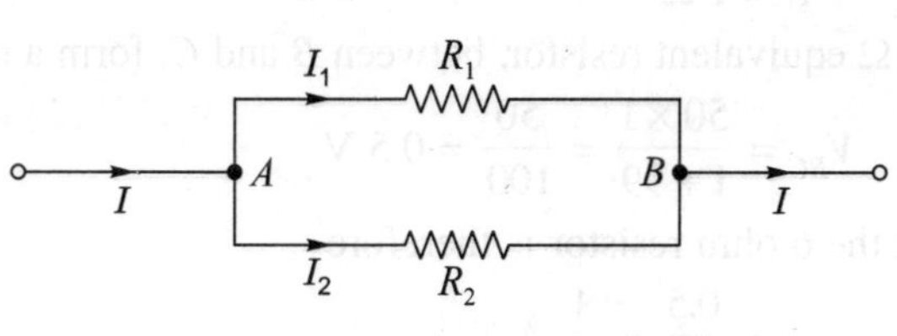

Fig. 2.11 *A current divider*

where R_{eq} is the combination of R_1 and R_2 in parallel.

Substituting for V_{AB} from Eqns. 2.15 and 2.16 in Eqn. 2.17, we obtain

$$I = \frac{I_1(R_1 + R_2)}{R_2} \qquad ...(2.18)$$

and
$$I = \frac{I_2(R_1 + R_2)}{R_1} \qquad ...(2.19)$$

Solving for I_1 and I_2,

$$I_1 = \frac{I R_2}{R_1 + R_2} \qquad ...(2.20)$$

$$I_2 = \frac{I R_1}{R_1 + R_2} \qquad ...(2.21)$$

Equations 2.20 and 2.21 may be used to find the current flow in two resistors connected in parallel given the total current entering the parallel circuit. It is possible to deal with situations with more than two resistors in parallel in a similar fashion.

Example 2.3. *In the circuit (Fig. 2.12), find the current through the 6 Ω resistor using the voltage divider principle.*

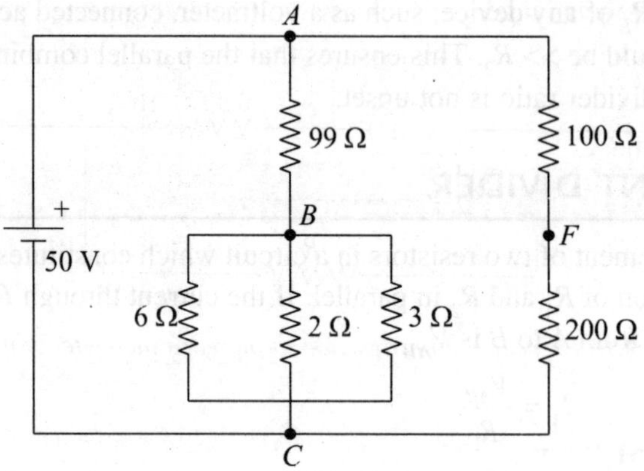

Fig. 2.12

Solution. We notice that the three resistors connected between nodes B and C are in parallel and are equivalent to a single resistor of value R ohms where

$$\frac{1}{R} = \frac{1}{6} + \frac{1}{2} + \frac{1}{3} = \frac{1+3+2}{6} = 1$$

Therefore $R = 1\ \Omega$

The 99 Ω and the 1 Ω equivalent resistor, between B and C, form a divider circuit.

$$V_{BC} = \frac{50 \times 1}{1 + 99} = \frac{50}{100} = 0.5 \text{ V}$$

The current through the 6 ohm resistor is therefore

$$= \frac{0.5}{6} = \frac{1}{12} \text{A.}$$

Note that the 100 and 200 ohm resistors also form a divider circuit. In this example neither of the dividers is being used to measure the voltage; the purpose of the example is to illustrate the application of the voltage divider principle in solving the circuits.

Example 2.4. *It is required to measure a current of 100 A but the only ammeter available has a range of 10A. (Inserting this ammeter in a branch where the current exceeds 10 A will damage the meter). In order to use the ammeter it is decided to connect a resistor in parallel with it. Find the value of this parallel resistor given that the resistance of the meter of 0.5 Ω.*

Solution. The situation is depicted in Fig. 2.13. A denotes the ideal ammeter with zero resistance. The actual instrument is composed of this ideal instrument and a 0.5Ω resistor in series with it. Since the meter can tolerate only 10A, by KCL, the remaining 90A should flow through *R*. Using the current divider principle,

$$90 = 100\frac{0.5}{R+0.5}$$

From the above relation,

$$R = \frac{5}{90}\Omega$$

The resistance *R* is known as a shunt resistor. Precision shunts are connected in parallel with ammeters in order to extend their range.

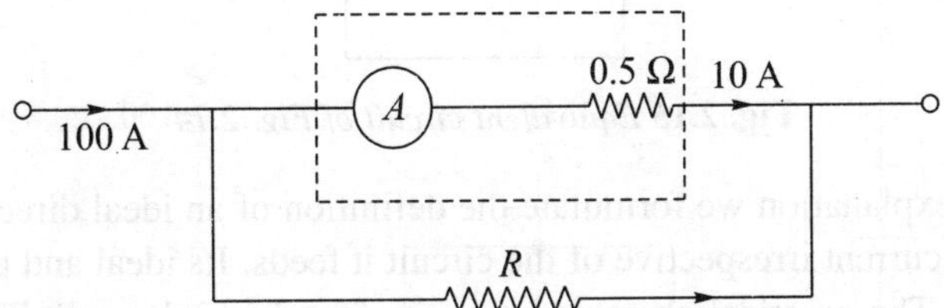

Fig. 2.13 *Precision shunt resistor to increase the meter range*

2.10 CURRENT SOURCES

Since voltage sources are more common place we will explain the concept of a current source with reference to them. Consider the simple circuit of Fig. 2.14 with two resistors R_1 and R_2 in series, the combination being connected to an ideal dc voltage source. The current *I* delivered by the source and flowing through R_1 and R_2, which are in series, is

$$I = \frac{V}{R_1 + R_2} \quad \text{...(2.22)}$$

if $R_1 >>> R_2$ $$I \approx \frac{V}{R_1} \quad \text{...(2.23)}$$

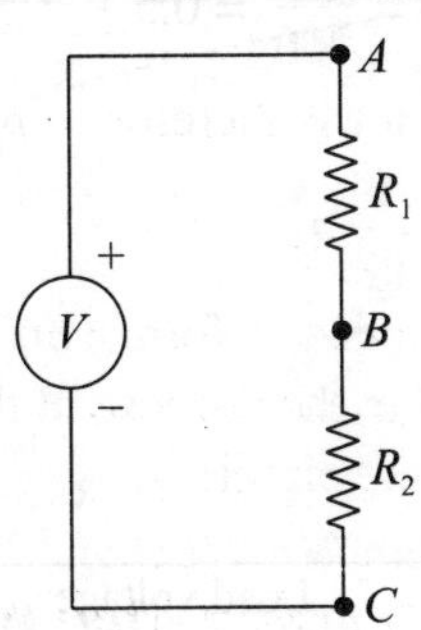

Fig. 2.14 *Series connection of two resistors to an ideal voltage*

If $R_1 >>> R_2$, variation of the value of resistor R_2 will not result in a change in the value of the current flowing through R_2. In other words the arrangement of Fig. 2.14 is equivalent to that in

Fig. 2.15. As far as R_2 is concerned it is connected to a direct current source. The voltage drop across $R_2 = IR_2$

$$= \left(\frac{V}{R_1}\right) R_2 \qquad \text{...(2.24)}$$

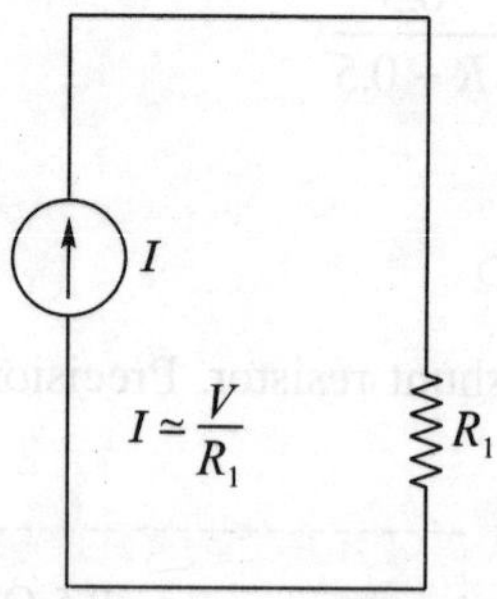

Fig. 2.15 *Equivalent circuit of Fig. 2.14*

From the above explanation we formulate the definition of an ideal direct current source as one which delivers constant current irrespective of the circuit it feeds. Its ideal and practical characteristics are shown in Fig. 2.16. The practical characteristics are found in solar cell. This is a semiconductor device which generates direct current of the order of 25 mA/cm^2 of surface area of the cell when exposed to sunlight. The efficiency of a solar cell is about 10 to 15%.

The practical characteristics of Fig. 2.16 may be explained by taking into account the finite resistance in parallel with such sources, i.e., the internal resistance of the cell, R_i. Let the load resistance be R_L. R_L is in parallel with R_i; as R_L increases, the total resistance increases. The maximum value of the total resistance is R_i and this occurs when $R_L = \infty$. It is clear that with an increase in R_L, the load voltage increases. Also, by application of the current divider rule, the load current decreases. An ideal direct current source, whose symbol is shown in Fig. 2.17, possesses an internal resistance of infinite value; hence it is capable of delivering constant current to any external load connected across it. Fig. 2.17 also shows that a practical current source is modelled by paralleling a resistor of suitable value across an ideal current source.

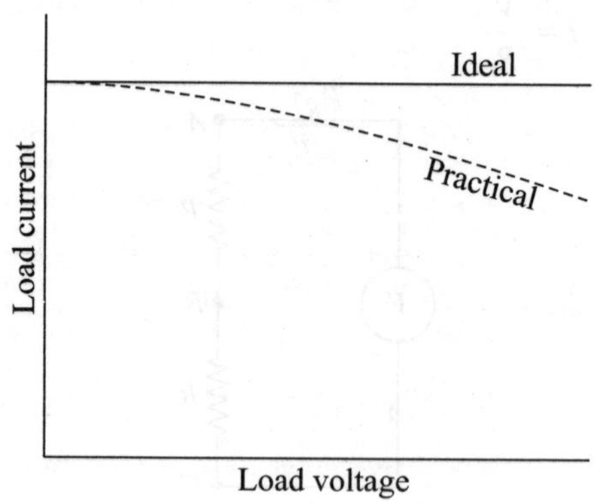

Fig. 2.16 *Ideal and practical characteristics of ideal current source*

Fig. 2.17 *Representation of ideal and practical current sources*

2.11 STAR (WYE) TO DELTA TRANSFORMATIONS

We have seen that resistors connected in series or parallel may be replaced by an equivalent single resistor. What of the arrangement of three resistors shown in Fig. 2.18? The resistors R_1, R_2 and R_3 are neither in series nor in parallel. They are said to be connected in Wye or star (λ) formation. Note that the two diagrams in Fig. 2.18 really represent the same situation. While it is not possible to reduce this arrangement to a single equivalent resistor, it is possible to transform it into another arrangement of three resistors connected between nodes A, B and C as shown in Fig. 2.19. The connection scheme shown by the diagrams in Fig. 2.19 is known as the Δ or delta connection. We will now derive the equivalence between the star and the delta connection schemes.

Since each scheme has three nodes (terminals), we have, in each case, three sets of two terminals. The resistance between one such set say AB in Fig. 2.18 is $= R_1 + R_2$.* If Fig. 2.19 is equivalent to Fig. 2.18, the resistance between terminals A and B in both figures should be the same. In Fig. 2.19, this resistance is the parallel combination of R_C with the series combination of R_A and R_B and is

$$= \left[\frac{1}{R_C} + \frac{1}{(R_A + R_B)}\right]^{-1}$$

$$= R_C\,(R_A + R_B)/((R_A + R_B) + R_C) \qquad \text{...(2.25)}$$

We may therefore write that

$$R_1 + R_2 = \frac{R_C(R_A + R_B)}{(R_A + R_B) + R_C} \qquad \text{...(2.26)}$$

Considering the two remaining terminal pairs, i.e., BC and CA, we obtain

$$R_2 + R_3 = \frac{R_A(R_B + R_C)}{(R_B + R_C) + R_A} \qquad \text{...(2.27)}$$

and

$$R_1 + R_3 = \frac{R_B(R_A + R_C)}{(R_A + R_C) + R_B} \qquad \text{...(2.28)}$$

---

*This may be understood by connecting a voltage source across AB. Since the other end of R_3 (*i.e.*, node C) is not part of the circuit, R_1 and R_2 are effectively in series.

Regarding R_1, R_2 and R_3 as the unknowns, we have three equations in three unknowns. After some algebra we obtain

$$R_1 = \frac{R_B R_C}{R_A + R_B + R_C} \quad ...(2.29)$$

$$R_2 = \frac{R_A R_C}{R_A + R_B + R_C} \quad ...(2.30)$$

$$R_3 = \frac{R_A R_B}{R_A + R_B + R_C} \quad ...(2.31)$$

From the above three equations one can find the values of the resistors in star formation given a set of three connected in delta. To enable the converse, we should express R_A, R_B and R_C in terms of R_1, R_2 and R_3. Again, after some algebra, one obtains

$$R_A = \frac{R_1 R_2 + R_1 R_3 + R_2 R_3}{R_1} \quad ...(2.32)$$

$$R_B = \frac{R_1 R_2 + R_1 R_3 + R_2 R_3}{R_2} \quad ...(2.33)$$

$$R_C = \frac{R_1 R_2 + R_1 R_3 + R_2 R_3}{R_3} \quad ...(2.34)$$

If all the values of the resistors in a star or delta connection are identical,

$$\left.\begin{aligned} R_A = R_B = R_C = R_\Delta \\ R_1 = R_2 = R_3 = R_\lambda \end{aligned}\right\} \quad ...(2.35)$$

and

It is easily shown that, in this case,

$$R_\lambda = \frac{R_\Delta}{3} \quad ...(2.36)$$

The star connection is sometimes referred to as the tee (T) connection; the delta connection is sometimes referred to as the *Pi* (π) connection although it does not resemble a π.

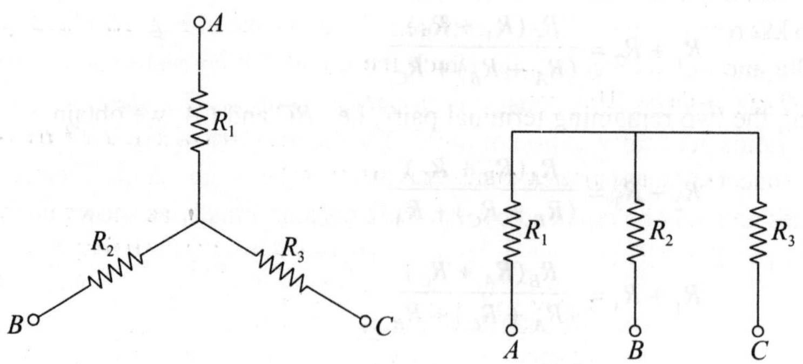

Fig. 2.18 *Resistors connected in star formation*

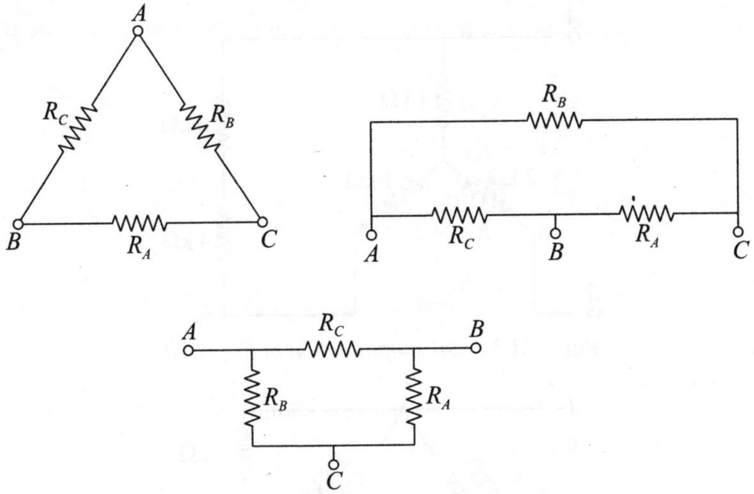

Fig. 2.19 *Resistors connected in delta formation*

Example 2.5. *Reduce the circuit of Fig. 2.20 to one equivalent resistor connected between A and B.*

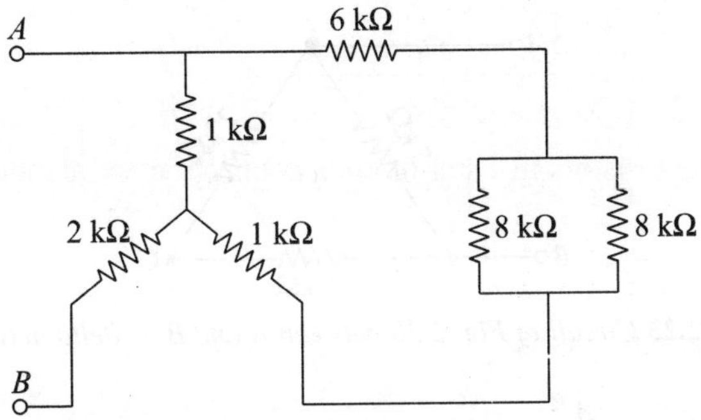

Fig. 2.20 *Problem involving star-delta transformation*

Solution. We notice that the two 1 kΩ resistors and a 2 kΩ resistor are connected in a star configuration. The two 8 kΩ resistors are in parallel and may be replaced by one 4 kΩ resistor which is in series with the 6 kΩ resistor. The circuit therefore reduces to that in Fig. 2.21. In Fig. 2.21 we replace the star with a delta and obtain Fig. 2.22 in which the 6 and 4 kΩ resistors are in series and may be replaced by one 10 kΩ resistor. This resistor is in parallel with the 2.5 kΩ resistor; combining these latter two resistors yields the configuration of Fig. 2.23. The resistors of Fig. 2.23 are connected in delta but node *C* is not connected to any branch other than the branches of the delta. Therefore the 2 and 5 kΩ resistors are in series and may be replaced by one 7 kΩ resistor. Finally as shown in Fig. 2.24 the 5 and 7 kΩ resistor are in parallel. The equivalent resistor between *A* & *B* is therefore

$$\frac{7.10^3 5.10^3}{12.10^3} = \frac{35}{12} \text{ k}\Omega.$$

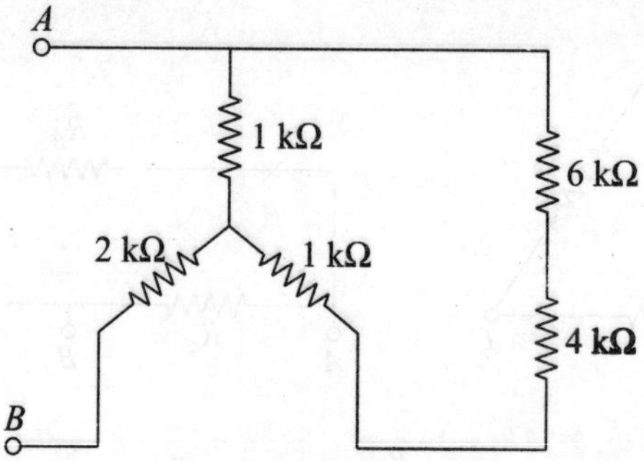

Fig. 2.21 *Partial simplification of Fig. 2.20*

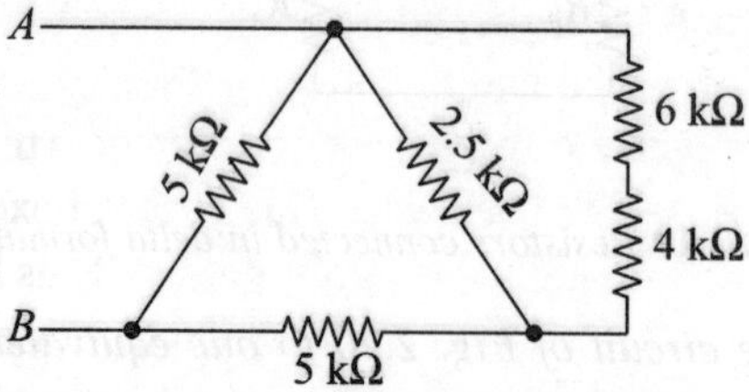

Fig. 2.22 *Conversion of star into its equivalent delta*

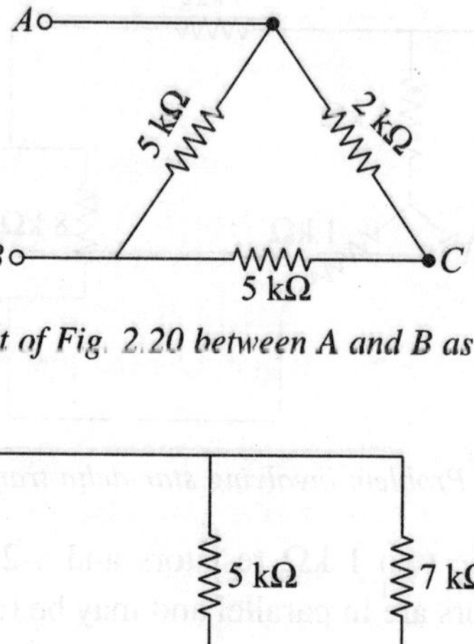

Fig. 2.23 *Circuit of Fig. 2.20 between A and B as delta network*

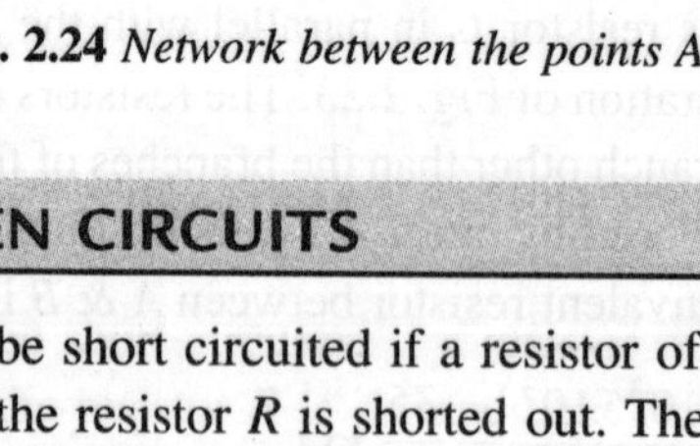

Fig. 2.24 *Network between the points A and B*

2.12 SHORT AND OPEN CIRCUITS

An element or branch is said to be short circuited if a resistor of zero ohms is connected across that element or branch. In Fig. 2.25, the resistor R is shorted out. The two resistors (R Ω and 0 Ω) are in parallel and the effective resistance between points A and B is

$$= (R^{-1} + 0^{-1})^{-1} = 0$$

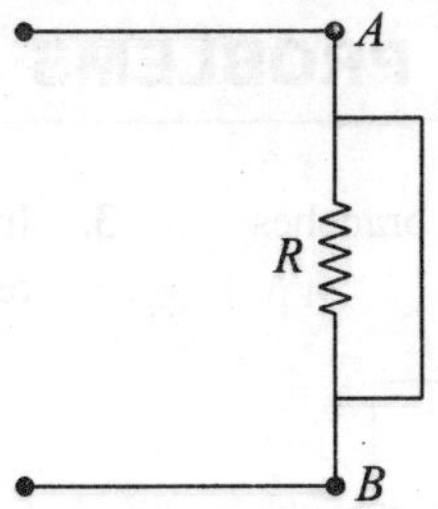

Fig. 2.25 *Connecting a short across a resistor*

Short circuits may be dangerous. Consider the circuit of Fig. 2.10 with V = 100 volts and R_1 = 1 Ω and R_2 = 99 Ω. The current in the circuit flowing through R_1 and R_2 is = 100/(99 + 1) = 1 A. Thus the power dissipation in R_1 is 1 watt and that in R_2 is 99 watts and the resistors have to be rated accordingly. If the R_2 resistor is accidentally shorted out, the current in the circuit becomes 100/1 = 100 A. The power dissipated in the R_1 resistor is 10^4 watts. This is far in excess of its rating and may cause much damage. Furthermore the source is strained severaly, perhaps to its limit, and its useful life shortened. Circuit breakers and fuses protect an installation from the dangerous effects of short circuits.

An open circuit is said to exist when current flow is interrupted either by an accidental break in the circuit or due to the opening of a switch located in the circuit. Any of these actions is the equivalent of inserting a resistor of value infinity ohms in the circuit.

In Eqn. 2.12, V_{ideal} is the open circuit voltage measured at the terminals of the practical voltage source.

2.13 RATINGS OF DC MACHINES AND BATTERIES

A dc machine converts mechanical energy to electrical energy or vice versa. The input to an electric motor is in the form of electrical energy which is converted into mechanical energy and may be used, for example, to drive a lathe.

Direct current operated machines are rated in volts and watts. For example a 50 kW 200 V dc generator can deliver a maximum of $50.10^3/200$ = 250 A at a voltage of 200 volts. A motor rated at 50 kW 200V takes 250 A, from a 200 V dc supply, when it is working at full load. The power input to the motor is the power output divided by the efficiency factor. In the case of the dc generator the electrical power delivered is equal to the mechanical power input multiplied by the overall efficiency.

The full load or nameplate rating of a machine may be exceeded but only for short times in accordance with short time ratings specified by the manufacturer.

In contrast to dc generators, batteries have limited life and due to this reason they are rated in volts and ampere hours rather than volts and watts. A battery rated at 12 V, 250 ampere hours can supply a steady current of 1 A at 12 V for 250 hours or 5 A at 12 V for 50 hours. The ampere hour rating increases with temperature of the electrolyte and decreases with increasing current supplied by the battery.

As a battery's life approaches the end, its internal resistance increases and the output voltage for a specified load current is lesser than the corresponding value of the same battery in a fully charged state.

PROBLEMS

1. In Fig. P.2.1 find the number of nodes, branches and loops.

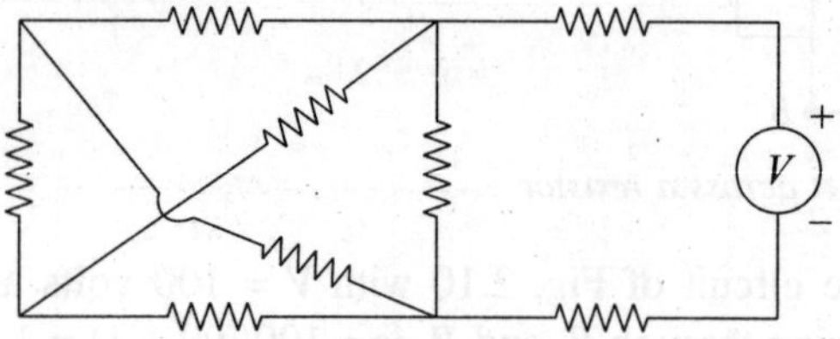

Fig. P.2.1

2. In Figs. P2.2*a* to *c* find the current through all the resistors, voltage across them and the power dissipated.

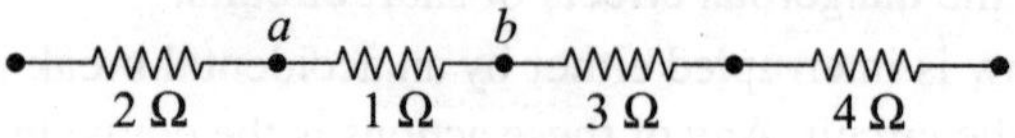

$V_{ab} = 4$ V

Fig. P.2.2a

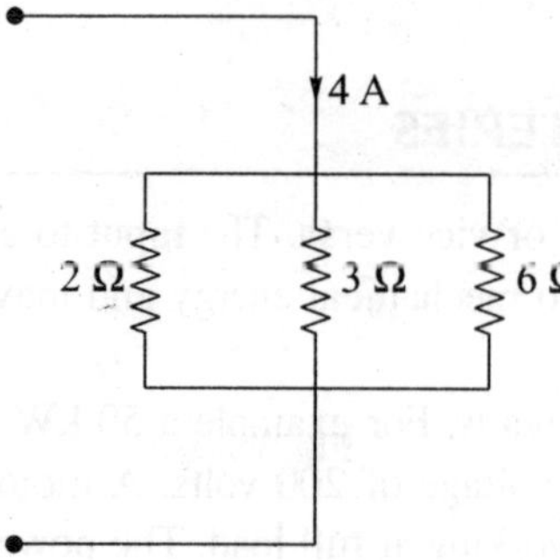

Fig. P.2.2b

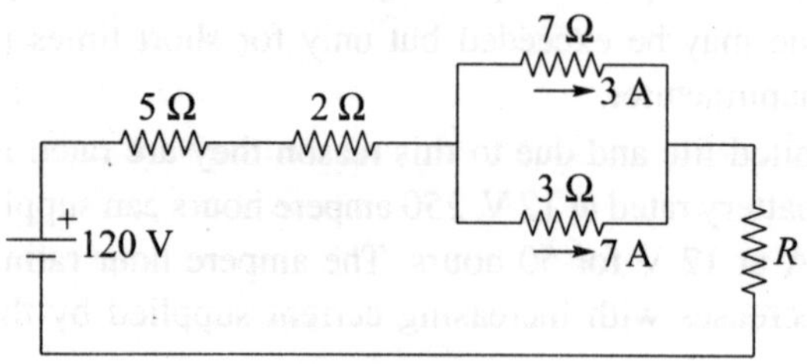

Fig. P.2.2c

3. In Fig. P.2.3 estimate the voltage across the resistor R_4.

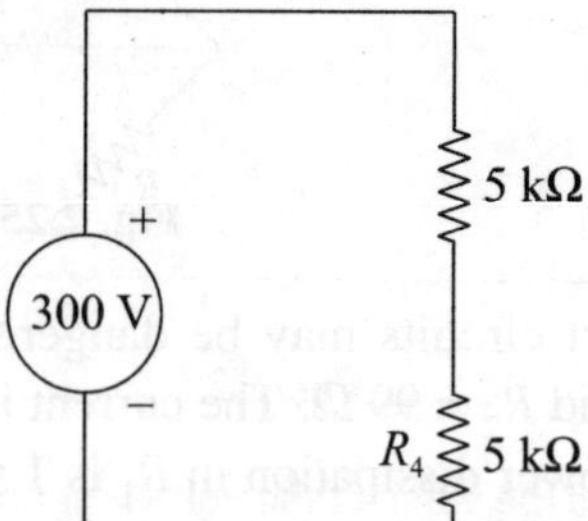

Fig. P.2.3

4. In Fig. P.2.4 make an estimate of the current division a many resistors assuming the resistors to have ohmic values R_1, R_2 and R_3.

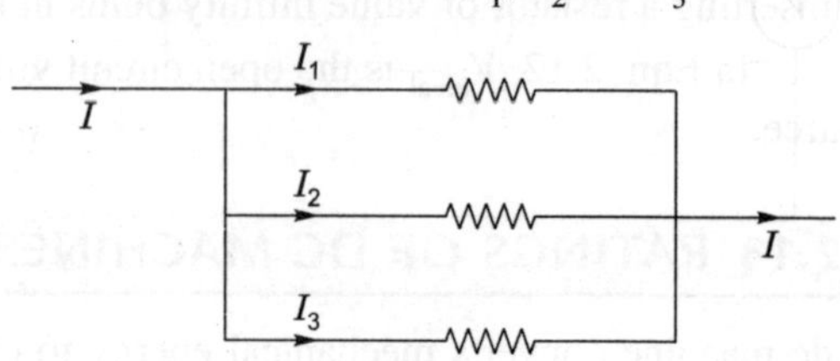

Fig. P.2.4

5. In Fig. P2.5 find the value of the source voltage such that a current of 2A flows through 6Ω resistor.

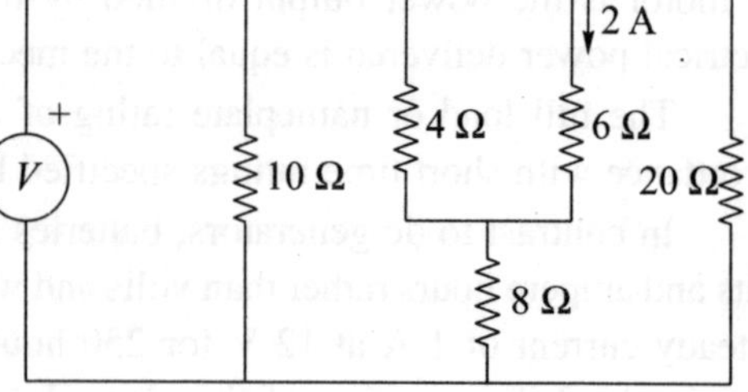

Fig. P.2.5

6. Find the current through the resistance R of Fig. P.2.6.

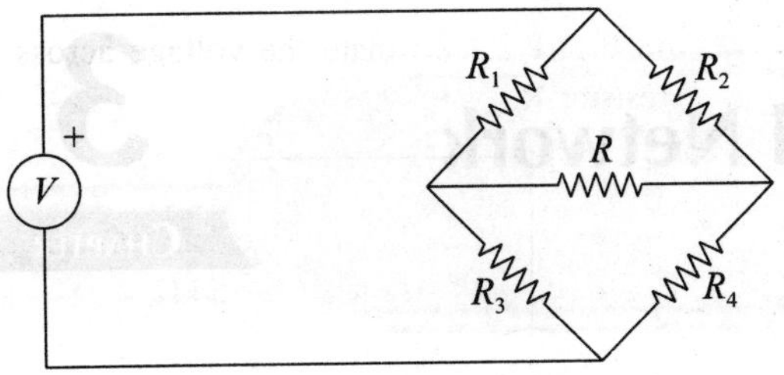

Fig. P.2.6

7. Find the value of the voltage source in Fig. P.2.7 which will drop 20V across 10Ω resistance.

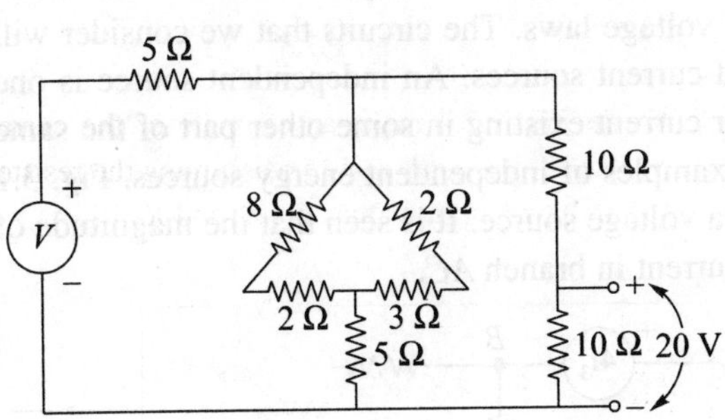

Fig. P.2.7

8. Find the value of the equivalent resistance between the points AB and CD in Figs. P.2.8a

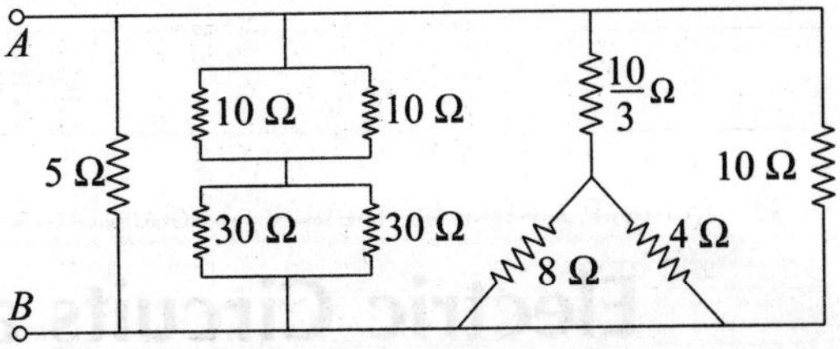

Fig. P.2.8a

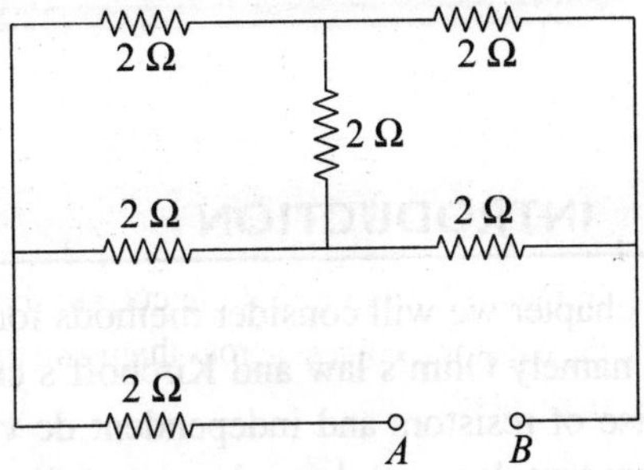

Fig. P.2.8b

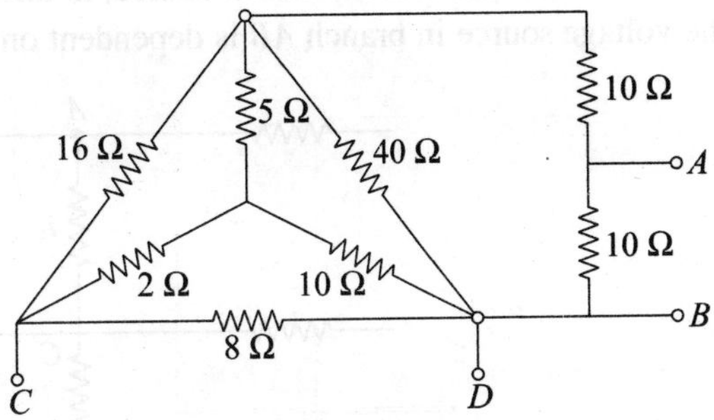

Fig. P.2.8c

CHAPTER 2

Electric Circuits and Network Theorems

3

CHAPTER

3.1 INTRODUCTION

In this chapter we will consider methods for solving the electric circuits using the basic laws of circuit theory namely Ohm's law and Kirchoff's current and voltage laws. The circuits that we consider will comprise of resistors and independent dc voltage and current sources. An independent source is one whose output does not depend on any other voltage or current existing in some other part of the same circuit. Batteries, power supplies and solar cells are examples of independent energy sources. Fig. 3.1 shows an example of a dependent source, in this case a voltage source. It is seen that the magnitude of the voltage source in branch *AB* is dependent on the current in branch *AC*.

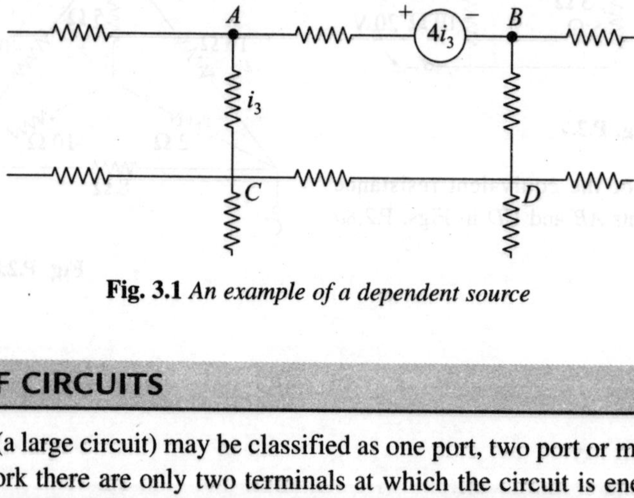

Fig. 3.1 *An example of a dependent source*

3.2 TYPES OF CIRCUITS

Circuits, or networks (a large circuit) may be classified as one port, two port or multi-port. In a one port or two terminal network there are only two terminals at which the circuit is energized by an external source. The response to such a stimulus is measured at the same two terminals only. An example of a one port network is shown in Fig. 3.2*a*. If the response is measured at another pair of terminals, the circuit is known as a two port or four terminal network. Such a circuit is shown in Fig. 3.2*b*. If terminals *B* and *D* in Fig. 3.2*b*, are joined together the circuit becomes a two port three terminal circuit. Most problems in circuit theory involve the solution of one and two port circuits. A circuit is said to be solved when all branch currents and voltages are known; further calculations such as amount of power dissipated etc. may be carried out if called for.

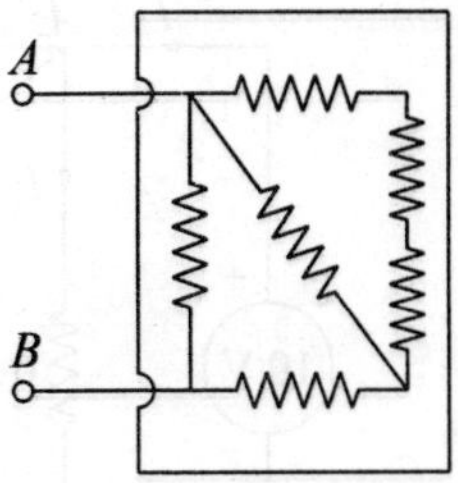

Fig. 3.2*a* A *one port circuit*

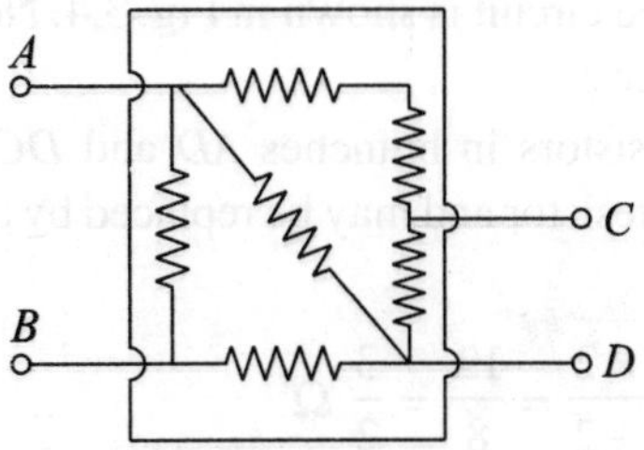

Fig. 3.2*b* A *two port network*

3.3 NETWORK REDUCTION METHOD

Consider a one port network comprised only of resistors as in Fig. 3.2*a*. The only energy source is external to the network and connected between *A* and *B* . In order to solve the circuit the following steps may be followed:

1. Reduce the resistive network to an equivalent resistor between nodes *A* and *B*. To accomplish this, use appropriate series and parallel combinations or star delta transformations or both.
2. The circuit is now reduced to one resistor across a current or a voltage source and the current flowing through the equivalent resistor and the voltage across it are easily found.
3. Next, we work our way backwards retracing the steps we took in step 1. By use of the current divider rule and basic laws we find the current and voltage associated with all the other branches of the circuit.

The following example serves to illustrate the procedure outlined above.

Example 3.1. *In the one port circuit of Fig. 3.3, find the current in the 2 Ω resistors in branches BD and DC by network reduction.*

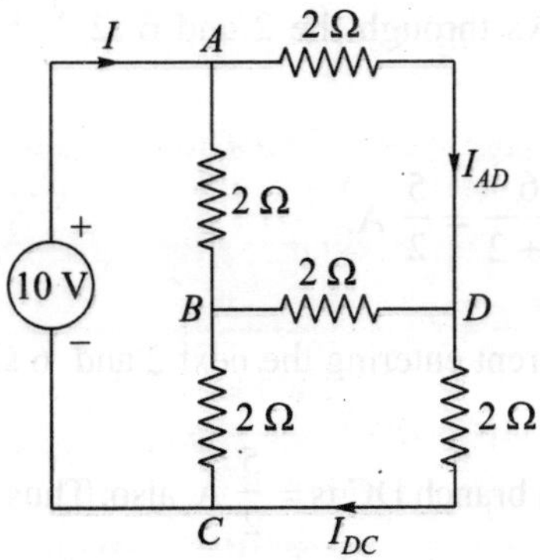

Fig. 3.3 *A one port network*

Solution. The three 2 Ω resistors which share node *B* are connected in star. Convert this to a delta connection.

From Eqn. 2.36 $R_\Delta = 3\ R_\lambda = 6\ \Omega$

The modified circuit is shown in Fig. 3.4. Note that node B is lost in the process.

The 6 Ω resistors in branches AD and DC are each in parallel with a 2 Ω resistor and may be replaced by an equivalent resistor of value

$$\frac{6\times 2}{6+2}=\frac{12}{8}=\frac{3}{2}\ \Omega.$$

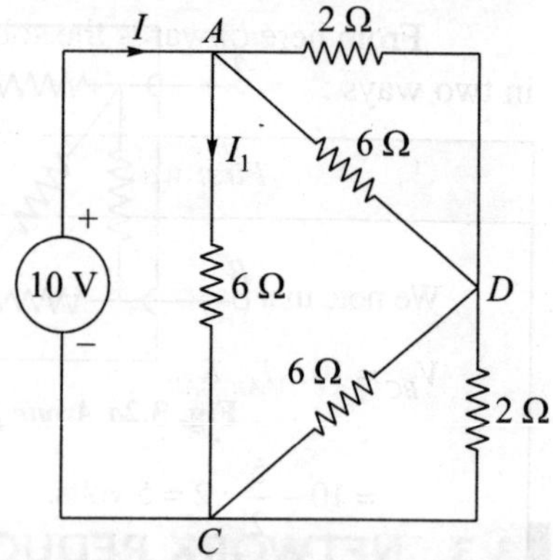

Fig. 3.4 *Reduction of network in Fig. 3.3*

Figure 3.4 therefore reduces to Fig. 3.5. In Fig. 3.2*a* 10 V drop occurs from A to C along the 6Ω resistor and from A to C along the two $\frac{3}{2}$ Ω resistors in series. From Fig. 3.5,

$$I_2 = I_{AD} = I_{DC}$$

$$=\frac{10}{\frac{3}{2}+\frac{3}{2}}=\frac{10}{3}\ \text{A.}$$

I_{DC} obtained in this step is not the current in the 2Ω resistor joining nodes D and C.

From Fig. 3.5,

$$I_1=\frac{10}{6}=\frac{5}{3}\ \text{A}$$

The current delivered by the source is

$$I = I_1 + I_2 = 5\ \text{A}$$

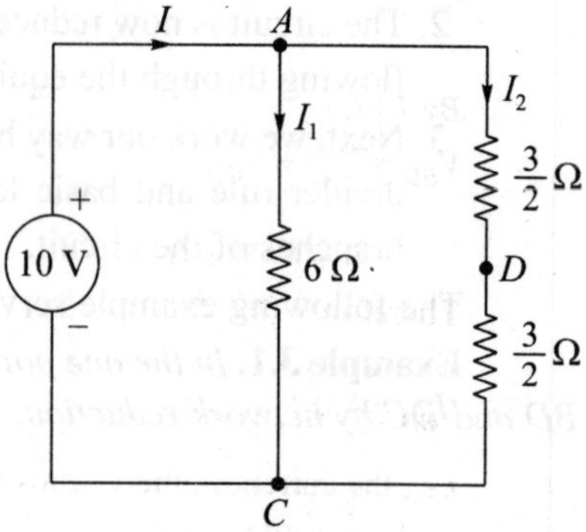

Fig. 3.5 *Further reduction of network of Fig. 3.4*

The currents I and I_1 are identified in Fig. 3.4. We know that $I_2 = I - I_1 = \frac{10}{3}$ A. This flows through the 2 and 6 Ω combination at node A. Thus,

$$I_{2\Omega}=\frac{10}{3}\cdot\frac{6}{6+2}=\frac{5}{2}\ \text{A.}$$

At node D, Fig. 3.4, the current entering the next 2 and 6 Ω combination is $=\frac{10}{3}$ A.

and the current in the 2Ω resistor in branch DC is $=\frac{5}{2}$ A also. Thus $I_{AD} = I_{DC} = \frac{5}{2}$ *A in Figs. 3.3 and 3.4.*

From Fig. 3.3 at node A

$$I_{AB} = I - \frac{5}{2}$$

$$= 5 - \frac{5}{2}$$

$$= \frac{5}{2}\ \text{A}$$

From here onwards the solution for the current in the 2Ω resistor in branch *BD* may be obtained in two ways :

First way	*Second way*
We note that $V_{BC} = 10 - I_{AB} R_{AB}$ $= 10 - \frac{5}{2} \cdot 2 = 5$ volts.	We know that $I_{AB} = \frac{5}{2}$ *A*. This current divides at node B into branches *BD* and *BC*. Using the current divider rule.
Also $V_{DC} = 10 - I_{AD} R_{AD}$ $= 10 - \frac{5}{2} \cdot 2 = 5$ volts.	$I_{BD} = \frac{5}{2} \frac{2}{2+2} = \frac{5}{4}$ *A* from *B* to *D*. The current I_{AD} divides at node *D* into branches *DB* and *DC*. The current in branch *BD* due to I_{AD} is $I_{BD} = -\frac{5}{2} \frac{2}{2+2} = \frac{5}{4}$ A
By KVL $V_{BD} = V_{BC} + V_{CD}$ $= 5 + (-5) = 0$ Therefore, $I_{BD} = -0$	The –ve sign signifies that current flows from node *D* to node *B*. The total current in branch *BD* is therefore $\frac{5}{4} - \frac{5}{4} = 0$
i.e., the current in the 2 Ω resistor in branch BD is = 0.	*i.e.*, the current in the 2 Ω resistor in branch *BD* = 0.

The method of network reduction is best applied to one port passive networks (*i.e.*, no energy sources inside).

Before we proceed to discuss another method of circuit solution we will study the solution obtained in example 3.1 shown in Fig. 3.6 in order to highlight a few important points. First, KCL is satisfied at all nodes. Second, KVL is true for any closed loop. Taking loop *A′ABDCC′A′* and traversing it in the clockwise sense, one obtains.

$$V_{C'A'} + V_{A'A} + V_{AB} + V_{BD} + V_{DC} + V_{CC'}$$

$$= -10 + 5(0) + \frac{5}{2}(2) + 0(2) + \frac{5}{2}(2) + 5(0)$$

$$= -10 + 5 + 5 = 0$$

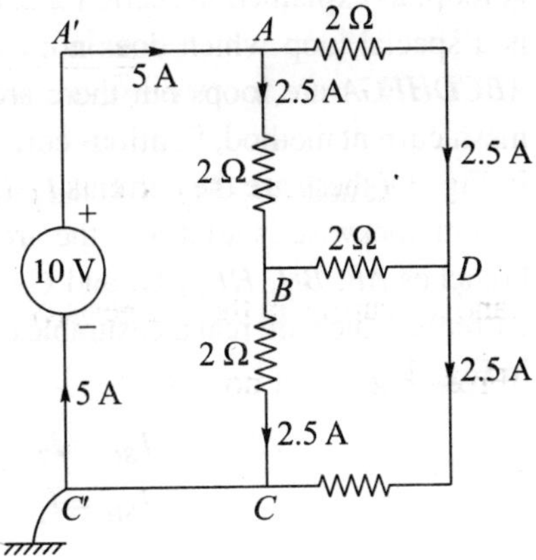

Fig. 3.6 *Network of Fig. 3.3*

Thirdly, in most circuits, the voltages at various nodes are measured with respect to a common node or reference, usually grounded, and therefore at zero potential. In Fig. 3.6 we choose C' to be ground. In circuit diagrams the connection of a node to ground is represented by connecting to that node the symbol ⏚ or ⏊.

We obtain, $$V_{A'C'} = V_{A'} = 10 \text{ V} = V_A$$
$$V_B = V_A - 2.5(2) = 5 \text{ V} = V_D$$
and $$V_C = V_{C'} = 0$$

The voltage drop across any branch is the difference in the nodal voltages of that branch

$$V_{AB} = V_A - V_B = 10 - 5 = 5 \text{ V}$$
and $$V_{CB} = V_C - V_B = 0 - 5 = -5 \text{ V}$$

If we choose to ground some other node in the circuit, the nodal voltages change but the voltage drops across each branch remain the same. For example, if we ground node D, the nodal voltages at the various nodes are

If we choose to ground some other node in the circuit, the nodal voltages change but the voltage drops across each branch remain the same. For example, if we ground node D, the nodal voltages at the various nodes are

$$V_{A'} = V_{A'C'} + V_{C'C} + V_{CD}$$
$$= 10 + 0 - 5 = 5 \text{ V}$$
$$V_C = -5 \text{ V}$$
$$V_B = 0$$
$$V_A = V_{A'} = 5 \text{ V}$$

For the branch drops we obtain

$$V_{AB} = V_A - V_B = 5 - 0 = 5 \text{ V and so on.}$$

3.4 THE MESH CURRENT METHOD

A loop, as explained in section 2.2, consists of branches of a circuit which form a closed path. A mesh is a special loop which does not contain any other loop. In Fig. 3.7, for example, *ABCDEFGA* and *ABCDHFGA* are loops but there are only three meshes, i.e., *ABHFGA*, *BCDHB* and *HDEFH*. In the mesh current method, fictitious currents known as mesh currents are assumed to circulate in the meshes. In Fig. 3.7 these are the currents I_1, I_2 and I_3. The direction of the assigned mesh current flow, clockwise or anticlockwise is arbitrary; the arrow head indicates the assumed direction. Thus current I_1 flows in branches *AB*, *BH*, *HF*, *FG*, and *GA*. Likewise I_2 flows in branches *BC*, *CD*, *DH* and *HB*. The branch currents, which are real measurable currents, may be obtained in terms of the mesh currents. For example, in Fig. 3.7

$$\left.\begin{aligned} I_{BC} &= I_2 \\ I_{BH} &= I_1 - I_2 = -I_{HB} \end{aligned}\right\} \qquad \text{...(3.1)}$$

and so on.

Let us suppose that in a circuit there exists a total of m meshes ($m = 3$ in Fig. 3.7). Kirchoff's voltage law is written for each of the m meshes to yield m equations in the m unknown mesh currents. Solving the set of simultaneous equations one obtains all the mesh currents and therefore all branch currents and voltages. Since the KVL equations are written for all the meshes in the circuit it is important to know how many meshes exist. Fortunately, application of a simple rule determines this. The total number of meshes, m in a circuit is given by

$$m = b - n + 1 \quad \text{... (3.2)}$$

where b = # of branches

and n = # of nodes

In Fig. 3.7, $b = 10$, $n = 8$ and therefore $m = 3$. If we decide to eliminate node C by combining the resistors in branches BC and CD we obtain

$$b = 9, n = 7 \text{ and once again, } m = 3.$$

The steps involved in the solution of a circuit by the mesh current method are as follows:

(1) Mark all nodes clearly. Find out the total number of nodes, n, the total number of branches, b, and use Eqn. 3.2 to find m, the total number of meshes.

(2) Identify the meshes and assign mesh currents in any direction (clockwise or anticlockwise).

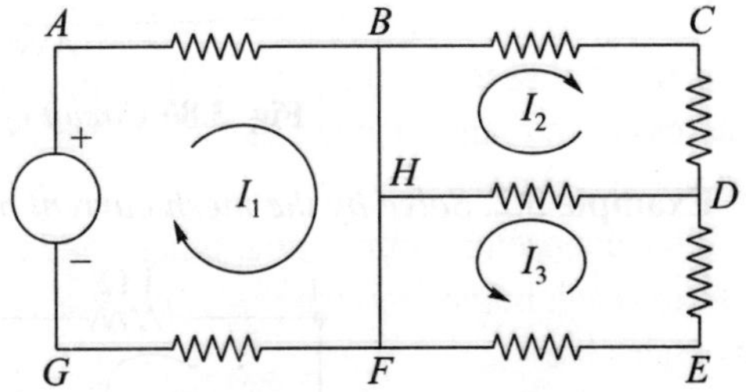

Fig. 3.7 *A circuit with 6 loops with only 3 meshes*

(3) Write down KVL for each mesh.

(4) Solve the simultaneous equations obtained in step 3, for all mesh currents.

(5) Obtain all branch currents from the mesh currents; perform further calculations if necessary.

Before we illustrate the method with examples, it is worth mentioning that often, and especially for simple circuits, the total number of mesh equations (meshes) may be found by inspection. To do this.

(1) Draw the circuit so that no branches intersect one another except at nodes.

(2) The number of meshes, m, is equal to the number of windows in the two dimensional drawing of the circuit.

For example, Fig. 3.8a shows a circuit with intersecting branches. This is redrawn in Fig. 3.8b so that these intersections are eliminated. The meshes are numbered in the same figure.

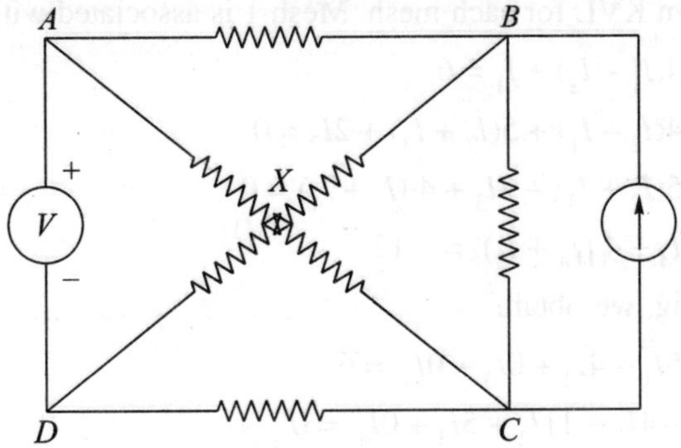

Fig. 3.8a *A nonplanar circuit*

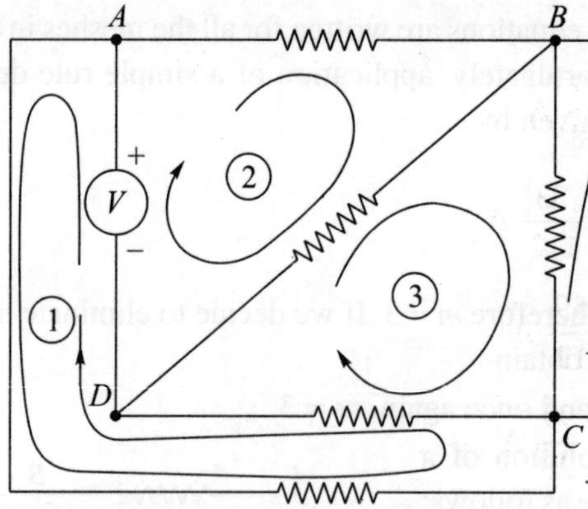

Fig. 3.8*b* *Circuit of Fig. 3.8 (a) rearranged*

Example 3.2. *Solve by the mesh current method the circuit of Fig. 3.9.*

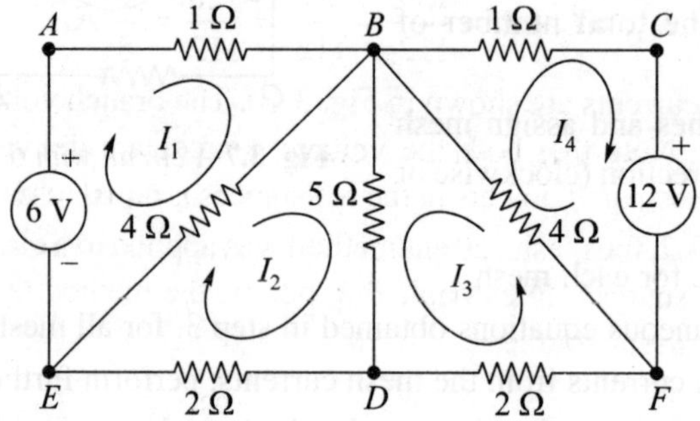

Fig. 3.9

Solution.

Step 1 $n = 6$

$b = 9$

$m = 9 - 6 + 1 = 4$

Step 2 The mesh currents are I_1, I_2, I_3, and I_4.

Step 3 Write down KVL for each mesh. Mesh 1 is associated with current I_1 and so on.

Mesh 1 $4(I_1 - I_2) + I_1 = 6$

Mesh 2 $4(I_2 - I_1) + 5(I_2 + I_3) + 2I_2 = 0$ ...(3.3)

Mesh 3 $5(I_2 + I_3) + 2I_3 + 4(I_3 + I_4) = 0$

Mesh 4 $I_4 + 4(I_4 + I_3) = -12$

Simplifying, we obtain

Mesh 1 $5I_1 - 4I_2 + 0I_3 + 0I_4 = 6$

Mesh 2 $-4I_1 + 11I_2 + 5I_3 + 0I_4 = 0$ ...(3.4)

Mesh 3 $0I_1 + 5I_2 + 11I_3 + 4I_4 = 0$

Mesh 4 $0I_1 + 0I_2 + 4I_3 + 5I_4 = -12$

Step 4 Solving Eqns. 3.4,

$$I_1 = \frac{27}{28} \text{ A}$$

$$I_2 = -\frac{33}{112} \text{ A}$$

$$I_3 = \frac{159}{112} \text{ A}$$

and $$I_4 = -\frac{99}{28} \text{ A}$$

Note that I_2 and I_4 are negative. This means that the directions of flow of these mesh currents is opposite to that indicated in Fig. 3.9.

Step 5 The branch currents are obtained as explained in Eqn. 3.1. For example,

$$I_{5\,\Omega} = I_2 + I_3 = \frac{159}{112} - \frac{33}{112} = \frac{126}{112} = \frac{9}{8} \text{ A.}$$

The branch currents are shown in Fig. 3.10. The branch voltages and powers may now be obtained. Note that both the voltage sources are delivering power. Naturally the sum of the dissipated powers in the resistances is equal to that delivered by the sources. In example 3.2, the mesh current method was applied to a circuit comprising of resistors and voltage sources. In example 3.3, below, the method is applied to a circuit which contains a current source.

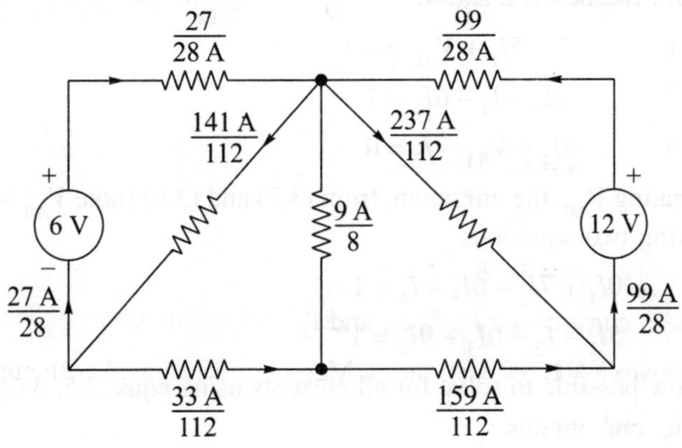

Fig. 3.10 *Branch currents of circuit in Fig. 3.9*

Example 3.3. *Solve the circuit of Fig. 3.11 by the mesh current method.*

Solution

Step 1 $n = 5 \quad b = 8 \quad m = 4$

Step 2 The assumed mesh currents are shown in Fig. 3.11.

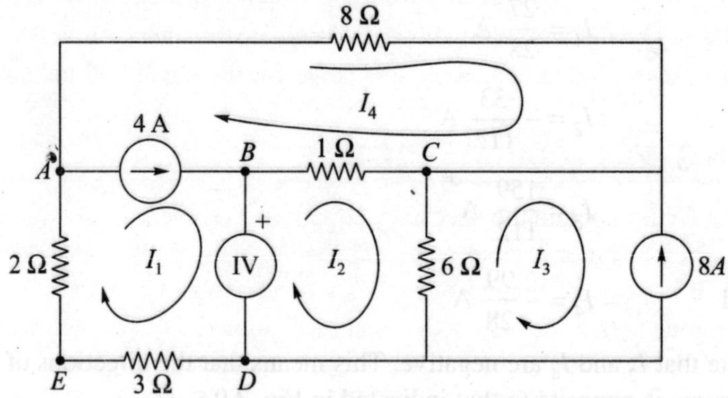

Fig. 3.11 *Illustration of mesh current method, Ex. 3.3*

Step 3 Write down KVL for each mesh. Since the voltage drop across the current sources, in the meshes 1, 3 and 4 are not known, we are unable to write down KVL for these without introducing two more unknowns.

However, we notice that

$$I_3 = -8 \quad ...(3.5)$$

Also $I_1 - I_4 = 4$ ...(3.6)

Thus one mesh current is already solved for. We now proceed with the writing of KVL eqns. for meshes 1, 2 and 4.

Mesh 1 $5I_1 + V_{AB} = -1$ ...(3.7)

Mesh 2 $7I_2 - I_4 - 6I_3 = 1$ ...(3.8)

Mesh 4 $9I_4 + V_{BA} - I_2 = 0$ ...(3.9)

Eliminating V_{AB}, the unknown, from (3.7) and (3.9) (note $V_{AB} + V_{BA} = 0$) we obtain the following two equations

$$0I_1 + 7I_2 - 6I_3 - I_4 = 1 \quad ...(3.10)$$

and $5I_1 - I_2 + 0I_3 + 9I_4 = 1$ ...(3.11)

It is now possible to solve for all currents using eqns. 3.5, 3.6, 3.10 and 3.11.

Step 4 Solving, one obtains

$$I_1 = 2\text{A}$$
$$I_2 = -7\text{A}$$
$$I_3 = -8\text{A} \quad ...(3.12)$$
$$I_4 = -2\text{A}$$

Step 5 The branch currents are obtained as in the previous case and further calculations may be performed.

The application of the mesh current method to problems involving current sources is summarized in the following:

(1) Look for relations between mesh currents or mesh currents that are obtainable by inspection.

(2) Write down KVL (step 3) for all meshes with unknown currents. The voltage drop across current sources are additional unknowns. Eliminate the unknown voltage drop and introduce the relations identified in (1) above, and solve for the remaining unknowns.

3.5 THE NODE VOLTAGE METHOD

This method relies on KCL to obtain the necessary equations to solve for the unknowns. In a circuit one node is chosen as the reference or ground node and the voltages of all other nodes are measured with respect to this node. It is possible that a voltage source connects one or more nodes to the reference node. In this case the node voltage at such nodes is known. At nodes whose voltages are unknown, KCL is written in terms of the node voltages and the branch resistances. This process yields a system of simultaneous equations involving the unknown nodal voltages. Solution of the equations yields these voltages. Branch currents etc. may then be found and further calculations performed if necessary. The steps involved in application of the node voltage method are:

(1) Identify the nodes of a circuit. Choose one node as a reference node. Preferably this should be one which has the most number of branches emanating from it.

(2) Identify nodes at which the node voltage (voltage at the node with respect to reference node) is known.

(3) Write down KCL for the remaining nodes in terms of the unknown nodal voltages.

(4) Solve the system of equations obtained in step 3.

(5) Solve for branch currents: perform additional calculations if necessary.

Example 3.4. *Solve the circuit of Fig. 3.12 using the node voltage method.*

Solution.

Step 1 $n = 4$

Choose D as the reference node. All node voltages are now measured with respect to D.

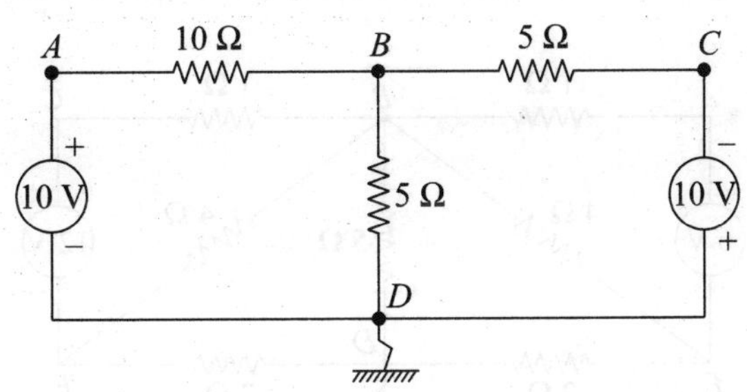

Fig. 3.12 *Solving network problem using node voltage method*

Step 2 We notice that $V_{AD} = V_A = +\,10\text{ V}$

and $V_{CD} = V_C = -\,10\text{ V}$

Step 3 The only remaining node is node B.

At this node by KCL,

$$I_{BC} + I_{BD} + I_{BA} = 0 \qquad \text{...(3.13)}$$

In eqn. 3.13 I_{BA} means the current flowing from B to A and so on

but $$I_{BA} = \frac{V_B - V_A}{10} = \frac{V_B - 10}{10}$$

Similarly $$I_{BD} = \frac{V_B}{5}$$

and $$I_{BC} = \frac{V_B - V_C}{5} = \frac{V_B + 10}{5} \text{ as } V_C = -10 \text{ V}$$

Substituting in Eqn. 3.13,

$$\frac{V_B + 10}{5} + \frac{V_B}{5} + \frac{V_B - 10}{10} = 0 \quad ..(3.14)$$

Step 4 In this case there is only one equation and one unknown. From Eqn.3.14,

$$V_B = -2 \text{ volts.}$$

Step 5 The branch currents are

$$I_{BA} = \frac{-2 - 10}{10} = -1.2 \text{ A}$$

$$I_{BD} = \frac{-2}{5} = -0.4 \text{ A}$$

and $$I_{BC} = \frac{-2 + 10}{10} = +1.6 \text{ A}$$

Additional computations *i.e.*, calculation of branch voltages and powers may now be performed. Note that we could have written, in step 3,

$$I_{CB} + I_{DB} + I_{AB} = 0 \quad ...(3.15)$$

instead of Eqn. 3.13. In any event the same result is obtained.

Example 3.5. *In this example we solve the circuit of example 3.2 shown in Fig. 3.13 using the node voltage method.*

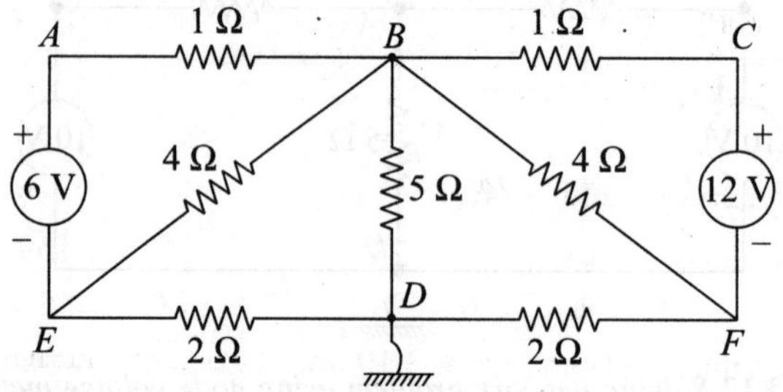

Fig. 3.13

Solution. We shall solve this problem using two approaches.

Approach I

Step 1 Here we treat the 1 Ω resistors in branches AB and BC as internal resistances of the 6 volt and the 12 volt voltage source respectively. Nodes A and C disappear and with D chosen as the reference node the nodes at which the voltages have to be solved for are B, E and F.

Step 2 We do not know the voltages at any node with respect to node D but we do know that

$$V_{AE} = V_A - V_E = 6 \quad ...(3.16)$$

and $$V_{CF} = V_C - V_F = 12 \quad ...(3.17)$$

Step 3 At node B, KCL yields

$$I_{BAE} + I_{BE} + I_{BD} + I_{BF} + I_{BCF} = 0 \quad ...(3.18)$$

In Eqn. 3.18 note that I_{BAE} and I_{BCF} are currents flowing away from node B, through sources, to nodes E and F, respectively

Now $$I_{BAE} = \frac{V_{BA}}{1} = V_{BA}$$

and $V_B - V_{BA} - V_{AE} = V_E$ ...(3.19)

Substituting V_{AE} from Eqn. 3.16 in 3.19,

$$V_B - V_{BA} - 6 = V_E \quad \text{or} \quad I_{BAE} = V_{BA} = V_B - V_E - 6 \quad ...(3.20)$$

Similarly,

$$I_{BCF} = \frac{V_{BC}}{1} = V_{BC} = V_B - V_F - 12 \quad ...(3.21)$$

Inserting I_{BAE} and I_{BCF} from Eqns. 3.20, 3.21 in Eqn. 3.18 and inserting suitable expressions for the remaining currents, I_{BE}, I_{BD} and I_{BF},

$$V_B - V_E - 6 + \frac{V_B - V_E}{4} + \frac{V_B}{5} + \frac{V_B - V_F}{4} + V_B - V_F - 12 = 0$$

or $$54\,V_B - 25\,V_E - 25\,V_F = 360 \quad ...(3.22)$$

At node E, application of KCL yields

$$\frac{V_E + 6 - V_B}{1} + \frac{V_E - V_B}{4} + \frac{V_E}{2} = 0$$

or $$7V_E - 7V_B = -24 \quad ...(3.23)$$

Lastly, at node F

$$\frac{V_F + 12 - V_B}{1} + \frac{V_F - V_B}{4} + \frac{V_F}{2} = 0$$

or $$V_F - 5\,V_B = -48 \quad ...(3.24)$$

Step 4 Solving 3.22, 3.23 and 3.24,

$$V_B = \frac{45}{8}\text{ V},\ V_E = \frac{23}{56}\text{ V} \quad \text{and} \quad V_F = \frac{-159}{56}\text{ V}.$$

V_A and V_C may be found from 3.19 and 3.20 and additional calculations performed if necessary.

Approach II

Step I We retain nodes A and C. Choose D as the reference node. We need to solve for the node voltages V_A, V_B, V_C, V_E and V_F.

Step II None of the node voltages are known but

$$V_A - V_E = 6 \quad ...(3.25)$$

and $$V_C - V_F = 12 \quad ...(3.26)$$

CHAPTER 3

Step III At node B we obtain

$$54V_B - 20V_A - 5V_E - 5V_F - 20V_C = 0 \qquad ...(3.27)$$

Using Eqns. 3.25 and 3.26 in Eqn. 3.27 we eliminate V_A and V_C and obtain

$$54V_B - 25V_E - 25V_F = 360 \qquad ...(3.28)$$

We need two more equations but find it difficult to obtain them at nodes A, E, C and F. This is because at each of these nodes we have a problem in writing down the expression for the current flowing through the voltage source. At node A, for example, $I_{AE} \dfrac{V_A - V_E}{0} = \infty$ but $I_{AE} \neq \infty$. In fact $I_{AE} = I_{BA}$ by KCL! To overcome this difficulty we write KCL in another fashion. Use is made of the fact that the current entering the source is equal to that leaving it or, the sum of the currents entering or leaving the source is = 0. For the 6V source,

$$\frac{(V_B - V_A)}{1} + \frac{V_B - V_E}{4} + \frac{0 - V_E}{2} = 0$$

or

$$5V_B - 4V_A - 3V_E = 0 \qquad ...(3.29)$$

Using Eqn. 3.25 in 3.29,

$$5V_B - 7V_E = 24 \qquad ...(3.30)$$

The 12 V source is handled similarly and we obtain

$$5V_B - 7V_F = 48 \qquad ...(3.31)$$

Eqns. 3.28, 3.30 and 3.31 may be used to solve for V_B, V_E and V_F. The solution then proceeds as usual.

In the above example, Eqn. 3.29 may be considered to have been obtained at the super node shown in Fig. 3.14. KCL is written for this giant node as for any other node.

We conclude our discussion of the node voltage method by considering the circuit of example 3.3.

Example 3.6. *Solve the circuit of Fig. 3.11 using the node voltage method.*

Solution.

Step 1 Choose node D as reference.

Step 2 Note that V_B is known. $V_B = 1$.

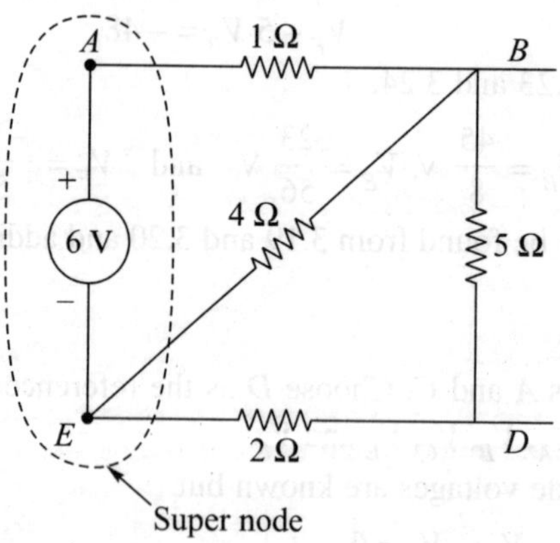

Fig. 3.14 *Illustrating the super node concept*

Step 3 KCL equations

Node A: $$\frac{V_A}{3+2} + \frac{V_A - V_C}{8} + 4 = 0$$

or $$13V_A - 5V_C = -160 \quad ...(3.32)$$

Node C: $$\frac{V_C}{6} + \frac{V_C - V_B}{1} + \frac{V_C - V_A}{8} = 8$$

using $V_B = 1$ in the above,

$$31V_C - 3V_A = 216 \quad ...(3.33)$$

Step 4 From Eqns. 3.32 and 3.33,

$$V_A = -10 \text{ volts}$$
$$V_C = +6 \text{ volts.}$$

The solution may now be completed.

Example 3.7. *The figure below indicates two batteries connected in parallel. The emf and internal resistance of batteries are indicated in the figure. A resistance of 20 ohms is connected across the parallel combination. Calculate the value and direction of current in each battery and voltage across the load resistance.*

Solution. Loop 1 and loop 2 are identified and shown in the circuit

Applying KVL to loop 1

$$110 - 6I_1 + 4I_2 - 130 = 0$$
$$-6I_1 + 4I_2 = 20 \quad ...(1)$$

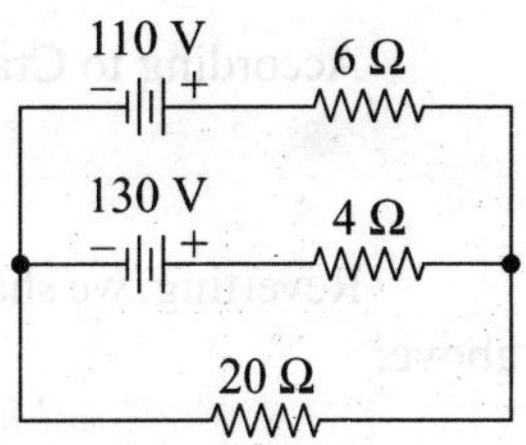

Applying KVL to loop 2

$$130 - 4I_2 - 20(I_1 + I_2) = 0$$
$$10I_1 + 12I_2 = 65 \quad ...(2)$$

Equations (1) and (2) may be solved by the elimination of variables one at a time. This procedure is lengthy. As such determinants and Cramer's method are adopted for solving equations. Method focuses on the manipulation of coefficients attached to variables.

Determinants in Retrospect: (Concise representation of the given problem)

$$\begin{vmatrix} a & b \\ c & d \end{vmatrix}$$

Representation is called determinant 2 × 2. a, b, c and d are the elements of the determinant and is a 2nd order determinant value is $\Delta = ad - bc$

$$\begin{vmatrix} a_1 & b_1 & c_1 \\ a_2 & b_2 & c_2 \\ a_3 & b_3 & c_3 \end{vmatrix}$$

On similar lines is a 3rd order determinant and expanding the above results in

$$= a_1\begin{vmatrix} b_2 & c_2 \\ b_3 & c_3 \end{vmatrix} - b_1\begin{vmatrix} a_2 & c_2 \\ a_3 & c_3 \end{vmatrix} + c_1\begin{vmatrix} a_2 & b_2 \\ a_3 & b_3 \end{vmatrix}$$

$$= a_1(b_2c_3 - b_3c_2) - b_1(a_2c_3 - a_3c_2) + c_1(a_2b_3 - a_3b_2)$$

CHAPTER 3

Solving equations with unknowns using determinants – Cramer's rule:

Consider equations $ax + by + cz = d$

$$ex + fy + gz = h$$

$$jx + ky + lz = m$$

The above three equations are written in the matrix form as below:

$$\begin{bmatrix} a & b & c \\ e & f & g \\ j & k & l \end{bmatrix} \begin{bmatrix} x \\ y \\ z \end{bmatrix} = \begin{bmatrix} d \\ h \\ m \end{bmatrix}$$

the value of the determinant is given by

$$\begin{vmatrix} a & b & c \\ e & f & g \\ j & k & l \end{vmatrix}$$

Expanding $= a(fl - kg) - b(el - gi) + c(ek - jf)$

The determinant for x is found by replacing coefficients of x in the original matrix by constants

i.e., $$\Delta_1 = \begin{vmatrix} d & b & c \\ h & f & g \\ m & k & l \end{vmatrix} \quad \Delta_2 = \begin{vmatrix} a & d & c \\ e & h & g \\ j & m & l \end{vmatrix} \quad \Delta_3 = \begin{vmatrix} a & b & d \\ e & f & h \\ j & k & m \end{vmatrix}$$

According to Cramer's rule

$$x = \frac{\Delta_1}{\Delta}; y = \frac{\Delta_2}{\Delta}; z = \frac{\Delta_3}{\Delta}$$

Reverting, we shall solve the two simultaneous equations (1) and (2) using the method mentioned above:

$$I_1 = \begin{vmatrix} 20 & 4 \\ 65 & 12 \end{vmatrix} \div \begin{vmatrix} -6 & 4 \\ 10 & 12 \end{vmatrix}$$

$$= (240 - 260) \div (-72 - 40) = 20 \div 112 = \frac{20}{112} = 0.178 \text{ A}$$

$$I_2 = \frac{(20 + 6I_1)}{4} = \frac{(20 + 6 \times 0.178)}{4} = 5.267 \text{ A}$$

$$I_1 + I_2 = 0.178 + 5.267 = 5.445\text{A}$$

V_L = Voltage across the load = 5.445 × 20 = 108.9 V.

Example 3.8. *If the total power dissipated in the circuit shown is 18 watts, find the value of R and the current through each component.*

Solution. R equivalent $= \left(\frac{8 \times R}{8 + R} + \frac{4 \times 16}{4 + 16}\right) = \left(\frac{8 \times R}{8 + R} + 3.2\right)$

$$R \text{ equivalent} = \left(\frac{8R}{8 + R} + 3.2\right) \quad \text{...(1)}$$

$P = V^2/$ Req. = 18 ($V = IR$ Ohms Law, Power = $VI = V^2/R$)

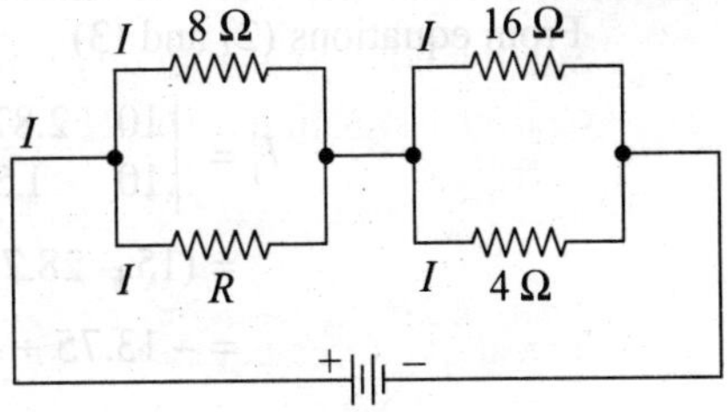

$$\text{Req.} = \frac{V^2}{18} = \frac{12^2}{18} = \frac{12 \times 12}{18} = 8\ \Omega$$

$$\text{Req} = 8\ \Omega = \frac{(8R)}{8 + R} + 3.2$$

Thus $$\frac{8R}{8 + R} = 8 - 3.2 = 4.8$$

$$8R = 4.8 \times 8 + 4.8\,R$$

$$R = \frac{4.8 \times 8}{3.2} = 12\ \Omega$$

$$\text{Req.} = \frac{(8 \times 12)}{8 + 12} + 3.2 = 4.8 + 3.2 = 8\ \Omega \text{ from equation (1)}$$

Thus $$I = \frac{V}{\text{Req.}} = \frac{12}{8} = 1.5\text{ A}$$

$$I_1 = 1.5 \times \frac{12}{20} = 0.9\text{ A}$$

$$I_2 = 0.6\text{ Amp}$$

$$I_3 = 1.5 \times \frac{16}{20} = 1.2\text{ A}$$

and $I_4 = 0.3$ Amps.

Example 3.9. *Find the value of the currents flowing through each of the resistors in the circuit shown when the current in the branch OA is zero.*

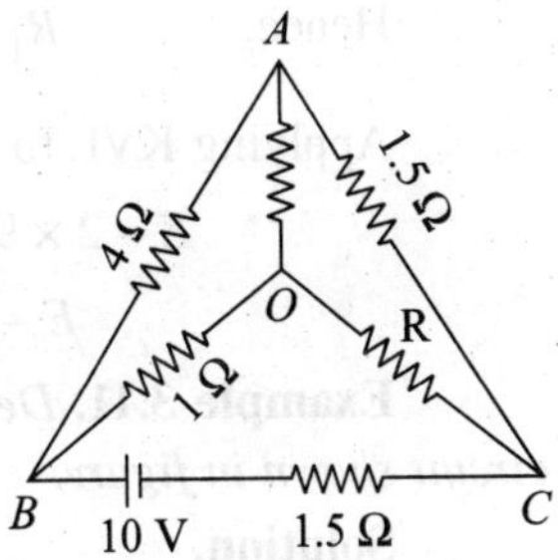

Solution. Applying KVL to loop *AOBA*

$$0 - 4I_1 + I_2 = 0$$

Thus, $$I_1 = I_2/4 \qquad ...(1)$$

Applying KVL to loop *ACOA*

$$-1.5\,I_1 + R\,I_2 = 0$$

Thus, $$R = \frac{1.5_1}{I_2} = \frac{1.5I_1}{4\,I_1} = 0.375$$

KVL equation for loop *BOCB*

$$-1I_2 - 0.375I_2 - 1.5\,(I_1 + I_2) + 10 = 0$$

i.e., $$1.5I_1 + 2.875I_2 = 10 \qquad ...(2)$$

KVL for loop *BACB*

$$-4I_1 - 1.5I_1 - 1.5\,(I_1 + I_2) + 10 = 0$$

$$7\,I_1 + 1.5\,I_2 = 10 \qquad ...(3)$$

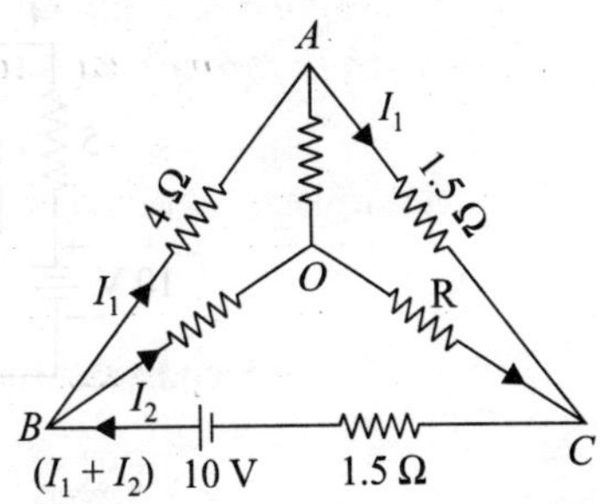

From equations (2) and (3)

$$I_1 = \begin{vmatrix} 10 & 2.875 \\ 10 & 1.5 \end{vmatrix} \div \begin{vmatrix} 1.5 & 2.875 \\ 7 & 1.5 \end{vmatrix}$$

$$= (15 - 28.75) \div (2.25 - 20.125)$$

$$= -13.75 \div -17.875 = 0.769 \text{ Amp.}$$

And $$I_1 = \begin{vmatrix} 1.5 & 10 \\ 7 & 10 \end{vmatrix} \div \begin{vmatrix} 1.5 & 2.875 \\ 7 & 1.5 \end{vmatrix}$$

$$= (15 - 70) \div (2.25 - 20.125) = 3.0769 \text{ A}$$

I_2 is the current through Resistance $R = 3.0769$ A.

Example 3.10. *In the circuit shown in the figure, determine the values E, R_1 and R_2 Applying* KCL *at junction A.*

Solution. $9 = I_1 + 4$

Hence, $I_1 = 9 - 4 = 5$ A

Applying KCL at junction *B*

$$I_1 = 2 + I_2$$

Thus, $5 = 2 + I_2$ and $I_2 = 3$A

Voltage across 8 ohms Resistor = $V = I_2 R = 3 \times 8 = 24$ V

Same voltage appear across R_2 and R_1 also

Hence $V = I \times R_2$

Thus, $R_2 = \dfrac{24}{2} = 12$ ohms

$V = 4 \times R_1$

Hence, $R_1 = \dfrac{V}{4} = \dfrac{24}{4} = 6$ ohms

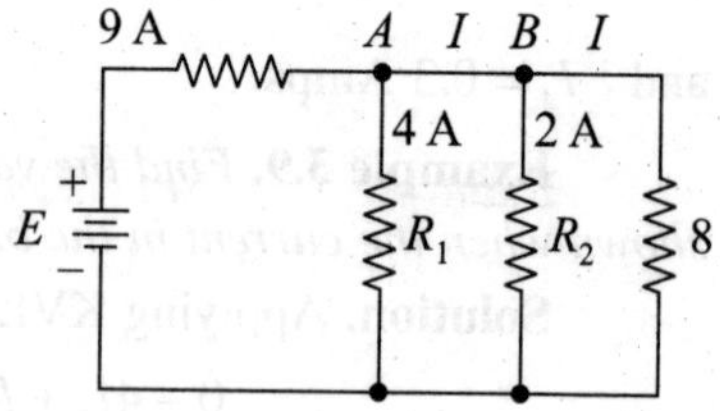

Applying KVL to the loop $EA R_1 E$

$$E - 2 \times 9 - 4 \times 6 = 0$$

$$E - 18 - 24 = 0 \quad \text{and} \quad E = 42 \text{ V}$$

Example 3.11. *Determine the potential difference between the points A and B for the electric circuit shown in figure.*

Solution.

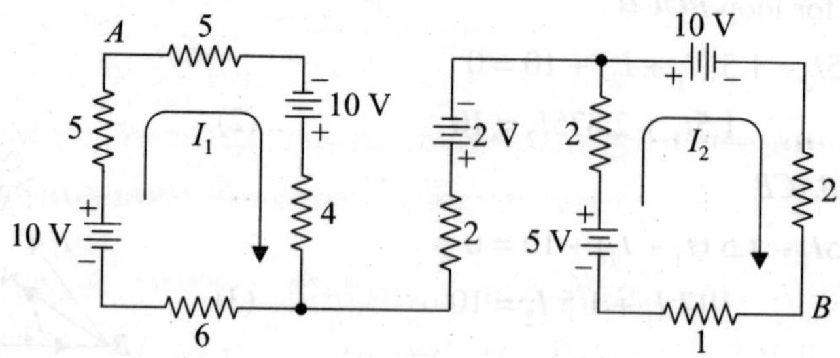

Applying KVL is loop 1

$$-5I_1 + 10 - 4I_1 - 6I_1 + 10 - 5I_1 = 0$$

$$I_1 = 20/20 = 1 \text{ A}$$

Applying KVL is loop 2

$$-2I_2 - 5 - I_2 - 2I_2 + 10 = 0$$

$$I_2 = 5/5 = 1 \text{ A}$$

$$V_{AB} = (-5I_1 + 10 - 4I_1 - 2 - 2I_2 - 5 - I_2)$$

$$= (-5 \times 1 + 10 - 4 \times 1 - 2 - 2 \times 1 - 5 - 1)$$

$$= (-5 + 10 - 4 - 2 - 2 - 5 - 1)$$

$$V_{AB} = -9 \text{ V} \quad \boxed{V_{BA} = +9 \text{ V}} \text{ volts.}$$

Example 3.12. *A current of 20 A flows through two ammeters A and B connected as shown in figure. The potential difference across A is 0.2 V and across B is 0.3 V. Find how the same current will divide between A and B when they are connected in parallel.*

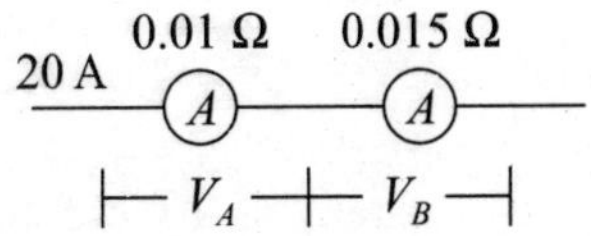

Solution. $R_A = \frac{V_A}{I} = \frac{0.2}{20} = 0.01$ ohms

$$R_B = \frac{V_B}{I} = \frac{0.3}{20} = 0.015 \text{ ohms}$$

When A and B connected in parallel as shown

Total current of $I = 20$ A will divide in the Ammeters according to their resistances.

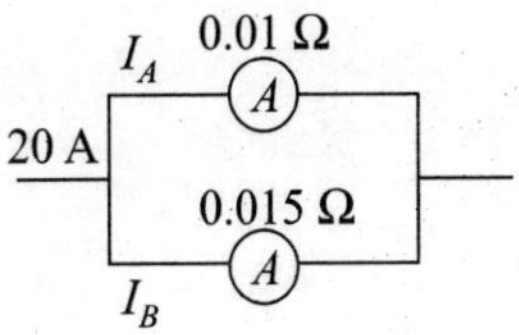

$$I_A = I \frac{R_B}{R_A + R_B} = \frac{(20 \times 0.015)}{0.025} = 12 \text{ A}$$

$$I_B = I \frac{(R_A)}{R_A + R_B} = \frac{(12 \times 0.015)}{0.025} = 8 \text{ A.}$$

Example 3.13. *Find the current in all branches of the network shown in figure.*

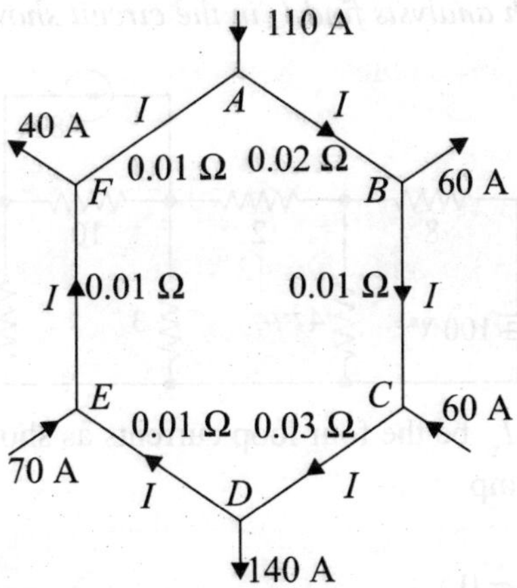

Solution. Let the current in any branch of the network is assumed as I with certain direction. Apply KCL at every junction and find out the branch currents of the network.

Applying KVL to the loop

$$-0.02\,I - 0.01\,(I - 60) - 0.03\,I - 0.01\,(I - 140) - 0.01\,(I - 70) - 0.02\,(I - 110) = 0$$

$$-0.02\,I - 0.01\,I + 0.6 - 0.03\,I - 0.01\,I + 140 - 0.01\,I + 0.70 - 0.02\,I + 1.1 = 0$$

$$0.1\,I = 3.8$$

Hence $I = \frac{3.8}{0.1} = 38$ A

The current in each branch is calculated as follows:

$$I_{AB} = I = 38 \text{ A}$$
$$I_{BC} = I = 60 = 38 - 60 = -22 \text{ A}$$
$$I_{CD} = I = 38 \text{ A}$$
$$I_{DE} = I - 140 = 38 - 140 = -102 \text{ A}$$
$$I_{EF} = I - 70 = 38 - 70 = -32 \text{ A}$$
$$I_{FA} = I - 110 = 38 - 110 = -72 \text{ A}$$

The currents in various branches are as marked below:

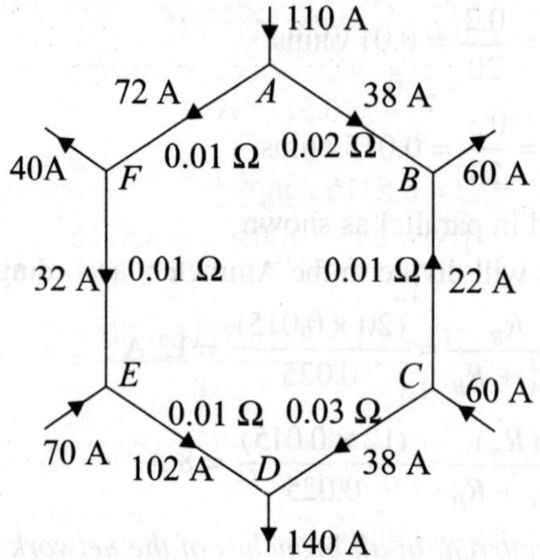

Example 3.14. *Using mesh analysis find I_x in the circuit shown in figure.*

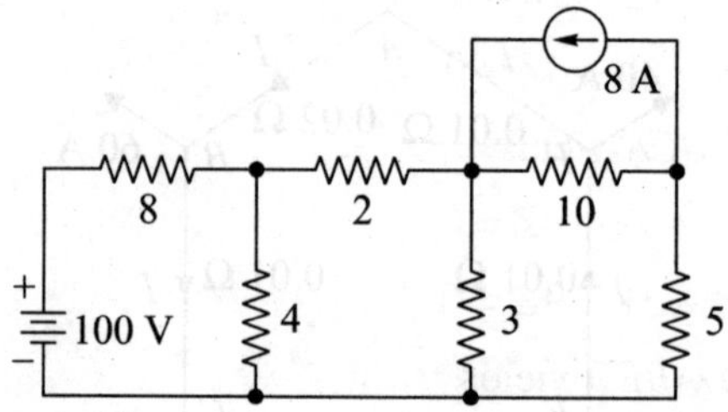

Solution. Let I_1, I_2, I_3 and I_x be the four loop currents as shown in the circuit diagram.

By observation $I_4 = -8$ Amp

Applying KVL to loop 1

$$100 - 8I_1 - 4(I_1 - I_2) = 0$$
$$-12I_1 + 4I_2 = -100$$
$$12I_1 - 4I_2 = 100 \quad \text{...(1)}$$

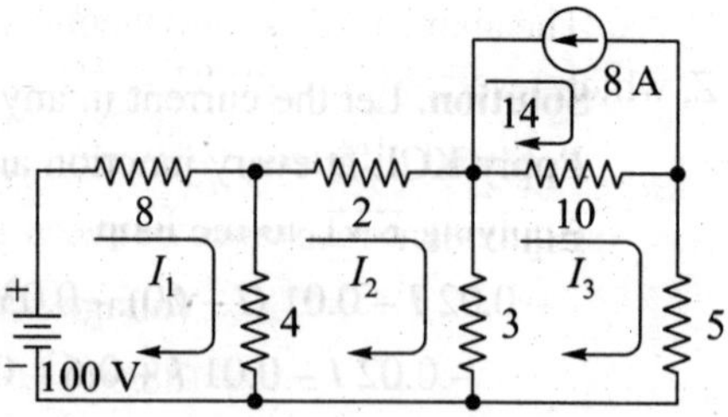

Applying KVL to loop 2

$$-2I_2 - 3(I_2 - I_3) - 4(I_2 - I_1) = 0$$
$$4I_1 - 9I_2 + 3I_3 = 0 \quad \text{...(2)}$$

Applying KVL to loop 3

$$-10(I_3 - I_4) - 5I_3 - 3(I_3 - I_2) = 0$$

$$3I_2 - 18I_3 = -80 \qquad ...(3)$$

Thus $$I_3 = \frac{3I_2 + 80}{18} \qquad ...(4)$$

Substituting the equation (4) in equation (2)

$$4I_1 - 9I_2 + 3I_3 = 0$$

$$4I_1 - 9I_2 + 3 \times \frac{3I_2 + 80}{18} = 0$$

$$24I_1 - 54I_2 + 3I_2 + 80 = 0$$

$$24I_1 - 51I_2 = -80 \qquad ...(5)$$

$$12I_1 - 4I_2 = 100 \text{ ...... from (1)}$$

From (1) and (5), we get $I_2 = \frac{-280}{-43} = 6.5116$ A

$$I_x = I_2 = 6.5116 \text{ Amps}$$

$$I_1 = \frac{100 + 4I_2}{12} = \frac{100 + 4 \times 6.5116}{12} = 10.5 \text{ A}$$

$$I_3 = \frac{3I_2 + 80}{18} = \frac{3 \times 6.5116 + 80}{18} = 5.5 \text{ A.}$$

Example 3.15. *Determine the current in the unbalanced bridge shown in the figure. Also determine the voltage across BD and the resistance from B to D.*

Solution. Current flow is marked in the figure.

Applying KVL to loop *DACD*, we get

$$-X - 4Z + 2Y = 0$$

$$X - 2Y + 4Z = 0 \qquad ...(1)$$

Applying KVL to loop *ABCA* yields

$$-2(X - Z) + 3(Y + Z) + 4Z = 0$$

$$2X - 3Y - 9Z = 0 \qquad ...(2)$$

Applying KVL to loop *DABED* yields,

$$-X - 2(X - Z) - 2(X + Y) + 2 = 0$$

$$5X + 2Y - 2Z = 2 \qquad ...(3)$$

The above three simultaneous equations (1), (2) and (3) may be solved for the variables *X*, *Y* and *Z*, which results in $X = 30/91$ A ; $Y = 17/91$ A and $Z = 1/91$A.

Potential difference between *D* and *B* is $2 - (X + Y) \times 2 = 88/91$ V

Equivalent resistance between *B* and *D* is

= Voltage across *B* and *D*/Current between *B* and *D*

= (88/91) / (47/91) = 1.87 ohms

We shall also solve equations (1), (2) and (3) by Determinants (as was done in previous

The matrix form of the three simultaneous equations is

$$\begin{bmatrix} 1 & -2 & 4 \\ 2 & -3 & -9 \\ 5 & 2 & -2 \end{bmatrix} \begin{bmatrix} X \\ Y \\ Z \end{bmatrix} = \begin{bmatrix} 0 \\ 0 \\ 2 \end{bmatrix}. \text{ Write the equations in matrix form}$$

$$\Delta = \begin{vmatrix} 1 & -2 & 4 \\ 2 & -3 & -9 \\ 5 & 2 & -2 \end{vmatrix}. \text{ Therefore } \Delta = 1(6+18) + 2(-4+45) + 4(4+15) = 182$$

$$\text{Similarly } \Delta_1 = \begin{vmatrix} 0 & -2 & 4 \\ 0 & -3 & -9 \\ 2 & 2 & -2 \end{vmatrix}. \text{ Therefore } \Delta_1 = 0(6+18) + 2(0+18) + 4(0+6) = 60$$

$$\text{Similarly } \Delta_2 = \begin{vmatrix} 1 & 0 & 4 \\ 2 & 0 & -9 \\ 5 & 2 & -2 \end{vmatrix}. \text{ Therefore } \Delta_2 = 1(0+18) + 0(-4+45) + 4(4+0) = 34$$

$$\Delta_3 = \begin{vmatrix} 1 & -2 & 0 \\ 2 & -3 & 0 \\ 5 & 2 & 2 \end{vmatrix}. \text{ Therefore } \Delta_1 = 1(-6+0) + 2(4+0) + 0(4+15) = 2$$

Then $X = \Delta_1/\Delta$ $= 60/182 = 30/91$ $Y = \Delta_2/\Delta$ $= 34/182 = 17/91$ $Z = \Delta_3/\Delta$ $= 2/182 = 1/91.$

Example 3.16. *Using Kirchhoff's current law, find the values of currents i_1 and i_2 in the circuit below. Resistances are in ohms.*

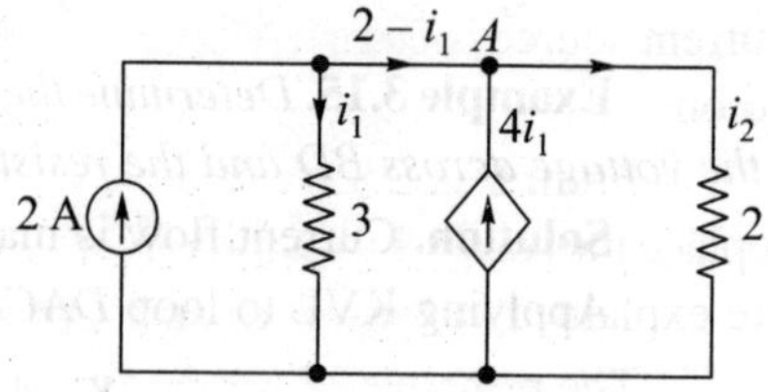

Solution. Applying KCL to node *A*

$$2 - i_1 + 4\,i_1 - i_2 = 0$$

i.e., $$-3\,i_1 + i_2 = 2 \quad ...(1)$$

By Ohms law, $i_1 = V/3$ and $i_2 = V/2$ ...(2)

Substituting equation (2) in (1), we get $V = -4$ Volts

Thus $i_1 = -4/3$ A and $i_2 = -2$ A

Value of the dependent current source is $4\,i_1 = -16/3$

Since i_1 and i_2 are –ve values, current flow in the given diagram may be marked as below.

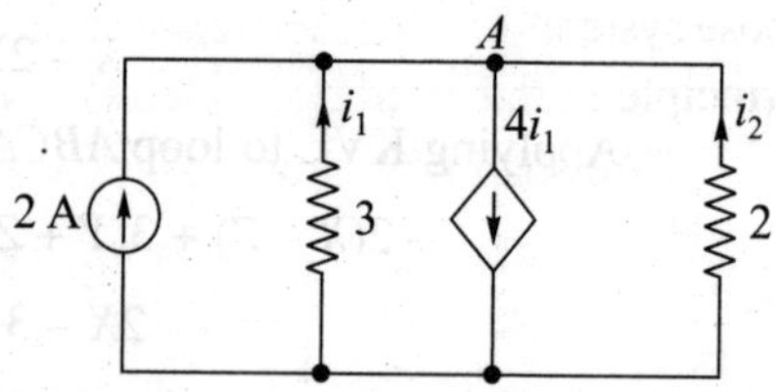

Example 3.17. *Using KCL find V_{AB}, I_1, I_2 and I_3 in the circuit shown below. All resistances are in ohms.*

Solution. Applying KCL at first junction

$$I_1 = I_1 + I_2 + 8 + I_3$$

$$I_1 + I_2 + I_3 = 3 \quad ...(1)$$

By Ohms law $I_1 = V_{ab}/18$; $I_2 = V_{ab}/12$ $I_3 = V_{ab}/9$

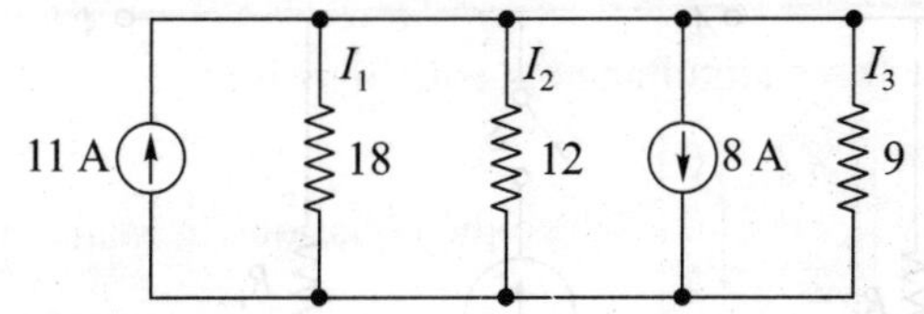

Substituting the above values in equation (1)

$$V_{ab} = 3 \times 36/9 = 12 \text{ V}$$

$$I_1 = 12/18 = 2/3 \text{ A} ; \; I_2 = 12/12 = 1 \text{ A}; \; I_3 = 12/9 = 4/3 \text{ A}.$$

3.6 NETWORK THEOREMS

It is possible that the solution of certain problems associated with networks can be made simpler by use of network theorems. We shall consider three such theorems—the therorem of superposition, and the Thevenin and Norton theorems.

3.6.1 The Superposition Theorem

Consider the circuit of Fig. 3.11 which contains three energy sources. Suppose we wish to find the current in the 2 ohm resistor. We may proceed to use either the mesh current or the node voltage method or use the principle of superposition. According to this principle we consider the sources one at a time, replacing the remaining sources by their internal resistance, and solve for the required quantity. The contributions of all the sources, considered turn by turn, are summed algebraically. In applying this principle to the circuit of Fig. 3.11 we would have to perform three sets of calculations. Thus, when the current source is being considered the voltage sources must be replaced by their internal resistances and so on.

From Fig. 2.9 we see that in order to replace a voltage source by its internal resistance we must replace the source by a short circuit. Fig. 2.17 shows that current sources must be opened. These concepts are explained in Figs. 3.15 and 3.16.

The principle of superposition is a universal principle which is applicable to linear systems, *i.e.*, those systems in which the relationship between cause and effect is linear. Application of the superposition principle in the nonlinear case results in erroneous values as shown in Fig. 3.17.

We shall now illustrate the application of the superposition principle by means of an example.

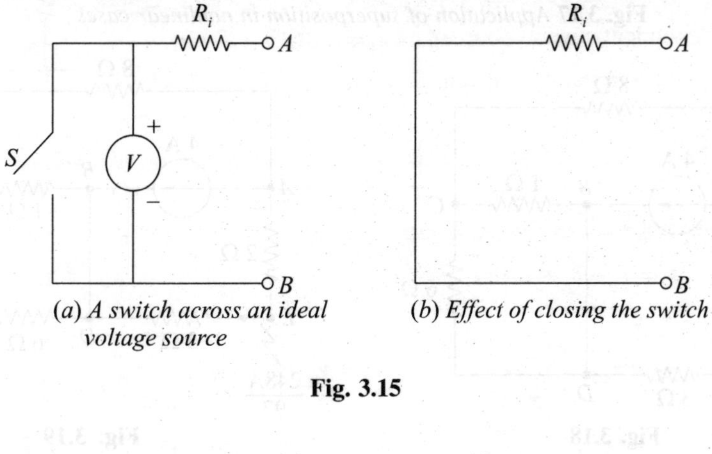

(*a*) *A switch across an ideal voltage source*

(*b*) *Effect of closing the switch*

Fig. 3.15

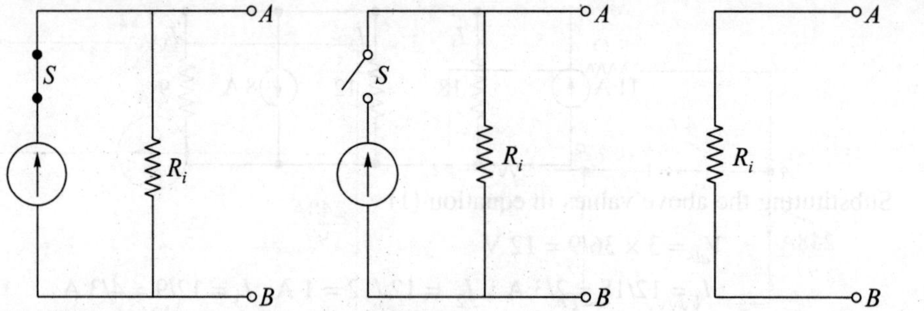

(a) *A switch in series with an ideal current source* (b) *Effect of opening the switch* (c) *Equivalent circuit*

Fig. 3.16

Example 3.18. *Solve for the current in the 2 Ω resistor in Fig. 3.11 using the principle of superposition.*

Solution. Let us consider the 4A source first. We replace the remaining voltage sources with short circuits and obtain Fig. 3.18. To solve for the current in the 2 Ω resistor we choose the method of network reduction. The successive steps in the solution are indicated in Figs. 3.19 to 3.21 and are self explanatory.

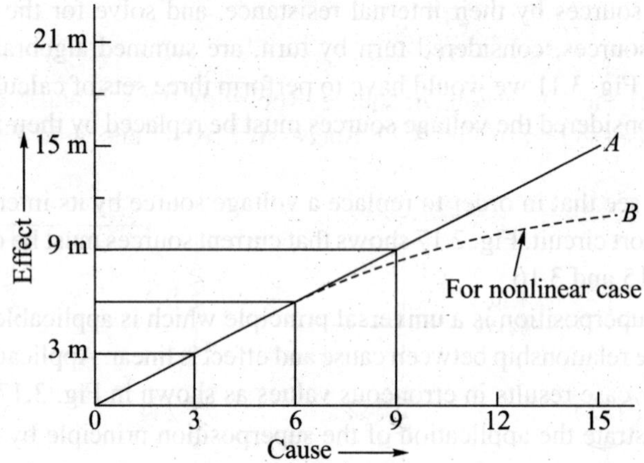

Fig. 3.17 *Application of superposition in nonlinear cases*

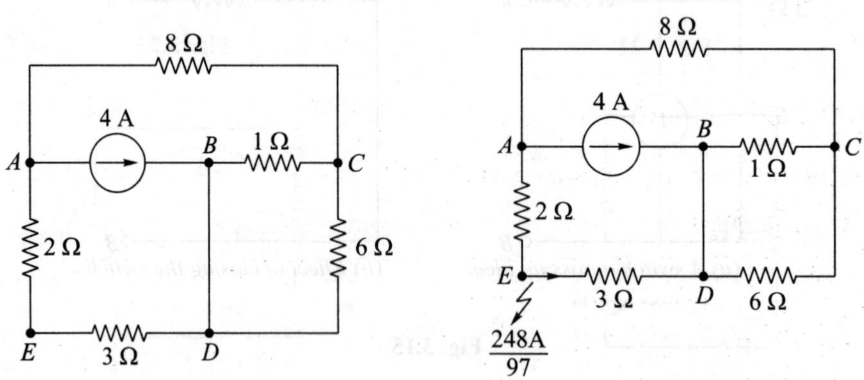

Fig. 3.18 **Fig. 3.19**

Figures for Ex. 3.18

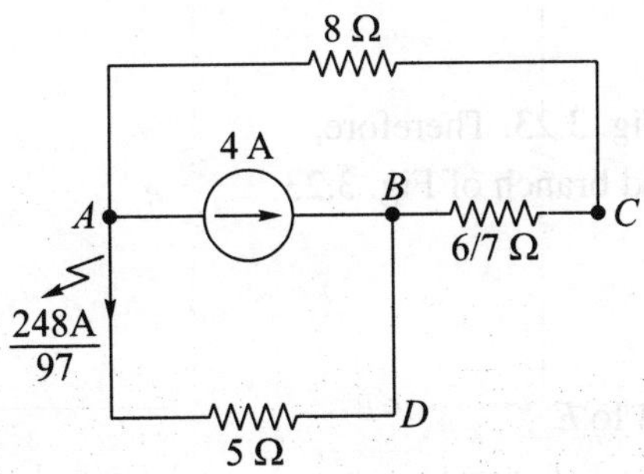

Fig. 3.20

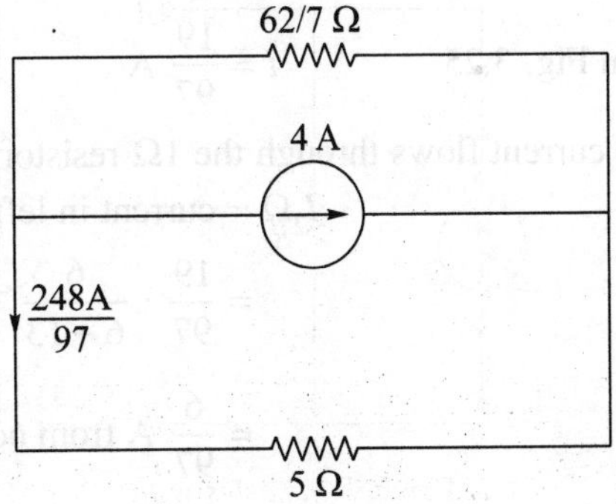

Fig. 3.21

From Fig. 3.21, $$I_{5\,\Omega} = \frac{4 \times 62/7}{5 + 62/7} = \frac{248}{97} \text{ A.}$$

The current of $\frac{248}{97}$ A flows from node A through the source and the 5 ohm resistor and therefore from A to E through the 2 ohm resistor as well. Denoting the current through the 2 Ω resistor due to the 4 A current source by I'_{AE}, we have,

$$I'_{AE} = -\frac{248}{97} \text{ A.} \qquad ...(3.34)$$

Next, we consider the 1 volt voltage source. Replacing the 4 A and the 8 A sources with open circuits, the circuit reduces to that of Fig. 3.22. Successive reductions yield Figs. 3.23, 3.24 and 3.25.

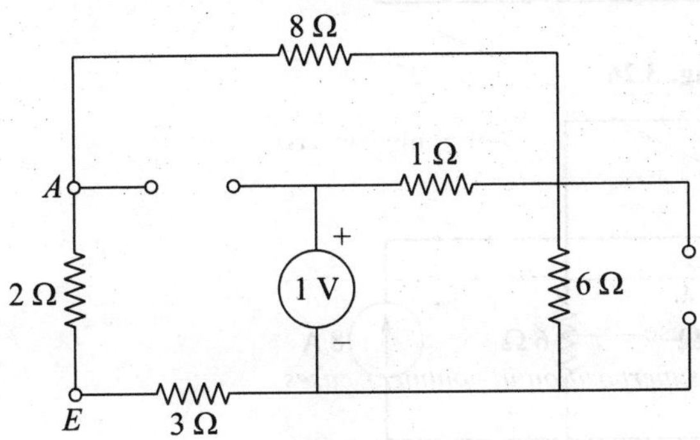

Fig. 3.22

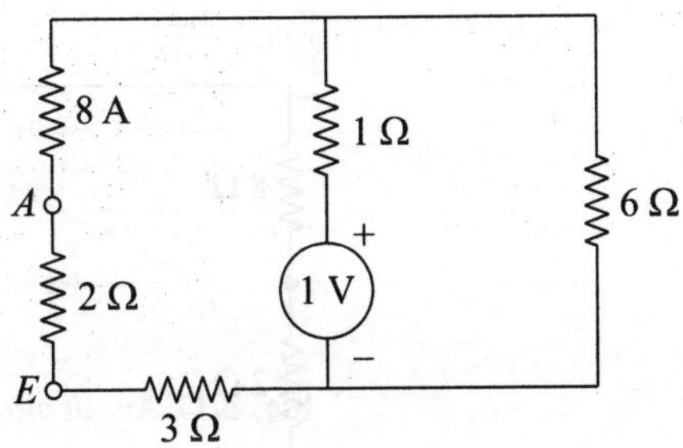

Fig. 3.23

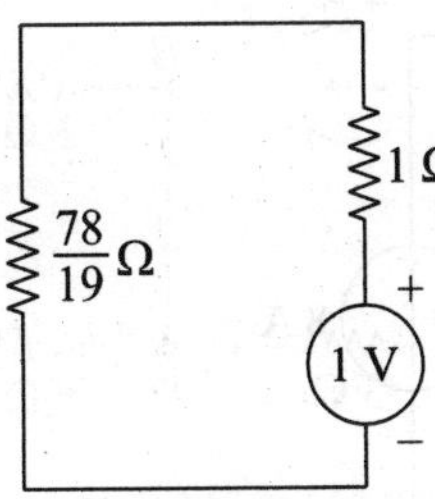

Fig. 3.24

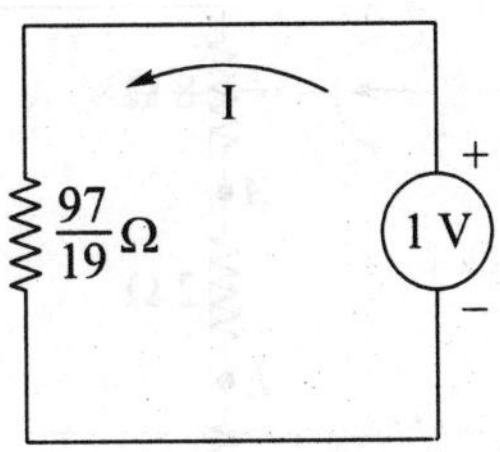

Fig. 3.25

CHAPTER 3

From Fig. 3.25 $I = \dfrac{19}{97}$ A

This current flows through the 1Ω resistor in Fig. 3.23. Therefore,

$$I_2\Omega = \text{current in left hand branch of Fig. 3.23}$$

$$= \frac{19}{97} \cdot \frac{6}{6+13}$$

$$= \frac{6}{97} \text{ A from node } A \text{ to } E$$

Denoting the current through the 2Ω resistor due to the 1 V voltage source by I''_{AE}

$$I''_{AE} = \frac{6}{97} \text{ A} \qquad \text{...(3.35)}$$

Lastly, we consider the 8A current source. The other 2 sources are treated as usual and the circuit of Fig. 3.26 results. Once again, using network reduction we obtain the circuits of Figs. 3.27 and 3.28.

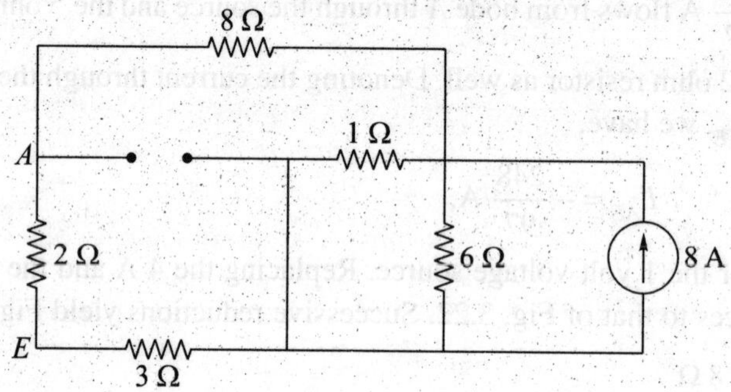

Fig. 3.26

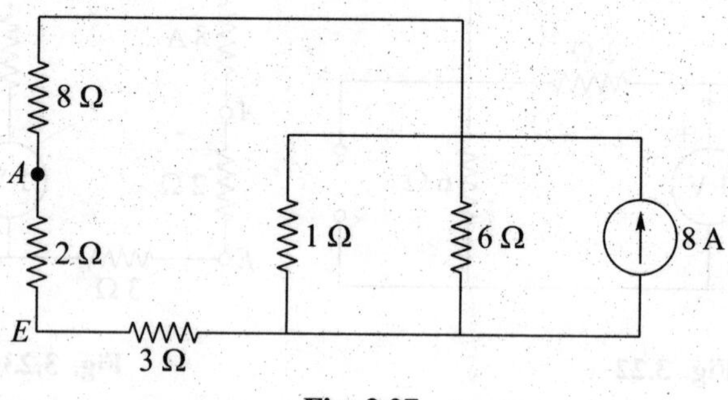

Fig. 3.27

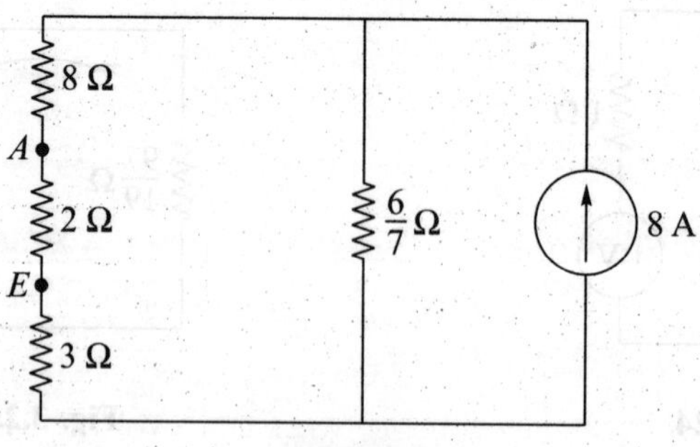

Fig. 3.28

From Fig. 3.28 $$I_{2\,\Omega} = I_{AE} = \frac{8.\frac{6}{7}}{13+\frac{6}{7}} = \frac{48}{97}\text{ A} \qquad ...(3.36)$$

Denoting this last current by I'''_{AE}, the total current flowing in the 2Ω resistor is

$$I'_{AE} + I''_{AE} + I'''_{AE}$$

$$= -\frac{248}{97} + \frac{6}{97} + \frac{48}{97} \text{ (from 3.34, 3.35 and 3.36)}$$

$$= -2\text{A}$$

i.e., the current in the 2 Ω resistor is 2A from *E* to *A*.

Before we pass on to Thevenin's theorem we wish to stress that the principle of superposition does not apply to power because power is not related linearly to either voltage or current. It is left as an exercise for the student to check, in example 3.7, that the powers dissipated in the 2 Ω resistor by the component currents I'_{AE}, I''_{AE} and $+ I'''_{AE}$ do not add up to $2I^2_{AE}$.

3.6.2 Thevenin's Theorem

In the method of circuit solution by network reduction, we saw that it is always possible to reduce a one port network, comprising only of resistors, to an equivalent resistor connected across the two terminals of the one port. Should the network contain energy sources in addition to resistors, Thevenin's theorem affords a way of replacing the network, at its terminals, by an equivalent voltage source in series with an equivalent resistor as shown in Figs. 3.29*a* and 3.29*b*. What is the meaning of the word "equivalent" as applied to electric circuits? If the network of Fig. 3.29*a* can be replaced at *AB* by the Thevenin equivalent of Fig. 3.29*b* we expect the current *I* through *R* and the voltage drop *V* across *R* to be the same in both circuits for all values of *R*.

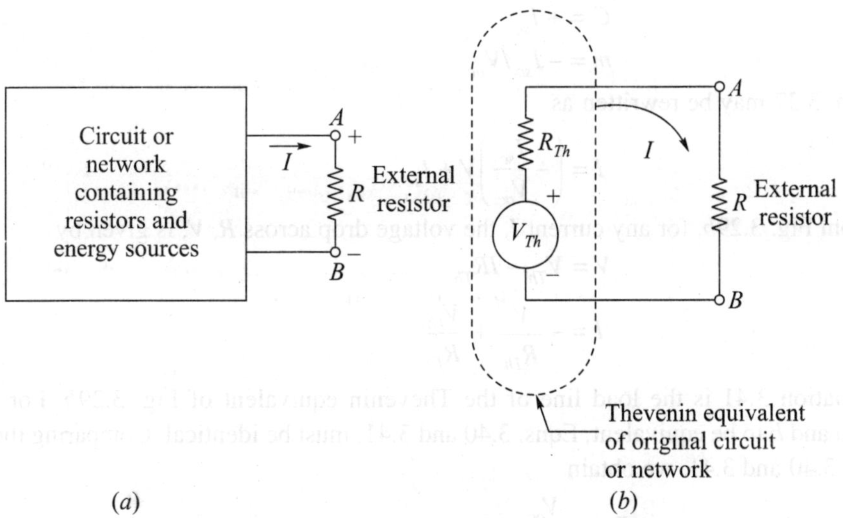

Fig. 3.29 *(a) Circuit with energy sources and resistors*
(b) Thevenin equivalent of original circuit or network

In the original network of Fig. 3.29*a* as *R* is varied, we expect both *I* and *V* to vary. When *R* = ∞, *I* = 0. However *A* and *B* are two terminals of the network and a voltage will exist between them. We call this the open circuit voltage, V_{oc}. Thus corresponding to the case *R* = ∞, open circuit, *I* = 0 and $V = V_{oc}$.

If we short circuit AB then clearly, $V_{AB} = V = 0$; but I is now non-zero and is what we may term the short circuit current, I_{sc}. Corresponding to $R = 0$, short circuit, $I = I_{sc}$ and $V = 0$.

We may plot the above pair of points (V_{oc}, 0), (0, I_{sc}) on a graph as in Fig. 3.30. Since the circuit is linear we expect all other values of I and V, corresponding to cases $0 < R < \infty$, to fall on the line CD and in between C and D. The graph of Fig. 3.30 is known as a "load *V-I* characteristic" or a "load line". The term 'load' has come about as the resistor R may represent a load such as an electric heater or loudspeaker coil, etc.

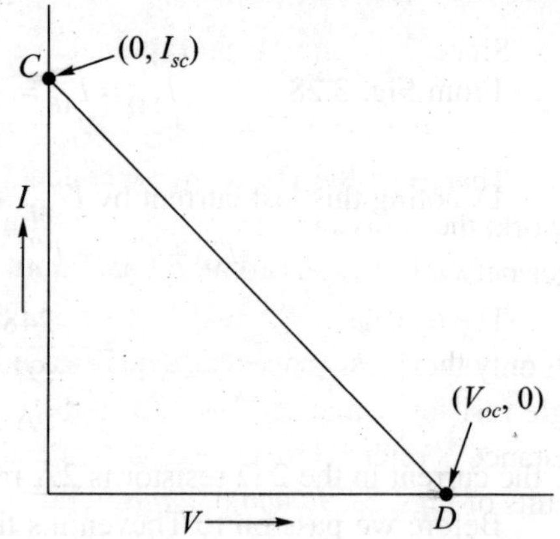

Fig. 3.30 *Voltamp characteristic of network in Fig. 3.29(a)*

Clearly, equivalence of Figs. 3.29*a* and *b* demands that their *V*-I characteristics or load lines be identical. We shall use this principle to find the Thevenin equivalent voltage source and resistance in terms of the parameters of the original network.

From Fig. 3.30 the *V-I* characteristics of the original network is described by the load line

$$I = mV + C \qquad \text{...(3.37)}$$

where m and C are constants.

To find the constants m and C, we note from Fig. 3.30 that when $V = 0$, $I = I_{sc}$ and $V = V_{oc}$ if $I = 0$. Therefore,

$$I_{sc} = 0 + C \qquad \text{...(3.38)}$$

and

$$0 = m\,V_{oc} + C \qquad \text{...(3.39)}$$

i.e.

$$C = +\,I_{sc}$$

and

$$m = -\,I_{sc}/V_{oc}$$

Eqn. 3.37 may be rewritten as

$$I = \left(-\frac{I_{sc}}{V_{oc}}\right)V + I_{sc} \qquad \text{...(3.40)}$$

From Fig. 3.29*b*, for any current I, the voltage drop across R, V, is given by

$$V = V_{Th} - IR_{Th}$$

or

$$I = -\frac{V}{R_{Th}} + \frac{V_{Th}}{R_{Th}} \qquad \text{...(3.41)}$$

Equation 3.41 is the load line of the Thevenin equivalent of Fig. 3.29*b*. For the circuits of Figs. 3.29*a* and *b* to be equivalent, Eqns. 3.40 and 3.41, must be identical. Comparing the coefficient of V in Eqns. 3.40 and 3.41, we obtain

$$R_{Th} = \frac{V_{oc}}{I_{sc}} \qquad \text{...(3.42)}$$

Comparison of the constant term (C in Eqn. 3.37) yields

$$\frac{V_{Th}}{R_{Th}} = I_{sc}$$

Since $I_{sc} = \frac{V_{oc}}{R_{Th}}$ from Eqn. 3.42,

$$V_{Th} = V_{oc} \quad ...(3.43)$$

Therefore, the Thevenin equivalent voltage source is the open circuit voltage at *AB* in the oringinal network; the equivalent resistance is the ratio of the open circuit voltage to the short circuit current. The larger network is replaced by a very simple equivalent circuit.

The resistance R_{Th} may be found in an alternative way. Replace all sources in the original network with only their resistances, as explained in section 3.61, and reduce the resulting resistive network to a single resistor connected between the terminals of the one port. This resistance is equal to R_{Th}. This resistance is referred to as the resistance at *AB*, looking into the network. The equivalence between the circuits of Figs. 3.29*a* and 3.29*b* is valid only for a circuit external to the one port, *i.e.*, a load resistor *R*, connected across *AB* as in Fig. 3.29. As far as this resistor is concerned, Figs. 3.29*a* and 3.29*b* are identical and one may find the current through *R*, the voltage drop across *R* or the power dissipated in *R* using the simpler circuit of Fig. 3.39*b*. The power delivered by the Thevenin equivalent is equal to the power dissipated in the external circuit plus that in the equivalent resistance. This is not equal to the total power delivered by all the sources in the original network when connected to the same external circuit.

The Thevenin equivalent is especially useful when a solution is sought for different values of the load resistor *R* or in the analysis of large networks. There are many useful applications of this theorem both in electronic circuits and in power system network calculations.

The steps to be followed to arrive at a Thevenin equivalent are:

(1) Identify the one port network/circuit and remove any resistor/circuit external to the one port and connected to its terminals.

(2) Find, using any convenient method, the open circuit voltage, V_{oc}.

(3) Find (*a*) I_{sc} and $R_{Th} = \frac{V_{oc}}{I_{sc}}$ or (*b*) R_{Th} directly using the alternative technique.

(4) The Thevenin equivalent is then a voltage source of magnitude V_{oc} (polarity determined in step 2) in series with R_{Th}.

(5) Reconnect the resistor/circuit disconnected in step 1 and perform the necessary calculations.

Example 3.19. *Find using Thevenin's theorem, the current in the 2 ohm resistor in Fig. 3.11.*

Solution.

Step 1 The circuit is redrawn in Fig. 3.31, for convenience. In this example, nodes *A* and *E* are the two terminals of the one port which is enclosed by the dotted line. The 2 Ω resistor is removed to yield Fig. 3.32.

Step 2 We now have to find V_{AE}. This is equal to V_{oc}. To solve the circuit of Fig. 3.32, we note that the current through the 8 Ω resistor must be equal to 4A. Further, since an open circuit exists at *AE*, the potenials of nodes *D* and *E* are equal. We choose *D* as reference. Therefore,

$$V_D = V_E = 0 \quad ...(3.44)$$

Writing the node voltage equations at *A* and *C*,

$$\frac{V_A - V_C}{8} + 4 = 0 \quad ...(3.45)$$

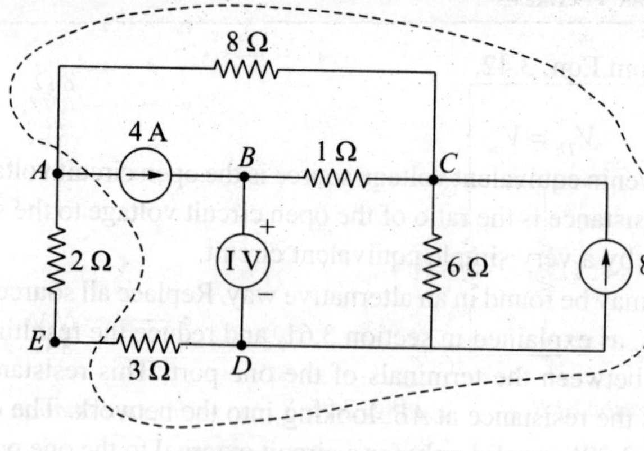

Fig. 3.31 *Network for Ex. 3.19.*

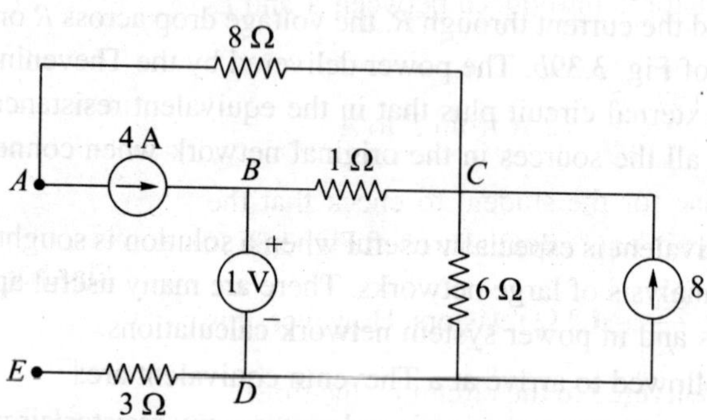

Fig. 3.32 *Network with open circuited terminals*

and $$4+\frac{V_C}{6}+\frac{V_C-1}{1}=8 \quad \text{...(3.46)}$$

From Eqn. 3.46, $V_C=\frac{30}{7}$. Substituting in Eqn. 3.45, ...(3.47)

$$V_A=V_C-32=-\frac{194}{7}=V_D=V_{AE}=V_{oc} \quad \text{...(3.48)}$$

Note that V_{AE} is –ve.

Step 3 To find R_{Th}, replace the sources in Fig. 3.32 with their internal resistances and obtain Fig. 3.33. Reduce the network to one resistor across AE as shown in Figs. 3.34 to 3.36.

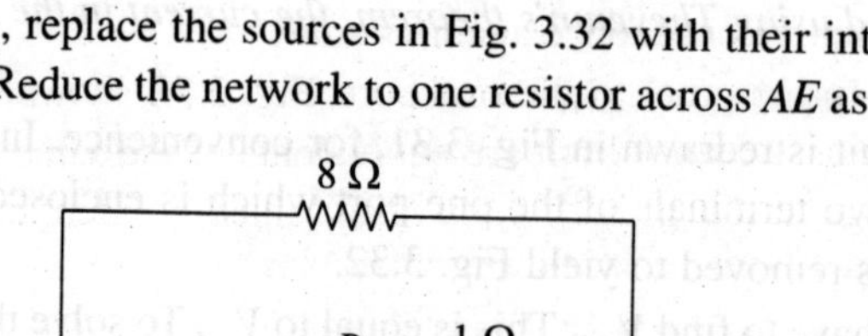

Fig. 3.33 *Preliminary to determination of R_{Th}*

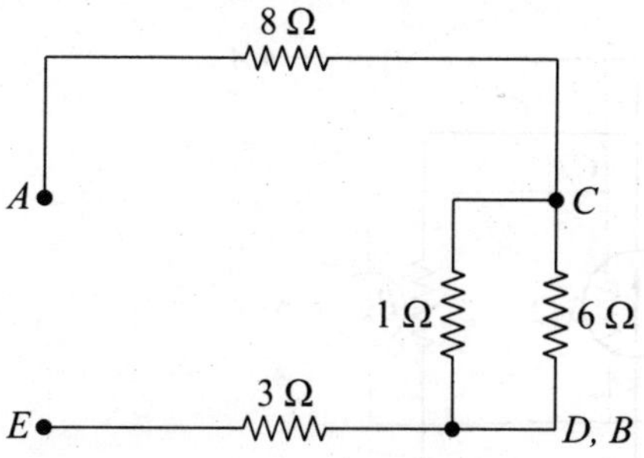

Fig. 3.34 *Determination of* R_{Th}

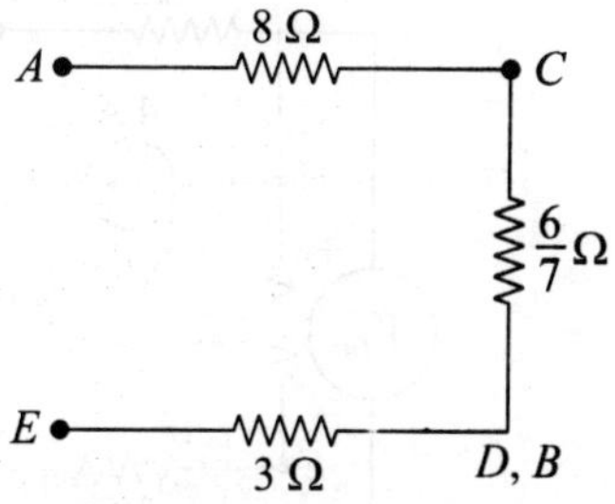

Fig. 3.35 R_{Th} *as series combination of resistors*

Step 4 The Thevenin equivalent is shown in Fig. 3.37.

Step 5 The 2 Ω resistor is introduced between *A* and *E*, and

$$I_{2\,\Omega} = \frac{197}{7} \cdot \frac{7}{97} = 2 \text{ A from } E \text{ to } A.$$

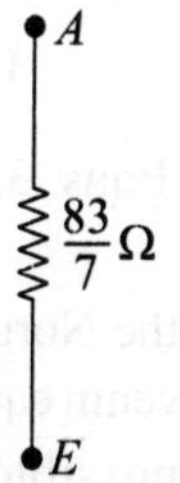

Fig. 3.36 *Computation of* R_{Th}

It is left as an exercise for the student to check that the power delivered by the Thevenin equivalent source in Fig. 3.37 is equal to that dissipated in the $\frac{83}{7}$ and 2 Ω resistors. However, it is not equal to the total power delivered to the circuit by the three sources in the original circuit of Fig. 3.31.

In attempting to derive Thevenin equivalents experimentally, introduction of a short circuit, to measure I_{SC}, is not recommended. A safer method exists and is brought out in problem 8 at the end of this chapter.

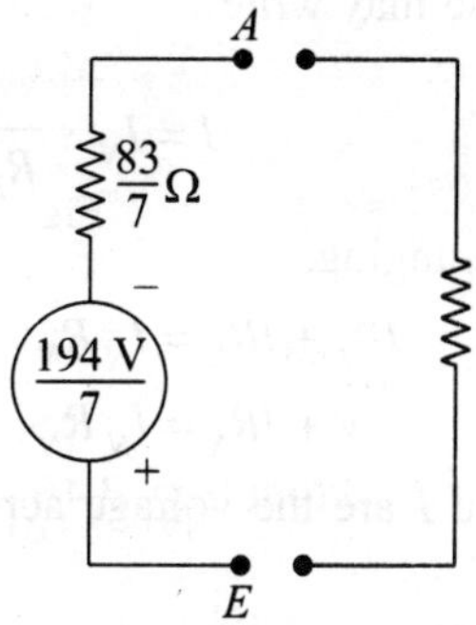

Fig. 3.37 *Thevenin's equivalent circuit of network in Fig. 3.31*

3.6.3 Norton's Theorem

According to this theorem any one port network consisting of resistors and energy sources may be replaced, at its terminals, by an equivalent consisting of a current source in parallel with an equivalent resistance. This equivalence, once again, is valid only for a circuit or load resistor external to the one port. Fig. 3.38 shows the Thevenin and Norton equivalents of a one port. Obviously, since both are equivalents of the same one port, the short circuit current and open circuit voltage at *AB* in both equivalents must be identical. Thus, for short circuit conditions at *AB* from Fig. 3.38,

$$I_N = \frac{V_{Th}}{R_{Th}} \qquad \text{...(3.49)}$$

where the subscript *N* stands for "Norton". Under conditions of open circuit at *AB*, from Fig. 3.38,

$$V_{Th} = I_N R_N \qquad \text{...(3.50)}$$

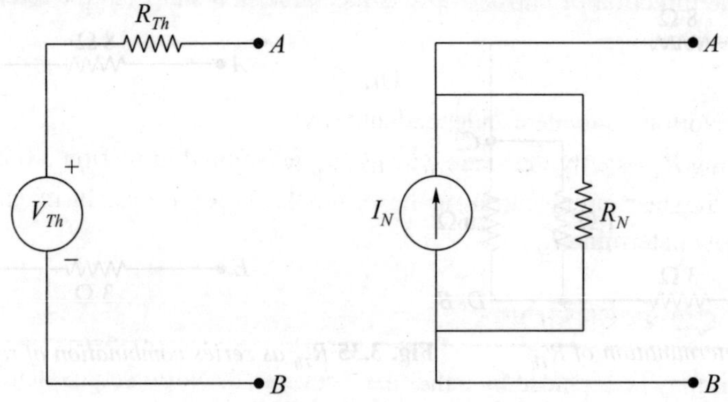

Fig. 3.38 *Thevenin's and Norton's equivalents of a one port network*

From Eqns. 3.49 and 3.50, we obtain that

$$R_N = R_{Th} \qquad ...(3.51)$$

Thus the Norton equivalent circuit may be derived from the Thevenin equivalent by using Eqns. 3.49 and 3.51.

It is possible to derive the Norton equivalent independently of the Thevenin equivalent. Consider Fig. 3.39. We may write

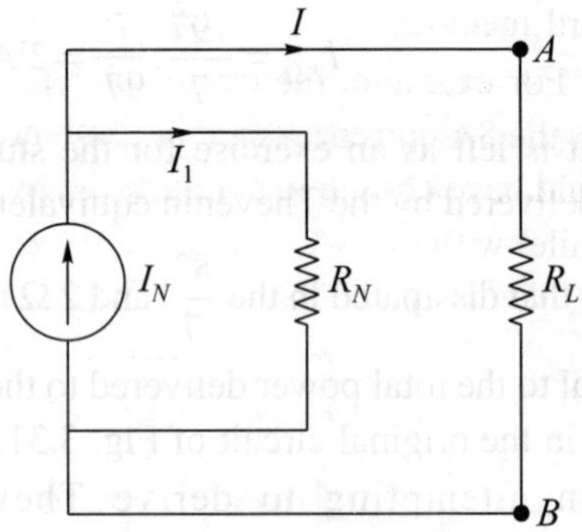

Fig. 3.39 *The Norton's equivalent circuit feeding a load resistor*

$$I = I_N \cdot \frac{R_N}{R_L + R_N} \qquad ...(3.52)$$

Rearranging,

$$IR_L + IR_N = I_N R_N$$

or

$$V + IR_N = I_N R_N \qquad ...(3.53)$$

where V and I are the voltage across and the current through the load resistor R. Eqn. 3.53 may be written as

$$I = -\frac{V}{R_N} + I_N \qquad ...(3.54)$$

Following a procedure identical to that used in deriving the Thevenin equivalent, Eqn. (3.54) is compared with Eqn. (3.40) to yield

$$R_N = \frac{V_{oc}}{I_{sc}} \qquad ...(3.55)$$

and

$$I_N = I_{sc} \qquad ...(3.56)$$

The magnitude and direction of the current source in the Norton equivalent is obtained by finding the short circuit current at the terminals of the one port.

The steps in determining the Norton equivalent are:

(1) Identify the one port network/circuit and remove any resistor/circuit external to the one port and connected to its terminals. Next, either

(2*a*) Obtain the Thevenin equivalent and find I_N and R_N using Eqns. 3.49 and 3.51. The direction of current flow in the source is assigned by noting that current flows out of the positive terminal; the direction of current flow is the same in a short circuit across the terminals of either equivalent.

Or,

(2*b*) Obtain the Norton equivalent independently by:

(*i*) Finding R_N exactly the same way as R_{Th} was found in section 3.6.2.

(*ii*) Find the short circuit current at the terminals of the one port. Its magnitude and direction of flow determine I_N.

3.7 SOURCE CONVERSIONS

The fact that a one port may be replaced by either the Thevenin or Norton equivalent yields a method of converting a voltage source in series with a resistance to a current source in parallel with a resistance. Thus an 8V source in series with 2 Ω is equivalent to, using Eqns. 3.49 and 3.51, a 4A current source in parallel with 2 Ω. This technique may be employed, in a circuit, prior to its solution by any of the standard methods.

For example, the circuit of Fig. 3.40*a* is equivalent to that of Fig. 3.40*b*. To obtain the latter circuit, the 8A current source is combined with one of the 4 Ω resistors in parallel with it. Alternatively we could have chosen to combine the two 4 Ω resistors in parallel to yield one 2 Ω resistor, this resistor in parallel with the 8A current source is equivalent to a 16 volt voltage source in series with 2 Ω.

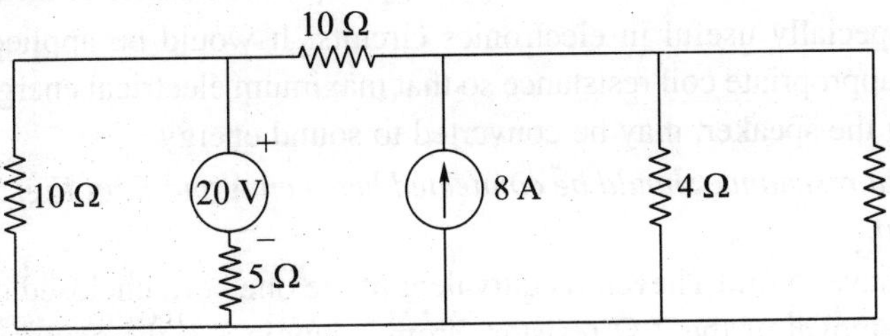

Fig. 3.40 (*a*) *An example involving source conversion*

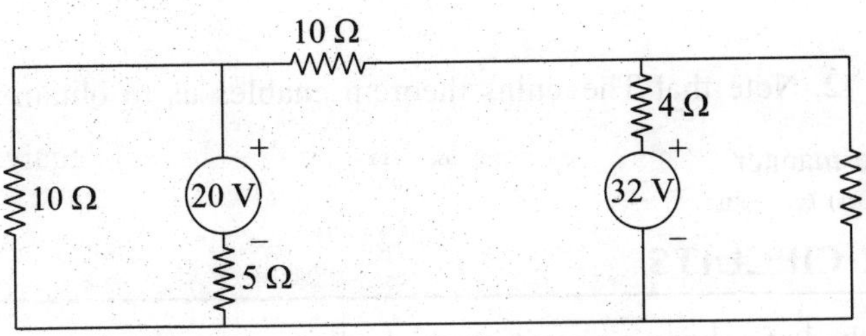

Fig. 3.40 (*b*) *Source conversions*

3.8 MAXIMUM POWER TRANSFER THEOREM

This theorem states that: "For maximum power dissipation in a load, the resistance is equal to the Thevenin equivalent resistance of the source".

We wish to find the value of R in 3.29*b* for maximum power dissipation in R.

In this circuit, $$I = \frac{V_{Th}}{(R + R_{Th})}$$

The power dissipated in the load, P_R, is given by

$$P_R = I^2 R = \frac{V_{Th}^2 R}{(R + R_{Th})^2}$$

To find the value of R which makes P_R a maximum, we set $\frac{dp_R}{dR} = 0$ and obtain

$$V_{Th}^2 (R + R_{Th})^2 - 2\,(R + R_{Th}) V_{Th}^2 R = 0$$

Simplification of the above expression yields the condition

$$R = R_{Th} \qquad ...(3.57)$$

This proves the statement of the theorem. Note that it applies to a load connected across a practical source or a load resistor in a circuit. In the latter case the Thevenin equivalent is found at the terminals of the load resistor after its removal from the circuit.

As a direct consequence of the theorem, under conditions of maximum power transfer half the available power is dissipated in the internal resistance of a generator or the Thevenin equivalent resistor and the remaining half expended in the load. The efficiency of power transfer is therefore 50%.

This theorem is especially useful in electronics circuits. It would be applied for example, to choose a speaker with the appropriate coil resistance so that maximum electrical energy, supplied by the power amplifier preceding the speaker, may be converted to sound energy.

Example 3.20. *What resistance should be connected between A and E, in Fig. 3.31 for maximum power to be dissipated in it.*

Solution. First we have to find Thevenin equivalent of the one port, enclosed by the dotted lines in Fig. 3.31, at *AE* after removal of the 2 Ω resistor. From example 3.8, the equivalent consists of a voltage source of $\frac{194}{7}$ volts in series with a resistor of $\frac{83}{7}$ ohms. The external resistor required between *A* and *E* is therefore $\frac{83}{7}$ Ω. Note that Thevenins theorem enables us to obtain the solution in a straightforward and simple manner.

3.9 NONLINEAR CIRCUITS

We will now present a method of solving a circuit in which all the components but one are linear. The sole device by virtue of being nonlinear posesses a nonlinear *V-I* characteristic. Examples of devices with nonlinear characteristics include nonlinear resistors, the diode, the transistor, dc generators, etc.

The situation is depicted in Fig. 3.41. Fig. 3.42 shows the nonlinear characteristic. This can be solved as follows. First, the device *D* is disconnected at *AB* (Fig. 3.41) and the Thevenin equivalent of the one port is obtained. The circuit of Fig. 3.41 is therefore transformed to that of Fig. 3.43. From Eqn. 3.41, the load line of Thevenin equivalent at *AB* is

$$I = \frac{V}{R_{Th}} + \frac{V_{Th}}{R_{Th}} \qquad ...(3.58)$$

For any load current, *I*, delivered by the equivalent source, the voltage across its terminals (*AB*) is realated to *I* by the expression in Eqn. 3.58. But, this voltage and current are also related by the equation which relates the current through and the voltage across the nonlinear device *D*. The latter equation, if available, should be solved simultaneously with Eqn. 3.58 in order to obtain a solution. This latter equation has to be formulated so that it expresses the *V-I* relationship of Fig. 3.42. On the other hand, the solution may be obtained graphically by finding the point of intersection of Eqn. 3.58 and the *V-I* characteristic of Fig. 3.42. The voltage and current corresponding to this point yield the solution.

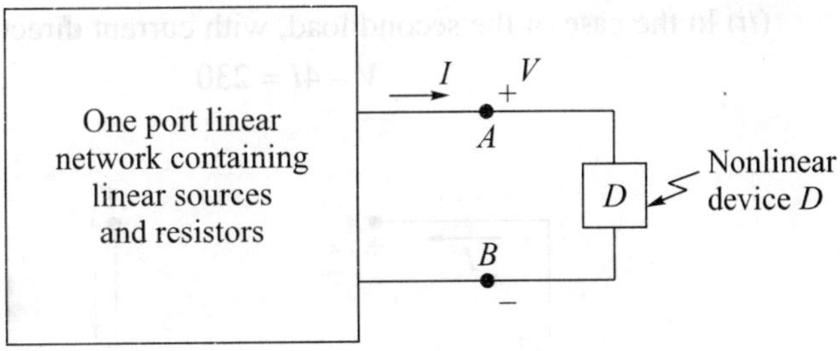

Fig. 3.41 *A nonlinear device connected at the terminals of a one port network*

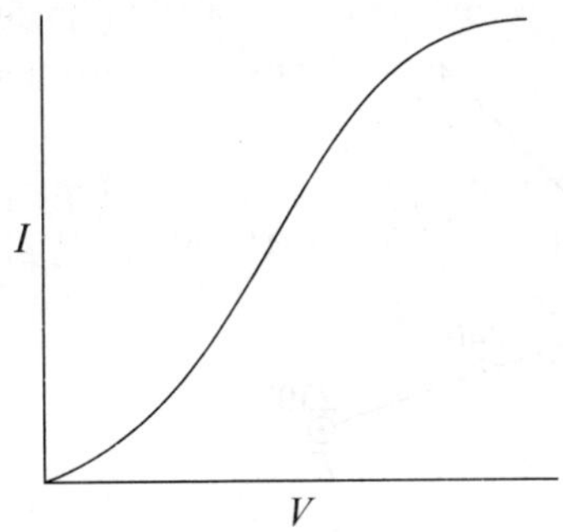

Fig. 3.42 *VI characteristic of the nonlinear device D of Fig. 3.41*

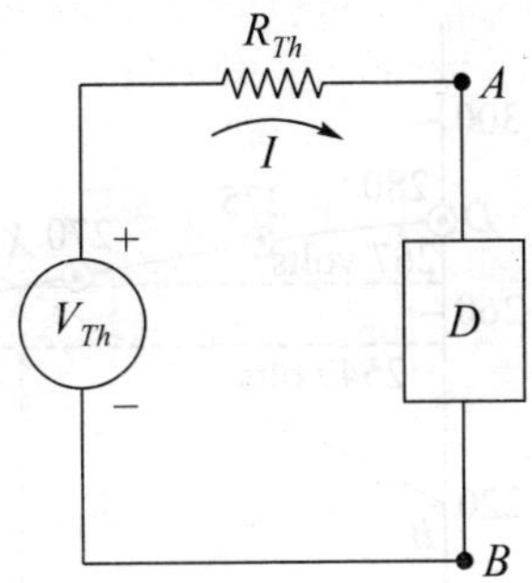

Fig. 3.43 *One port network of Fig. 3.41 replaced by its Thevenin's equivalent*

Example 3.21. *Table 3.1 shows the variation of the terminal voltage of a dc generator with load current. Find the terminal voltage and current supplied to a load comprising of*

(*i*) *a 18 ohm resistor*

(*ii*) *a 4 ohm resistor in series with a 230V battery as shown in Fig. 3.44c.*

Table 3.1. DC generator characteristics

Terminal voltage (V)	*280*	*275*	*270*	*260*	*250*	*240*	*230*
Load current (A)	*0*	*5*	*10*	*15*	*20*	*25*	*30*

Solution. Except for the DC generator, all other components are linear.

(*i*) First the generator characteristics are plotted to yield the curve *DXE*, Fig 3.45. The *V-I* characteristics of the 18Ω resistor (load line) is a line through the origin with a slope of 18 units, line *DA*. The point of intersection yields the answer, 19A and 254 volts.

(*ii*) In the case of the second load, with current direction as indicated, the load line equation is

$$V - 4I = 230 \qquad \text{...(3.59)}$$

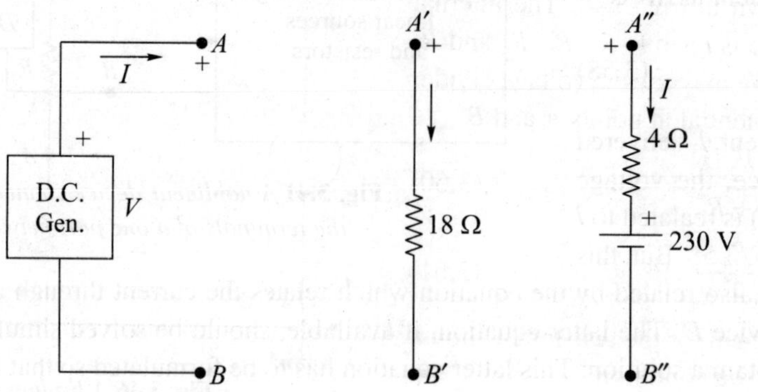

(*a*) *DC generator* (*b*) *Load across A′B′* (*c*) *Load across A″B″*

Fig. 3.44

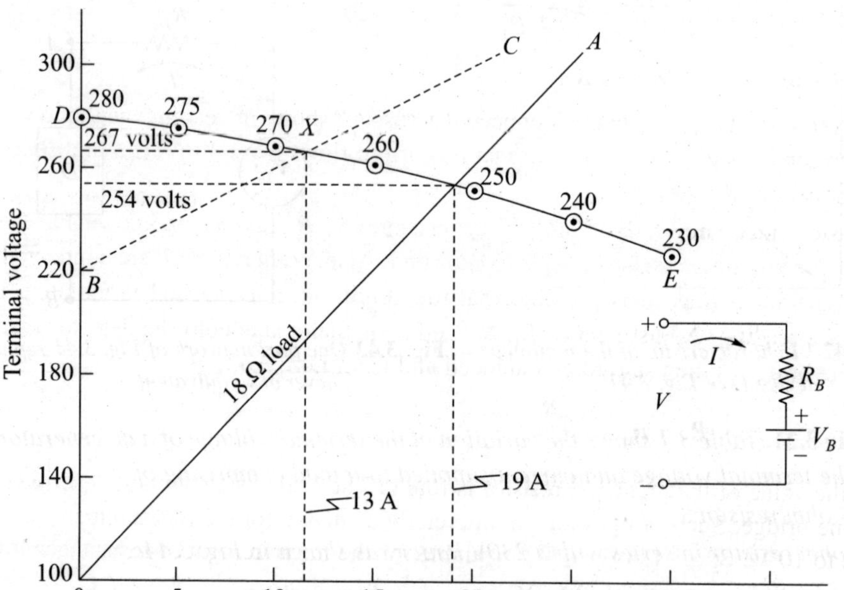

Fig. 3.45 *Generator characteristics*

Note that this equation differs from Eqn. 3.58, the load line of the Thevenin equivalent. The difference is due to the different directions of current flow. The Thevenin equivalent is a source whereas in the example at hand the combination of the battery and the resistor comprise a "live load".

To continue with the solution, Eqn. 3.59 is plotted on Fig. 3.45, line *BXC*, intersecting the generator characteristic at point *X*. The terminal voltage and load current in this case are 13A and 267 volts.

3.10 THE BRIDGE CIRCUITS

Consider the arrangement of four resistors across a voltage source as shown in Fig. 3.46. The internal resistance of the source is r while R_1, R_2, R_3 and R_4 are external resistors. We may use the voltage divider principle to find the potential at points A and B.

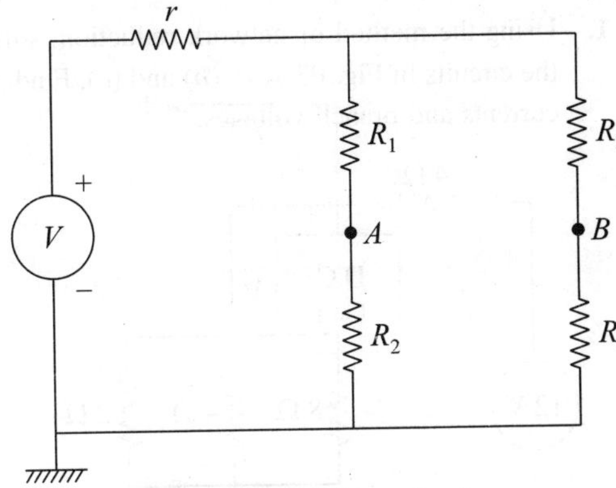

Fig. 3.46 *A bridge circuit*

Thus $$V_A = \frac{R_2}{R_1 + R_2} V \quad ...(3.60)$$

and $$V_B = \frac{R_4}{R_3 + R_4} V \quad ...(3.61)$$

Through adjustment of the resistors it should be possible to achieve the condition

$$V_A = V_B \quad ...(3.62)$$

When Eqn. 3.62 holds,

$$\frac{R_2}{R_1 + R_2} = \frac{R_4}{R_3 + R_4}$$

which simplifies to $$R_2 R_3 = R_1 R_4 \quad ...(3.63)$$

Under this condition, a voltmeter connected across AB shows no reading; neither does an ammeter connected between the same two points. In fact no current flows from A to B if A and B are joined by a resistor of R ohms, $0 \le R \le \infty$.

In a basic bridge circuit, three of the four resistors, R_1, R_2, and R_3 are known and the fourth one, say $R_4 = R_X$ is the unknown whose value is to be found. Also, points A and B are connected together by a voltmeter (detector). Since it is possible that the condition of Eqn. 3.63 is violated, initially, the detector shows a reading. Adjustment of R_1, R_2, and R_3 is then made until the detector reads zero (null condition). The bridge is then said to be balanced and from Eqn. 3.63,

$$R_X = R_4 = \frac{R_2 R_3}{R_1} \quad ...(3.64)$$

Thus the value of the unknown resistor is found. The basic bridge circuit described is known as the Wheatstone bridge. Such bridges are commercially available for the measurement of resistances in the range 1Ω to 10^9Ω. Special bridges are available for the measurement of resistances lower than 1Ω and higher than 10^9Ω.

The principle of the Wheatstone bridge is used in the measurement of torque, pressure, strain, vacuum, etc.

In the strain gauge a resistive wire experiences changes in resistance due to elongation as a result of mechanical forces. The change in resistance is measured and calibrated in terms of the mechanical force causing it. The changes in resistance are quite small and can be detected only with the aid of electronic amplifiers.

In a Pirani type vacuum gauge the unknown resistor, a heating element, is connected to the vacuum chamber the degree of vacuum in which is desired to be measured. The resistance of the element depends on its temperature and therefore on the heat loss from it to its surroundings which in turn depends on pressure. Thus resistance changes are related to pressure. A Pirani gauge measures pressure in the range 10 to 10^{-4} Torr (1 Atmosphere = 760 Torr = 760 mm Hg). Some Pirani gauges use thermistors.

PROBLEMS

1. Using the method of network reduction, solve the circuits in Fig. P3.1(*a*), (*b*) and (*c*). Find all currents and branch voltages.

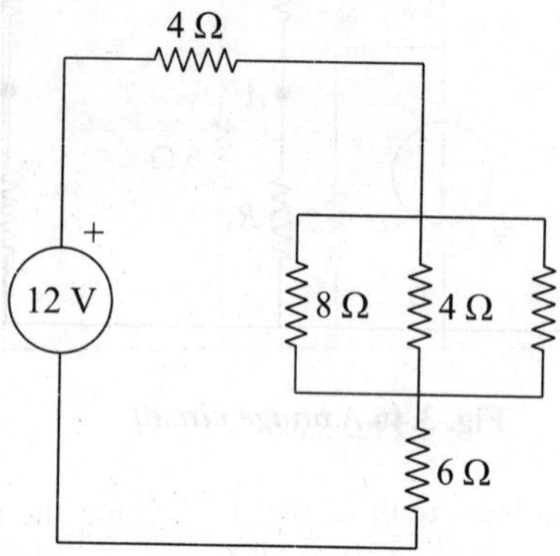

Fig. P.3.1(*a*)

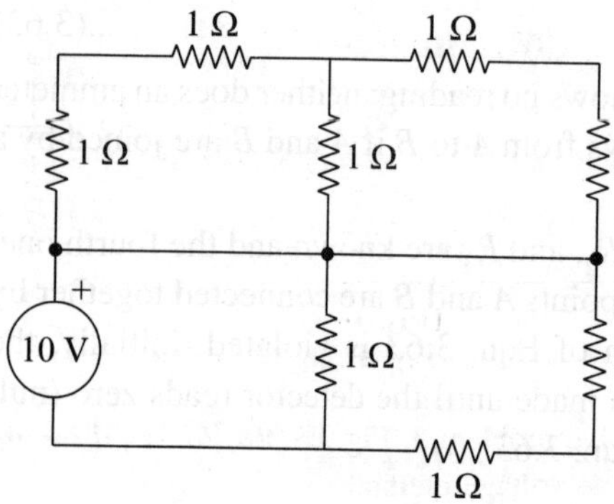

Fig. P.3.1(*b*)

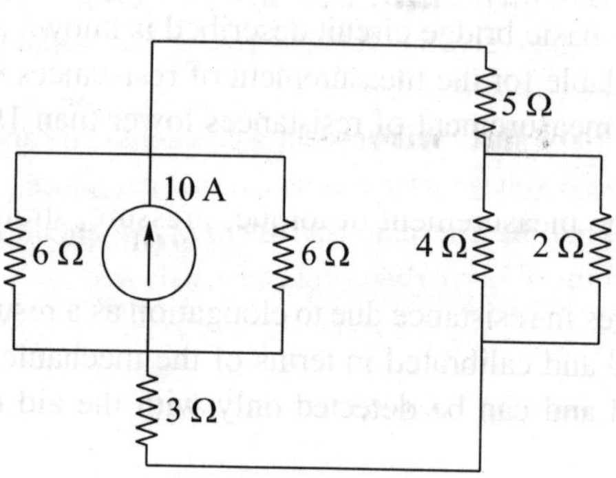

Fig. P.3.1(*c*)

2. Solve for all branch currents problem P2.8 of Chapter 2, using the method of network reduction, after connection of 20 volt source across *AB* with terminal *A* as positive.

3. Solve the circuits below, Figs. P3.3(*a*) to (*f*), using the method of mesh currents. Find all branch currents and node voltages.

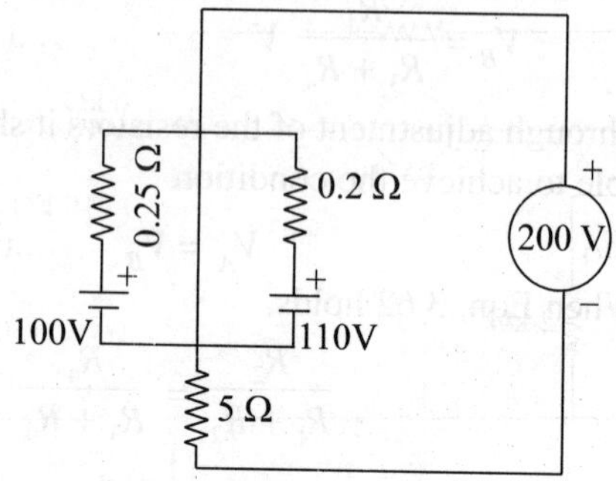

Fig. P.3.3(*a*)

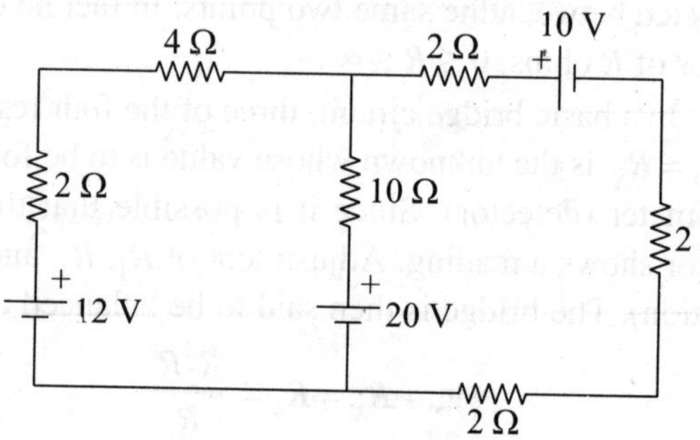

Fig. P.3.3(*b*)

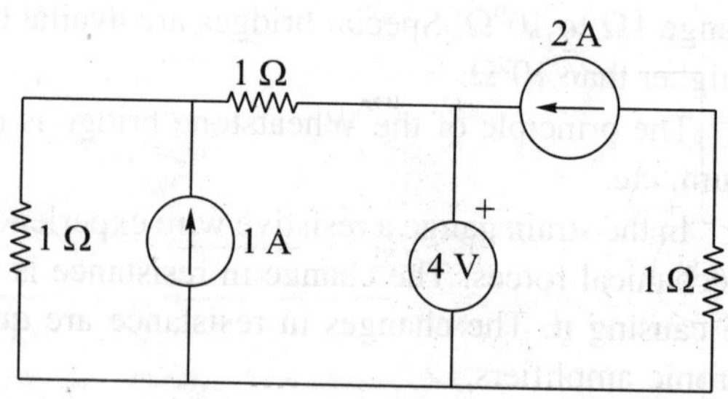

Fig. P.3.3(*c*)

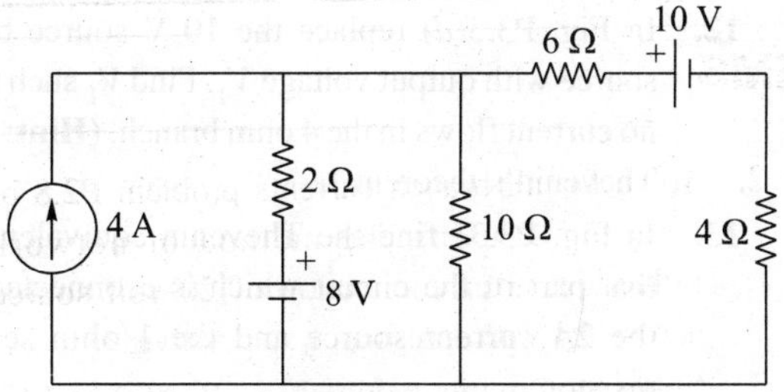

Fig. P.3.3(*d*)

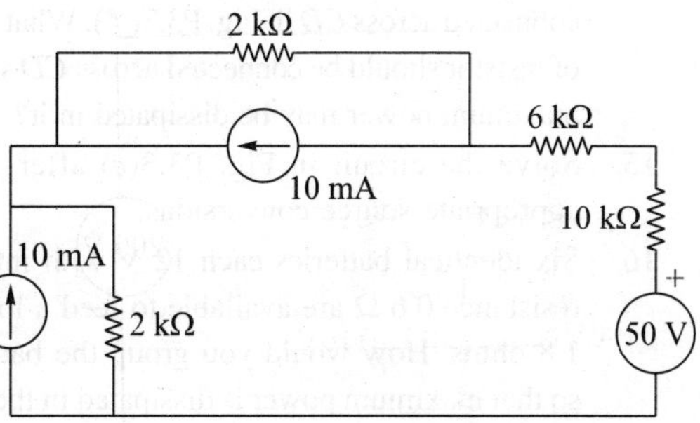

Fig. P.3.3(*e*)

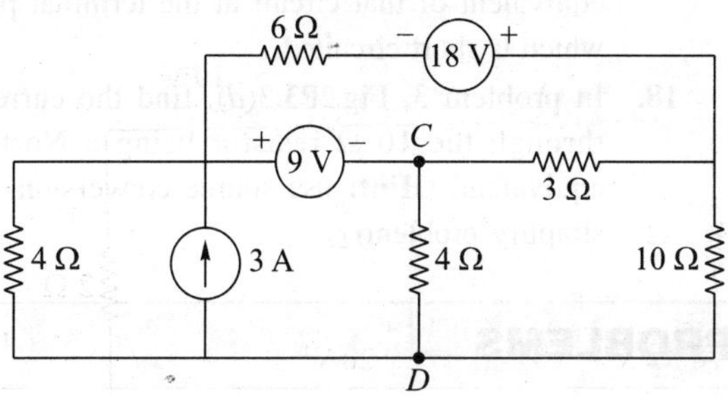

Fig. P.3.3(*f*)

4. In Fig. P3.4 find the current flowing through the detector using the mesh current method.

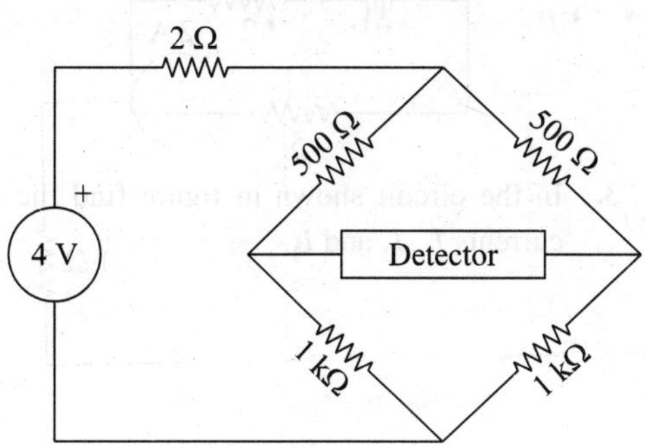

Fig. P.3.4

5. In Fig. P3.5 find I_{SC}, the short circuit current, using the mesh current method.

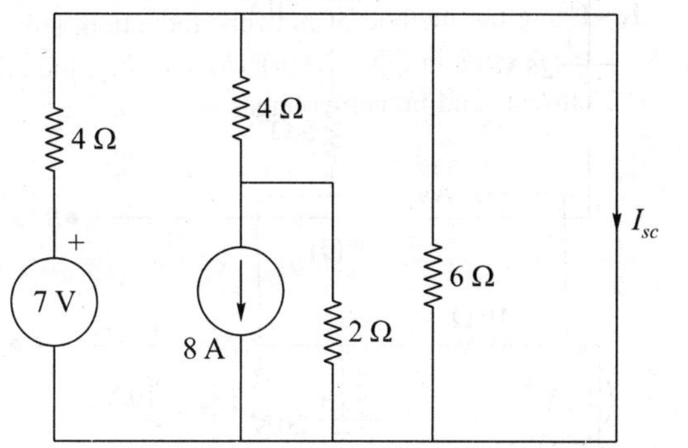

Fig. P.3.5

6. Solve the circuit of Fig. P3.6 using the node voltage method. Find all branch currents and node voltages.

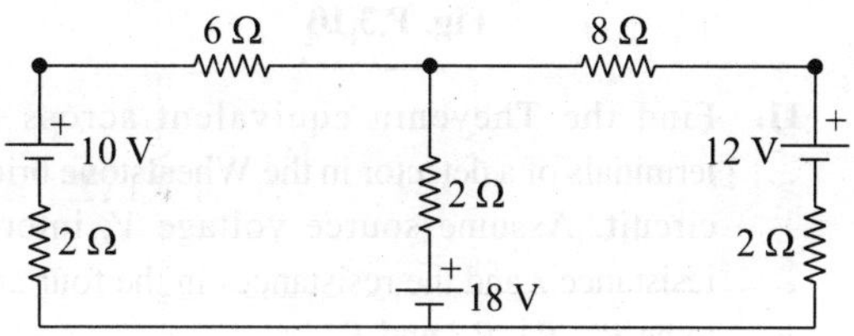

Fig. P.3.6

7. Solve problem 3, Fig. P3.3(*b*) to (*f*) using the node voltage method.

8. Show that the Thevenin equivalent of a source may be found by measuring the open circuit voltage and the voltage drop across a known load resistor.

9. Show that the Thevenin equivalent resistance of a voltage source is its internal resistance.

10. Find the Thevenin equivalent of the circuit of Figs. P3.10(*a*) and (*b*) at terminals *AB*.

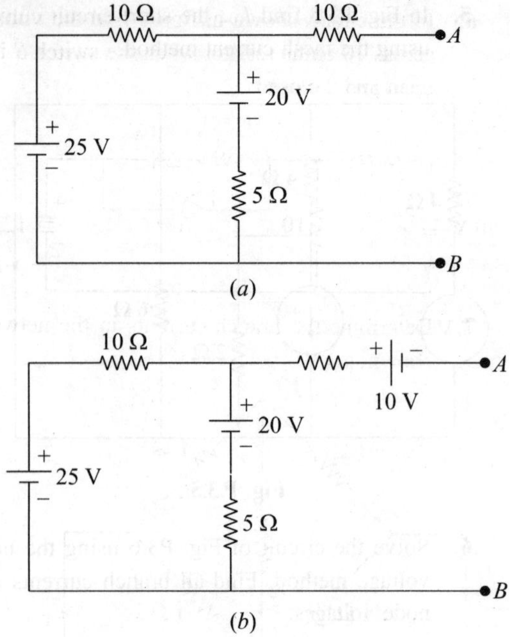

Fig. P.3.10

11. Find the Thevenin equivalent across the terminals of a detector in the Wheatstone bridge circuit. Assume source voltage V, internal resistance r and the resistances in the four arms to be R_A, R_B, R_C, and R_D.

12. In Fig. P3.3(d) replace the 10 V source by a source with output voltage V_1. Find V_1 such that no current flows in the 4 ohm branch. (**Hint:** use Thevenin's theorem).

13. In Fig. P3.3c find the Thevenin equivalent of that part of the circuit which is cconnected to the 2A current source and the 1 ohm series resistor.

14. Using Thevenin's theorem find the power dissipated in resistors of value 4, 8 and 12 ohms connected across CD in Fig. P3.3(f). What value of resistor should be connected across CD so that maximum power may be dissipated in it?

15. Solve the circuit in Fig. P3.3(e) after using appropriate source conversions.

16. Six identical batteries each 12 V with internal resistance 0.6 Ω are available to feed a load of 1.8 ohms. How would you group the batteries so that maximum power is dissipated in the load resistor?

17. Using the result of problem 5, find the Norton equivalent of that circuit at the terminal pair which is short circuited.

18. In problem 3, Fig. P3.3(d), find the current through the 10 Ω resistor using a Norton equivalent. (**Hint:** use source conversions to simplify problem).

EXERCISE PROBLEMS

1. Two batteries of 24 V and 20 V with internal resistance of 0.4 ohms and 0.25 ohms respectively are connected in parallel across a load of 4 ohms. Calculate the current supplied by each battery and the voltage across the land. [I_1 = 8.148 A, I_2 = – 2.96 A, V_L = 20.74 V].

2. In the circuit shown in figure find E_1, E_2 and I when the power dissipated in 5 ohms resistor is 125 watts. [E_1 = 32.5 V, E_2 = 30 V, I = 5A]

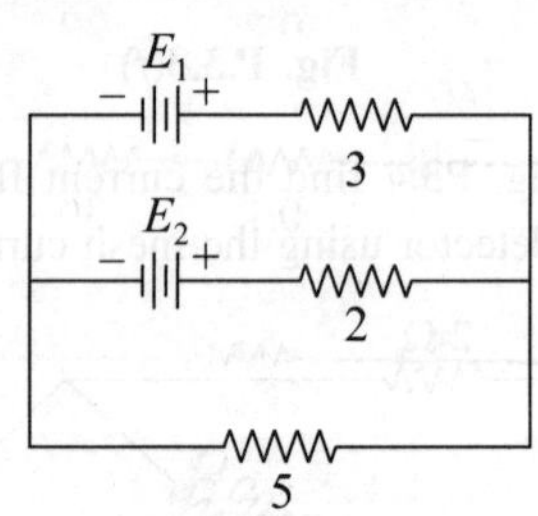

3. In the circuit shown in figure find the mesh currents I_1, I_2 and I_3.

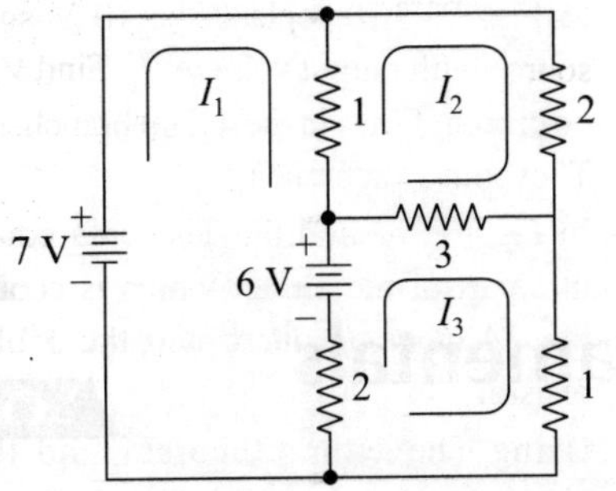

4. In the circuit shown, determine the value of R, if the power consumed in the 10 ohm resistor is 90 watts. [77.42 Ω].

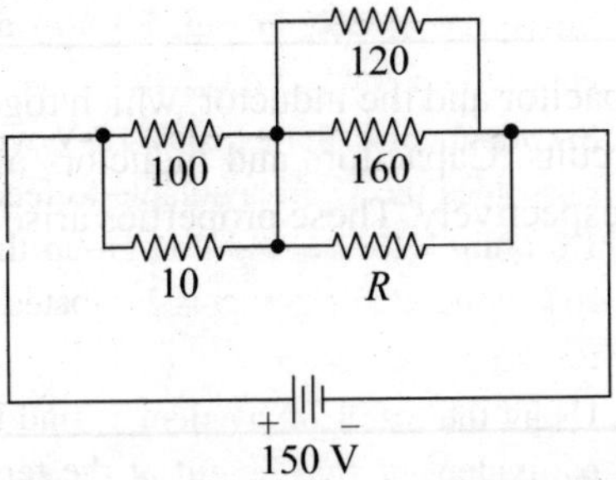

5. Find the current in each battery and in the 16 ohms resistor using branch current method for the circuit given in figure.

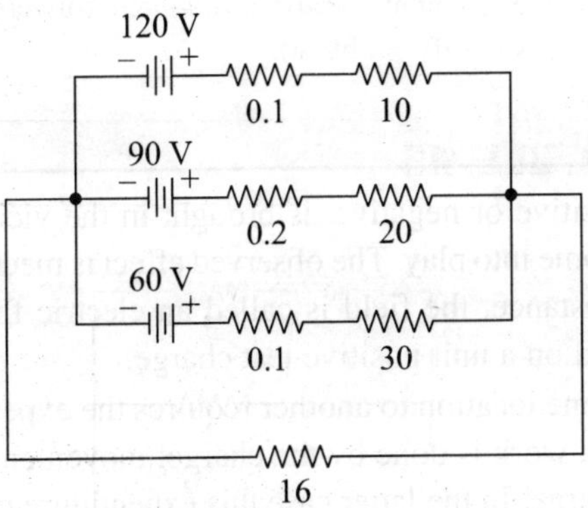

6. In the circuit shown in figure find the voltage across 10 ohms resistor when the switch S is 1 open and 2 closed.

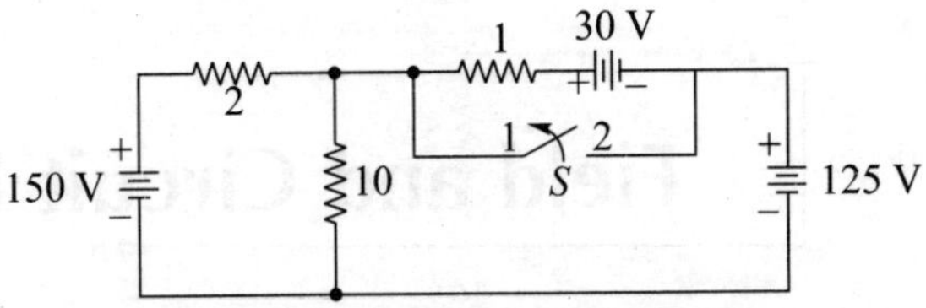

7. Determine the branch currents in the network shown.

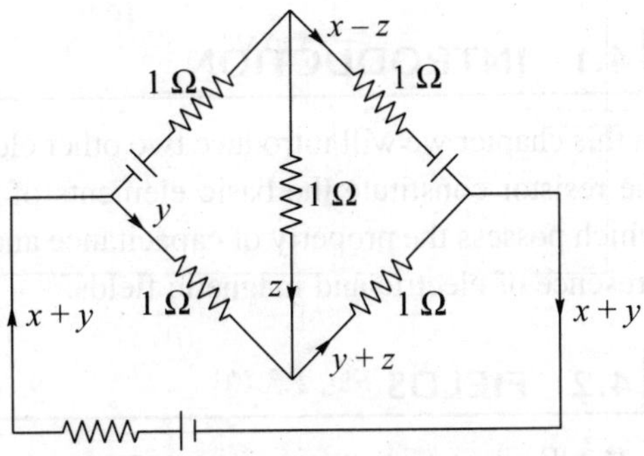

8. Use KCL to find the value of V in the circuit shown below.

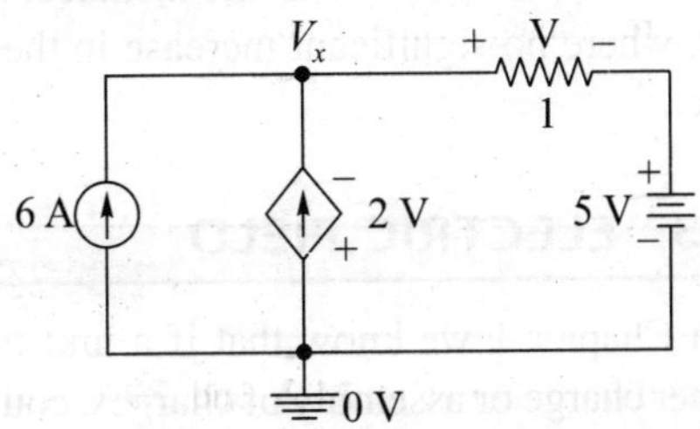

Field and Circuit Fundamentals

4

CHAPTER

4.1 INTRODUCTION

In this chapter we will introduce two other elements, the capacitor and the inductor, which together with the resistor constitute the basic elements of all electric circuits. Capacitors and inductors are devices which possess the property of capacitance and inductance respectively. These properties arise out of the presence of electric and magnetic fields.

4.2 FIELDS

A field is a region where certain effects may be observed. For example, if a body is maintained at a temperature higher than ambient, its presence is felt in the surrounding space by an increase in temperature which can be measured. In this instance, the field is a heat or thermal field. At some distance from the body, where no significant increase in the ambient temperature may be recorded, the field is said to be weak.

4.3 ELECTRIC FIELD

From Chapter 1 we know that if a unit test charge, positive or negative, is brought in the vicinity of another charge or assembly of charges, coulomb forces come into play. The observed effect is mechanical force due to the presence of electric charges. In this instance, the field is called an electric field. Its magnitude and direction are defined by the force exerted on a unit positive test charge.

Movement of a charge, in an electric field, from one location to another requires the expenditure of work. If the movement is in the direction of the force, work is done by the charge; movement in the opposite direction demands that work be done on the charge. In the latter case this expenditure of work increases the potential. In other words, the presence of an electric field is indicated by the existence of potential or voltage. In fact (section 1.8)

$$\text{Potential} = \frac{\text{Work}}{\text{Unit charge}} = \frac{\text{Force} \times \text{Distance}}{\text{Unit charge}}$$

$$= \text{Electric field} \times \text{Distance} \qquad \text{...(4.1)}$$

Thus potential and electric field are related.

In a battery, for example, an electric field exists between the positive and negative plates. An electric field also exists in the wires of an electric circuit and is responsible for the movement of charges which we call electric current.

4.4 CAPACITANCE, CAPACITORS

Consider an arrangement of two parallel plates separated by some distance in air. When the two plates are connected to the two terminals of a battery, electrons leave one plate, travel through the battery to the other plate. The two plates, therefore, get charged to opposite polarities. Work is necessary to establish these charges and is expended external to the battery. (Recall that in the case of a battery, this work is expended chemically within the battery.) The work done goes to increase the energy stored in the parallel plate arrangement. In general, the work done is proportional to the charge separated.

Therefore, charge separated, $Q \propto$ work done

$\propto$ potential (potential difference between the plates)

$\propto V$

or $$Q = CV \qquad ...(4.2)$$

In Eqn. 4.2, C is a constant and is called the capacitance of the parallel plate system. The capacitance property arises out of a separation of electric charge. In fact, any two oppositely charged bodies separated by a distance possess capacitance. The greater the capacitance, the greater the charge separation for the same potential difference and the stored energy is correspondingly greater.

In the parallel plate arrangement, if the space between the two plates is filled with an insulator (solid or liquid) it is found that the capacitance increases. The ratio $\frac{C_{\text{insulator}}}{C_{\text{air}}}$ is characteristic for each insulator and is known as the *permittivity* of the insulator in question. The higher this value, the greater the capacitance for the same electrode arrangement. The capacitance of the parallel plate arrangement also increases if the area of the plates is increased or if the distance separating them is decreased.

From Eqn. 4.2, the units of capacitance are Coulomb/Volt or $(\text{Coulomb})^2$/Joule; this is known as a Farad, and is denoted by F. The Farad is a rather large quantity and is therefore not a practical unit. For example, two metallic plates of size 60 m × 26 m (this areas is approximately that of an ice hockey rink) separated by a distance of 1 meter in air possess a capacitance of 1.38×10^{-8} F. If the distance separating the plates is decreased to 1 millimeter the capacitance becomes 1.38×10^{-5} F.

A practical unit is the microfarad (μF). Capacitors with values in the picofarad (pF) to microfarad range are common.

4.5 CAPACITOR TERMINAL VOLT-CURRENT RELATION

From Eqn. 4.2, $$Q = CV$$

Since $$I = \frac{dQ}{dt},$$

we obtain $$I = C\frac{dV}{dt} \qquad ...(4.3)$$

Equation 4.3 relates the voltage across the capacitor terminals to the current flowing through it. This is analogous to Ohm's law, Eqn. 1.4, for a resistor. Equation 4.3 shows that the voltage across a

CHAPTER 4

capacitor cannot change instantaneously. If it did, it implies that $\frac{dV}{dt} = \infty$ and this would demand infinite current flow through it. Clearly, such a situation is not physically possible.

4.6 ELECTROMAGNETISM

Electromagnetism deals with the relationship between electricity and magnetism. Electromagnetism is essentially the foundation for all electrical engineering. We use electromagnetism to generate electricity, store memory on our computers, generate pictures on a television screen, diagnose illnesses and in all aspects of lives that depends on electricity.

Principle of electromagnetism is that when an electric current flows through a wire, generates magnetic field. This magnetic field is that force which makes the metal objects stick to permanent magnets.

In a bar magnet, the magnetic field runs from the north to the south pole. In a wire, magnetic field forms around the wire. In fact, the magnetic field can be thought of as consisting of lines of force. The force of attraction and repulsion move along the magnetic force. When a magnet is placed on a paper where iron filings are spread, the orientations of the filings are as shown:

It is worth noting the circular pattern of the field lines. By convention, we say that field lines (lines of force) emanate from the north pole and re-enter the magnet through the south pole. More iron filings are attracted to the poles than else where—indicating the strength of the field is more at the poles.

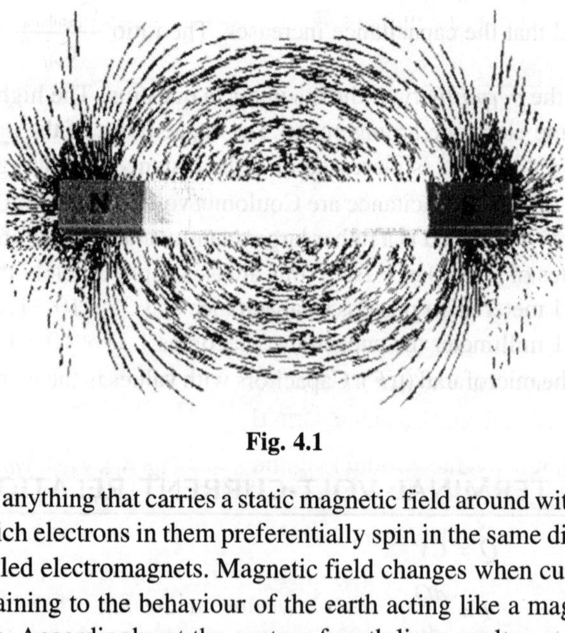

Fig. 4.1

Thus, a **magnet** is anything that carries a static magnetic field around with it. **Permanent magnets** are those materials in which electrons in them preferentially spin in the same direction. Magnets needing electricity to flow are called electromagnets. Magnetic field changes when current in the wire changes. Indeed, explanation pertaining to the behaviour of the earth acting like a magnetic has attracted many scientists and technicians. Accordingly, at the center of earth lies a molten metallic iron rich core. The outer portion of this core is molten. This core is spinning. The metals in the core have many loosely bound electrons and that these particles can conduct electricity. It is this mass of moving electrons which produces the magnetic field due to dynamo action. As such, when a compass is held, in the hand, it points to the earth's north pole. This is because, as said earlier, earth is like one giant magnet and the compass points to the magnetic north pole.

4.6.1 Magnetic Fields

We have seen that an electric field may be visualized to exist in the region surrounding charges at rest. It is observed that in the vicinity of a current carrying wire (charges in motion), a force is exerted on other charges in motion. This force cannot be accounted for by the presence of the Coulomb force alone. The additional force arises due to the presence of a magnetic field. Magnetic field are associated with current flow. The student is, no doubt, familiar with bar magnets. A magnetic field exists in the vicinity of a bar magnet; in this case the field is created by the cumulative effect of the flow of electronic currents in the atoms of the bar magnet.

Consider a bar magnet on top of which a smooth plane insulating surface is laid horizontally. The student has probably performed the experiment in which iron filings are sprinkled on the plate which is then tapped gently. It is seen that the fillings arrange themselves in the form of lines emanating from one pole of the magnet and terminating at the opposite pole. This situation is visualized as the flow of magnetic flux from one pole to the other. Where the lines are bunched close together, the flux density is greater and the observed magnetic forces are greater. Flux density is identified by the symbol $\overline{\mathbf{B}}$ and is defined by the equation

$$\overline{\mathbf{F}} = q\,(\overline{\mathbf{v}} \times \overline{\mathbf{B}}) \qquad \text{...(4.4)}$$

where $\overline{\mathbf{F}}$ is the force exerted on a charge of magnitude q coulombs, moving with velocity $\overline{\mathbf{v}}$ in a magnetic field where the flux density is $\overline{\mathbf{B}}$. Note that $\overline{\mathbf{F}}$, $\overline{\mathbf{v}}$ and $\overline{\mathbf{B}}$ are vectors and the cross product of $q\,\overline{\mathbf{v}}$ and $\overline{\mathbf{B}}$ yields $\overline{\mathbf{F}}$. From Eqn. 4.4, the units of $\overline{\mathbf{B}}$ are

$$\frac{\text{Newton } s}{\text{Coulomb } m} = \frac{\text{Newton } ms}{\text{Coulomb } m^2} = \frac{\text{Joule } s}{\text{Coulomb } m^2} = \frac{\text{Volt sec}}{m^2} \qquad \text{...(4.5)}$$

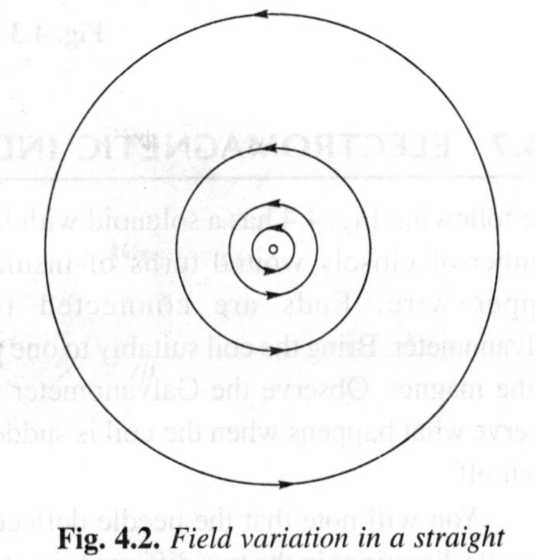

Fig. 4.2. *Field variation in a straight current carrying conductor*

A volt-second is known as a Weber and is denoted by Wb. Magnetic flux density is measured in Webers per m^2. A Weber per square meter is known as a Tesla. The actual quantity of flux, Φ, flowing through an area normal to the direction of $\overline{\mathbf{B}}$ is given by the product of the magnitudes of flux density and the area.

Thus

$$\Phi = BA \text{ Webers} \qquad \text{...(4.6)}$$

Consider a straight wire isolated in space carrying dc current. This situation has cylindrical symmetry and we expect the associated flux lines to be located concentrically about the wire. Naturally the field decays with distance from the wire. The situation is shown in Fig. 4.2.

If the same current carrying wire is coiled, the magnetic field pattern around each turn of the coil will be as shown in Fig. 4.3(*a*) and the fluxes due to each turn add algebraically. The net result is a strengthening of flux within the coil. The flux pattern now looks like that associated with a bar magnet, as shown in Fig. 4.3(*b*).

The flux entering the cross-sectional area of a coil along its axis and parallel to it is known as flux linking the coil.

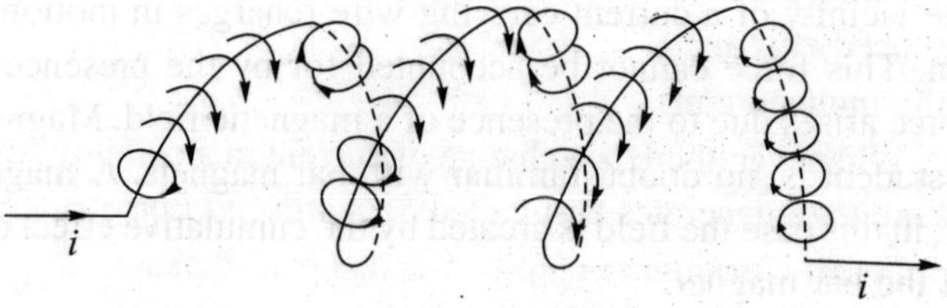

Fig. 4.3 (*a*) *Flux pattern*

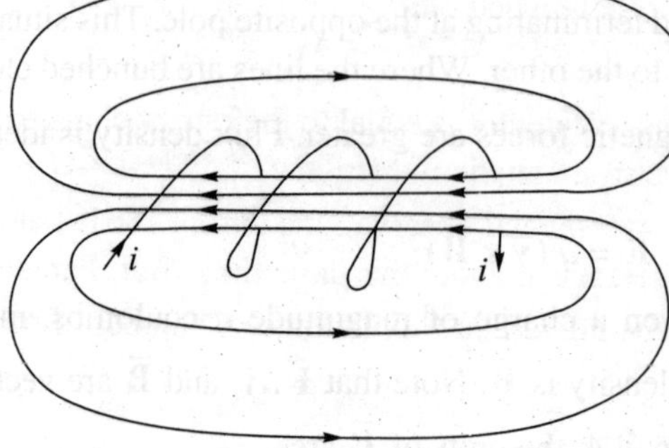

Fig. 4.3 (*b*) *Magnetic field pattern*

4.7 ELECTROMAGNETIC INDUCTION

The following Fig. 4.4 has a solenoid with large number of closely wound turns of insulated copper wire. Ends are connected to a Galvanometer. Bring the coil suitably to one pole of the magnet. Observe the Galvanometer also observe what happens when the coil is suddenly taken off.

You will note that the needle deflects to opposite directions in the two different situations and suddenly comes back to the initial position.

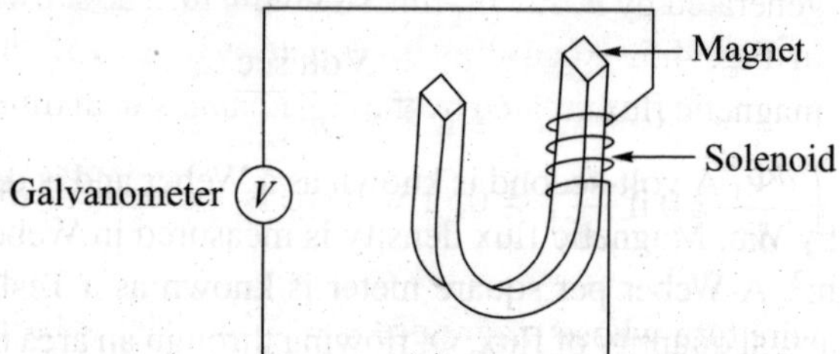

Fig. 4.4

In this situation, a temporary electric current was generated either because the flux lines were cut by the moving coil or the flux lines with the coil were changed.

The process of inducing an emf in a conductor whenever the magnetic flux linked with it changes, is known as **Electromagnetic Induction**. The emf is induced emf and current induced current. The induced emf depending on the rate at which the magnetic pole is introduced into a solenoid and withdraw from it. In fact, the induced emf increases when the speed of motion increases, so also with an increase in the number of turns and the strength of the magnetic field.

4.7.1 Classification of Induced emfs

Induced emfs are classified as

(*i*) Statically induced emf and

(*ii*) Dynamically induced emf.

Further statically induced emfs are classified into

(*i*) Self-induced emf and

(*ii*) Mutually induced emf.

Self-Induced emf: Whenever, there is a change of current in a coil it produces magnetic field and as seen it cuts the coils and then generates emf called *Self-Induced Emf.*

Mutually induced emf: Consider two coils *A* and *B* placed near to each other. Let coil *A* carry a uniformly changing current I_1 and the flux produced in the coil is ϕ_1. The entire flux ϕ_1 links with coil *B* and as ϕ_1 is changing at every instant, hence there will be induced emf in coil *B*. This emf is termed as 'mutually induced emf .'

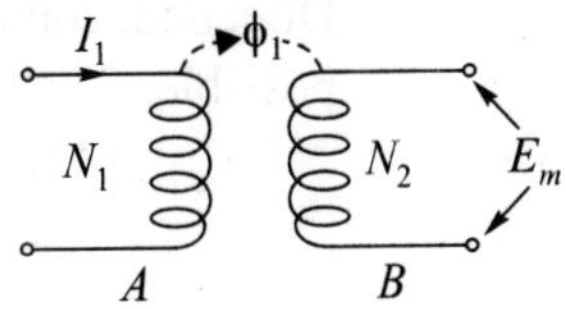

4.7.2 Induced emf

"The induced emf developed in a conductor is equal to the rate of change of flux linked with it." This is known as Faraday's law of electro magnetic induction.

Faraday's law was by experimental observations during 1831. Later it was formalized the effect was also discovered by Joseph Henry at about the same time. But, Faraday published it first.

From the above, it may be noted that flux linkage = Number of turns × flux linking these turns. Unit is Weber-turn.

4.7.3 Faraday and Lenz Laws

Consider a coil carrying dc current. It creates a magnetic field whose pattern will be as shown in Fig.4.3(*b*). Suppose, now, a wire turn is placed in the vicinity of the coil so that some of the flux generated by it, say Φ_1 links the wire turn as shown in Fig. 4.5. According to **Faraday's law,** if the magnetic flux created by the coil changes with time, $\left(\frac{d\Phi_1}{dt} \neq 0 \text{ if } \frac{di}{dt}\right) \neq 0$, a voltage is induced in the wire turn whose magnitude is = $\frac{d\Phi_1}{dt}$. The polarity of the induced voltage is obtained by application of **Lenz's law** which states that the induced voltage ends to cause current flow in the wire turn in such a direction so that its magnetic flux opposes the changing parent magnetic flux.

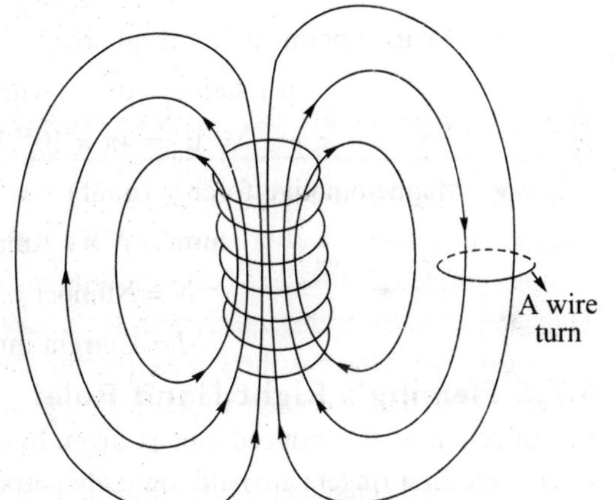

Fig. 4.5 *Flux generated by coil A linking the wire turn*

Generally, we may combine the Faraday and Lenz laws into one statement as follows:

"The induced voltage in a circuit is proportional to the rate of change of magnetic flux which links it; the polarity of the induced voltage is such that it tends to cause current flow which oppose the changing magnetic flux."

Suppose a flux Φ_2, arising out of current flow in a coil, links another coil which comprises of many wire turns. In each turn the induced voltage, by Faraday's law, is $\frac{d\Phi_2}{dt}$. The total magnitude of induced voltage in this coil is therefore $N\frac{d\Phi_2}{dt}$. The total effective flux linkage is therefore $N\phi_2$ Webers.

4.7.4 Definitions of Some Common Terms Used

Magnetic flux ϕ (Weber)

- Flux lines have the following characteristics:
  Direction, continuous, flux lines repel each other they arrange themselves to be as short as possible.

$$\phi = \frac{F}{R} \text{ where } \phi = \text{Wb}, F = \text{MMF in Amp-turns}, R = \text{Reluctance.}$$

$$(1 \text{ Wb} = 10^8 \text{ lines})$$

- Flux density = B (Wb/m^2) Tesla

$$B = \phi/A$$

B = Magnetic flux density, ϕ = Flux in Wbs, A = Area in sq mt.

- Permeability : μ (Wb/Amp-turn-meter)
  Ease with which flux lines may be established within a material.

$\mu = B/H$ where μ = Permeability

B = Flux density

H = Magnetic field intensity

- Relative permeability μ relative

μ relative = μ / μ_0 where μ_0 = Permeability of vacuum

$\mu_0 = 4\pi \times 10^{-7}$ Wb/A-m

- Magnetomotive force χ (mmf)

mmf = $N \times I$ Amp turns

N = Number of turns of a conductor

I = Current through the N turns.

4.7.5 Fleming's Right Hand Rule

The direction of the induced emf is given by **Fleming's right hand rule**. This law can be stated as, when three-first fingers are held mutually perpendicular to each other and if the fore finger is placed in the direction of current and thumb in the direction of motion of the conduct then the middle finger points out the direction of induced emf.

This emf is also called as *dynamically induced emf.*

Hold the three fingers as shown below, Then Thumb – Direction of Motion

Fore Finger – Field direction, Middle Finger – Induced emf

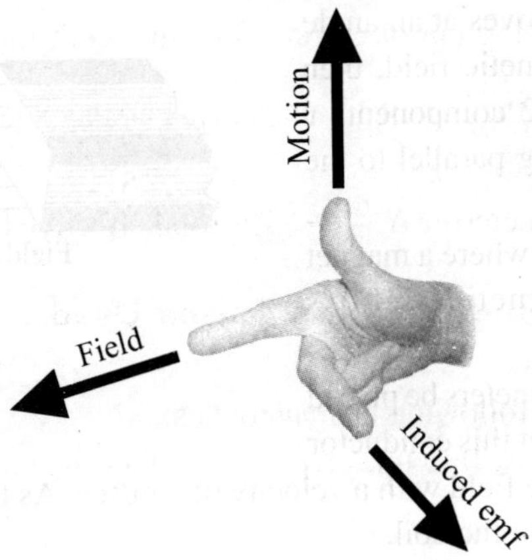

Fig. 4.6 *Fleming's right hand rule*

Generator Rule

If the coil has N turns, then

$$E_s = \text{N}.\ \frac{d\phi}{dt} = N\cdot\frac{dI}{dt}\left(\frac{\phi}{I}\right)$$

I and ϕ vary continuously keeping $\left(\frac{\phi}{I}\right)$ constant.

As such,
$$E_s = \left(N\cdot\frac{\phi}{I}\right)\cdot\frac{dI}{dt} \text{ Volts}$$

$\left(N\cdot\frac{\phi}{I}\right)$ is known as sub-inductance of a coil or inductance denoted as L.

Hence,
$$E_s = L\frac{dI}{dt} \text{ (as } \phi \text{ is proportional to } I)$$

where, $L = \dfrac{N\,.\,\phi}{I}$ Unit of L is Henry.

A coil is said to have an inductance of 1H, if an emf of 1 volt is generated in it, when a current through it is changing at the rate of 1 A/sec. If may also be noted that

$$L = N\cdot\frac{\phi}{I}.\ \text{However, } \phi = \frac{NI}{S}$$

$$= \left(\frac{N^2}{S}\right)$$

or
$$L = \frac{N^2}{(l/a\mu_0\mu_R)} \text{ Henry Since } S = \left(\frac{l}{a\mu_0\mu_R}\right).$$

4.7.6 Dynamically Induced emf

When a magnetic field is stationary and the conductor is in motion, then the induced emf is called dynamically induced emf.

Suppose the conductor moves at an angle α with the direction of the magnetic field, then the velocity V is resolved into 2 components $v \cos \alpha$ and $v \sin \alpha$. $v \cos \alpha$ being parallel to the field doesn't induce any voltage.

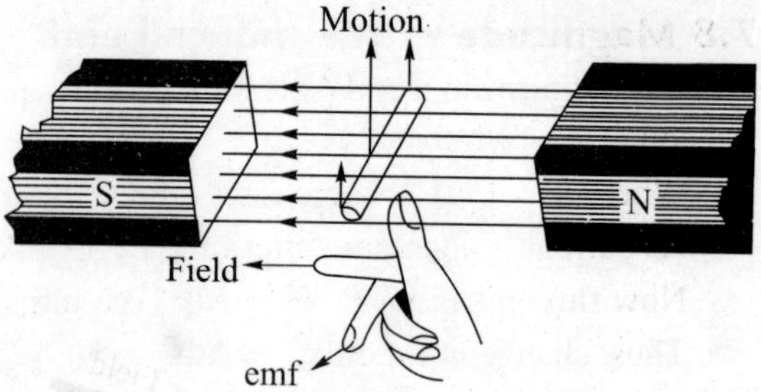

Fig. 4.7

Consider the above figure where a magnet with B Wb/m^2 uniform magnetic field is considered.

Let a conductor AB with L meters be placed in the magnetic field as shown. Let this conductor AB be moved perpendicular to the field with a velocity of v m/sec. As the coil moves, it cuts the lines of force and thus emf is developed in the coil.

Let the voltage developed be E volts.

Let A' B' be quite near AB *i.e.*, AB has been moved through a small distance of dx in a time of say dt.

Hence, total area cut by the conductor = $(dx \cdot l)$ m^2

Thereby flux cut = $(dx \cdot x)\, B$ Webers

Also, $\dfrac{d\phi}{dt} = B.l\,\dfrac{dx}{dt}$ $\dfrac{dx}{dt}$ = Velocity

Hence, $\dfrac{d\phi}{dt} = B.l.v$ volts

Thus, voltage induced = $B.l.v$ volts

If, however, as mentioned above, conductor moves at an angle α, then $\mathbf{E = B\, \mathit{l}\, \mathit{v} \sin \theta}$ volts.

4.7.7 Fleming's Left Hand Rule

The direction of motion of the conductor is given by **Fleming's Left Hand Rule.** This law can be stated as, when first-three fingers of left hand are held perpendicular to each other and if the fore finger points in the direction of field and middle finger points in the direction of current then the thumb gives the direction of the motion of the conductor.

Hold the three fingers as above, Then Thumb – Direction of Motion

Fore Finger – Field direction and Middle Finger points the direction of – Induced Current

Motor Rule

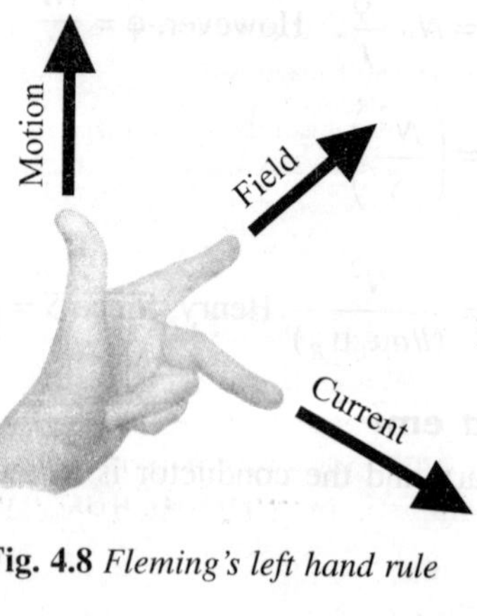

Fig. 4.8 *Fleming's left hand rule*

4.7.8 Magnitude of the Induced emf

Let N = No. of turns in a coil /solenoid, I = Current flow through the coil (ac) at any inst; flux linkages of the coil = $N\phi_1$ Wb-turns.

Where ϕ_1 = Flux at some arbit time t_1 (with a current say I_1)

As current is changing; after time t_1, it could be say I_2 and thus Φ_2 = Flux set up by it.

Now flux linkages $= N\Phi_2$ Wb-turns.

Thus, change in the flux $= N\Phi_2 - N\Phi_1$

$= N(\Phi_2 - \Phi_1)$ Wb-turns

Rate of change of flux $= \dfrac{N(\Phi_2 - \Phi_1)}{t}$ Wb-turns/sec

and this is the average induced voltage according to Farady

$$\text{Thus,} \qquad E = \text{Induced voltage} = \frac{N(\Phi_2 - \Phi_1)}{t} \text{ volts}$$

As $(\phi_2 - \phi_1)/t$ is the rate of change of flux, we may also write

$$E = \text{Induced voltage} = \left(N\frac{d\Phi}{dt}\right) \text{ volts}$$

Indeed, the direction of the induced voltage is according to (Russian physicist Heinrich Friedrich Emil Lenz) Lenz's law (1834) which states that the induced emf is in such a direction as to oppose the cause producing it.

$$\text{Thus, we write} \qquad E = -N\frac{d\Phi}{dt}$$

Lenz's law is also connected with the conservation of energy: To see this point, move a magnet towards a closed loop of wire-say a solenoid. An electric current is induced in the solenoid. This produces an emf that acts upon them. The direction of the induced current depends on whether the south or the north pole approaching the solenoid, an approach of north pole will produce an current is induced in the solenoid. This produces an emf that acts upon them. The direction of the induced current depends on whether the south or the north pole approaching the solenoid, an approach of north pole will produce an counter-clockwise current, and the south pole approaching will produce a clockwise current to understand the implications of conservation of energy, suppose the induced current directions were opposite to those joint described. Then the north pole of an approaching magnet would induce a south pole in the near face of the loop. These N-S poles attract and accelerate magnets approach. This would make the magnetic field increase more quickly, which in turn would increase the loop's current, strengthening the magnetic field, increasing the attraction and acceleration and so on. Both the kinetic energy of the magnet and the rate of energy dissipation in the loop would increase. A small energy input produces a large energy output, violating the law of conservation of energy.

4.8 SELF-INDUCTANCE AND INDUCTORS

If dc current flows through a coil of wire of zero resistance and if the magnitude of the current increases with time the following events occur. Since the current is increasing, so does the magnetic flux Φ linking the coil. By Faraday's law, a voltage is induced which appears across the terminals of the coil.

Since an electric circuit exists, the induced voltage tends to produce current flow which, by Lenz's law, should be opposite in direction to the parent current. The polarity of the induced voltage must therefore be as shown in Fig. 4.9. We may therefore regard this induced voltage as a voltage drop whose magnitude is equal to $N\dfrac{d\Phi}{dt}$. If the magnetic flux, Φ, linking the coil and the current, i, causing it are linearly related, we may write

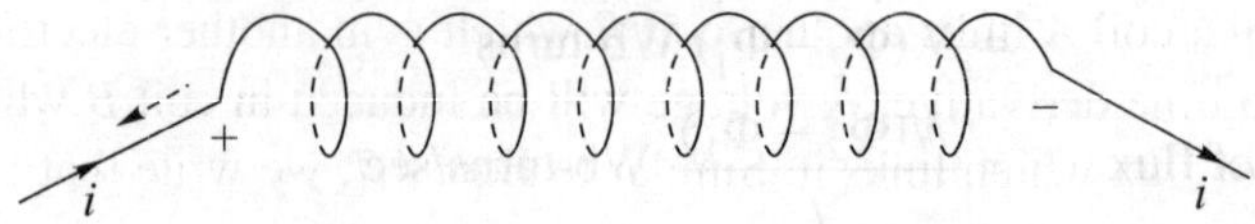

Fig. 4.9 *Voltage induced in a current carrying conductor*

$$N\,\Phi \propto i$$

or $$N\,\Phi = \text{L}i \qquad \text{...(4.7)}$$

The constant of proportionality, L, is known as self-inductance. Coils possessing the property of self-inductance are known as inductors.

From Eqn. 4.7, the unit of inductance is Weber/amp. This is known as a Henry, abbreviated H.

The Henry is a large and, therefore, impractical unit. For example, if number 18 AWG solid copper wire (1.0 mm diameter) is used to wind a single layer air core coil on an insulating tube 1 cm diameter and 5 cm long, one obtains approximately 50 turns; the inductance of this coil is about 5 μH.

The inductance of a single layer coil is directly proportional to the square of the number of turns and the coil area (flux linkage area) and it is inversely proportional to the length of the coil. In the above example, if the coil radius and length are doubled are the same wire used to wind it, the resulting inductance will be 40 μH.

The inductance of a coil increases if the material of the core over which it is wound is magnetic in nature. The increase is proportional to a property of magnetic materials called the permeability. For example, if the 5 cm long coil is wound on a ferrite core whose permeability is 1500, the inductance of the coil increases from 5 μH to 7500 μH or 7.5 mH.

4.9 INDUCTOR TERMINAL VOLT-CURRENT RELATION

From the considerations of Section 4.7 and Eqn. 4.7, the voltage drop across an inductor due to current flow i through it is

$$v = \frac{d}{dt}[N\phi] = \frac{d}{dt}[Li] = L\frac{di}{dt} \qquad \text{...(4.8)}$$

Should the inductor coil possess finite resistance, Eqn. 4.8 should be modified to

$$v = L\frac{di}{dt} + Ri \qquad \text{...(4.9)}$$

From Eqn. 4.8 one can draw conclusions similar to that drawn from consideration of Eqn. 4.3. The current through an inductor cannot change instantaneously as this would demand an infinite voltage drop across it. Also, the voltage drop is zero if $\frac{di}{dt}$ is zero.

4.10 MUTUAL INDUCTANCE

Suppose flux Φ from a coil A links another coil B which is in another electric circuit. Further, let this flux have a non-zero time derivative. A voltage will be induced in coil B which is proportional to the time rate of change of flux which links it. Similar to Eqn. 4.7, we write that

$$N\Phi = Mi \qquad ...(4.10)$$

In Eqn. 4.10, $N\Phi$ is the total flux linkage of coil B and i is the current in coil A. The voltage induced in coil B is therefore $\frac{d}{dt}[N\Phi]$ or $M\frac{di}{dt}$. The constant M has the units of inductance and is known as mutual inductance. Naturally, M is equal to zero if none of the flux from coil a links coil B.

4.10.1 Mutual Inductance and Coefficient of Coupling

Consider two coils A and B placed near to each other as shown in figure. Let the coil A carry the current I_1 and produces a flux Φ_1 in the winding. This flux link with the coil B entirely if there is no magnetic leakage. As Φ_1 is changing or varying with time the flux linking with coil B also changes and induces an emf Em. in the coil B.

$$E_m = N_2\frac{(d\Phi_1)}{dt}$$

$$= N_2\frac{d\Phi_1}{dI_1} \times \frac{dI_1}{dt}$$

$$= \frac{N_2\Phi_1}{I_1} \times \frac{dI_1}{dt}$$

$$Em = M\frac{dI_1}{dt} \quad \text{where } M = \frac{(N_2\Phi_1)}{I_1}$$

M is called coefficient of mutual inductance or mutual inductance between the coils A and B and is defined as the number of flux linkages of one coil due to unit current in the other coil.

$$M = \frac{(N_2\Phi_1)}{I_1} = \frac{(N_1\Phi_2)}{I_2}$$

Similarly if Φ_2 is the flux in the second coil and Φ_1 is the flux linking with coil A then the induced emf Em in coil 'A' is

$$Em = \frac{d\Phi_2}{dt} = N_1\frac{d\Phi_2}{dI_2}\frac{dI_2}{dt}$$

$$= N_1\frac{\Phi_2}{I_2}\frac{dI_2}{dt}$$

$$Em = M\frac{dI_2}{dt}$$

CHAPTER 4

Also, we have $M = N_2 \dfrac{\Phi_1}{I_1}$; where $\Phi_1 = \dfrac{N_1 I_1}{S}$

where $S = 1/\mu_0 \, \mu_r \, A.$ Therefore $\dfrac{\Phi_1}{I_1} = \dfrac{N_1}{S}$

Substituting it, we get

$$M = \frac{N_2 N_1}{S} = \frac{(N_2 N_1)}{1/\mu_0 \mu_r A}$$

$$\boxed{M = \frac{\mu_0 \, \mu_r \, A N_1 N_2}{l}}$$

Mutual inductance between two coils is defined as the number of flux lines linking with the second coil due to the current in the first coil. If N_1 and N_2 are the number of turns in first and second coils and I_1 and I_2 are the current through the coils 1 and 2. Then the flux generated by the coil 1 which is Φ_1 may not link completely with second coil due to leakage and hence the flux linking with coil 2 which is Φ_2 will always less than Φ_1.

The emf induced in the second coil due to the flux Φ_2 is

$$Em = \frac{N_2 d\Phi_2}{dt} = \frac{(N_2 d\Phi_2)}{dI_1}\left(\frac{dI_1}{dt} E_m = M_{21}\frac{dI_1}{dt}\right)$$

$$\boxed{M_{21} = \frac{N_2 \Phi_2}{I_1}}$$

is the flux linkage in second coil due to the current in first coil.

Similarly if we write the equation for mutual inductance referred to first coil due to the current in second coil.

$$M_{12} = \frac{N_1 \Phi_1}{I_2}$$

$$M_{12} \times M_{21} = \frac{(N_2 \Phi_2)}{I_1} \times \frac{(N_1 \Phi_1)}{I_2} = \frac{(N_1 \Phi_1)}{I_1} \times \frac{(N_2 \Phi_2)}{I_2}$$

$$M_{12} \times M_{21} = L_1 \, L_2, \quad \text{where} \quad L_1 = \frac{(N_1 \Phi_1)}{I_1} \quad \text{and} \quad L_2 = \frac{(N_2 \Phi_2)}{I_2}$$

If $\quad M_{12} = M_{21} = M$

$\therefore \quad M^2 = L_1 \, L_2$

$$M = \sqrt{L_1 L_2}$$

If K's fraction of Φ_1 is linked with coil 2. Then $\Phi_2 = K\Phi_1$

Similarly if K's fraction of Φ_2 is linked with coil 1. Then $\Phi_1 = K\Phi_2$

$$M_{12} = \frac{N_2 \Phi_2}{I_2} = \frac{N_1 K \Phi_1}{I_2} = \frac{K N_1 \Phi_1}{I_2}$$

$$M_{21} = \frac{N_2 \Phi_1}{I_1} = \frac{N_2 K \Phi_2}{I_1} = \frac{K N_2 \Phi_2}{I_1}$$

$$M_{12} = M_{21} = \frac{KN_1\Phi_1}{I_2} \times \frac{KN_2\Phi_2}{I_1} = \frac{K'N_1\Phi_1}{I_1} \times \frac{N_2\Phi_2}{I_2} = K^2 (L_1 L_2)$$

If $M_{12} = M_{21} = M$

$$M^2 = K^2 L_1 L_2$$

$$K^2 = \frac{M^2}{L_1 L_2} \qquad \boxed{K = \frac{M}{\sqrt{L_1 L_2}}}$$

where K is called **coefficient of magnetic coupling.**

4.11 THE BASIC ELEMENTS AND ENERGY STORAGE

Resistors, capacitors and inductors are bilateral, linear and passive elements. The first-two attributes imply that current may flow in either direction through these elements; further the volt-amp characteristics are linear. Passive elements do not create energy.* Although all the three elements are passive, inductors and capacitors differ from resistors in that energy may be stored in them. This is easily seen by consideration of the terminal volt-current characteristics. In the case of an inductor,

$$v = L\frac{di}{dt}$$

and

$$E = \int_0^t P\,dt$$

In the above equation, E is the energy delivered to the inductor in time t; P is the power delivered to it.

Since $P = v\,i$, we obtain

$$E = \int_0^t v\,i\,dt$$

Use of the terminal volt current relationship of an inductor in the above expression yields

$$E = \int_0^t L\frac{di}{dt}i\;dt = \int_0^t L\,i\;di$$

where it is assumed that at $t = 0$, $i = 0$ and that at time t $i = I$.

The energy given to the inductor as the current increases from zero to a value I in time t is

$$E = \frac{1}{2}L\,I^2 \qquad \text{...(4.11)}$$

This energy is stored by the inductor; if the current is now decreased to zero, the energy given to the inductor is

$$= \int_1^0 L\,i\;di = -\frac{1}{2}LI^2$$

which indicates that all the energy stored by the inductor is now returned. Thus, when current is increasing, the inductor acquires and stores energy; this energy is returned to the source when current decreases. It is important to note that in Eqn. 4.11, I is the final value of current. Thus, if the current through an inductor increases from 0 to 4A the energy stored is 8L joules when $i = 4$A. If the current is decreased to 3A, the inductor gives up 3.5L joules of energy and the energy stored in it is 4.5 joules when $i = 3$A.

CHAPTER 4

Note that if current increases in the negative sense, say from 0 to – 6A, the energy stored in the inductor is 18L joules when $i = -6A$.

From Eqn. 4.11, we see that the energy stored is directly proportional to the inductance value for a given value of I. Also, since instantaneous changes of energy are not allowed in a physical system*, we infer that the current flowing through an inductor cannot change its value instantaneously – a conclusion which was arrived at in Section 4.8 by consideration of Eqn. 4.8. This conclusion implies that inductors have an inertial or flywheel effect on the current flowing in a branch which contains the inductor. If the absolute value of the circuit current is decreased the inductor gives up some of its stored energy and tends to slow down current decay.

Example 4.1. *A current of 10 Amps has established a flux of 1000 μWb in a coil of 1000 turns. Current is reversed to – 10Amp in 0.01 sec. Calculate (i) the emf induced and (ii) Energy stored.*

Solution. Emf induced $= E = L\dfrac{di}{dt}$ where $L = N \cdot \dfrac{\phi}{I} = \dfrac{1000 \times 1000 \times 10^{-6}}{10} = 0.1$ H

Thus, $$E = 0.1\frac{20}{0.01} = 200 \text{ volts}$$

$$\text{Energy stored} = \frac{1}{2}LI^2 = \frac{1}{2}(0.1)(10^2) = 5 \text{ joules.}$$

Exercise. On an iron core are wound two coils 50 and 1000 turns, iron core has a coils of 100 cm^2 and a mean length of 200 cm. Find (*i*) Inductance of coils, (*ii*) Mutual Inductance between coils—when the permeability of iron is 2000 and (*iii*) If the current in the first coil increases from zero to 20 Amp in 0.02 sec, find the emf induced in the other coil.

Example 4.2. *A coil consists of 1000 turns. A current of 10 Amp through it produces a magnetic flux of 1000 μ Wb. Find the inductance and the average emf induced in the coil, when this current is reversed in 0.01secs.*

Solution. $$L = N \cdot \frac{\phi}{I} = \frac{1000 \times 1000 \times 10^{-6}}{10} = \frac{1}{10} = 0.1 \text{ Henry.}$$

Also, $$E = L\frac{dI}{dt} = 0.1\, x\, \frac{20}{0.01} \quad \text{[Change from 10 to –10 is change of 20]}$$

$$= 200 \text{ volts.}$$

A similar analysis can be carried out using the terminal volt current relation of a capacitor. In this case,

$$E = \int_0^t P\,dt$$

$$= \int_0^t C\frac{dv}{dt}\,v dt = \int_0^v Cv\,dv$$

Once again, it is assumed that $v = 0$ at $t = 0$ and that $v = V$ at time t. The energy given to the capacitor as the voltage is increased from zero to a value V in time t is therefore given by

$$E = \frac{1}{2}CV^2 \qquad ...(4.12)$$

*Since $P = \dfrac{d}{dt}$ [energy], instantaneous changes in energy imply the flow of infinite power, a physical impossibility.

This energy is stored in the capacitor; if the voltage is now decreased to 0 the energy given to the capacitor is

$$= \int_v^0 Cv\, dv = -\frac{1}{2}CV^2$$

which indicates that all the energy stored is now returned.

All the considerations which apply to inductors apply to capacitors as well with 'voltage' replacing 'current'. Thus the energy stored in a capacitor depends only on the terminal voltage which cannot change instantaneously. Capacitors too have an inertial or flywheel effect but on the voltage at a node in the circuit to which they are connected.

Example 4.3. *3000 turns of wire is wound uniformly on an air cored cylinder of 50 cm in diameter and 2 mt long. A second layer of wire of 150 turns uniformly is wound over the first. Calculate the Mutual inductance between the coils.*

Solution. $d = 50$ cm $\quad 1 = 2$ mt $\quad N_1 = 3000 \quad N_2 = 150 \quad \mu_0 = 4\pi \times 10^{-7}\ \mu_r = 1$

Area of cross-section of the air core is $= \pi d^2/4 = \pi \times 0.5^2/4 = 0.19634$ m^2

Mutual Inductance

$$M = \frac{\mu_0 \mu_r A N_1 N_2}{1}$$

$$= 4\pi \times 10^{-7} \times 1 \times 3000 \times 150 \times 0.19634/2$$

$$= 55.51 \text{ mH.}$$

Example 4.4. *If the mutual inductance between two coils is 0.1 H, calculate the emf induced in one coil when the current in the other coil is increased from 1 to 5 amps in 0.05 seconds uniformly.*

Solution. $di_1/dt = (5 - 1)/0.05 = 80$ amps/sec

$$Em = M\, di_1/dt = 0.1 \times 80 = 8 \text{ volts.}$$

Example 4.5. *One 10 H coil and one 20 H coil are connected in series and are physically close to each other so that their coefficient of coupling is 0.5. What is the mutual inductance between the coils?*

Solution. $L_1 = 10$ H, $\quad L_2 = 20$ H $\quad$ and $\quad K = 0.5$

$$M = K\sqrt{L_1 L_2} = 0.5 \times \sqrt{10 \times 20} = 7.07 \text{ H.}$$

Example 4.6. *Coil 1 of a pair of coupled coils has a continuous current of 5.A and the corresponding fluxes Φ_{11} and Φ_{12} are 0.2 and 0.4 mWB respectively. If the turns are N_1 = 500 and N_2 = 1500, find L_1, L_2, M and K.*

Solution. Total flux linking with first coil $= \Phi_1 = \Phi_{11} + \Phi_{12}$

$$= 0.2 + 0.4 = 0.6 \text{ mWb}$$

$$= 6 \times 10^{-4} \text{ Wb}$$

The self-inductance of coil 1 $= L_1 = \dfrac{N_1 \Phi_1}{I_1} = \dfrac{500 \times 6 \times 10^{-4}}{5} = 0.06$ H $= 60$ mH

Mutual inductance between the two coils $= M = \dfrac{N_2 \Phi_{12}}{I_1}$

CHAPTER 4

$$= \frac{500 \times 0.4 \times 10^{-3}}{5} = 0.12 \text{ H} = 120 \text{ mH}$$

Coefficient of coupling $K = \frac{\Phi_{12}}{\Phi_1} = \frac{0.4}{0.6} = 0.667$

Mutual inductance $M = K\sqrt{(L_1 L_2)}$

$$M^2 = K^2 (L_1 L_2)$$

$$L_2 = \frac{M^2}{K^2 L_1} = \frac{(0.12)^2}{(0.667)^2 \times 0.06} = 0.539 \text{ H.}$$

Example 4.7. *Two coupled coils with turns $N_1 = 100$ and $N_2 = 800$ are wound with a coupling coefficient of 0.85. With coil 1 open, and a current of 5 Amps in coil 2, flux produced is $\Phi_2 = 0.35$ mWb. Find L_1, L_2 and M.*

Solution.

$$\Phi_2 = 0.35 \text{ mWb}$$

$$K = 0.85$$

$$N_1 = 100$$

$$N_2 = 800$$

$$I_2 = 5 \text{ Amps}$$

The self-inductance of coil

$$2 = L_2 = \frac{N_2 \Phi_2}{I_2} = \frac{800 \times 0.35 \times 10^{-3}}{5} = 56 \text{ mH}$$

The coefficient of coupling

$$K = \frac{\Phi_{21}}{\Phi_2} = 0.85$$

$\therefore$

$$\Phi_{21} = 0.85\ \Phi_2 = 0.85 \times 0.35 \times 10^{-3}$$

$$\Phi_{21} = 0.2975 \text{ mWb}$$

$\therefore$ The mutual inductances coil 1 $= M = \frac{N_2 \Phi_{21}}{I_2} = \frac{100 \times 0.975}{5} = 0.00595 \text{ H} = 5.95 \text{ mH.}$

The self-inductance of coil 1 (L_1)

$$M = K\sqrt{L_1 L_2}$$

$$M_2 = K^2 (L_1 L_2)$$

$$L_1 = \frac{M^2}{K^2 L_2} = \frac{(5.95 \times 0.10^{-2})^2}{(0.85)^2 \times (56 \times 10^{-3})} = 0.875 \times 10^{-3}$$

$$L_1 = 0.875 \text{ mH.}$$

Example 4.8. *Two coils with 50 and 500 lines are wound on a closed magnetic circuit side by side of cross-sectional area 100 sq. cm and mean length = 500 cm. The magnetic circuit has relative permeability of 2000. Find the mutual inductance. Also calculate the self-induced emf and the mutually induced emf when the current in the coil with 50 turns grows from zero to 25 A in a line of 0.025 sec.*

Solution.

Mean length $l = 500$ cm

Cross-sectional area $A = 100\ cm^2$

$N_1 = 50, N_2 = 500$

$\mu_r = 2000\ \mu_0 = 4\pi \times 10^{-7}$

Mutual inductance
$$M = \frac{(\mu_0 \mu_r A N_1 N_2)}{l}$$
$$= \frac{4\pi \times 10^{-7} \times 2000 \times 100 \times 10^{-4} \times 50 \times 5000}{500 \times 10^{-2}}$$
$$= 0.12566\ H = 0.1257\ H$$

Self-induced emf
$$= e_1 = L_1 \frac{(di_1)}{dt}$$
$$L_1 = \frac{\mu_0 \mu_r N_1^2 A}{l} = \frac{4\pi \times 10^{-7} \times 2000 \times 50^2 \times 100 \times 10^{-4}}{500 \times 10^{-2}}$$
$$e_1 = L_1 \frac{(di)}{dt} = \frac{0.0125 \times 25}{0.025} = 12.5 \text{ volts}$$

Mutually induced emf $Em = M \dfrac{(di)}{dt}$
$$= 0.01256 \times \frac{25}{0.025} = 125.6 \text{ volts.}$$

Example 4.9. *An iron ring of having a mean length of 50 cm and a uniform cross-section of 5 cm² is wound with 240 turns. A current of 2 Amps in the winding produces a flux of 0.4 mWb. Calculate the relative permeability of the iron and the relative of the magnetic paths.*

Solution. $l = 50$ cm Wb/m² $\qquad B$ = Flux density $= \dfrac{\Phi}{A} = 0.4 \times 10^{-3} = 0.8$

$A = 5\ cm^2$ $\qquad$ H = Magnetic field intensity $= \dfrac{NI}{l}$

$N = 240$

$I = 2$ A $\qquad = \dfrac{240 \times 2}{50 \times 10^{-2}} = 960$ AT/mt

$\Phi = 0.4$ mWb $\qquad B = \mu H$

*If the insulation is air, as in an air capacitor, the losses are = 0.

Permeability $\mu = \frac{B}{H} = \frac{0.8}{960} = 8.33 \times 10^{-4}$

$$\mu = \mu_0 \mu_r$$

$$\therefore \quad \mu_r = \frac{\mu}{\mu_0} = \frac{8.33 \times 10^{-4}}{4\pi \times 10^{-7}} = 663.14$$

Reluctance $S = \frac{1}{\mu_0 \mu_r A} = \frac{50 \times 10^{-2}}{4\pi \times 10^{-7} \times 663.14 \times 5 \times 10^{-4}} = 12 \times 10^{-5}$ AT/Wb.

or $\phi = \frac{\text{MMF}}{\text{Reluctance}}$

$$\therefore \quad \text{Reluctance} = \frac{\text{MMF}}{\Phi} = \frac{NI}{\Phi} = \frac{240 \times 2}{0.4 \times 10^{-3}} = 12 \times 10^{-5} \text{ AT/Wb.}$$

Example 4.10. *An iron ring has a mean length of 60 cm cross-sectional area of 1 cm². It is wound with 1000 turns. If a current of 1.5 Amps flows through the coil, find the flux density in the ring. Assume relative permeability of iron as 300. Also, calculate the current in the coil, if 1 mm airgap is created in the ring to have the same flux density in the ring.*

Solution. l = 60 cm; $I = 1.5$ A

$A = 1 \text{ cm}^2$; $\mu_r = 300$

$N = 1000$; $B = ?$

$$\text{MMF} = NI = 1000 = 1000 \times 1.5 = 1500$$

Reluctance, $S = \frac{1}{\mu_0 \mu_r A} = \frac{60 \times 10^{-2}}{4\pi \times 10^{-7} \times 300 \times 1 \times 10^{-4}} = 15915494.31$

$$\text{Flux } \Phi = \frac{NI}{S} = \frac{1500}{15915494.31} = 94.24 \ \mu\text{Wb}$$

$$\text{Flux density} = B = \frac{\Phi}{A} = \frac{94.24 \times 10^{-6}}{1 \times 10^{-4}} = 0.9424 \text{ Wb/m}^2$$

l_g = Air gap length = 1 mm = 1×10^{-3} mt

$l_i = 60 - 1 = 59 \text{ cm} = 59 \times 10^{-2}$ mt

$$S_i = \frac{l_i}{\mu_0 \mu_r A} = \frac{59 \times 10^{-2}}{4\pi \times 10^{-7} \times 300 \times 1 \times 10^{-4}} = 15650236.07$$

$$S_g = \frac{l_g}{\mu_0 A} = \frac{1 \times 10^{-3}}{4\pi \times 10^{-7} \times 1 \times 10^{-4}} = 7957747.155$$

$$S = S_i + S_g = 15650236.07 + 7957747.155 = 23607983.22$$

$$\Phi = \frac{NI}{S}$$

$$B = \frac{\Phi}{A} = \frac{NI}{SA}$$

$$I = \frac{(B.S.A)}{N} = \frac{0.9424 \times 23607983.22 \times 1 \times 10^{-4}}{1000} = 2.225 \text{ Amp.}$$

If we consider a solid state amplifier rated at 250 W rms per channel, runs at about ± 75 volts. If they are advertising 100,000 μF, then they are saying is they have 50,000 μF operations at +75 volts and 50,000 μF operating or – 75 volts.

If we calculate the energy storage, we end up with the following:

$$E = \left(\frac{1}{2} \times 0.05 \times 75^2\right) \times 2 = 281.25 \text{ joules (for both channels)}$$

Energy storage in capacitors is a convenient method of storing electrical energy. This energy stored can be released, as required for a very short duration of time under controlled conditions. It produces high peak current and power under discharge conditions.

These capacitors are extremely useful in controlled Nuclear Fusion, Lasers, Impulse generators etc.

Energy stored in a capacitor

$$E = \frac{1}{2}\frac{Q^2}{C} = \frac{1}{2}QV = \frac{1}{2}CV^2 \text{ joules (watt/sec)}$$

This is the energy stored in the electric field.

where C = Farads

V = Volts

Q = Coulombs

E = Joules.

Example. When C = 1,00,000 μF

V = 10 V

$$\text{Energy} = \frac{1}{2}CV^2$$

$$= \frac{1}{2} \times 0.1 \times 10^2 = 5 \text{ joules.}$$

If a company advertises their amplifier has over 100,000 micro farads of capacitance, they mean:

$$E = \frac{1}{2}CV^2 = \text{w/sec, if } c = 0.1\text{F}, V = 10 \text{ V}$$

$$= 0.5 \times 0.1 \times 10^2 = 5 \text{ joules,}$$

if $$V = 100 \text{ V}$$

then $$E = 500 \text{ joules.}$$

We now turn our attention to resistors and carry out a similar analysis. In this case,

$$P = vi = i^2 R$$

and $$= \int_0^t P\,dt = \int_0^t i^2 R\,dt$$

If R is a constant, $$E = R\int_0^t i^2\,dt \qquad \text{...(4.13)}$$

Equation 4.13 involves the integral of a square of a function. The energy E calculated using Eqn. 4.13 can never be negative. This dismisses the possibility of a return of energy from the resistor. A resistor is a device which can only dissipate energy. The energy dissipated is directly proportional to the resistance for constant current.

On the other hand, ideal inductors and capacitors are lossless as the foregoing considerations have shown. Practical inductors and capacitors do exhibit some losses. For example, non-zero winding resistance is a source of power loss in inductors. Losses also occur in the magnetic cores of inductors and in capacitor insulation*.

The presence of losses in inductors and capacitors may be accounted for in calculations by the inclusion of a suitable resistor placed in series with the ideal inductor or capacitor. It is also quite common to model a lossy capacitor by including a suitable resistor in parallel with the ideal lossless capacitor.

Example 4.11. *The current waveform of Fig. 4.10(a) is passed through an inductor of 0.2H. Plot to scale the voltage developed across it, the power delivered to the inductor and the energy stored in the inductor.*

Solution. From the current waveform of Fig. 4.10(*c*) the voltage waveform is obtained by finding $L\frac{di}{dt}$. The variation of power is obtained by plotting the product of the volt and the current waveforms. Lastly, the energy plot is a plot of $\int P\,dt$ versus time. Note that the energy at any instant of time may also be found by application of the formulae $\frac{1}{2} \cdot L_i^2$.

4.12 TRANSIENT AND STEADY-STATE SOLUTIONS

In the previous chapters, we considered dc circuits comprising of energy sources and resistors. We now turn our attention to dc circuits which may contain either inductors or capacitors in addition to resistors. Before we do so, however, we must learn to distinguish between transient and steady-state solutions.

*If the insulation is air, as in an air capacitor, the losses are ≈ 0.

Ohms law provides the volt-current relationship of a resistor which responds immediately to either voltage or current sources. In other words, instantaneous changes in voltage and current are permitted in the resistor. Therefore, when an energy source is switched on to a resistive circuit, the initial and final solutions are the same.

In circuits containing inductors and capacitors there are restrictions imposed (by Eqns. 4.3 and 4.8) on the build-up of current and voltage associated with them.

When an energy source is switched on to a circuit containing such elements, the initial solution will differ from the final solution. The initial period of the solution when the currents and voltages have not settled to a steady value is known as the *transient period*. After some time, which depends on the circuit parameters, solution down to a steady value is achieved and the solution at this stage is known as the steady-state solution. A solution which comprises of both the transient and steady-state solutions is known as the *complete solution*. We shall derive the complete solution of series *RC* and *RL* circuits when switched on to dc sources.

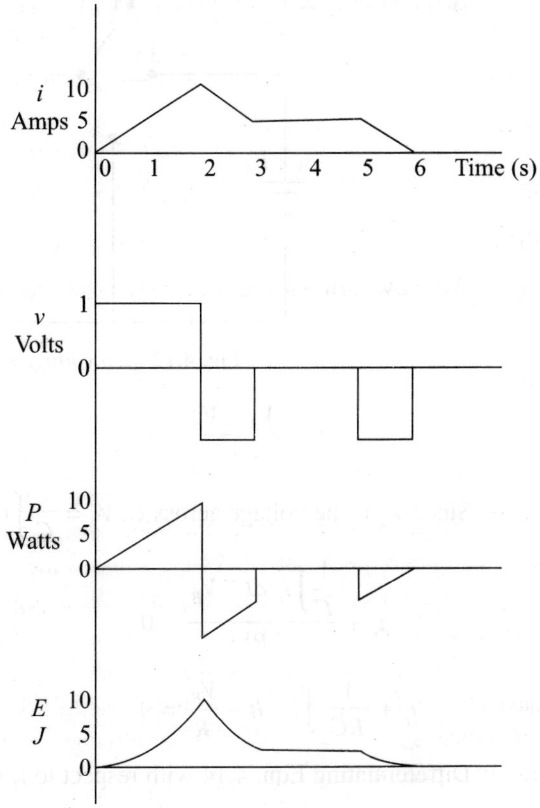

Fig. 4.10 *Current through an inductor in Ex. 4.11.*

4.13 SERIES RC CIRCUITS AND STEP RESPONSE

When dc voltage is applied suddenly to a circuit, an instantaneous change in voltage level takes place at the moment of switching, $t = 0$, as shown in Fig. 4.11. Such a voltage waveshape is referred to as a step voltage. Figure 4.12 shows the circuit arrangement. At time $t = 0$ the switch is moved from position 1 to 2 to complete the circuit. We assume that the capacitor is initially uncharged; the initial voltage across the capacitor is therefore zero. We shall use the node voltage method to obtain the complete solution when the switch is in position 2. At node A,

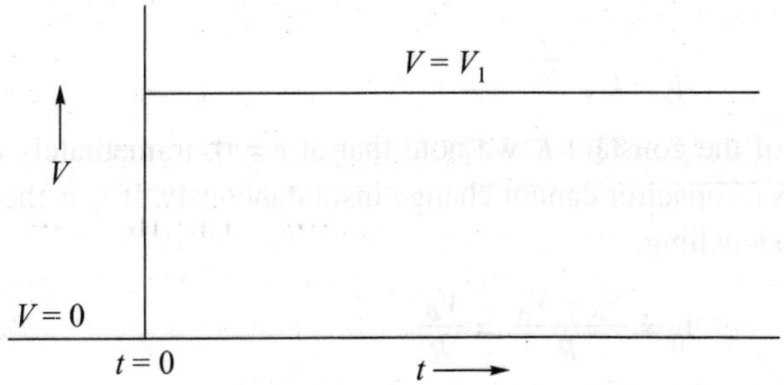

Fig. 4.11 *A voltage step*

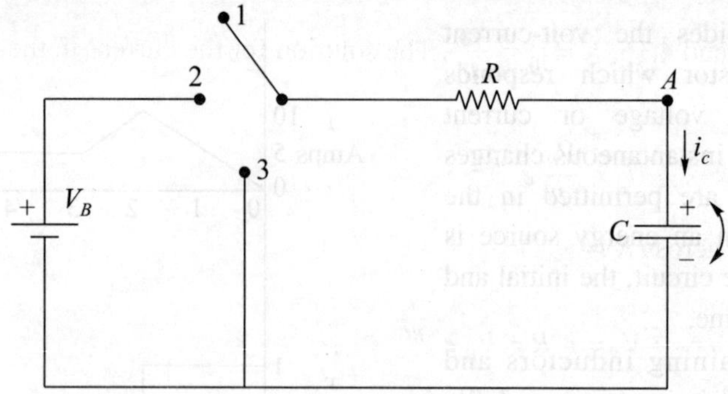

Fig. 4.12 *Step voltage as applied to an RC circuit*

$$i_c + \frac{V_A - V_B}{R} = 0$$

Since V_A is the voltage across C, $V_A = \frac{1}{C}\int i_c \, dt$ and we have

$$i_c + \frac{\frac{1}{C}\int i_c \, dt - V_B}{R} = 0$$

or $$i_c + \frac{1}{RC}\int i_c \, dt - \frac{V_B}{R} = 0 \qquad \text{...(4.14)}$$

Differentiating Eqn. 4.14 with respect to t, we obtain

$$\frac{di_c}{dt} + \frac{i_c}{RC} = \frac{d}{dt}\left(\frac{V_B}{R}\right) = 0$$

Rearranging $$\frac{di_c}{i_c} = -\frac{dt}{RC}$$

The solution is given by

$$\log_e i_c = \frac{t}{RC} + \log(K)$$

where K is a constant.

Expressing the solution in a more convenient form,

$$i_c = k\, e^{-\frac{t}{RC}} \qquad \text{...(4.15)}$$

To find the value of the constant K we note that at $t = 0$, immediately after switching $V_A = 0$ because the voltage across a capacitor cannot change instantaneously. If i_0 is the value of current in the circuit immediately after switching.

$$i_0 = \frac{V_B - V_A}{R} = \frac{V_B}{R} \qquad \text{...(4.16)}$$

From Eqns. 4.15 and 4.16, $K = i_0 = \frac{V_B}{R}$. The solution for the current in the circuit is given by

$$i_c = \frac{V_B}{R} e^{-\frac{t}{RC}} \quad ...(4.17)$$

The voltage drop across R is

$$V_R = i_c R = V_B e^{-\frac{t}{RC}} \quad ...(4.18)$$

and the voltage across the capacitor is

$$v_c = V_B - V_R = V_B \left[1 - e^{-\frac{1}{RC}}\right] \quad ...(4.19)$$

Equation 4.19 may also be obtained by integration of 4.17 using $v_c = \frac{1}{C}\int_0^t i\, dt$ and the fact that at $t = 0$, $v_c = 0$.

At time $t = \infty$, $i_c = 0$, $V_R = 0$ and $v_c = V_B$, indicating that the capacitor is charged to the battery voltage. In this time, the total charge delivered to the capacitor is

$$\int_0^\infty i_c\, dt = \int_0^\infty \frac{V_B}{R} e^{-\frac{t}{RC}} dt = C V_B \quad ...(4.20)$$

Also, the total energy delivered to the capacitor is

$$= \int_0^\infty V_B \left[1 - e^{-\frac{1}{RC}}\right] \frac{V_B}{R} e^{-\frac{t}{RC}} dt$$

$$= \frac{1}{2} C V_B^2 \quad ...(4.21)$$

Figure 4.13 shows a plot of v_c and i_c versus time. Both v_c and i_c vary exponentially and settle to their final values after infinite time at which point, theoretically, the steady-state is reached.

From Eqns. 4.16, 4.17 and 4.19, we see that when $t = RC$*,

$$i_c = i_0 e^{-1} = \frac{i_0}{e} = 0.37 i_0 \quad ...(4.22)$$

and $$v_c = V_B[1 - e^{-1}] = V_B[1 - 0.37] = 0.63 V_B \quad ...(4.23)$$

The time taken for the current to decay to 37% of its initial value and for the voltage across the capacitor to rise to 63% of its final value is known as the time constant. The time constant of the RC circuit in Fig. 4.12 is equal to RC seconds; the time constant is denoted by the symbol τ.

---

*The product RC has the dimensions of time as the following dimensional analysis shows. $RC \rightarrow$ ohm farad $\rightarrow \frac{\text{volt}}{\text{amp}} \frac{\text{coul}}{\text{volts}} \rightarrow$ sec.

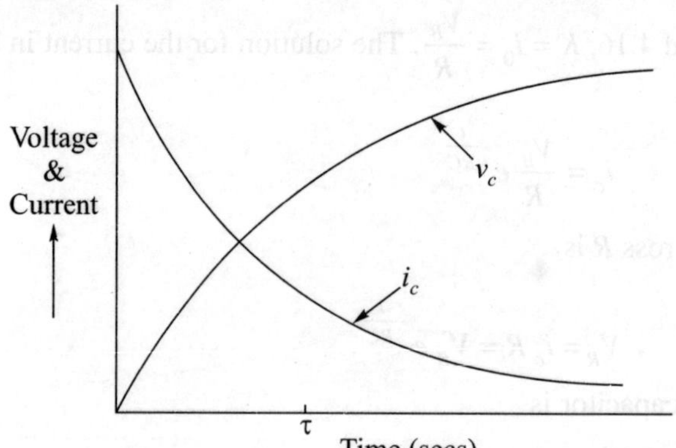

Fig. 4.13 *Plot of v_c and i_c versus time*

Mention was made earlier that the steady-state is reached only after infinite time. Practically, however, after five time constants, $i_c = 0.00674\ i_0$ and $v_c = 0.9933\ V_B$ and steady-state conditions may be considered to have been attained. If the time constant is shorter, we may consider, therefore, that steady-state conditions will be attained sooner.

Suppose that, after 5 time constants, the switch in Fig. 4.12 is moved to position 3 from 2. To solve the resulting circuit we resort to the node voltage method again and obtain at node *A*.

$$i_c + \frac{V_A}{R} = 0$$

or

$$C\frac{dv_c}{dt} + \frac{v_c}{R} = 0$$

Rearranging,

$$\frac{dV_c}{V_c} = -\frac{dt}{RC}$$

The solution is given by

$$v_c = K_1\, e^{-\frac{t}{RC}} \qquad \text{...(4.24)}$$

where K_1 is a constant.

At $t = 0$, $v_c = V_B$. Thus, $K_1 = V_B$ and the complete solution is

$$v_c = V_B e^{-\frac{t}{RC}} \qquad \text{...(4.25)}$$

For the complete solution of the current i_c,

$$i_c = c\frac{dv_c}{dt} = -C\frac{1}{RC}V_B e^{-\frac{t}{RC}} = -\frac{V_B}{R}e^{-\frac{t}{RC}} \qquad \text{...(4.26)}$$

The negative sign in Eqn. 4.26 indicates that when the switch is in position 3, the direction of current flow is opposite to that assumed. Fig. 4.13 shows a plot of v_c and i_c as described by Eqns. 4.25 and 4.26.

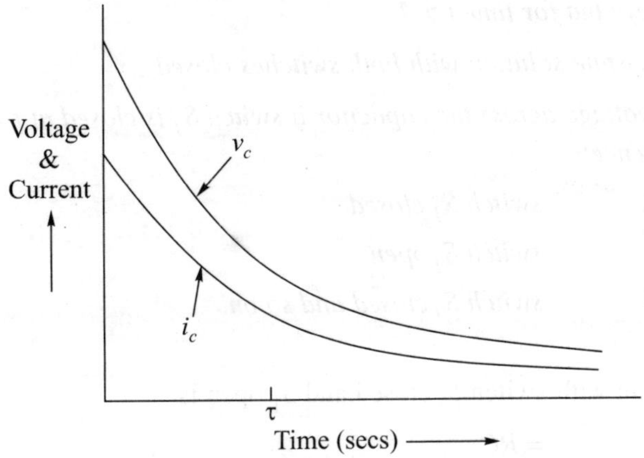

Fig. 4.14 *Decay of voltage and current in the RC circuit of Fig. 4.12 with switch in position 3*

The charged capacitor, with node *A* positive, behaves like an energy source. With the passage of time, however, the source voltage decreases exponentially as charge and energy are drained from the capacitor. Once again it takes infinite time for the capacitor to discharge fully but from a practical standpoint the voltage across it is negligibly small and may be considered to be zero after 5 time constants.

From the above analysis, we see that initially, immediately after switching, the uncharged capacitor behaves like a short circuit. After attainment of the steady-state, the capacitor behaves like an open circuit and blocks the flow of dc current. In fact, capacitors are used for this purpose in electronic circuits.

4.14 BLOCKING CAPACITORS

Consider the circuit of Fig. 4.15. Suppose that the voltage applied at node *A* is of the form $[v(t) + V_1]$ where $v(t)$ is a voltage whose magnitude varies with time and V_1 a constant dc voltage. Suppose the output is tapped across resistor R_2 at node *B*. To find the current flow through R_2 we may use the theorem of superposition by summing the responses due to the two sources $v(t)$ and V_1. The current flow through R_2 due to V_1, in the steady-state, is zero. The voltage drop across R_2, due to source V_1, is therefore zero. However, since $v(t)$ varies with time a current can flow through the capacitor and R_2 and set up a time varying voltage drop across the output resistor R_2. The output voltage, therefore, is solely in response to the time varying voltage $v(t)$. Thus, the dc voltage is effectively blocked by the capacitor. In such an application the capacitor is referred to as a blocking capacitor.

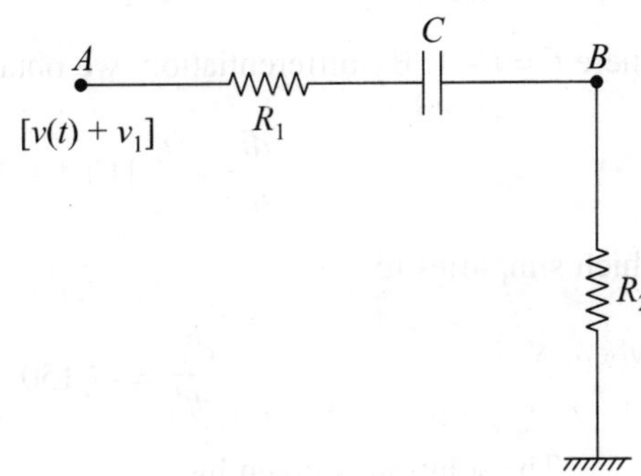

Fig. 4.15 *Blocking capacitor*

Example 4.12. *In the circuit of Fig. 4.16 switch S_1 is initially open, and switch S_2 is closed. The initial charge on the 2 μF capacitor is 0. After 1 second switch S_1 is closed.*

Find:

(i) the expression for voltage across and current through the capacitor in time $0 \le t \le 1$

(ii) same as (i) above but for time $t > 1$

(iii) the final steady-state solution with both switches closed

(iv) the pattern of voltage across the capacitor if switch S_1 is closed at $t = 1$ and then obeys the following sequence:

$1 \le t \le 2$	*switch S_1 closed*
$2 \le t \le 3$	*switch S_1 open*
$3 \le t \le 4$	*switch S_1 closed and so on.*

Solution.

(*i*) The time constant with switch S_2 closed and S_1 open is

$$= RC$$

$$= 10 \times 10^3 \times 2 \times 10^{-6}$$

$$= 0.02 \text{ sec}$$

It may be noted that after 1 sec, 50 time constants will have elapsed. From Eqn. 4.17, for $0 \le t \le 1$

$$i_c = \frac{10}{10.10^3} e^{-\frac{t}{RC}} = 10^{-3}\, e^{-50t} \quad ...(4.27)$$

From Eqn. 4.19, $\quad v_c = 10[1 - e^{-50t}] \quad ...(4.28)$

(*ii*) During time $t > 1$ both switches are closed. Writing the node voltage equations at node *A*,

$$i_c + \frac{\frac{1}{c}\int i_c dt' - 10}{10^4} + \frac{\frac{1}{c}\int i_c dt' - 5}{5.10^3} = 0$$

where $t' = t - 1$. By differentiation, we obtain

$$\frac{di_c}{dt'} + \frac{i_c}{C}[10^{-4} + 2.10^{-4}] = 0$$

which simplifies to

$$\frac{di_c}{dt'} = -i_c 150$$

The solution is given by

$$i_c = K_1\, e^{-150t'} \quad ...(4.29)$$

where k_1 is constant.

At $t = 1$, the capacitor may be considered to be charged up to 10V. Immediately after closure of switch S_2, the capacitor voltage, which cannot change instantaneously, remains at 10V. Therefore no current can flow in the left hand mesh, *i.e.* in the 10 kΩ resistor. However, current can flow through the 5 kΩ resistor and the initial value of this current is

$$= \frac{10 - 5}{5.10^3} = 10^{-3} \text{ A}$$

The current flows in a direction opposite to that indicated by i_c in Fig. 4.16. Therefore, when

$t = 1, t' = t - 1 = 0$ and $i_c = -10^{-3}$ A.

Using this fact in Eqn. 4.29, the constant K_1 is found to be $= -10^{-3}$. The solution for i_c may therefore be written as

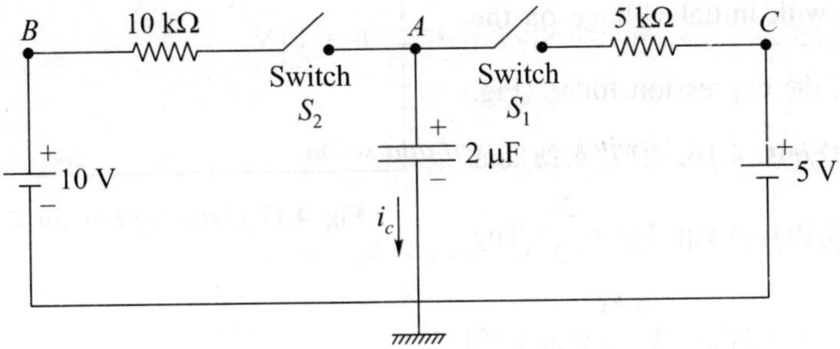

Fig. 4.16 *Circuit of Fig. for Ex. 4.12*

$$i_c = -(10^{-3})e^{-150t'} \quad ...(4.30)$$

v_c for $t > 1$ ($t' > 0$) may be found from

$$v_c = \frac{1}{C}\int i_c dt'$$

Substituting for i_c from Eqn. 4.30 and integrating,

$$v_c = \frac{-10^{-3}}{2.10^{-6}}\frac{e^{-150t'}}{(-150)} + K_2 \quad ...(4.31)$$

When $t' = 0$, $v_c = 10$ volts. Thus,

$$K_2 = \left(10 - \frac{10}{3}\right) \quad ...(4.32)$$

From Eqns. 4.31 and 4.32, we obtain that

$$v_c = \left\{\frac{20}{3} + \frac{10}{3}e^{-150t'}\right\} \quad ...(4.33)$$

(*iii*) With both switches closed the final steady-state value of i_c and v_c is obtained by putting $t = \infty$ in Eqns. 4.30 and 4.33.

i_c (steady-state value) = 0 volts

v_c (steady-state value) = $\frac{20}{3}$ volts

This last answer could have been deduced by noting that in the steady-state, the capacitor behaves like an open circuit; the potential at node *A* is then found using the voltage divider principle.

(*iv*) At $t = 1$, $t' = 0$ and the initial voltage on C is 10V which decays exponentially to $\frac{20}{3}$V at $t = 2$. At $t = 2$ switch S_1 opens. Solving the resultant RC circuit with initial voltage on the capacitor $= +\frac{20}{3}$ V, the expression for v_c (Fig. 4.17) is found from Eqns. 4.16, 4.17, 4.18 and 4.19 with V_A in Eqn. 4.16 now equal to $+\frac{20}{3}$. The expression for v_c is

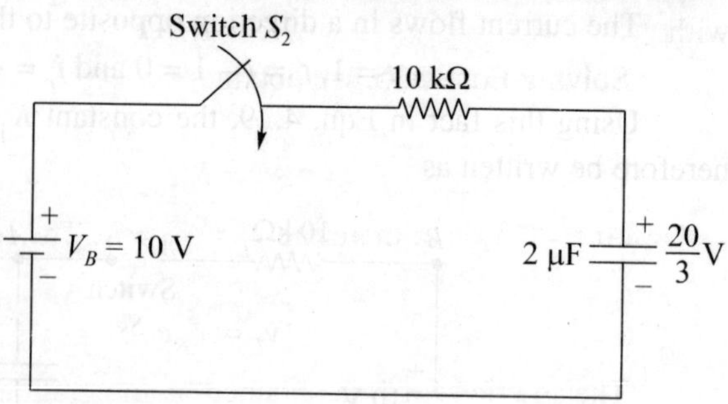

Fig. 4.17 *Circuit of Fig. for Ex. 4.12 part (iv)*

$$v_c = [V_B - (V_B - V_C)e^{-t'/RC}]$$

$$= \left[10 - \left(10 - \frac{20}{3}\right)e^{-50t'}\right] \qquad ...(4.34)$$

where $t'' = t - 2$.

When $t = 3$, $t'' = 1$ and $v_c = 10$ volts as $e^{-50} \approx 0$.

At $t = 3$ switch S_1 closes and the process repeats. The waveform of the voltage across the capacitor will be as shown in Fig. 4.18.

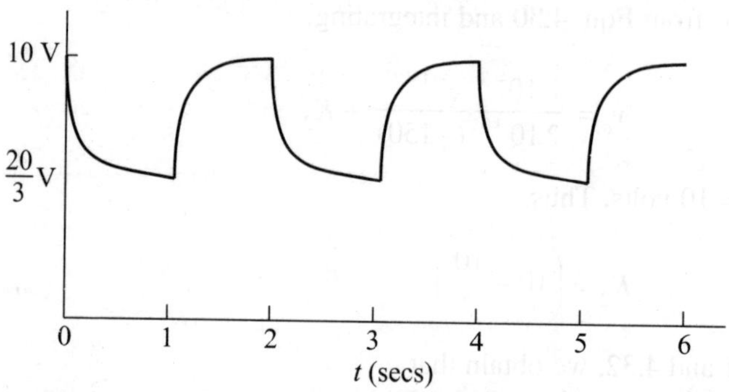

Fig. 4.18 *Voltage waveform across 2 μF capacitor in Ex. 4.12.*

4.15 THE SERIES RL CIRCUIT; STEP RESPONSE

The analysis is quite similar to that carried out for the RC circuit with the exception that

(*i*) the initial current in the inductor is assumed to be zero

(*ii*) to obtain the value of constant we use the fact that the current in an inductor cannot change its value instantaneously.

Referring to Fig. 4.19, the differential equation to be solved with the switch in position 2, obtained by application of the node voltage method at node A is

$$\frac{dv_L}{dt} = -\frac{R'}{L}V_L \qquad ...(4.35)$$

with $$R' = R + r \qquad \text{...(4.36)}$$

Solving Eqn. 4.35, we obtain

$$v_L = K\,e^{-\frac{R't}{L}}$$

At $t = 0$, $i_L = 0$; therefore $v_L = V_B = K$. The solution is

$$v_L = V_B e^{-\frac{R'}{L}} \qquad \text{...(4.37)}$$

The solution for i_L is obtained by integration of v_L in Eqn. 4.37

$$i_L = \frac{V_B}{R'}\left[1 - e^{-\frac{R't}{L}}\right] \qquad \text{...(4.38)}$$

The ratio *L*/*R* has the dimensions of time and is known as the time constant denoted by the symbol τ. After five time constants steady-state conditions may be assumed to have been established and the current in the circuit is limited solely by the resistor. Therefore

$$i_L \text{ (steady-state)} = \frac{V_B}{R'}. \qquad \text{...(4.39)}$$

It is therefore seen that initially, at $t = 0$, immediately after switching, the inductor behaves like an open circuit and in the steady-state, it behaves like a short circuit.

The total energy delivered by the source and stored in the inductor is

$$= \int_0^{\infty} \frac{V_B}{R'}\left[1 - e^{-\frac{R't}{L}}\right] V_B e^{-\frac{R't}{L}}\,dt$$

$$= \frac{1}{2} L \left(\frac{V_B}{R'}\right)^2$$

$$= \frac{1}{2} L (i_L)^2_{\text{steady-state}} \qquad \text{...(4.40)}$$

If we now attempt to move the switch from position 2 to position 3, we will be interrupting the electric circuit. This means that $\frac{di}{dt}$ takes on large values (theoretically infinity). By Lenz's law a large voltage is induced in the inductor with polarity opposite to that indicated in Fig. 4.19. It is this induced voltage which causes a spark upon the opening of a switch in an inductive circuit. Physically, it satisfies the requirement of continuity of current flow in the inductor. Such a situation did not arise in the case of the *RC* circuit because instantaneous changes in current are allowed in a capacitor.

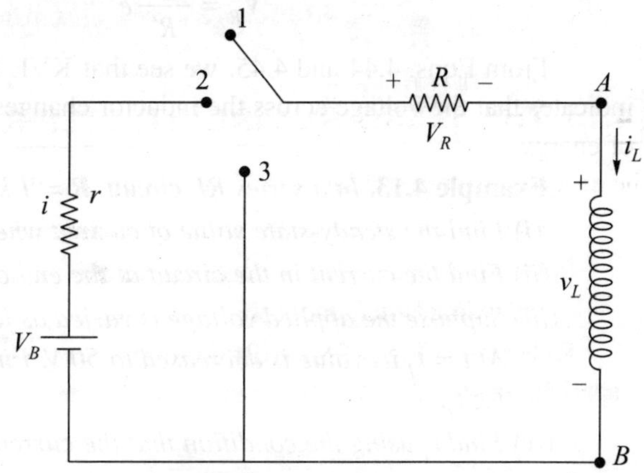

Fig. 4.19 *Series RL circuit*

We could avoid the occurrence of a spark by ensuring that the switch in Fig. 4.17 is of the "make before break" variety, *i.e.* the switch makes contact with position 3 and then breaks away from position 2. For some time the switch is in contact with both positions 2 and 3. Under these conditions the current in the inductor continues to flow upwards from node B to position 3. The battery is now shorted and supplies a current limited only by its internal resistance. The current delivered by V_B is $\frac{V_B}{R}$ and the current in the branch from node 2, 3 to ground is

$$\left(\frac{V_B}{r} - \frac{V_B}{R'}\right)$$

When the switch is in contact with position 3 only,

$$L\frac{di_L}{dt} + R_i = 0 \qquad \text{...(4.41)}$$

the solution is
$$i_L = K_1 e^{-\frac{Rt}{L}} \qquad \text{...(4.42)}$$

when $t = 0$, $i_L = \frac{V_B}{R'}$. The constant in Eqn. 4.41 can be found and

$$i_L = \frac{V_B}{R'} e^{-\frac{Rt}{L}} \qquad \text{...(4.43)}$$

Equation 4.43 indicates that the current in the inductor decays exponentially.

For the voltage across the inductor,

$$v_L = L\frac{di}{dt}$$

$$= -V_B\frac{R}{R'} e^{-\frac{Rt}{L}} \qquad \text{...(4.44)}$$

The voltage drop across the resistor is

$$V_R = \frac{V_B R}{R'} e^{-\frac{Rt}{L}} \qquad \text{...(4.45)}$$

From Eqns. 4.44 and 4.45, we see that KVL is verified in the RL loop. Furthermore, Eqn. 4.44 indicates that the voltage across the inductor changes polarity. The inductor now behaves like a source of energy.

Example 4.13. *In a series RL circuit, R = 1 kΩ and L = 40 H.*

(i) Find the steady-state value of current when the applied voltage is 50 V.

(ii) Find the current in the circuit at the end of five time constants.

(iii) Suppose the applied voltage is varied as follows. Initially, from t = 0 to t_1, its value = 100 V. At t = t_1 its value is decreased to 50 V. Find an expression for current in the circuit for time $t \geq t_1$.

(iv) Find t_1 using the condition that the current at t = t_1 is equal to that in part (ii).

(v) Suppose t_1 = 25 ms. Find the total time taken for the current to attain the value of part (ii).

Solution.

(*i*) the steady-state value is $= \dfrac{50}{10^3} = 50$ mA.

(*ii*) After five time constants, the current is

$$= 50 \times 10^{-3}\left[1 - e^{-\frac{R'}{L}}\right]$$

$$= 50 \times 10^{-3}\,[1 - e^{-5}]$$

The time corresponding to five time constants is

$$= 5\tau = 200 \text{ ms.}$$

(*iii*) at $t = 0$, $V = 100$ volts and the current at $t = t_1$ is

$$I_1 = 100 \times 10^{-3}[1 - e^{-25t_1}] \qquad ...(4.46)$$

At $t = t_1$ the 50 V source is applied. The expression for current in the *RL* series circuit with initial current I_i is (the student should device this expression)

$$i = 50.10^{-3}[1 - e^{25t'}] + I_1\, e^{-25t'} \qquad ...(4.47)$$

where $t' = t - t_1$ and I_i is defined by Eqn. 4.46.

At any time t after $t = t_1$ the current is given by

$$i = 50.10^{-3}\left[1 - e^{-25(t-t_1)}\right] + 100.10^{-3}\,[1 - e^{-25t_1}]\,e^{-25(t-t_1)}. \qquad ...(4.48)$$

(*iv*) In order to find t_1 so that the condition stated in this part of the problem is fulfilled the expression for i given by Eqn. 4.46 is equated to the value of current found in part (*ii*).

We obtain that

$$100.10^{-3}\left[1 - e^{-25t_1}\right] = 50.10^{-3}[1 - e^{-5}]$$

Simplifying, $$e^{-25t_1} = \frac{1 + e^{-5}}{2}$$

Therefore, $$t_1 = \frac{1}{25}\left\{\log_e\left[\frac{2}{1 + e^{-5}}\right]\right\}$$

$$= 27.46 \text{ ms.}$$

(*v*) Since $t_1 = 25$ ms which is < 27.46 ms, the current in the circuit at time t_1 will be less than that found in (*ii*). In order to find the total time taken to reach the current magnitude of part (*ii*) we equate Eqns. 4.48 with the value of current found in part (*ii*) and obtain that

$$e^{25t} = e^5\left[2 - e^{-25t_1}\right] \qquad ...(4.49)$$

Inserting $t_1 = 25$ ms in Eqn. 4.49, we obtain

$t = 118.9$ ms

In part (*ii*), we found that it takes 200 ms to attain the same value of current.

This example shows that it is possible to speed up the process of current build up in an inductor by overvolting it, *i.e.*, application of a voltage in excess of normal, for a suitable time period.

Example 4.14. *Explain how the connection of a capacitor across the terminals of a switch can prevent the occurrence of a spark due to the interruption of an inductive circuit.*

Solution. With switch S (Fig. 4.20) closed, steady-state conditions are reached and the inductor carries a steady current. When S is opened, as pointed out earlier, a spark occurs. This is due to the large induced voltage across the switch contacts. Physically, as pointed out earlier, it satisfies the condition of continuity of current flow in the inductor.

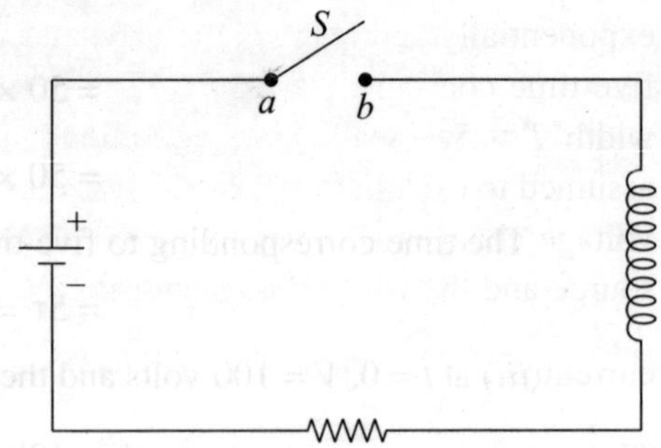

Fig. 4.20 *Circuit Fig. for Ex. 4.14*

When a capacitor is connected across S, no spark occurs as the current flows through C; this is because instantaneous changes in the value of i_c are allowed. The energy stored in the inductor is now transferred to the capacitor. Of course, some energy is also dissipated in the resistor R and the internal resistance of the source.

4.16 PULSE RESPONSE OF RC CIRCUITS

In the RC circuit of Fig. 4.21, the input is a pulse and the output is tapped off the capacitor. The input is defined in the same figure.

From $t = -\infty$ to $t = 0$ the voltage applied is $-v$; at $t = 0$ there is a sudden transition to $+V$ which lasts until $t = t_1$ at which time the applied voltage returns to its original value at $t < 0$. It is assumed that the pulse is ideal, *i.e.*, the time taken for the voltage to change at $t = 0$ and $t = t_1$ is equal to zero.

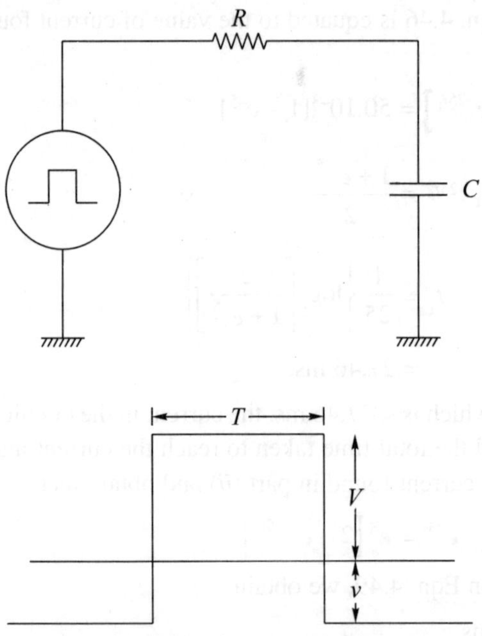

Fig. 4.21 *Pulse as applied to RC circuit*

To determine the response of this circuit we note that prior to $t = 0$, steady-state conditions prevail; no current flows in the circuit and the capacitor is charged to $-v$ volts which is the output. At $t = 0$, the voltage source jumps instantaneously to $+V$. Since the voltage across a capacitor cannot change instantaneously the current in the circuit at $t = 0$ is equal to $\frac{V+v}{R}$. This current decays exponentially and charges the capacitor, exponentially, to a voltage of V volts which is attained after five time constants, $5\tau = 5RC$. The pulse shape, across the output is therefore distorted. If the pulse width $T > 5\tau$, steady-state conditions (*i.e.*, the current in the circuit is zero and $v_c = +V$.) may be assumed to exist before the next step change in the voltage source at $t = t_1$. When this occurs the source voltage changes abruptly to $-v$ initial voltage on the capacitor V volts. The polarities of the voltage source and the charged capacitor determine the direction of current flow which reverses. Initially, the current is $\frac{V+v}{R}$ which decays exponentially to zero when the capacitor voltage attains a value of $-v$. The time constant is again equal to RC and the capacitor may be considered to be charged to $-v$ volts after 5τ seconds. Figure 4.22 shows the output under three different situations. It is seen that the least distortion occurs when $T >> 5\tau$.

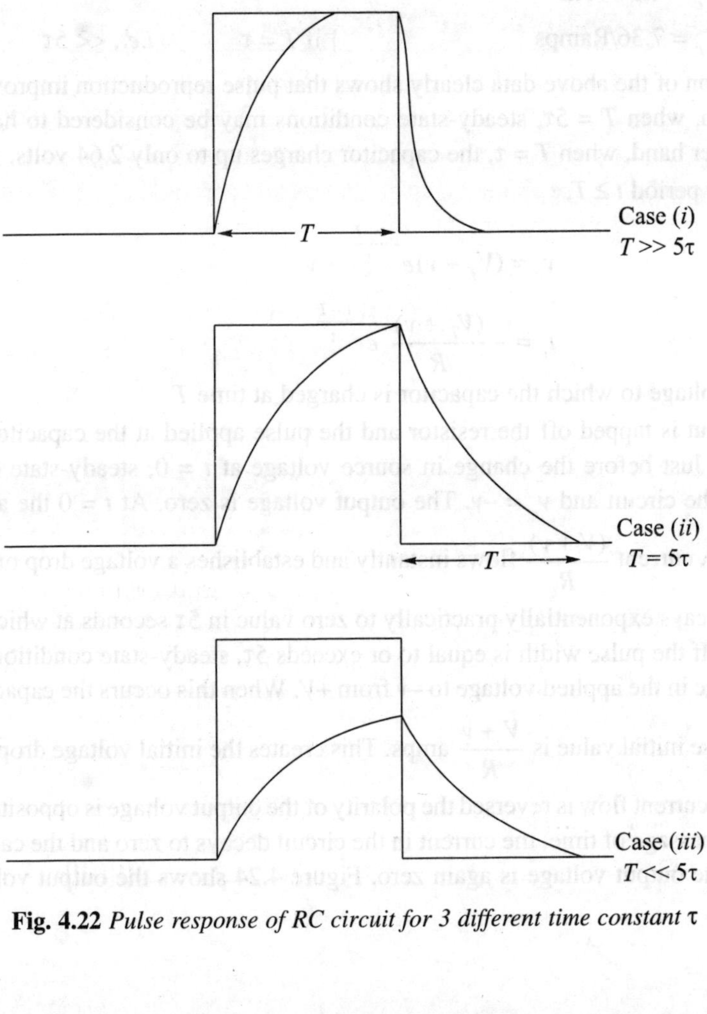

Fig. 4.22 *Pulse response of RC circuit for 3 different time constant* τ

CHAPTER 4

When $T << 5\tau$ the capacitor is not given sufficient time to charge fully. Since the input is a single pulse it does however discharge fully.

In time $0 \le t \le T$, the voltage across the capacitor is

$$v_c = V - (V + v)e^{-t/\tau} \quad ...(4.50)$$

where $\tau = RC$

The current through the capacitor during $0 \le t \le T$ is

$$i_c = \frac{V + v}{R} e^{-t/\tau} \quad ...(4.51)$$

As an example, if $V = v = 10$ volts, using Eqns. 4.50 and 4.51, one obtain at $t = T$

$v_c = 9.999$ volts
$i_c = 6.1 \times 10^{-6}$/Ramps } if $T = 15\tau$ *i.e.*, $>> 5\tau$

$v_c = 9.865$ volts
$i_c = 0.1348$/Ramps } if $T = 5\tau$

$v_c = 2.64$ volts
$i_c = 7.36$/Ramps } if $T = \tau$ *i.e.*, $<< 5\tau$

Examination of the above data clearly shows that pulse reproduction improves as T is increased relative to τ. Also, when $T = 5\tau$, steady-state conditions may be considered to have been attained at $t = T$. On the other hand, when $T = \tau$, the capacitor charges up to only 2.64 volts.

During the period $t \ge T$,

$$v_c = (V_T + v)e^{-\frac{t-T}{\tau}} - v \quad ...(4.52)$$

and

$$i_c = -\frac{(V_T + v)}{R} e^{-\frac{t-T}{\tau}} \quad ...(4.53)$$

where V_T is the voltage to which the capacitor is charged at time T.

If the output is tapped off the resistor and the pulse applied at the capacitor end, the circuit of Fig. 4.23 results. Just before the change in source voltage at $t = 0$, steady-state conditions exist; no current flows in the circuit and $v_c = -v$. The output voltage is zero. At $t = 0$ the applied voltage rises suddenly to $+ V$. A current $\frac{(V + v)}{R}$ flows instantly and establishes a voltage drop of $(V + v)$ volts across R. This current decays exponentially practically to zero value in 5τ seconds at which time the capacitor is charged to $+V$. If the pulse width is equal to or exceeds 5τ, steady-state conditions exists prior to the second step change in the applied voltage to $-v$ from $+V$. When this occurs the capacitor drives a current in the circuit whose initial value is $\frac{V + v}{R}$ amps. This creates the initial voltage drop across R. However, as the direction of current flow is reversed the polarity of the output voltage is opposite to that experienced at $t = 0$. With the passage of time, the current in the circuit decays to zero and the capacitor is charged to $-v$ once again. The output voltage is again zero. Figure 4.24 shows the output voltage waveshape for three cases.

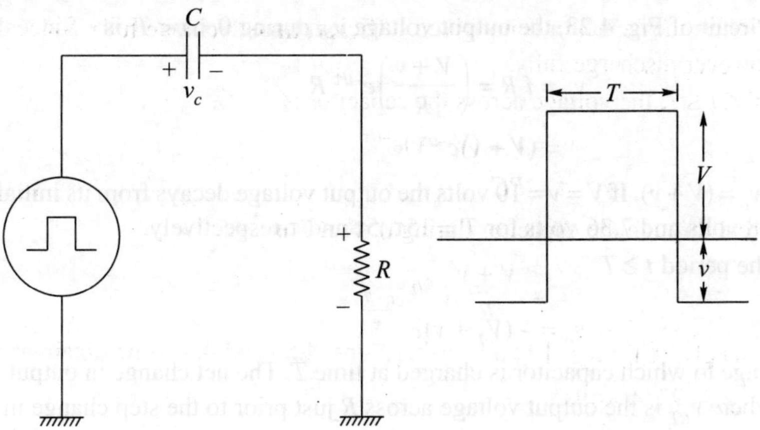

Fig. 4.23 *Pulse as applied to an RC High-Pass circuit*

In Fig. 4.24 the first-two cases, i.e., $T >> 5\tau$ and $T = 5\tau$ are straightforward. The third case, $T << 5\tau$ merits some explanation. In this case, the capacitor does not have enough time to charge up fully. Therefore, at $t = T$ the voltage drop across the resistor is not zero but some positive value, say v_1. The voltage to which C is charged is $(V - v_1)$, by application of KVL. At $t = T$, the applied voltage becomes $-v$. This creates a reverse current $\left(\frac{V - v_1 + v}{R}\right)$ and the magnitude of the initial voltage drop across R is $= (V + v - v_1)$ and of polarity opposite to that which existed initially. From Fig. 4.24 it may be seen that the net change in voltage at each transition of the applied voltage is $(V + v)$ volts in all cases.

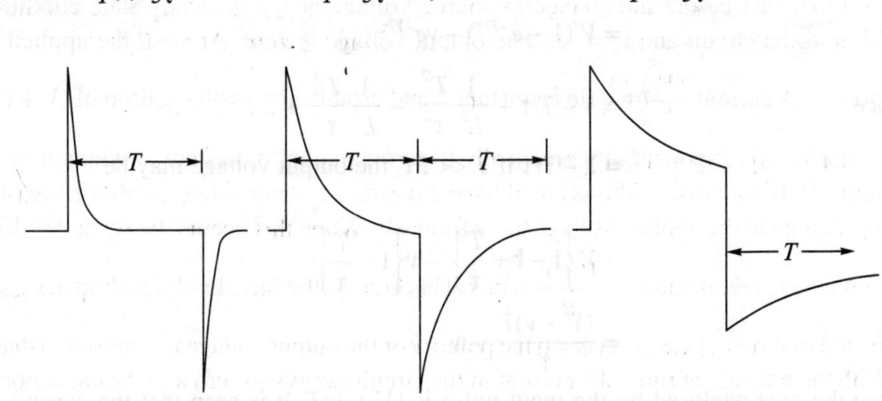

Fig. 4.24 *Pulse response of RC high-pass circuit*

CHAPTER 4

For the circuit of Fig. 4.23, the output voltage v_0, during $0 < t < T$, is

$$v_o = i_c R = \left(\frac{V+v}{R}\right)e^{-t/\tau} R$$

$$= (V + v)e^{-t/\tau} \qquad ...(4.54)$$

At $t = 0$, $v_o = (V + v)$. If $V = v = 10$ volts the output voltage decays from its initial value of 20 volts to 5.1 μv, 0.1348 volts and 7.36 volts for $T = 15\tau$, 5τ and τ respectively.

During the period $t \geq T$

$$v_o = -(V_T + v)e^{-\frac{t-T}{\tau}} \qquad ...(4.55)$$

where V_T = Voltage to which capacitor is charged at time T. The net change in output voltage at $t = T$ is $(V_T + v) + v_{RT}$ where v_{RT} is the output voltage across R just prior to the step change in source voltage at $t = T$.

Since $v_{RT} = V - V_T$ we obtain that

$$V_T + v + v_{RT} = V_T + v + V - V_T = V + v \qquad ...(4.56)$$

For example, if $T = \tau$ and $v = V = 10$ volts,

$$V_{RT} = 7.36 \text{ volts}$$

$$V_T = 2.64 \text{ volts}$$

$$v_o = -(2.64 + 10)e^{-\left(\frac{t-T}{\tau}\right)}$$

The net change in output voltage at $t = T$ is

$$= V + v = 20 \text{ volts.}$$

4.17 INTEGRATING AND DIFFERENTIATING CIRCUITS

Consider the circuit of Fig. 4.21. From Eqn. 4.50, the output voltage at $t = T$, for the pulse input voltage, is

$$= V - (V + v)e^{-T/\tau}$$

$$= V(1 - e^{-T/\tau}) - ve^{-T/\tau}$$

Since $$e^{-T/\tau} = 1 - T/\tau + \frac{1}{L^2}\frac{T^2}{\tau^2} - \frac{1}{L^3}\frac{T^3}{\tau^3} + ...$$

$= 1 - T/\tau$ if $T << 5\tau$, the output voltage may be written as

$$= V\left\{1 - 1 + \frac{T}{\tau}\right\} - v\left\{1 - \frac{T}{\tau}\right\}$$

$$= \frac{(V + v)T}{\tau} - v \qquad ...(4.57)$$

Since the area enclosed by the input pulse is $(V + v)T$, it is seen that the capacitor voltage is proportional to the area and therefore to the integral of the input.

In more general terms, we may write

$$V_{IN} = v_R + v_c \qquad ...(4.58)$$

where V_{IN} is the pulse input voltage and v_R and v_c are the voltage drops across the resistor and the capacitor. If $5RC >> T$ the capacitor voltage will be much less than the resistive voltage drop for all $t < T$. Therefore,

$$V_{IN} = v_R = iR \qquad ...(4.59)$$

But
$$i = C\frac{dv_c}{dt} \qquad ...(4.60)$$

Using Eqn. 4.60 in Eqn. 4.59, we obtain

$$RC\frac{dv_c}{dt} = V_{IN}$$

and therefore
$$v_c = \frac{1}{RC}\int V_{IN}\, dt \qquad ...(4.61)$$

Thus, the output, across the capacitor, is the integral of the input.

Referring to the circuit of Fig. 4.23, if $T >> 5\tau$ we see from Eqns. 4.54 and 4.55 that the output is of the form of short duration pulses at $t = 0$ and $t = T$. The magnitude, as may be seen from Fig. 4.24, is $(V + v)$ volts for both the positive and the negative going pulses. If the pulse voltage of Fig. 4.23 differentiated, one obtains zero duration pulses of infinite magnitude; these are called impulses. We see that the shape of output pulse for $T >> 5\tau$ approaches that obtained by differentiation of the input pulse. For this reason, the RC circuit of Fig. 4.23 is referred to as a differentiating circuit.

In more general terms,

$$V_{IN} = v_R + v_c \qquad ...(4.62)$$

where the symbols have the same significance as defined in Eqn. 4.58.

If $T >> 5\tau$, the capacitor charges up quickly and as the current decays rapidly we may write

$$V_{IN} \approx v_c \qquad ...(4.63)$$

The output voltage tapped across the resistor is

$$v_R = iR = C\frac{dv_c}{dt}R$$

Using Eqn. 4.63 in the above, we obtain

$$v_R = RC\frac{dv_{IN}}{dt} \qquad ...(4.64)$$

Eqn. 4.64 shows that the output is proportional to the derivative of the input.

4.18 DC CIRCUITS WITH INDUCTORS AND CAPACITORS

In the circuit of Fig. 4.25 assume that all capacitors are initially uncharged and that all initial inductor currents are zero prior to closing of switch S. Immediately after switching, the capacitors behave like short circuits and the inductors behave like open circuits. At this stage, the circuit may be reduced to that of Fig. 4.26 from which it is easily deduced that the total current delivered by the battery is 6 A. This initial current flows through the 2Ω resistor and the two capacitors C_A and C_B. After the steady-state has been reached, the capacitors behave like open circuits and the inductors like short circuits. The circuit now reduced to that in Fig. 4.27.

CHAPTER 4

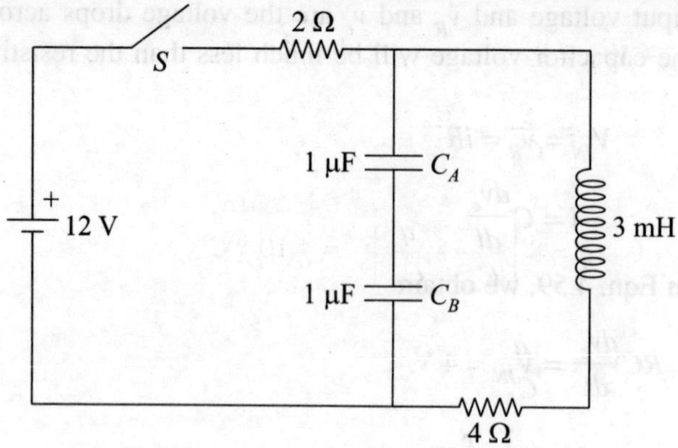

Fig. 4.25 *DC circuit with inductors and capacitors*

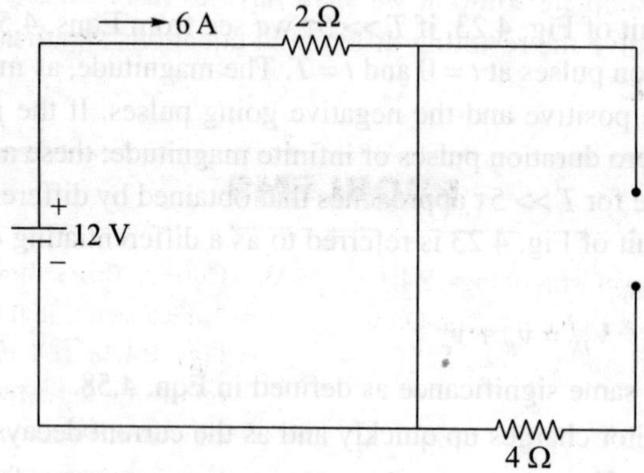

Fig. 4.26 *Circuit of Fig. 4.25 immediately after switching*

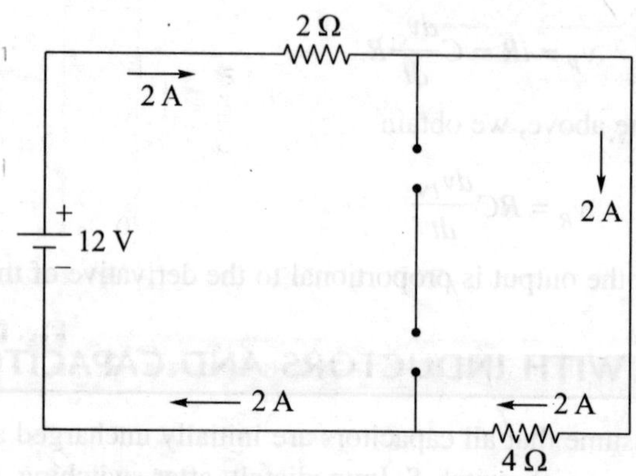

Fig. 4.27 *Circuit of Fig. 4.25 in the steady-state*

The battery now delivers 2 A which flows through the 2 and 4 Ω resistors. The voltage across the two capacitors in series is 8 V. Since C_A and C_B are in series, the same change q flows through both of them. Thus

$$V_{CA} + V_{CB} = 8$$

$$= \frac{q}{C_A} + \frac{q}{C_B}$$

Solving for q,
$$q = 8\left[\frac{q}{C_A} + \frac{q}{C_B}\right]^{-1} = 4.10^{-6}\ \text{C}$$

Therefore,
$$V_{C_A} = \frac{q}{C_A} = 4\ \text{V},$$

and
$$V_{C_B} = \frac{q}{C_B} = 4\ \text{V}.$$

In order to find the complete solution we shall have to resort to one of the standard methods discussed in Chapter 3 and solve the resulting differential equations simultaneously. This is, however, beyond the scope of this book.

PROBLEMS

1. The repetitive voltage waveforms of Figs. P.4.1*a* and P.4.1*b* are applied to a 1 μF capacitor. Draw the resulting current waveform.

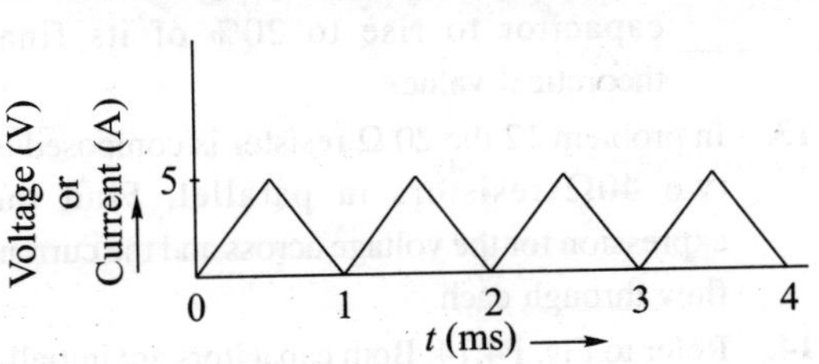

Fig. P.4.1(a)

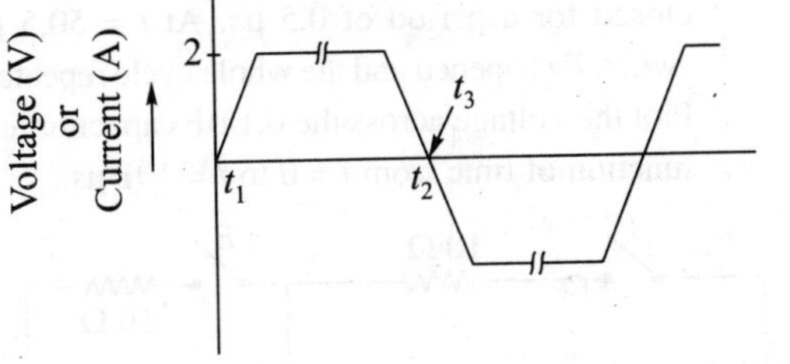

Fig. P.4.1(b)

2. Find the expression for current which flows through a 1μF capacitor if the voltage across it is given by $v_c = V \sin(400t)$.

3. Current flows through an initially uncharged 2μF capacitor in the form of pulses as shown in Figs. P.4.3*a*, *b*, *c* and *d*. In each case, draw the resulting waveform of voltage across the capacitor. What would your answer be if the initial charge on the capacitor is 2 volts?

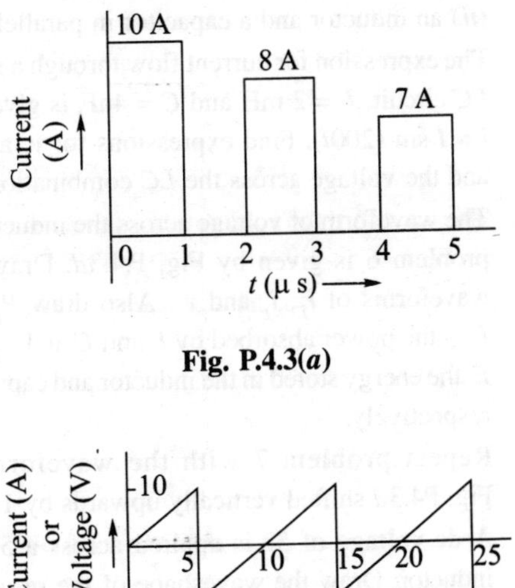

Fig. P.4.3(*a*)

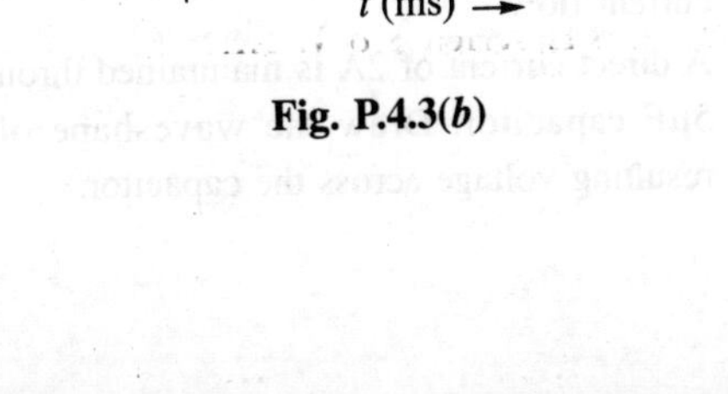

Fig. P.4.3(*b*)

CHAPTER 4

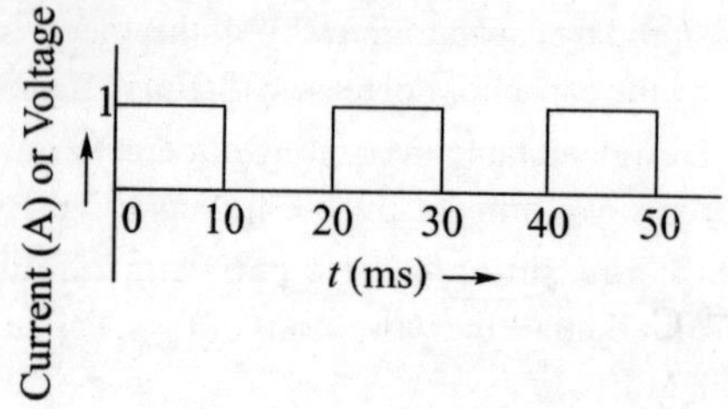

Fig. P.4.3(*c*)

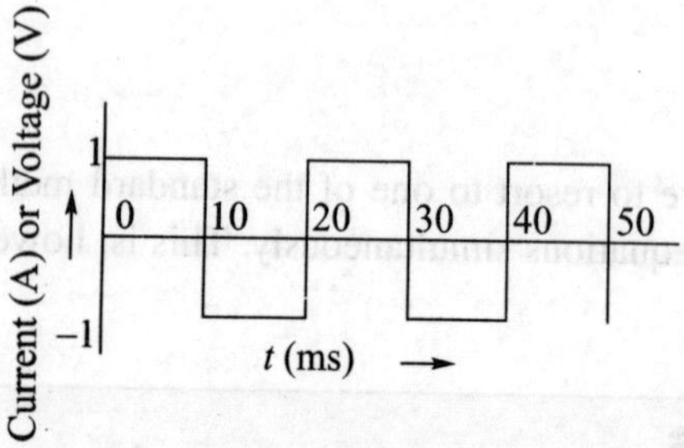

Fig. P.4.3(*d*)

4. Draw the waveform of current flow through a 10 mH inductor given that the voltage across it has the repetitive waveform of Fig. P.4.3*d*.

5. Can either voltage or current or both change instantaneously across a combination of
   (*i*) an inductor and a capacitor in series?
   (*ii*) an inductor and a capacitor in parallel?

6. The expression for current flow through a series *LC* circuit, $L = 2$ mH and $C = 4$nF, is given by $i = I \sin (200t)$. Find expressions for v_L and v_c and the voltage across the *LC* combination.

7. The waveform of voltage across the inductor in problem 6 is given by Fig. P.4.3*d*. Draw the waveforms of i_L, i_c and v_c. Also draw P_L and P_c – the power absorbed by *L* and *C* and E_L and E_c the energy stored in the inductor and capacitor respectively.

8. Repeat problem 7 with the waveform of Fig. P4.3*d* shifted vertically upwards by 1*v*.

9. A dc voltage of 5*v* is applied across a 5 mH inductor. Draw the waveshape of the resulting current flow.

10. A direct current of 2A is maintained through a 5μF capacitor. Draw the waveshape of the resulting voltage across the capacitor.

11. A lossy capacitor takes 10 μA in the steady-state from a 100 volt dc voltage source. Find the loss in watts. Derive a model for the lossy capacitor and find its self time constant.

12. Refer to Fig. P.4.12. The switch is closed at $t = 0$. Assume an initially uncharged capacitor. Find

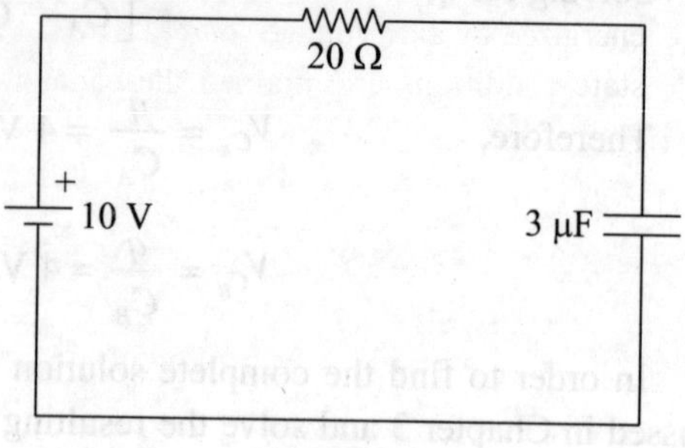

Fig. P.4.12

   (*i*) the current in the circuit at $t = 0$ immediately after switching.
   (*ii*) the current in the circuit at $t = \infty$.
   (*iii*) time taken (practically) to achieve steady-state conditions.
   (*iv*) time taken for the voltage across the capacitor to rise to 20% of its final theoretical value.

13. In problem 12 the 20 Ω resistor is composed at two 40Ω resistors in parallel. Find the expression for the voltage across and the current flow through each.

14. Refer to Fig. P4.14. Both capacitors are initially uncharged and both switches are open. Switch *A* is closed at $t = 0$ and held closed till $t = 50$ μs. At this time Switch *A* is opened and switch *B* is closed for a period of 0.5 μ*s*. At $t = 50.5$ μs switch *B* is opened and the whole cycle repeated. Plot the voltage across the 0.1 μF capacitor as a function of time from $t = 0$ to $t = 101$ μs.

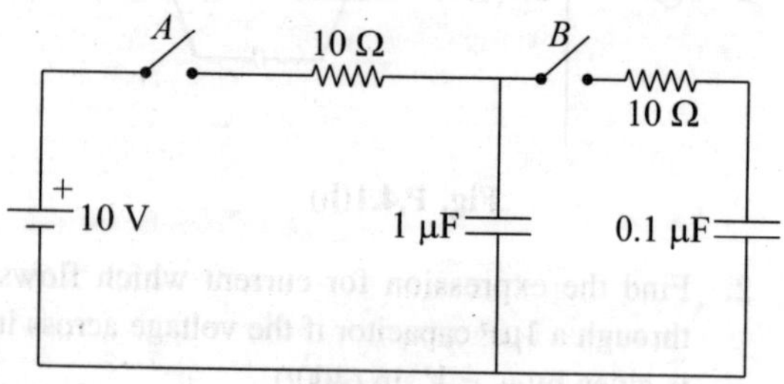

Fig. P.4.14

15. A 10V dc voltage source is to connected across a 1mH indicator. It is desired to limit the current magnitude to 5A. What resistance should be inserted in series with the inductor?
16. In problem 5, what are the times taken to establish 1A, 3A and 5A in the inductor?
17. A capacitor is inserted in series *RC* circuit energized by a dc voltage source. After steady-state conditions are attained the capacitor is disconnected from the circuit. What is the energy stored by capacitor now? Will the energy stored by the capacitor decrease with time? If so, why?
18. Design suitable integrating circuits to integrate the waveforms of Figs. P.4.1*a* and Fig. P.4.3*c*.
19. Design suitable differentiating circuits to differentiate the waveforms of Figs. P.4.1*a*, 4.1*b* and P.4.3*d*.

Alternating Current Circuits

5

CHAPTER

5.1 INTRODUCTION

In the previous chapters techniques for the transient and steady-state solution of dc circuits have been discussed. We now turn our attention to obtaining the steady-state solution of circuits energized by periodic time varying sources of the type shown in Fig. 5.1. Such a waveshape is time-varying because its amplitude is a function of time; furthermore it is periodic because it repeats itself in regular fashion. The waveshape of Fig. 5.1 is referred to as a sinusoid or a sinusoidal waveshape because its amplitude varies as a sine function of time. A source generating such a waveshape is referred to as a sinusoidal or ac source. The letters ac stand for alternating current and the word "alternating" is reserved to describe periodic sinusoidal waveshapes.

The study of techniques to solve circuits energized by ac sources is of practical importance because such voltages are common place; ac voltages are generated in power stations, transmitted via transmission lines to distribution centers to power various devices. In fact many devices such as motors etc. operate best when energized by an ac source.

5.2 REPRESENTATION OF AN AC SOURCE

The voltage output of the ac source, in Fig. 5.1, at any instant of time may be expressed by the equation

$$v(t) = V_m \sin(\omega t) \qquad ...(5.1)$$

In Eqn. 5.1 and Fig. 5.1 the symbol $v(t)$ represents the time varying source whose maximum value is V_m. The waveform of Eqn. 5.1 is periodic because sin (ωt) is periodic. Zeroes of this waveform occur at time $t = \dfrac{n\pi}{\omega}$ seconds where n takes on values 0, 1, 2, 3, ... The time period, $T = \dfrac{2\pi}{\omega}$, indicated in Fig. 5.1, is the time interval between any two similarly situated points such as A and B. The radian frequency, ω, has units of radians/s. If ω is large the number of repetitions of the waveform per second is large. In such a case the frequency is said to be high. From the definition of time period, it follows that the total number of repetitions per second is equal to $\dfrac{1}{T}$; this is the frequency denoted by the symbol f. Frequency is measured in Hertz, denoted by Hz, and has the dimensions of s^{-1}.

$$f = \frac{1}{T} = \frac{\omega}{2\pi}$$

and

$$\omega = 2\pi f \qquad ...(5.2)$$

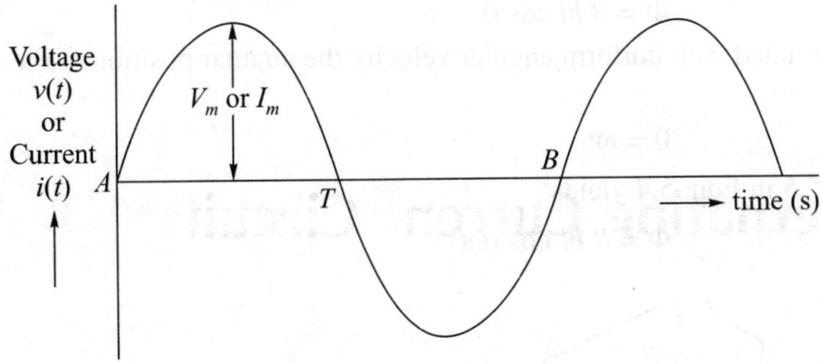

Fig. 5.1 *A sinusoidal time function*

5.3 POLARITY OF AC SOURCES

Figure 5.2 shows the symbolic representation of ac voltage and current sources. Since we admit the possibility of $v(t)$ and $i(t)$ changing polarity, what is the significance of the polarity markings in Fig. 5.2? With the top terminal marked positive, as in Fig. 5.2, it implies that when this terminal goes positive the voltage will be denoted by a positive number; otherwise it will be represented by a negative number. A similar explanation holds for the current source. If the direction of current flow at any instant coincides with that of the arrow, it shall be represented by a positive number. Referring to the voltage source, when the top terminal is positive, the positive direction of current flow is away from that terminal. Should the actual direction of current flow be towards the positive terminal, it shall be represented by a negative number.

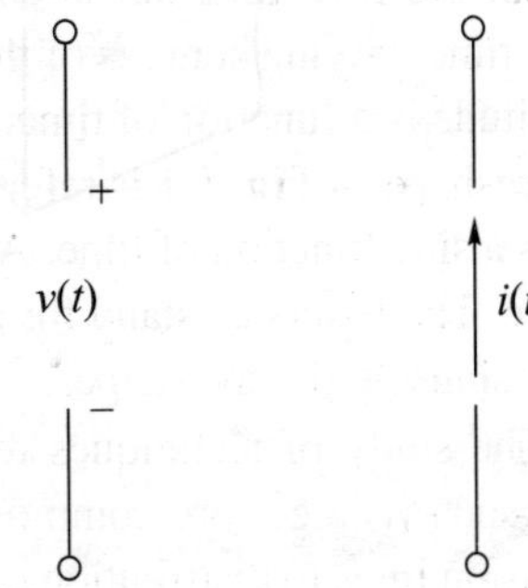

Fig. 5.2 *Symbolic representation of ac voltage and current sources*

5.4 GENERATION OF AC VOLTAGE

In this section the fundamental principle underlying the operation of ac generators will be described; the actual machines used in power stations are of more complex structure and design.

Figure 5.3 shows a rectangular shaped coil suspended between the poles of a horseshoe shaped magnet. The coil is rotated about axis AA' with uniform angular velocity ω. In the space between the poles of the magnet a magnetic field exists which is assumed to be uniform. This means that the magnetic flux density B is the same at all points in the gap between the poles. For the coil position shown, (*i.e.* coil sides xy and pq perpendicular to the direction of B) the flux linkage is given by the product of the flux density magnitude and the area of the coil.

$$\Phi = Bhl \text{ Wb} \quad \text{...(5.3)}$$

If the coil is turned through 90° the flux linkage is zero. Clearly, as the coil rotates about AA' there are two positions each of minimum and maximum flux linkage. The general expression for flux linkage may be derived from Fig. 5.4 which shows the cross-sectional view with coil sides xp and yq inclined at an angle $\phi°$ to the vertical. The flux linkage in this position is given by

$$\Phi = B\,hl\cos\theta \qquad ...(5.4)$$

If the coil is rotated with uniform angular velocity the angular position of the coil θ is related to the time t by

$$\theta = \omega t \qquad ...(5.5)$$

Use of Eqn. 5.5 in Eqn. 5.4 yields

$$\Phi = B\,hl\cos(\omega t) \qquad ...(5.6)$$

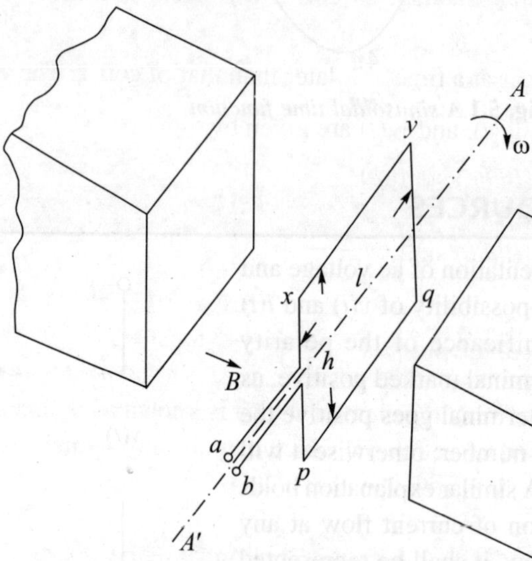

Fig. 5.3 *Illustrating the principle of operation of an ac generator*

Equation 5.6 shows that the flux linking the coil varies with time. By Faraday's law a voltage must be induced in it whose magnitude is given by

$$\left|\frac{d\Phi}{dt}\right| = Bhl\omega\sin(\omega t) \qquad ...(5.7)$$

Since B, h, l, and ω are constants, the arrangement generates a sinusoidal wave of voltage which may be tapped off the coil at its terminals, marked ab in Fig. 5.3.

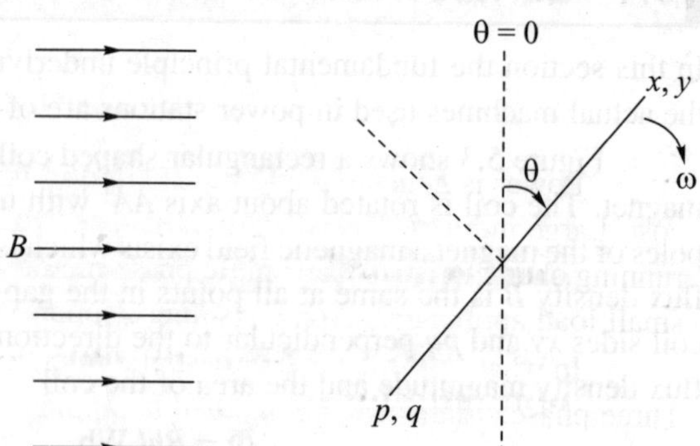

Fig. 5.4 *Deriving expression for flux linkage*

In an ac generator many such coils are wound suitably on a frame and interconnected in series and parallel to deliver the required power. The connection of coils in series increases the voltage delivered (very much like connecting batteries in series). On the other hand, connection of coils in parallel increases the current delivering capability and ensures that the available power can be utilized. Naturally, the power delivered by the generator is always less than the mechanical power input by the efficiency factor. The mechanical energy required to rotate the assembly of coils is derived from thermal or nuclear or the energy associated with a water fall.

5.5 SINGLE AND THREE PHASE GENERATORS

If instead of one coil, in Fig. 5.3 suppose that there are three identical coils, on the common axis AA′, each displaced from the other by 120°. If the assembly is rotated with uniform angular velocity, each coil will generate a sinusoidal waveshape of voltage at its terminals. However, due to the angular displacement of the coils, the maximum voltage of coil 2 will occur at a time $\frac{2\pi}{3\omega}$ later than that of coil 1. The maxima of coil 3 will occur at a time $\frac{4\pi}{3\omega}$ later than that of coil 1. The voltages produced at the terminals of the three coils $v_1(t)$, $v_2(t)$, and $v_3(t)$ are given by

$$v_1(t) = (Bhl\omega) \sin (\omega t)$$

$$v_2(t) = (Bhl\omega) \sin \left(\omega t - \frac{2\pi}{3}\right) \quad ...(5.8)$$

and

$$v_3(t) = (Bhl\omega) \sin \left(\omega t - \frac{4\pi}{3}\right)$$

Figure 5.5 shows the output of such a generator which is known as a three phase generator. On the other hand, the generator described in section 5.4 which outputs only a single waveform is known as a single phase ac generator.

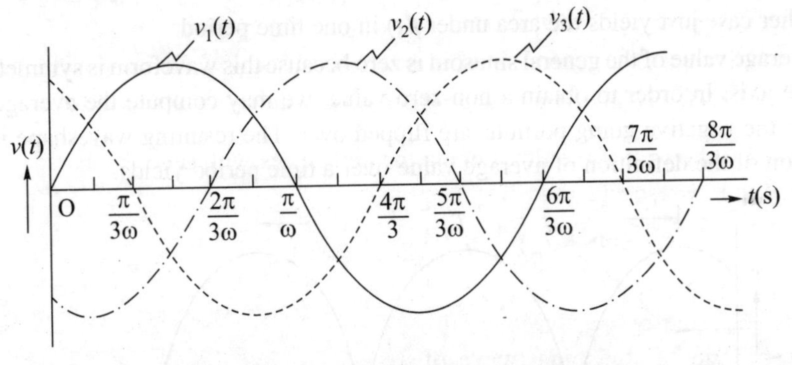

Fig. 5.5 *Output waveform of a 3–Φ generator*

Power is generated and transmitted in three phase form because of better efficiency and lesser cost. Large industrial loads are invariably of the three phase variety as three phase motors have better running characteristics than single phase motors. Single phase loads are common place in domestic and small load applications and consumer appliances.

In what follows, we will describe rules and techniques for handling single phase ac circuits only. Three phase circuits can be handled by application of similar rules.

5.6 AC WAVEFORM; PEAK, AVERAGE AND RMS VALUE

Figure 5.6 shows the general sinusoid whose equation is given by

$$v(t) = V_m \cos (\omega t - \theta_1) \quad ...(5.9)$$

At $\omega t = \theta_1$, $(\omega t - \theta_1) = 0$, and $v = V_m$, the maximum value. If $\theta_1 = \frac{\pi}{2}$, Eqn. 5.9 reduces to

$$v(t) = V_m \sin(\omega t) \quad ...(5.10)$$

θ_1 is known as the phase angle of $v(t)$.

The question to be answered now is — What quantities may we use to describe the magnitude of an ac waveform of the type represented by Eqn. 5.9? There are three quantities — namely the peak, average and effective (*RMS*) values.

Peak value: The peak value is simply the maximum value identified by V_m in Fig. 5.6 and Eqn. 5.9.

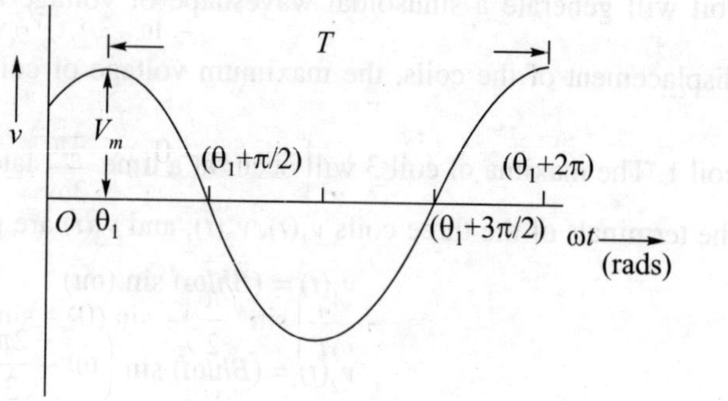

Fig. 5.6 *The general sinusoid*

Average value: By definition, the average value of a periodic waveform $f(t)$ with time period T is $= \frac{1}{T}\int_t^{t+T} f(t)\,dt$. We could make matters simple if we choose to evaluate the simpler integral $\frac{1}{T}\int_0^T f(t)\,dt$. Note that the integral in either case just yields the area under $f(t)$ in one time period.

The average value of the general sinusoid is zero because this waveform is symmetrically disposed about the time axis. In order to obtain a non-zero value, we may compute the average of the general sinusoid when the negative going portions are flipped over. The resulting waveshape is shown in Fig. 5.7. Application of the definition of average value over a time period yields.

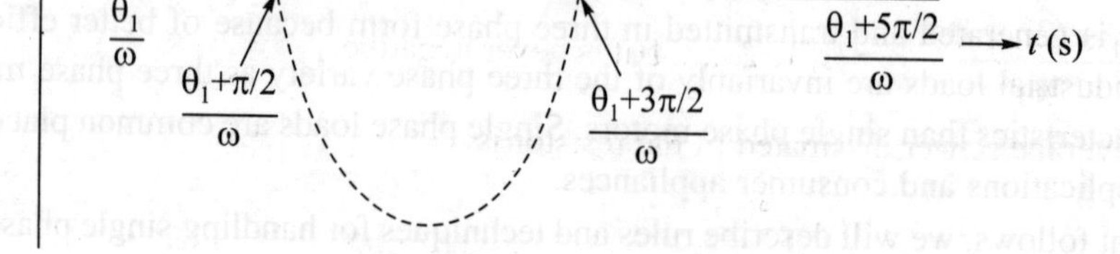

Fig. 5.7 *Flipping the –ve portion of the sinusoid to obtain a non-zero average value*

$$V_{avg} = \frac{1}{T}\int_{\frac{\theta_1}{\omega}}^{\frac{\theta_1+2\pi}{\omega}} v(t)\,dt$$

$$= \frac{1}{T}\int_{\frac{\theta_1}{\omega}}^{\frac{\theta_1+\pi/2}{\omega}} V_m \cos(\omega t - \theta_1)\,dt$$

$$- \int_{\frac{\theta_1+\pi/2}{\omega}}^{\frac{\theta_1+3\pi/2}{\omega}} V_m \cos(\omega t - \theta_1)\,dt + \int_{\frac{\theta_1+3\pi/2}{\omega}}^{\frac{\theta_1+2\pi}{\omega}} V_m \cos(\omega t - \theta_1)\,dt$$

$$= \frac{V_m}{T}\left[\frac{\sin(\omega t - \theta_1)}{\omega}\right]_{\frac{\theta_1}{\omega}}^{\frac{\theta_1+\pi/2}{\omega}} - \left[\frac{\sin(\omega t - \theta_1)}{\omega}\right]_{\frac{\theta_1+\pi/2}{\omega}}^{\frac{\theta_1+3\pi/2}{\omega}} + \left[\frac{\sin(\omega t - \theta_1)}{\omega}\right]_{\frac{\theta_1+3\pi/2}{\omega}}^{\frac{\theta_1+2\pi}{\omega}}$$

$$= \frac{V_m}{\omega T}\left[\sin\left(\frac{\pi}{2}\right) - \sin(0) - \sin\left(\frac{3\pi}{2}\right) + \sin\left(\frac{\pi}{2}\right) + \sin(2\pi) - \sin\left(\frac{3\pi}{2}\right)\right]$$

$$= \frac{2V_m}{\pi}$$

Thus $$V_{avg} = \frac{2V_m}{\pi} = 0.636\, V_m \qquad \text{...(5.11)}$$

Note that the same result is obtained by evaluating any of the following integrals.

$$\frac{1}{\pi/\omega}\int_{\frac{\theta_1}{\omega}}^{\frac{\theta_1+\pi}{\omega}} v(t)\,dt \qquad \text{...(5.12)}$$

$$\frac{1}{2\pi}\int_{\theta_1}^{\theta_1+2\pi} v(t)d(\omega t) \qquad \text{...(5.13)}$$

$$\frac{1}{\pi}\int_{\theta_1}^{\theta_1+\pi} v(t)d(\omega t) \qquad \text{...(5.14)}$$

Effective value, I_{eff}: Suppose an alternating current $i(t) = I_{max}\cos(\omega t - \theta_1)$ flows through a resistor of R ohms. The resulting voltage drop $v(t)$ is equal to $RI_{max}\cos(\omega t - \theta_1)$. The power dissipated in the resistor at any instant of time t is given by

$$p(t) = v(t)\, i(t) = RI_m^2 \cos^2(\omega t - \theta_1) \qquad \text{...(5.15)}$$

The last equation shows that the instantaneous power dissipated in the resistor is zero at times given by $\frac{2\theta_1 + (2n+1)\pi}{2\omega}$ $n = 0, 1, 2, ...$ but is never negative.

The average power dissipated in the resistor is

$$= \frac{1}{\pi/\omega}\int_{\frac{\theta_1}{\omega}}^{\frac{\theta_1+\pi}{\omega}} I_m^2\, R\cos^2(\omega t - \theta_1)\,dt \qquad \text{...(5.16)}$$

$$= \frac{\omega}{\pi}\int_{\frac{\theta_1}{\omega}}^{\frac{\theta_1+\pi}{\omega}} I_{m/2}^2\,[1 + \cos 2(\omega t - \theta_1)]\,dt$$

$$= \omega\frac{I_m^2 R}{2\pi}\left[t + \frac{\sin 2(\omega t - \theta_1)}{2\omega}\right]_{\frac{\theta_1}{\omega}}^{\frac{\theta_1+\pi}{\omega}}$$

CHAPTER 5

$$
\left.
\begin{aligned}
&= \frac{\omega I_m^2 R}{2\pi}\left[\frac{\theta_1+\pi}{\omega} - \frac{\theta_1}{\omega} + \frac{\sin 2\pi}{2\omega} - \frac{\sin 0}{2\omega}\right] \\
&= \frac{I_m^2 R}{2} \\
&= \left(\frac{I_m}{\sqrt{2}}\right)^2 R \\
&= I_{\text{eff}}^2 R
\end{aligned}
\right\} \qquad \text{...(5.17)}
$$

From Eqn. 5.17 one may infer that the same amount of average power is dissipated in the resistor whether a sinusoidal waveshape of current of peak value I_m or dc of value I_{eff} is passed through it. I_{eff} is known as the effective value or the Root Mean Square value. This name has come about because I_{eff} may be written as

$$
I_{\text{eff}} = \sqrt{\frac{1}{R}\frac{1}{\pi/\omega}\int_{\frac{\theta_1}{\omega}}^{\frac{\theta_1+\pi}{\omega}} I_m^2 R \cos^2(\omega t - \theta_1)\,dt}
$$

= square root of the mean of the square of the time function .

$= I_{\text{RMS}}$

From Eqn. 5.17,

$$
I_{\text{eff}} = I_{\text{RMS}} = \frac{I_m}{\sqrt{2}} = 0.707\, I_m \qquad \text{...(5.18)}
$$

This definition applies to voltage as well because, from Eq. 5.17,

$$
p_{\text{avg}} = \frac{I_m^2 R^2}{2R} = \frac{I_{\text{eff}}^2 R^2}{R} = \frac{V_{\text{eff}}^2}{R}
$$

Since p_{avg} is also equal to $\frac{V_m^2}{2R}$, we obtain that

$$
V_{\text{eff}} = V_{\text{RMS}} = \frac{V_m}{\sqrt{2}} = 0.707\, V_m \qquad \text{...(5.19)}
$$

In Electrical Engineering, it is common practice to describe the amplitudes of sinusoidally varying voltages and currents by mean of RMS values. In fact all meters are calibrated to read RMS values. They may, however, respond to the peak, average or the mean square.

In this book the symbols V and I will be used to represent RMS quantities. V_m and I_m will be used to represent maximum quantities. Time varying voltage and current sources will be denoted by the symbols $v(t)$ and $i(t)$ or v and i respectively.

5.7 PHASOR REPRESENTATION OF AC SOURCES

Consider the circuit of Fig. 5.8. To solve this by the mesh current method we write the two mesh equations

$$v(t) = L_1\frac{di_1}{dt} + R(i_1 - i_2) + \frac{1}{C}\int i_1\, dt \qquad ...(5.20)$$

and
$$0 = R(i_2 - i_1) + L_2\frac{di_2}{dt} \qquad ...(5.21)$$

The simultaneous solution of the above two integro differential equations yields the complete response of the circuit. There are two disadvantages associated with this approach. First, we may not be interested in the complete response but only in the steady-state response. Second, for more complicated circuits, the number of simultaneous equations to be solved increases.

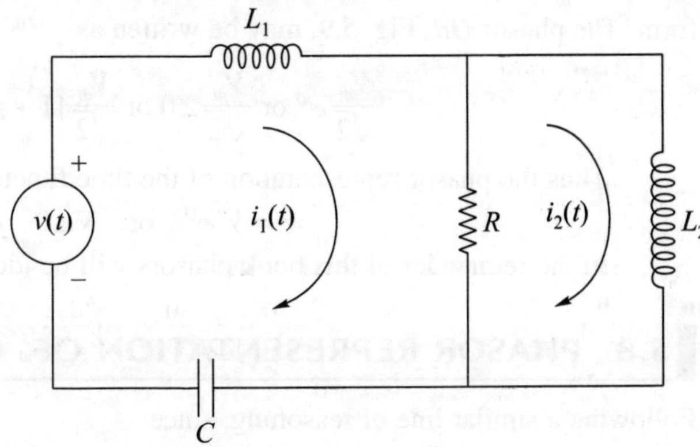

Fig. 5.8 *Mesh current method as applied to ac*

Such difficulties are avoided by resorting to what is known as the phasor representation. This technique reduces the integro differential equations to ordinary algebraic equations whose solution is much simpler.

Consider the complex number $V_m e^{j\omega t}$ where V_m is a constant voltage, t denotes time in seconds and ω a constant which has the dimensions of radians/s. For all t, the magnitude of the complex number $V_m e^{j\omega t}$ is equal to V_m. We may set θ = ωt and measure θ from the real axis in the anti-clockwise sense. At $t = 0$, θ = 0; as t increases, so does θ and the complex vector $V_m e^{j\omega t}$ rotates with uniform angular velocity ω in the anti-clockwise sense. The time taken to complete one revolution is the time period, T, which is found by setting θ = 2 π in θ = ωt *i.e.*, $T = \frac{2\pi}{\omega}$. The frequency of revolution is therefore $f = \frac{1}{T}$ Hz.

From Euler's identity,

$$V_m e^{j\omega t} = V_m\,[\cos \omega t + j \sin \omega t]$$
$$= V_m \cos \omega t + j\, V_m \sin \omega t$$

The time function of interest V_m cos (ωt) with maximum value V_m is in fact equal to the real part of $V_m e^{j\omega t}$. This gives rise to the possibility of representing the time function by a rotating vector in the complex plane. Since $V_m e^{j\omega t}$ and V_m cos ωt both vary with time in cyclic fashion, the time function V_m cos ωt may be represented by a vector in the complex plane, at a convenient instant of time such as $t = 0$. The complex vector OA (Fig. 5.9) of length V_m units therefore represents the time function V_m cost ωt. Note that

$$OA = V_m[e^{j(\omega t)}]_{t=0} = V_m$$

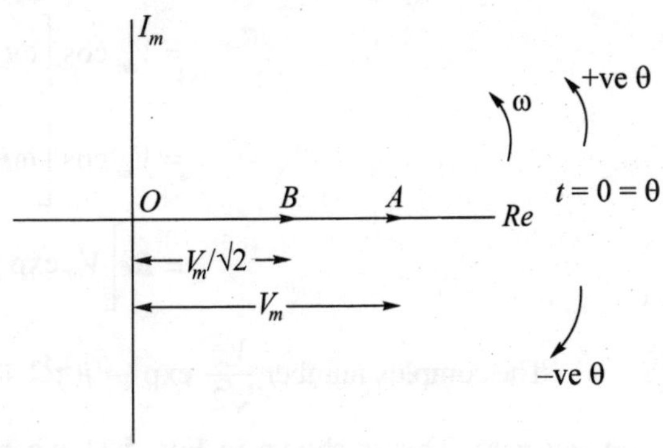

Fig. 5.9 *Rotating phase representation of* V_m *cos* (ωt)

We now introduce a rule the length of the complex vector which represents a sinusoidal time function shall be equal to the RMS value of that time function. Dividing OA by $\sqrt{2}$ we obtain the complex vector OB of length $\frac{V_m}{\sqrt{2}}$. In Fig. 5.9, OB is said to be rotating phasor representation of the time function $V_m \cos(\omega t)$. Since a phasor is a complex number it may be expressed in either polar or rectangular form. The phasor OB, Fig. 5.9, may be written as

$$\frac{V_m}{\sqrt{2}} e^{j0} \text{ or } \frac{V_m}{\sqrt{2}} \angle 0 \text{ or } \frac{V_m}{\sqrt{2}} [1 + j0]$$

Thus the phasor representation of the time function $v = V_m \cos(\omega t)$ is given by

$$V = V e^{j0} \quad \text{or} \quad V\angle 0 \quad \text{or} \quad V[1 + j0] \qquad ...(5.22)$$

In the remainder of this book phasors will be identified by use of boldface letters.

5.8 PHASOR REPRESENTATION OF COSINUSODIAL WAVEFORMS

Following a similar line of reasoning, since

$$V_m \cos(\omega t \pm \phi) = Re\,[e^{j(\omega t \pm \phi)}],$$

the complex number $\frac{V_m}{\sqrt{2}} e^{\pm j\phi}$ is the phasor representation of the time function $V_m \cos(\omega t \pm \phi)$. The rotating phasor representations of $V_m \cos(\omega t \pm \phi)$ are OC and OD respectively. The phasor representation of $v = V_m \cos(\omega t \pm \phi)$ is given by

$$V = V e^{\pm j\phi} \text{ or } V\angle \pm \phi \text{ or } V[\cos\phi \pm j \sin\phi] \qquad ...(5.23)$$

5.9 PHASOR REPRESENTATION OF THE GENERAL SINUSOIDAL WAVEFORM

We notice that

$$V_m \sin(\omega t + \phi) = V_m \cos\left[\frac{\pi}{2} - (\omega t \pm \phi)\right]$$

$$= V_m \cos\left[\omega t \pm \phi - \frac{\pi}{2}\right]$$

$$= V_m \cos\left[\omega t - \left(\frac{\pi}{2} \mp \phi\right)\right]$$

$$= Re\left[V_m \exp j\left[\omega t - \left(\frac{\pi}{2} \mp \phi\right)\right]\right]$$

The complex number $\frac{V_m}{\sqrt{2}} \exp(-j(\pi/2 \mp \phi))$ is the phasor representation of the time function $V_m \sin(\omega t \pm \phi)$. This is shown in Fig. 5.11 where the rotating phasors OE and OF represent the time functions $V_m \sin(\omega t + \phi)$ and $V_m \sin(\omega t - \phi)$ respectively. The phasor representation of these two time functions is given by

$$V = V \exp(\pm j(\phi \mp \pi/2)), \text{ or } V/\pm(\phi \mp \pi/2) \text{ or } V\{\pm(\sin\phi - j\cos\phi)\} \qquad ...(5.24)$$

5.10 A SIMPLE TECHNIQUE

From the foregoing it is readily seen that the phasors *OX* and *OY*, in Fig. 5.12 represent the time functions V_m cos ωt and V_m sin ωt respectively. The negative of these phasors *i.e.* *OZ* and *OT* therefore represent the time functions $-V_m \cos(\omega t)$ and $-V_m \sin(\omega t)$.

Recall that angles measured in the anti-clockwise sense, in the direction of rotation of the phasor, are positive. To obtain the rotating phasor representation of $V_m \cos(\omega t - \phi)$ displace the phasor *OX* (Fig. 5.12) in the clockwise sense by an angle ϕ and obtain *OD* in Fig. 5.10. Similarly, to obtain the representation of $V_m \sin(\omega t + \phi)$ displace the phasor *OY* in the anti-clockwise sense by the angle ϕ thus obtaining *OE*, (Fig. 5.11). Thus, the representation of any time function may be obtained from the representation of the basic functions V_m cos ωt and V_m sin ωt. Use of this simple technique enables one to draw the rotating phasor of a time function or derive the time function corresponding to a rotating phasor with ease. The phasor representation in either polar or rectangular form can be written once the position of the rotating phasor in the complex plane is identified.

5.11 INSTANTANEOUS VALUES OF A TIME FUNCTION

Consider the time function $v = V_m \cos(\omega t - \phi)$; V_2 in fact, is the instantaneous value. At $t = 0$, $v = V_m \cos \phi$ while at any time t_1, $v = V_m \cos(\omega t_1 - \phi)$. In particular, at $t = \frac{\phi}{\omega}$ v is a maximum and equals V_m while at $t = \frac{\frac{\pi}{2} + \phi}{\omega}$, v is 0.

The rotating phasor representation of v is *OD* in Fig. 5.10. From this figure we see that the horizontal projection of *OD* is $\frac{V_m}{\sqrt{2}} \cos \phi$. Since *OD* is a representation of the time function at $t = 0$ and since we have chosen to represent RMS rather than maximum values, the instantaneous value of v at $t = 0$ is the horizontal projection of *OD* multiplied by $\sqrt{2}$.

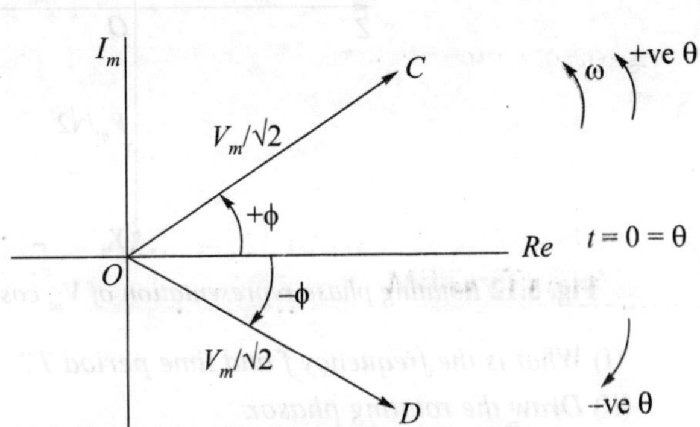

Fig. 5.10 *Rotating phase representation of* $V_m \cos(\omega t \pm \theta)$

To find the instantaneous value at any time *t*, the position of the rotating phasor at that time is located, and its horizontal projection is multiplied by $\sqrt{2}$.

When the phasor aligns itself with the +ve imaginary axis, the instantaneous value is zero. A negative maximum is recorded when it points in the direction of the negative real axis.

Example 5.1. *For the time functions*

(a) $i_1 = 2 \cos(300t + \pi/4)$ *amps and*

(b) $v_1 = 1.5 \sin(400t - \pi/3)$ *volts.*

CHAPTER 5

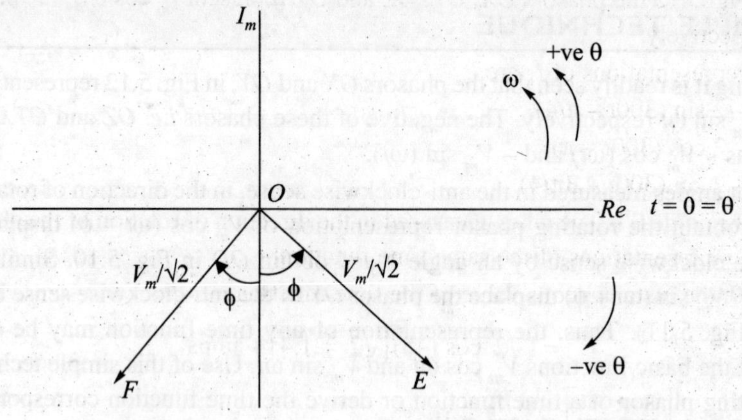

Fig. 5.11 *Rotating phase representation of V_m sin (ωt ± θ)*

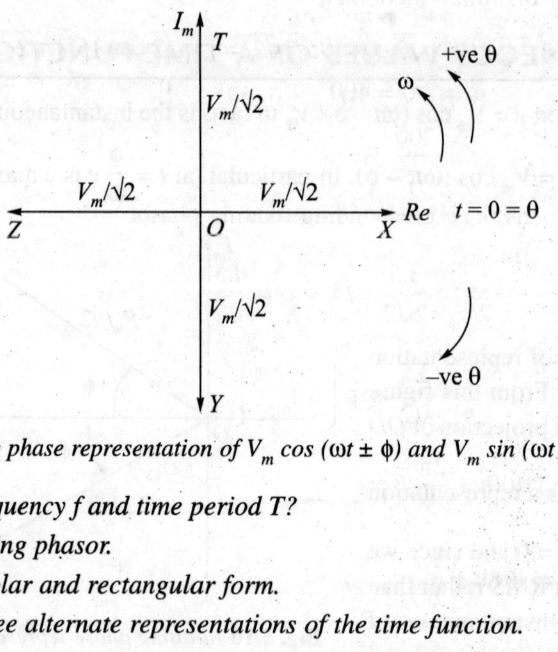

Fig. 5.12 *Rotating phase representation of V_m cos (ωt ± ϕ) and V_m sin (ωt ± ϕ) respectively*

(*i*) *What is the frequency f and time period T?*

(*ii*) *Draw the rotating phasor.*

(*iii*) *Express it in polar and rectangular form.*

(*iv*) *Write down three alternate representations of the time function.*

(*v*) *Find the instantaneous values of the time functions at t = 0 and $t = \dfrac{5\pi}{6\omega}$.*

Solution. (*a*) (*i*) $\omega = 2\pi f = 300$

$$f = \frac{300}{2\pi} \text{ Hz.}$$

(*ii*) The routing phasor is represented in Fig. 5.13.

(*iii*) $\sqrt{2}\left[\frac{1}{\sqrt{2}} + j\frac{1}{\sqrt{2}}\right] = (1 + j1)$

$$= \sqrt{2}\, e^{j\pi/4} \text{ or } \sqrt{2} \angle 45°.$$

(*iv*) From Fig. 5.12 the phasors *OX*, *OT*, *OZ* and *OY* represent $I_m \cos \omega t$, $-I_m \sin \omega t$, $-I_m \cos \omega t$ and $I_m \sin \omega t$ respectively.

Alternate representations of i_1 are

$$-2 \sin (300t - \pi/4)$$

$$-2 \cos (300t - \pi)$$

and $$-2 \sin (300t + 3\pi/4)$$

Note that the angle θ is +ve when measured in the direction of rotation of the phasor. In all, there are eight possible representations of the same time function.

(*v*) At $t = 0$, the instantaneous value of the time function i_1

$$= [\sqrt{2} \cos (45)]\sqrt{2} = 1.414 \text{ amps}$$

$$\text{At } t = \frac{5\pi}{6\omega} \quad \theta = \left[\frac{\pi}{4} + \frac{5\pi}{6}\right] = \frac{13\pi}{12} = 195°$$

the instantaneous value of the time function is

$$= [\sqrt{2} \cos 195°]\sqrt{2} = [-\sqrt{2} \cos 15°]\sqrt{2}$$

(*b*) (*i*) $$\omega = 2\pi f = 400$$

$$f = \frac{200}{\pi} \text{ Hz}$$

(*ii*) Figure 5.14 depicts the corresponding rotating phasor

(*iii*) $$\frac{1.5}{\sqrt{2}}\left[\frac{\sqrt{3}}{2} - j\frac{1}{2}\right] = \frac{1.5}{2\sqrt{2}}[\sqrt{3} - j] = \frac{1.5}{\sqrt{2}} \angle -150°$$

or $$= \frac{1.5}{\sqrt{2}} \exp\left[-j\frac{5\pi}{6}\right]$$

(*iv*) $$-1.5 \sin\left(400t + \frac{2\pi}{3}\right)$$

$$-1.5 \cos\left(400t + \frac{\pi}{6}\right)$$

$$+1.5 \cos\left(400t + \frac{5\pi}{6}\right)$$

At $t = 0$, the instantaneous value of v_1

$$= \left[-\frac{1.5}{\sqrt{2}} \cos 30\right]\sqrt{2}$$

$$= \frac{-1.5\sqrt{3}}{2\sqrt{2}}\sqrt{2} = -1.3 \text{ volts}$$

$$\text{At } t = \frac{5\pi}{6\omega}$$

CHAPTER 5

(v) θ, measured from the real axis is

$$= 210° + 150° = 360°$$

the instantaneous value is

$$= \left(\frac{1.5}{\sqrt{2}}\cos 0\right)\sqrt{2}$$

$$= 1.5 \text{ volts, a +ve maximum.}$$

Example 5.2. *A current I is calculated to be equal to (8 + j6) amps. Find the dial reading of an ammeter (which is calibrated in RMS values) which measures this current. Also, find the time function.*

Solution. $$I = 8 + j6 = 10 \angle \tan^{-1}\frac{3}{4}$$

$$I_m = 10\sqrt{2} \text{ amps}$$

The ammeter reads 10 amps.

From Fig. 5.15, the time function is $10\sqrt{2}\cos(\omega t + \theta)$. Note that we do not know the value of ω in this question.

5.12 CONCEPT OF LEAD AND LAG

Consider the phasors OX and OY in Fig. 5.12, which represent $V_m \cos(\omega t)$ and $V_m \sin(\omega t)$ respectively. The cosine wave attains its maximum value at time $t = \frac{\pi}{2\omega}$ before the sine wave registers its maximum. The phasor OX is said to lead the phasor OY by $\frac{\pi}{2}$ radians. Conversely the phasor OY lags OX by $\frac{\pi}{2}$ radians or 90 degrees.

The terms lead and lag are relative Phasor OX leads OY by 90° or OY leads OX by 270°. Once again, Fig. 5.16 confirms this. However, usually when one speaks of lead or lag, only angles < 180° are involved.

There is a very simple rule to determine the lead or lag angles. Referring to Fig. 5.12 an observer is stationed in the complex plane. As the phasors rotate, assuming he first observes OX, the phasor OY is observed 90° later in time. Therefore OX leads OY by 90°.

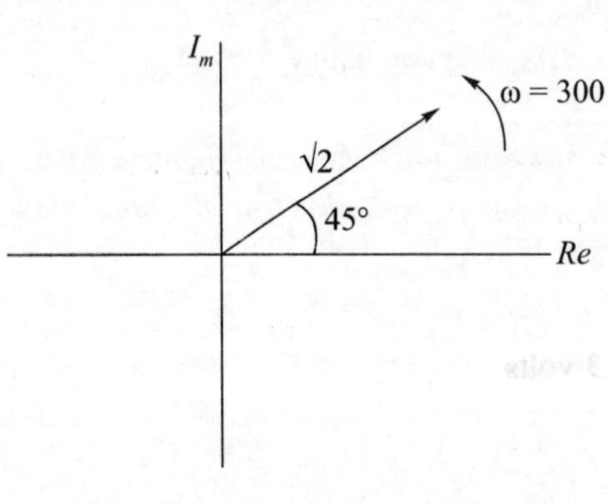

Fig. 5.13 *Rotating phasor of Ex. 5.1(a) part (ii)*

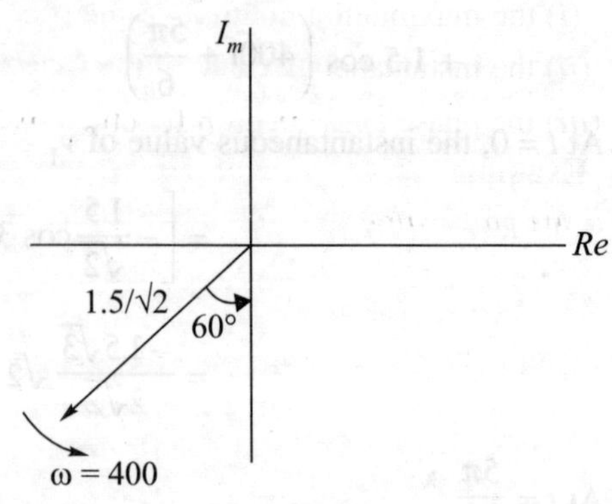

Fig. 5.14 *Rotating phasor of Ex. 5.1(b) part (ii)*

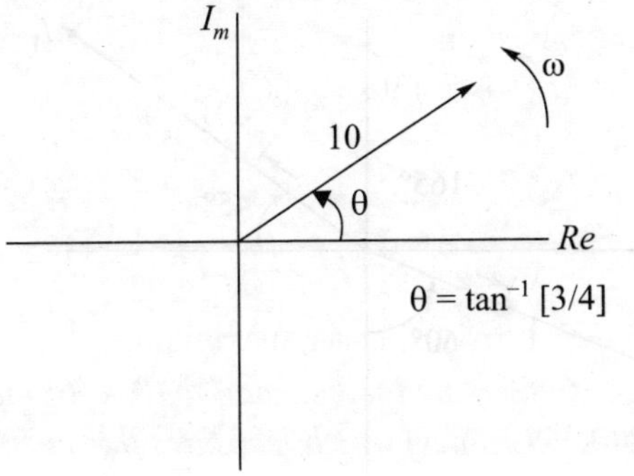

Fig. 5.15 *Rotating phasor of Ex. 5.2*

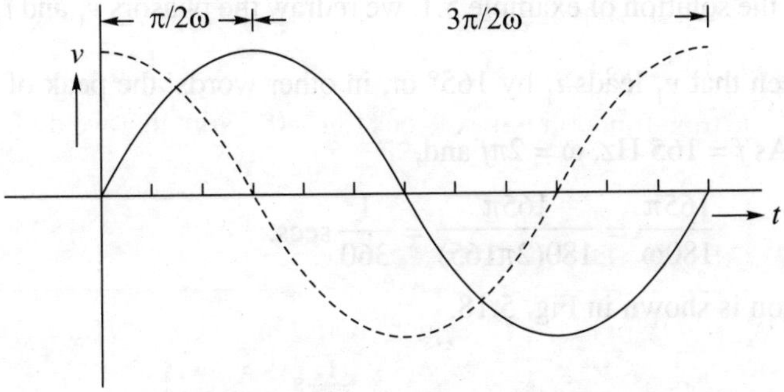

Fig. 5.16 *Concept of lead and lag*

The angle of lead or lag is called *phase difference.* If the phase difference is 90 degrees the phasors are said to be in quadrature. If the phase difference is zero, the phasors are said to be in phase. If the phase difference is 180° one phasor is the negative of the other; the phasors are said to be out of phase.

5.13 INFORMATION OBTAINED FROM A PHASOR DIAGRAM

When two or more phasors representing two or more sinusoidal functions of the same frequency are drawn on the same phasor diagram, one obtains information about

(*i*) the maximum amplitude of the time function.

(*ii*) the instantaneous value of the functions at $t = 0$ and at any time t.

(*iii*) the phase angle of each function and the phase difference.

Example 5.3. *In example 5.1 assume that both* i_1 *and* v_1 *have the same frequency* $f = 165$ *Hz. What is the phase difference between* v_1 *and* i_1*? Which phasor is leading? Draw the time functions.*

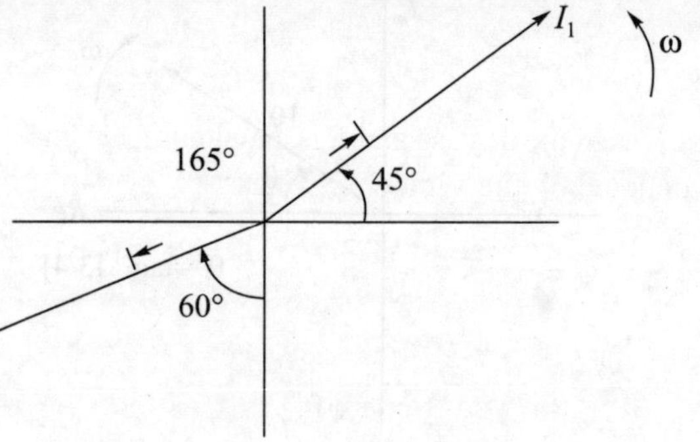

Fig. 5.17 *Phasor relation between V_1 and I_1*

Solution. From the solution of example 5.1, we redraw the phasors v_1 and i_1 on the same diagram as in Fig. 5.17. It is seen that v_1 leads i_1 by 165° or, in other words, the peak of v_1 occurs $\frac{165\pi}{180\omega}$ secs earlier than that of i_1, As $f = 165$ Hz, $\omega = 2\pi f$ and,

$$\frac{165\pi}{180\omega} = \frac{165\pi}{180(2\pi 165)} = \frac{1}{360} \text{ secs.}$$

The time function is shown in Fig. 5.18.

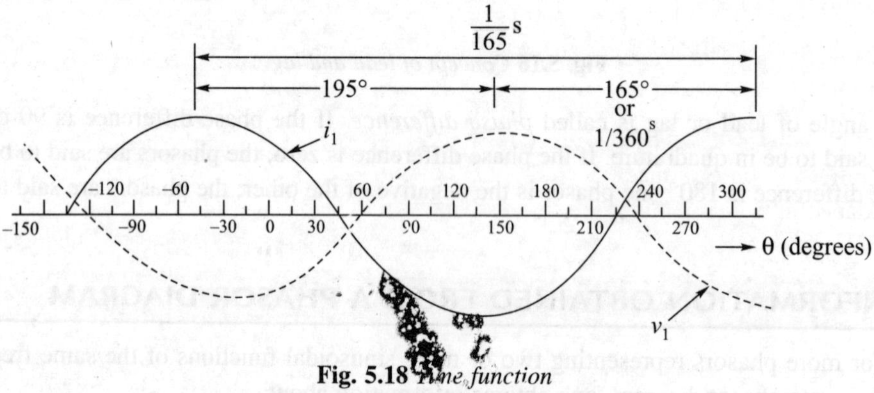

Fig. 5.18 *Time function*

5.14 AC STEADY-STATE RESPONSE OF THE BASIC ELEMENTS: IMPEDANCE

Resistor

Suppose a current $i = I_m \cos(\omega t + \phi)$ flows through a resistor R; the voltage drop at any time t, is given by

$$v = R\, I_m \cos(\omega t + \phi) \quad ...(5.25)$$

It is seen that the v and i are in phase. In phasor form

$$V = \frac{RI_m}{\sqrt{2}} \angle\phi = R\, I \angle\phi \quad ...(5.26)$$

and $$I = \frac{I_m}{\sqrt{2}} / \phi = I / \phi \quad ...(5.27)$$

The ratio of V to I is R as in the dc case and R is a real number. The inverse of R is the conductance G measured in mhos and denoted by the symbol Ω. Thus

$$G = \frac{1}{R} \Omega \quad ...(5.28)$$

Inductor

If the current $$i = I_m \cos(\omega t + \phi) \quad ...(5.29)$$

flows through an inductor of L Henries, the associated voltage drop is

$$= L \frac{d}{dt}[i(t)] = -\omega L I_m \sin(\omega t + \phi) \quad ...(5.30)$$

In phasor form $$I = I\angle\phi \quad ...(5.31)$$

and $$V = \omega L I \angle \frac{\pi}{2} + \phi \quad ...(5.32)$$

These two phasors are shown in Fig. 5.19. It is seen that the current through an inductor lags the voltage drop that it causes by 90º.

The ratio of V to I is

$$= \omega L I \angle \frac{\pi/2 + \phi}{I\angle\phi}$$

$$= \omega L \angle \pi/2 = j\omega L \quad ...(5.33)$$

The ratio is a purely imaginary number. This is called impedance; it is denoted by the symbol Z and has the units of ohms.

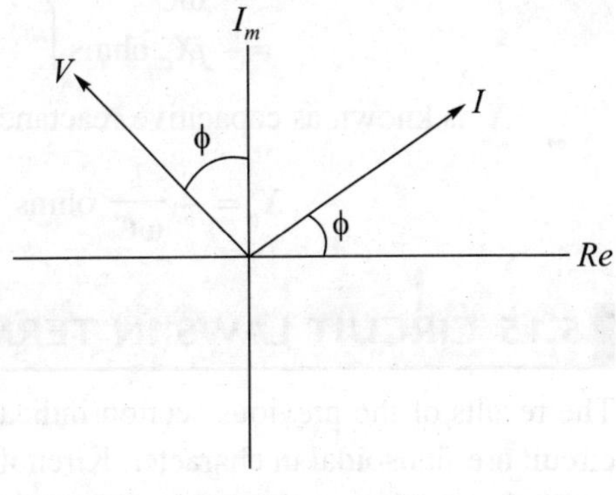

Fig. 5.19 *Phase relation following the ac steady state response*

Thus,

$$\left.\begin{aligned} Z &= j\omega L \text{ ohms} \\ &= jX_L \text{ ohms} \end{aligned}\right\} \quad ...(5.34)$$

X_L is known as reactance or inductive reactance

$$X_L = \omega L \text{ ohms} \quad ...(5.35)$$
$$= 2\pi f L \text{ ohms}$$

The inverse of the impedance Z is called admittance and is denoted by the symbol Y.

Thus $$Y = \frac{1}{Z} = \frac{1}{j\omega L} = \frac{-j}{\omega L} \quad ...(5.36)$$

Y is measured in mhos.

Capacitor

Let us assume that the voltage drop across a capacitor is given by

$$v = V_m \cos(\omega t + \phi) \quad ...(5.37)$$

CHAPTER 5

this must be due to a current flow

$$i = C\frac{d}{dt}[v(t)] = -\omega C\, V_m \sin(\omega t + \phi) \qquad ...(5.38)$$

In phasor form,

$$V = V\angle\phi \qquad ...(5.39)$$

and

$$I = \omega CV\left|\left(\frac{\pi}{2} + \phi\right)\right. \qquad ...(5.40)$$

It is seen that the current through a capacitor leads the voltage drop that it causes by 90º.

The ratio of V to I is

$$= \frac{V\angle\phi}{\omega CV\underline{|\ \pi/2 + \phi}} = \frac{1}{\omega C}\underline{|-\pi/2} \qquad ...(5.41)$$

As in the case of the inductor, this ratio is a purely imaginary value and is called impedance.

$$\left.\begin{aligned} Z &= \frac{-j}{\omega C}\text{ ohms} \\ &= -jX_c\text{ ohms}\end{aligned}\right\} \qquad ...(5.42)$$

X_c is known as capacitive reactance

$$X_c = -\frac{1}{\omega C}\text{ ohms} \qquad ...(5.43)$$

5.15 CIRCUIT LAWS IN TERMS OF PHASORS

The results of the previous section indicate that, in the steady-state, all currents and voltages in an ac circuit are sinusoidal in character. Kirchoff's current and voltage laws are valid in all circuits and when applied to ac circuits they are valid at all instants of time. Thus in a mesh with voltage drops v_1, v_2, ..., v_n, their sum must equal zero.

$$v_1 + v_2 + \ldots + v_n = 0 \qquad ...(5.44)$$

Since each of the above terms is a sinusoid, we may write

$$V_{m1}\cos(\omega t + \phi_1) + V_{m2}\cos(\omega t + \phi_2) + \ldots + \ldots + V_{mn}\cos(\omega t + \phi_n) = 0$$

Replacing each time function by a real part of a complex number, we obtain,

$$Re\left[V_{m1}e^{j(\omega t + \phi_1)}\right] + Re\left[V_{m2}e^{j(\omega t + \phi_2)}\right] + \ldots + Re\left[V_{mn}e^{j(\omega t + \phi_n)}\right] = 0$$

Since the sum of the real parts is equal to the real part of the sum, we write

$$Re\left[V_{m1}e^{j(\omega t + \phi_1)} + V_{m2}e^{j(\omega t + \phi_2)} + \ldots + \ldots V_{mn}e^{j(\omega t + \phi_n)}\right] = 0$$

Since $e^{j\omega t}$ is common to each term, we obtain

$$Re\left\{e^{j\omega t}\left[V_{m1}e^{j\phi_1} + V_{m2}e^{j\phi 2} + \ldots + V_{m''}e^{j\phi_n}\right]\right\} = 0$$

Each term in square brackets in the above equation may be expressed as a phasor of the corresponding time function. Thus,

$$Re\left\{e^{j\omega t}\left[V_1 + V_2 + \ldots + V_n\right]\right\} = 0$$

Since $e^{j\omega t}$ cannot equal zero, we obtain

$$V_1 + V_2 + \ldots + V_n = 0 \qquad \ldots(5.45)$$

This is Kirchoff's voltage law in terms of phasors.

Similarly, at a junction of n branches each carrying currents i_1, i_2, ... i_n, flowing towards the common node,

$$I_1 + I_2 + \ldots + I_n = 0 \qquad \ldots(5.46)$$

From the previous section it is seen that when ac current flows through an element it is related to the voltage drop it produces by a relation of the type

$$V = IZ \qquad \ldots(5.47)$$

which is ohms law in terms of phasors. Z is a complex number but not a phasor. The term phasor is used only to describe sinusoidally varying voltage and current. In this book the boldfaced symbol **Z** will be used to denote the magnitude of Z.

5.16 IMPEDANCES IN SERIES AND PARALLEL

If current I flows through n impedances $Z_1, Z_2, ..., Z_n$ in series, the total voltage drop is

$$= I\,(Z_1 + Z_2 + \ldots + Z_n) = I\,(Z_{eq})$$

The n impedances may be replaced by an equivalent impedance Z_{eq} whose value is

$$Z_{eq} = Z_1 + Z_2 + \ldots + Z_n \qquad \ldots(5.48)$$

The law of combination of impedances in series is identical to the one for combination of series resistors in series in dc circuits.

Should the impedances comprise of inductors only we have

$$Z_{eq} = j\omega L_{eq} = j\omega\,[L_1 + L_2 + \ldots + L_n]$$

The expression for the equivalent inductance is

$$L_{eq} = L_1 + L_2 + \ldots + L_n \qquad \ldots(5.49)$$

which is the law of combination of n inductors in series.

For the case of n capacitors in series

$$Z_{eq} = -j/\omega C_{eq}$$

$$= \frac{-j}{\omega}\left[\frac{1}{C_1} + \frac{1}{C_2} + \ldots + \frac{1}{C_n}\right]$$

The expression for the equivalent capacitance is

$$\frac{1}{C_{eq}} = \frac{1}{C_1} + \frac{1}{C_2} + \ldots + \frac{1}{C_n} \qquad \ldots(5.50)$$

It is seen that the law of combination of n capacitors is different from that for resistors and inductors.

In a similar manner, by consideration of n impedances in parallel each Z_i ($i = 1, 2, ..., n$) carrying current I_i ($i = 1, 2, ..., n$) with a common voltage drop V,

CHAPTER 5

$$I_{\text{total}} = I_1 + I_2 + \ldots + I_n$$

$$= \frac{V}{Z_1} + \frac{V}{Z_2} + \ldots + \frac{V}{Z_n} = \frac{V}{Z_{eq}}$$

The n impedances in parallel may be replaced by an equivalent impedance Z_{eq} whose value is

$$\frac{1}{Z_{eq}} = \frac{1}{Z_1} + \frac{1}{Z_2} + \ldots + \frac{1}{Z_n} \qquad \text{...(5.51)}$$

Starting from Eqn. 5.51 the laws of combination of n inductors in parallel and n capacitors in parallel may be deduced to be

$$L_{eq} = L_1 + L_2 + L_3 + \ldots + L_n \qquad \text{...(5.52)}$$

and $$\frac{1}{C_{eq}} = \frac{1}{C_1} + \frac{1}{C_2} + \frac{1}{C_3} + \ldots + \frac{1}{C_n} \qquad \text{...(5.53)}$$

5.17 GENERAL FORM OF IMPEDANCE AND ADMITTANCE

Consider a one port circuit comprising of impedances only and no sources. We may use series-parallel combinations and star delta transformations to reduce the circuit to an impedance connected across the terminals of the port. In general, the impedance will be of the form $Z = R + jX$ or $R - jX$. The real term representing resistance can never be negative. The imaginary term may be negative. This is because the impedances associated with inductors and capacitors carry opposite signs (Eqns. 5.34 and 5.42). When Z is of the type $(A_1 + jA_2)$ $A_1, A_2 > 0$ one infers that the impedance is inductive. In this case,

$$Z = (A_1^2 + A_2^2)^{1/2} \; Z = (A_1^2 + A_2^2)^{1/2} \angle\theta,$$

where $0 < \theta < 90°$ if $A_1 \neq 0 \neq A_2$. Also, $A_1 = Z\cos\theta$ and $A_2 = Z\sin\theta$. If $A_1 = 0$,

$$Z = A_2 \angle 90° = (0 + jA_2)$$

and the impedance is said to be purely inductive.

If $A_2 = 0, Z = A_1 \angle 0$

and the impedance is purely resistive.

Similarly, when Z is of the type $(A_1 - jA_2)$ the impedance is said to be capacitive and

$$Z = (A_1^2 + A_2^2)^{1/2}; \; Z = (A_1^2 + A_2^2)\angle\phi,$$

where $-90° < \phi < 0$ if $A_1 \neq 0 \neq A_2$. Now, $A_1 = Z\cos\phi$ and $A_2 = Z\sin\phi$.

If $\quad A_1 = 0, Z = A_2\angle -90° = -jA_2$

and the impedance is said to be purely capacitive.

If $A_2 = 0, \quad Z = A_1\angle 0 = A_1$

and the impedance is purely resistive.

Given an impedance Z defined by

$$Z = (A_1 \pm jA_2) \qquad \text{...(5.54)}$$

the admittance is defined to be the inverse of Z and is denoted by Y

$$Y = 1/Z = \frac{1}{(A_1 \pm jA_2)} = \frac{A_1}{A_1^2 + A_2^2} \mp j\frac{A_2}{A_1^2 + A_2^2} \qquad \text{...(5.55)}$$

Y is a complex number as Z is complex. The bold faced symbol Y will be used to denote the magnitude of Y.

The real part of Y is called conductance and the imaginary part is the susceptance. If the imaginary term is negative, it is called inductive susceptance (because, it arises from an inductive impedance $jA_1 + jA_2$, Eqn. 5.54). If the sign is positive, it is called capacitive susceptance. The units of both conductance and susceptance are in mhos.

Example 5.4. *For the circuit of Fig. 5.20, find the value of an equivalent impedance, which when connected across the terminals of the one port, replaces the original circuit, Assume $\omega = 10^6$ radians/s. What are the elements of this equivalent impedance? Also, find the equivalent admittance.*

Solution. The 1 μF capacitor and the resistor of conductance 0.2 Ω are in series. The total impedance of this branch is

$$Z_1 = \left(\frac{1}{.2}\right) - \frac{j}{10^6(10^{-6})}$$

$$= (5 - j\,1)$$

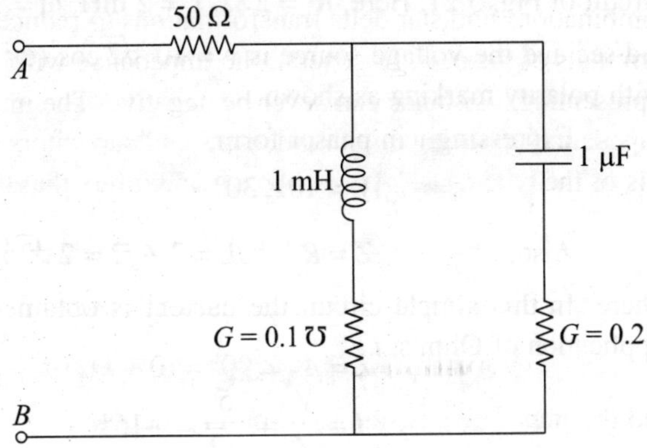

Fig. 5.20

Z_2, the impedance of the inductive branch is

$$= \left(\frac{1}{0.1}\right) + j\,(10^6)\,(10^{-3})$$

$$= (10 + j1000)$$

Z_1 and Z_2 are in parallel and are equivalent to an impedance Z' where

$$\frac{1}{Z'} = \frac{1}{Z_1} + \frac{1}{Z_2}$$

$$= \frac{1}{(10 + j1000)} + \frac{1}{(5 - j)}$$

$$= .1959\angle 11.14^\circ$$

$$Z' = 5.1\angle -11.14^\circ$$

The equivalent impedance is given by

$$Z_{eq} = 50 + 5.1\angle -11.14 = 50 + 5.0 - j.985$$

$$= (55 - j.985) \text{ ohms or } 55.01\angle -1.026^\circ$$

Z_{eq} is capacitive, and its elements are

$$R_{eq} = 55\ \Omega \text{ in series with } C_{eq}$$

where $$C_{eq} = \frac{1}{\omega(0.985)} = 1.015\ \mu F$$

The equivalent admittance is

$$Y_{eq} = \frac{1}{Z_{eq}} = \frac{1}{55.01\angle -1.026}$$

$$= 0.182\angle 1.026 = (0.01819 + j.00033)$$

The equivalent conductance and susceptance are 0.01819 and 0.00033 mho respectively.

Sometimes, when several branches are in parallel it may be more convenient to find the admittance of each branch and then find the total admittance of all the branches in parallel by summing the admittances. The total admittance may be converted to an impedance for further calculations.

5.18 STEADY-STATE SOLUTION OF AC CIRCUITS USING PHASORS

Method

We will explain the method of solution using the simple circuit of Fig. 5.21. Here, $R = 2\ \Omega$, $L = 2$ mH, $\omega = 1000$ rad/sec and the voltage source is $v = 10\sqrt{2}\cos(\omega t + \phi)$ with polarity marking as shown.

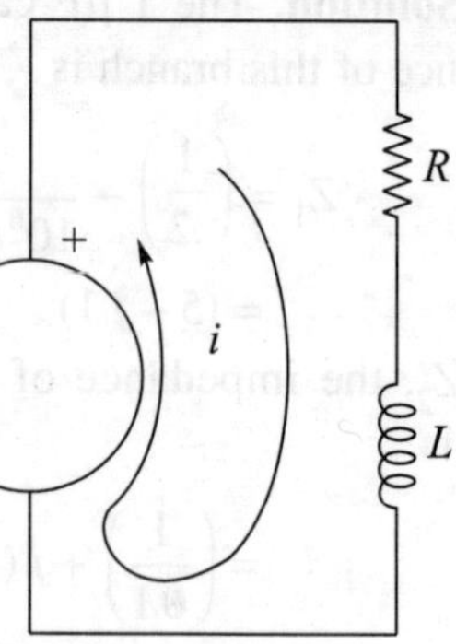

Fig. 5.21 *Solving ac circuit using phasors*

Expressing v in phasor form,

$$V = 10\angle 30°$$

Also, $$Z = R + j\omega L = 2 + j2 = 2\sqrt{2}\angle 45°$$

In this simple circuit the current is obtained by application of Ohm's, *i.e.*,

$$I = \frac{V}{Z} = \frac{5}{\sqrt{2}}\angle -15°$$

The current and voltage phasors are shown in Fig. 5.22. Note that the solution is valid at an instant of time when the voltage source is 30° or $\frac{\pi}{6\omega}$ ms away from its positive maximum value. Since the circuit is in the steady-state, the voltage and current phasors maintain their relative positions and magnitudes. The solution at any other instant of time may be obtained by rotating the phasors to the desired position. Alternatively we may also express the solution in the form of a time function, $i = 5\cos(\omega t - 15°)$. Thus, the phasor method allows us to obtain the steady- state solution without resorting to the solution of differential equations.

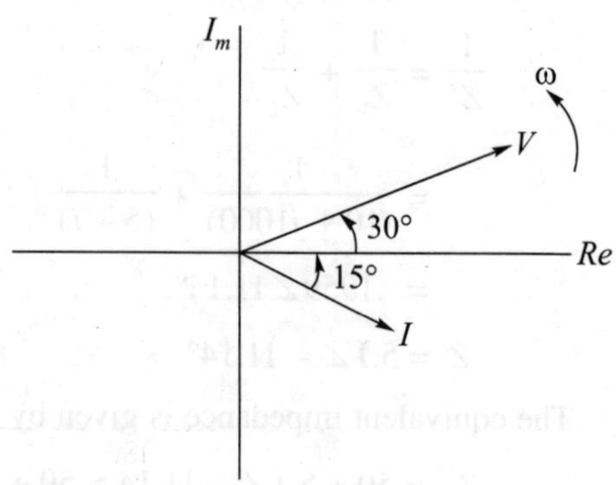

Fig. 5.22 *Current and voltage phasors of Fig. 5.21*

Source Polarity

If the polarity of the source is reversed nothing will change as far as the source is concerned. The current in the circuit, however, now in the opposite direction, *i.e.*,180° out of phase with the current in the circuit of Fig. 5.21. The concept of polarity is especially important when dealing with multiple sources. Consider the circuit of Fig. 5.23. If $v_1 = v_2 = 10\angle 30$, with polarity markings as shown, no current flows in the circuit as v_1 and v_2 oppose each other at all instants of time and are equal in magnitude. However, if the polarity of one of the sources is reversed, the current in the circuit is $10\angle 30°$ A. If v_1 were $= 10\angle 0$ and $v_2 = 10\angle 30°$ with polarities as shown in Fig. 5.23, it means that source v_2 registers a positive maximum at its +ve terminal at time $\frac{\pi}{6\omega}$ secs after v_1 has gone through a positive maximum at its +ve terminal. Should the polarity of v_2 be opposite to that shown in Fig. 5.23, the situation is totally different as shown in Fig. 5.24.

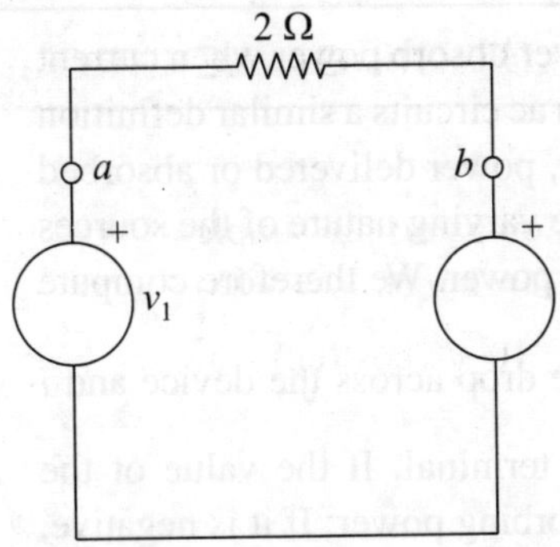

Fig. 5.23 *Polarity marking in case of ac sources*

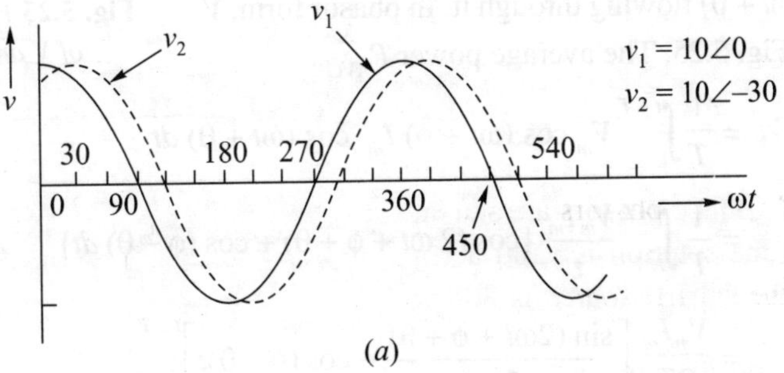

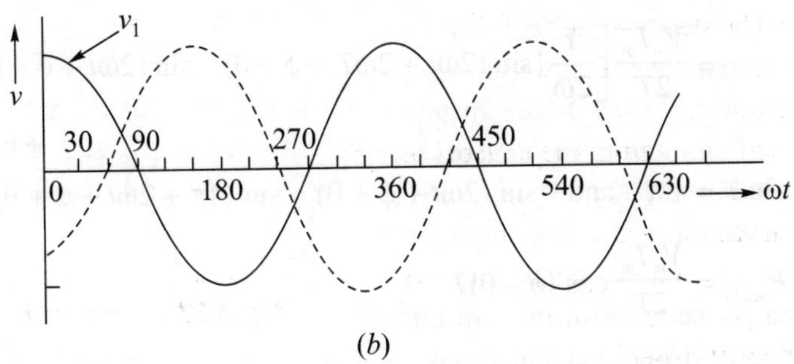

Fig. 5.24 (*a*) *Source waveforms at (a) and (b) of Fig. 5.23*

5.19 GENERAL METHOD OF SOLUTION OF AC CIRCUITS

The solution of circuits may be obtained by employing any of the techniques discussed in earlier chapters such as source transformations, mesh current analysis, node voltage analysis, the Thevenin or Norton equivalents, the theorem of superposition and star-delta transformations.

The steps involved in the solution of ac circuits are:

(*i*) Calculate the impedance in all branches.

(*ii*) Transform source voltages into phasors.

(*iii*) Solve the circuit using any of the known techniques; the solution is obtained in phasor form.

(*iv*) Transform phasors back to time functions if necessary.

5.20 POWER IN AC CIRCUITS

In dc circuits a device is said to deliver/absorb power when current leaves/enters its positive terminal. In ac circuits a similar definition applies for instantaneous power, *i.e.*, power delivered or absorbed at any given instant. Due to the time varying nature of the sources it is convenient to speak of average power. We therefore compute $\frac{1}{T}\int_t^{t+T} v\, i\, dt$ where v is the voltage drop across the device and i the current entering at its positive terminal. If the value of the integral is positive the device is absorbing power; If it is negative, power is being delivered.

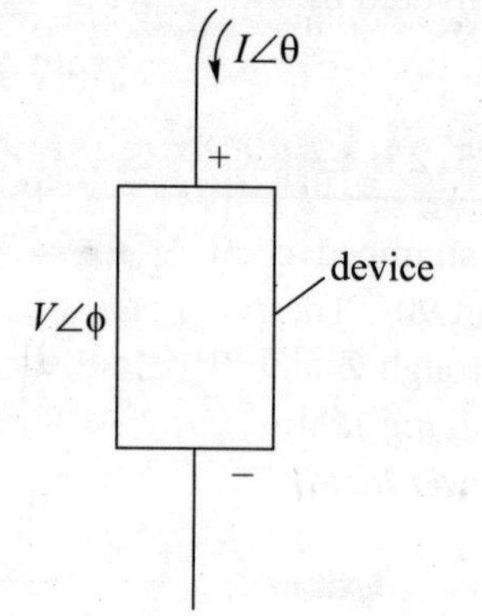

Fig. 5.25 *Phasor representation of V and I in ac circuits*

Let v, the voltage drop across a device by $V_m \cos(\omega t + \phi)$ due to current $I_m \cos(\omega t + \theta)$ flowing through it. In phasor form, $V = V\angle\phi$ and $I = I\angle\theta$, Fig. 5.25. The average power P_{AVG},

$$= \frac{1}{T}\int_t^{t+T} V_m \cos(\omega t + \phi)\, I_m \cos(\omega t + \theta)\, dt$$

$$= \frac{1}{T}\int_t^{t+T} \frac{V_m I_m}{2}\{\cos(2\,\omega t + \phi + \theta) + \cos(\phi - \theta)\, dt\}$$

$$= \frac{V_m I_m}{2T}\left[\frac{\sin(2\omega t + \phi + \theta)}{2\omega} + \cos(\phi - \theta)t\right]_t^{t+T}$$

$$= \frac{V_m I_m}{2T}\left[\frac{1}{2\omega}\{\sin(2\omega t + 2\omega T + \phi + \theta) - \sin(2\omega t + \phi + \theta)\}\right.$$

$$\left. + \cos(\phi - \theta)\{t + T - t\}\right]$$

but $\quad 2\omega T = 4\pi \quad$ and $\quad \sin(2\omega t + \phi + \theta) = \sin(4\pi + 2\omega t + \phi + \theta)$. Thus

$$P_{AVG} = \frac{V_m I_m}{2T}\cos(\phi - \theta)T$$

which simplifies to

$$P_{AVG} = VI\cos(\phi - \theta) \qquad ...(5.56)$$

In ac circuits the power is not the product of V and I but the product multiplied by a factor, cos $(\phi - \theta)$, whose value lies between 0 and 1; this is called *power factor*.

Let us review the power dissipated in the basic elements. The angle $(\phi - \theta)$ is the phase angle between the current flowing through a device and the voltage drop across it.

If the device is a resistor, $\phi - \theta = O$, $P_{AVG} = VI$ watts and the power factor (p.f.) is unity.

If the device is either an inductor or a capacitor $|\phi - \theta| = 90°$+* In this case,

$$P_{AVG} = VI\cos(\phi - \theta) = 0 \text{ watts}$$

and $\qquad$ p.f. = 0

It is therefore seen that ideal inductors and capacitors absorb no power, on the average. Equation 5.56 is also used to calculate the power delivered by a source. In the example of Fig. 5.21, the power delivered by the voltage source is $10.\frac{5}{\sqrt{2}}\cos(45°) = 25$ watts.

5.21 LAGGING AND LEADING POWER FACTOR

If an impedance Z is inductive the current through it lags the voltage across it by some angle between 0 and 90°. The power dissipated in Z is VI cos (angle between V and I) where I is the current flowing through Z and V the voltage drop across it (Fig. 5.25). The power factor in this case is said to be a *lagging power factor*. Similarly, the power factor associated with capacitive loads is called *leading power factor*.

Example 5.5. *In the circuit of Fig. 5.26, given* $f = \frac{5000}{2\pi}$ *Hz*

(i) Find the current in the 2 ohm resistor in branch ab.

(ii) Check that the power delivered by the source is dissipated only in the resistors.

(iii) Find the instantaneous value of $i_{ab}(\tau)$ *when the source labelled* $10\angle 0$ *has an instantaneous value of 6 volts.*

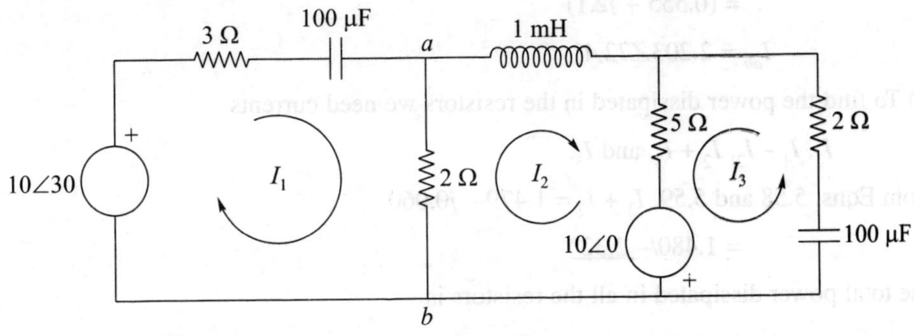

Fig. 5.26

---

*In the case of an inductor, $\phi - \theta = 90°$; for a capacitor $\phi - \theta = -90°$.

CHAPTER 5

Solution. Since $f = \frac{5000}{2\pi}$,

$$\omega = 2\pi f = 5000 \text{ radians/s.}$$

and $X_c = \frac{1}{\omega c} = \frac{-1}{5000.100\,10^{-6}} = -2$

The impedance of each of 100 μF capacitors is

$$Z_c = \frac{-j}{\omega c} = J X_c = -2j$$

The impedance of the 1 mH inductor is

$$Z_L = j\omega L = j(5000)(10^{-3}) = j5$$

Choose phasor currents I_1, I_2, I_3 as mesh currents. Note that the source voltage magnitudes indicated on the diagram are RMS quantities. The mesh equations are

$$I_1(5 - 2j) - I_2 2 + I_3(0) = 10\angle 30 = (8.66 + j5)$$

$$I_1(-2) + I_2(7 + 5j) + I_3 5 = 10\angle 0 = (10 + j0)$$

$$I_1(0) + I_2(5) + I_3(7 - 2j) = 10\angle 0 = (10 + j0)$$

Solving for I_1, I_2 and I_3 using the method of determinants, one obtains after some calculations

$$I_1 = 1.568 + j1.312 = 2.044\angle 39.92° \quad ...(5.57)$$

$$I_2 = (0.902 - 0.788j) = 1.198\angle 41.14° \quad ...(5.58)$$

$$I_3 = 0.577 + j0.728 = 0.929\angle 51.62° \quad ...(5.59)$$

The student is encouraged to check for himself the KVL holds for all closed loops and that KCL holds at all nodes.

(*i*) the current in the 2 ohm resistor in branch *ab* is

$$I_{ab} = I_1 - I_2 = (1.568 + j1.312 \; - 0.902 + 0.788j)$$

$$= (0.555 + j2.1)$$

$$I_{ab} = 2.203\angle 72.4°$$

(*ii*) To find the power dissipated in the resistors we need currents

$$I_1, I_1 - I_2, I_2 + I_3, \text{ and } I_3.$$

From Eqns. 5.58 and 5.59, $I_3 + I_2 = 1.479 - j0.060$

$$= 1.480/\underline{-2.32°}$$

The total power dissipated in all the resistors is

$$= I_1^2 + 2(I_1 - I_2)^2 + 5(I_3 + I_2)^2 + 2I_3^2$$

$$= 3(2.044)^2 + 2(2.203)^2 + 5(1.480)^2 + 2(0.929)^2$$

$$= 34.918 \text{ watts} \quad ...(5.60)$$

The total power delivered by the sources is

$$= \Sigma V_{source} I_{source} \text{ (power factor)}$$

$$= (10)(2.044)\,[\cos(30 - 39.92)°] + (10)\,(1.480)\cos(0 - (-2.32))°$$

$$= 34.922 \text{ watts} \quad ...(5.61)$$

The wattage figures in Eqn. 5.60 and 5.61 should agree. The slight difference is due to round-off error. Since the power delivered by the sources is equal to the total power dissipated in the resistors, we conclude that no power is dissipated in the inductors and capacitors. For example the power dissipated in the 1 mH inductor, P_L, is

$$= V_L I_L \cos(\theta_L) \text{ where } \theta_L \text{ is the angle between } V_L \text{ and } I_L$$

$$V_L = I_2(5j) = (1.198)\,5\angle 90 - 41.14$$

$$I_L = I_2 = 1.198\angle - 41.14$$

Since, $\cos\theta_L = \cos[90 - 41.14 - (-41.14)]$

$$= \cos[90] = 0,$$

$$P_L = 0$$

Example 5.6. *An impedance Z has for its value $Z_1\angle\psi$. Find the power dissipated in it if the voltage source connected across it is*

(i) $V = V_1\angle 0$ *(ii)* $V = V_1\angle\theta$.

Solution.

(i) $V = V_1\angle 0$

$$I = \frac{V_1/0}{Z_1\angle\psi} = \frac{V_1}{Z_1}\angle -\psi$$

$$P = V\,I(\text{power factor})$$

$$= V_1\frac{V_1}{Z_1}\cos(-\psi - 0) = \frac{V_1^2}{Z_1}\cos\psi$$

(ii) $V = V_1/\theta,$

and

$$I = \frac{V_1\angle\theta}{Z_1\angle\psi} = \frac{V_1}{Z_1}\underline{\left|\theta - \psi\right.}$$

$$P = V\,I\,(\text{power factor})$$

$$= \frac{V_1}{Z_1}V_1\cos[\theta - (\theta - \psi)] = \frac{V_1^2}{Z_1}\cos(\psi).$$

CHAPTER 5

Example 5.7. *In example 5.4, a sinusoidal source of 120 volts peak value is connected across the terminals of the one port. Find the power dissipated.*

Solution. The RMS value of the source voltage

$$= \frac{120}{\sqrt{2}} = 84.85 \text{ volts}$$

From example 5.4 for the 1 port,

$$Z_{eq} = 55.01\angle -1.026°$$

From example 5.6 we see that the power factor angle is contained in Z. Therefore, the power dissipated

$$= V\,I \text{ (power factor)}$$

$$= 84.85\left(\frac{84.85}{55.01}\right)\cos(-1.026°) = 130.9 \text{ watts.}$$

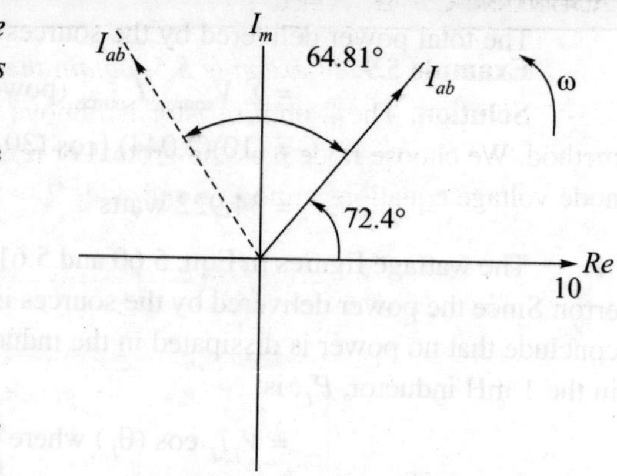

Fig. 5.27 *Phasor representation of I_{ab}*

Example 5.8. *Consider the bridge circuit, in Fig. 5.28; the bridge is fed by an ac source. Derive the balance condition.*

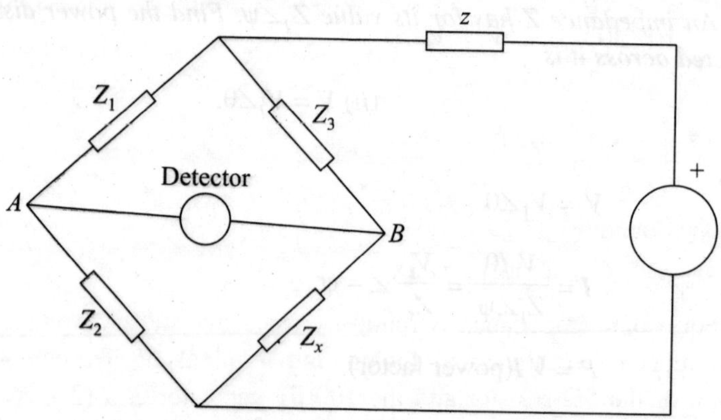

Fig. 5.28 *Bridge circuit fed by an ac source*

Solution. We proceed as we did with the dc bridge circuit. When no current flows through the detector the potentials at nodes *A* and *B* are equal, i.e. $Z_1Z_x = Z_2Z_3$ is the balance condition. Since an impedance is a complex number, the above balance condition is in fact equivalent to two balance conditions. Expressing the balance condition to include phase angles,

$$Z_1\angle\theta_1 Z_x\angle\theta_x = Z_2\angle\theta_2 Z_3\angle\theta_3.$$

From the above expression, separating real and imaginary parts, we obtain the two balance conditions.

i.e., $$Z_1Z_x = Z_2Z_3$$

and $$\theta_1 + \theta_x = \theta_2 + \theta_3$$

where θ_1, θ_2, θ_3, θ_x are the angles associated with Z_1, Z_2, Z_3 and Z_x respectively.

Example 5.9. *In example 5.5, obtain the current in branch ab by use of Thevenin's theorem.*

Solution. The 2 ohm resistor is removed and the voltage V_{ab} is found using the node voltage method. We choose node *b* as the ground or reference node. Referring to Fig. 5.29, we obtain the two node voltage equations at node *a* and node 2.

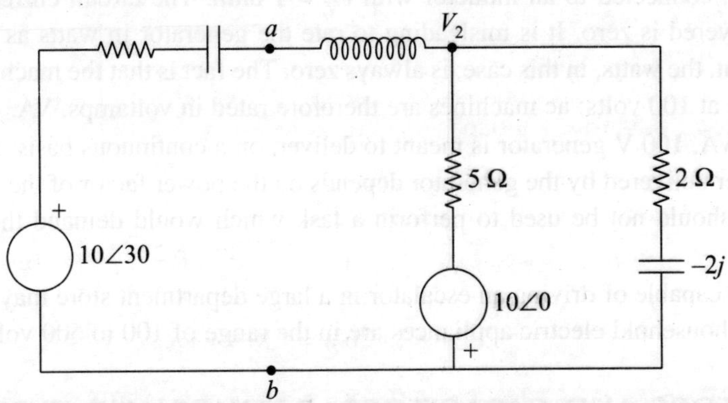

Fig. 5.29 *Node voltage method as applied to ac network*

$$\frac{10\angle 30 - V_a}{3-2j} + \frac{V_2 - V_a}{j5} = 0$$

and
$$\frac{V_a - V_2}{j5} + \frac{-V_2 - 10\angle 0}{5} + \frac{-V_2}{2-2j} = 0$$

Solving for V_a one obtains

$$V_a = 11.181\angle 78.43$$

The Thevenin equivalent impedance is found by replacing the two voltage sources by short circuits and finding the impedance of the circuit looking into terminals *ab*. The combined impedance of the parallel combination of the 5Ω resistor and the 100 μF capacitor is 5 (2 – 2*j*) / (7– 2*j*). This is combined in series with the inductive impedance of 5*j*. This impedance is then combined in parallel with (3 – 2*j*). This latter quantity is obtained by the series combination of the 3Ω resistor and the 100 μF capacitor. The Thevenin impedance is

$$\frac{\dfrac{(20+25j)}{(7-2j)}(3-2j)}{\dfrac{(20-25j)}{(7-2j)}+(3-2j)} = 3.09/\underline{9.954}\Omega$$

The current in branch *ab* is therefore

$$\frac{11.181/\underline{78.43}}{3.09\angle 9.954 + 2} = 2.203/\underline{72.4}\text{ A}$$

CHAPTER 5

5.22 AC MACHINE RATINGS

Direct current machines are rated in watts which is equal to the product of volts and amps. In the ac case the product is not a watt but a voltamp. Consider the case of an ac generator, which develops 100 volts across its terminals, connected to an inductor with ω_L = 1 ohm. The circuit current is 100 A but the average power delivered is zero. It is misleading to rate the generator in watts as no matter what the magnitude of current, the watts, in this case, is always zero. The fact is that the machine must be capable of delivering 100 A at 100 volts; ac machines are therefore rated in voltamps, VA.

Thus a 10 kVA, 100 V generator is meant to deliver, on a continuous basis, a maximum current of 100 A. The power delivered by the generator depends on the power factor of the load. A motor rated at 10 kVA, 100 V should not be used to perform a task which would demand the supply current to exceed 100 A.

An ac motor capable of driving an escalator in a large department store may be rated at 500, 50 kVA. The rating of household electric appliances are in the range of 100 to 500 volt amperes.

5.23 INDUCTORS AND CAPACITORS—RATINGS AND TYPES

Inductors and capacitors, like ac machines, are rated in volts and voltamps. A capacitor rated at x kVa, y kV has a capacitance of $\dfrac{x\,10^{-3}}{y^2\omega}$ F. An inductor with the same rating has an inductance value of $\dfrac{10^3 y^2}{x\omega}$ H.

Inductors consist of turns of insulated wire wound on cores of magnetic material. If the core is in the shape of a donut it is called a *toroidal inductor*. Inductors are also wound on cylindrical formers. The core may consist of magnetic material, such as Silicon Steel, Ferrites and Nickel-Iron alloys. Variable inductors may be constructed in which the magnetic core is movable and slides in and out of a coil.

Capacitors are classified according to the insulating material employed, *i.e.*, paper, plastic film, mica and electrolytic. In paper capacitors, alternate layers of special paper and metallic foil are rolled into a cylindrical shape. Special electrical grade oil is introduced into all the air spaces by a process known as impregnation and the assembly is sealed. The construction of plastic film capacitors is similar with the plastic film replacing the paper as insulation. Popular plastics are polypropylene, polythene, polystyrene teflon and mylar. Mica capacitors are formed by alternate layers of mica and metal electrodes; the assembly is then encapsulated to provide mechanical strength and prevent ingress of moisture.

Electrolytic capacitors possess a large capacitance/volume ratio as compared to other capacitor types. The basic construction consists of two electrodes in an electrolyte. The insulation is provided by a thin oxide layer on one or both electrodes. Polar electrolytic capacitors are polarity sensitive; such capacitors bear polarity markings which must be observed and therefore can not be used in ac circuits. Non-polar electrolytic capacitors do not have any polarity restrictions.

5.24 THE RESONANT SERIES RLC CIRCUIT

Figure 5.30 shows, a series RLC circuit energized by an ac voltage source. The total impedance in the circuit is

$$Z = R + j\left(\omega L - \frac{1}{\omega C}\right) \qquad ...(5.62)$$

If either L or C or ω is adjusted so that the condition

$$\omega L = \frac{1}{\omega C} \qquad ...(5.63)$$

is satisfied, Z is a maximum and becomes purely resistive, *i.e.*, $Z = R$; the circuit is said to be in resonance. The condition for resonance in a series RLC circuit is expressed by Eqn. 5.63. At resonance, if R is small, large currents will flow and the voltages developed across L and C will be large and exceed the supply voltage.

Since $\omega L = \dfrac{1}{\omega C}$ the voltages across L and C will be equal but out of phase and therefore cancel; the supply voltage is dropped entirely across R. Thus, KVL is not violated!

If the current flowing in the circuit at resonance is $i = I_m \sin \omega t$, the voltage across the capacitor is $-\dfrac{I_m}{\omega C}\cos(\omega t)$. The maximum energy stored in the inductor is $\dfrac{1}{2}LI_m^2$ and that in the capacitor is $\dfrac{1}{2}$ $C\dfrac{I_m^2}{\omega^2 C^2}$. Equating the two, we obtain

$$\frac{1}{2}L\,I_m^2 = \frac{1}{2}\frac{CI_m^2}{\omega^2}$$

The above expression yields the condition

$$\omega = \sqrt{\frac{1}{LC}} \qquad ...(5.64)$$

This is identical to the condition of Eqn. 5.63. At resonance, the stored energies in L and C are equal. When one element is experiencing a decrease in tis energy the other is gaining it; the sum of the energies stored in L and C at any instant is

$$= \frac{1}{2}LI_m^2 \quad \text{or} \quad \frac{1}{2}CV_m^2 \text{ with } V_m = \frac{I_m}{\omega C}.$$

In the steady-state, therefore, the source needs to supply only the energy expended in R.

At resonance, the current in the circuit reaches its maximum value and is given by

$$I = \frac{V}{R} \qquad ...(5.65)$$

The voltage drop across the inductor is

$$V_L = I\omega_R L = \frac{V\omega_R L}{R} = VQ \qquad ...(5.66)$$

where $$Q = \frac{\omega_R L}{R} = \frac{1}{\omega_R CR} \qquad ...(5.67)$$

CHAPTER 5

From Eqn. 5.66 the inductor voltage drop is Q times the supply voltage. Q is usually $>> 1$ as R in resonant circuits is kept small. Equation 5.67 defines Q which is known as the quality factor of the resonant circuit. ω_R is the resonant frequency; the subscript R stands for resonance

The voltage across the capacitor is

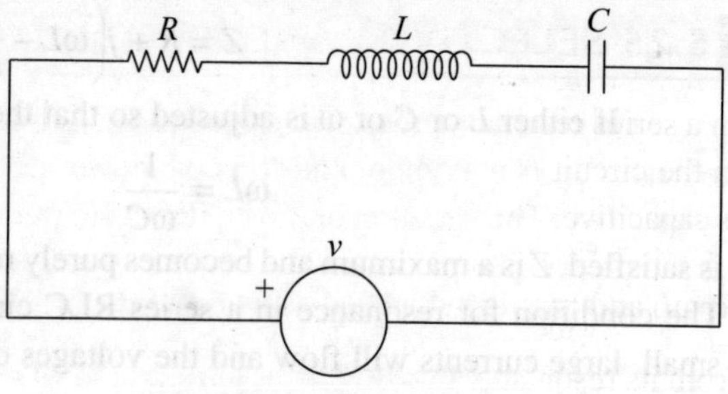

Fig. 5.30 *Series RLC circuit*

$$V_C = \frac{1}{\omega_R C} = I\omega_R L \qquad \text{(from Eqn. 5.63)}$$

$$= \frac{V}{R}\omega_R L = QV \qquad \text{(from Eqn. 5.67)}$$

$$= V_L.$$

Example 5.10. *In the series circuit of Fig. 5.30 R = 1 Ω, L = 1 m H and C = 1 μF and the source voltage has a peak value of 10* $\sqrt{2}$ *volts.*

Find

(*i*) *the resonant frequency*

(*ii*) *the value of Q*

(*iii*) V_L, V_C *at resonance*

(*iv*) *the net watts consumed by the circuit*

(*v*) *the overall power factor at resonance.*

Solution. (*i*) $\omega_R^2 = \frac{1}{LC} = \frac{1}{10^{-4} 10^{-6}}$

$$\omega_R = 10^5 \text{ rad/s}$$

(*ii*) $Q = \frac{\omega_R L}{R} = \frac{10^5\ 0.1\ 10^{-3}}{1} = 10$

(*iii*) $V_L = QV = 10.10 = 100$ volts $= V_C$

Alternative, at resonance, the circuit current is

$$= \frac{V}{R} = 10\text{A} \quad \text{and} \quad V_L = I\,(\omega_R L)$$

$$= 10\ (10^5 10^{-4}) = 100 \text{ volts} = V_C$$

(*iv*) the net watts consumed by the circuit

$$= I^2R = 10^2\ 1 = 100 \text{ watts}$$

(*v*) the overall p.f. = 1 as the impedance is purely resistive at resonance.

5.25 SELECTIVITY AND BANDWIDTH OF THE SERIES RESONANT CIRCUIT

In a series resonant circuit, the impedance Z is minimum at $\omega = \omega_R$, the resonant frequency. The current in the circuit is maximum and so is the power dissipated. For $\omega > \omega_R$, Z is inductive and for $\omega < \omega_R$, Z is capacitive. The variation of Z with respect to frequency is shown in Fig. 5.31 where its three components R, ωL and $\dfrac{1}{\omega C}$ are sketched as well. It is seen that Z increases when ω is either increased or decreased from its resonant value. In fact as $\omega \to 0$ or $\omega \to \infty$, $Z \to \infty$. The variation of Z with ω is not symmetrical about ω_R except for small changes on either side of ω_R. As Z increases, the circuit current decreases and the power dissipated in the resistor also decreases.

The variation of Z with ω depends on R as shown by the curves labelled 1 and 2 in Fig. 5.31. The R associated with curve 2 is much larger than that with curve 1; the result is that curve 2 is less peaky, *i.e.,* the minimum value is not as well defined as by curve 1. The circuit corresponding to curve 2 is said to be less selective than the circuit corresponding to curve 1.

A good measure of the selectivity of the circuit is the bandwidth which is defined as the range of frequency over which the power dissipated in the series RLC circuit is greater than or equal to half the maximum possible value. The maximum power dissipation occurs at $\omega = \omega_R$ and is $\left(\dfrac{V^2}{R^2}\right) R = \dfrac{V^2}{R}$. At half this value, since R is constant, the current is $= \dfrac{V}{\sqrt{2}R}$. Further, as the applied voltage V is constant this means that the circuit impedance $= \sqrt{2}\,R$ ohms. In other words, bandwidth is the range of frequencies over which $Z \leq \sqrt{2}\,R$. If the $Z - \omega$ curve is peaky, Z increases rapidly as one strays away from ω_R and the condition $Z = \sqrt{2}\,R$ will be reached after only a small change in ω.

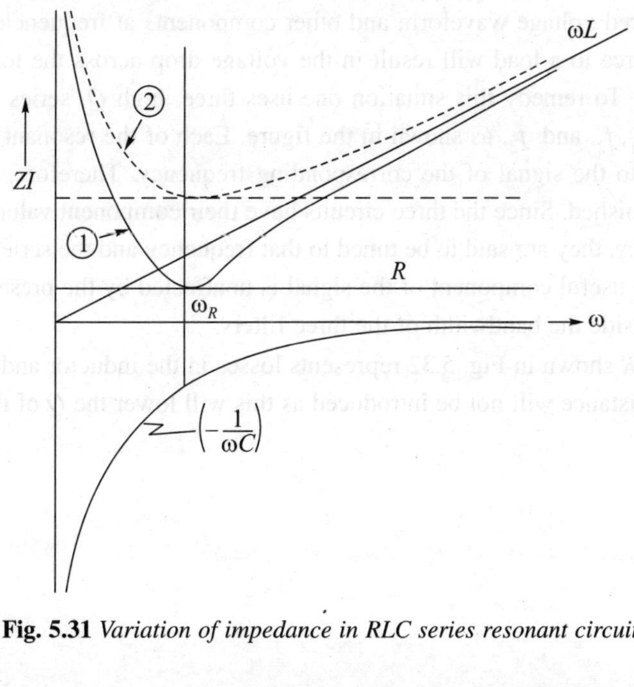

Fig. 5.31 *Variation of impedance in RLC series resonant circuit*

CHAPTER 5

From Eqn. 5.62, $Z = \sqrt{2}\,R$ when $\pm\left(\omega L - \dfrac{1}{\omega C}\right) = R$ ...(5.68)

Corresponding to the +ve sign, one obtains ω_1 ($> \omega_R$); ω_2 ($< \omega_R$) is obtained by solution of Eqn. 5.68 when the negative sign is taken into accounts. The two frequencies ω_1 and ω_2, at which the power dissipation is half that at the resonant frequency, are known as the half power frequencies. Solving Eqn. 5.68 twice, one obtains

$$\omega_1 = \frac{R + \sqrt{R^2 + 4L/C}}{2L}$$

and

$$\omega_2 = \frac{-R + \sqrt{R^2 + 4L/C}}{2L} \qquad ...(5.69)$$

Bandwidth, $\quad$ **B.W.** $= f_1 - f_2$

$$= \frac{\omega_1 - \omega_2}{2\pi} = \frac{R}{2\pi L}$$

Multiplying the numerator and the denominator by f_R, and using Eqn. 5.67, one obtains

$$\textbf{B.W.} = \frac{f_R}{Q} \qquad ...(5.70)$$

Equation 5.70 shows that the selectivity of a series resonant circuit is high (low B.W.) when Q is high (low R).

5.26 AN EXAMPLE OF THE USE OF A SERIES RESONANT CIRCUIT

High Q, series resonant circuits find application as tuned filters. Suppose the voltage at node A in Fig. 5.32 contains the desired voltage waveform and other components at frequencies f_1, f_2, and f_3. Direct connection of this source to a load will result in the voltage drop across the load consisting of these unwanted frequencies. To remedy this situation one uses three, high Q, series resonant circuits with resonant frequencies f_1, f_2, and f_3, as shown in the figure. Each of the resonant circuits present a low impedance path only to the signal of the corresponding frequency. Therefore, the unwanted voltage drops are greatly diminished. Since the three circuits have their component values adjusted to resonate at a particular frequency, they are said to be tuned to that frequency and the series RLC circuit behaves like a *tuned filter*. The useful component of the signal is unaffected by the presence of the filters if its frequency lies will outside the bandwidth of the three filters.

The resistance R shown in Fig. 5.32 represents losses in the inductor and capacitors. Normally, additional external resistance will not be introduced as this will lower the Q of the circuit.

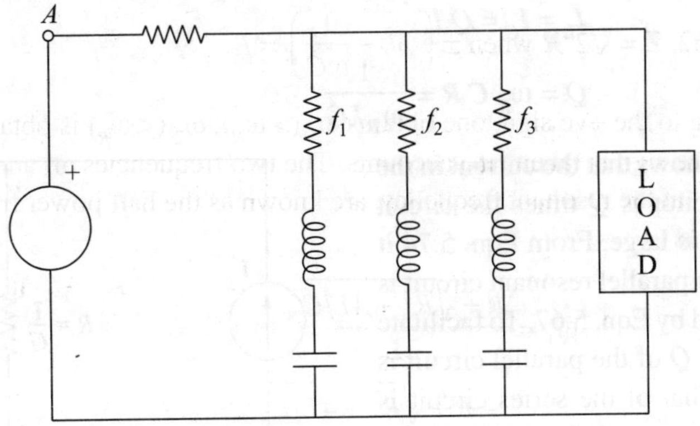

Fig. 5.32 *An application of a series resonant circuit*

5.27 THE RESONANT PARALLEL RLC CIRCUIT

Figure 5.33 shows the elements R, L and C connected in parallel across a current source. The total admittance is

$$Y = G + j\left(\omega C - \frac{1}{\omega L}\right) \quad ...(5.71)$$

When $$\omega_L = \frac{1}{\omega C} \quad ...(5.72)$$

$$Y = G = \frac{1}{R}$$

and $Z = R$; Z is large if R is large.

The impedance is now purely resistive and the circuit is said to be in resonance: the resonant condition is expressed by Eqn. 5.72.

It can be shown that, at resonance, the maximum stored energies in L and C are equal; also, at any instant of time the sum of the stored energies in L and C is equal to the maximum value stored in either L or C.

At resonance, the current flowing into the parallel LC combination is a minimum and is small if R is large. In the parallel LC circuit, however, there is an exchange of energy. The inductor and capacitor swap their stored energies in an oscillating manner. The current flow in L and C resulting out of this energy exchange may be many times the total circuit current. However, KCL is not violated as the currents in L and C are out of phase and cancel each other.

At resonance, $$I_L = I_C \left\{\text{as } \omega L = \frac{1}{\omega C}\right\} = \frac{V}{\omega_R L}$$

where V is the voltage across the parallel circuit and ω_R is the resonant frequency.

Since $$V = IR$$

$$I_L = L_C = \frac{1}{\omega_R L/R} = I\,\omega_R\,C\,R$$

We may write $$I_L = I_C = Q\,I \qquad \text{...(5.73)}$$

where $$Q = \omega_R\, C\, R = \frac{1}{\omega_R LG} \qquad \text{...(5.74)}$$

Equation 5.73 shows that the current in the inductor and the capacitor is Q times the circuit current; Q is >> 1 if R is large. From Eqn. 5.74 it is seen that the Q of the parallel resonant circuit is the inverse of Q defined by Eqn. 5.67. To facilitate easy identification, the Q of the parallel circuit is denoted by Q_p while that of the series circuit is represented by Q_s. Thus,

$$Q_p = \frac{1}{Q_s} \qquad \text{...(5.75)}$$

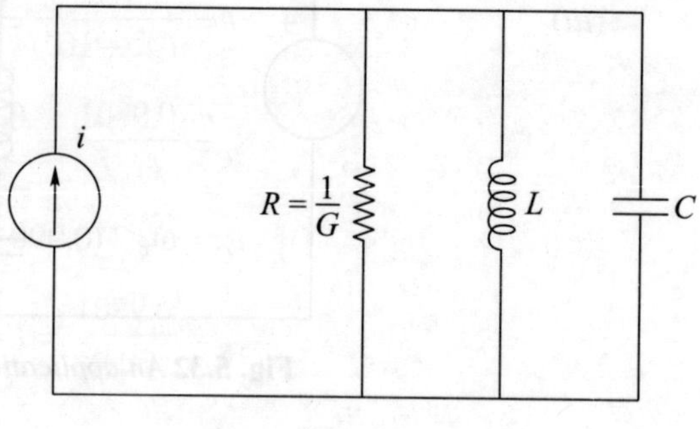

Fig. 5.33 *A parallel RLC circuit*

Example 5.11. *In the circuit of Fig. 5.34, find*

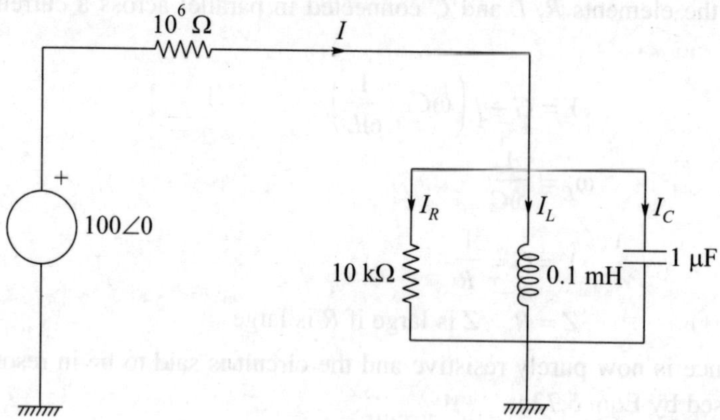

Fig. 5.34 *Circuit*

(i) the resonant frequency

(ii) the voltage across the parallel circuit at resonance

(iii) the currents I, I_R, I_L, I_C at resonance

(iv) show that $I_C = I_L = Q_P I$.

(v) Solve the circuit for ω = 100 radians/s. Find the voltage drop across the parallel circuit and the currents I, I_R, I_L and I_C.

(vi) Why is the 10^6 ohm series resistance necessary?

Solution. (*i*) $$\omega_R = \frac{1}{\sqrt{LC}} = \frac{1}{\sqrt{10^{-4}\,10^{-6}}} = 10^5 \text{ radians/s.}$$

(*ii*) At $\omega = \omega_R$, the impedance of the parallel RLC combination is

$$Z = 10^4\ \Omega$$

V, the voltage across the parallel circuit is

$$= \frac{100.10^4}{10^4 + 10^6} = 0.9901 \text{ volts}$$

(iii)
$$I = \frac{100}{10^6 + 10^4} = 99.01 \ \mu\text{A} \approx 99 \ \mu\text{A}$$

$$I_L = \frac{0.9901}{\omega_R L} \approx \frac{0.99}{10} = 99 \text{ m A}$$

$$I_C = \omega_R C\,(0.9901) = (.99)\,(10^{-1}) = 99 \text{ mA}$$

$$I_R = \frac{0.9901}{10^4} = I \approx 0.99 \ \mu\text{A}$$

(iv)
$$Q_P = \frac{R}{\omega L} = \frac{10^4}{10} = 10^3$$

$$I_C = I_L = 10^3 I \text{ is verified}$$

(v) at $\omega = 10^2$ rad/sec

$$Y = \frac{1}{Z} = 10^{-4} + j\left[10^2 10^{-6} - \frac{1}{10^2 10^{-4}}\right]$$

$$= (10^{-4} - 10^2 j)$$

$$Z \approx 10^{-2} j$$

$$Z_{\text{total}} = 10^6 + 10^2 j \approx 10^6 \ \Omega$$

and the circuit current is

$$I = 100 \ \mu\text{A}$$

V, the voltage drop across the parallel circuit is

$$= (j\,10^2)\,(100.10^{-6}) = j\,10^{-6} \text{ volts}$$

$$I_R = \frac{j10^{-6}}{10^4} = j\,10^{-10} \text{ A}$$

$$I_L = \frac{j10^{-6}}{j10^{-2}} = 10^{-4} \text{ A}$$

$$I_C = \frac{j10^{-6}}{-j} 10^2 10^{-6} = -10^{-10} \text{ A}$$

(vi) The 10^6 ohm series resistance is necessary as otherwise the source voltage appears directly across the resonant circuit.

The voltage across the parallel RLC circuit will be independent of ω in the absence of a suitable series resistor.

5.28 SELECTIVITY AND BANDWIDTH OF THE PARALLEL RESONANT CIRCUIT

Using Eqn. 5.71, one may plot the variation of Y with ω. We notice that this equation is similar to Eqn. 5.62 with L and C intercharged, G replacing R and Y replacing Z. Figure 5.31 is therefore valid for the parallel resonant circuit with the above changes. The selectivity of the parallel resonant circuit therefore increases as G decreases or R increases. The resistor R may not be an external resistor but one that accounts for power loss in C. Since this loss is usually small, R is high.

It can be shown that the bandwidth, B.W., of the parallel resonant circuit is

$$= \frac{f_R}{Q_P} \quad \text{...(5.76)}$$

Example 5.12. *Find the bandwidth of the parallel resonant circuit in example 5.11. What should be the value of R so that the bandwidth is 100 Hz?*

Solution $\quad \text{B.W.} = \frac{f_R}{Q_P}\text{Hz} = \frac{\frac{10}{2\pi}}{10^3} = 15.92 \text{ Hz}$

If B.W. = 100,

$$Q_p = \frac{f_R}{100} = \frac{1000}{2\pi} = \frac{R}{\omega L} = \frac{R}{10}$$

and
$$R = \frac{10000}{2\pi} = 1591.55 \text{ ohms.}$$

In a practical parallel resonant circuit, some resistance has to be introduced in series with L to account for losses in the inductor's magnetic core and the fact that the wire used to wind the inductor possesses some finite resistance. To find the resonant frequency of such a circuit, shown in Fig. 5.35, one uses the principle that the impedance, at resonance, is purely resistive.

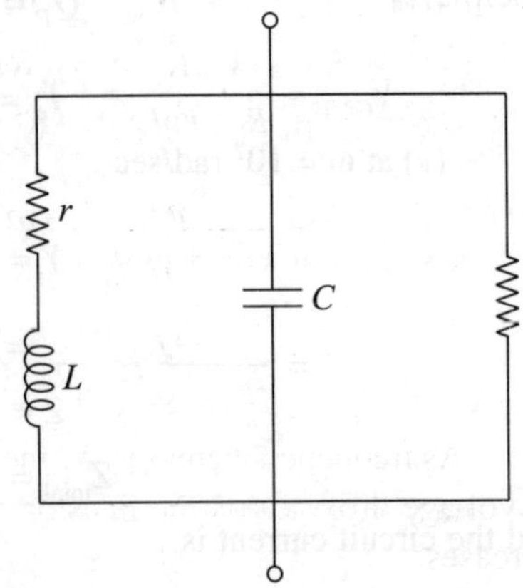

Fig. 5.35 *A parallel resonant circuit*

5.29 APPLICATION OF THE PARALLEL RESONANT CIRCUIT

Like its series counterpart, the parallel resonant circuit is used where frequency selectivity is desired. Consider the block diagram in Fig. 5.36.

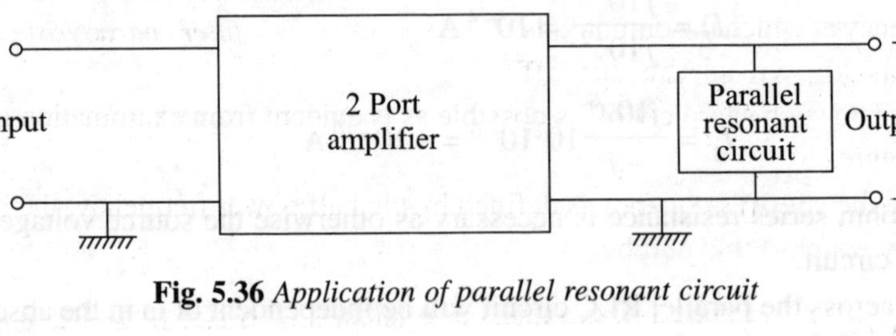

Fig. 5.36 *Application of parallel resonant circuit*

Here, the input signal may consist of many frequency components all of which are amplified by the voltage amplifier. One may, however, be interested only in a particular frequency component, say f_1, at the output. Introduction of a parallel LC resonant circuit, tuned to the frequency f_1, at the amplifier output–ensures a high impedance load over a range of frequencies determined by the bandwidth of the resonant circuit. If Q_p is large, the circuit becomes very selective and the system, as a whole, amplifies only that component of the input signal which has a frequency f_1. Such an amplifier is known as a *tuned voltage amplifier.*

5.30 RL AND RC FILTERS

In the previous sections we have seen how a resonant circuit may be used as tuned filter. *RL* and *RC* circuits may be used as filters as well but they will be of the bandpass variety *i.e.* such filters transmit a range of frequencies. Consider the *RL* two port circuit of Fig. 5.37. Let the input voltage V_{IN} be held constant in magnitude and its frequency *f* varied. Using the voltage divider principle,

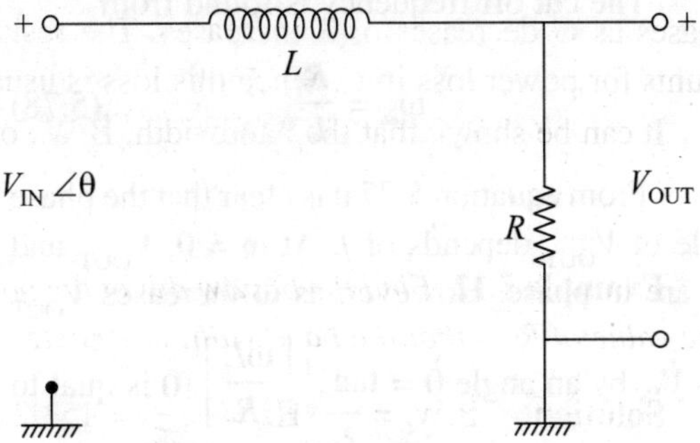

Fig. 5.37 *An RL two-port circuit*

$$V_{OUT} = \frac{V_{IN} R}{R + j\omega L} = \frac{V_{IN} R (R - j\omega L)}{(R^2 + \omega^2 L^2)}$$

$$= \frac{V_{IN} R}{(R^2 + \omega^2 L^2)} (R^2 + \omega^2 L^2)^{1/2} \angle \tan^{-1} \frac{-\omega L}{R}$$

$$= \frac{V_{IN} R}{(R^2 + \omega^2 L^2)^{1/2}} \angle \tan^{-1} \frac{-\omega L}{R} \quad ...(5.77)$$

As frequency increases, X_L increases, and the voltage drop across the resistor, the output, decreases.

As $\omega \to \infty$ $V_{OUT} \to 0$ and as $\omega \to 0$ $V_{OUT} \to V_{IN}$, the d.c. value. The arrangement works as a *low pass filter*; the *RL* two port allows the transmission of low frequency signals more readily than high frequency signals.

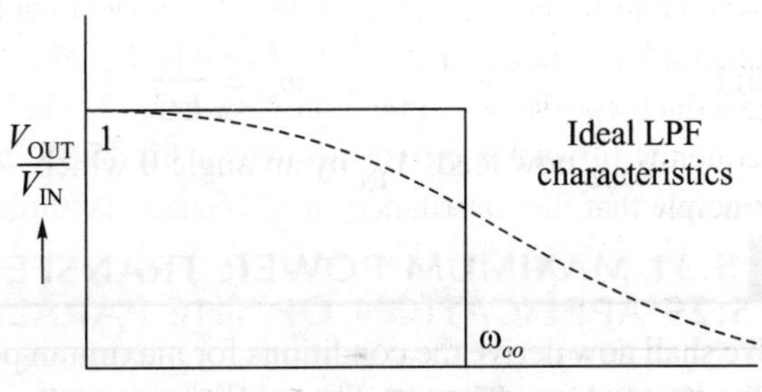

Fig. 5.38 *Ideal and practical low pass filter characteristics*

An ideal low pass filter exhibits the characteristics shown by the solid line in Fig. 5.38. The frequency at which the output falls suddenly to zero is known as the cut off frequency. In practice no such sharp cut off is possible as is evident from examination of the dotted line curve in the same figure.

In such a case the cut off frequency is defined by the half power frequency; the bandwidth of the circuit is numerically equal to this number.

Maximum power is dissipated in the resistor *R* when $\omega = 0$ and is $= \frac{V_{IN}^2}{R}$ watts. The current corresponding to this power is $\frac{V_{IN}}{R}$ amps.

If the power dissipated is half of the maximum, the circuit current should be $\frac{V}{\sqrt{2}R}$ amperes.

This is possible only if

$$Z = |R + j\omega L| = \sqrt{2}R \quad \text{or} \quad \omega L = R$$

The cut off frequency is found from

$$\omega_{\infty} = \frac{R}{L} \qquad ...(5.78)$$

From equation 5.77 it is clear that the phase angle of V_{OUT} depends of f. At $\omega = 0$, V_{OUT} and V_{IN} are in phase. However, as ω increases V_{OUT} lags V_{IN} by an angle $\theta = \tan^{-1}\left[\frac{\omega L}{R}\right]$. θ is qual to 45° at the cut off frequency and $\rightarrow$ 90° as $\omega \rightarrow \infty$.

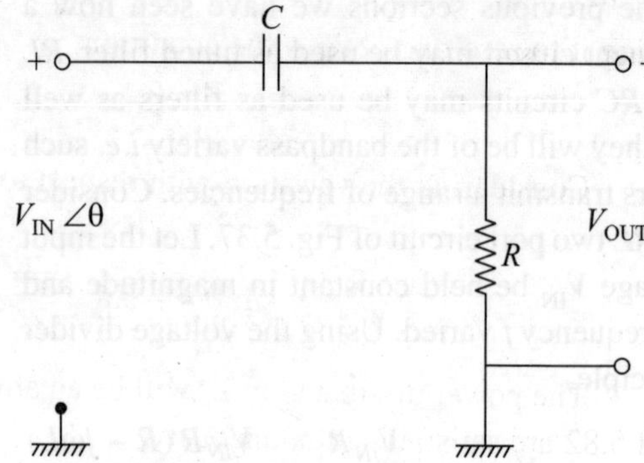

Fig. 5.39 *An RC high pass circuit*

The *RC* circuit of Fig. 5.39 constitutes another filter arrangement. The student should check for himself that this arrangement works as a high pass filter with

$$V_{OUT} = \frac{V_{IN}\,R}{\left(R^2 + \frac{1}{\omega^2 C^2}\right)^{1/2}} \angle \tan^{-1}\left[\frac{1}{\omega CR}\right] \qquad ...(5.79)$$

and

$$\omega_{\infty} = \frac{1}{RC} \qquad ...(5.80)$$

V_{OUT} now leads V_{IN} by an angle θ which $\rightarrow 0$ as $\omega \rightarrow \infty$ and equals 45° at ω_{co}.

5.31 MAXIMUM POWER TRANSFER THEOREM—AC CASE

We shall now derive the conditions for maximum power transfer in the ac case when a load of impedance $Z_L\angle\theta$ is fed by a Thevenin equivalent source, $Z_G\angle\phi$. The square of the total impedance Z in the circuit is

$$= |Z_G\angle\phi + Z_L\angle\phi|^2$$

$$= (Z_G \cos\phi + Z_L \cos\phi)^2 (Z_G \sin\phi + Z_L \sin\theta)^2$$

$$= Z_G^2 + Z_L^2 + Z_G Z_L \cos(\phi - \theta)$$

The power dissipated in the load, P,

$$= \frac{V^2}{Z^2} \text{(Resistive part of load)}$$

$$= \frac{V^2}{Z^2} Z_L \cos\theta = \frac{V^2 Z_L \cos\theta}{Z_G^2 + Z_L^2 + 2Z_G Z_L} \cos(\phi - \theta)$$

where V is the magnitude of the Thevenin equivalent voltage. To find maximum power transfer we get both $\frac{dP}{dZ_L}$ and $\frac{dP}{d\theta}$ to zero to yield two conditions both of which have to be satisfied. Finding $\frac{dP}{dZ_L}$ and setting it to zero one obtains the condition

$$Z = Z_G \quad \text{...(5.81)}$$

Considering the variation with respect to θ one obtains that $\frac{dP}{d\theta} = 0$, if

$$\sin\theta = -\sin\phi \frac{2Z_G Z_L}{Z_G^2 + Z_L^2} \quad \text{...(5.82)}$$

The power dissipated in Z_L will be an absolute maximum if both conditions given by Eqns. 5.81 and 5.82 are satisfied simultaneously

i.e., and

$$\left.\begin{aligned} Z_L &= Z_G \\ \theta &= -\Phi \end{aligned}\right\} \quad \text{...(5.83)}$$

Therefore, the load for maximum power dissipation is = $Z_G \angle -\phi$. *i.e.* the Thevenin equivalent impedance is in the form $(R + jX)$, the load impedance should be of the form $(R - jX)$.

As in the dc case, under these conditions, half the available power is dissipated in the load and the efficiency is therefore 50%.

5.32 CIRCUIT AND DEVICE CHARACTERIZATION

Of the many parameters used to describe the behaviour of a device or circuit, four are more common and will be described here.

Input Impedance

Consider an ac source with an internal impedance Z feeding a circuit which may contain sources and active and passive elements. Connection of the source causes a current, I, to flow. Representing the effect of the entire circuit by Z_i, we may write

$$I = \frac{V}{Z + Z_i} \quad \text{...(5.84)}$$

Z_i is known as the input impedance of the circuit or device. Clearly, the greater the magnitude of Z_i the lesser the current drain from the source. Also, by voltage divider action, V_i the voltage across the input terminals of the circuit is

$$= \frac{VZ_i}{Z_i + Z}$$

and ≈ V if $Z_i >> Z$. Thus, the larger the input impedance, the greater is the proportional of the voltage appearing across the input terminals of the device. This is important especially in the case of amplifiers where the input voltage V_i and not V is recognized and amplified.

CHAPTER 5

Gain

In a two port circuit or device, the ratio of the open circuit output voltage to the input voltage is known as the *gain* of the circuit. The gain of a circuit usually varies with frequency. It is possible to determine the gain-frequency characteristic by calculating or measuring the output voltage as the magnitude of the input signal is kept constant while its frequency is varied.

Equations 5.77 and 5.79 are the expressions to gain of a *RL* and *RC* filter respectively. Of course, in this instance, the magnitude of the gain is less than or equal to one. More importantly, we notice that the gain is a complex number. In other words, the output voltage is not in phase with the input, the phase angle changes with frequency. Likewise, for most devices the gain is a complex number and both its magnitude and phase vary with frequency.

Bandwidth

This information is obtained directly from a gain frequency plot. The bandwidth, in Hz, defines the useful range of frequencies over which the gain magnitude is not too different from its maximum value. These frequencies are usually the half power frequencies and the bandwidth is therefore the range of frequencies over which the voltage gain magnitude, G, is ≥ 0.707 or $\frac{1}{\sqrt{2}}$ of its maximum value G_{max}. At the half power frequencies points,

$$\frac{G}{G_{max}} = \frac{1}{\sqrt{2}}$$

choosing G_{max} as the reference value, the gain at the half power points is $20 \log_{10}\left[\frac{1}{\sqrt{2}}\right]$ dB below G_{max} *i.e.*, 3 dB below G_{max}.

The limiting frequencies which define bandwidth are therefore those frequencies at which the gain is 3 dB lower than the maximum gain. At these frequencies the power dissipated in a load is one half of the maximum value.

Output Impedance

Given a two port circuit or device, one can always find a Thevenin equivalent at the output terminals. The Thevenin equivalent impedance is called the *output impedance*.

Suppose the device is fed at its input terminals by a voltage source with internal impedance Z_S. Let the device, in turn, feed a load of impedance Z_L. By voltage divider action only a portion of the open circuit output voltage appears across the load. A low output impedance ensures that a large proportion of the open circuit output voltage appears appears across the load. Naturally this is also true if the load impedance is much larger than the output impedance.

On the other hand, as shown earlier, in section 5.30, maximum power is dissipated in the load if its impedance is the complex conjugate of the output impedance of the device.

The concepts of gain, input and output impedance also apply to dc circuits with the word impedance replaced by resistance.

5.33 POWER TRANSMISSION AND DISTRIBUTION

The first scheme suggested for urban electrification employed direct current. Direct current transmission and distribution systems were then developed. It was soon realized that it is not possible to transmit large blocks of power over large distances unless the voltage drop in the transmission line is reduced by decreasing the current flow. This was made possible after the discovery of ac, ac machines, and the transformer.* A transformer is a two port device which provides either a voltage gain or voltage reduction. The voltage gain or reduction is accompanied by a reduction or increase in the current in the same ratio. Thus the law of conservation of energy is not violated. In practical transformers, there are losses and the power output is related to the power input by the efficiency factor.

In modern power systems, power is generated at a voltage of the order of 30 kV which is then stepped upto transmission levels using transformers.

The transmission voltage depends upon the power being transmitted and the distance over which it has to be transmitted. The highest ac transmission voltage now in existence is 765 kV.

All transmission is carried out using three phase ac at a frequency of 60 Hz. It turns out that for the same power transfer, a three phase' scheme is more economical than three single phase schemes. There are a few other advantages as well. Near load centers, the voltages are stepped down and distributed at various levels ranging from 110 volts to a few hundred kilovolts. The latter voltages are used to feed large industrial loads while the 110 V system is meant for residential use.

Although dc was discarded in favour of ac many years ago, dc transmission has made a comeback as it is now recognized that it is more economical to use high voltage dc for transmitting large quantities of power over large distances. Such schemes employ ac generation; the voltages are then stepped up using transformers and converted to dc which is then reconverted to ac (inverted) at the load end of the transmission line.

It should be pointed out that in a power system, the theorem of maximum power transfer is not applicable. All loads *i.e.* appliances, industrial machines etc., are voltage sensitive devices and need the maintenance of a specified constant voltage at their terminals for proper operation. The power transmission and distribution network therefore served as a means of efficient voltage transfer.

5.34 MORE ON AC CIRCUITS

In previous sections of this chapter, introduction to ac circuits was done. Some more details are as below:

5.34.1 Alternating Current Circuit Containing Pure Resistance

When a sinusoidal emf is applied across a pure Resistance an alternating current sine wave will pass through the resistance of same frequency and of same phase as that of AC voltage applied. Resistance has no capacity to store power and as such, is also called a Linear Element. (The relationship between voltage and current is linear).

*For example, if a generator is rated is 100 MVa, 20 kV, delivery of 100 MVa to a load center entails a current flow of 5000 A in the transmission line. If the line has an impedance of j 0.25 Ω/km (a representative figure; the series impedance of transmission lines is mostly reactive) and is 400 km long the corresponding voltage drop is 500 kV. Clearly this is absurd and shows that the above transmission scheme is not possible. Use of a transformer allows the transmission voltage to be raised to, say, 400 kV; the current in the line is now reduced to 250 A and the accompanying voltage drop is only 25 kV.

$$I = \frac{V}{R}$$

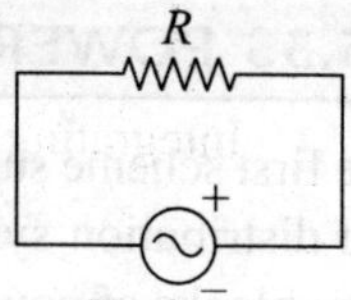

Fig. 5.40

Where I and V are R.M.S. values of current and voltage applied.

In terms of instantaneous values

$$i = \frac{v}{R} = \frac{V_m \sin \omega t}{R} = \frac{V_m}{R} \sin \omega t = I_m \sin \omega t$$

$$i = I_m \sin \omega t \quad \text{Where } I_m = V_m/R$$

Fig. 5.41

The phasor representation is as shown in Fig. 5.41

The graphical representation of voltage and current waveforms are shown in Fig. 5.42 and indicates that the current and voltage are in phase.

Power Consumed = $vi = V_m \sin \omega t \times I_m \sin \omega t$

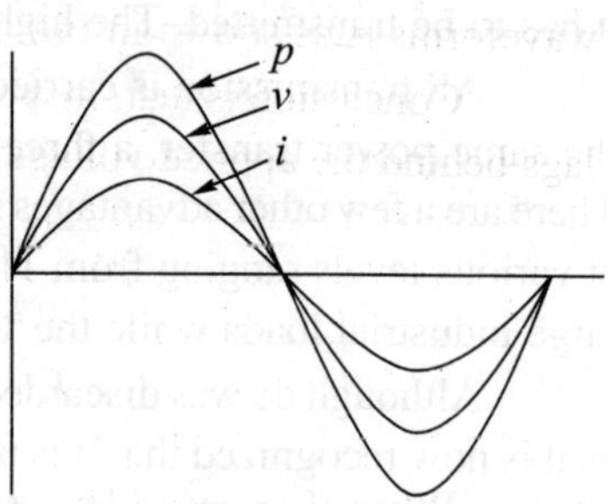

Fig. 5.42

$$P = V_m I_m \sin^2 \omega t$$

$$= V_m I_m \frac{(1 - \cos 2\omega t)}{2} = \frac{V_m I_m}{2} - \frac{V_m I_m \cos 2\omega t}{2}$$

It consists of two parts $\frac{V_m I_m}{2}$ is a fixed value which is time invariant.

The second term is time variant and its value over one cycle is zero.

Power consumed in one cycle

$$P = \int V_m I_m \sin^2 \omega t \, dt = \int V_m I_m \frac{(1 - \cos 2\omega t)}{2} dt$$

$$P = \int \left(\frac{V_m I_m}{2} - \frac{V_m I_m \cos 2\omega t}{2} \right) dt$$

The second component is time dependent and when evaluated over one cycle (integrated between 0 and 2π) its value is zero.

Therefore $\quad P = \frac{V_m I_m}{2} = \frac{V_m I_m}{\sqrt{2} \times \sqrt{2}} = VI$ = Power Consumed

5.34.2 AC through an Inductance

When an alternating emf is applied across a pure inductive coil, an alternating current will flow through it and induces an emf across the inductive coil.

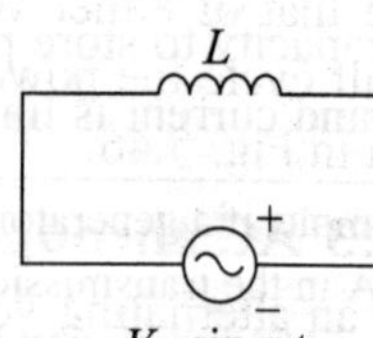

Fig. 5.43

Since the induced emf always oppose the applied voltage,

We have, $\quad e = -v = -L \frac{di}{dt}$;

Therefore $\quad v = L \frac{di}{dt}$

$$di = \frac{v}{L}\,dt = \frac{V_m \sin \omega t}{L}\,dt$$

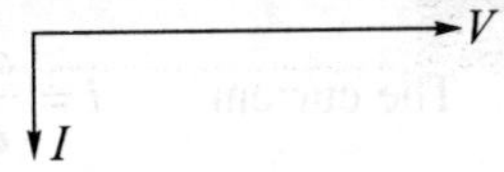

Fig. 5.44

Integrating yields

$$\int di = \int \frac{V_m \sin \omega t}{L}\,dt$$

$$i = \frac{V_m}{\omega L}(-\cos \omega t) = \frac{V_m}{X_L}(-\cos \omega t)$$

$$i = I_m \sin(\omega t - \pi/2)$$

This indicates that the current lags the voltage by $\pi/2$.

$X_L = \omega L = 2\pi f L$ $\quad$ X_L is called Induction Reactance.

The phase relationship between voltage and current is as shown in Fig. 5.44

The graphical representation of voltage and current waveforms is as shown in Fig. 5.45.

Conclusion is that, in a pure inductive circuit the current lags behind the applied voltage by $\pi/2$ radians or 90° degrees.

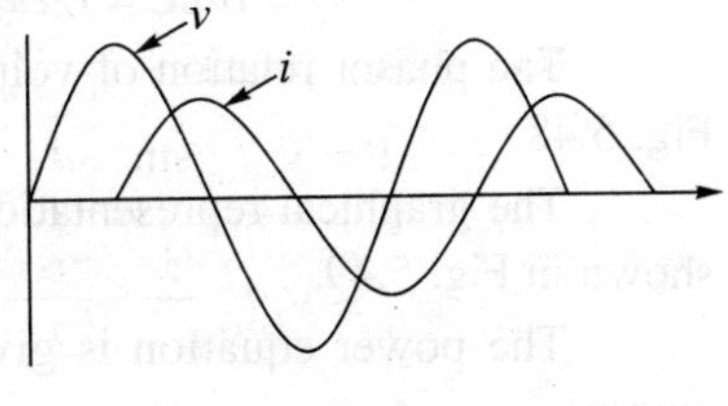

Fig. 5.45

$$i = \frac{V_m}{\omega L}(-\cos \omega t) = \frac{V_m}{X_L}(-\cos \omega t)$$

$$= I_m \sin(\omega t - \pi/2)$$

Where $I_m = \frac{V_m}{X_L}$ (The relationship between the voltage and current in an inductor is non-linear).

Power $\quad P = v.i = V_m \sin \omega t \,.\, I_m \sin(\omega t - \pi/2) = V_m I_m \sin \omega t \cos \omega t = V_m I_m \frac{\sin 2\omega t}{2}$

Power $\quad P = \int_0^{2\pi} V_m I_m \frac{\sin 2\omega t}{2}\,dt = \frac{V_m I_m}{2}\int_0^{2\pi} \sin 2\omega t\,dt = \frac{V_m I_m}{2}\Big[\cos 2\omega t/2\omega\Big]_0^{2\pi}$

$$P = \frac{V_m I_m}{4\omega}[\cos 4\pi - \cos 0]$$

$$= \frac{V_m I_m}{4\omega}[1 - 1] = 0$$

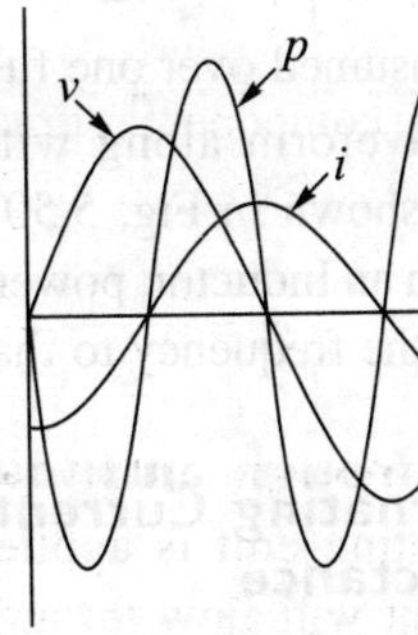

The power consumed in one cycle by a pure induction coil is zero. The power variation frequency is double that of either voltage or current and hence over one half cycle the power consumed goes to zero. It is as shown in Fig. 5.46.

Fig. 5.46

5.34.3 AC through Capacitance

When an alternating voltage is applied across a pure capacitance there will be flow of current in the capacitor.

The current $\quad i = \dfrac{dq}{dt} = \dfrac{d(Cv)}{dt} = C\dfrac{dv}{dt}$

$$i = C\frac{dv}{dt} = C\frac{d(V_m \sin \omega t)}{dt} = CV_m(\cos \omega t)\omega$$

$$i = V_m\,(\omega C)\cos \omega t = \frac{V_m}{1/\omega C}\cos \omega t$$

$$i = \frac{V_m}{X_C}\sin(\omega t + \pi/2)$$

$$i = I_m \sin(\omega t + \pi/2)$$

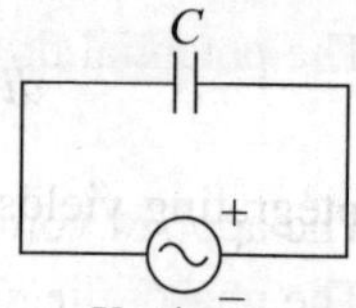

Fig. 5.47

This indicates that the current leads the voltage by $\pi/2$.

ω = Angular frequency = $2\pi f$

$X_C = 1/\omega C = 1/2\pi fC$ is called capacitive reactance.

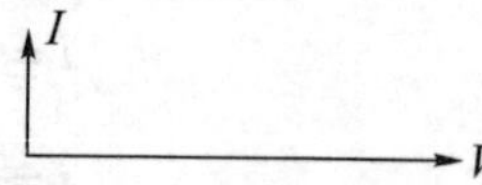

Fig. 5.48

The phasor relation of voltage and current is as shown in Fig. 5.48.

The graphical representation of voltage and current are as shown in Fig. 5.49.

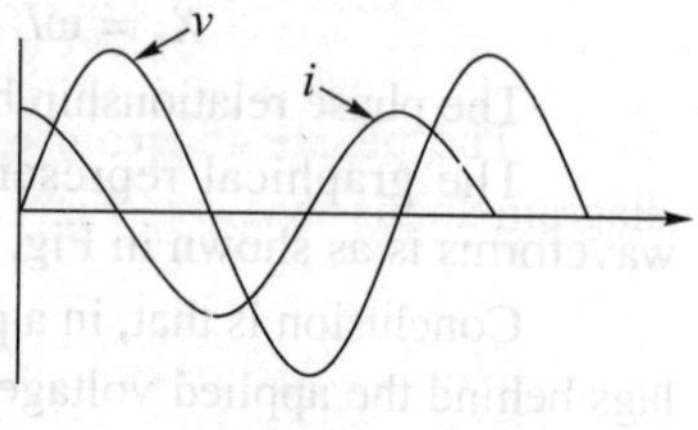

Fig. 5.49

The power equation is given by product of voltage and current.

$$\text{Power } P = v.i = V_m \sin \omega t.\ I_m \sin(\omega t + \pi/2) = V_m I_m \sin \omega t \cos \omega t = V_m I_m \frac{\sin 2\omega t}{2}$$

$$\text{Power } P = \int_0^{2\pi} V_m I_m \frac{\sin 2\omega t}{2}\,dt = \frac{V_m I_m}{2}\int_0^{2\pi} \sin 2\omega t\,dt = \frac{V_m I_m}{2}\Big[\cos 2\omega t/2\omega\Big]_0^{2\pi}$$

$$P = \frac{V_m I_m}{4\omega}[\cos 4\pi - \cos 0]$$

$$= \frac{V_m I_m}{4\omega}[1 - 1] = 0$$

Power consumed over one full cycle is zero.

Power waveform along with voltage and current waveforms is as shown in Fig. 5.50. (Similar to that of the power variation in an Inductor, power variation in a capacitor is also at double the frequency to that of the voltage/current waveforms).

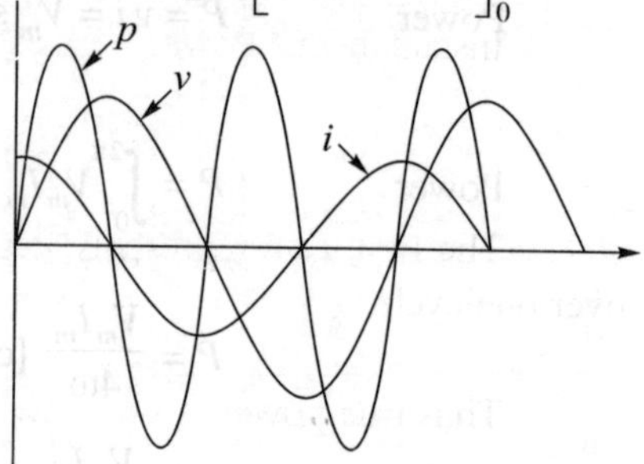

Fig. 5.50

5.34.4 Alternating Current through a Series Combination of Resistance and Inductance

Consider an alternating current circuit having resistance and inductance connected in series across a voltage source having an RMS value of V volts. This develops an rms value of current I.

The potential drop across resistance

$$V_R = IR$$

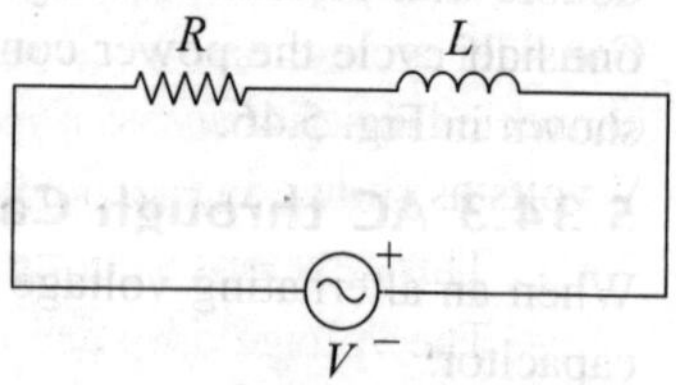

Fig. 5.51

The potential drop across inductance

$$V_L = IX_L$$

The applied voltage is vectorial sum of V_R and V_L.

The phasor diagram for the circuit is as shown in Fig. 5.52 taking current as reference phasor.

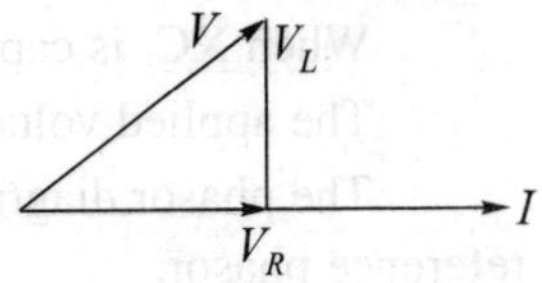

Fig. 5.52

$$V = V_R + V_L = | V_R | \angle 0 + | V_L | \angle 90° = V_R + jV_L$$

$$= IR + jIX_L = I (R + jXL) = I Z$$

where $Z = (R + j X_L) = | Z | \angle \phi$

$$V = | I | \ | Z | \angle \phi$$

$$V = | V | \angle \phi$$

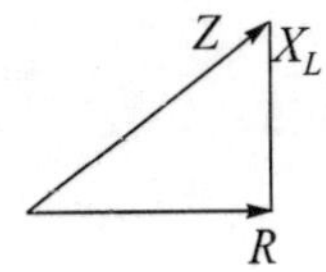

Fig. 5.53

The phasor diagram of voltages can be converted into impedance diagram and is shown in Fig. 5.53.

$$Z = R + j XL \ ; \tan \phi = \frac{X_L}{R}$$

$$Z = | Z | \angle \phi \quad \phi = \tan (X_L/R)$$

Power factor $\cos \phi = R/Z$

Voltage loads the current by angle ϕ radians.

or Current lags the voltage by an angle of ϕ radians.

$$v = V_m \sin \omega t$$

$$i = I_m \sin (\omega t - \phi)$$

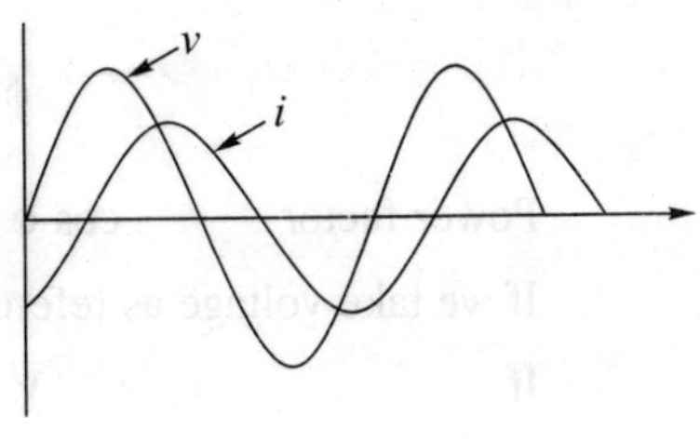

Fig. 5.54

Instantaneous Power $= v.i = V_m \sin \omega t \, I_m \sin (\omega t - \phi)$

$$= \frac{V_m I_m}{2} \cos \phi - \frac{V_m I_m}{2} \cos (2\omega t - \phi)$$

The first term represents steady power, the second term is the fluctuating power which is zero over one cycle.

Thus true power $P = \dfrac{V_m I_m}{2} \cos \phi = \dfrac{V_m I_m}{\sqrt{2} \times \sqrt{2}} \cos \phi = VI \cos \phi$

Where V and I are RMS values of voltage and current.

The waveforms of voltage, current and power have been shown in Fig. 5.54.

5.34.5 Alternating Current through a Series Combination of Resistance and Capacitance

Consider an alternating current circuit having resistance and capacitance connected in series across a voltage source having an RMS value of voltage V volts as shown in Fig. 5.55.

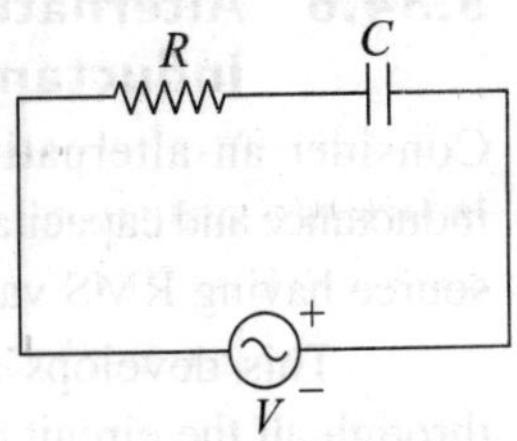

Fig. 5.55 *RC cirucit*

This develops a current I which passes through the circuit elements.

The voltage drop across the Resistance $= V_R = IR$

The voltage drop across the capacitance $= V_C = IX_C$

When XC is capacitive reactance of capacitance '*C*'.

The applied voltage is vectorial sum of V_R and V_C.

The phasor diagram is as shown in Fig. 17 taking current as reference phasor.

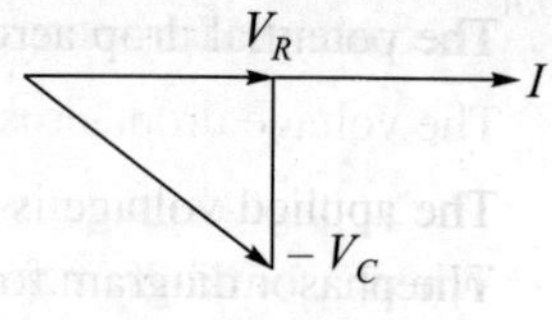

Fig. 5.56

$$\overline{V} = \overline{V}_R + (-\overline{V}_C)$$

$$= |V_R| \angle 0 + (V_C) \angle -90°$$

$$= V_R - j\,V_C$$

$$= IR - j\,IX_L$$

$$= I\,(R - JX_C)$$

The phasor diagram of voltages can be converted into impedance diagram as in Fig.5.57.

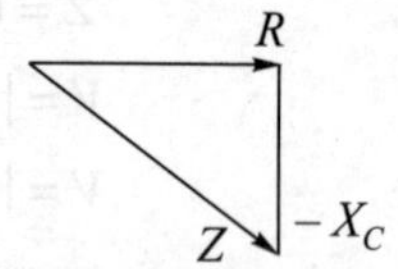

Fig. 5.57 *Impedance vector diagram*

$$Z = R - j\,XC = |Z| \angle -\phi$$

$$\therefore \qquad \tan\phi = -\frac{X_C}{R}$$

$$\phi = \tan^{-1}\left(-\frac{X_C}{R}\right)$$

Power factor $\qquad \cos\phi = (R/Z)$

If we take voltage as reference phasor then this current will be leading the voltage by ϕ.

If $\qquad V = |V| \angle 0 \quad \text{then} \quad I = |I| \angle \phi$

If $\qquad v = V_m \sin \omega t$

$$i = I_m \sin(\omega t + \phi)$$

Instantaneous Power $\qquad = v.i = V_m \sin \omega t I_m \sin(\omega t + \phi)$

$$= \frac{V_m I_m}{2}\cos\phi - \frac{V_m I_m}{2}\cos(2\omega t + \phi)$$

The first term represents steady power, the second term is the fluctuating power which is zero over one cycle.

Thus true power $\qquad P = \frac{V_m I_m}{2}\cos\phi = \frac{V_m I_m}{\sqrt{2}\times\sqrt{2}}\cos\phi = VI\cos\phi$

where *V* and *I* are RMS values of voltage and current.

5.34.6 Alternating Current through a Series Combination of Resistance, Inductance and Capacitance

Consider an alternating current circuit having resistance, inductance and capacitance connected in series across a voltage source having RMS value of *V* volts.

This develops an alternating current *I* which passes through all the circuit elements.

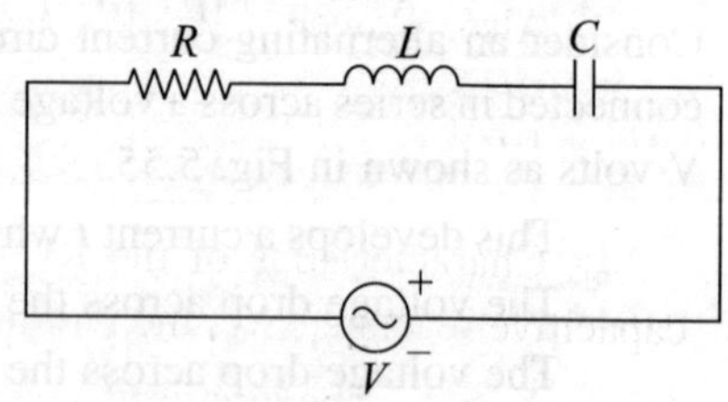

Fig. 5.58 *RLC series circuit*

The voltage drop across resistance $R = V_R = IR$

The voltage drop across inductance $L = V_L = IX_L$

The voltage drop across capacitance $C = V_C = IX_C$

When X_L and X_C represents the inductive reactance and capacities reactance respectively.

The phasor sum of V_R, V_L and V_C gives applied voltage

$$\bar{V} = \bar{V}_R + \bar{V}_L + \bar{V}_C$$

$$= V_R + jV_L - jV_C$$

$$V = V_R + j(V_L - V_C)$$

$$|V| = \sqrt{V^2{}_R + (V_L - V_C)^2}$$

$$\tan\phi = \frac{(V_L - V_C)}{V_R}$$

Phase angle $\phi = \tan^{-1}\frac{(V_L - V_C)}{V_R}$

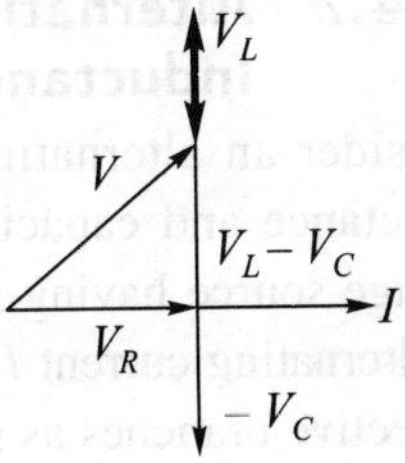

Fig. 5.59 *Phasor diagram of series RLC circuit*

The phasor diagram of voltage can be counted into impedance vector diagram

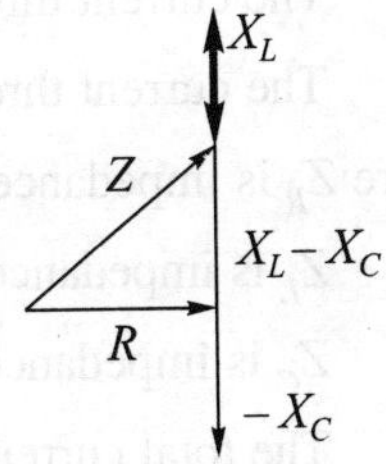

Fig. 5.60 *Phasor diagram of series RLC circuit*

$$Z = R + jX_L - jX_C$$

$$Z = R + j(X_L - X_C)$$

$$Z = |Z| \angle\phi$$

$\therefore$ When $\phi = \tan^{-1}\frac{(X_L - X_C)}{R}$;

$$\cos\phi = \frac{R}{Z} = \frac{R}{\sqrt{R^2 + (X_L - X_C)^2}}$$

In case if X_C is greater than X_L

$$Z = R + (jX_L - jX_C)$$

$$Z = R - j(X_C - X_L)$$

$$|Z| = \sqrt{R^2 + (X_C - X_L)^2}$$

$$\cos\phi = \frac{R}{Z} = \frac{R}{\sqrt{R^2 + (X_C - X_L)^2}}$$

Also, Power $V = V \times I \times \cos$ (angle between V and I)

$$\boxed{P = VI\cos\phi}$$

Characteristics of the RLC circuit depends on the magnitudes of inductor reactance X_L and capacitive reactance X_C, the circuit may be inductive or capacitive.

$X_L > X_C$ The circuit behaves like an inductive circuit.

$X_C > X_L$ The circuit behaves like a capacitive circuit.

If the circuit is inductive, current lags behind voltage by an angle ϕ_1. If the circuit is capacitive current leads the voltage by an angle ϕ_2.

5.34.7 Alternating Current through a Parallel Combination of Resistance, Inductance and Capacitance

Consider an alternating current circuit having resistance, inductance and capacitance connected in parallel across a voltage source having RMS value of *V* volts. This develops an alternating current *I* which will divide into I_1, I_2 and I_3 in respective branches as shown in Fig. 5.61.

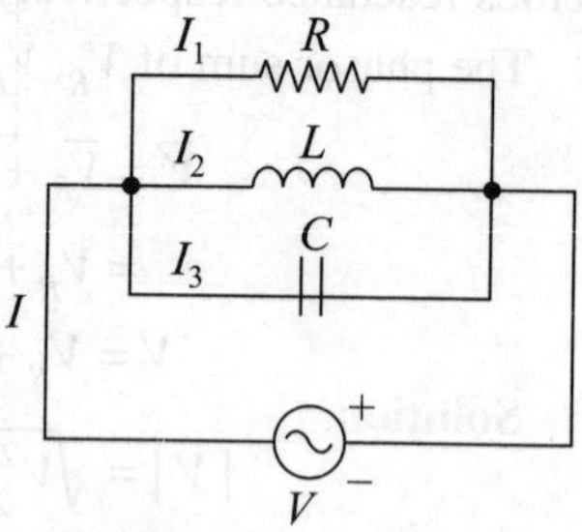

Fig. 5.61 *RLC parallel circuit*

As the voltage across each branch is same

The current through Resistance branch = $I_1 = V/Z_R$

The current through Inductance coil branch, $I_2 = V/Z_L$

The current through Capacitance branch = $I_3 = V/Z_C$

where Z_R is impedance of Resistance branch $Z_R = (R + j0) = R$

Z_L is impedance of Inductive branch $= Z_L = (r_1 + jX_L)$

Z_C is impedance of capacitive branch $= Z_C = (r_2 - jX_C)$

The total current *I* is the vectorial sum of I_1, I_2 and I_3

$$\bar{I} = \bar{I}_1 + \bar{I}_2 + \bar{I}_3$$

$$I = \frac{V}{Z_R} + \frac{V}{Z_L} + \frac{V}{Z_C} = V\left(\frac{1}{Z_R} + \frac{1}{Z_L} + \frac{1}{Z_C}\right) = \frac{V}{Z}$$

$$\frac{1}{Z} = \left(\frac{1}{Z_R} + \frac{1}{Z_L} + \frac{1}{Z_C}\right)$$

$$Y = Y_R + Y_L + Y_C$$

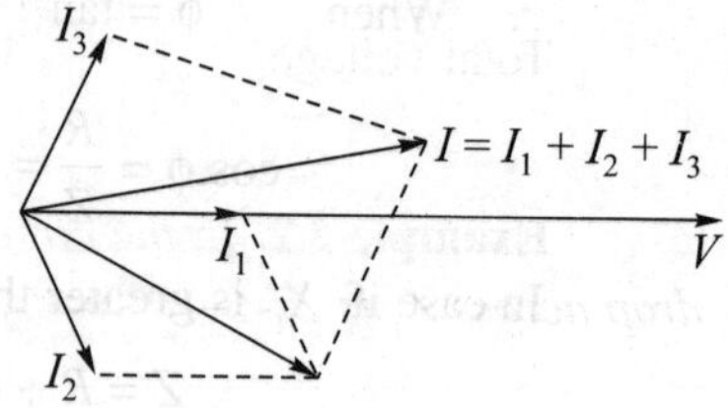

Fig. 5.62

where *Y* represents the admittance of the circuit

$Y_R = 1/Z_R$ – Admittance of the Resistance branch

$Y_L = 1/Z_L$ – Admittance of the Inductance branch

$Y_C = 1/Z_C$ – Admittance of the Capacitance branch

Total admittance $Y = Y_R + Y_L + Y_C$

current distribution

$$I_1 = VY_R\,;\ I_2 = VY_L\,;\ I_3 = V\,Y_C$$

The vector diagram is as shown in Fig. 5.62 taking voltage as reference vector.

When the parallel circuit is having more than two branches then admittance method is suggested for finding the distribution of current.

Example 5.1. *Figure (5.1) shows an ac series circuit. Find the voltage across each impedance. Show that the sum of $V_1 + V_2 + V_3$ is equal to the applied voltage $V = 100\ \angle 0°$ V.*

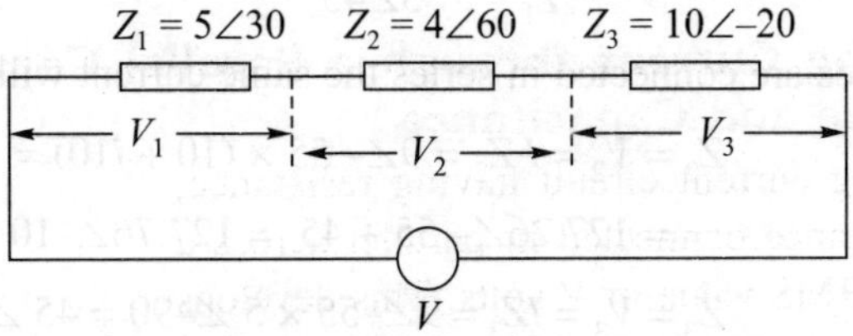

Fig 5.1

Solution. $Z_1 = 5\ \angle 30 = 4.33 + j2.5$

$Z_2 = 4\angle 60 = 2 + j3.464$

$Z_3 = 10\angle -20 = 9.396 - j3.4202$

As the impedance are in series $Z = Z_1 + Z_2 + Z_3$

Total impedance of the circuit $Z = 15.726 + j\ 2.543$

$Z = 15.93\ \angle 9.185°$

The current through the circuit $I = \dfrac{V}{Z} = \dfrac{100\angle 0}{15.93\angle 9.185} = 6.277\ \angle -9.185$

Voltage across $Z_1 = V_1 = IZ_1 = 6.2775\ \angle -9.185 \times 5\ \angle 30\ = 31.387\ \angle\ 20.815$

Voltage across $Z_2 = V_2 = I\ Z_2 = 6.2775\ \angle -9.185 \times 4\ \angle 60\ =\ 25.11\ \angle 50.815$

Voltage across $Z_3 = V_3 = I\ Z_3 = 6.2775\ \angle -9.185 \times 10\angle -20\ = 62.775\ \angle -29.815$

Total voltage $V = V_1 + V_2 + V_3 = 31.387\ \angle 20.815 + 25.11\ \angle 50.815 + 62.775\ \angle -29.815$

$= 100$ V.

Example 5.2. *In the circuit shown below (Fig. 5.2), find the applied voltage 'V', if the voltage drop across Z_1 is $27\angle -10°$ volts.*

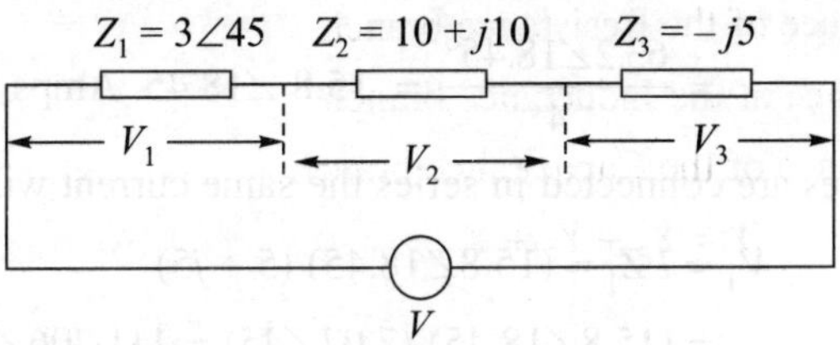

Fig. 5.2

Solution. Voltage across $Z_1 = V_1 = 27\angle -10$ $\quad Z_2 = 10 + j10 = 14.142\ \angle 45°$

$Z_1 = 3\angle 45 \qquad Z_3 = -j\ 5 = 5\ \angle -90°$

CHAPTER 5

The current through the impedance

$$Z_1 = I = \frac{V}{Z_1} = \frac{27\angle -10^\circ}{3\angle 45} = 9\angle -10-45 = 9\angle -55$$

As the impedances are connected in series the same current will flow through them.

Voltage across $\quad Z_2 = V_2 = I\,Z_2 = 9\angle -55 \times (10 + j10) = 9\angle -55 \times (14.14\angle 45)$

$$= 127.26\angle -55 + 45 = 127.76\angle -10$$

Voltage across $\quad Z_3 = V_3 = IZ_3 = 9\angle -55 \times 5\angle -90 = 45\angle -145^\circ$

$$V = V_1 + V_2 + V_3$$

$$= 27\angle -10 + 127.26\angle -10 + 45\angle -145^\circ$$

$$= 26.59 - j\,4.69 + 125.326 - j22.10 - 36.86 - j\,25.81$$

$$= 115.56 - j52.6 = 126.51\angle -24.57.$$

Example 5.3. *Three impedances $Z_1 = 5 + j5\ \Omega$, $Z_2 = -j8\ \Omega$ and $Z_3 = 4\ \Omega$ are connected in series to an unknown voltage source V. Find I and V if the voltage drop across Z_3 is 63.2 ∠18.45° volts.*

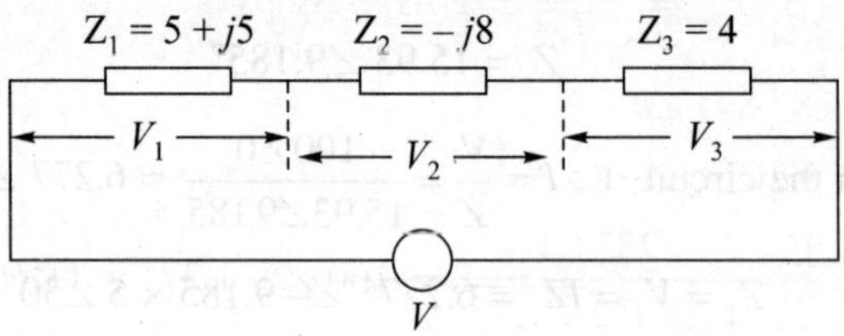

Fig. 5.3

Solution. The Fig. 5.3 shows how the impedances are connected across the voltage source of unknown voltage V.

Voltage across $\quad Z_3 = V_3 = 63.2\angle 18.45\ ;\ Z_3 = 4\ \Omega;$

$$Z_2 = j8 = 8\angle -90\ \Omega;\ Z_1 = 5 + j\,5 = 7.07\angle 45$$

The current through $\quad Z_3 = I = V_3/Z_3$

$$= \frac{63.2\angle 18.45^\circ}{4} = 15.8\angle 18.45 \text{ Amps}$$

As all the impedances are connected in series the same current will pass through them.

$$V_1 = I\,Z_1 = (15.8\angle 18.45)\,(5 + j5)$$

$$= (15.8\angle 18.45)\,(7.07\angle 45) = 111.706\angle 63.45$$

$$V_2 = I\,Z_2 = (15.8\angle 18.45)\,(-j8)$$

$$= (15.8\angle 18.45)\,(8\angle -90) = 126.4\angle 71.55$$

$$V = V_1 + V_2 + V_3 = 111.706\angle 63.45 + 126.4\angle -71.55 + 63.2\angle 18.45$$

$$= (49.93 + j\,99.92 + 33.67 - j\,121.83 + 59.95 + j\,20)$$

$$= (143.67 - j\,1.83) = 143.68\angle 0.729$$

Another approach of calculating the total voltage $= V = IZ$.

Where $Z = Z_1 + Z_2 + Z_3 = 5 + j5 - j8 + 4 = (9 - j13) = 9.4868\angle 18.43$

$$V = I\,Z = 15.8\angle 18.45 \times 9.4868\angle -18.43 = 149.89 = 150 \text{ V.}$$

Example 5.4. *An emf of 400 sin (314 t) is applied to a series circuit and the resulting current is 2.5 sin (314 t – 1.37°). Find the (1) frequency (2) Phase angle between voltage and current and (3) circuit parameters.*

Solution. $v = V_m \sin \omega t = 400 \sin (314\, t)$

$$V_m = 400 \quad \omega = 314$$

$$V_{rms} = \frac{V_m}{\sqrt{2}} = \frac{(400)}{\sqrt{2}} = 282.84 \quad \omega = 2\pi f = 314$$

$$f = \frac{314}{2\pi} = 50 \text{ Hz}$$

$$i = I_m \sin (\omega t - \phi) = 2.5 \sin (314\, t - 1.37°)$$

$$\therefore \quad I_m = 2.5 \quad I_{rms} = \frac{(2.5)}{\sqrt{2}} = 1.7677 \text{ Amps}$$

$$\therefore \quad V = 282.84 \angle 0$$

$$I = 1.7677 \angle -1.37°$$

$$\therefore \quad Z = \frac{V}{I} = \frac{282.84}{1.7677\sqrt{-1.37°}} = 160 \angle -1.37° = (159.95 + j\,3.825)$$

$$R = 159.95; \qquad X = 3.825 \quad \therefore \quad X = 2\pi fL = 3.825$$

$$L = \frac{3.825}{2\pi f} = \frac{3.825}{2\pi \times 50} = 0.0122 \text{ H.}$$

Example 5.5. *A coil having an inductance of 200 mH and a resistance of 4 Ω is connected in series with a capacitor across a 50 Hz supply. Calculate the capacitance required to give the circuit a power factor of 0.5 lagging and 0.5 leading.*

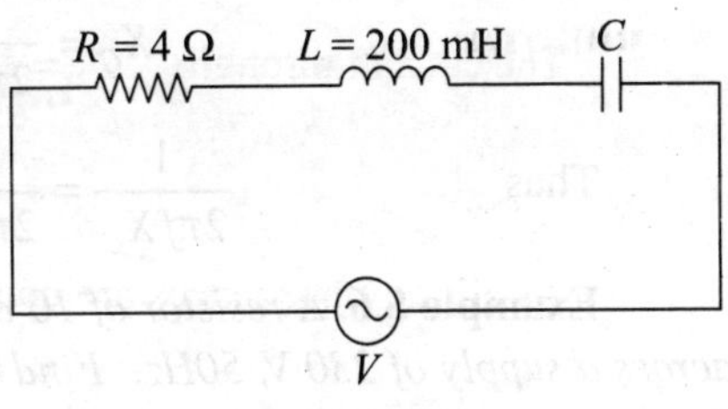

Fig. 5.4

Solution. $R = 4 \quad L = 200 \text{ mH} \quad C = ?$

Inductive reactance $X_L = 2\pi f L$

$$= 2\pi \times 50 \times 200 \times 10^{-3}$$

$$= 62.83 \ \Omega$$

The circuit diagram is as shown in Fig. 5.4.

Capacitive reactance of C is X_C

Total impedance of the series circuit

$$= R + j\,X_L - j\,X_C = R + j\,(X_L - X_C)\Omega$$

If $\cos \phi = 0.5$ lagging

$$\phi = \cos^{-1}(0.5) = +\,60° \text{ (lag)}$$

∴ If p.f . is lagging the circuit is an inductive circuit.

$$Z = R + j\,(X_L - X_C) = 4 + j\,(62.80 - X_C)$$

$$\tan\phi = \tan 60 = 1.732$$

$$\tan\phi = \frac{(X_L - X_C)}{R} = 1.732$$

$$(X_L - X_C) = 1.732 \times R$$

$$(62.83 - X_C) = 1.732 \times 4$$

$$62.83 - 1.732 \times 4 = X_C$$

$$\therefore \quad X_C = 55.90$$

$$X_C = \frac{1}{2\pi fC}; \text{ Thus } C = \frac{1}{2\pi f X_C} = \frac{1}{2\pi \times 50 \times 55.90} = 56.94\ \mu\text{f}$$

If the $\cos\phi = 0.5$ leading

$$\therefore \quad \phi = \cos^{-1} 0.5 = 60° \text{ lead}$$

Then the circuit will be capacitive. Hence $X_C > X_L$

$$Z = R - j\,(X_C - X_L)$$

$$\tan\phi = -\frac{(X_C - X_L)}{R} = \tan -60 = -\sqrt{3}$$

$$\frac{(X_C - X_L)}{R} = \sqrt{3}$$

$$-X_C - X_L = \sqrt{3} \times R = \sqrt{3} \times 4$$

$$X_C = X_L + \sqrt{3} \times 4 = 62.83 + \sqrt{3} \times 4$$

$$X_C = 69.758\ \Omega$$

$$X_C = \frac{1}{2\pi fC}$$

Thus

$$\frac{1}{2\pi f X_C} = \frac{1}{2\pi \times 50 \times 69.78} = 4.563 \times 10^{-5}\ F = 45.63\ \mu\text{F}.$$

Example 5.6. *A resistor of 10 ohms an inductor of 0.1H and a capacitor of 50 µf an in series across a supply of 230 V, 50Hz. Find (i) the impedance of the circuit, (ii) the current (iii) Power and Power factor (iv) Voltage across capacitor.*

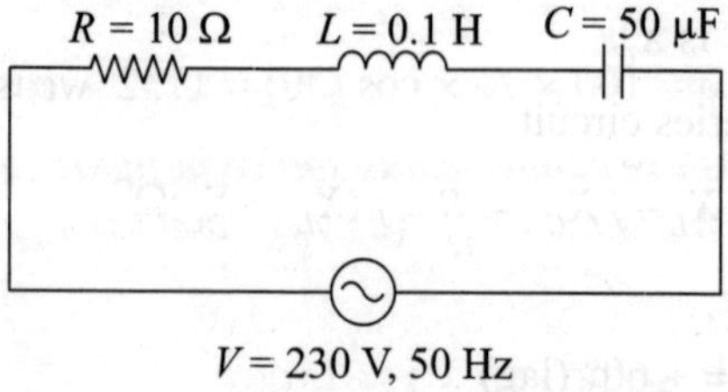

Fig. 5.5

Solution. $R = 10\ \Omega \quad L = 0.1\text{ H} \quad C = 50\ \mu\text{F}$

$X_L = 2\pi f \quad L = 2\pi \times 50 \times 0.1 = 31.4\ \Omega$

$X_C = 1/2\pi fC = 1/2\pi \times 50 \times 50 \times 10^{-6}$

$= 63.66\ \Omega$

The circuit diagram is as shown in Fig. 5.5

$$Z = R + j\,(X_L - X_C) = 10 + j\,(31.4 - 63.66) = 10 + j\,(-32.26)$$

$$Z = 10 - j32.26 = 33.77\angle{-72.77}$$

Impedance $= 33.77\ \Omega$, power factor $\cos(72.77) = 0.296$

The current $I = \dfrac{V}{Z} = \dfrac{230\angle 0}{33.77(\angle -72.77)} = 6.810\angle 72.77$ A leading current

Power $= P = VI\cos\phi$

$= 230 \times 6.81 \times 0.296 = 463.67$ watts

p.f. $= \cos\phi = \cos(72.77) = 0.296.$

Voltage across the capacitance $V_C = IX_C$

$= 6.810 \times 63.66$

$= 433.5246$ volts.

Example 5.7. *A current of average value 18.099A is flowing in a circuit to which a voltage of peak value 141.42V is applied. Determine (i) $Z_1 = R \pm jX$ (ii) Power. V lags I by (π/6) radians.*

Solution. $I_{av} = 18.019$ A; $V_m = 141.42$ V $\quad Vrms = V_m/\sqrt{2} = 141.41/\sqrt{2} = 100$ V

$$I_{av} = \frac{2I_m}{\pi} = 18.019\text{ A} \qquad I_m = \frac{I_{av} \times \pi}{2} = \frac{18.019 \times \pi}{2} = 28.304\text{ A}$$

$$Z = \frac{V_m}{I_m} = \frac{141.42}{28.304} = 4.996\ \Omega = 5\ \Omega$$

$$I_{rms} = \frac{I_m}{\sqrt{2}} = \frac{28.304}{\sqrt{2}} = 20\text{ A}$$

V lags I by $\pi/6$ radians. This indicates that the angle lag is $\left(\dfrac{\pi}{6} \times \dfrac{180°}{\pi}\right) = 30°$

$\therefore \quad V = 100\angle -30°,\ I = 20\angle 0$

$\therefore \quad Z = \dfrac{V}{I} = \dfrac{100\angle -30}{20\angle 0} = 5\angle -30 = 4.33 - j\,2.5$

Power $= VI\cos\phi = 100 \times 20 \times \cos(30) = 1732$ watts.

Example 5.8. *Three voltages are connected as shown in figure (5.6). If $V_a = (17.32 + j10)$ V, $V_b = 30\angle{+80}°$V; $V_c = 15\angle{-100}°$V. Find (1) V_{12} (2) V_{23} and (3) V_{34}.*

Solution. $V_{12} = V_{14} + V_{42}$

$= -V_b + V_c = -30\angle 80 + 15\angle{-100}$

$= -(5.209 + j\,29.544) + (-2.604 - j\,4.772)$

$= (-5.209 - j\,29.544 - 2.604 - j\,14.772)$

$= (-7.813 - j\,44.316)$

$= 45\angle -100$

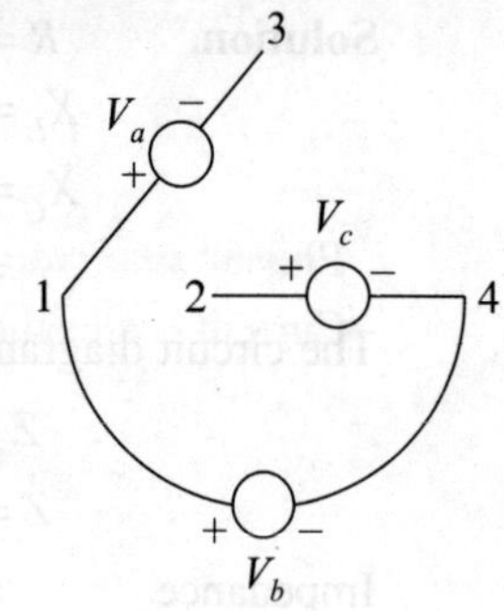

Fig. 5.6

$V_{23} = (V_{24} + V_{41} + V_{13})$

$V_{23} = -V_C + V_b - V_a$

$= -15\angle -100 + 30\angle -80 - (17.32 + j10)$

$= -(-2.6047 - j14.772) + (5.2094 + j\,29.544) - (17.32 + j10)$

$= 2.6047 + j14.772 + 5.2094 + j29.544 - 17.32 - j10$

$= -9.5059 + j\,34.316 = 35.608\angle 105.48$

$V_{34} = V_{31} + V_{14}$

$= V_a - V_b = 17.32 + j10 - (5.209 + j\,29.54)$

$= 17.32 + j10 - 5.209 - j\,29.54$

$= 12.111 - j\,19.54 = 22.988\angle -58.211.$

Example 5.9. *A choke coil of inductance 0.08 H and a resistance of 12 ohms, is connected in parallel with a capacity of 120 μF. The combination is connected to a supply of 240 V, 50 Hz. Find the total current and the power factor. Draw the phasor diagram.*

Solution. The circuit diagram is as shown in Fig. 5.7

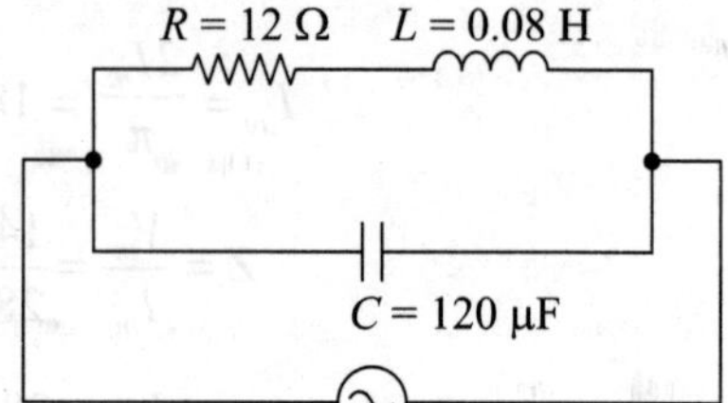

Fig. 5.7

The impedance of branch 1

$Z_1 = 12 + j\,X_L$

When $X_L = 2\pi f_L = 2\,\pi \times 50 \times 0.08$

$= 25.132\ \Omega$

$Z_1 = 12 + j25.132 = 27.85\angle 64.47$

$$\therefore \quad X_C = \frac{1}{2\pi fC} = \frac{1}{2\pi \times 50 \times 120 \times 15^{-6}} = 26.526$$

$Z_2 = R_2 - jX_C = 0 - j\,26.526 = 26.526\angle -90$

$$I_1 = V/Z_1 = \frac{240\angle 0}{27.85\angle 64.47} = 8.6176\ \underline{\angle -64.47}\ \text{Amps}$$

$$I_2 = V/Z_2 = \frac{240\angle 0}{26.526\angle -90} = 9.047\ \underline{\angle 90}\ \text{Amps}$$

$I = I_1 + I_2 = 8.6176\ \underline{\angle -64.47} + 9.047\ \underline{\angle 90}$

$= 3.714 - j\,7.776 + j\,9.047 = (3.714 + j\,1.2708) = 3.925\ \ \underline{\angle +18.88^\circ}$

Power factor = cos (Angle between V and I)

$= \cos (18.88)$

$= 0.946$

Phasor diagram

Current I is leading the voltage V by an angle of 18.88°

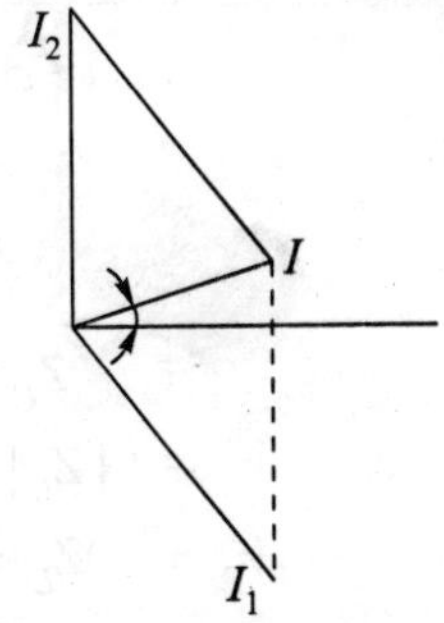

Fig. 5.8 *Vector diagram*

Example 5.10. *A choke coil having a resistance of 20 ohms and an inductance of 0.07 H is connected in parallel with a capacitor of 60 μF capacitance which is in series with a resistor of 50 ohms. Calculate the total current and phase angle when this arrangement is connected to 200 V, 50 Hz*

Solution.

$$Z_1 = R + j\,X_L$$

$$X_L = 2\pi f\,L = 2\pi \times 50 \times 0.07 = 22\ \Omega$$

$$Z_2 = R - jX_C$$

$$X_C = \frac{1}{2\pi fC} = \frac{1}{2\pi \times 50 \times 60 \times 10^{-6}} = 53\ \Omega$$

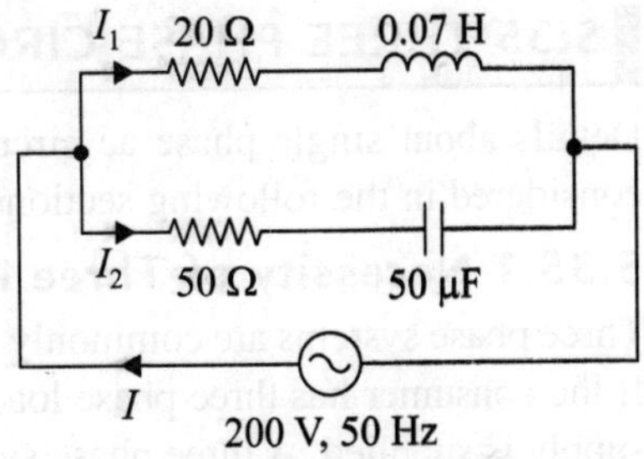

Fig. 5.9

The circuit diagram is as shown in Fig. 5.9.

$$\therefore \quad Z_1 = 20 + j\,22 = 29.732\,\angle 47.73$$

$$Z_2 = 50 - j53 = 72.862\angle -46.66$$

$$I_1 = V/Z_1 = \frac{200\angle 0}{29.732\angle 47.73} = 6.726\angle -47.73° = 4524 - j\,4.977$$

$$I_2 = V/Z_2 = \frac{200\angle 0}{72.862\angle -46.66} = 2.745\angle 46.66° = 1.884 + j1.996$$

$$I = I_1 + I_2 = 4.524 - j\,4.977 + 1.884 + j\,1.996 = (6.408 - j2.98) = 7.07\angle -25°\text{Amps.}$$

Example 5.11. *A coil of power factor 0.6 is in series with 100 μF capacitor when connected to a 50 Hz supply, the potential drop across the coil is equal to the potential drop across the capacitor. Find the resistance and inductance of the coil.*

Solution. $\cos \phi_L$ = p.f. of the coil = 0.6

$$Z_L = (R + jX_L)$$

$$R = Z_L \cos \phi$$

$$X_L = Z_L \sin \phi$$

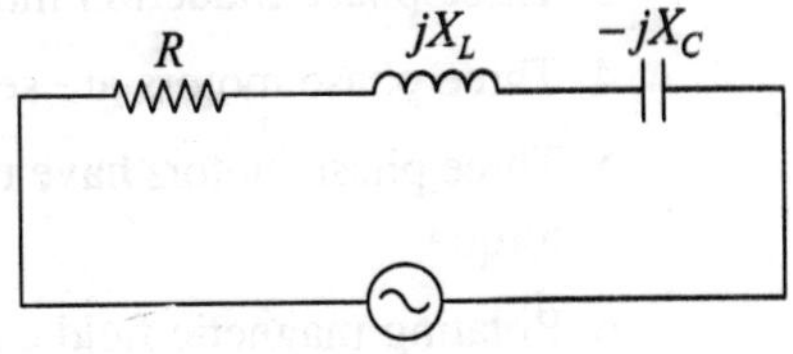

Fig. 5.10

The circuit diagram is as shown in Fig. 5.10.

$$V_L = V_C; \quad IZ_L = I\,(Z_C)$$

$$|Z_L| = |Z_C|$$

CHAPTER 5

$$Z_C = (0 - j\,X_C) = 0 - j\,\frac{1}{2\pi f C}$$

$$= 0 - j\,\frac{1}{2\pi \times 50 \times 100 \times 10^{-6}}$$

$$Z_C = 0 - j\,31.83\,;\ |Z_C| = (31.83)\ \Omega$$

$$\therefore \quad |Z_L| = |Z_C| = 31.83\ \Omega$$

$$Z_L = R + j\,X_L$$

$$R = Z_L \cos\varphi = 31.83 \times 0.6 = 19.09\ \Omega$$

$$X_L = Z_L \sin\varphi = 31.83 \times 0.8 = 25.46\ \Omega$$

$$X_L = 2\pi f L;\ L = \frac{X_L}{2\pi f} = \frac{25.46}{2\pi \times 50} = 0.0814\text{ H.}$$

5.35 THREE PHASE CIRCUITS

Details about single phase ac circuits was considered. In continuation of it, 3 phase ac circuits are considered in the following sections.

5.35.1 Necessity of Three Phase System

Three phase systems are commonly used for generation, transmission and distribution of electric power. If the consumer has three phase load or consumer requires large amount of power then the three phase supply is supplied. A three phase system is essentially the same as three ordinary single phase systems with 3 voltages of the 3 single phase systems out of phase with each other by 1/3 of cycle (120°) as in Fig. 5.65.

Advantages of Poly Phase Systems

The poly phase system has more advantages over single phase system.

The following are the list of advantages of 3 phase system over single phase system.

1. To supply the same amount of power at the same voltage 3 phase system requires less conductor material than the single phase system, due to less conductor size, transmission losses are less.
2. The 3 phase machine gives higher output over the single phase machine of same frame size. 3 phase motor gives 1.5 times the output of single phase motor.
3. Three phase Induction motors are more efficient than single phase induction motor.
4. Three phase motors are self starting and are more efficient than single phase motors.
5. Three phase motors have uniform torque where as the single phase motors have the pulsating torque.
6. Rotating magnetic field can be set up by passing current through the stationary winding.
7. If neutral point is available, we can supply single phase loads as well along with 3 phase loads.

5.35.2 Generation of Three Phase Voltages

Consider a three phase two pole alternator as shown in Fig. 5.63. The armature is having three coils named as aa', bb', and cc' and their axis is displaced by 120° in space with each other.

When the field winding is excited and rotated it produces a rotating magnetic flux and when this flux was cut by the armature conductor an emf is induced in them according to Faradays laws of Electromagnetic induction. The field structure is so designed that flux is distributed sinusoidally over the poles and the flux linkages also vary sinusoidally with any of the armature winding. Hence the induced emf is sinusoidal and displaced from each phase by 120°.

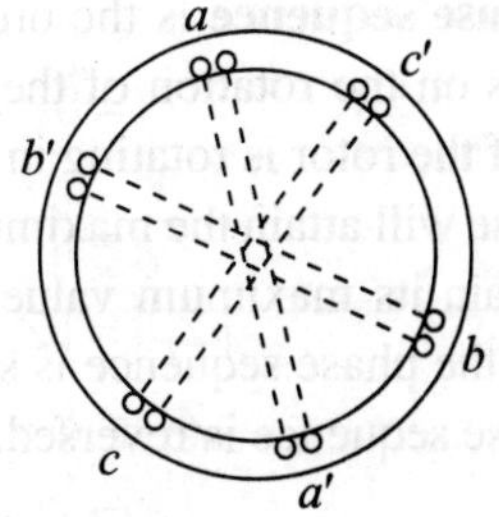

Fig. 5.63 *Three phase two pole alternator*

The three instantaneous voltages induced in the stator windings are

$$e'_{aa} = E_{max} \sin \omega_t$$
$$e'_{bb} = E_{max} \sin (\omega_t - 120°)$$
$$e'_{cc} = E_{max} \sin (\omega_t - 240°)$$

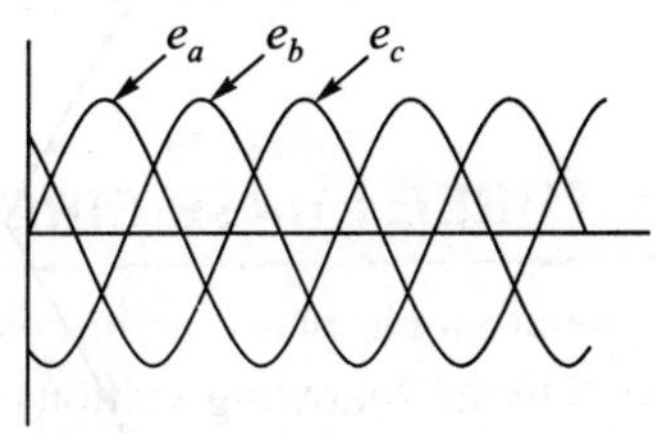

Fig. 5.64 *Three phase voltage waveforms*

These voltages can be represented graphically as shown in Fig. 5.64.

The same voltages can be represented in phasor form as

The sum of three emfs at any instant is equal to zero. (this may easily be seen from the phasor diagram — add E'_{aa} and E'_{bb} and to the resultant add E'_{cc} what is the result).

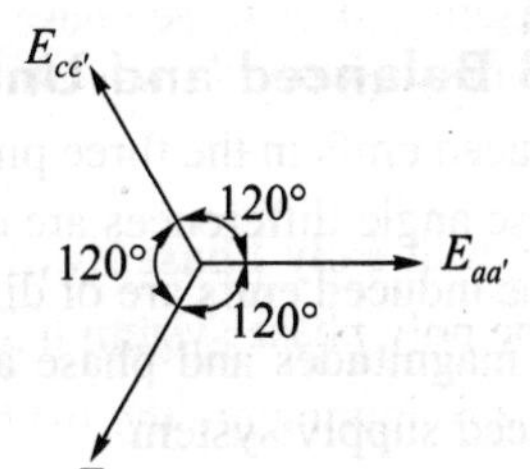

Fig. 5.65 *Phasor diagram of generated voltages*

$$e'_{aa} = E_{max} \sin \omega t$$
$$e'_{bb} = E_{max} \sin (\omega t - 120)$$
$$e'_{cc} = E_{max} \sin (\omega t - 240)$$
$$= E_{max} \sin(\omega t + 120)$$

The resultant emf at any instant is

$$e_r = e'_{aa} + e'_{bb} + e'_{cc'}$$
$$= E_m \sin \omega t + E_m \sin (\omega t - 120) + E_m \sin (\omega t + 120)$$
$$= E_m [\sin \omega t + \sin (\omega t - 120) + \sin (\omega t + 120)]$$
$$= E_m [\sin \omega t + \sin \omega t \cos 120 - \cos \omega t \sin 120 + \sin \omega t \cos 120 + \cos \omega t \sin 120]$$
$$= E_m [\sin \omega t + 2 \sin \omega t \cos 120]$$
$$= E_m \left[\sin \omega t + 2 \sin \omega t \frac{(-1)}{2}\right]$$
$$= E_m [\sin \omega t - \sin \omega t] = 0$$

CHAPTER 5

5.35.2.1 *Phase Sequence*

The **phase sequence** is the order in which the three phases attain their maximum induced voltage. It depends on the rotation of the rotor in the clockwise or in anticlockwise direction. As shown in Fig. (5.63) if the rotor is rotating in the clockwise direction then the sequence is *a*, *b*, *c*. It indicates that first '*a*' phase will attain the maximum value of induced emf and after 120° phase displacement the '*b*' phase will attain its maximum value and after 120° displacement '*c*' phase will attain its maximum value. Hence, the phase sequence is said to be *abc*. If the rotor is rotating in the anticlockwise direction, then the phase sequence is reversed. Meaning thereby the voltages attain their maximum values in the order *acb*.

In any three phase system only two possible sequences either *a b c* or *a c b* and they are termed as positive sequence or negative sequence which have been shown in Fig. 5.66.

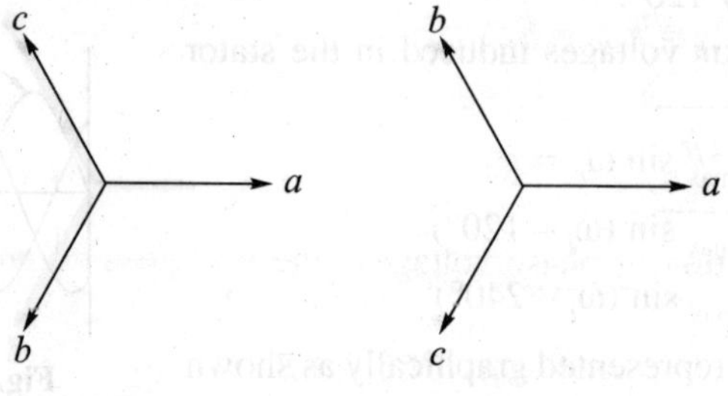

Fig. 5.66 *Different sequences of three phase voltages*

5.35.3 Balanced and Unbalanced Supply

The induced emfs in the three phases of alternator are said to be **balanced** if their magnitudes are equal and phase angle differences are equal to 120° in space. The induced emfs are said to be **unbalanced** if either the induced emfs are of different magnitudes or if the phase angle difference is not equal to 120° or both magnitudes and phase angle differences are different. In such cases the supply is said to be unbalanced supply system.

5.35.3.1 *Types of Three Phases Connection*

The three phases of the stator winding will have three individual phase windings with a start and finish end. If individual load is connected across each phase then it gives an non-inter connected three phase system.

If these three individual phases are interconnected then there will be a saving in copper with a higher power output.

The possible interconnections are:

1. Star or Wye (*Y*) connection
2. Delta or Mesh (Δ) connection.

1. Star or Wye Connection

The similar ends of the three phases (either start or end points) are joined together to form the common point '*N*' which is called **star point** or **neutral point**. Other three ends are connected to the external circuit. The **star connection** with neutral wire, form three phase four wire system where single phase loads can be connected between line and neutral. If neutral wire is not connected then it will become three phase three wire system. The star connection is as shown in Fig. 5.67.

The voltage between the line terminals is called line voltage and the voltage between line and neutral point is called phase voltage.

The line voltages are E_{RY}, E_{YB} and E_{BR}

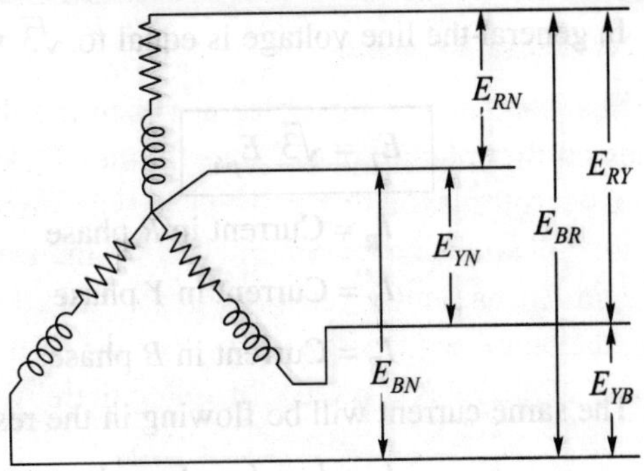

Fig. 5.67 *Star connection of three phases with phase and line voltages marked*

The phase voltages are E_{RN}, E_{YN}, E_{BN}

$$E_{RN} = E_{YN} = E_{BN} = E_{ph}$$

$$E_{RY} = E_{YB} = E_{BR} = E_L$$

$$\boxed{E_L = \sqrt{3}E_{ph}} \quad I_L = I_{ph}$$

The vector representation of phase voltages, line voltages and phase current are shown in the Fig. 5.68.

The line voltage E_{RY} is vectorial sum of E_R and E_Y.

$$E_{RY} = E_{RN} + E_{NY}$$

$$= E_{RN} - E_{YN}$$

$$E_{RY} = OB = OA + AB$$

$$= OA + OA = 2(OA)$$

$$= 2E_{RN} \cos 30 = 2\,E_{RN}\frac{\sqrt{3}}{2}$$

$$E_{RY} = \sqrt{3}\;E_{RN}$$

or $\boxed{E_L = \sqrt{3}\;E_{ph}}$

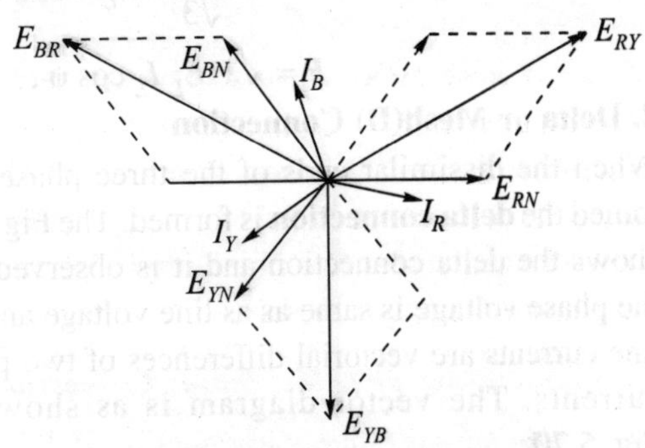

Fig. 5.68 *Phasor representation of three-phase voltages*

Similarly $E_{YB} = E_{YN} + E_{NB}$

$$= E_{YN} - E_{BN}$$

$$E_{YB} = (OC + CD) = (OC + OC)$$

$$= 2(OC) = 2\,E_{YN} \cos 30° = 2E_{YN}\frac{\sqrt{3}}{2} = \sqrt{3}\,E_{YN},$$

$$E_{YB} = \sqrt{3}\;E_{YN} \quad \text{or} \quad \boxed{E_L = \sqrt{3}\;E_{ph}}$$

In general the line voltage is equal to $\sqrt{3}$ times phase voltage-star connection

$$\boxed{E_L = \sqrt{3}\ E_{ph}}$$

I_R = Current in R phase

I_Y = Current in Y phase

I_B = Current in B phase

The same current will be flowing in the respective lines of RYB

$$I_R = I_Y = I_B = I_{Ph} = I_L$$

$$\boxed{I_L = I_{ph}}$$

Power: The phase power is the product of phase voltage multiplied phase current and cosine of angle between voltages and current of that phase.

Phase power = $E_{RN} \times I_R \times \cos$ (angle between E_{RN} and I_R)

$$P_{Ph} = E_{RN} I_R \cos \phi.$$

Total power = 3 times the phase power

$$= 3\ E_{RN}\ I_R \cos \phi = 3\ E_{PH} \times I_{Ph} \cos \phi$$

$$P = 3\ \frac{E_L}{\sqrt{3}} \times I_L \times \cos \phi$$

$$P = \sqrt{3}\ E_L\ I_L \cos \phi\ .$$

2. Delta or Mesh(D) Connection

When the dissimilar ends of the three phases are joined the **delta connection** is formed. The Fig. (30) shows the delta connection and it is observed that the phase voltage is same as as line voltage and the line currents are vectorial differences of two phase currents. The vector diagram is as shown in Fig. 5.70.

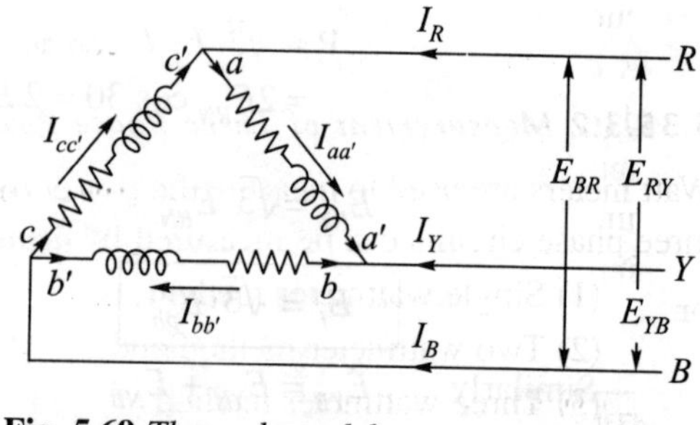

Fig. 5.69 *Three phase delta connected circuit*

Applying KCL at junction R

$$I_R + I_{c'c} = I_{d'a}$$

$$I_R = I_{d'a} - I_{c'c}$$

Similarly
$$I_Y = I_{b'b} - I_{a'a}$$

$$I_B = I_{c'c} - I_{b'b}$$

$$I_R = I_{a'a} - I_{c'c}$$

$I_R = OA + AB$. $\therefore$ A is midpoint of OB

$$= 2(OA) = 2\,I_{a'a} \cos 30 = 2\,I_{a'a}\,\frac{\sqrt{3}}{2}$$

$$= \sqrt{3}\,I_{a'a}$$

If $I_{a'a} = I_{b'b} = I_{c'c} = I_{ph}$

and $I_R = I_Y = I_B = I_L$

$$\boxed{I_L = \sqrt{3}\,I_{ph}}$$

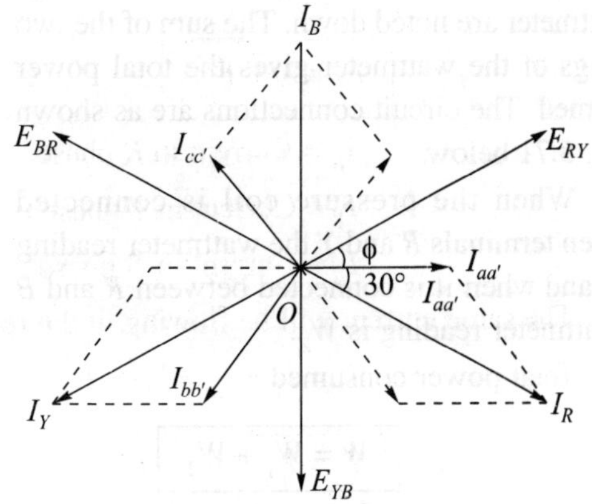

Fig. 5.70 *Phasor representation of three phase voltages*

Regarding voltages, Phase voltage is same as Line voltage;

$$E_{ph} = E_L\ ;\ E'_{aa} = E_{RY}\ ;$$

$$E_{b'b} = E_{YB}\ ;\ E_{c'c} = E_{BR}$$

The phase power is the product of phase voltage multiplied by phase current and cosine of angle between voltage and current.

$$\text{Phase Power} = E_{ph}\,I_{ph} \cos(\text{angle between } E_{ph} \text{ and } I_{ph})$$

$$= E_{ph}\,I_{ph} \cos \phi.$$

$$\text{Total 3 phase power} = 3 \times \text{phase power}$$

$$= 3\,E_{ph}\,I_{ph} \cos \phi$$

$$= 3\,\frac{E_L I_L}{\sqrt{3}} \cos \phi$$

$$P = \sqrt{3}\,E_L\,I_L \cos \phi.$$

5.35.3.2 *Measurement of Three Phase Power*

Watt meters are used to measure the power consumed in the electrical circuits. The power consumed in three phase circuits can be measured by using the following methods:

(1) Single wattmeter method

(2) Two wattmeter method and

(3) Three wattmeter method.

A wattmeter is having two coils: (1) current coil (2) pressure coil. The current coil is always connected in series with the line or load whose current is need for measurement. The current coil will have low Resistance.

The pressure coil is always connected across the terminals or load terminals whose potential difference is need for measurement. The wattmeter shows the reading which is proportional to the product of current through its current coil and potential difference across its pressure coil and cosine of the angle between voltage and current.

W = (Current through current coil) × (Potential difference across the voltage coil) × cos (Angle between V and I)

***(a)* Single wattmeter method:** This method is used to measure the power in balanced three phase circuits only. The current coil is connected in any one of the lines and the pressure coil is connected

CHAPTER 5

between two lines alternately and two readings of wattmeter are noted down. The sum of the two readings of the wattmeter gives the total power consumed. The circuit connections are as shown in Fig. 5.71 below.

When the pressure coil is connected between terminals R and Y the wattmeter reading is W_1 and when it is connected between R and B the wattmeter reading is W_Z.

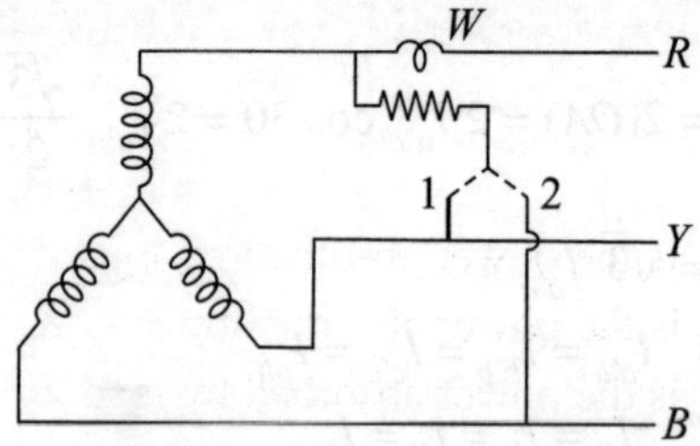

Fig 5.71 *Circuit diagram for measurement of three phase power using single wattmeter*

Total power consumed

$$\boxed{W = W_1 + W_2}$$

***(b)* Two wattmeter method:** The connection diagram of two watt meters across a three phase unbalanced load is as shown in Fig. 5.72. The current coils are connected in the two lines of the three phase circuit. The pressure coils of each are connected in between the respective line and third line.

The wattmeter W_1 connected in line R carries the current I_R and pressure coil is connected across R and B lines measures V_{RB}.

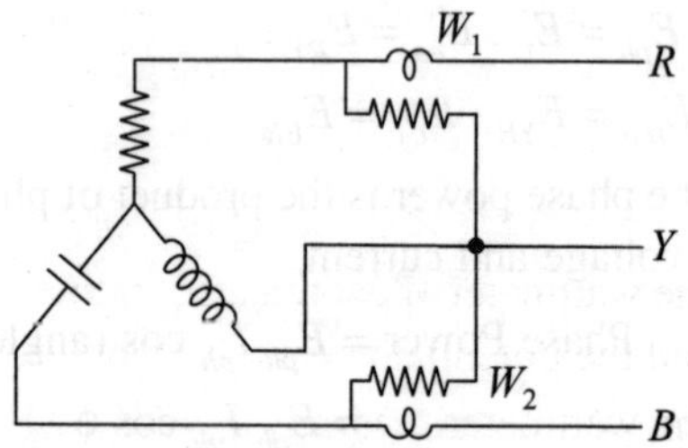

Fig. 5.72 *Connection diagram of two watt meters for a star connected load*

$$V_{RB} = V_{RN} + V_{NB}$$
$$= (V_{RN} - V_{BN})$$

Instantaneous power read by

$$W_1 = (V_{RN} - V_{BN})\, I_R$$

In wattmeter W_2, current coil carries a current of I_Y and pressure coil is connected across Y and B lines (V_{BY})

$$V_{YB} = V_{YN} + V_{NB}$$
$$= (V_{YN} - V_{NB})$$

The instantaneous power read by

$$W_2 = (V_{YN} - V_{BN})\, I_Y$$

Total power consumed by the load

$$= W_1 + W_2$$
$$= (V_{RN} - V_{BN})\, I_R + (V_{YN} - V_{BN})\, I_Y$$
$$= V_{RN}\, I_R - V_{BN}\, I_R + V_{YN}\, I_Y - V_{BN}\, I_Y$$
$$= V_{RN}\, I_R + V_{YN}\, I_Y - V_{BN}\,(I_R + I_Y)$$

∴ In a three phase circuit the sum of phase currents meeting at the neutral is equal to zero.

$$I_R + I_Y + I_B = 0$$
$$(I_R + I_Y) = -I_B$$

$\therefore \quad = V_{RN} I_R + V_{YN} I_Y - V_{BN}(-I_B)$

$= (V_{RN} I_R + V_{YN} I_Y + V_{BN} I_B)$

$= P_1 + P_2 + P_3$

Where P_1 is the power absorbed by load Z_1

P_2 is the power absorbed by load Z_2

P_3 is the power absorbed by load Z_3

$\therefore \quad W_1 + W_2 =$ Total power absorbed.

If the load is delta connected then the circuit diagram for measuring power is as shown in Fig. 5.73 below.

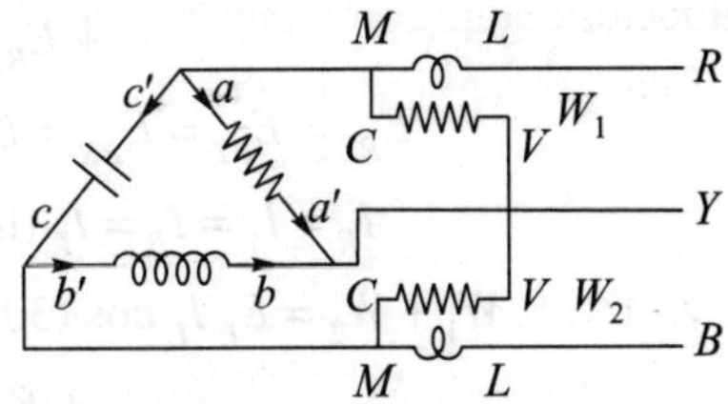

Fig. 5.73 *Connection diagram of two watt meters for a delta connected load.*

$$I_R + I_{BB'} = I_{RR'}$$

$$I_R = (I_{RR'} - I_{BB'})$$

$$I_B + I_{YY'} = I_{BB'}$$

$$I_B = I_{BB'} - I_{YY'}$$

The wattmeter W_1 connected in line R carries I_R current and the potential across the pressure coil is $V_{RY'}$.

The wattmeter reading $W_1 = V_{RY} I_R = V_{RY}(I_{RR'} - I_{BB'})$

Similarly the wattmeter W_2 is connected in line B carries I_B current and the potential across the pressure coil is V_{BY}

$$W_2 = V_{BY}(I_B) = V_{BY}(I_{BB'} - I_{YY'})$$

The total power $\quad W = W_1 + W_2 = V_{RY}(I_{RR'} - I_{BB}) + V_{BY}(I_{BB'} - I_{YY'})$

$$= V_{RY} I_{RR'} - V_{RY} I_{BB'} + V_{BY} I_{YY'} - V_{BY} I_{BB'}$$

$$= V_{RY} I_{RR'} - V_{BY} I_{YY'} - I_{BB'}(V_{RY} - V_{BY})$$

$$= V_{RY} I_{RR'} + V_{BY} I_{YY'} - I_{BB'}(V_{RY} + V_{BY})$$

$\therefore$ The sum of the three phase voltage is equal to zero

$$V_{RY} + V_{YB} + V_{BR} = 0$$

$$V_{RY'} + V_{YB} = -V_{BR}$$

$\therefore \quad W_1 + W_2 = V_{RY} I_{RR'} + V_{BY} I_{YY'} - I_{BB'}(-V_{BR})$

$$\boxed{W_1 + W_2 = V_{RY} I_{RR'} + V_{YB} I_{YY'} + V_{BR} I_{BB'}}$$

$$P_1 = V_{RY} I_{RR'},\ P_2 = V_{YB} I_{YY'},\ P_3 = V_{BR} I_{BB'}$$

(c) If the load is balanced and connected in star: The load impedance in each phase of the three phase system will be same. Let E_R E_Y and E_B represent the phase voltages in RMS value. The current I_R, I_Y and I_B represent the rms value of line current. The current lags behind the phase voltage if the load is assumed to be inductive.

CHAPTER 5

As per the phasor diagram (Fig. 5.74) the potential E_{RB} is

$$E_{RY} = E_{RN} - E_{YN}$$

$$E_{BY} = E_{BN} - E_{YN}$$

$$W_1 = E_{RY} I_R \,.\, \cos (30° + \phi)$$

$$W_2 = E_{BY} I_B \cos (30° - \phi)$$

$$W_1 + W_2 = E_{RY} I_R \cos (30 + \cos \phi)$$

$$+ E_{BY} I_B \cos (30 - \phi)$$

$$E_{RY} = E_{BY} = E_{BR} = E_L \text{ (line voltage)}$$

$$I_R = I_Y = I_B = I_L \text{ (line current)}$$

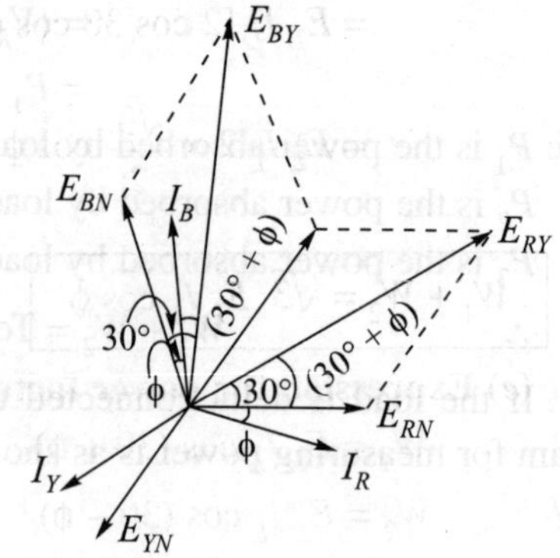

Fig. 5.74 *Phasor diagram of three phase voltage and current*

$$\therefore \quad W_1 + W_2 = E_L I_L \cos (30° + \phi)$$

$$+ E_L I_L \cos (30° - \phi)$$

$$= E_L I_L [\cos (30° + \phi) + \cos (30° - \phi)]$$

$$= E_L I_L [\cos 30° + \cos \phi - \sin 30° \sin \phi + \cos 30° \cos \phi + \sin 30° \sin \phi]$$

$$= E_L I_L (2 \cos 30° \cos \phi)$$

$$= E_L I_L \times 2 \times \frac{\sqrt{3}}{2} \cos \phi = \sqrt{3}\, E_L I_L \cos \phi \,.$$

$$\therefore \quad W_1 + W_2 = \text{Total power} = \sqrt{3}\; E_L I_L \cos \phi$$

(*d*) **If the load is delta connected:** The two watt meters are connected in *R* and *B* lines. The voltage E_{RY} and E_{BY} gives the potentials across potential coils. Phasor diagram is shown in Fig. 5.75 (*a*)

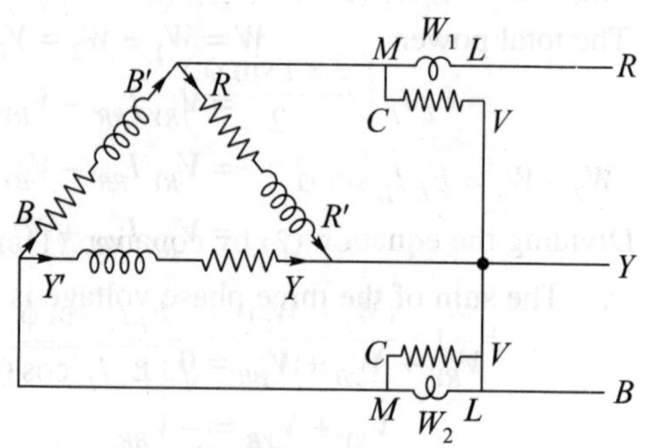

Fig 5.75 *Circuit diagram of two watt meters for a delta connected balanced load*

The wattmeter W_1 reading is $= W_1 = E_{RY} I_R \cos$ (Angle between E_{RY} and I_R)

$$W_1 = E_{RY} I_R \,.\, \cos$$

$$\text{(Angle between } E_{RY} \text{ and } I_R)$$

$$W_1 = E_{RY} I_R \cos (30 + \phi)$$

$$I_R = I_{RR'} = I_{BB'}$$

$$W_2 = E_{BY} I_B \cos \text{ (Angle between } E_{BY} \text{ and } I_B)$$

$$W_2 = E_{BY} I_B \cos (30 - \phi)$$

$$I_Y = I_{YY'} - I_{RR'}$$

$$\therefore \quad W_1 = E_{RY} I_R \cos (30 + \phi) = E_L I_L \cos (30 + \phi)$$

$$W_2 = E_{BY} I_B \cos (30 - \phi) = E_L I_L \cos (30 - \phi)$$

$$W_1 + W_2 = E_L I_L[\cos(30+\phi) + \cos(30-\phi)]$$
$$= E_L I_L [2\cos 30 \cos\phi]$$
$$= E_L I_L 2 \times \frac{\sqrt{3}}{2} \cos\phi$$
$$\boxed{W_1 + W_2 = \sqrt{3}\, E_L I_L \cos\phi}$$

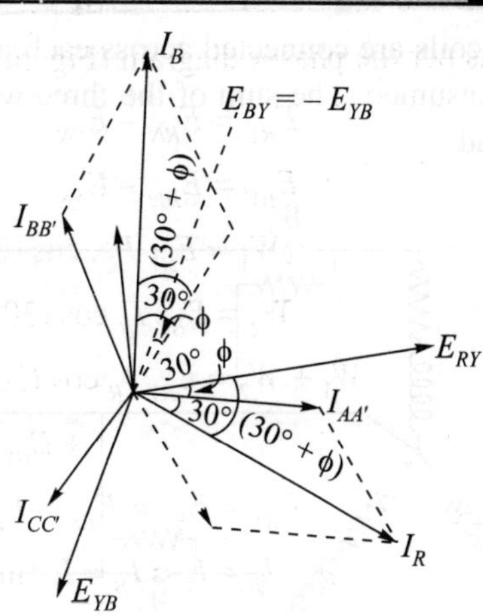

Fig. 5.75 *(a) Phasor diagram of 3 phase voltage and current*

(e) Expression for power factor

$$W_1 = E_L I_L \cos(30+\phi)$$
$$W_2 = E_L I_L \cos(30-\phi)$$
$$W_1 + W_2 = E_L I_L [\cos(30+\phi) + \cos(30-\phi)]$$
$$= E_L I_L [2\cos 30\cos\phi]$$
$$= E_L I_L 2\times\frac{\sqrt{3}}{2}\cos\phi$$
$$= \sqrt{3} E_L I_L \cos\phi \qquad \text{...(1)}$$
$$W_2 - W_1 = E_L I_L \cos(30-\phi) - V_L I_L \cos(30+\phi)$$
$$= E_L I_L [\cos(30-\phi) - \cos(30+\phi)]$$
$$= E_L I_L [\cos 30\cos\phi + \sin 30\sin\phi - \cos 30\cos\phi + \sin 30\sin\phi]$$
$$W_2 - W_1 = E_L I_L (2\sin 30\sin\phi)$$
$$= E_L I_L \left(\frac{2\times 1\sin\phi}{2}\right)$$
$$W_2 - W_1 = E_L I_L \sin\phi \qquad \text{...(2)}$$

Dividing the equation (2) by equation (1)

$$2 \div 1;\ \frac{(W_2 - W_1)}{W_1 + W_2} = \frac{E_L I_L \sin\phi}{\sqrt{3} E_L I_L \cos\phi} = \frac{\tan\phi}{\sqrt{3}}$$

$$\tan\phi = \frac{\sqrt{(W_2 - W_1)}}{(W_1 + W_2)} \qquad \phi = \tan^{-1}\left[\frac{\sqrt{(W_2 - W_1)}}{(W_1 + W_2)}\right]$$

$$\phi = \tan^{-1}\left[\frac{\sqrt{(W_2 - W_1)}}{(W_1 + W_2)}\right] \quad \therefore \quad \cos\phi = \cos\left[\tan^{-1}\frac{\sqrt{(W_2 - W_1)}}{(W_1 + W_2)}\right]$$

***(f)* Measurement of three phase power using three wattmeters:** This method of power measurement is used to measure the three phase power of any type of loads within balanced or unbalanced. The current coils of the watt meters are connected in series in respective line and the pressure coils are connected across the line and neutral if the load is star connected. If the load is delta connected the pressure coils are connected across each phase. So that each wattmeter measures the individual phase power consumed. The sum of the three watt meter readings gives the total power consumed by the 3 phase load.

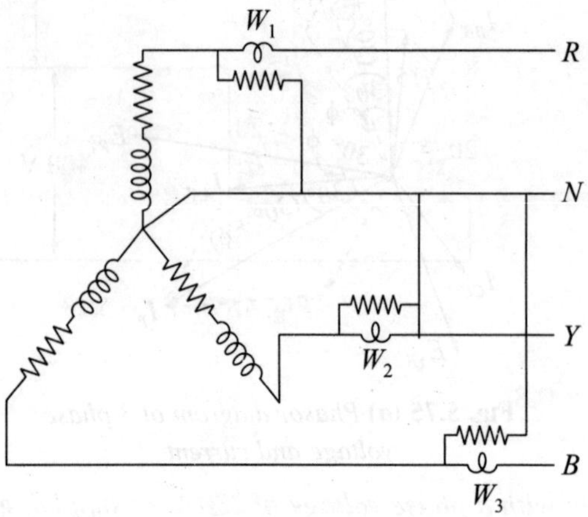

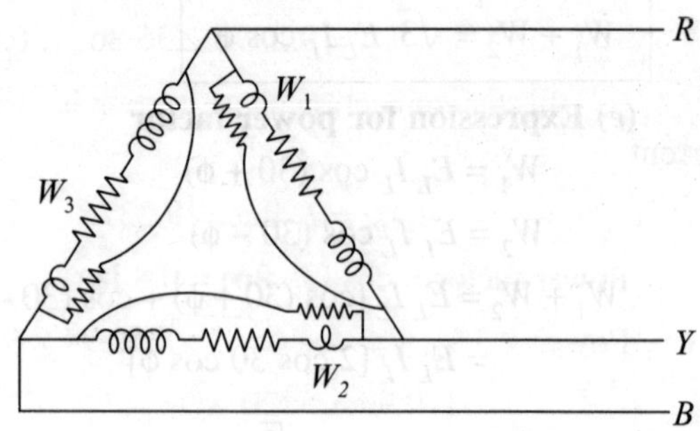

Total power consumed by the load = $W_1 + W_2 + W_3$

Example 5.12. *Determine the line currents in an unbalanced star connected load supplied from a symmetrical 3 phase 440 V system. The branch impedances of the load are* $Z_R = 5 \angle 30\ \Omega$,

Solution. $Z_Y = 10\angle 45°$, $Z_B = 10\angle 60\ \Omega$. The phase sequence is R_{YB}.

Figure 5.76 shows the arrangement of star connected load connected to the supply of 440V.

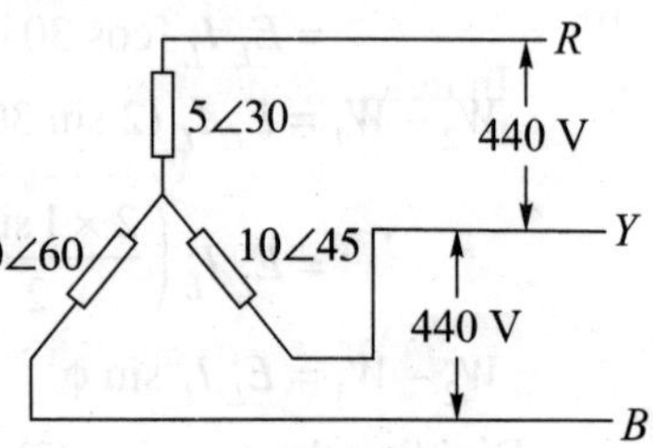

Fig. 5.76 *for Ex. 5.12*

$$\text{The phase voltage} = \frac{440}{\sqrt{3}} = 254.03 \text{ V}$$

$$I_R = \frac{E_{RN}}{Z_R} = \frac{254.03 \angle 0}{5 \angle 30}$$

$$= 50.806 \angle -30$$

$$I_Y = \frac{E_{YN}}{Z_Y} = \frac{254.03 \angle -120°}{10 \angle 45} = 25.4\angle -165°$$

$$I_B = \frac{E_{BN}}{Z_B} = \frac{254.03 \angle +120}{10 \angle 60} = 25.4\angle +60°.$$

Example 5.13. *Three equal impedances each having a resistance of 20 ohms and reactance of 15 ohms are connected in star to a 400V, 3 phase, 50 Hz system. Calculated (1) Line current (2) Power factor (3) Power consumed.*

Solution. Figure 5.77 shows the arrangement of star connected load connected to the supply of 400 V.

$$V_L = 400 \text{ V}$$

$$V_{Ph} = \frac{400\text{ V}}{\sqrt{3}} = 230.94 \text{ Volts/ph}$$

$$Z = 20 + j\,15 = 25\angle 36.86$$

$$(I_1)_{Ph} = V_{Ph}/Z = \frac{230.94\angle 0}{25\angle 36.86}$$

$$= 9.2376\angle 36.86 - 36.86°$$

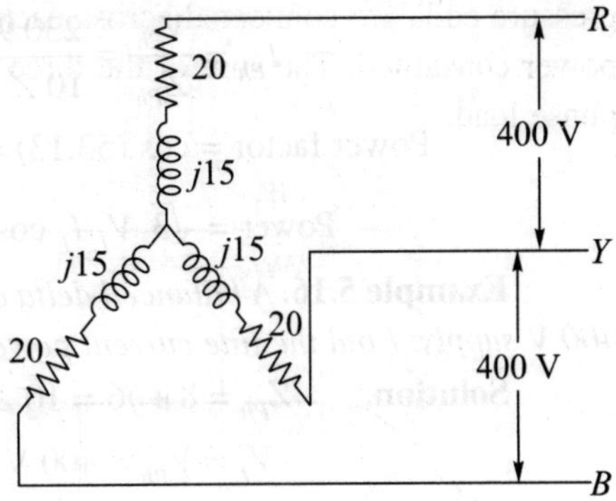

Fig. 5.77 *for Ex. 5.13*

$\therefore$ In star connection phase current is same as line current

$$(I_1)_{Ph} = I_1 \text{ line} = 9.2376$$

Power factor = cos (36.86) = 0.8 lag

$$\text{Power} = 3\,V_{Ph}\,I_{Ph}\cos\phi = 3 \times 230.94 \times 9.2376 \times 0.8$$

$$= 5119.99 = 5120 \text{ watts.}$$

Example 5.14. *A 3 phase star connected supply with a phase voltage of 230 V, is supplying a balanced Δ load. The load is drawing 15 kW at 0.8 pf lagging. Find the line current and the current in each phase of the load. What is load impedance per phase ?*

Figure 5.78 shows the arrangement of star connected load connected to the supply of phase voltage 230V.

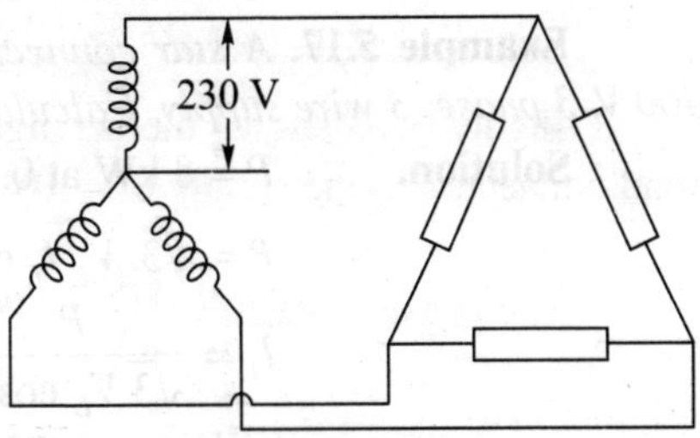

Fig. 5.78 *for Ex. 5.14*

$$V_{Ph} = 230 : V_L = \sqrt{3}\,V_{Ph} = 400 \text{ V}$$

In delta connection

$$V_L = V_{Ph} = 400 \text{ V}$$

Load Power = 15 kW at 0.8 pf lag.

$$\sqrt{3}\;V_L I_L \cos\varphi = 15 \times 10^3$$

$$I_L = \frac{15 \times 10^3}{\sqrt{3} \times 400 \times 0.8} = 27.06$$

$$I_{Ph} = I_L/\sqrt{3} = \frac{27.06}{\sqrt{3}} = 15.625 \text{ Amps}$$

$$Z_{Ph} \text{ phase} = \frac{V_{Ph}}{I_{Ph}} = \frac{400}{15.625} = 25.6\ \Omega$$

Example 5.15. *A balanced star connected load of (6 + j8) ohms is connected to a 3 phase 400 V supply. Find the line current, power and power factor.*

Solution. $Z_{Ph} = (6 + j8) = 10\angle 53.13°$

$$V_L = 400$$

$$V_{Ph} = 400/\sqrt{3} = 230.94$$

$$I_{Ph} = \frac{V_{Ph}}{Z_{Ph}} = \frac{230.94400}{10 \angle 53.13} = 23.09 \angle -53.13$$

Power factor = cos (53.13) = 0.6 lag

$$\text{Power} = \sqrt{3}\, V_L I_L \cos\phi = \sqrt{3} \times 400 \times 23.09 \times 0.6 = 9598.35 \text{ watts.}$$

Example 5.16. *A balanced delta connected load of (8 + j6)Ω per phase is connected to a 3 phase 400 V supply. Find the line current power and power factor.*

Solution. $Z_{Ph} = 8 + j6 = 10 \angle 36.86$

$$V_L = V_{Ph} = 400 \text{ V}$$

$$I_{Ph} = \frac{V_{Ph}}{Z_{Ph}} = \frac{400}{10 \angle 36.86} = 40 \angle -36.86 \text{ Amps}$$

$$\therefore \quad I_L = \sqrt{3}\, I_{Ph} = \sqrt{3} \times 40 = 69.28 \text{ Amps}$$

Power factor = cos φ = cos (36.86) = 0.8

$$\text{Power} = \sqrt{3}\, V_L I_L \cos\phi$$

$$= \sqrt{3} \times 400 \times 69.28 \times 0.8$$

$$= 38400 \text{ watts} = 38.4 \text{ kW.}$$

Example 5.17. *A star connected Inductive load takes 8 kW at 0.8 pf lag when connected to 460 V, 3 phase, 3 wire supply. Calculate the readings of two wattmeters used to measure the power.*

Solution. $P = 8$ kW at 0.8 pf lag

$$P = \sqrt{3}\, V_L I_L \cos\phi$$

$$I_L = \frac{P}{\sqrt{3}\, V_L \cos\phi} = \frac{8 \text{ kW}}{\sqrt{3} \times 460 \times 0.8} \text{ Amps}$$

$$= \frac{8000}{\sqrt{3} \times 460 \times 0.8} = 12.55 \text{ Amps}$$

$$\cos\phi = 0.8. \quad \therefore \quad \phi = \cos^{-1} 0.8 = 36.86$$

The wattmeter reading are

$$W_1 = V_L I_L \cos(30 + \phi)$$

$$= 460 \times 12.55 \times \cos(30+36.86)$$

$$= 2268.66 \text{ watts}$$

$$W_2 = V_L I_L \cos(30 - \phi)$$

$$= 460 \times 12.55 \times \cos 30 - 36.86$$

$$= 5731.67 \text{ watts.}$$

Example 5.18. *A balanced 3 phase star connected load draws power from a 440V, 3 phase supply. Two wattmeters connected to indicate W_1 = 4.2 kW W_2 = – 0.8 kW. Calculate the power and power factor.*

Solution. $W_1 = 4.2$ kW $\quad W_2 = -0.8$ kW

Total power $P = W_1 + W_2 = 4.2 + (-0.8) = 4.2 - 0.8 = 3.4$ kW

Power factor [(*pf*) – cos ϕ = cos $\tan^{-1}\left(\sqrt{3}\,\dfrac{(W_1 - W_2)}{(W_1 + W_2)}\right)$

$$\tan\phi = \sqrt{3}\,\frac{(W_1 - W_2)}{(W_1 + W_2)} = \sqrt{3}\,\frac{(4.2 - 0.8)}{4.2 + (-8)} = \sqrt{2}\,\frac{(4.2 - 0.8)}{4.2 - (0.8)}$$

$$\tan\phi = \frac{\sqrt{3}\times 5}{3.4} = 2.547$$

$$\phi = \tan^{-1}(2.547) = 68.565$$

$$\text{pf} = \cos\phi = \cos(68.565) = 0.3654.$$

Example 5.19. *Power is measured in a 3 phase balanced load using three wattmeters. The line voltage is 400 V. The load and its pf is so adjusted that the line current is 10 Amps. Find the readings of the wattmeters when the pf is (1) Unity (2) 0.866 (3) 0.5 (4) zero.*

Solution. $W_1 = V_L\,I_L\cos(30 + \phi)$

$$W_2 = V_L\,I_L\cos(30 - \phi)$$

If pf is unity,

$$\cos\phi = 1,\ \phi = \cos^{-1}(1) = 0°$$

$$W_1 = 400 \times 10 \times \cos(30) = 34364.1\text{ W}$$

$$W_2 = 400 \times 10 \times \cos(30) = 34364.1\text{ W}$$

If pf is 0.866

$$\cos\phi = 0.866,\ \phi = \cos^{-1}(0.866) = 30°$$

$$W_1 = 400 \times 10 \times \cos(30° + 30°) = 2000$$

$$W_2 = 400 \times 10\cos(30° - 30°) = 4000$$

If pf is 0.5 $\cos\phi = 0.5;\ \phi = \cos^{-1}0.5 = 60°$

$$W_1 = 400 \times 10 \times \cos(30° + 60°) = 0$$

$$W_2 = 400 \times 10 \times \cos(30° - 60°) = 3464$$

If pf is 0 $\cos\phi = 0;\ \phi = \cos^{-1}(0) = 90°$

$$W_1 = 400 \times 10 \times \cos(30° + 90°) = -2000\text{ W}$$

$$W_2 = 400 \times 10 \times \cos(30° - 90°) = 2000\text{ W}.$$

Example 5.20. *A 3 phase, 440 V motor has a power factor of 0.8. Two wattmeters are used to measure the power input 35 kW. Find the readings of the wattmeters.*

Solution. $V = 440$ V ; $\cos\phi = 0.8$; $W = 35$ kW

The current drawn by the load = $I = \dfrac{W}{\sqrt{3}\,V\cos\phi}$

$$I = \frac{35\times 10^3}{\sqrt{3}\times 440\times 0.8} = 57.41\text{ Amps}$$

$$\cos\phi = 0.8,\ \phi = \cos^{-1}0.8 = 36.86°$$

CHAPTER 5

First wattmeter readings

$$W_1 = V.I \cos (30 + \phi)$$
$$= 440 \times 57.41 \times \cos (30 + 36.86)$$
$$= \underline{35079.56} \text{ watts}$$

Second wattmeter of reading of

$$W_2 = V . I \cos (30 - \phi)$$
$$= 440 \times 57.41 \times \cos (30 - 36.86)$$
$$= 9926.3 \text{ Watts.}$$

Example 5.21. *Three coils each of impedance 25∠– 60° ohms are connected in delta across a 400 V, 3 phase 50 Hz supply. Find*

1. *The current in each phase*
2. *The line current*
3. *Total Power consumed*
4. *Power read by each wattmeter.*

Solution.

$$Z_{PH} = 25\angle -60°$$
$$E_L = E_{PH} = 400\angle 0. \quad \therefore \quad \text{delta connected.}$$

$$I \text{ phase} = I'_{aa} = ° \frac{E'_{aa}}{Z'_{aa}} = \frac{400 \angle 0}{25\angle -60} \; 16\angle\underline{60°} \text{ Amps}$$

$$I'_{bb} = \frac{E'_{bb}}{Z'_{bb}} = \frac{400 \angle -120}{25\angle -60} \; 16\angle\underline{-60°} \text{ Amps}$$

$$I'_{cc} = \frac{E'_{cc}}{Z'_{cc}} = \frac{400 \angle +120}{25\angle -60} \; 16\angle\underline{180°} \text{ Amps}$$

$$I \text{ line} = \sqrt{3}\; I_{PH} = \sqrt{3} \times 16 = 27.712 \text{ Amps}$$

$$\text{Power consumed} = \sqrt{3}\; V_L I_L \cos \phi$$
$$= \sqrt{3} \times 400 \times 27.712 \times \cos (60)$$
$$= 9600 \text{ watts}$$

First wattmeter readings

$$W_1 = V_L R_L \cos (30 + \phi)$$
$$= 400 \times 27.712 \times \cos (30 + 60)$$
$$= 0 \text{ watts}$$

Second wattmeter of reading of

$$W_2 = V_L R_L \cos (30 - \varphi)$$
$$= 400 \times 27.712 \times \cos (30 - 60)$$
$$= 9600 \text{ Watts.}$$

PROBLEMS

1. For each of the following time functions, find f, T, ω the RMS, average and peak values. Also sketch one complete cycle of each time function.
   (i) $v_1(t) = 300 \sin (200t + 50°)$
   (ii) $i_1(t) = 10 \sin (377t - 10°)$
   (iii) $v_2(t) = 100\sqrt{2} \sin (10^6 t + 200°)$
   (iv) $i_2(t) = -20 \cos (2t + 60°)$
2. Find the RMS and average value of the time function
   $$v(t) = 50 \sin (10^4 t + 120°) + 10.$$
3. Does your answer to problem 2 depend on ω?
4. Draw the rotating phasors corresponding to the time functions of problem 1.
5. Express each of the phasors in problem 4 in both polar and rectangular form. Can all these phasors be drawn on the same phasor diagram? If not, why not?
6. Given that all the time functions in problem 1 have the same time period of 10ms, write down the time functions. By how many degrees v_1 lead i_1? v_2 lead i_2?
7. In problem 6 find the instantaneous values of v_1 and i_1 when v_2 goes through a zero through a zero with a positive slope and when i_2 goes through a negative maximum.
8. Express the phasors $V_1 = 10\angle 20$ $V_2 = 20\angle 300$
   $V_3 = \frac{10}{\sqrt{2}}\angle -200$ as time functions given that ω = 400 rad/s. Write down each time function as a sine as well as a consine time function.
9. In problems 8 find $V_1 + V_2$ and $V_2 - V_3$. Express your answer in the form of sinusoidal time functions.
10. Given $\omega = 10^4$ rad/s, $L = 20$ μH, $C = 10$ nF, $R = 500\Omega$ find X_L, X_C, Z_L and Z_C. Find also the impedance of the series and parallel combinations of L and C.
11. If $Z_1 = 3 - 4j$, $Z_2 = 8 + 6j$, $Z_3 = 10 - 5j$, find Y_1, Y_2, Y_3, G_{11}, G_2, G_3, B_1, B_2, B_3. Find Z_{eq} when Z_1, Z_2, and Z_3 are connected in series. Also find Y_{eq}, B_{eq} and G_{eq}. Is Y_{eq} inductive or capacitive?
12. Repeat problem 11 with the three impedances connected in parallel.
13. If the impedances Z_1, Z_2, and Z_3 of problem 11 are connected in star formation find the impedances of the delta connected equivalent.
14. In the circuits of Fig. P14.1 and P14.2 find all branch current using any method.

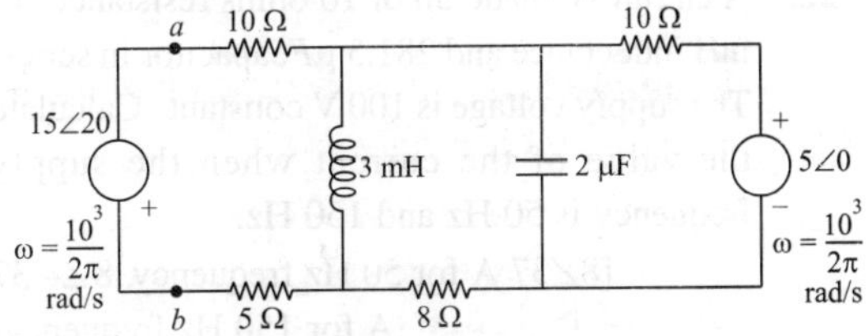

Fig. P.14.1

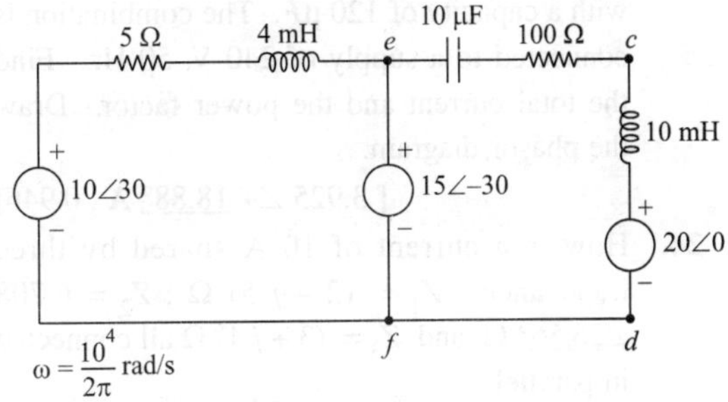

Fig. P.14.2

15. For the circuit of Fig. P14.1 find the power dissipated in the 8Ω resistor.
16. In Fig. P14.2 find a voltage source which should replace the 15∠–30 source so that no current flows through branch ef.
17. Given $C = 5$ μF design series and parallel resonant circuits with $f_R = 5$ kHz and a bandwidth of 100 Hz. What are the impedance magnitudes of the two resonant circuits at a frequency 5 kHz ± 100 Hz.
18. For the circuit of Fig. P14.1, find the input impedance of the circuit to the right of the terminals ab.
19. Break the circuit of Fig. P14.2 at terminals cd and find the output impedance of the circuit to the left of cd.

20. Design a *RL* filter with a cut off frequency of 2kHz. Chose $R = 5\text{k}\Omega$.

21. In a series of $R = 5\ \Omega$ and $L = 0.06$ H circuit the voltage across the inductance is $V_L = 15 \sin 200\, t$ volts. Find the total voltage, the current, the angle by which *I* lags V_T and the magnitude of impedance.

[16.25 ∠157.38 V, 1.25 ∠– 90 A, *i* lags $(V_T)m$ is 157.38]

22. A circuit is made up of 10 ohms resistance, 12 mH inductance and 281.5 μF capacitor in series. The supply voltage is 100 V constant. Calculate the value of the current when the supply frequency is 50 Hz and 150 Hz.

[8∠37 A for 50 Hz frequency, 8∠– 37 A for 150 Hz frequency]

23. A Choke coil of inductance 0.08 H and a resistance of 12 ohms, is connected in parallel with a capacity of 120 μ*F*. The combination is connected to a supply of 240 V, 50 Hz. Find the total current and the power factor. Draw the phasor diagram.

[3.925 ∠+ 18.88° A , 0.946]

24. How is a current of 10 A shared by three impedances $Z_1 = (2 - j\,5)\ \Omega$; $Z_2 = 6.708 \angle 26.56°\ \Omega$ and $Z_3 = (3 + j\,4)\ \Omega$ all connected in parallel.

[5.687∠77.868 A, 4.563 ∠– 16.89 A, 6.1256∠– 43.46 A]

25. For the two branch parallel circuit shown in Fig. 5.12. Compute the current in each branch and the total current.

[8.94 ∠– 63.43 A, 9.43 ∠45 A, 10.75∠– 7.117 A]

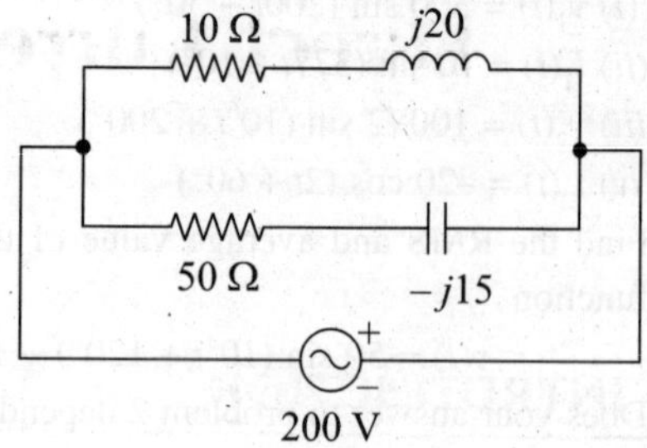

Fig. P.25

26. Two circuits, the impedances of which are given by $Z_1 = (10 + j\,15)\ \Omega$, and $Z_2 = (6 - j\,8)$ ohms are connected in parallel. If the total current supplied is 15 A, what is the power taken by each branch.

[8.575 ∠– 76.828°A, 15.479∠32.902°A, 735.3 watts, 1437.6 watts]

27. A resistance of 10 ohms and inductive reactance of 8 ohms and capacitive reactance of 15 ohms are connected in parallel across 120 V, 50 Hz main. Determine (1) the total current (2) power factor of the circuit and (3) the power.

[12∠– 0°A, 15∠– 90°A and 13.89∠– 30.25°]

6 CHAPTER

Direct Current Machines

6.1 INTRODUCTION

A coil with current passing through it exhibits the same magnetic behaviour as a bar magnet, thus electric current produces magnetic effect. By utilizing the magnetic properties of ferromagnetic materials, the pattern of the magnetic flux can be suitably guided by special shaping of the iron core. Due to this reason, the essential magnetic components of electric machines are made of iron. The space in which magnetic flux exists is the *Magnetic Circuit*.

The various stages of the magnetic flux are shown in Fig. 6.1. Certain portion of the flux, *leakage flux* is lost and does not contribute to the intended effect.

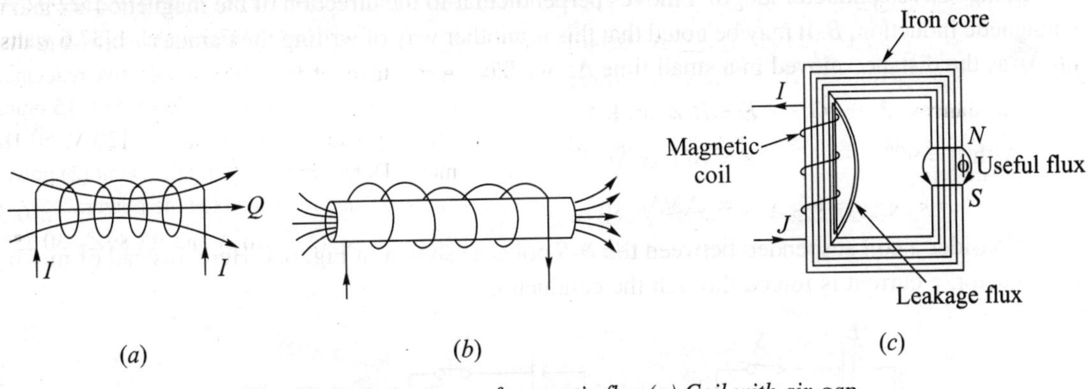

Fig. 6.1 *Various stages of magnetic flux (a) Coil with air-gap (b) Coil with iron core (c) Guided magnetic flux*

The reversal of this process was thought of by Michael Faraday. Under certain conditions, a magnetic field can produce electric current. The basis of conversion of mechanical energy into electrical energy is precisely this—whether it is the small bicycle dynamo or the large power stations. These laws were enunciated by Michael Faraday during 1831 and are known as *Laws of Induction*. The following experiment describes the basics of the law.

A coil as shown in Fig. 6.2, is moved from position *A* through *C*. Voltmeter shows a deflection. This is due to the coil cutting the magnetic field. This induced voltage is generally termed, *electromotive force* (EMF, E). This makes a current, *I* to flow through the coil, which in turn produces a flux affecting the original magnetic flux ϕ as indicated in Fig. 6.3.

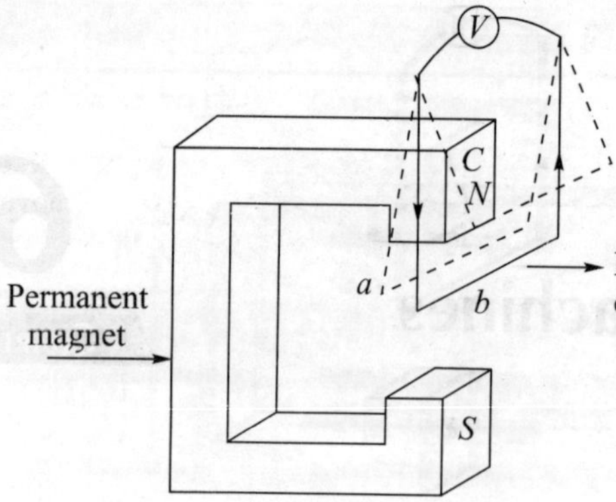

Fig. 6.2 *Basics of the law of induction*

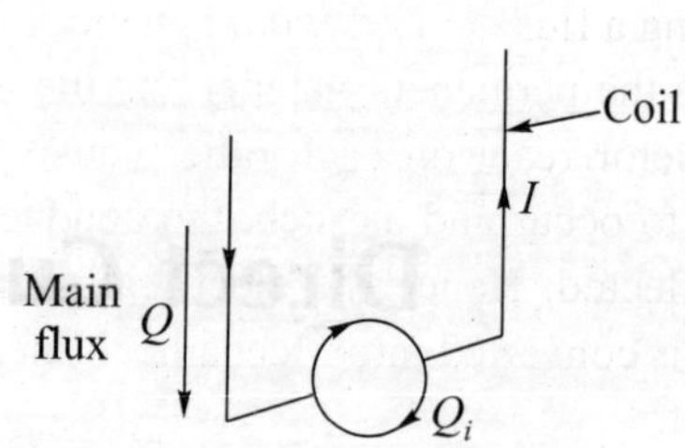

Fig. 6.3 *Induced flux affecting the flux causing it*

The amount of flux cut by the conductor, $\Delta\phi$ in a small time, Δt depends on the velocity, v with which the conductor moves perpendicular to the flux. Thus,

Rate of change of flux $= \Delta\phi/\Delta t$

Induced emf, $E = (-N)\ \Delta\phi\ \Delta t$ ...(6.1)

The negative sign is due to Lenz law, which states that, *E always has a direction such that the flux* ϕ_i *opposes the flux cutting process.*

Further investigations showed that the induced voltage is directly proportional to the velocity, v at which the active conductor length, l moves perpendicular to the direction of the magnetic flux and to the magnetic induction, B. It may be noted that this is another way of writing the Faraday's law, and thus with Δx as the distance moved in a small time Δt, we have

$$E = Bl\ v \sin\theta \qquad ...(6.2)$$

With $\theta = 90°$, $E = Bl\ (\Delta x/\Delta t)$

$$= \Delta\phi/\Delta t \qquad ...(6.3)$$

Consider a coil suspended between the N-S poles as shown in Fig. 6.4. Here, instead of moving the conductor, a current is forced through the conductor.

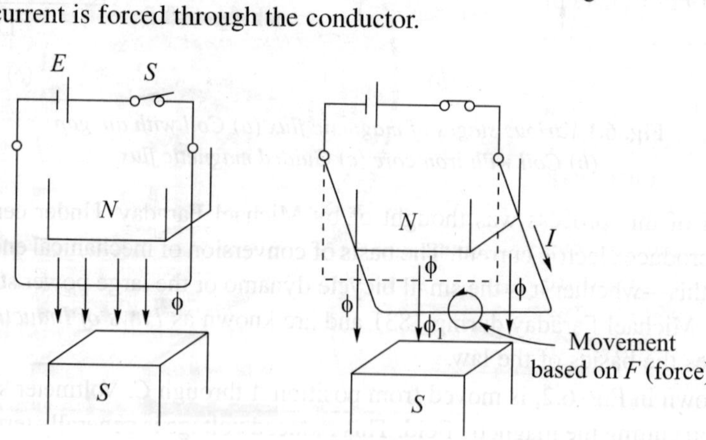

Fig. 6.4 *Force due to flow of current*

Once the switch, S is closed, current flows through the conductor thereby creating a flux ϕ_i. The two magnetic fields due to the permanent magnet and the live conductor react on each other causing a force to occur and as such, the conductor is deflected. Hence the electrical energy input is converted into Mechanical Energy output.

The force on the conductor may be conceived by replacing the coil in the diagrams considered so far by a loop which can rotate about its axis as in Fig. 6.5.

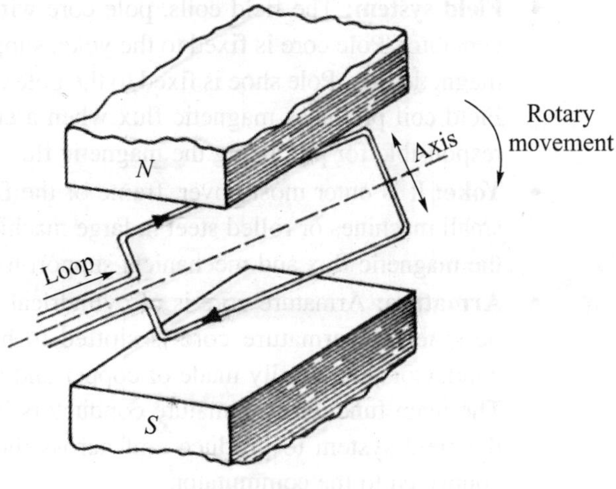

Fig. 6.5 *Rotation of a coil*

Since the forces act on a radius of $d/2$, the torque is given by,

$$T_d = F.\,d/2 + F.d/2 = F.\,d \qquad \text{...(6.4)}$$

where F is the force acting on the conductor forming a couple. This makes the loop to rotate.

6.2 CONSTRUCTIONAL FEATURES

DC machine is a highly versatile energy conversion device. It can thus be regarded as a transducer. As a generator, it is capable of providing a constant voltage power supply to loads and as a motor, it is provides wide range of speed control and high starting torque. There are no constructional differences between Generators and Motors and as such can be used interchangeably.

A DC machine consists of *stationary parts*: field coils, yoke, pole shoe, pole core and *rotating parts*—armature core, armature winding, commutator, shaft. The schematic diagram is shown in Fig. 6.6 with the various parts as under:

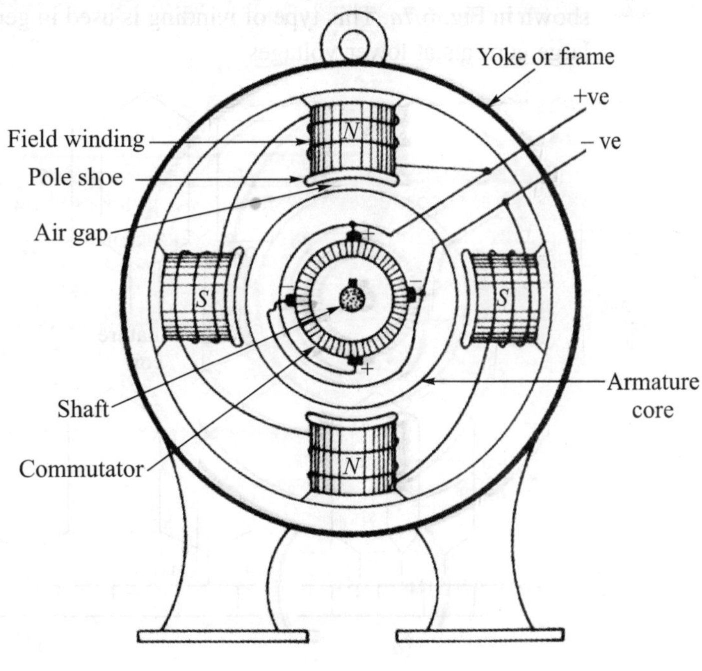

Fig. 6.6 *Constructional features of DC machines*

CHAPTER 6

- **Field system:** The field coils, pole core with the pole shoe from the field system of a DC generator. Pole core is fixed to the yoke, supports field coil and permits the establishment of magnetic flux. Pole shoe is fixed to the pole core to provide large area under the pole system. Field coil produces magnetic flux when a current is passed through it. The field system is responsible for producing the magnetic flux in the generator.
- **Yoke:** It is outer most cover, frame of the DC generator. It is usually made of cast iron in small machines or rolled steel in large machines, which provides a path of low reluctance to the magnetic flux and mechanical support to the poles.
- **Armature:** Armature core is of cylindrical structure and is made of high grade steel. The periphery of armature core is slotted to house the armature conductors. The armature conductors are usually made of copper and they are joined at both ends to form a winding. The main function of armature conductors is to cut the magnetic lines of flux produced by the field system to produce emf across the armature winding. The armature winding is connected to the commutator.
- **Armature winding:** The armature conductors are placed in the slots provided on the periphery of the armature core. The armature conductors are connected together to form armature winding. The basic rule for forming an armature coil is to join two conductors which come under poles of opposite polarity. Based on the method of grouping of armature coils, two types of armature windings *viz., Lap winding* and *Wave winding*, are used in practice. The number of parallel paths in lap winding is equal to the number of poles where as in wave winding the number of parallel paths is equal to two.
- **Lap winding:** Here, the coils are connected is such a way that they overlap each other as shown in Fig. 6.7*a*. This type of winding is used in generators which are designed to deliver large currents at lower voltages.

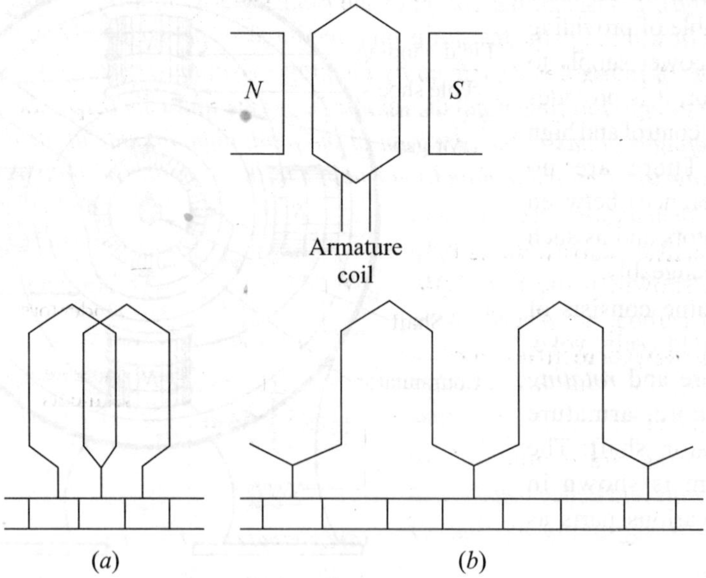

Fig. 6.7 *Armature windings of DC machine (a) Lap winding (b) Wave winding*

- **Wave winding:** Here, the armature coils are connected in a wave pattern as shown in Fig. 6.7*b*. This type of winding is used in generators which are designed to deliver lower currents at higher voltages.

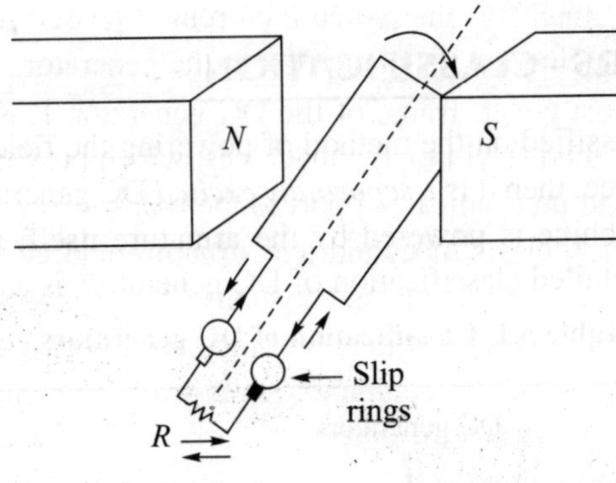

Fig. 6.8 *Performance of slip-rings*

- **Commutator and brush:** The coil when rotated under the influence of a magnetic field, induces a current in it. If the coil ends are connected to two slip-rings as shown in Fig. 6.8, which are rotating along with the coil, each coil is in contact with the same slip-rings and hence, as the coil rotates by 180°, the generated emf will reverse in each coil and as such, current flowing through the circuit is of the nature as shown in Fig. 6.9(*a*). If instead, the coil ends are connected to split-rings rather than slip-rings, the current flow through the resistor is unidirectional, as per the details shown in Fig. 6.9(*b*). The direction of induced emf is given by Fleming's right hand rule: stretch your right hand such that the thumb, forefinger and the middle finger are mutually perpendicular to one another. *If the forefinger points in the direction of the field, thumb points in the direction of motion of the conductor, then the middle finger points to the direction of the induced emf.*

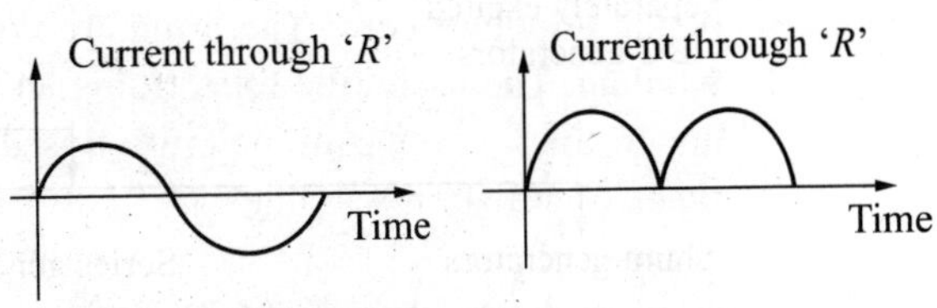

Fig. 6.9 *Rectification of ac*

Thus, the Commutator is a cylindrical core performing rectifier action with the help of split-rings as shown in the Fig. 6.10. Brushes, made of carbon, are placed above the commutator to collect rectified current from the commutator. The commutator segments are insulated from each other. The armature coils/turns are connected to commutator segments and hence there are as many commutator segments as that of armature winding.

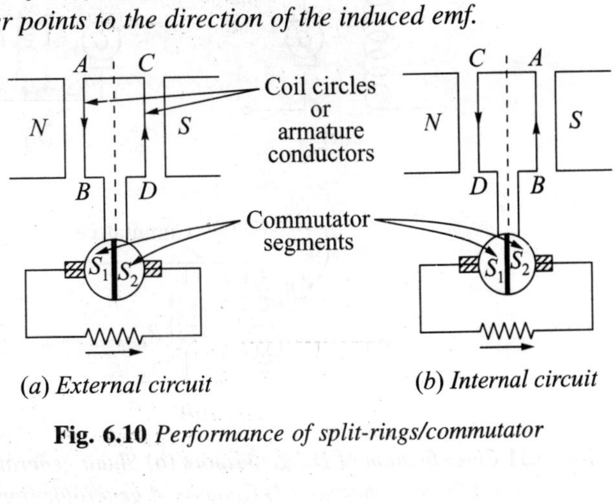

(*a*) *External circuit* (*b*) *Internal circuit*

Fig. 6.10 *Performance of split-rings/commutator*

Shaft: It is a cylindrical structure on which both the armature core and the commutator are mounted. The shaft is supported at both end by bearings and is used for coupling the DC generator to the prime mover.

6.3 DC GENERATORS—CLASSIFICATION

DC generators are basically classified on the method of powering the field coil. If the field winding is powered, by a separate DC source, then it is a *separately excited* DC generator [Fig. 6.11 (*a*)]. Similarly, if the field winding of the machine is powered by the armature itself, then it is a self excited DC generator [Fig. 6.11(*b*)]. The detailed classification of DC generators is as in Table 6.1

Table 6.1. Classification of DC generators

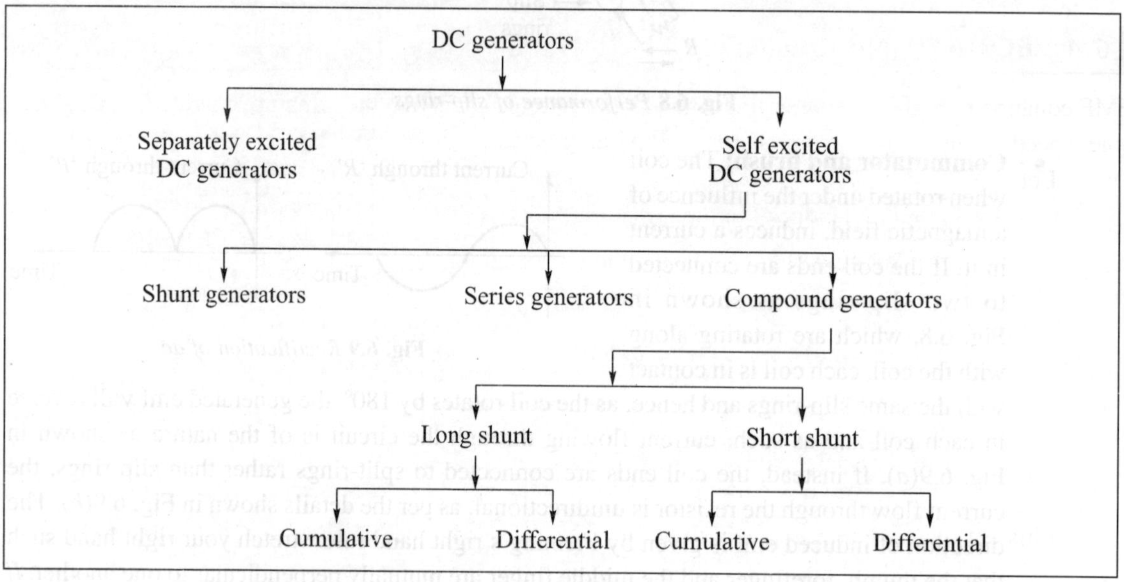

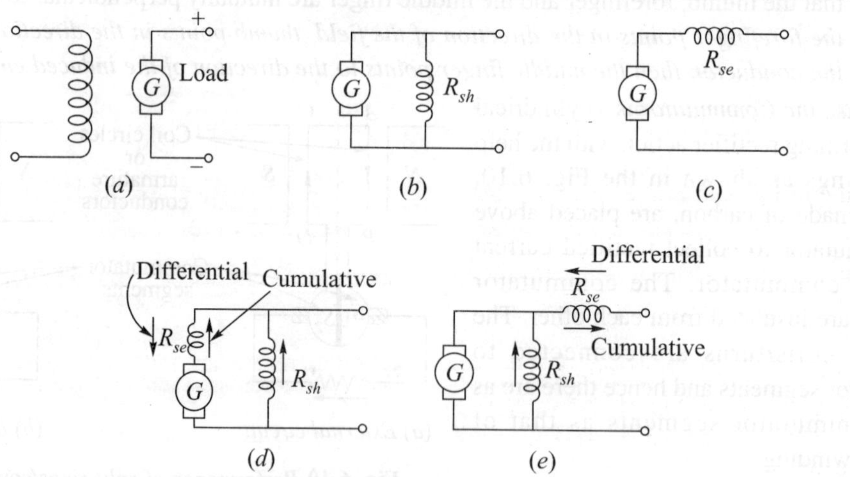

Fig. 6.11 *Classification of DC generators (a) Shunt generator (separately excited) (b) Shunt generator (self excited) (c) Series generator (d) Compound generator (long shunt) (e) Compund generator (short shunt).*

Self excited DC generators are further classified in to two groups based upon the method of connecting the field winding to the armature: *shunt generator* — field winding is connected in parallel with the armature winding, *series generator* — field winding is connected in series with the armature winding and *compound generator* — two field windings, one connected in series with the armature and the other connected in parallel with it. The main objective of compounding of DC machines is to combine the features of both the types of generators in a dingle generator. The compound generator is said to be *long shunt* if the shunt field winding is connected in parallel with the armature and the series field winding. It is referred to as *short shunt* if the shunt field winding is in parallel with armature and series field winding is in series with the parallel combination. Also, the compound generator is a *cumulative machine* if the magnetic flux produced in shunt and series field windings aid each other, while it is a *differential machine* if the magnetic flux values oppose each other.

6.4 EQUATION FOR INDUCED EMF

EMF equation of a DC generator gives the amount of emf induced in the armature conductors, flux per pole, speed, number of poles and number of parallel paths.

Let

E = *EMF* induced in the armature, Volts

p = Total number of poles in the DC generators

ϕ = Average flux per pole in Webers

N = Speed of the generator in RPM

Z = Total number of armature conductors

A = No. of parallel paths.

= 2 (Wave winding), P (Lap winding)

Flux cut by conductor in one revolution = (No. of poles) Average flux per pole = $p\,\phi$ Webers ...(6.5)

Time taken by the conductor to complete one revolution = (60/N) secs. ...(6.6)

Average EMF induced in one conductor per revolution

= Flux cut by one conductor in one revolution/time taken for one revolution

$$= P\phi/\,(60/N) = (P\phi\, N/60) \text{ volts} \quad ...(6.7)$$

Total emf induced in Z conductors = (No. of conductors) (Avg. emf/conductor)

$$E = (\phi ZN\,/\,60) \text{ volts} \quad ...(6.8)$$

EMF across generator terminals = total emf induced in Z conductors / parallel paths

$$E = (\phi ZN\,/\,60)\,(P/A) \text{ volts} \quad ...(6.9)$$

For a given DC generator, P, A and Z are fixed and therefore emf induced $\propto \phi\, N$.

Thus, at constant fixed excitation, (EMF $\propto N$). *i.e.*,

$$E_1/E_2 = N_1/N_2 \quad ...(6.10)$$

Further, when the armature conductor carries current and sets up a magnetic field, the field interacts with the main magnetic flux/field produced by the current in the field winding, which is known

CHAPTER 6

as *armature reaction.* The immediate effect of armature reaction is to reduce the total flux resulting in a voltage drop known as armature reaction drop.

6.5 DC GENERATORS—PERFORMANCE CHARACTERISTICS

The three important performance characteristics of DC generators are:

- *Open Circuit Characteristics (OCC)*: It is a graph showing the relationship between no-load induced emf and field current at constant speed.
- *External characteristics or voltage regulation characteristics*: It is a graph showing the relationship between terminal voltage and load current.
- *Internal characteristics*: It is a graph showing the relationship between induced emf and armature current.

These characteristics are briefly discussed for each type of generators below.

6.5.1 Shunt Generator

OCC: The emf induced in a DC generator is given by (6.9). Further, from (6.10), if the generator is run at a constant speed, then, $E \alpha \phi$. The value of ϕ (flux/pole) directly depends on the field current and hence, ($\phi \alpha I_f$). Thus, by neglecting the magnetic saturation of the poles.

$$E \alpha \phi \alpha I_f \quad ...(6.11)$$

For this condition, the plot of E_o *vs.* I_f is a straight line, which is referred as OCC. However in practice, OCC is not a straight line and also it does not pass through the origin, owing to magnetic saturation and residual flux in the poles respectively. On account of magnetic saturation in the poles, $I_f \alpha \phi$ initially and further increase in field current does not increase flux. The OCC of a typical DC generator is shown in Fig. 6.12.

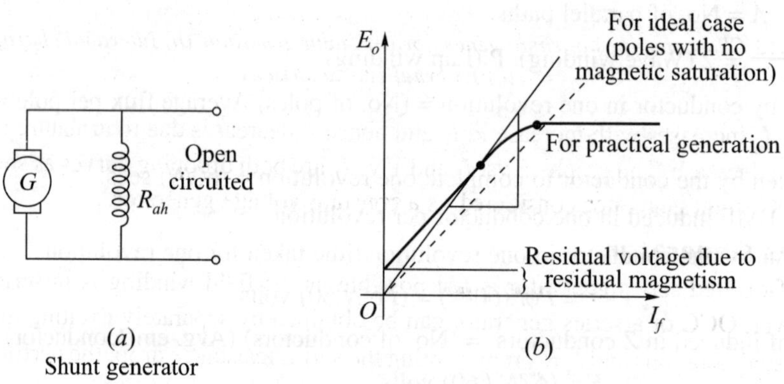

Fig. 6.12 *Determination of OCC of DC generators*

It is to be noted from Fig. 6.12, that the value of field circuit resistance at which the machine just fails to build up voltage is called *Critical resistance*. It corresponds to the slope of the line drawn tangential to the OCC from the origin. A self excited DC shunt generator builds up the voltage as follows.

- When the armature is rotated at constant speed, initially the armature conductors cut the residual magnetic lines of flux, however small it is, a small induced emf appears across the armature. This emf drives a small current through the field winding thus producing small additional flux.

- If the polarity of the field winding is such that the additional flux adds the residual flux then the net flux increases. When this flux is cut by the armature conductors, a larger emf is induced across the armature.
- This process of more emf, more field current, more flux continues and becomes cumulative. The net result is that the machine develops a voltage which is limited by the field circuit resistance and speed:

External and internal characteristics: When the shunt generator is loaded, its terminal voltage decreases due to armature resistance and armature reaction. For a loaded DC shunt generator, the performance equations are:

$$E = V + \text{armature resistance drop} + \text{armature reaction drop} + \text{brush contact drop}$$

$$= V + I_a R_a + ARD + BCD \quad ...(6.12)$$

and $$I_a = I_f + I_L \quad ...(6.13)$$

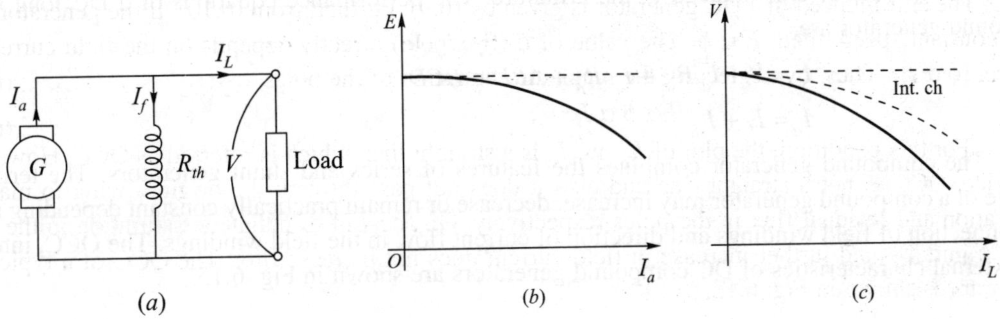

Fig. 6.13 *Characteristics of shunt generator (a) Shunt generator (b) Interanal characteristics (c) External characteristics*

Clearly I_a increases with increase in I_L and hence E decreases due to armature reaction which in turn forces V to decrease. The graphs E vs. I_a and V vs I_L are both drooping curves as shown in Fig. 6.13. Usually, the DC shunt generator considered as a constant voltage generator.

6.5.2 Series Generator

OCC of a self-excited series generator is not possible as the field winding is in series with the open circuit. However, OCC of a series generator can be obtained by separately exciting the field winding.

With usual notations and $I_a R_{se}$ representing the series resistance drop, the performance equations of a series generator are:

$$E = V + I_a R_a + I_a R_{se} + ARD + BCD \quad ...(6.14)$$

and $$I_a = I_f = I_L \quad ...(6.15)$$

The internal and external characteristic of DC series generators are raising curves as shown in Fig. 6.14.

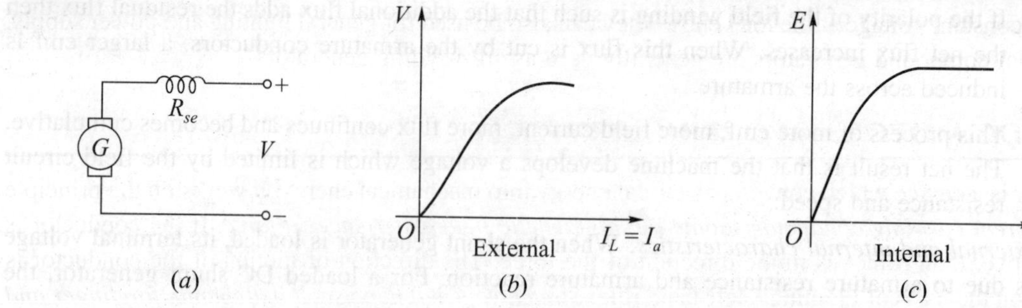

Fig. 6.14 *Characteristics of series generator (a) Series generator (b) Internal characteristics (c) External characteristics*

6.5.3 Compound Generator

The OCC of a compound generator is similar to that of a shunt generator. The net flux across the air gap decides the amount of emf induced in the armature. The performance equations of a DC long shunt compound generator are,

$$E = V + I_a R_{sc} + I_a R_a + ARD + BCD \quad \text{...(6.16)}$$

and

$$I_a = I_L + I_{sh} \quad \text{...(6.17)}$$

The compound generator combines the features of series and shunt generators. The terminal voltage of a compound generator may increase, decrease or remain practically constant depending upon the connection of field windings and direction of current flow in the field windings. The OCC, internal and external characteristics of DC compound generators are shown in Fig. 6.15.

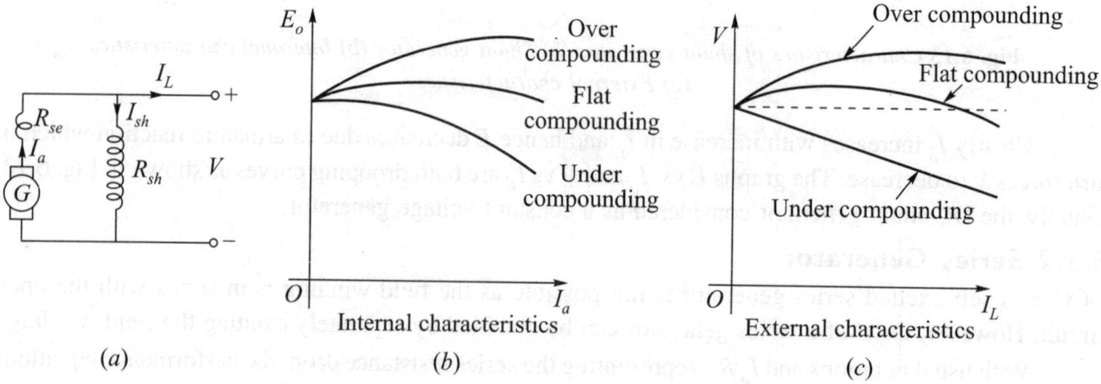

Fig. 6.15 *Characteristics of compound generator (long shunt) (a) Compound generator (b) Internal characteristics (c) External characteristics*

6.6 DC GENERATORS—APPLICATIONS

DC shunt generators are extensively used for general lighting, power supply and charging of batteries as they maintain constant terminal voltage when used in conjunction with a field regulator. Series generators are mainly used as boosters in DC transmission system in order to compensate for drop in voltage during transmission. Compound generators are used in DC transmission, when it is required to maintain constant voltage at the load ends. They can also be used for general lighting and power supply. Differential compound generators are generally used as arc-welding generators.

6.7 DC MOTORS—WORKING PRINCIPLE

DC motor is a device which converts electrical energy into mechanical energy. It works on the principle that *a current carrying conductor situated in a magnetic field experiences a force.* If the conductor is free to move, then it moves in the direction of the force. The direction of motion of the conductor is obtained on the basis of Fleming's left-hand rule: *Stretch your left hand such that thumb, forefinger and middle finger are mutually perpendicular to each other. If the forefinger points in the direction of the field and the middle finger points in the direction of current, then the thumb would point in the direction of force experienced by the conductor.*

Consider a 2-pole DC motor as shown in Fig. 6.16. Let the armature and field windings be connected to a DC voltage source. The voltage source will drive currents in the armature and field conductors which produce flux in the machine. These two react with each other and result in higher flux on one side. The ultimate effect is that the conductor is pushed in the direction of higher flux to lower flux.

Further, when the power supply is on, current flows in both armature and field windings of the DC motor, resulting in a driving torque. This puts the armature into motion. As the armature rotates, the armature conductors cut across magnetic flux in the air gap. Due to magnetic induction, an emf is induced in the armature, which acts in opposite direction to the applied voltage and is referred to as *back emf*, E_b (Fig. 6.17).

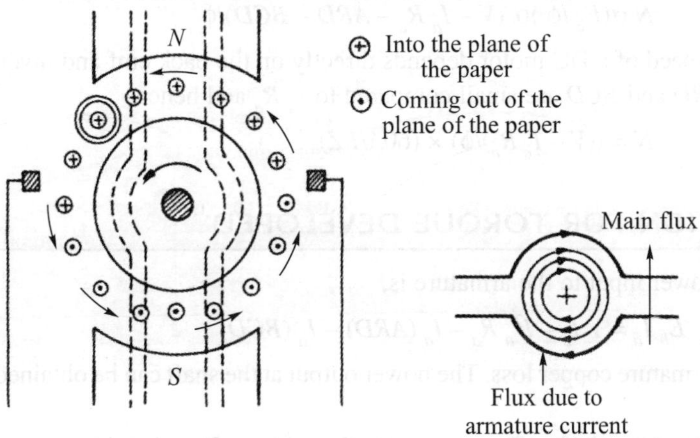

Fig. 6.16 *2-pole DC motor*

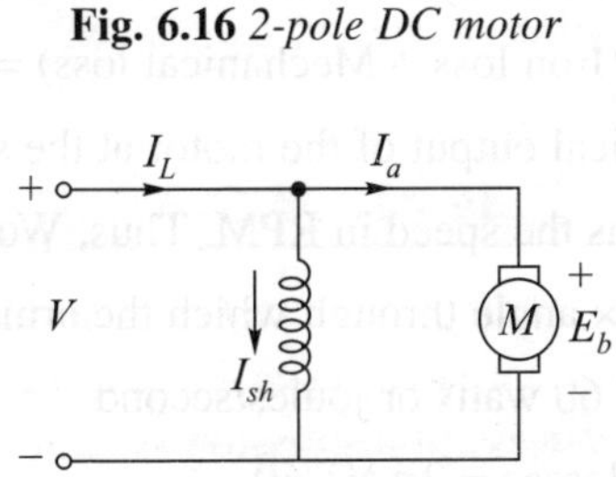

Fig. 6.17 *Significance of back emf*

Let V = Applied Voltage

E_b = Back emf

I_a = Armature current

I_L = Line current

R_a = Armature resistance

I_{sh} = Shunt field current

R_{sh} = Shunt field resistance

ARD = Armature reaction drop

BCD = Brush contact drop

Applying *KVL* to the loop in Fig. 6.17, we get

$$E_a = V - I_a R_a - ARD - BCD \quad ...(6.18)$$

Since E_b is the emf induced in the armature on account of flux cut by the armature conductors, it is also given by equation (6.9), and hence

$$E_b = \frac{Z N\phi}{60}\left(\frac{P}{A}\right) = V - I_a R_a - ARD - BCD \quad ...(6.19)$$

$$\therefore \quad N = [(V - I_a R_a - ARD - BCD)/\phi]\,(60A/PZ) \quad ...(6.20)$$

For a given motor P, Z and A are fixed.

$$N \,\alpha (E_b/\phi)\, \alpha\, (V - I_a R_a - ARD - BCD)/\phi \quad ...(6.21)$$

Therefore, speed of a DC motor depends directly on the back emf and inversely on the flux per pole. Generally, ARD and BCD are small compared to $I_a R_a$ and hence

$$N = ((V - I_a R_a)/\phi) \times (60A/PZ) \quad ...(6.22)$$

6.8 EQUATION FOR TORQUE DEVELOPED

From (6.19), the power input to the armature is,

$$E_b I_a = V I_a - I^2_a R_a - I_a (ARD) - I_a (BCD) \quad ...(6.23)$$

where $I^2_a R_a$ is the armature copper loss. The power output at the shaft can be obtained from the following relation:

Power output at the shaft = Power input to the motor – Rotational losses

$= E_b I_a$ – (Iron loss + Mechanical loss) = $2\pi NT/60$

= Mechanical output of the motor at the shaft in watts. ...(6.24)

where, T is the torque in Nm and N is the speed in RPM. Thus, Work done per second,

W = Torque × angle through which the armature moves/second = $T\theta$

$= 2\pi NT/60$ watts or joules/second ...(6.25)

$$\therefore \quad E_b I_a - \text{Rotational losses} = 2\pi NT/60 \quad ...(6.26)$$

or $$T = [(E_b I_a - \text{Rotational losses}) 60] / 2\pi NT \quad ...(6.27)$$

Neglecting rotational losses, we have

$$T = 60\ E_b I_a / 2\pi N \quad ...(6.28)$$

From (6.9) we get, after simplification,

$$T = 0.159\ \phi\ Z I_a\ (P/A) \text{ N-m}$$
$$= 0.0165\ \phi\ Z I_a\ (P/A) \text{ kg-m} \quad ...(6.29)$$

Since, for a given DC motor Z, P and A are constants,

$$T\ \alpha\ \phi\ I_a \quad ...(6.30)$$

Thus the torque developed by the motor depends on both flux/pole (or field current) and armature current I_a.

6.9 DC MOTORS—CLASSIFICATION

Based on the interconnection of field windings and the armature, DC motors can be classified as *Series, Shunt and Compound motors*. The connection diagrams for these motors are given in Fig. 6.18.

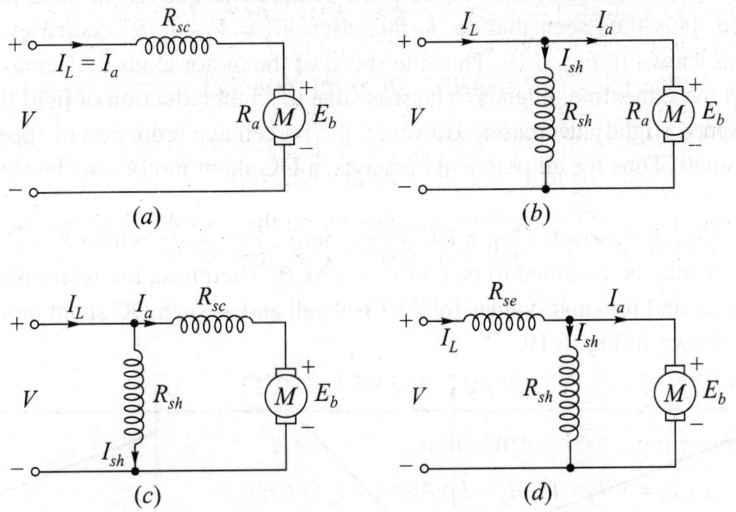

Fig. 6.18 *Types of DC motors: (a) Series motor (b) Shunt motor (c) Compound motor (Long shount) (d) Compound motor (Short shunt)*

In series motors, the field winding is connected in series with the armature. The performance equations are:

$$E_b = V - I_a R_{se} - I_a R_a - ARD - BCD \text{ and } I_L = I_{se} = I_a \quad ...(6.31)$$

In shunt motors, the field winding is connected in parallel with the armature. The performance equations are:

$$E_b = V - I_a R_a - ARD - BCD \text{ and } I_{sh} = V / R_{sh} \quad ...(6.32)$$

A compound motor has two field windings — a shunt field winding connected across the armature and a series field winding connected in series with the armature. Depending on these connections, they can be long shunt or short shunt. The performance equations are:

(*a*) *Long shunt:*

$$E_b = V - I_a R_{se} - I_a R_a - ARD - BCD \text{ and } I_{sh} = V / R_{sh};\ I_L = I_a + I_{sh} \quad ...(6.33)$$

(*b*) *Short shunt:*

$$E_b = V - I_L R_{se} - I_a R_a - ARD - BCD \text{ and}$$

$$I_{sh} = (V - I_L R_{se}) / R_{sh} \text{ and } I_L = I_a + I_{sh} \quad ...(6.34)$$

6.10 DC MOTORS—PERFORMANCE CHARACTERISTICS

The important performance characteristic of DC motors include Speed *vs.* Armature Current characteristics, Torque *vs.* Armature Current characteristics and Speed *vs.* Torque Characteristics. These characteristics in respect of shunt, series and compound motors are briefly discussed below.

6.10.1 Shunt Motor

Speed vs. Armature current: For a DC shunt motor, we know that $E_b = KN\phi$ where $K = ZP / 60A$ so that

$$N \alpha E_b/\phi \quad \text{or} \quad N\alpha(V - I_a R_a)/\phi \quad ...(6.35)$$

When a shunt motor is loaded, it draws current from the supply mains. It is evident that the motor draws more and more current to develop the required torque as the load increases. Hence I_a increase with load. It is thus seen that, as I_a increases, $E_b = V - I_a R_a$ decreases. Hence the speed characteristics is as shown in Fig. 6.19. Thus the speed of the motor tends to decrease due to reduction of back emf and at the same time, it tends to increase due to slight reduction of field flux. The combined effect is that the speed slightly decreases. However, the percentage reduction of speed from no-load to full load is quite small. Thus for all practical purposes, a DC shunt motor may be treated on a constant speed motor.

Torque vs. Armature current: For a DC shunt motor, $T = K\phi I_a$, where $K = (1/2\pi)\ ZP/A$, so that $T \alpha \phi I_a$. Since, flux may be assumed to be constant, $T \alpha I_a$. Therefore, the relationship between T and I_a is practically linear and for small values for I_a, T is small and as such DC shunt motor has a very poor starting torque as shown in Fig. 6.19.

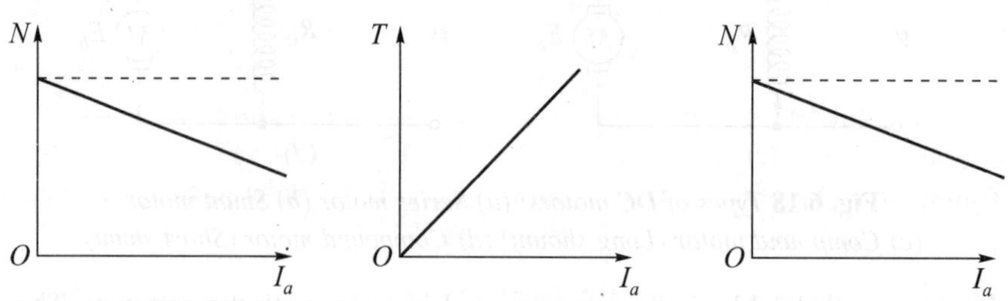

(*a*) Speed *vs.* Arm current (*b*) Torque *vs.* Arm current (c) Speed *vs.* Torque

Fig. 6.19 *DC shunt motor characteristics*

Speed vs. Torque: Since $T\ \alpha\ (\phi I_a)$, as the load increases, I_a increases and E_b decreases. It is thus clear that T increases and N decreases as load increases.

$$\therefore \qquad N\ \alpha E_b/(T/I_a) \quad \text{and} \quad N\ \alpha 1/T \quad ...(6.36)$$

Also $T\alpha\ \phi$ and $N\alpha\ (1/\phi)$. Therefore, N varies inversely with T. The graph of N *vs.* T is drooping curve shown in Fig. 6.19.

6.10.2 Series Motor

In a DC series motor, the field current is the same as armature current and hence both the field current and armature current increase as the load on the motor increases.

Speed vs. Armature current: For a DC series motor we have

$$N \propto E_b / \phi = (V - I_a R_a) / \phi \quad ...(6.37)$$

As I_a increases, E_b decreases and hence N decreases. Also, the field current increases as ϕ increases. Since $N \propto 1/\phi$, the speed further decreases. The combined effect is that the speed of the motor drastically reduces with the increase of load as shown in Fig. 6.20. Thus, DC series motor is essentially a *variable speed motor.* Even small changes of load cause large changes in speed.

Torque vs. Armature current: We know that, $T \propto \phi I_a$. Since $\phi \propto I_a$ and $I_f = I_a$, $T \propto I_a^2$. Thus the torque current characteristic is parabolic as shown in Fig. 6.20. This is valid until the magnetic saturation of poles. After saturation, ϕ does not increase appreciably even if I_f (*i.e.*, I_a) increases considerably. A DC series motor should not be started under light load, as T is quite small for smaller values of I_a. Speed $N \propto 1/T$ and hence the speed may become dangerously high which may damage the motor.

Speed vs. Torque: We know that $N \propto E_b / \phi$, and $T \propto I_a \phi$, and hence $N \propto 1/T$. The speed of DC series motor decreases with the increase in torque which in turn increases with load. The typical characteristics are as in Fig. 6.20.

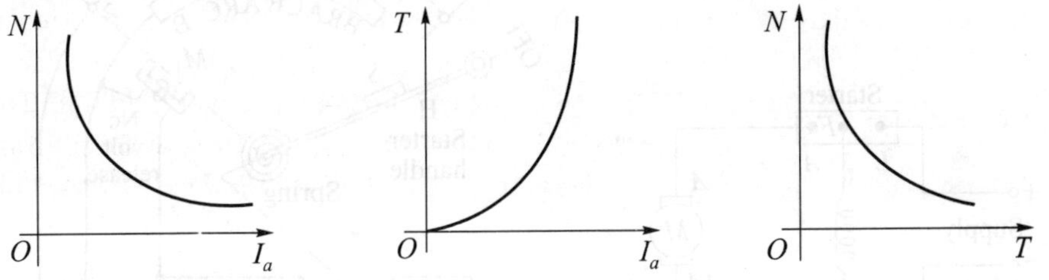

(a) Speed vs. Current (b) Torque vs. Current (c) Speed vs. Torque

Fig. 6.20 *DC series motor characteristics*

6.10.3 Compound Motor

A compound motor may be cumulatively or differentially compounded. In a cumulative compound motor, the series flux and shunt flux are additive. In a differential compound motor, the net flux is the difference of series and shunt flux values. Differential compound motors do not find wide applications in practice. Cumulative compound motors exhibit the characteristics of both shunt and series motors. The typical characteristics are indicated as in Fig. 6.21.

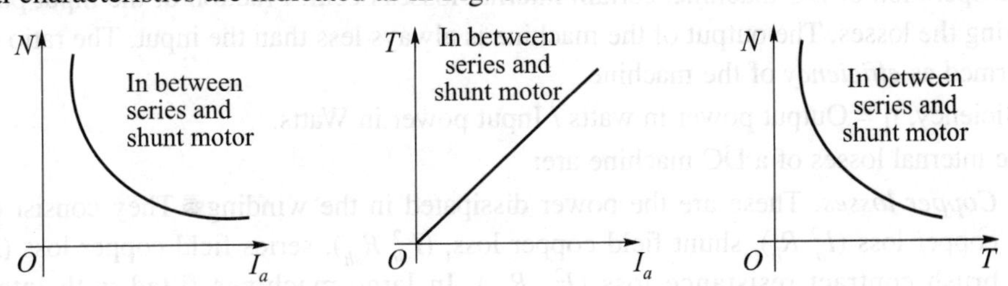

(a) Speed vs. Arm current (b) Torque vs. Arm current (c) Speed vs. Torque

Fig. 6.21 *DC Compound motor characteristics*

6.11 DC MOTOR–STARTERS

DC motor should never be started by applying full voltage across its armature as it results in very large current through the armature. This large in-rush of current can be avoided by using a starter. Consider the relation between the supply voltage and the back emf of a DC shunt motor:

$$V = E_b + I_a R_a \quad \text{or} \quad I_a = (V - E_b)/R_a \qquad ...(6.38)$$

When the armature is at rest, the back emf E_b is zero that, $I_a = V/R_a$. As R_a is very small, I_a becomes alarmingly large for rated voltage of the motor. Therefore, care should be taken to ensure that I_a does not go beyond the rated current of the motor. This can be achieved by initially inserting a starting resistance and cutting out this resistance, once E_b is developed in the motor. A properly designed, continuously variable resistance along with other protective mechanisms are incorporated in a starter. A three point starter is widely used in this context which incorporates not only the starting resistance but also no-volt and over-load release mechanisms as shown in Fig. 6.22.

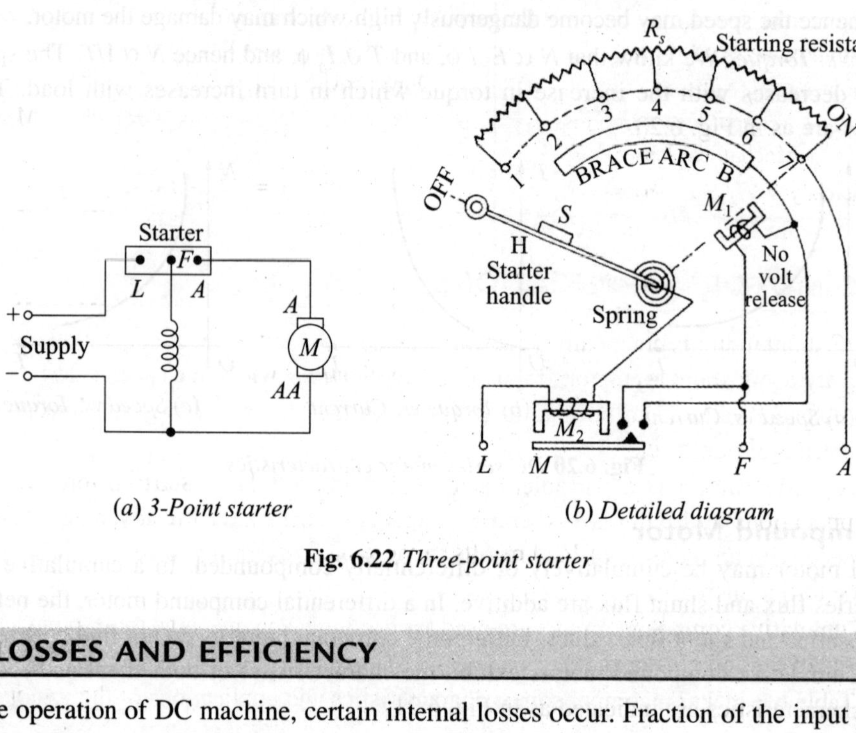

(a) 3-Point starter (b) Detailed diagram

Fig. 6.22 *Three-point starter*

6.12 LOSSES AND EFFICIENCY

During the operation of DC machine, certain internal losses occur. Fraction of the input power is used for supplying the losses. The output of the machine is always less than the input. The ratio of output to input is termed as *efficiency* of the machine.

Efficiency, η = Output power in watts / Input power in Watts.

The internal losses of a DC machine are:

- *Copper losses*: These are the power dissipated in the windings. They consist of armature copper loss ($I_a^2 R_a$), shunt field copper loss, ($I_{sh}^2 R_{sh}$), series field copper loss ($I_{se}^2 R_{se}$) and brush contract resistance loss ($I_{br}^2 R_{br}$). In large machines fitted with interlopes and compensating windings, there is additional copper loss due to their winding resistances.

- *Iron or Core losses*: These occur in the armature core and have two components: hysteresis losses and eddy current losses. When the machine is in operation, armature core is subjected to magnetic hysteresis. The hysteresis power loss is found to be proportional to $B_{max}^{1.6} f$. Also, when the machine is in operation, the armature core cuts the magnetic flux traversing through it. As a result, an eddy emf is induced in it. Since the armature core forms a closed circuit, there will be $B^2_{max} f^2 t^2$, where t is the thickness of core laminations.
- *Mechanical losses*: These are due to rotation of the armature core and they consist of bearing friction loss, brush friction loss, windage loss etc. These are assumed to be constant.

In summary, the relations between the various parameters as referred to a DC generators

Table 6.2 Efficiency of DC machines

Generator	*Motor*
If V = terminal voltage I_L = load current then output power = VI_L Input power = VI_L + losses = VI_L + (copper loss + iron loss + Mechanical losses) ∴ Efficiency = VI_L (VI_L + Losses)	If V = supply voltage I_L = line current then output power = VI_L Input power = VI_L + losses = VI_L – (copper loss + iron loss + Mech. losses) ∴ Efficiency = (VI_L – Losses) / VI_L

6.13 DC MOTORS—APPLICATIONS

- DC shunt motor is practically a constant speed motor and its speed regulation may be obtained easily using shunt regulator. It thus finds applications where the speed is to be maintained at a constant value from no-load to full load such as lathes, driving machine tools, blowers, centrifugal pumps etc.
- DC series motor is a variable speed motor and has large starting torque. It thus finds applications in driving hoists, cranes, trams etc. These have the advantage that decrease of speed with an increase of load results in the motor absorbing power not at the rate at which the torque increases.
- Cumulative compound motors are used for driving heavy machine tools, punches and planes, conveyers and elevators etc.

The Table 6.3 makes a comparison of characteristics and applications of the various generators/ motors.

Table 6.3 Comparison of DC machines

Type	*Characteristics*	*Applications*
Shunt Generator	Terminal voltage is almost constant with load	• Used for lighting and power supply purposes • Used for charging batteries
Shunt Motor	Constant speed characteristics	• Driving constant speed lathes • Driving *CF* pumps, Machine tools

(*Contd.*)

Type	*Characteristics*	*Applications*
Series Generator	Rising characteristics	• Not used for power supply • Due to rising characteristics, used as boosters
Series Motor	Variable Speed, High starting torque	• Where heavy starting torque is required – such as in traction, Trolley cars, Conveyors
Compound Generator	Almost constant terminal voltage over a wide range	• Used for power supply purposes
Compound Motor	Variable/Adjustable speed, High starting torque	• Used in places where heavy intermittent torque is required as in elevators, Conveyors and Rolling Mills

ILLUSTRATIVE EXAMPLES

Problems on DC Generators

1. A 2 pole, wave wound, generator has 51 slots, 24 conductors/slot. If the flux/pole is 0.01 wbs. Determine the speed at which the armature be driven to give an induced emf of 220 V.

Solution: $\phi = 0.01$ Wb, $P = A = 2$, $Z = (51 \times 24) = 1224$

$E = (\phi\, ZN/60) \times (P/A)$ Volts

Plugging the values of all the known quantities, we arrive at $N = 1078$ RPM.

2. A wave wound 4-pole, 750 RPM shunt generator has armature and field resistance of 0.4 Ω and 200 Ω respectively. The armature has 720 conductors and the flux/pole is 0.029 Wbs. If the load resistance is 10 Ω, determine the terminal voltage.

Solution: [Refer Fig. 6.11(*b*)]

Given $E = (\phi ZN/60)\,(P/A) = 522$ Volts

Terminal voltage = Generated voltage – ARD

Armature current $= I_{sh} + I_L = (522/200) + (522/10) = 54.81$ A

Armature drop $= 54.81\,(0.4) = 21.92$ V

Terminal voltage $= 522 - 21.92 = 510.08$ V

3. An 8-pole, lap connected, armature has 960 conductors, flux/pole of 40 mWb a speed of 400 RPM. Find the emf generated in the armature. Determine the speed at which the armature is to be driven to maintain a voltage of 400 V if it is wave connected.

Solution: ***Case 1. Lap Wound armature:***

Given $P = 8$, $N = 400$ RPM, $Z = 960$, $\phi = 0.004$ Wb., $A = P = 8$ (lap)

$E = ZN\phi/60\,A = 256$ Volts.

Case 2. Wave Wound armature:

$$E = 400, A = 2$$

$$\therefore \quad N = 60\ AE/Z\ \phi\ P = 156 \text{ RPM}$$

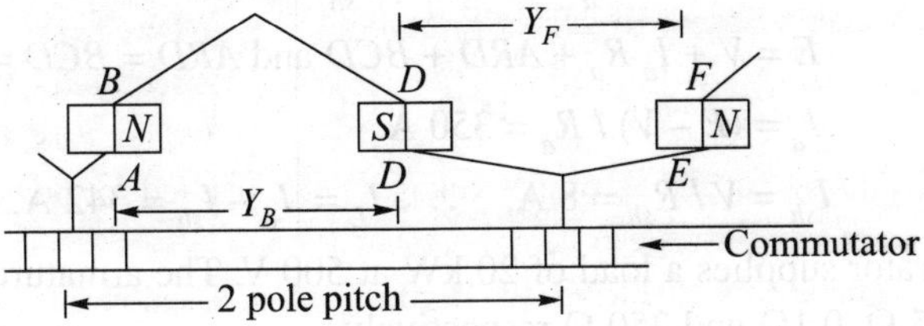

Fig. 6.23 (*a*) *Design of wave winding*

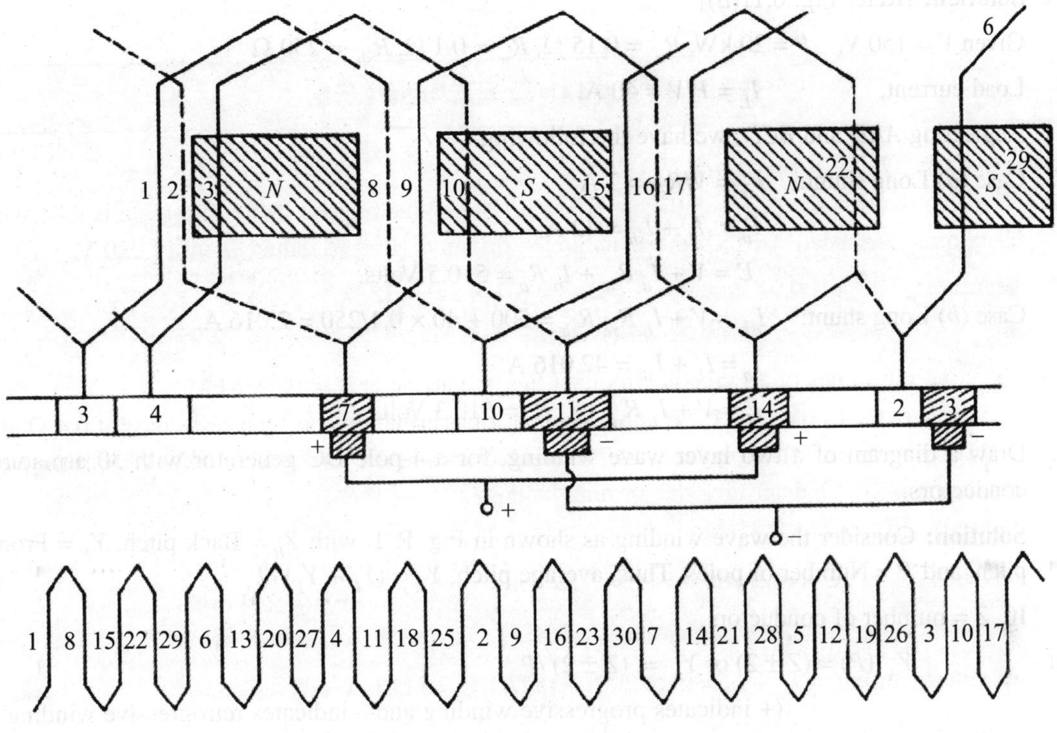

Fig. 6.23 (*b*) *Wave winding diagram*

4. Calculate the flux/pole of a DC generator developing 500 Volts at 1500 RPM. The generator is lap connected with 83 slots and 12 conductors/slot.

Solution:

Given $E = 500$ V, $N = 1500$ RPM, $Z = 83$ slots (12 conductors/slot) $= 996$

$$A = P \text{ (lap connection)}$$

$$E = ZN\phi P/60A$$

$$\therefore \quad \phi = 60\ E/ZN = 0.02 \text{ Wb.}$$

5. A DC Shunt generator has an induced voltage of 127 V. When it is on load, the voltage is 120 V. Find the load current if $R_{sh} = 15\ \Omega$ and $R_a = 0.02\ \Omega$. Neglect armature reaction.

Solution: [Refer Fig. 6.11(*b*)]

Given $E = 127$ V, $V = 120$ V, $R_a = 0.02\ \Omega$, $R_{sh} = 15\ \Omega$

$$E = V + I_a R_a + ARD + BCD \text{ and } ARD = BCD = 0$$

$$\therefore \quad I_a = (E - V) / R_a = 350 \text{ A.}$$

$$I_{sh} = V / R_{sh} = 8 \text{ A}, \quad \therefore \quad I_L = I_a - I_{sh} = 342 \text{ A.}$$

6. A compound generator supplies a load of 20 kW at 500 V. The armature, series and shunt field resistances are 0.15 Ω, 0.1Ω and 250 Ω respectively.

Find the induced voltage.

Solution: [Refer Fig. 6.11(*b*)]

Given $V = 150$ V, $P = 20$ kW, $R_a = 0.15\ \Omega$, $R_{se} = 0.1\ \Omega$, $R_{sh} = 250\ \Omega$

Load current, $I_L = P/V = 40$ A.

Neglecting *ARD* and *BCD*, we have the following:

Case (*a*) Long shunt: $I_{sh} = V/R_{sh} = 2$ A.

$$\therefore \quad I_a = I_L + I_{sh} = 42 \text{ A.}$$

$$E = V + I_a R_{se} + I_a R_a = 510.5 \text{ Volts.}$$

Case (*b*) Long shunt: $I_{sh} = V + I_L R_{se}/R_{sh} = 500 + 40 \times 0.1/250 = 2.016$ A.

$$I_a = I_L + I_{sh} = 42.016 \text{ A}$$

$$E = V + I_L R_{se} + I_a R_a = 510.3 \text{ Volts.}$$

7. Draw a diagram of a two layer wave winding, for a 4-pole DC generator with 30 armature conductors.

Solution: Consider the wave winding as shown in Fig. P. 1, with Y_B = Back pitch, Y_F = Front pitch, and P = Number of poles. Thus, average pitch, $Y_A = (Y_B + Y_F) / 2$

If Z = number of conductors,

$$Y_A (P) = (Z \pm 2) \text{ or } Y_A = (Z \pm 2) / P$$

(+ indicates progressive winding and—indicates retrogressive winding).

In the light of the above, $Y_A = (30 \pm 2)/4 = 8$ or 7. Say $Y_B = Y_F = 7$. Thus the wave winding diagram is as shown in Fig. P.2. The Brush positions are fixed as under:

As $Y_A = 7$, conductors (effective) = (7) (4) = 28. In each path there are 14 conductors to be considered. As such, in the coil wave diagram, count 14 from the start and it lands in 2. As such, combination is as below:

2-25-18-11-4-27-20-13-6-29-22-15-8-1-24-17 and

9-16-23-30-7-14-21-28-5-12-19-26-3-10

The points of interest are: Only two brushes are required, Number of parallel paths are only two, voltage induced E = (average induced in a conductor) $Z/2$ and current flow in each path = $I_a/2$.

8. Draw a winding diagram of a two layer, lap winding, 4 pole, DC generator with 16 coil segments.

Solution: Number of commutator segments = 16, Number of conductors = (16) (2) = 32 and Pole pitch = 32\4 = 8. Y_B and Y_F are to be odd for the lap winding and differ by 2. Thus, $Y_B = 9$ and $Y_F = 7$ (Retrogressive) or $Y_B = 7$ and $Y_F = 9$ (Progressive). The lap winding diagram is given in Fig. P.3. Division of the conductors in parallel division is as shown in Fig. P.4.

Generated emf, E = (Average induced emf/conductor) Z/P.

For finding the total armature resistance, let

l = length of the armature conductor

S = area of cross-section

$A = P$ = number of parallel paths

R = resistance of the whole winding = $(\rho \times l/S) \times Z$.

Resistance of each parallel path = $\rho lZ/SA$.

With $A = P$ paths in parallel, the equivalent resistance is = $\rho lZ/SA^2$.

If I_a is the total armature current, then current per parallel path = I_a/P.

9. A 4 pole lap wound, DC generator has 42 coils with 8 turns per coil. It is driven at a speed of 1120 RPM. If useful flux per pole is 21mWb, calculate the generated EMF. Find the speed at which it is to be driven to generate the same EMF with wave wound armature.

Solution: No of coils = 42; 8 turns per coil; $\Phi = 21 \times 10^{-3}$ Wb; N = 1120 RPM; P = 4;

Lap winding $A = P = 4$

$Z = 42 \times 8 \times 2 = 672$ (Number of conductors)

$E = (\Phi ZN/60) \times (P/A)$

$$E = \left(\frac{21 \times 10^{-3} \times 672 \times 1120}{60} \times \frac{4}{4}\right) = 263.42 \text{ V}$$

To develop 263.42 Volts when the armature is wave wound the required speed is

$N = (E \times 60 \times A)/(\Phi ZP)$ rpm

$$N = \left(\frac{263.42 \times 60 \times 2}{21 \times 10^{-3} \times 672 \times 4}\right)$$

= 560 RPM (Note $A = 2$ for wave winding = P for lap winding)

10. A 4 pole DC generator has a wave wound armature with 792 conductors. If it is driven at a speed of 750 RPM. Calculate the necessary flux per pole to generate 240 Volts on no load.

Solution: $E = 240$ Volts; $N = 750$ RPM; $P = 4$; $Z = 792$; A = 2

$\Phi = (E \times 60 \times A)/(ZNP)$

$$\phi = \left(\frac{240.42 \times 60 \times 2}{792 \times 750 \times 4}\right) = 0.01212 \text{ Wb} = 12.12 \text{ mWb}$$

11. A 4 pole DC generator having wave wound armature has 50 slots and 25 conductors per slot. Find the generated EMF. If it is driven at 25 RPS and useful flux in the machine is 0.03 Wb.

Solution: $P = 4$; slots = 50; conductors/slot = 25; $N = 25$ RPS;

$\Phi = 0.03$ Wb; $A = 2$ (Wave winding)

$N = 25 \times 60 = 1500$ RPM, $Z = 50 \times 25 = 750$

$$E = (\Phi ZN/60) \times (P/A) = \left(\frac{0.03 \times 750 \times 1500}{60} \times \frac{4}{2}\right) = 1125 \text{ Volts}$$

12. A 4 pole DC machine has a lap connected armature having 60 slots and 8 conductors per slot. The flux per pole is 30 mWb. If the armature is rotated at 1000 RPM, find the *EMF* available across its armature terminals. Also, calculate the frequency of EMF in the armature coils.

Solution: $P = 4$; $A = 4$; Slots = 60; conductors/slot = 8; $\Phi = 0.03$ Wb; $N = 1000$ RPM

$Z = 60 \times 8 = 480$;

$$E = (\Phi ZN/60) \times (P/A) = \left(\frac{0.03 \times 480 \times 1000}{60} \times \frac{4}{4}\right) = 240 \text{ V}$$

Frequency $f = PN/120 = 4 \times 1000/120 = 33.33$ Hz.

13. A 4 pole lap connected shunt generator delivers 200 amp at terminal voltage of 250 Volts. It has field and armature resistance of 50 ohms and 0.05 ohms respectively. Neglecting brush drop, determine armature current, current per armature parallel path, EMF generated and power developed.

Solution: $P = 4$; $I_1 = 200$ amps; $R_{sh} = 50$ ohms; $R_a = 0.05$ ohms; $A = 4$ (lap wound)

$I_{sh} = V_1/R_{sh} = 250/50 = 5$ amps.

$I_a = I_1 + I_{sh} = 200 + 5 = 205$ *A*; Current per parallel path $= I_a/A = 205/4 = 51.25$ amps

$E = V_1 + I_a R_a = 250 + 205 \times 0.05 = 260.25$ volts.

14. A short shunt cumulatively compounded DC generator supplies 7.5 kW at 230 volts. The shunt field, series field and armature resistances are 100, 0.3 and 0.4 ohms respectively. Calculate the induced EMF and Load resistance.

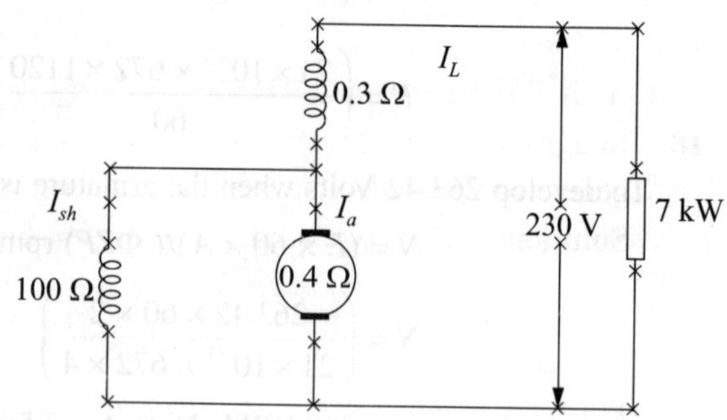

Solution: Output power = 7.5 kW;

$V_1 = 230$ volts;

$R_{sh} = 100$ ohms;

$R_{se} = 0.4$ ohms; $R_a = 0.3$ ohms

$$I_1 = \left(\frac{O/P}{V_1}\right) = \left(\frac{7.5 \times 1000}{230}\right)$$

$= 32.60$ A

$E = V_1 + I_1 R_{se} = 230 + 32.6 \times 0.4 = 243.04$ V

$I_{sh} = E/R_{sh} = 243.04/100 = 2.4304$ A

$I_a = I_1 + I_{sh} = 32.6 + 2.3 = 34.9$ A

$E_g = E + I_a R_a = 243.04 + 34.9 \times 0.4 = 257$ V.

15. A 4 pole DC shunt generator has 36 slots with ten conductors/slot. The flux is 0.03 Wb and the speed is 750 RPM. Calculate the EMF generated if the armature is (*i*) lap wound and (*ii*) wave wound.

Solution: $P = 4; Z = 36 \times 10 = 360; \Phi = 0.03$ Wb; $N = 750$ RPM

Lap winding $A = P = 4;$

$$E = (\Phi ZN/60) \times (P/A) = E = \left(\frac{0.03 \times 360 \times 750}{60} \times \frac{4}{4}\right) = 135 \text{ Volts}$$

Wave winding $A = 2; E = (\Phi ZN/60) \times (P/A) = \left(\frac{0.03 \times 360 \times 750}{60} \times \frac{4}{2}\right) = 270$ Volts.

16. A 4 pole DC shunt generator has a wave wound armature with 792 conductors. The flux per pole is 12.1 mWb; calculate the speed at which it should be run to generate 240 Volts on No load.

Solution: $E_g = 240$ Volts; $Z = 792; \Phi = 12.1$ mWb; $P = 4; A = 2$

$$N = (E \times 60 \times A)/(\Phi ZP) = \left(\frac{240 \times 60 \times 2}{0.0121 \times 792 \times 4}\right) = 751.35 \text{ RPM.}$$

17. A DC generator generates an EMF of 520 volts. It has 2000 armature conductors. Flux per pole is 0.013 Wb, Speed of 1200 RPM and the armature winding has 4 parallel paths. Find the number of poles and the type of winding.

Solution: $E_g = 520$ Volts; $Z = 2000$ conductors; $\Phi = 0.013$ Wb; $N = 1200$ RPM, $A = 4$

$$P = (E \times 60 \times A)/(\Phi ZN) = \left(\frac{520 \times 60 \times 4}{0.013 \times 2000 \times 1200}\right) = 4 \text{ Poles}$$

As **A = P** the winding is lap wound.

18. In a given DC machine of $P = 8; Z = 400; N = 300$ RPM; $\Phi = 0.9$ Wb, calculate the voltage generated when the winding is lap and wave connected.

Solution: For lap wound $A = P = 8$; $E = (\Phi ZN/60) \times (P/A)$

$$= \left(\frac{0.9 \times 400 \times 300}{60} \times \frac{8}{8}\right) = 1800 \text{ Volts}$$

For wave winding $A = 2$; $E = (\Phi ZN/60) \times (P/A)$

$$= \left(\frac{0.9 \times 400 \times 300}{60} \times \frac{8}{2}\right) = 7200 \text{ RMM.}$$

19. When driven at 1000 RPM with a flux per pole of 0.02 Wb a DC generator has an EMF of 200 V. If the speed is increased to 1100 RPM and at the same time the flux per pole is reduced to 0.019 Wb per pole. What is the Induced EMF?

Solution: When $N_1 = 1000$ RPM; $\Phi_1 = 0.02$ Wb; $E_1 = 200$ V

When $N_2 = 1100$ RPM; $\Phi_2 = 0.019$ Wb; $E_2 = ?$

$$E_1 \,\alpha\, N_1\Phi_1; \quad E_2 \,\alpha\, N_2\Phi_2$$

$$\left(\frac{E_2}{E_1} = \frac{N_2\phi_2}{N_1\phi_1}\right)$$

$$\left(E_2 = \frac{E_1 N_2 \phi_2}{N_1 \phi_1}\right) = \frac{200 \times 0.019 \times 1100}{1000 \times 0.02} = 209 \text{ V.}$$

20. Calculate the flux per pole required on full load for a 50 kW, 400 V, 8 Pole, 600 RPM, DC shunt generator with 256 conductors arranged in lap connected winding. The armature winding resistance is 0.1Ω and the shunt field resistance is 200 Ω. There is brush contact voltage drop of 1 V at each brush on Full load.

Solution: V_L = 400 Volts; Power = 50 kW; P = 8; N = 600 RPM; Z = 256; A = 8 winding is lap

R_{sh} = 200 Ω R_a = 0.1 Ω Brush drop = 1 × 2 = 2 volts.

$I_L = O/P / V_L = 50 \times 1000/400 = 125$ amps.

$I_{sh} = V_L / R_{sh} = 400/200 = 2$ amps. $I_a = I_1 + I_{sh} = 125 + 2 = 127$ amps

$E = V_L + I_a R_a + B.D = 400 + 127 \times 0.1 + 2 = 414.7$ volts

$E = (\Phi ZN/60) \times (P/A)$; $\Phi = (E \times 60 \times A) / (ZNP)$

$= (414.7 \times 60 \times 8)/(256 \times 600 \times 8)$

$= 0.1659$ Wb.

21. Calculate the flux in a 4 pole dynamo with 722 armature conductors generating 500 V when running at 1000 RPM. When the armature is (*i*) Lap connected (*ii*) wave connected.

Solution: $P = 4$; $Z = 722$; $E = 500$ V; $N = 1000$ RPM; $A = 4$ (if Lap connected)

= 2 (if Wave connected)

$E = (\Phi ZN/60) \times (P/A)$;

$\Phi = (E \times 60 \times \text{A}) / (ZNP)$

$= (500 \times 60 \times 4) / (722 \times 1000 \times 4) = 41.55$ mWb.

$E = (\Phi ZN/60) \times (P/A)$;

$\Phi = (E \times 60 \times \text{A}) / (ZNP)$

$= (500 \times 60 \times 2) / (722 \times 1000 \times 4) = 20.78$ mWb.

22. A 4 pole generator having two circuit armature has 51 slots. Each slot contains 20 conductors. What will be the voltage generated in the machine when driven at 25 RPS and useful flux is 0.025 Wb.

Solution: $P = 4$; $A = 2$; Slots = 51; Conductors/slot = 20; Speed = 25 RPS; $\Phi = 0.025$ Wb.

$Z = 51 \times 20 = 1020$; $N = 25 \times 60 = 1500$ RPM

$E = (\Phi ZN/60) \times (P/A) = (0.025 \times 1020 \times 1500/60) / (4/2) = 1275$ volts.

23. A 4 pole machine running at 1500 RPM has an armature with 90 slots and 6 conductors per slot. The flux per pole is 10 mWb. Determine the terminal EMF as DC generator if the coils are lap connected. If the current per conductor is 100 A determine the electrical power.

Solution: $P = 4$; $A = 4$; Slots = 90; Conductors/slot = 6; Speed = 1500 RPM; $\Phi = 10$ mWb.

$E = (\Phi ZN/60) \times (P/A) = (0.01 \times 540 \times 1500/60)/(4/4) = 135$ volts.

The electrical power developed in the armature $P_a = E \times I_a = 135 \times 100 = 13.5$ kW.

Problems on DC Motors

24. A DC shunt motor has armature and field resistance of 0.6 Ω and 100 Ω respectively. If the motor is connected to 230 V supply, it draws a full load armature current of 30 A and no load armature current of 4 A. Find the change in back emf from no-load to full load.

Solution: (Refer Fig. 6.18(*b*))

$$E_b = V - I_a R_a$$
$$= 212 \text{ volts on full-load}$$
$$= 227.6 \text{ volts on no-load}$$

Thus change in voltage = 15.6 volts.

25. A 100 kW, 500 V, 750 RPM DC shunt generator connected to constant voltage bus bars has field and armature resistances of 100 Ω and 0.1 Ω respectively. If the prime mover fails and the machine continues to run taking 50 A from the bus bars, calculate its speed. Neglect brush contact drop and armature reaction effects.

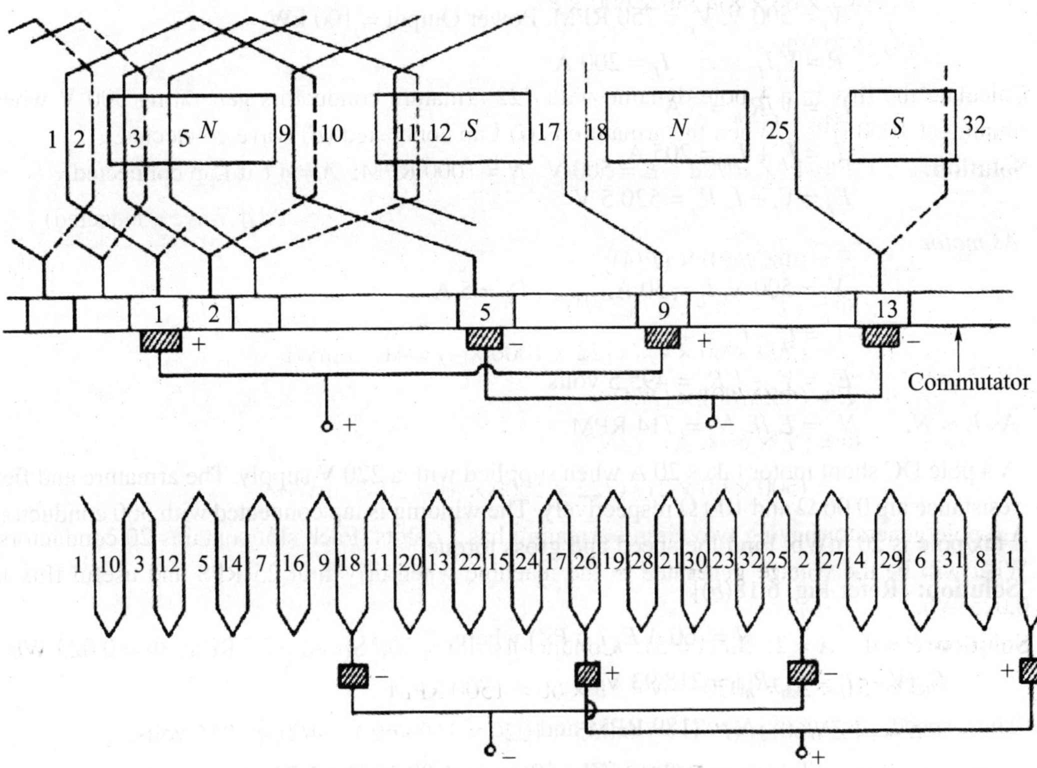

Fig. 6.24 (*a*) *Lap winding diagram*

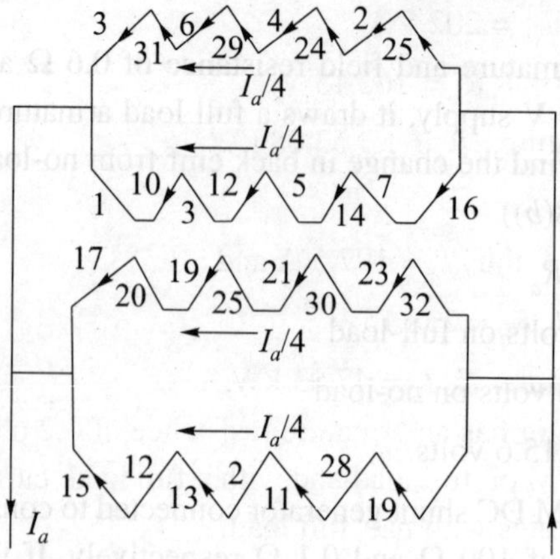

Fig. 6.24 (*b*) *Parallel division of conductors*

Solution: *As generator*

$V_t = 500$ V, $V_g = 750$ RPM, Power Output = 100 kW

$P = V_t I_L$, $\therefore$ $I_L = 200$ A

$I_{sh} = V_t / R_{sh} = 5$ A

$I_a = I_L + I_{sh} = 205$ A

$\therefore$ $E_g = V_t + I_a R_a = 520.5$ V

As motor

$V_t = 500$ V, $I_L = 50$ A, $\therefore$ $I_{sh} = 5$ A

$I_a = I_L - I_{sh} = 45$ A

$E_b = V_s - I_a R_a = 495.5$ volts

As $E \propto N$, $N_m = E_b / E_g N_g = 714$ RPM.

26. A 4 pole DC shunt motor takes 20 A when supplied with a 220 V supply. The armature and field resistance are 0.06 Ω and 100 Ω respectively. The winding is lap connected with 300 conductors. Flux/pole is 20 mWb. Find the speed and gross torque.

Solution: [Refer Fig. 6.18(*b*)]

$N = (60\, A\, E_b / \phi\, PZ)$ where,

$E_b\, [V - (I_L - I_{sh}) R_a] = 218.93$ V.

Thus, speed, $N = 2189$ RPM and

Torque = $(1/2\pi)\, (\phi Z I_a)\, (P/A) = 16.99$ Nm or 1.73 kg-m.

27. A 250 kW, 250 V, DC shunt generator has an armature resistance of 0.06 Ω and a field resistance of 100 Ω. Determine the total armature power developed when working as a generator delivering 50 kW output and a motor taking 50 kW input.

Solution: *As generator.* [Refer Fig. 6.18(*b*)]

$I_L = 50{,}000/250 = 200$ A, $I_{sh} = 250/100 = 2.5$ A

$I_a = I_L + I_{sh} = 202.5$ A

Generated emf, $E_g = 250 + I_a R_a = 262.15$ V

Power developed in armature, $(E_g I_a) = 53.08$ kW

As motor:

$I_L = I_{sh} + I_a$ thus $I_a = 197.5$ A and

$E_b = V - I_a R_a = 238.15$ V

Power developed in armature, $E_b I_a = 47.03$ kW.

28. A 120 volt, DC shunt motor has an armature resistance of 0.2 ohms and a field resistance of 60 ohms. It runs at 1800 RPM on full load and with a full load current of 40 amps. Find the speed of the motor when it operates with half full load.

Solution: Case 1: At full load

$V = 120$ V, $R_{sh} = 60$ ohms,

$R_a = 0.2$ ohms, $N_1 = 1800$ rpm, $I_1 = 40$ amps

$I_{sh} = V/R_{sh} = 120/60 = 2$ amps.

$I_{a_2} = I_1 - I_{sh} = 40 - 2 = 38$ amps

$E_{b_1} = V - I_{a_1} R_a = 120 - 38 \times 0.2 = 112.4$ V

Case 2: At half full load

$I_2 = 20$ amps,

$I_{sh} = V/R_{sh} = 120/60 = 2$ amps, $I_{a_2} = I_2 - I_{sh}$

$I_{a_2} = 20 - 2 = 18$ amps

$E_{b_2} = V - I_{a_2} R_a = 120 - 18 \times 0.2 = 116.4$ V

$N_2/N_1 = E_{b_2}/E_{b_1}$ $N_2 = N_1 \times E_{b_2}/E_{b_1}$

$= 1800 \times 116.4/ 112.4 = 1864$ RPM.

29. A 4 pole lap wound DC motor has 40 slots, each housing 20 conductors on its armature. It runs at 360 RPM and carries an armature current of 40 amps with a flux per pole of 45 mWb. Calculate the torque.

Solution: $P = 4; A = 4; N = 360$ RPM;

slots = 40; conductors/slot = 20; $I_a = 40$ A;

$\Phi = 45$ mWb.

$Z = 40 \times 20 = 800.$

$E_b = (\Phi ZN/60) \times (P/A)$

$= (45 \times 10^{-3} \times 800 \times 360/60) \times (4/4)$

$= 216$ V

$T_a = E_b I_a / 2\pi N$ Nw-m

where N in RPS = 360/60 = 6 rps

$= 216 \times 40/ 2\pi \times 6 = 229.18$ Nw-m.

30. The current drawn from the mains by a 200 V DC shunt motor is 3 A on no-load. The armature and field resistance are respectively 0.5 Ω and 200 Ω. If the line current on-load is 51 A at a speed of 1200 rpm, find the no-load speed.

Solution: $V = 200$ V; $R_a = 0.5\ \Omega$; $R_{sh} = 200\ \Omega$;

$I_0 = 3$ A; $I_1 = 51$ A; $N_1 = 1200$; $N_0 = ?$

$I_{sh} = V/R_{sh} = 200/200 = 1$ A ;

$I_a = I_0 - I_{sh} = 3 - 1 = 2$ A

$E_{b_0} = V - I_a R_a = 200 - 2 \times 0.5 = 199$ V

$I_{a_1} = I_1 - I_{sh} = 51 - 1 = 50$ A;

$E_{b_1} = V - I_{a_1} R_a = 200 - 50 \times 0.5 = 175$ V

As flux is constant $E_{b_0} / E_{b_1} = N_0 / N_1$

$N_0 = (E_{b_0} / E_{b_1}) \times N_1$

$= (199/175) \times 1200 = 1364.57$ RPM.

31. A 10 HP, 230 V shunt motor takes an armature current of 6 A from 230 V mains at no-load and runs at 1200 RPM. The armature resistance is 0.25 Ω. Determine the speed and electromagnetic torque when the armature takes 36 amps with the same flux.

Solution: Output = 10 HP = 10 × 735 = 7350 watts.

$V = 230$ V; $R_a = 0.25\ \Omega$; $I_{a_0} = 6$ A;

$I_{a_1} = 36$ A; $N_0 = 1200$; $N_1 = ?$

$E_{b_0} = V - I_{a0} R_a = 230 - 6 \times 0.25 = 228.5$ V

$E_{b_1} = V - I_{a_1} R_a = 230 - 36 \times 0.25 = 221$ V

$\Phi_0 = \Phi_1$, $E_{b_0} / E_{b_1} = N_0/N_1$;

$N_1 = (E_{b1} / E_{b_0}) \times N_0$

$= (221/228.5) \times 1200 = 1160.6$ RPM

$T_a = (E_{b1} \times I_{a_1}) / 2\pi N$ where N is in RPS

$= (221 \times 36)/ (2\pi \times 1160.0/60)$

$= 65.46$ Nw-mt.

32. A shunt generator delivers 100 kW at 250 V, when running at 400 RPM. The armature resistance is 0.01 Ω and field resistance is 100 Ω. If the same machine is run as a shunt motor with an input of 100 kW at 250 V, calculate the speed of the machine as a motor. Contact drop per brush is 1 volt.

Solution: Output power = 100 kW; $V = 250$ V;

$N = 400$ RPM; $R_a = 0.01\ \Omega$; $R_{sh} = 100\ \Omega$;

$I_1 = \text{Output}/V_1 = 100 \times 1000/250 = 400$ A

$I_{sh} = V_1/R_{sh} = 250/100 = 2.5$ A;

$I_a = I_1 + I_{sh} = 400 + 2.5 = 402.5$ A

$E_g = V_1 + I_a R_a + \text{Brush Drop}$

$= 250 + 402.5 \times 0.01 + 2 \times 1 = 256.025$ V

If the same machine acts as a motor:

$I_1 = \text{Input}/V_1 = 100 \times 1000/250 = 400$ A

$I_{sh} = V_1/R_{sh} = 250/100 = 2.5$ A;

$I_a = I_1 - I_{sh} = 400 - 2.5 = 397.5$ A

$E_b = V_1 - I_a R_a - B.D$

$= 250 - 397.5 \times 0.01 - 2 \times 1 = 244$ V

In both the cases the shunt field current is same and hence the flux.

$E_b/E_g = N_m/N_g$;

$N_m = (E_b/E_g) \times N_g = (244/256.025) \times 400$

$N_m = 381.25$ RPM.

33. A DC shunt motor runs at 1000 RPM on 200 Volts supply. Its armature resistance is 0.8 ohms and the current taken is 40 amps in addition to the field current. What resistance do you connect in series with the armature to reduce the speed to 600 RPM. The current in the armature remaining the same. Neglect armature reaction.

Solution: $I_{a_1} = 40$ A; $N_1 = 1000$ RPM; $V = 200$ V;

$R_a = 0.8$ ohms; R extra = ?

to carry the same armature current.

$I_{a_2} = 40$ amps ; $N_2 = 600$ RPM;

$E_{b_1} = V - I_a R_a - BD$

$= 200 - 40 \times 0.8 = 168$ V.

$E_{b_2} = V - I_{a_2}(R_a + R_{\text{extra}})$

$E_{b_2}/E_{b_1} = N_2/N_1$

CHAPTER 6

$$E_{b_2} = E_{b_1} \times (N_2 / N_1)$$
$$= 168 \times (600 / 1000) = 100.8 \text{ volts.}$$

Substituting in the equation of E_{b_2},

$$100.8 = 200 - 40(0.8 + R_{extra});$$
$$40 \times R_{extra} = 200 - 100.8 - 32 = 67.2$$
$$R_{extra} = 67.2 / 40 = 1.68 \text{ ohms.}$$

34. Determine the total torque developed in a 250 volts, 4 pole DC shunt motor with lap winding accommodated in 60 slots each containing 20 conductors. The armature current is 50 amps and the flux per pole is 23 mWb.

Solution: $\Phi = 23 \text{ mWb} = 23 \times 10^{-3}$ Wb;

$$Z = 60 \times 20 = 1200 \text{ conductors;}$$
$$P = 4; \ A = P = 4 \ \text{(since it is lap wound);}$$
$$I_a = 50 \text{ amps}$$
$$T_a = 0.159 \, \Phi \, Z \, I_a \, (P/A)$$
$$= 0.159 \times 1200 \times 23 \times 10^{-3} \times 50 \times (4/4)$$
$$= 219.42 \text{ Nw-mt.}$$

35. A 15 HP, 4 poles, 250 V lap connected DC shunt motor has 48 slots, each containing 20 conductors. It draws a current of 80 A from the supply. The field and armature resistances are 125 and 0.2 ohms respectively. The total flux per pole is 100 m Wb. Calculate the speed and the torque developed by armature.

Solution: $P = 4 \, ; \, A = 4 \, ;$

$$\text{slots} = 48; \text{ conductors / slot} = 20;$$
$$\Phi = 100 \text{ mWb} = 0.1 \text{ Wb}$$
$$\text{Total conductors} = 48 \times 20 = 960;$$
$$I = 80 \text{ A} \, ; \, R_a = 0.2 \, \Omega; \, R_{sh} = 125 \, \Omega;$$
$$I_{sh} = V / R_{sh} = 250 / 125 = 2 \text{ A};$$
$$I_a = I - I_{sh} = 80 - 2 = 78$$
$$E_{b_1} = V - I_a R_a - BD = 250 - 78 \times 0.2$$
$$= 234.4 \text{ V.} \quad B.D = \text{Brush drop} = 0$$
$$E_b = (\Phi ZN/60) \times (P/A)$$
$$= (100 \times 10^{-3} \times 960 \times N/60) \times (4/4)$$
$$1.6\,N = 234.4;$$

Hence $N = 234.4 / 1.6 = 146.5$ RPM

$$T_a = (E_b \times I_a) / 2\pi N \quad \text{where } N \text{ is in RPS}$$

$= 234.4 \times 78 / 2\pi \times (146.5/60)$

$= 1191.787$ Nw-mt.

36. The armature resistance of a 25 HP, 250 V DC series motor is 0.2 ohms and the series field resistance is 0.05 ohms. When the series motor takes 80 A the speed is 600 RPM. Calculate the speed when the current is 50 A.

Solution: $V = 250$ V; $R_a = 0.2\ \Omega$;

$R_{se} = 0.05\ \Omega$; $I_{a_1} = 80\ A$; $N_1 = 600$ RPM;

$E_{b_1} = V - I_{a_1}(R_a + R_{se}) - BD$

$= 250 - 80 \times (0.2 + 0.05) = 230$ V.

$E_{b_2} = V - I_{a_2}(R_a + R_{se}) - BD$

$= 250 - 50 \times (0.2 + 0.05) = 237.5$ V.

$E_{b_1}\ \alpha\ \Phi_1 N_1\ \alpha\ I_{a_1} N_1$

$E_{b_2}\ \alpha\ \Phi_2 N_2\ \alpha\ I_{a_2} N_2$ [α = Proportional]

$E_{b_2} / E_{b_1} = I_{a_2} N_2 / I_{a_1} N_1$

$N_2 = (E_{b_2} / E_{b_1}) \times (I_{a_1} / I_{a_2}) \times N_1$

$= (237.5 / 230) \times (80 / 50) \times 600$

$= 991.3$ RPM.

PROBLEMS

1. A DC generator has an armature resistance of 0.1 Ω and the OCC at 800 RPM is as given in table below. The generator is run as a shunt machine at 1000 RPM. Determine the total resistance of the field circuit for obtaining an emf of 250 V on no-load. Calculate the terminal voltage and field current when armature current is 80 A.

Field current	0.5	1.0	1.5	2.0	2.5	3.0
Emf	70	118	155	186	211	232

2. A 230 V, series motor takes 50 A current. Armature and series field winding resistances are 0.15 Ω and 0.1 Ω respectively. Calculate Brush voltage, Back emf, Power wasted in armature and Mechanical power developed.

3. A shunt develops 23 HP at 200 V, while consuming 20.2 kW of power. The armature resistance is 0.06 Ω and the field resistance is 50 Ω. Find the efficiency and power input when the output is 10 HP.

4. A 220 V DC shunt motor takes 5 A at no-load and runs at 700 RPM. The armature resistance is 0.1 Ω and field resistance is 100 Ω. Find the efficiency, speed and torque developed when the motor input is 8 kW.

5. A 500 V series motors has a resistance of 0.2 Ω and runs at 400 RPM. When taking a current of 60 A, calculate the speed when taking a current of 30 A, if the flux is 35% less than that at 60 A.

CHAPTER 6

Alternating Current Machines

7

CHAPTER

7.1 INTRODUCTION

An AC machine is one that operates on AC supply. AC machines may be classified as: Transformers, Induction machines and Synchronous machines. They can work on either single phase or three phase. The generating plants, generating the bulk of AC power, are concentrated in a few, large, favorably situated stations. The power generated is then transmitted to various parts of the power system. Large power should be transmitted at appreciably high voltage to reduce the amount of copper material and to increase the efficiency of transmission. However, the distribution of power in a given area should be carried out at a suitably low voltage for various reasons concerned with safety, use of small apparatus, etc. Hence the generated energy needs to be transformed. Such transformation of AC from one voltage level to another is done by a *transformer*.

A transformer is a static, electromagnetic device that transforms one AC system into another of different voltage and current, the power and frequency remaining constant. Thus, transformers play a major role in transmission and distribution of AC power. The transformers are also used in rectifiers, starters (auto-transformer starters), furnaces, welding, traction systems, testing units, etc. A transformer basically works on the mutual induction between the two circuits electrically isolated from each other and linked by a common magnetic field.

Thus, in brief, a transformer is a device that:

- transfers electric power from one circuit to another
- it does so without a change in frequency
- it accomplishes this by electromagnetic induction, and where the two electric circuits are in mutual inductive influence of each other.

7.2 TRANSFORMERS

7.2.1 Construction

Transmission of electrical energy from generation station to the consumer premises results in the losses and depends on the magnitude of the current flow. In order to minimize these losses higher voltages are used and thus lower currents are needed for the same energy. However, on the distribution end, high voltage is to be returned to low voltages depending on the various purposes/requirements. The priority that the AC gets over DC is due to the fact that the former can be more easily transformed. Thus transformers are used for transmitting electric energy from systems with a given voltage to systems with a different voltage (higher/lower). One of the main advantages of AC transmission and distribution is the ease with which an AC voltage can be increased or reduced. Transformers are the devices used for conversion of voltage levels but the power transmitted/distributed remains the same. It should be noted that the transmission of power at high voltage levels incur low currents and hence low copper loss.

Transformer may be defined as a static device which works on the principle of mutual induction to transfer electrical power from one circuit to another. In this process of power transfer, the voltage may be stepped up or down without change in frequency level. Transformer essentially consists of two windings mounted on a laminated magnetic core. The winding to which supply is connected is *primary* and the other winding to which load is connected is *secondary*.

Depending upon the construction of core and the way in which windings are mounted on it, transformers are classified as: *Core type* and *Shell type*. In core type, the core is rectangular and the windings are mounted on the two limbs. The main magnetic feature of core transformer is that the core is surrounded by the coils. On the other hand in shell type, the core has three limbs and two window. In this case, it appears as if the coils are surrounded by the core. All primary and secondary coils are mounted only on the central limb. The details are indicated in Fig. 7.1.

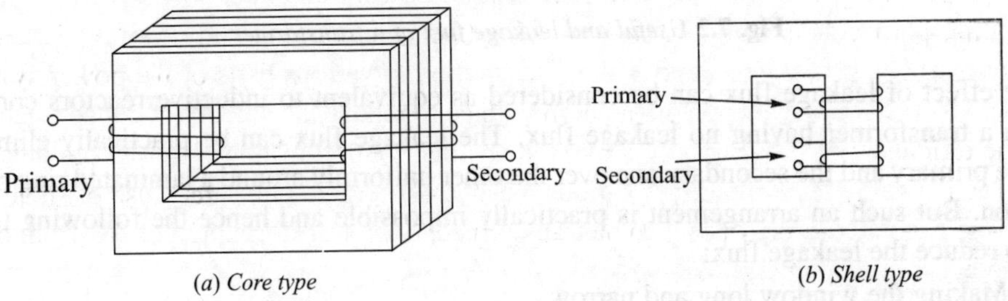

Fig. 7.1 *Types of transformers based on construction*

Transformers can operate on single phase or three phase systems. They can be oil filled self cooled, oil filled water cooled, air blast type etc. Also, they can be step-up or step-down transformers depending on the ratio of number of turns on primary and secondary windings.

7.2.2 Principle

Two windings of a transformer are magnetically connected and are electrically isolated. The transformer core provides a path of low reluctance for the flux. When the primary winding is applied with the alternating voltage is produces a current in the primary winding. This current produces a flux in the transformer core which then links with the secondary winding. The flux linking with the secondary winding induces an emf in the secondary winding on account of mutual induction. This secondary emf supplies the load connected to it. The flux in the transformer core also links with the primary winding and induces an emf in the primary winding on account of self induction.

Certain amount of current flows in the primary depending on the load at secondary. This current in the primary windings produces a flux which is responsible for inducing a voltage across the primary and the secondary windings. The secondary induced voltage then pumps certain amount of current in the load. This process of drawing current from the primary and producing an equivalent amount of current in the secondary continues throughout the operation of a transformer.

The actual flux in the transformer can be regarded as a combination of two components: (Fig. 7.2).

- The useful flux linked with both windings and remaining practically constant at all loads.
- The leakage flux links only with the winding by which it is produced. The reluctance of the paths of the leakage flux is almost entirely due to the long air paths. The value of the leakage flux is proportional to the load current.

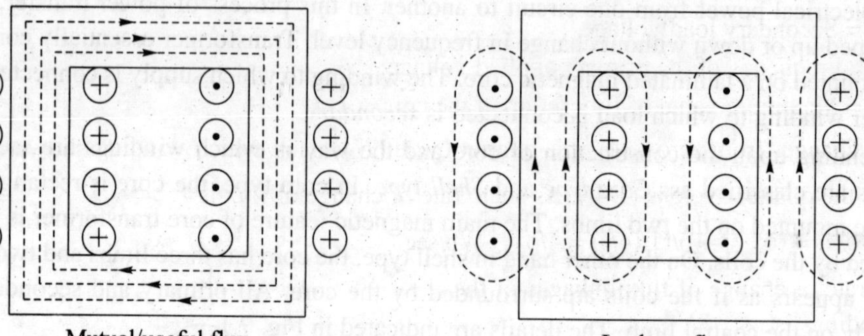

Fig. 7.2 *Useful and leakage flux of a transformer*

The effect of leakage flux can be considered as equivalent to inductive reactors connected in series with a transformer having no leakage flux. The leakage flux can be practically eliminated by winding the primary and the secondary one over the other uniformly around a laminated ring of uniform cross-section. But such an arrangement is practically impossible and hence the following techniques are used to reduce the leakage flux:

- Making the window long and narrow,
- Arranging primary and secondary windings concentrically and
- Sandwitching the primary and secondary windings.

7.2.3 Equation for Induced EMF

When AC voltage is applied to primary winding, it produces a self induced emf in the primary and a mutual induced emf across the secondary winding. Consider the parameters corresponding to primary and secondary circuits of a single phase transformer, represented by the circuit symbol in Fig. 7.3.

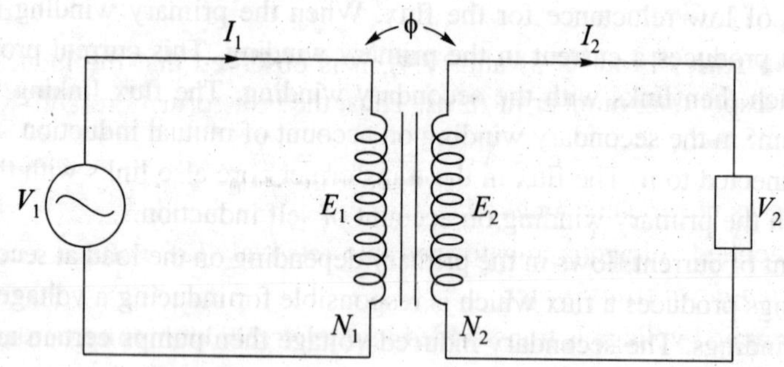

Fig. 7.3 *Transformer-circuit symbol*

N_1 = Number of turns in the primary winding
N_2 = Number of turns in the secondary winding
E_1 = Primary induced EMF
E_2 = Secondary induced EMF
V_1 = Primary supply voltage
V_2 = Secondary load voltage
f = Frequency of the primary applied voltage
ϕ_{max} = Maximum value of flux set up in the core

Flux changes from zero to ϕ_m in a quarter cycle ($T/4$). However, $T = 1/f$, as shown in Fig. 7.4.

Thus the quarter cycle is ($1/4f$). As such, rate of change of flux is

$$d\phi/dt = (\phi_{max} - 0)/(1/(4f)) = 4f\phi_{max} \text{ Wb/sec} \quad ...(7.1)$$

The rate of change of flux linkages of the primary windings is

$$4\phi_{max} f N_1 \text{ Wb-Turns/sec} \quad ...(7.2)$$

This must be equal to the average magnitude of the induced emf as per the Faraday's law of induction. Thus, the average value of the induced emf in the primary is given by

$$E_{av} = 4\phi_{max} f N_1 \text{ volts} \quad ...[7.2(a)]$$

∴ RMS value of induced emf E_1 is the product of form factor of a sine wave and the average value *i.e.*,

$$E_1 = (1.11)\, 4\phi_{max} f N_1$$
$$= 4.44\phi_{max} f N_1 \text{ volts} \quad ...(7.3)$$

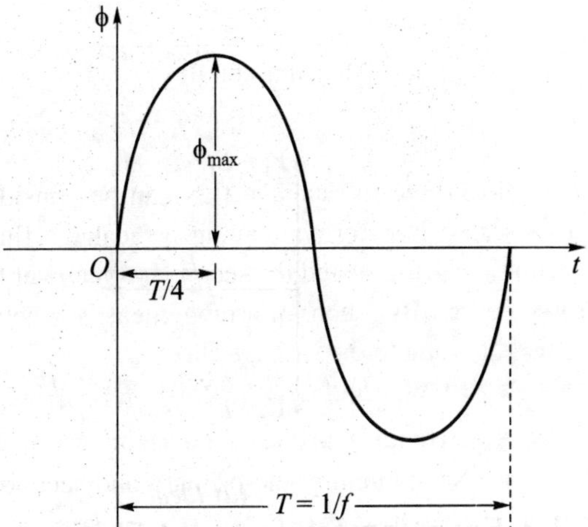

Fig. 7.4 *Variation of input voltage*

Similarly, the RMS value of the induced emf in the secondary is

$$E_2 = 4.44\phi_{max} f N_2 \text{ volts.} \quad ...(7.4)$$

Transformation ratio: From (7.3) and (7.4), it is observed that the induced emf values are proportional to the corresponding number of turns. Thus, the transformation ratio, K is defined as

$$K = E_2/E_1 = N_2/N_1 = V_2/V_1 = I_1/I_2 \quad ...(7.5)$$

Indeed, three cases may be encountered:

- For $K < 1$, applied voltage is transformed into relatively low voltage. Such a transformer is known as *Step-down transformer.*
- For $K > 1$, applied voltage is transformed into relatively high voltage. Such a transformer is known as a *Step-up transformer.*
- For $K = 1$, the turns ratio is unity and the secondary voltage is at the same level as that of the primary voltage. Such transformers are used whenever electrical isolation is required.

7.2.4 Transformers Under No-Load

When the secondary of the transformer is open circuited, then it is said to be under no-load condition. Let ϕ be the total flux (mutual flux) produced in the primary. When the transformer is ideal (loss less) then, $V_1 = E_1$ and $V_2 = E_2$. On the other hand, for a practical transformer:

$V_1 = E_1$ + drop across primary impedance

$V_2 = E_2$ – drop across secondary impedance ...(7.6)

When the secondary of the transformer is open circuited, then there will be a no-load current I_0 lags behind V_1 by 90° as shown in Fig. 7.5.

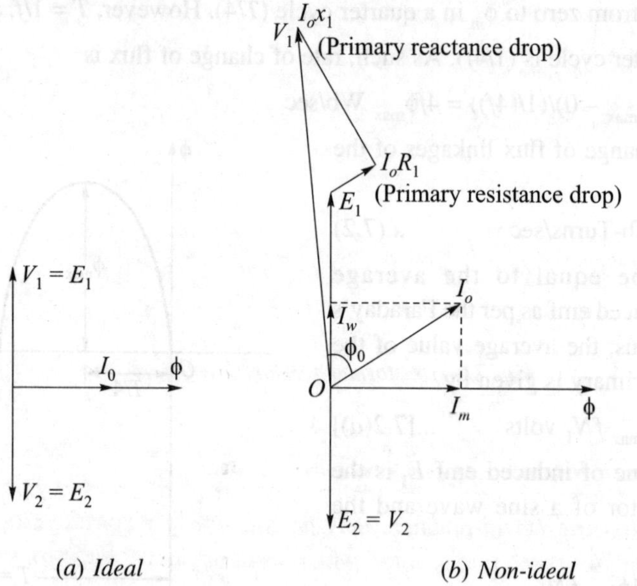

Fig. 7.5 *Transformer phasor diagram on no load*

However, in practice, even on no-load, there are core losses and a small amount of copper loss due to resistance and reactance of the primary winding. In order to supply these losses, enough power must be drawn from the supply. The no-load current I_0 lags behind V_1 by an angle less than 90°. I_0 can be resolved into two components I_w along V_1 and I_m in quadrature, lagging. I_w, the working component, supplies the core-loss and primary copper loss. I_m, the magnetizing component, sets up mutual flux ϕ. *i.e.*,

$I_w = I_0 \cos \phi_0$, core-loss component,

$I_m = I_0 \sin \phi_0$, magnetizing component and

$\cos \phi_0$ is the no-load power factor. ...(7.7)

7.2.5 Transformers on Load

When a load is connected to the secondary of transformer, then it draws secondary load current, I_2. This current would cause, by transformer action, an additional current I_1^1 to be drawn from the supply in addition to the no-load current I_0. Hence total primary current $I_1 = I_1^1 + I_0$. The current I_1^1 is such that the mmf established by it would just balance the secondary mmf, *i.e.*, $N_1 I_1^1 = N_2 I_2$. The phasor diagram of the transformer is shown in Fig. 7.6.

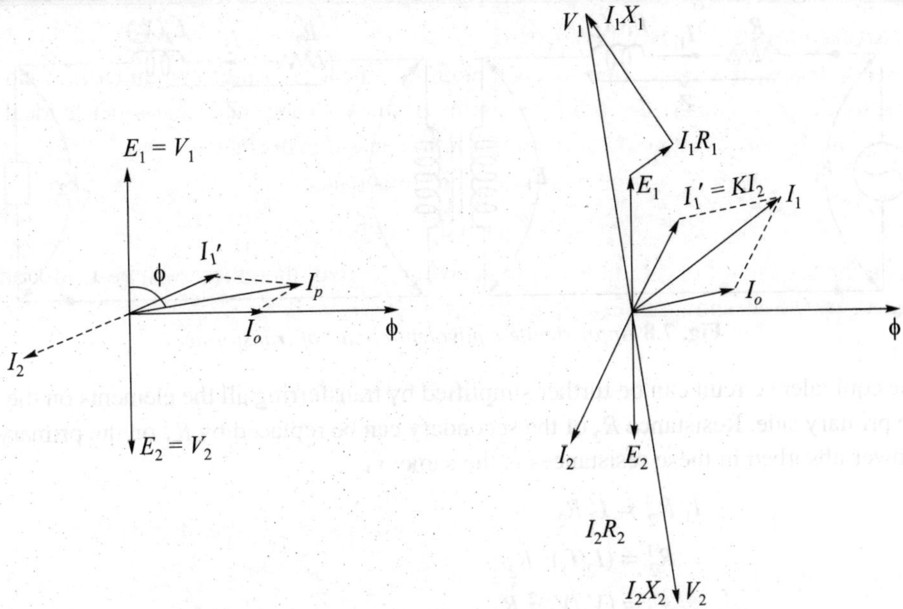

(a) Ideal (b) Non-ideal

Fig. 7.6 *Transformer phasor diagram on-load*

7.3 TRANSFORMERS—EQUIVALENT CIRCUIT

The behaviour of a transformer in practice, may be conveniently considered by referring to an ideal transformer with all losses taken into account which were neglected hitherto. Considering the winding resistance and reactances, magnetic leakage reactances and core loss effects of the transformer, the equivalent circuit can be arrived at as in Fig. 7.7.

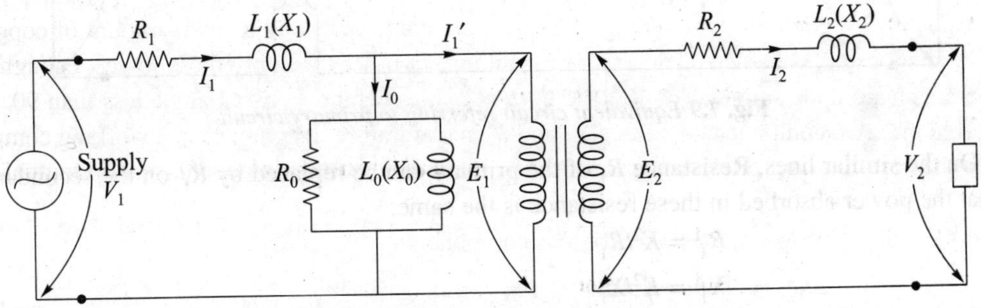

Fig. 7.7 *Equivalent circuit of a transfomer*

Since the no-load current I_0 of a transformer is about 3 to 5% of the full load primary current, the parallel circuit consisting of R_0 and X_0 can be omitted. Thus, the approximate equivalent circuit of a transformer simplifies to the one shown in Fig. 7.8.

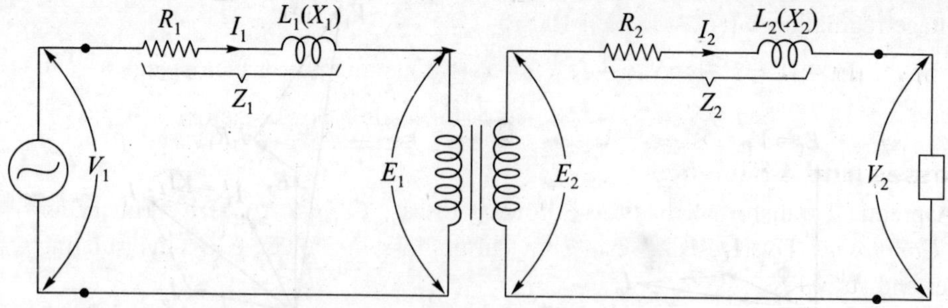

Fig. 7.8 *Approximate equivalent circuit of transformer*

The equivalent circuit can be further simplified by transferring all the elements on the secondary side to the primary side. Resistance R_2 of the secondary can be replaced by R_2^1 on the primary side such that the power absorbed in these resistances is the same. *i.e.*,

$$I_1^2 R_2^1 = I_2^2 R_2$$

$$R_2^1 = (I_2/I_1)^2 R_2$$

$$= (V_1/V_2)^2 R_2$$

$$= R_2/K^2$$

Similarly, $$X_2^1 = X_2/K^2 \qquad ...(7.8)$$

The equivalent circuit with the secondary values referred to the primary circuit is shown in Fig. 7.9.

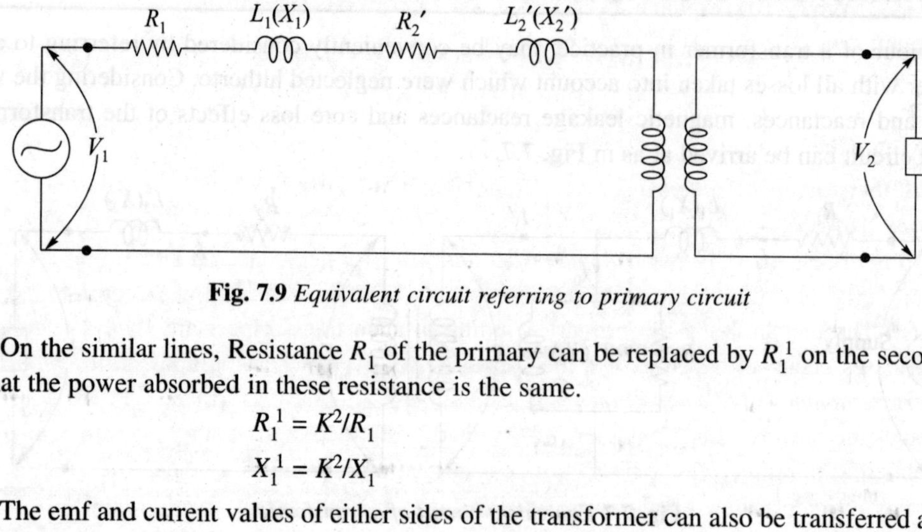

Fig. 7.9 *Equivalent circuit referring to primary circuit*

On the similar lines, Resistance R_1 of the primary can be replaced by R_1^1 on the secondary side such that the power absorbed in these resistance is the same.

$$R_1^1 = K^2/R_1$$

and $$X_1^1 = K^2/X_1 \qquad ...(7.9)$$

The emf and current values of either sides of the transformer can also be transferred as required on similar lines.

7.3.1 Voltage Regulation

It is defined as the change in secondary voltage from no-load to full load expressed as either a per unit or a percentage of the no-load voltage, primary voltage remaining constant.

Voltage regulation = $[(E_2 - V_2)/E_2]$ 100%

where, $E_2 - V_2 = I_2 R_2 \cos\phi + I_2 X_2 \sin\phi$ (for lagging power factor) and

$= I_2 R_2 \cos\phi - I_2 X_2 \sin\phi$ (for leading power factor) ...[7.9(*a*)]

7.3.2 Losses and Efficiency

Looses: A practical transformer has the following losses: *Copper losses* in primary and secondary windings, *Core losses* (Hysteresis losses + Eddy current losses), dielectric loss in insulating walls of the transformer and stray losses.

Efficiency, η: It is defined as the ratio of output power to the input power *i.e.*

$$\eta = (\text{Output/Input})\ 100\%$$
$$= [(\text{Input} - \text{Losses})\ (\text{Input})]\ 100\%$$
$$= [(\text{Output})/(\text{Output} + \text{Losses})]\ 100\%$$

$$\eta = \frac{V_2 I_2 \cos\phi}{V_2 I_2 \cos\phi + W_i + I_2^2 (R_1^1 + R_2)} \quad ...(7.10)$$

Efficiency at any fraction of full load, x, η_x (for instance, full load – $x = 1$, 3/4 full load – $x = 0.75$ and so on) can be obtained as follows:

$$\eta_x = (x\text{KVA} \cos\phi)/(x\text{KVA} \cos\phi + W_i + x^2 W_{cu})\ 100\% \quad ...(7.11)$$

where, KVA = rating of the transformer, $\cos\phi$ = power factor of the load, W_i = core losses (kW) and W_{cu} = full load copper losses (kW).

Condition for maximum efficiency: The efficiency of a transformer is maximum when $d\eta/dI_2 = 0$ *i.e.*, from (7.10), we have,

$$\frac{d\eta}{dI_2} = \frac{\{V_2 I_2 \cos\phi + W_i + I_2^2 (R_1^1 + R_2)\}\{V_2 \cos\phi\} - (V_2 I_2 \cos\phi)\{V_2 \cos\phi + 2I_2 (R_1^1 + R_2)\}}{\{V_2 I_2 \cos\phi + W_i + I_2^2 (R_1^1 + R_2)\}^2} = 0$$

Solving which we get, $W_i = I_2^2\ (R_1^1 + R_2)$ ...(7.12)

Thus, the efficiency of the transformer is maximum when the iron loss (constant loss) equals the copper losses (variable losses).

All-day efficiency: The performance of certain transformers (such as distribution transformer) cannot be properly judged by using power efficiency (in which input and output are represented in watts or kilowatts). The reason being the primary winding of such transformers are always energized and hence core losses occur all the time. But the copper losses occur when the transformer supplies load. Hence, *energy efficiency* or *all-day efficiency* is used for assessing the performance of such transformers. It is defined as the ratio of the output energy (*i.e.*, energy supplied to the load) to the input energy (*i.e.*, energy supplied to the transformer) both being considered for a period of one day (*i.e.*, for 24 hours).

All-day efficiency, $\eta_{\text{all-day}}$ = (Output in kWh/Input in kWh) 100% (over 24 hours)

7.4 TRANSFORMERS—TESTS

The actual loading of transformers involve wastage of power and arrangement of large loads for testing large transformers. Hence, to *predetermine* their efficiency and voltage regulation, tests are conducted without actually loading them. The tests conducted include the *open circuit* and *short circuit* tests, discussed below:

7.4.1 Open Circuit Test

In open circuit (OC) test, the secondary side (usually *HV* side) is open circuited and rated voltage is applied on the primary side. Power drawn from the supply is equal to the core losses in the transformer as there are no-copper losses in the secondary winding (no current flow) and the copper losses in the primary winding are very small. No-load current is about 3 to 5% of full load current. The current, power and voltage are measured on the primary side using the respective meters connected as shown in Fig. 7.10.

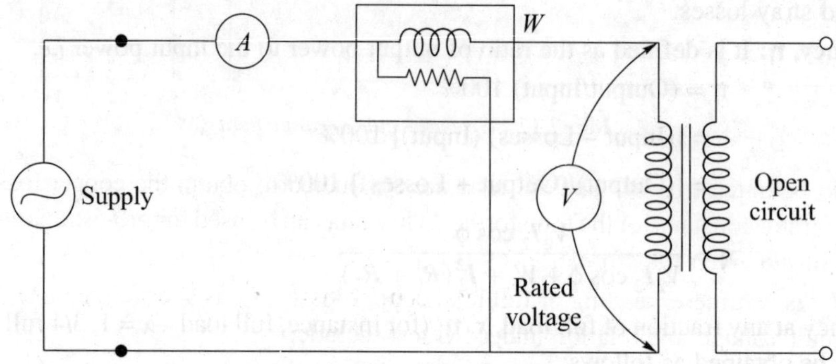

Fig. 7.10 *Test-circuit arrangement*

With V_0, I_0 and W_0 as the Voltmeter, Ammeter and Wattmeter readings respectively, the no-load power loss (core loss) is given by,

$$W_0 = V_0 I_0 \cos \phi_0 \qquad ...(7.13)$$

Thus the no-load power factor is

$$\cos \phi_0 = W_0/V_0 I_0 \qquad ...(7.14)$$

The vector diagram under OC condition is as shown in Fig. 7.11, where,

Core loss component

$$I_w = I_0 \cos \phi_0$$

Magnetizing component

$$I_m = I_0 \sin \phi_0$$

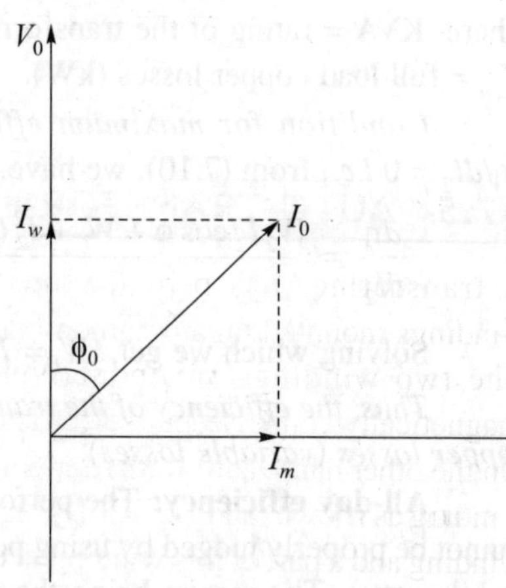

Fig. 7.11 *Vector diagram–OC test*

$$R_0 = V_0/I_w \quad \text{and} \quad X_0 = V_0/I_m \qquad ...(7.15)$$

7.4.2 Short Circuit Test

In short circuit (SC) test, the secondary (usually LV) side is short circuited and a small voltage is applied to the primary side such that rated current flows through it. The voltage, current and power are measured on the primary side using voltmeter, ammeter and wattmeter respectively. As the applied voltage and hence flux are only about 1/20 to 1/30 of the rated voltage and core losses are approximately proportional to the square of the flux, the power drawn from the supply in this test completely represents the copper loss of the transformer (as the core losses are negligible). The circuit arrangement for the test is as shown in Fig. 7.12.

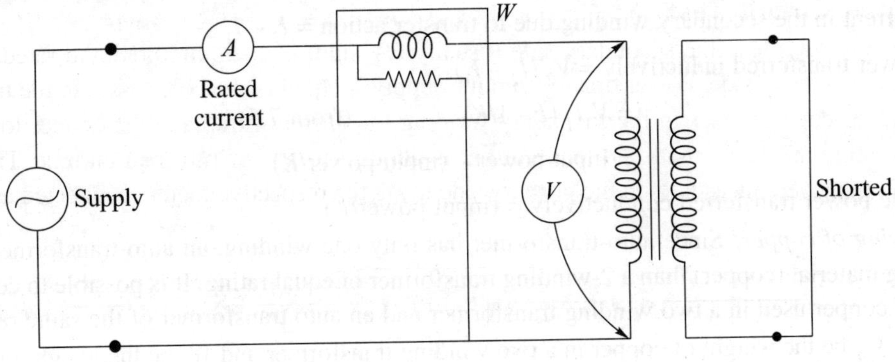

Fig. 7.12 *SC test-circuit arrangement*

It should be noted that OC and SC tests are conducted to obtain the copper losses, core losses and equivalent circuit constants of the transformer. This data can be used for pre-estimating the efficiency and regulation of the given transformer.

With W_{sc} as wattmeter reading or full load copper losses, I_{sc} as short circuit or rated current and V_{sc} as short circuit voltage, the relation under SC test include:

$$R_{eq} = (R_1 + R_2^1) = W_{sc}/I_{sc}^2$$

$$Z_{eq} = (Z_1 + Z_2^1) = V_{sc}/I_{sc}$$

$$X_{eq} = (X_1 + X_2^1) = \sqrt{Z_{eq}^2 - R_{eq}^2} \quad ...(7.16)$$

7.5 AUTO-TRANSFORMERS

A transformer has primary and secondary windings mounted on a common magnetic core. The two windings are inductively coupled, magnetically connected and electrically isolated. On the other hand, auto-transformer has only one winding as shown in Fig. 7.13. This is the primary winding and a part of this winding itself functions as secondary winding. In an auto-transformer, transfer of power from primary to secondary winding takes place both inductively and conductively. Auto-transformers are used for smooth and continuous variation of voltage as a starter for induction motors and to supply power to arc furnaces at the desired voltage level.

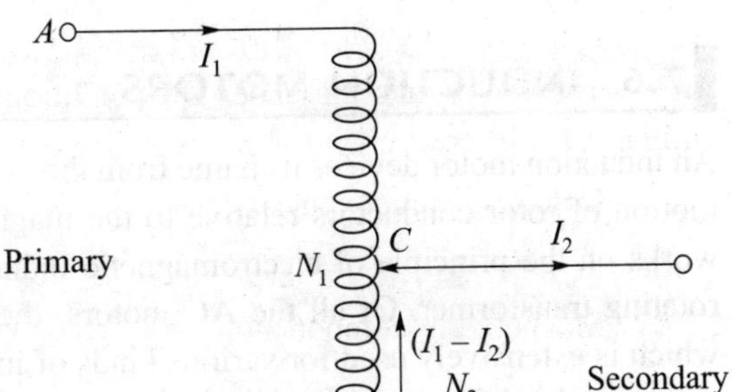

Fig. 7.13 *Auto-transformer*

Transfer of power: Consider the input and output power values given by,

Input power = $V_1 I_1$

Output power = $V_2 I_2$

where, V_2 = Secondary induced emf ...(7.17)

Current in the secondary winding due to transfer action = $I_2 - I_1$ ...(7.18)

Power transferred inductively = $V_2 (I_2 - I_1)$

$= V_1 I_1 (I - 1/K)$ (from 7.5)

= Input power – (input power/K) ...(7.19)

and the power transferred conductively = (input power/K). ...(7.20)

Saving of copper: Since auto-transformer has only one winding, an auto-transformer uses less conducting material (copper) than a 2-winding transformer of equal rating. It is possible to compare the amount of copper used in a two winding transformer and an auto transformer of the same rating.

Let W_1 be the weight of copper in a two winding transformer and W_2 be the weight of copper in an auto-transformer. As weight is proportional to volume, it varies in proportion to the product of number of turns and current.

$$W_1 \alpha (N_1 I_1 + N_2 I_2)$$

and $$W_2 \alpha (N_1 - N_2) I_1 + N_2 (I_2 - I_1)$$

$$\therefore \quad W_1/W_2 = (N_1 I_1 + N_2 I_2)/(N_1 - N_2) I_1 + N_2 (I_2 - I_1))$$

$$= (N_1 I_1 + N_2 I_2)/(N_1 I_1 + N_2 I_2 - 2N_2 I_1) \quad ...(7.21)$$

However, $N_1/N_2 = I_2/I_1 = K$, the above may be written as,

$$W_1/W_2 = (N_1/N_2 I_1 + I_2)/(N_1/N_2) I_1 + I_2 - 2I_1)$$

$$= (KI_1 + I_2)/(KI_1 + I_2 - 2I_1) \quad ...(7.22)$$

Dividing the numerator and denominator by I_1 and noting that $I_2/I_1 = K$ yields, $W_1/W_2 = K/(K-1)$. As $K > 1$, $W_1 > W_2$ and a saving of (1/K) times the weight of copper of two winding transformer is realizable.

7.6 INDUCTION MOTORS

An induction motor devices its name from the fact that the current in the rotor winding is induced by the motion of rotor conductors relative to the magnetic field produced by the stator currents. The motor works on the principle of electromagnetic induction. In fact, an induction motor can be viewed as a rotating transformer. Of all the AC motors, the poly-phase (three phase) induction motor is the one which is extensively used for various kinds of industrial drives. The three phase induction motor is the most popular AC motor. This is because of the fact that the motor has several advantages over the other types of motors.

The induction motors can be operated as single phase or three phase systems. Single phase induction motors are much inferior in performance compared to three phase induction motors. These motors are not self starting. Still, these motors are very much used for domestic and commercial purposes, where only single phase supply is available. The important features of the motor are:

- *Rugged construction*
- *Low cost and reliable operation*
- *High efficiency and high power factor especially at full load*
- *Maintenance free operation*
- *Self starting and simple starting arrangement*

- *Efficiency decreases when the speed variation is opted*
- *Speed versus Load is a drooping characteristic.*

7.6.1 Construction

A three phase induction motor mainly consists of two parts: stator and rotor. The schematic diagram showing the constructional details of a three phase induction motor is shown in Fig. 7.14.

Fig. 7.14 *Induction motor-construction*

Stator: It is the static member of the machine. It forms the outermost covering. The stator core is cylindrical and is made of cast iron or cast steel. The stator core has slots on its inner surface to house stator windings. The core is laminated to reduce iron losses. The stator carries three independent windings which may be interconnected either in Δ or Y. The windings are prepared for a fixed number of poles and the exact number of poles is decided on the basis of speed requirement. Greater the number of poles, lower the speed and vice versa.

Rotors: It is the rotating member of the motor which is a closed set of conductors wound on an iron core. The rotor emf produces rotor currents. The rotating field due to stator currents and the rotor currents react to produce forces on the rotor conductors and hence the torque. Based on the method of rotor construction, there are three types of rotor construction for induction motor which are commonly used for commercial purposes: *Squirrel cage, Slip ring* or *Phase wound* and *Double-cage rotors.*

Squirrel cage rotor: Motors using this type of rotor are known as squirrel cage induction motors. Here, the rotor core is cylindrical and built up of laminations. It has slots on its outer surface and usually made up of cast iron or cast steel with conductors in the form of thick bars of copper or aluminium. The rotor conductors are connected to copper end-rings at both the ends. The arrangement of conductors with end-rings appears like a cage for squirrels as shown in Fig. 7.15 and hence the name squirrel cage rotor. It may be noted that as the rotor bars are short circuited on themselves, it is not possible to add any external resistance in the rotor circuit either for starting, or for speed control purposes. Rotor slots are usually skewed (slots are not parallel to the shaft) which results in the smooth running of the motor without any magnetic hum and reducing the tendency of the rotor teeth to remain under the stator teeth due to direct magnetic attraction between the two, called *locking tendency* of the rotor.

Slip-ring or phase-wound rotor: In this type of rotor, core is cylindrical and its periphery has slots to house rotor windings. The rotor windings are prepared for the same number of poles and phases as that of stator windings. The three ends of the three phases are connected in star and the other three ends are brought out and connected to the slip rings mounted on the shaft of the motor as shown in Fig. 7.16. The slip-rings are connected to the external circuit through carbon brushes placed on the slip rings. This facilitates the introduction of external resistance in the rotor circuit during the starting process of the motor, thereby increasing the starting torque of the motor and for achieving different speed-load characteristics. While the machine is running under normal conditions, slip rings are automatically short circuited by a metal collar connecting all the rings together. Brushes are automatically lifted from slip rings, thereby reducing the frictional losses and the wear and tear. As such, under normal conditions, a wound rotor motor runs as a squirrel-cage motor only.

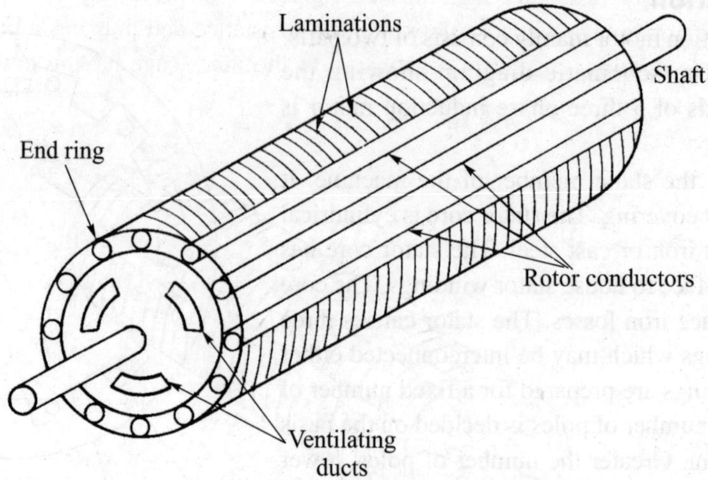

Fig. 7.15 *Squirrel-cage rotor*

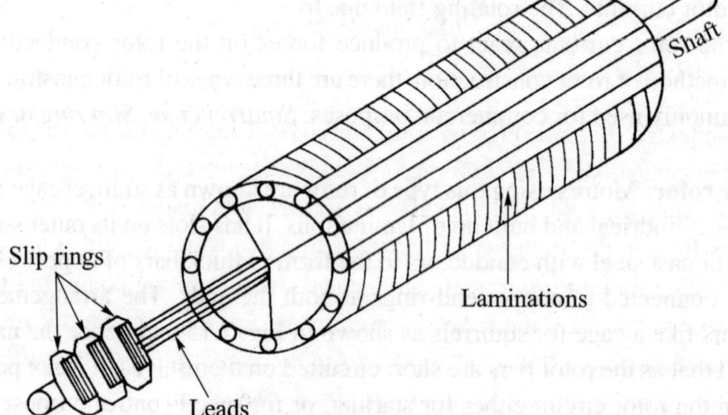

(a) Construction

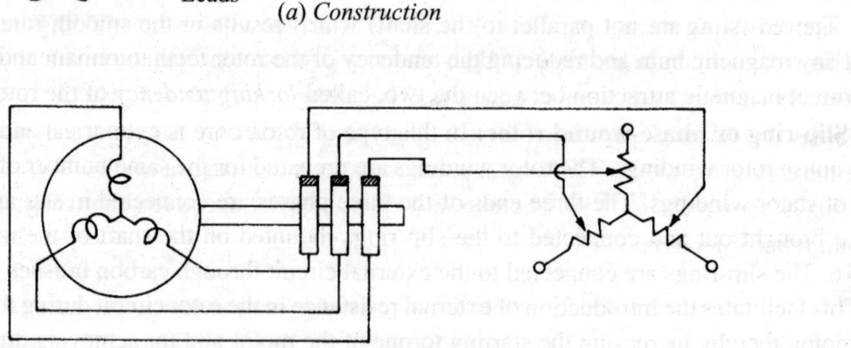

(b) Connection diagram

Fig. 7.16 *Slip-ring rotor*

Double-cage rotor: Here, there are two cages for the production of high starting torque. The outer cage winding is made up of high resistance material like aluminum or brass and the inner cage winding is made up of low resistance material like copper as shown in Fig. 7.17. As such, when the motor is started, the upper cage plays a role which has resistance and thus has a high starting torque. When the machine is running, current is constrained to the inner cage having low resistance, which results in low losses.

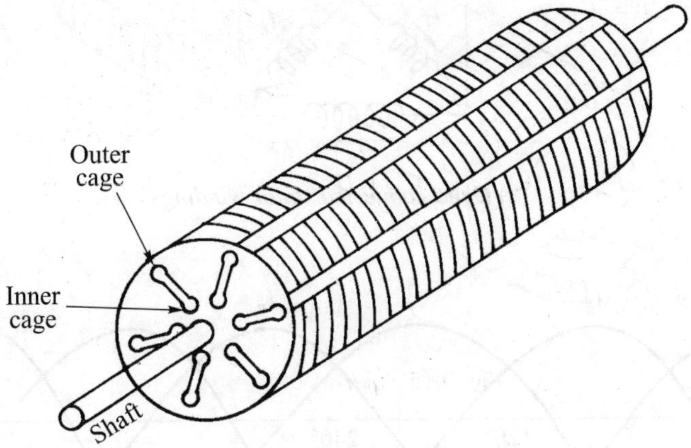

Fig. 7.17 *Double-cage rotor*

7.6.2 Principle

The induction motor consists of a *stator* (fixed core) and *rotor*. The stator carries the three phase winding, while the rotor carries a cage, slip-ring winding or a double cage. The rotor is free to rotate inside the stator. The air-gap between the rotor and the stator is uniform and made as small as possible. When the power is on, currents flow in the stator windings and a uniform rotating field is produced as follows.

Consider an induction motor with delta connected stator winding connected to supply resulting in currents as indicated in Fig. 7.18. It can be observed from mmf diagram that the resultant mmf would be rotating in space at a constant speed called *synchronous speed*, $N_s = (120\ f/p)$ RPM where f is the frequency of supply in Hz, and P is the number of poles of the stator.

The revolving stator flux is cut by the stationary rotor conductors and thereby emfs are induced, producing rotor currents in the rotor conductors, by electromagnetic induction. The rotor currents produce magnetic flux around the rotor conductors. The interaction between rotor flux and the stator flux strengthens the flux on one side of the conductor and simultaneously weakness the flux on the other side of the conductor. On account of this, rotor starts rotating in the same direction as that of the rotating stator flux as shown in Fig. 7.19. The rotor always rotates at a speed less than the speed of stator flux to maintain relative motion.

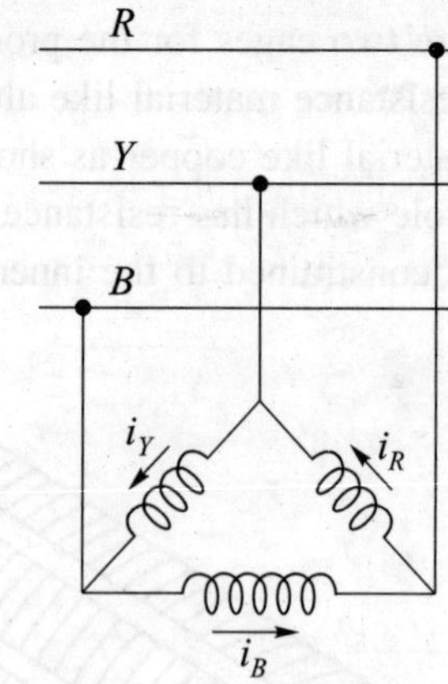

(a) *Delta connected stator windings*

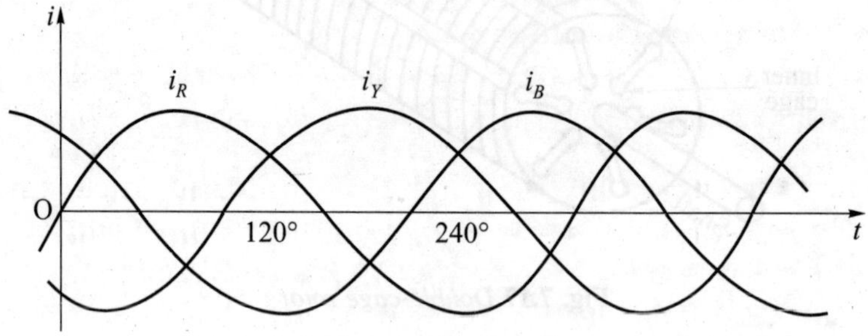

(b) *Induced current*

Fig. 7.18 *Principle of induction motor*

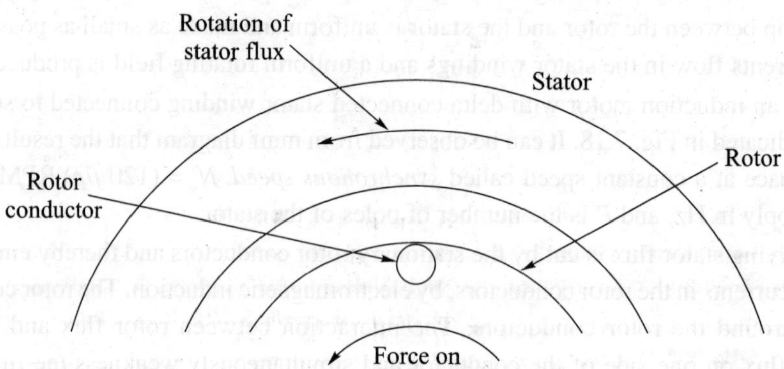

Fig. 7.19 *Production of force*

7.6.3 Slip and Slip Speed

Slip: The rotor can never run at synchronous speed, since the relative motion is required for inducing emf in the rotor conductors which is turn is responsible for producing the driving torque. The difference between the synchronous speed and rotor speed is termed as *slip speed*. The slip speed expressed as a fraction of synchronous speed is referred to as *slip*. *i.e.*,

Slip speed = $(N_s - N)$ RPM

and Slip, $s = [(N_s - N)/N_s]$ 100% ...(7.23)

Frequency of rotor induced emf: When the rotor is at rest, there is maximum relative motion between the rotor and the stator field and slip is 100%. Obviously maximum emf is induced in the rotor. At this position, the frequency of the rotor induced emf is same as that of supply frequency. When the rotors starts rotating, the relative motion decreases which in turn reduces the indeed emf and its frequency.

Since, $N_s = 120\, f/P$ and $N = 120\, f_r/P$, the slip is given by

$$s = (N_s - N)/N_s$$
$$= (f - f_r)/f$$

where f = stator frequency and f_r = rotor frequency ...(7.24)

Frequency of the rotor current, $f^1 = sf.$ ...(7.25)

7.6.4 Equation for Torque Developed

The torque developed in induction motors is a function of rotor current at stand still – I_2, magnitude of the rotating flux per stator pole-ϕ and power factor of the rotor circuit-cos ϕ_2. Thus

$$T \,\alpha\, I_2\, \phi \cos \phi_2$$
$$\alpha\, E_2 I_2 \cos \phi_2 \text{ (as } E_2\text{, the rotor emf at standstill } \alpha\, \phi)$$
$$= K\, E_2 I_2 \cos \phi_2$$

where K is a constant ...(7.26)

Starting torque: With R_2 and X_2 representing the per phase rotor resistance and reactance at stand still, the rotor impedance/phase at stand still is given by

$$Z_2 = \sqrt{R_2^2 + X_2^2} \text{ so that}$$

$$\cos \phi_2 = R_2/Z_2 \quad \text{and} \quad I_2 = E_2/\sqrt{R_2^2 + X_2^2}$$

Thus, $$T_S = KE_2\left[E_2/\sqrt{R_2^2 + X_2^2}\right]\left[R_2/\sqrt{R_2^2 + X_2^2}\right]$$

$$= KE_2^2 R_2/(R_2^2 + X_2^2)$$ ...(7.27)

Running torque: Under running conditions, rotor induced emf is sE_2, frequency of rotor induced emf is sf_2 and rotor reactance/phase is sX_2. As such, the running torque is given by

$$T_r = (K\phi s E_2 R_2)/[R_2^2 + (sX_2)^2]$$ ...(7.28)

In a squirrel cage motor, at stand still, rotor, resistance is low compared to the reactance. As such, the starting current I_2 is very high. However, the power factor is very low and hence the starting torque is poor. Starting current is 5-7 times full load current, and torque produced is about 1-5 times the full load torque. As such, squirrel cage motors are not suitable for starting heavy loads.

Conditions for maximum torque: The condition for obtaining maximum torque is got differentiating the torque equation (7.28) with respect to slip and then equating it to zero, *i.e.*,

$$dT_r/ds = [(R_2^2 + s^2X_2^2)](K\phi E_2R_2) - (K\phi sE_2R_2)(2sX_2^2)]/(R_2^2 + s^2X_2^2)^2 = 0$$

which after simplification yields the condition for maximum torque under running condition : *i.e.*, $R_2 = sX_2$ or $s = R_2/X_2$. Interestingly, at stand-still, the condition for maximum torque is : *rotor resistance equals rotor reactance*.

Torque-slip characteristics: The torque-slip cure of an induction motor is as shown in Fig. 7.20. Initially, the torque increases linearly with slip until it becomes maximum. After T_{max}, if the load is further increased, the motor operation becomes unsuitable, as it cannot develop the required electromagnetic torque. It is important to note that the motor would stop beyond a certain load.

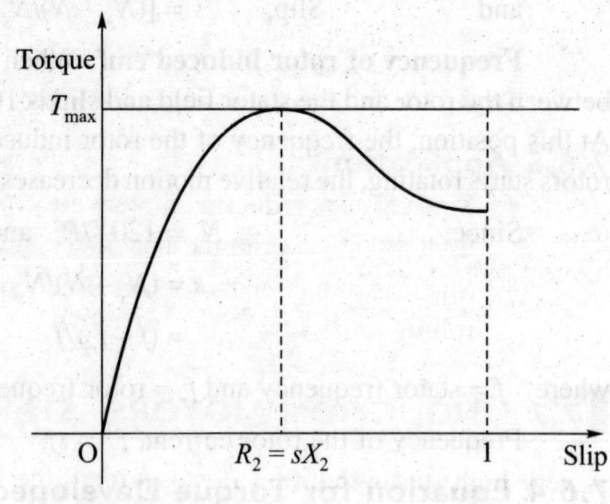

Fig. 7.20 *Torque-slip characteristics*

Rotor input and rotor copper losses: The power transfer cycle of an induction motor involves the different losses at various stages of transformation as shown in Fig. 7.21.

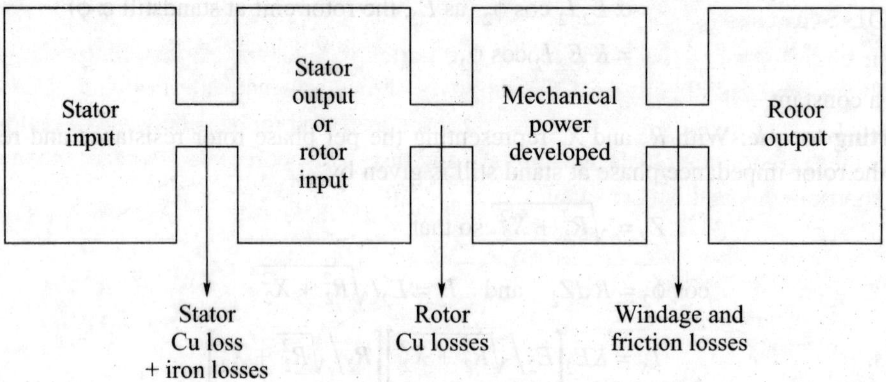

Fig. 7.21 *Power transfer diagram*

With T_g as gross rotor torque, N_s as synchronous speed in RPM and N as rotor speed in RPM, the following relations can be obtained with respect to an induction motor (Fig. 7.21).

$$\text{Rotor input} = \text{Stator input} - \text{Stator losses}$$
$$= 2\pi N_sT_g/60$$
$$\text{Rotor gross output} = \text{Rotor input} - \text{Rotor Cu losses}$$
$$= 2\pi NT_g/60$$
$$\text{Rotor copper losses} = \text{Rotor input} - \text{Rotor gross output}$$
$$= [2\pi N_sT_g/60] - [2\pi NT_g/60]$$
$$= [2\pi(N_s - N)T_g]/60$$

$$\text{Rotor Cu losses/Rotor input} = \{[2\pi(N_s - N)T_g]/60\}/\{[2\pi N_s T_g]/60\}$$
$$= (N_s - N)/N_s$$
$$= s$$

Thus, *Rotor Cu losses = s (Rotor input)* ...(7.29)

7.6.5 Applications

- Squirrel cage induction motors are constant speed motors having low starting torque and are used in lathes, printing machinery, flour mills, saw mills etc.
- Slip ring induction motors are used where high starting torque is required such as lifts, cranes, rolling mills, etc.

7.7 INDUCTION MOTORS—STARTERS

A very high starting current flows through the winding causing damage to the stator winding, when rated voltage is applied to the stator winding of induction motor. This current may be limited by applying reduced voltage at starting. Normally, starters are used in conjunction with motors of higher rating. Some protective devices are also incorporated in starters to protect motors against electrical faults. Various types of starters used for starting induction motors are discussed below:

7.7.1 DOL Starters

Owing to the cost of starters, low rating motors are started without any starters. Motors of lower rating (up to 5 HP) are switched directly onto the supply as shown schematically in Fig. 7.22. Although the starting current is very high there is no damage caused as the motor accelerates very rapidly which is turn reduces the current. Suitably designed relays and fuses are incorporated to guard the motor against overloads, short circuits and under voltages.

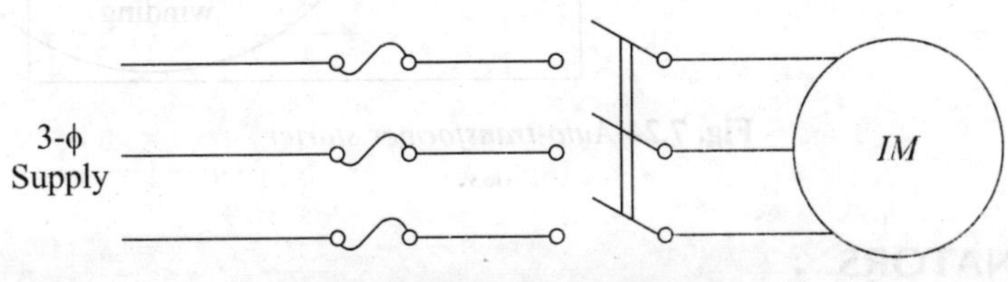

Fig. 7.22 *DOL starters*

7.7.2 Y-Δ Starters

A star-delta starter is shown in Fig. 7.23. In this case, the starter windings are connected in star and hence only $1/\sqrt{3}$ times full line voltage is applied across each windings. This limits the starting current. When the motor accelerates, the motor windings are connected in delta so that full line voltage is applied across each winding/phase.

7.7.3 Auto-Transformer Starters

This type of starter consists of a 3 ϕ auto-transformer with a number of tappings as shown in Fig. 7.24. The auto-transformer is connected to a balanced three-phase supply and it can produce any reduced voltage available at its output terminals. The motor is started at reduced voltage and the voltage across the motor is gradually increased, and finally full time voltage is applied.

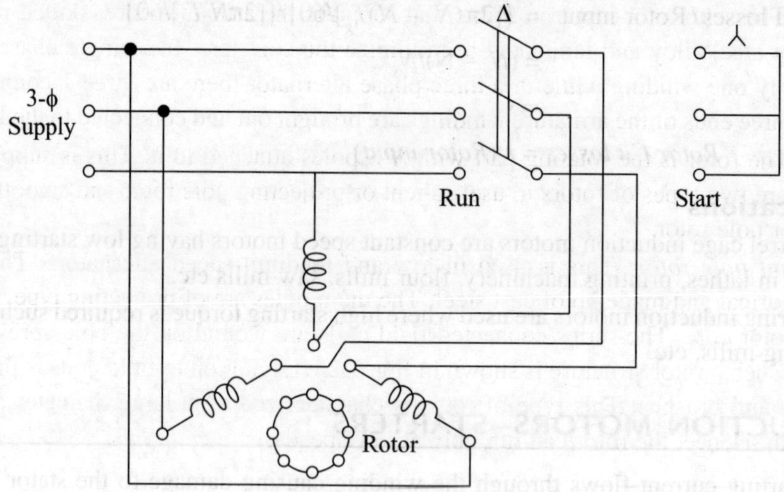

Fig. 7.23 *Y-Δ starters*

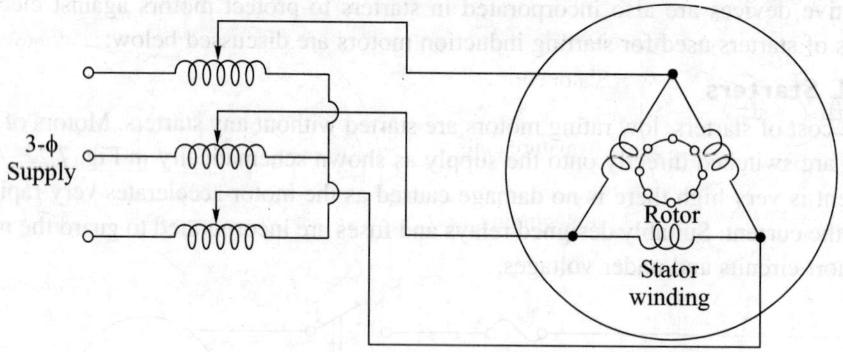

Fig. 7.24 *Auto-transformer starter*

7.8 ALTERNATORS

The alternator is an AC generator working on the principle of electromagnetic induction. It is an electrical machine which converts mechanical energy into electrical energy. Unlike the DC generator, the alternator has a stationary armature. The following are the advantages of having the stationary armature.

- Insulation of stationary armature conductors working at high voltage is easier.
- Tapping of electrical energy from a stationary armature is simpler.
- The use of slip rings and brushes are eliminated as the load is directly connected to the alternator terminals, and
- The machine can operate at higher speeds enabling a larger output from the alternator.

7.8.1 Construction

An alternator basically consists of a single armature winding mounted on the *stator* and field windings mounted on the *rotor* to provide the required magnetic field.

Stator: The stator is a cast iron frame that supports the armature core, slotted made of special magnetic iron or steel alloy and laminated to minimize the core loss. In a single phase alternator, the stator carries only one winding while in a three phase alternator there are three *Y*-connected armature windings. The three ends of the armature windings are brought out and connected to the fixed terminals.

Rotor: The rotor is the rotating part with *N-S* poles attached to it. This is supplied with a DC voltage. There are two types of rotors in use: salient or projecting pole rotor and smooth cylindrical or non-salient rotor pole rotor.

- *Salient pole rotor:* This is used in low and medium speed alternators. The rotor core is cylindrical and made up of cast steel. The main poles are of projecting type, rigidly fixed to the rotor core. The series connected field coils are wound on the pole cores. An alternator with such a rotor structure is shown in Fig. 7.25. Excitation to field coils is provided via slip rings and brushes. This type of rotor is characterized by a large diameter and small axial length. Hence, the rotor can run only at low speeds.

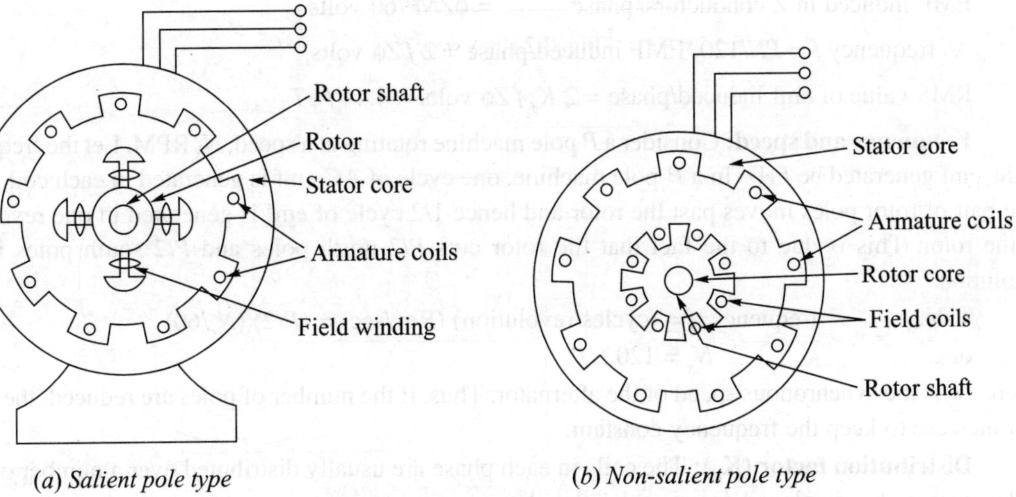

(a) Salient pole type *(b) Non-salient pole type*

Fig. 7.25 *Rotors of an alternator*

- *Non-salient pole rotor:* This is used in high speed alternators. The rotor consists of a smooth solid forged-steel cylinder having a number of slots, to accommodate filed coils. The excitation is supplied to the filed coils through brushes and slip rings. The cylindrical rotor is characterized by small diameter and large axial length. This makes the rotor to run at high speeds. A typical structure is as shown in Fig. 7.25.

7.8.2 Equation for Induced EMF

The emf equation of an alternator can be derived by assuming the following parameters:

Z — Number of conductors/phase

T — Number of stator turns/phase = $Z/2$

P — Number of poles

f — Frequency of induced emf

N — Speed of rotor in RPM

K_d — Distribution factor

K_p — Pitch factor or coil span factor

K_f — Form factor (1.11 for a sinusoidal waveform)

ϕ — Flux per pole.

To begin with, assume that all stator coils are full pitched ($K_c = 1$), all coils are placed in one slot instead of being distributed in several slots ($K_d = 1$) and field flux is sinusoidal. In one complete rotation of the field system each stator conductor passes through each of the poles. Thus,

Total flux cut by one conductor in one rotation = $P\phi$ Wb.

Time for one full rotation = $1/N$ minutes

= $60/N$ seconds

Rate of change of flux by one conductor = $d\phi/dt = p\phi/(60/N)$.

EMF induced in Z conductors/phase = $\phi ZNP/60$ volts.

As frequency $f = PN/120$, EMF induced/phase = $2 f Z\phi$ volts.

RMS value of emf induced/phase = $2\, K_f f Z\phi$ volts = $4.44\, f\phi T$ ...(7.30)

Frequency and speed: Consider a P pole machine rotating at a speed, N_5 RPM. Let the frequency of the emf generated be f Hz. In a P-pole machine, one cycle of AC emf is generated in each coil as one pole pair of rotor poles moves past the rotor and hence 1/2 cycle of emf is generated in one revolution of the rotor. This is due to the fact that the rotor cuts $P/2$ north poles and $P/2$ south poles in one revolution.

Thus, frequency, f = (cycles/revolution) (Rev/sec) = $(P/2)\,(N_s/60)$

or $N_s = 120\, f/P$ ...(7.31)

where, N_s is the synchronous speed of the alternator. Thus, if the number of poles are reduced, the speed will increase to keep the frequency constant.

Distribution factor (K_d): The coils in each phase are usually distributed over a number of slots under each pole, displaced from each other by a certain angle β. As such, the induced emfs in different coils of one phase under each pole are not in phase but differ from each other by a certain angle depending on the number of slots. Thus, the total emf is the vector sum of the individual components. This is taken care of by the distribution factor or breadth factor defined as:

K_d = ratio of (vector sum of emfs of all coils under each pole) to (arithmetic sum of emfs, had all coils were concentrated in one slot)

= $\sin(m\beta/2)/m \sin(\beta/2)$ ...(7.32)

where, m is the number of slots/pole/phase, $\beta = 180°/$ No. of slots per pole = $180°/s$, with s = number of slots/pole.

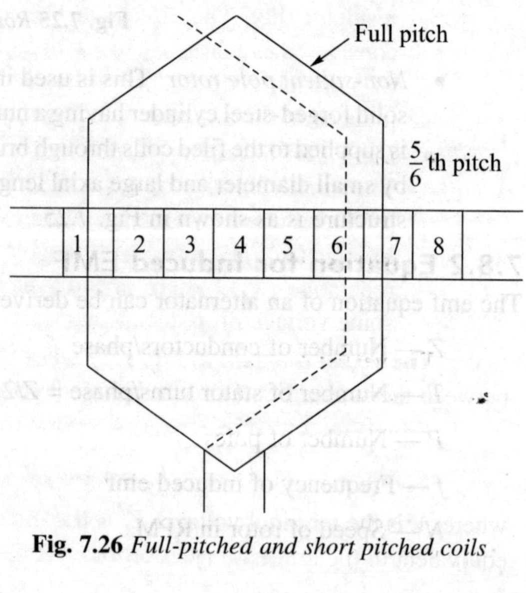

Fig. 7.26 *Full-pitched and short pitched coils*

Pitch factor K_p : Full pitched coils are those having a span of one pole pitch *i.e.* spanning 180° electrical. As a typical example, consider a slotted armature as shown in Fig. 7.26. If the conductors are placed in slots 1 and 7, it is said to be full pitched. If the conductors are placed between 1 and 6, then it becomes short pitched. It is indeed equal to $(5/6)^{th}$ of the pole pitch. It falls short by $(1/6)^{th}$ pole pitch or it is equivalent to a pole span of 30° (180/6). The advantages of the short pitched coils are saving in copper of end connections and improvement in the waveform generated which could be made nearer to sine wave.

The total emf generated is thus found to be less due to the effect of short pitched coils. This is taken care by the pitch factor or coil span factor defined as:

K_p = ratio of vector sum of the induced emfs per coil to the Arithmetic sum of the induced emfs per coil (usually <1).

$$= \cos(\alpha/2) \quad ...(7.33)$$

where, α is the short pitch angle.

7.8.3 Principle

The alternator basically works on the principle of electromagnetic induction. While on single phase, voltage is induced in the stator coils as they intercept the magnetic field of the rotor. An alternator, while working as a poly-phase machine, AC voltages are generated in different coils of the stator, staggered in phase. The voltages are of the same amplitude and frequency as the rotor is rotating at a constant speed. Typically, in a three phase alternator, voltages are generated with a phase difference of 120° electrical.

The terminal voltage of an alternator drops as the load is increased on account of the following reasons:

- *Drop due to armature resistance:* Whenever current flows in the armature winding, there is a small drop in voltage due to armature resistance, thereby reducing the terminal voltage.
- *Drop due to armature reaction:* The stator currents produce their own flux which will react with the main flux and hence reduce the resultant flux. The effect may be considered as a drop in a resistance (X_a) which reduces the voltage induced in the armature windings.
- *Drop due to leakage reactance:* The small amount of main flux produced due to the field system, leakage flux gives rise to leakage reactance (X_L). There is always some voltage drop due to this.

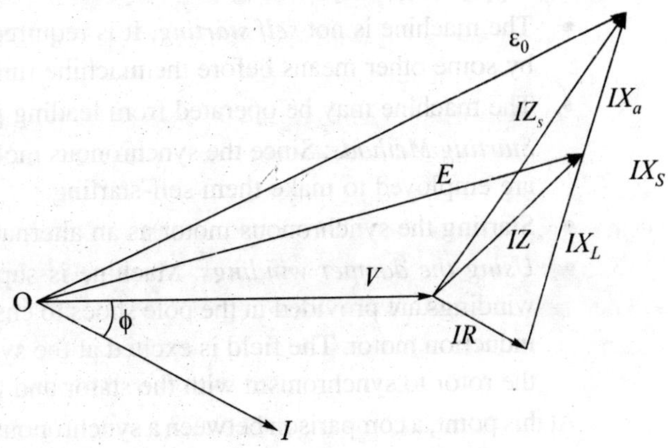

Fig. 7.27 *Vector diagram*

The vector diagram in Fig. 7.27 takes these factors into consideration and show the relationship between the induced emf and the terminal voltage.

From Fig. 7.27,

$$E_0 = V + I\,[R + j\,(X_L + X_a)] \quad ...(7.34)$$

where, V is the terminal voltage, E_0 is the induced voltage, X_L is the leakage reactance, X_a is reactance equivalent to the armature reaction and I is the load current.

Voltage regulation: The voltage regulation of the alternator is defined as the drop in voltage from no-load to full-load expressed as a percentage of full-load voltage, *i.e.*,

$$\text{Voltage regulation} = [(E_0 - V)/V]100\ \% \quad \text{...(7.35)}$$

7.8.4 Synchronization

Whenever a single alternator is unable to meet the load demand, it is required that two or more alternators will have to supply the load together. Under such conditions, the alternators will be connected in parallel to meet the load requirements. This method of connecting them in parallel is known as *synchronization*. For proper synchronization, the following conditions are to be met:

- The terminal voltage of all alternators must be same.
- The speed of the alternators must be such that the frequencies of emfs of alternators are equal.
- It is also required that the phase sequence of all alternators should be the same.

There are two methods of synchronizing the alternators: *Synchronizing lamp method* and using *synchroscopes*.

7.9 SYNCHRONOUS MOTORS

A synchronous motor is electrically identical to that of an alternator. Indeed, an alternator may be driven as a synchronous motor and vice-versa. Clearly, an alternator at synchronous speed, if synchronized with the supply or with another alternator, continues to run by taking the required power from the supply, even if the prime mover is disconnected. The alternator will then be running as a *synchronous motor* at synchronous speed. The salient features of such motors are:

- Machine always runs at synchronous speed and only way to change its speed is to vary the supply frequency.
- The machine is not *self starting*. It is required to run the motor up to the synchronous speed by some other means before the machine runs on its own taking power from the supply.
- The machine may be operated from leading power factor to lagging power factor.

  Starting Methods: Since the synchronous motors are not self-starting, the following methods are employed to make them self-starting.
- Starting the synchronous motor as an alternator and running it as a synchronous motor.
- *Using the damper windings*: Machine is supplied with no field excitation and the damper windings are provided in the pole shoes to ensure the starting of the synchronous motor as an induction motor. The field is excited at the synchronous speed of the machine. This will pull the rotor to synchronism with the stator and the motor then runs at synchronous speed.

At this point, a comparison between a synchronous motor and an induction motor may be relevant:

Synchronous motor	*Induction motor*
• It is not self-starting.	It is self-starting.
• It runs at constant speed even if it is loaded.	The speed decreases with the increase in load.
• It takes leading current when over excited.	It takes lagging current under all conditions.
• It is used in power factor improvement applications and clock mechanisms.	It is used in lathes, flour mills, saw mills, lifts, cranes and rolling mills.

ILLUSTRATIVE EXAMPLES

Examples on Transformers

1. A 20 KVA, 2200/200 V, 50 Hz Transformer has the following test data:

   OC Test-220 V, 4.2 A, 148 W

   SC Test-86 V, 10.5 A, 360 W

   Find the equivalent circuit parameters, Regulation and efficiency at full load and half load at 90.8 pf lagging.

   Solution: (*a*) *Equivalent circuit parameters*

   Core Losses = 148 Watts, I^2R = 360 W. Thus the value of the resistance in the equivalent circuit referred to primary is $R_1 = 360/(10.5)^2 = 3.26\ \Omega$.

   Hence with $K = 2200/220,\ R_2 = R_1/K^2 = 3.26/10^2 = 0.033\ \Omega.$

   Further, $Z_1 = V_{sc}/I_{sc} = 86/10.5 = 8.19\ \Omega$

   and $X_1 = \sqrt{(Z_1^2 - R_1^2)} = 7.51\ \Omega$

   $$X_2 = X_1/K^2 = 0.075\ \Omega$$

   (*b*) *Regulation*: (Refer to Fig. P.1)

   Primary current = 20,000/2,200 = 9.1 A.

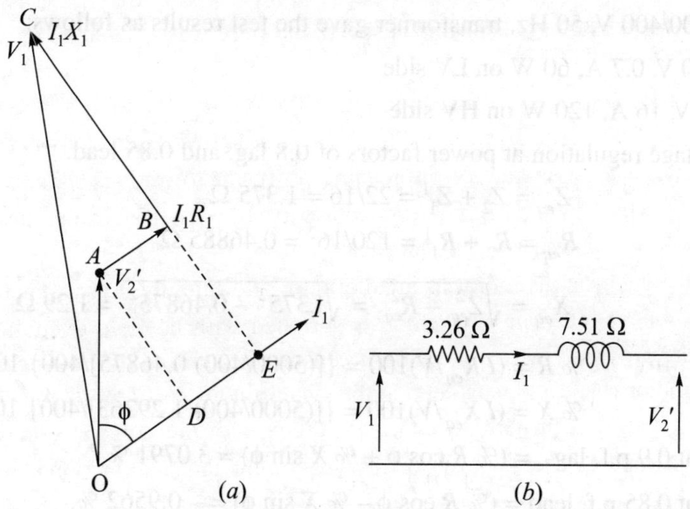

Fig. 7.28 *Phasor diagram*

$$V_1^2 = OC^2 = OE^2 + EC^2$$

$$\approx (OD + DE)^2 + (EB + BC)^2$$

$$= (2200 \times 0.8 + 9.1 \times 3.26)^2 + (2200 \times 0.6 + 9.1 \times 7.51)^2$$

$\therefore \quad V_1 = 2265$ V

Regulation = (2265 – 2200) × 100/2200 = 2.95%.

(*c*) *Efficiency*:

Iron losses = 148 W (same at all loads).

Cu-losses at full load = $I_1^2 R_1 = 9.1^2 \times 3.26 = 270$ W

Cu-losses at half load = $(9.1/2)^2 \times 3.26 = 67.5$ W

$\eta_{FL} = 20{,}000 \times 0.8/(20{,}000 \times 0.8 + 148 + 270) = 97.4\%$

$\eta_{HL} = 10{,}000 \times 0.8/(10{,}000 \times 0.8 + 148 + 67.5) = 97.3\%$

2. A 50 KVA, 6360/240 V transformer is tested on OC and SC and the results are:

OC test: Primary voltage = 6360 V, Primary current = 1 A, Power input = 2 kW

SC test: Primary voltage = 180 V, Secondary current = 175 A, Power input = 2 kW

Find efficiency of the transformer at full load and 0.8 lagging power factor.

Solution: Core losses = W_i = 2000 watts

Full load primary current of the transformer = (50)1000/6360 = 7.86 A

SC current referred to the primary = I_{sc}/K = 175/(6360/240) = 6.6 A

Full load copper losses = $(7.86/6.6)^2$ 2000 = 2836.53 watts

$\eta_{FL} = (50 \times 0.8)/(50 \times 0.8 + 2.0 + 2.8365) = 89.21\%$

3. A 5 KVA, 200/400 V, 50 Hz. transformer gave the test results as follows:

OC test : 220 V, 0.7 A, 60 W on LV side

SC test : 22 V, 16 A, 120 W on HV side

Find the voltage regulation at power factors of 0.8 lag. and 0.85 lead.

Solution: $Z_{eq} = Z_2 + Z_1^1 = 22/16 = 1.375\ \Omega$

$R_{eq} = R_2 + R_1^1 = 120/16^2 = 0.46885\ \Omega$

$$X_{eq} = \sqrt{Z_{eq}^2 - R_{eq}^2} = \sqrt{1.375^2 - 0.46875^2} = 1.29\ \Omega$$

$\% R = (I R_{eq}/V)100$ = {[(5000/400) 0.46875]/400} 100 = 1.4648

$\% X = (I X_{eq}/V)100$ = {[(5000/400) 1.29263]/400} 100 = 4.0395

Regulation at 0.9 p.f. lag = (% $R \cos \phi$ + % $X \sin \phi$) = 3.0791 %

Regulation at 0.85 p.f. lead = (% $R \cos \phi$ – % $X \sin \phi$) = – 0.9562 %.

4. Find the all-day efficiency of a 500 KVA distribution transformer whose iron and copper losses at full load are 3.5 kW and 4.5 kW respectively. During a day of 24 hours, it is loaded as under:

No. of hours	6	10	4	4
Load in kW	400	300	100	0
Power factor	0.8	0.75	0.8	–

Solution: The iron loss is constant at all loads and the copper loss α KVA_2 *i.e.*,

Copper losses at 400 kW = $((400/0.8)/500)^2 \times 4.5 = 4.5$ kW

Copper losses at 300 kW = $((300/0.75)/500)^2 \times 4.5 = 2.48$ kW

Copper losses at 100 kW = $((100/0.8)/500)^2 \times 4.5 = 0.281$ kW

Total copper losses over 24 Hrs = $4.5 \times 6 + 2.48 \times 10 + 0.281 \times 4 = 52.92$ kWh

Iron loss for 24 hours = $3.5 \times 24 = 84$ kWh

Total energy losses = $52.92 + 84 = 136.92$ kWh

Output per day = $(400 \times 6 + 300 \times 10 + 100 \times 4) = 5800$ kWh

$$\therefore \quad \eta_{\text{All day}} = 5800/(5800 + 36.9)$$

$$= 97.7\%.$$

Additional Examples on Transformers

5. A 25 KVA, transformer has 500 turns on the primary and 50 turns on the secondary winding. The primary is connected to a 3.3 KV, 50 Hz supply. Calculate the full load primary and secondary currents, the EMF in the secondary and the maximum flux in the core. Neglect leakage and magnetization current.

Solution: KVA rating = 25 KVA = 25000 VA

Primary turns $= N_1 = 500$

Secondary turns $= N_2 = 50$

Primary voltage $= V_1 = E_1 = 3.3$ KV = 3300 V

Frequency of supply $= f = 50$ Hz.

$$\text{KVA rating} = \text{KVA} = 25 = V_1 I_1 \times 10^{-3}$$

Then,
$$I_1 = \frac{25 \times 1000}{V_1} = \frac{25 \times 1000}{3300} = 7.576 \text{ amp}$$

$$E_1 = 4.44 f \Phi_m N_1$$

Hence
$$\Phi_m = \frac{E_1}{4.44 f N_1} = \frac{3300}{4.44 \times 50 \times 500} = 0.02973 \text{ Wb}$$

EMF induced in the secondary $= E_2$

$$\frac{E_2}{E_1} = \frac{N_2}{N_1}$$

$$E_2 = \frac{N_2}{N_1} \times E_1 = \frac{50}{500} \times 3300 = 330 \text{ V.}$$

6. A single phase transformer has turns ratio of 1 : 15 and a secondary winding of 1500 turns. The primary winding is connected to a 25 volts sinusoidal supply. If the maximum core flux is 2.25 mWb. Find (1) the frequency of the supply (2) The number of primary turns (3) The secondary voltage on open circuit.

Solution:

Given $\frac{N_1}{N_2} = \frac{1}{15}$ where $N_2 = 1500$ turns and

Then Primary turns $N_1 = N_2 \times \frac{1}{15} = 1500 \times \frac{1}{15} = 100$ turns

Also $E_1 = 25\text{ V} = 4.44\, f\, \Phi_m N_1$

$$f = \frac{E_1}{4.44\,\Phi_m N_1} = \frac{25}{4.44 \times 2.25 \times 10^{-3} \times 100}$$

$$f = 25\text{ Hz}$$

$$\frac{E_2}{E_1} = \frac{N_2}{N_1}$$

$$E_2 = E_1 \frac{N_2}{N_1} = 25 \times \frac{15}{1} = 375\text{ V.}$$

7. A 125 KVA, transformer has a primary voltage of 2000 V at 60 Hz. Primary turns 182 and secondary turns 40. Neglecting losses calculate:

(1) No load secondary EMF

(2) Flux in the core

(3) The full load secondary and primary current.

Solution: We know that $\frac{E_2}{E_1} = \frac{N_1}{N_1}$

$$E_2 = E_1 \times \frac{N_2}{N_1} = 2000 \times \frac{40}{182} = 439.56\text{ V}$$

Also $E_1 = 4.44\, f\Phi_m N_1$

Hence $\Phi_m = \frac{E_1}{4.44\, fN_1} = \frac{2000}{4.44 \times 60 \times 182} = 0.04125\text{ Wb}$

$$E_1 \times I_1 = \text{KVA} \times 10^{-3}$$

$$I_1 = \frac{125000}{E_1 \times 1000} = \frac{125000}{2000} = 62.5\text{ amps}$$

$$\frac{I_1}{I_2} = \frac{N_2}{N_1}$$

$$I_2 = \frac{I_1 N_1}{N_2} = \frac{62.5 \times 82}{40} = 284.375\text{ amps.}$$

8. A 10 KVA, 400/230 Volts, single phase transformer gave the following test results.

OC test: Power input at rated voltage on LV side 80 W

SC test: Supply on HV side with LV shorted 24 volts, 25 Amps, 120 watt.

Determine percentage regulation and efficiency at half full load at 0.8 p.f. lag and lead.

Solution: Iron loss = from OC Test = 80 watts

$$\text{Full load current on primary} = \frac{KVA \times 1000}{E_1} = \frac{10 \times 1000}{400} = 25 \text{ A}$$

∴ Full load copper loss = 120 watts

i.e., $$I_1^2 R_{01} = 120; R_{01} = \frac{120}{I_1^2} = \frac{120}{25^2} = 0.192 \text{ ohms}$$

$$Z_{01} = \frac{Vsc}{I_{SC}} = \frac{24}{25} = 0.96 \text{ ohms}$$

$$X_{01} = \sqrt{Z_{01}^2 - R_{01}^2}$$

$$\sqrt{0.96^2 - 0.192^2}$$

$$X_{01} = 0.9406 \text{ ohms}$$

$$\% \text{ Regulation} = I_1 \frac{(R_{01} \cos \Phi \pm X_{01} \sin \Phi)}{E_1} \times 100 \begin{bmatrix} + \text{(for lag)} \\ - \text{(for lead)} \end{bmatrix}$$

% Regulation at F.L. at 0.8 p.f. lag

$$= 25 \frac{(0.192 \times 0.8 + 0.9406 \times 0.6)}{400} \times 100 = 4.487\%$$

% Regulation at F.L. at 0.8 p.f. lead

$$= 25 \frac{(0.192 \times 0.8 - 0.9406 \times 0.6)}{400} \times 100 = 2.56\%$$

% Regulation at $\frac{1}{2}$ F.L. 0.8 p.f. lag

$$= 12.5 \frac{(0.192 \times 0.8 + 0.9406 \times 0.6)}{400} \times 100 = 2.2435\%$$

% Regulation at $\frac{1}{2}$ F.L. 0.8 p.f. lead

$$= 12.5 \frac{(0.192 \times 0.8 - 0.9406 \times 0.6)}{400} \times 100 = 1.28\%$$

$$\eta = \frac{O/P \times 100}{O/P + \text{losses}}$$

$$\eta \text{ at } X \text{ load} = \frac{X\,(KVA \times 1000) \cos \Phi}{X\,(KVA \times 1000) \times \cos \Phi + W_i + X^2\, W_{sc}} \times 100$$

$$\eta \text{ at F.L.} = \frac{1 \times 10 \times 1000 \times 0.8}{1 \times 10 \times 1000 \times 0.8 + 80 + 1^2 \times 120} \times 100 = 97.56\%$$

$$\eta \text{ at } \frac{1}{2} \text{ F.L.} = \frac{\frac{1}{2} \times 10 \times 1000 \times 0.8}{\frac{1}{2} \times 10 \times 1000 \times 0.8 + 80 + \left(\frac{1}{2}\right)^2 \times 120} = 97.32\%$$

9. The primary winding of a transformer is connected to a 240V, 50 Hz, supply. The secondary winding has 1500 turns. If the maximum value of the core flux is 0.00207 Wb. Determine (*i*) the secondary induced EMF (*ii*) number of times in the primary (*iii*) In area of cross section if the flux density has a maximum value of 0.465 Tesla.

Solution: $E_1 = 240\text{V} \quad f = 50 \text{ Hz}, \quad N_2 = 1500, \Phi_m = 0.00207 \text{ Wb}$

$$E_2 = 4.44 f \Phi_m N_2$$

$$= 4.44 \times 50 \times 0.00207 \times 1500 = 689.31 \text{ volts}$$

$$\frac{E_2}{E_1} = \frac{N_2}{N_1}$$

$$N_1 = \left(\frac{I_1}{I_2}\right) N_2 = \frac{240}{689.3} \times 1500 = 522.26 \text{ turns}$$

Also, $\Phi_m = B_m \times A$

$$A = \frac{\Phi_m}{B_m} = \frac{0.00207}{0.465}$$

$$A = 4.45 \times 10^{-3} \text{ m}^2.$$

10. A 40 KVA transformer has a iron loss of 450 watts and a full load copper loss of 850 watts. If the full load power factor is 0.8, calculate: (1) efficiency at full load (2) load at which copper loss equal to iron loss (3) efficiency at this load.

Solution: $W_i = 450$ watts, W_{cu} at $FL = 850$ watts, $\cos \Phi = 0.8$, KVA= 40 KVA

$$\eta \text{ at F.L. at 0.8 p.f.} = \frac{\text{KVA} \times 1000 \times \cos \Phi}{\text{KVA} \times 1000 \times \cos \Phi + W_i + W_{cu}} \times 100$$

$$= \frac{40 \times 1000 \times 0.8}{40 \times 1000 \times 0.8 + 450 + 850} \times 100 = 96.9\%$$

The load at which copper loss equal to iron loss is

$$x = \sqrt{\frac{\text{Iron loss}}{\text{Copper loss}}} = \sqrt{\frac{450}{850}} = 0.7276$$

At 72.76% of the load iron loss = copper loss

$$\therefore \quad \eta \text{ at 72.76\% at 0.8 p.f.} = \frac{0.7276 \times 40 \times 1000 \times 0.8}{0.7276 \times 40 \times 1000 \times 0.8 + 450\,(0.7276)^r\ 850} \times 100$$

$$= \frac{23283.2}{23283.2 + 900} \times 100 = 96.27\%.$$

11. A 50 KVA transformer has $N_1 : N_2 = 300 : 20$. The primary winding is connected to 2200 V, 50 Hz supply. Calculate

(*i*) Secondary voltage on No load

(*ii*) Approximate values of primary and secondary currents on full load.

(*iii*) The maximum value of the flux.

Solution: $E_1 = 2200$ V $N_1 : N_2 = 300 : 20$ $f = 50$ Hz

$$\frac{E_2}{E_1} = \frac{N_2}{N_1}$$

$$E_2 = E_1 \frac{(N_2)}{N_1} = 2099 \times \frac{(20)}{3000} = 133.33 \text{ V}$$

$$\text{KVA rating} = 50 \text{ KVA} = E_1 \times I_1 \times 10^{-3}$$

$$I_1 = \frac{50}{E_1 \times 10^{-3}} = \frac{50}{2000 \times 10^{-3}} = 25 \text{ amps}$$

$$\frac{I_1}{I_2} = \frac{N_2}{N_1}$$

$$I_2 = I_1 \frac{(N_1)}{N_2} = 25 \times \frac{(300)}{20} = 375 \text{ amps}$$

$$E_1 = 4.44 f \phi_{m1} N_1$$

$$\therefore \quad \Phi_m = \frac{E_1}{4.44 f N_1} = \frac{2000}{4.44 \times 50 \times 300}$$

$$\Phi_m = 0.03 \text{ Wb}$$

12. A transformer working at unity power factor has an efficiency of 90% at both one half load and at the full load of 500 W. Determine the efficiency at 75% of F.L.

Solution: Given the full load output of the transformer = 500 W = VI Cos Φ

$$\% \eta \text{ at } x \text{ load at u.p.f.} = \frac{X \text{ KVA} \cos \varphi \times 1000}{X \text{ KVA} \cos \phi \times 1000 + W_i + X^2 W_{cu}} \times 100$$

$$\eta_{\text{at F.L. at u.p.f.}} = \frac{500}{500 + W_i + W_{cu}} \times 100 = 90$$

$$500 = 0.9 [500 + (W_i + W_{cu})]$$

$$500(1 - 0.9) = 0.9 (W_i + W_{cu})$$

$$(W_i + W_{cu}) = 50/0.9 = 55.55 \text{ W} \quad \text{...(Eqn. 1)}$$

$$\eta_{\text{at1/2 F.L. at u.p.f.}} = \frac{250}{250 + W_i + \frac{1}{2^2} W_{cu}} \times 100 = 90$$

$$250 = 0.9 [250 + (W_i + (1/4)W_{cu})]$$

$$(W_i + (1/4) W_{cu}) = 25/0.9 = 27.78 \text{ W} \quad \text{...(Eqn. 2)}$$

$$W_i + W_{cu} = 55.55$$

$$W_i + \frac{W_{cu}}{4} = 27.78$$

Solving for W_{cu}

$$\frac{3}{4} W_{cu} = 27.78$$

$$\boxed{W_{cu} = 37.04 \text{ W}}$$

$$\therefore \quad W_i = 55.55 - W_{cu} = 55.55 - 37.04$$

$$W_i = 18.51 \text{ W}$$

$$\% \, \eta \text{ at } 75\% \text{ of load at upf} = \frac{0.75 \times 500}{0.75 \times 500 + 81.51 + (0.75)^2 \times 37.04} \times 100 = 90.49\%.$$

13. A 20 KVA, 2000/200 V, single phase 50 Hz transformer has a primary resistance of 2.5 ohms and reactance of 4.8 ohms. The secondary resistance and reactance are 0.01 ohms and 0.018 ohms respectively. Find

(1) The equivalent impedance referred to secondary

(2) The equivalent impedance referred to primary.

Solution: $R_1 = 2.5 \, \Omega \qquad X_1 = 4.8 \, \Omega$

$R_2 = 0.01 \, \Omega \qquad X_2 = 0.018 \, \Omega$

$$K = \frac{N_2}{N_1} = \frac{E_2}{E_1} = \frac{200}{2000} = \frac{(1)}{10}$$

Equivalent Resistance referred to primary $R_{01} = R_1 + R_2^1$

$$= R_1 + \frac{R_2}{K^2} = 2.5 + \frac{0.01}{(1/10)^2} = 2.5 + 0.01 \times 100 = 3.5 \, \Omega$$

Equivalent Reactance referred to primary

$$X_{01} = X_1 + X_2^1 = X_1 + \frac{X_2}{K^2} = 4.8 + \frac{0.018}{(1/10)^2} = 6.4 \, \Omega$$

Equivalent Impedance referred to primary

$$Z_{01} = R_{01} + J X_0^1 = (3.5 + J \, 6.4)$$

Equivalent Resistance referred to secondary

$$R_{02} = R_2 + R_1^1 = R_2 + K^2 R_1$$

$$= 0.01 + \frac{(1)^2}{10} \times 2.5 = 0.035 \Omega$$

Equivalent Reactance referred to secondary

$$X_{02} = X_2 + X_1^1 = X_2 + K^2 X_1$$

$$= 0.018 + (1/10)^2 \times 4.8 = 0.064 \, \Omega$$

Equivalent Impedance referred to secondary

$$Z_{02} = R_{02} + J\,X_{02} = (0.035 + J\,0.064)$$

14. Determine the equivalent circuit of a 200/400 Volts, 50 Hz, single phase transformer from the following test data.

OC test: (LV side): 200 V, 0.7 A, 70 W

SC test: (HV side): 15 V, 10 A, 85 W

$$\text{Primary} = \text{LV} = 200 \text{ V}$$

$$\text{Secondary} = \text{HV} = 400 \text{ V}$$

Solution: OC test: Meters are on LV side HV side is kept open

$$V_1 = 200, \quad I_0 = 0.7, \quad W_0 = 70$$

$$\therefore \quad W_0 = V_1 I_0 \cos \Phi_0$$

$$\cos \Phi_0 = \frac{W_0}{V_1 I_0} = \frac{70}{200 \times 0.7} = 0.5$$

$$\cos \Phi_0 = 0.5, \quad \sin \Phi_0 = 0.866$$

Working component or loss component $I_W = I_0 \cos \Phi_0 = 0.7 \times 0.5 = 0.35$ A

Magnetizing component $I_\mu = I_0 \sin \Phi_0 = 0.7 \times \sin (60) = 0.7 \times 0.866 = 0.606$ A

$$R_0 = \frac{V_1}{I_W} = \frac{200}{0.35} = 571.4 \text{ ohms}$$

$$X_0 = \frac{V_1}{I_\mu} = \frac{200}{0.6062} = 330 \text{ ohms}$$

SC test: (HV Side) LV side is shorted, meters on secondary side.

$$V_{SC} = 15 \text{ V}, I_2 = 10\text{A}, W_{SC} = 85 \text{ W}$$

$$W_{SC} = \text{Copper loss in the transformer} = I_2^2 \; R_{02} = W_{SC}$$

$$R_{02} = \frac{W_{SC}}{I_2^2} = \frac{85}{(10)^2} = 0.85 \text{ ohms}$$

$$Z_{02} = \frac{V_{SC}}{I_2^2} = \frac{15}{10} = 1.5 \text{ ohms}$$

$$X_{02} = \sqrt{Z_{02}^2 - R_{02}^2} = 1.236 \text{ ohms}$$

$$K = \frac{E_2}{E_1} = \frac{(400)}{200} = 2$$

$$\therefore \quad R_{01} = (R_{02}/K_2) = \frac{0.85}{(2^2)} = 0.2125 \text{ ohms}$$

$$X_{01} = (X_{02}/K^2) = \frac{1.236}{2^2} = 0.3089 \text{ ohms}$$

Thus the equivalent circuit of the transformer referred to primary is as below:

Example: Calculate if η at F.L., $\frac{1}{4}$ load: Regulation at F.L., $\frac{1}{2}$ load.

We have already noted certain important features about η and regulation in previous sections. We see more about these aspects before solving the problem:

Efficiency: In general efficiency is defined as the ratio of the output to input. In case of Transformers power is inputted to the primary. Out of this power a fraction is utilized for the supply of losses. Remaining gets transferred to the output.

$$\text{Input} = \text{Output} + \text{Losses}$$

$$\text{Losses} = \text{Copper loss} + \text{Iron loss (ore loss)}$$

Now if the transformer is supplying a load with a current of I_2 at voltage V_2 with power factor of load cos Φ

$$W_i = \text{Iron loss and } W_{cu} = \text{Copper loss} = I_2^2 R_{02}.$$

Output of the transformer = $V_2 I_2 \cos \Phi$ watts

Hence $$\% \eta = \frac{\text{Output}}{\text{Input}} \times 100$$

$$= \frac{V_2 I_2 \cos \phi}{V_2 I_2 \cos \phi + W_i + I_2^2 R_{02}} \times 100$$

If the current I_2 is full load current, then we have full load efficiency.

If the efficiency at (X . Rated KVA) is required where X is a fraction of the load may be 1/4, 1/2, 3/4. ......

Then Efficiency is defined as

$$\% \eta = \frac{X (V_2 I_2 \cos \phi)}{X (V_2 I_2 \cos \phi) + W_i + (X I_2)^2 R_{02}} \times 100$$

Regulation: Due to the internal resistance and leakage reactance of the transformer, there occurs certain amount of drop in the voltage which dependent on the current flow (load supplied).

If V_2 = Secondary terminal voltage on full load.

${}_0V_2$ = Secondary voltage on no load.

Then % Regulation $$= \frac{{}_0V_2 - V_2}{{}_0V_2} \times 100$$

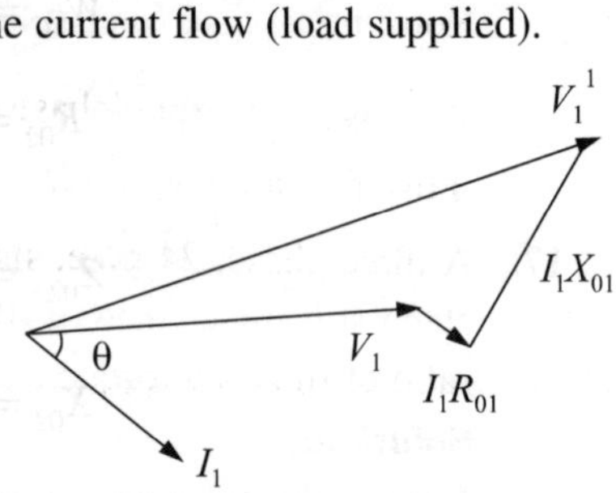

Pictorially the above may be understood as below:

Approximate equation of a transformer from the phasor diagram

$$V_1 - V_2^1 = I_1 R_{01} \cos \Phi + I_1 X_{01} \sin \Phi \quad \text{for lagging power factors}$$

$$\% \text{ Regulation} = \frac{V_1 - V_2^1}{V_1} \times 100 = \frac{I_1 R_{01} \cos \phi + I_1 X_{01} \sin \phi}{V_1} \times 100$$

It may be noted that in the above definition primary voltage is kept constant while the secondary voltage was varying depending on the load.

Indeed, when the transformer is loaded terminal voltage at the secondary falls (lagging p.f.), As such to keep the secondary voltage constant it is required to raise the primary voltage. The raise required to maintain the voltage at the load end constant is expressed as Regulation.

$$\text{Thus \% Regulation} = \frac{V_1^1 - V_1}{V_1} \times 100$$

Primary voltage has to be raised from V_1 to V_1^1 to keep secondary voltage constant.

Examples on Induction Motors

15. A 6 pole induction motor supplied at 50 Hz has a full load slip of 3%. Find the full load speed of the induction motor and the frequency of its rotor emf.

Solution: $f = sf = 0.03 \times 50 = 1.5$ Hz

$N_s = 120\, f/P = 1000$ RPM

Actual speed, $N = N_s (1 - s) = 970$ RPM.

16. A three phase slip-ring induction motor has a star connected secondary. It has an induced emf of 80 V between slip-rings at stand still on open circuit. The rotor resistance and reactance are 1 Ω and 4 Ω. Find the current/phase and power factor when

(*i*) slip-rings are shorted

(*ii*) slip-rings are connected to a rheostat of 4 Ω per phase.

Solution:

Case 1. Stand still emf/phase = $80/\sqrt{3} = 46.2$ volts

Rotor impedance/phase, $Z = \sqrt{1^2 + 4^2} = 4.12\ \Omega$

∴ Rotor current/phase = $(46.2)/Z = 11.2$ amps

Power factor, $\cos \phi = R/Z = 0.243$.

Case 2. Rotor resistance/ phase = (Rotor resistance + External resistance) = 5 Ω

Rotor impedance/phase, $Z = \sqrt{5^2 + 4^2} = 6.4\ \Omega$

∴ Rotor current/phase = $46.2/Z = 7.215$ amps

Power factor, $\cos \phi = R/Z = 0.781$.

17. A three phase, 24 pole, slip-ring induction motor running on 3300 V, 50 Hz mains has a rotor stand still impedance of $(0.016 + j\, 0.265)$ Ω/phase. Find (*i*) the speed at maximum torque (*ii*) ratio of full load torque to maximum torque, is the full load torque is obtained at 247 RPM.

Solution:

Case 1. Synchronous speed, $N_s = 120\, f/P = 250$ RPM.

$s = R_2/X_2 = 6\%$ (as maximum torque occurs when: $R_2 = sX_2$)

Rotor speed, $N = (1 - s)\, N_s = 235$ RPM

Case 2. Full load slip, $S_{FL} = 1.2\%$

Since, $T_{FL} \propto sR_2/[R_2^2 + (sX_2)^2]$ and

$$T_{\max} \; \alpha \; \frac{SR_2}{2(sX_2)} \quad \text{(as maximum torque occurs when: } R_2 = sX_2)$$

$$\therefore \quad T_{FL}/T_{\max} = 2/1 + (R_2/sX_2)^2 = 0.077.$$

18. A 4 pole, 50 Hz Induction motor on full load runs at 1440 RPM. Calculate the synchronous speed and % slip and frequency of the rotor.

Solution: Given data: $P = 4, f = 50$ Hz, $N = 1440$ RPM

$$N_S = \frac{120\,f}{P} = \frac{120 \times 50}{4} = 1500 \text{ RPM}$$

$$\%\text{ Slip} = \frac{N_S - N}{N_S} \times 100 = \frac{1500 - 1440}{1500} \times 100 = 4\%$$

$$f' = Sf = 0.04 \times 50 = 2 \text{ Hz.}$$

19. The frequency of the EMF in the stator of a 4 pole Induction motor is 50 Hz and that of rotor is 1½ Hz. What is the slip and what is the speed of the motor.

Solution: Given data: $P = 4, f = 50 \text{ Hz}, f' = 1\frac{1}{2}$ Hz

$$N_S = \frac{120\,f}{P} = \frac{120 \times 50}{4} = 1500 \text{ RPM}$$

$$S = \frac{f'}{f} = \frac{1.5}{50} = 0.03 \text{ or } 3\%$$

$$N = N_S\,(1 - S) = 1500\,(1 - 0.03) = 1455 \text{ RPM.}$$

20. A 6 pole Induction motor is connected to a 50 Hz supply. It is running at a speed of 970 RPM. Find the synchronous speed and the slip.

Solution: Given data: $P = 6, f = 50$ Hz, $N = 970$ RPM

$$N_S = \frac{120 f}{P} = \frac{120 \times 50}{6} = 1000 \text{ RPM}$$

$$\%\text{ Slip} = \frac{N_S - N}{N_S} \times 100 = \frac{1000 - 970}{1000} \times 100 = 3\%$$

21. A 4 pole, 50 Hz induction motor has a slip of 1% at No load. When operated at full load the slip is 2.5%. Find the change in speed from No load to full load.

Solution: On No Load: $P = 4,\ f = 50$ Hz, $S = 1\%$

$$N_S = \frac{120\,f}{P} = \frac{120 \times 50}{4} = 1500 \text{ RPM}$$

$$N = N_s\,(1 - S) = 1500\,(1 - 0.01) = 1485 \text{ RPM}$$

On Load: $P = 4, f = 50$ Hz, $S = 2.5\%$

$$N = N_S (1 - S) = 1500 (1 - 0.025) = 1462.5 \text{ RPM}$$

The change in speed from no load to full load = 1485 – 1462.5 = 22.5 RPM.

22. A 10 pole induction motor is supplied by a 6 pole alternator which is driven at 1200 RPM. If the motor runs with a slip of 3%, what is its speed. If the slip is 5% what is the speed.

Solution: Data: $P = 6$, $N_S = 1200$ RPM – of the alternator.

From, $f = \dfrac{PN_S}{120} = \dfrac{6 \times 1200}{120}$; Frequency input of I.M. = 60 Hz

Induction motor data: $P = 10$

Synchronous speed of I.M. = $\dfrac{120 f}{P} = \dfrac{120 \times 60}{10} = 720$ RPM

If $S = 3\%$ $N = N_S (1 - S) = 720 (1 - 0.03) = 698.4$ RPM

If $S = 5\%$ $N = N_S (1 - S) = 720 (1 - 0.05) = 684$ RPM.

23. An 8 pole alternator runs at 750 RPM and supplies power to a 6 pole induction motor which has a slip of 3% at full load. Find the full load speed of Induction motor and frequency of rotor EMF.

Solution: Alternator data: $P = 8$, $N_s = 750$ RPM

$$f = \frac{PN_S}{120} = \frac{8 \times 750}{120} = 50 \text{ Hz}$$

Induction motor data: $P = 6$ and $S = 3\%$

Synchronous speed of I.M. = $N_S = \dfrac{120 f}{P} = \dfrac{120 \times 50}{5} = 1000$ RPM

If $S = 3\%$ $N = N_s (1 - S) = 1000 (1 - 0.03) = 970$ RPM

$$f' = Sf = 0.03 \times 50 = 1.5 \text{ Hz.}$$

24. An 8 pole three phase alternator is coupled to an engine running at 750 RPM and supplies a three phase Induction motor having a full load speed of 1440 RPM. Find the percentage slip and number of poles of the motor.

Solution: Alternator data: $P = 8$, $N_s = 750$ RPM

$$f = \frac{PN_s}{120} = \frac{8 \times 750}{120} = 50 \text{ Hz.}$$

To calculate N_s assume different values of poles and select the number of poles such that the synchronous speed will be near to the running speed of the Induction motor.

If $P = 2$ then $N_s = \dfrac{120 f}{P} = \dfrac{120 \times 50}{2} = 3000$ RPM

If $P = 4$ then $N_s = \dfrac{120 f}{P} = \dfrac{120 \times 50}{4} = 1500$ RPM

If $P = 6$ then $N_s = \dfrac{120 f}{P} = \dfrac{120 \times 50}{6} = 1000$ RPM

Therefore P should be 4 and $N_s = 1500$ RPM.

$$\%\text{Slip} = \frac{N_s - N}{N_s} \times 100 = \frac{1500 - 1440}{1500} \times 100 = 4\%.$$

Examples on Alternators

25. Find the winding factor of a three phase AC generator having 24 stator slots and 4 poles. The coil span is 1 : 4.

Solution: Slots/poles/phase, $m = 2$, Slots/pole, $s = 6$, short chording angle, $\beta = 180°/s = 30°$.

$$\therefore \quad K_d = \sin (m\beta/2)/\ m \sin (\beta/2) = 0.966$$

Full pitch is for 180°, difference in coil span is 3 and thus the coil span is less by 3 slots, so that $\alpha = 180°(3/6) = 90°$

$$\therefore \quad K_p = \cos (\alpha/2) = 0.707.$$

26. A 220 V, 24 pole, three phase alternator is running at 300 RPM. Find the number of stator conductors. if the magnetic flux is 0.05 Wb/pole and $K_d = K_p = 1.0$.

Solution: $f = PN_s/120 = 60$ Hz.

$E_{ph} = 4.44\ K_d K_p f\phi T$ Substituting for all the values, we get

$$220/\sqrt{3} = 4.44\ (60)\ 0.05T$$

Solving ; $T = Z/2 = 19/2$ so that $Z = 19$ conductors/phase and 57 conductors for the three phase machine.

27. A three phase, 4 pole, 50 Hz, alternator has 2 slots/pole/phase and 40 conductors/slot. The winding is *Y*-connected. Find the generated emf, if the flux/pole is 60 m Wb.

Solution: Assume $K_p = 1.0$, Slots/pole/phase, $m = 2$; Slots/pole, $s = 6$,

$\beta = 180°/s = 30°$ and $Z = (2 \times 4 \times 3)\ (40) = 960$. Thus,

$$K_d = \sin (m\beta/2)/m \sin (\beta/2) = 0.966$$

$\therefore$ Number of turns per phase,

$$T = 960/(3 \times 2) = 160 \text{ turns}$$

$E_{\text{Line}} = \sqrt{3}(4.44\ K_d K_p f\phi T)$ Substituting for all the values, we get

$$= \sqrt{3}(4.44)\ (0.966)\ (1.0)\ (50)\ (60 \times 10^{-3})\ (160) = 3.535 \text{ kV}.$$

28. A 8 pole AC generator is running at 750 RPM. Find the frequency and determine the speed at which the generator must be run so that the frequency be 40 Hz.

Solution: $f = PN_s/120 = 50$ Hz

and $N_s = 120 f/P = 600$ RPM.

29. A 12 pole, single phase, AC generator has 144 slots, 2/3rd of which are wound with 8 conductors/slot. The flux per pole is 42 mWb, sinusoidally distributed. The factors K_d and K_p are 0.829 and 1.0 respectively. If the speed is 500 RPM, find the frequency of the generated emf.

Solution: $f = PN_s/120 = 50$ Hz

No. of turns/phase, $T = Z/2 = 1/2\ [8 \times 144(2/3)] = 3.84$

Voltage induced, E/phase 4.44 $K_d K_p f \phi T = 2.968$ kV

so that $E_{\text{Line}} = 5.14$ kV

30. **A three phase, 50 Hz, 16 pole alternator with *Y*-connected, winding has 144 slots and 10 conductors/slot. The flux per pole is 0.03 Wb, sinusoidally distributed. The coil span is 160° electrical. Find synchronous speed, winding factors and line emf.**

Solution: $N_s = 120\, f/P = 375$ RPM, $m = 144/(16 \times 3) = 3$;

$s = 144/16 = 9$ so that, $\beta = 180°/9 = 20°$ and $\alpha = 180° - 160° = 20°$

$K_d = \sin(m\beta/2)/m \sin(\beta/2) = 0.96$

$K_p = \cos(20°/2) = 0.9848$, $T = (144 \times 10)/(3 \times 2)$ 240 turns

$E_{\text{Line}} = \sqrt{3}\,(0.44\ K_d K_p f \phi T) = 2.2$ kV.

31. **A 500 V, 50 KVA, single phase alternator has an effective resistance of 0.2 Ω. A field current of 10 A produces an armature current of 200 A on short circuit and an emf of 450 V on open circuit. Calculate**

(*a*) the synchronous impedance and reactance and

(*b*) the full load regulation with 0.8 power factor lagging.

Solution: (Ref. Fig. 7.27)

Z_s = (Open circuit voltage/SC current) = 2.52 Ω and R_a = 0.2 Ω so that

X_s = 2.24 Ω. From the vector diagram for lagging loads.

$$E_0 = \sqrt{(V\cos\phi + IR_a)^2 + (V\sin\phi + IX_s)^2}$$

With cos ϕ = 0.8, full load current = 100 Amps, we get E_0 = 672 V and Regulation

= [(672 – 500/)/500] 100 = 34.4%.

32. **A three phase 400 V, synchronous motor takes 52.5 A at a power factor of 0.8 leading. Calculate the power supplied and the induced emf, if the motor impedance per phase is (0.25 + *j* 3.2) Ω.**

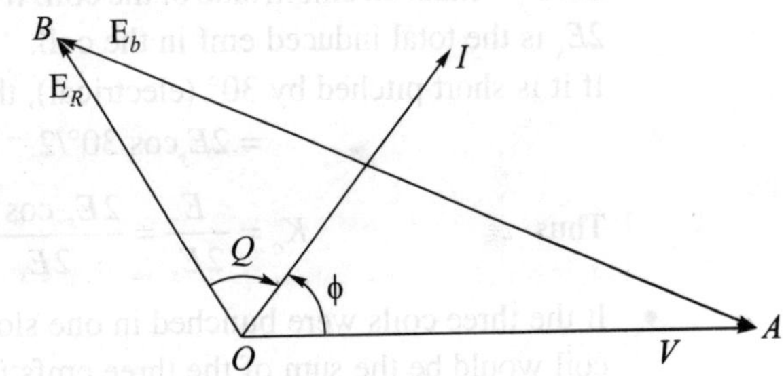

Solution: $P_L = \sqrt{3}\, V_L I_L \cos\phi$

= 29.1 kW.

Impedance angle, $\theta = \tan^{-1}(X/R) = 85°$, Power factor angle, $\phi = 36°$

As such, the vector diagram may be drawn as in Fig. P.1.

$E_R = IZ_s = 52.5 \times 3.21 = 168.5$ volts.

$$E_b = \sqrt{(V^2 + E_R^2 - 2VE_R\cos(180 - (\theta + \phi))} = 350.5 \text{ volts}$$

Thus, $E_{\text{line}} = \sqrt{3}\, E_b = 670$ V. It is to be noted that if $E_b > V$, the motor power factor leading and if $E_b < V$, it is lagging.

33. Calculate the line and phase voltages and also the speed of a 4 pole, 3 phase, 50 Hz, star connected alternator with 36 slots and 30 conductors per slot. Flux per pole 50 mWb sinusoidally distributed.

Solution: We know that $f = \dfrac{PN}{120}$ and hence $N = 1500$ rpm.

$$E_{ph} = 4\, K_f K_c K_d f \phi T \text{ volts}$$

where K_c = Pitch or coil-span factor and is defined as

$$= \frac{\text{Vector sum of induced emfs per coil}}{\text{Arithmatic sum of the induced emfs per coil}}$$

- Full pitch coils have spans equal to one pole pitch *i.e.*, spanning over 180 electrical (Placed in slots 1 and 7).
- If coils are placed in slots 1 and 6 it is a short pitched coil it is equal to 5/6th of a pole pitch. *i.e.*, it falls short by 180/6 = 30°.

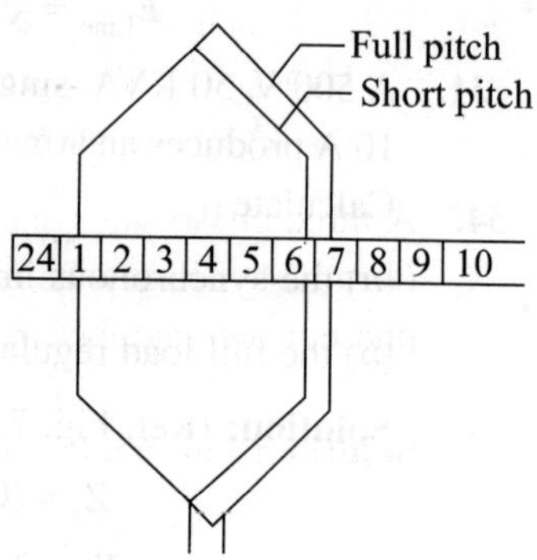

- Short pitch coils are deliberately used for the reasons 1. save copper of end connection. 2. Improve the waveform of the generated emf thereby reducing harmonics as efficiency is increased.
- Disadvantage being, the overall voltage around the coil is reduced. Due to this the voltage induced in the two sides of the short pitched coil are out of phase, their resultant is less than their arithmetic sum and thus,

$$\text{Pitch factor } (K_c \text{ or } K_p) = \frac{\text{Vector sum of induced emfs per coil}}{\text{Arithamatic sum of the induced emfs per coil}}.$$

- This can be more easily seen from the diagram below.
  Let E_s = Induced emf in side of the coil. If the coil is full pitched, $2E_s$ is the total induced emf in the coil.
  If it is short pitched by 30° (electrical), then emf induced $= 2E_s \cos 30°/2$

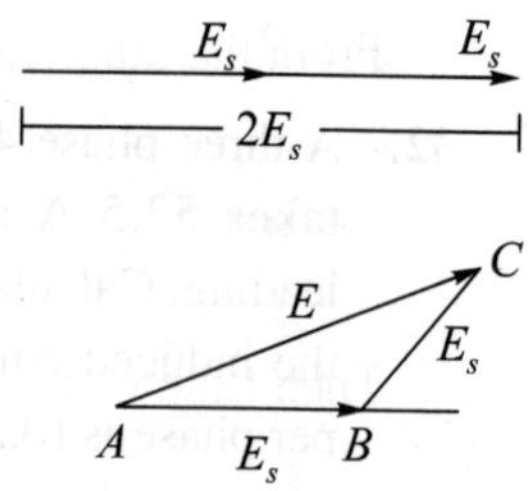

Thus $$K_c = \frac{E}{2E_s} = \frac{2E_s \cos 15}{2E_s} = \cos 15° = 0.966.$$

- If the three coils were bunched in one slot, then the total emf generated in the 3 sides of the coil would be the sum of the three emfs *i.e.*, $=3E_s$.
  Since the coils are distributed, difference of 20° with each other (9 slots per pole *i.e.*, 3 slots /pole/phase *i.e.*, 1, 2 and 3 belong to *R* phase. But these coils are not bunched in one slot but are distributed in 3 different slots. Angular displacement between any two adjacent slots is 180/9 = 20° Electrical). Their vector sum is less than 3 E_s.

$$= E_s \cos 20° + E_s + E_s \cos 20° = 2.88E_s$$

$$\text{Thus the distribution factor} = \frac{\text{Emf in the distributed windings}}{\text{Emf with concentrated windings}}$$

$$= 2.88E_s/3E_s = 0.96$$

And indeed, $K_d = \dfrac{\sin \beta/2}{m \sin \beta/2}$, where m = Phases ; β = chording angle

With all the above $E_{ph} = 4K_f K_c K_d f \phi T$ volts

- Substituting the values given in the above expression,

$$\beta = \frac{180}{\text{No. of slots per pole}} = \frac{180}{36/4} = 20°;\ m = 36/4/3 = 3$$

$$K_d = \frac{\sin m\beta/2}{m \sin \beta/2} = \frac{\sin 3 \times 20/2}{3 \sin 20/2} = 0.96 \quad K_f = 1.11$$

$K_c = 1$ assumed

$Z = 36 \times 30/3 = 360$; T per phase $=360/2 = 180$

Hence $E_{ph} = 4 \times 1.11 \times 1 \times 0.96 \times 50 \times 0.05 \times 180 = 1920$ V

$E_l = \sqrt{3}\, E_{ph} = 3320$ volts

34. A three phase star connected alternator supplies a load of 10 MW at p.f. 0.8 lag and at 11 kV (terminal voltage). Its resistance is 0.1 ohm per phase and synchronous reactance 0.66 ohm per phase. Calculate the line value of emf generated. Find also the regulation.

Solution: Full load current $= \dfrac{10 \times 10^6}{\sqrt{3} \times 11000 \times 0.85} = 618$ A

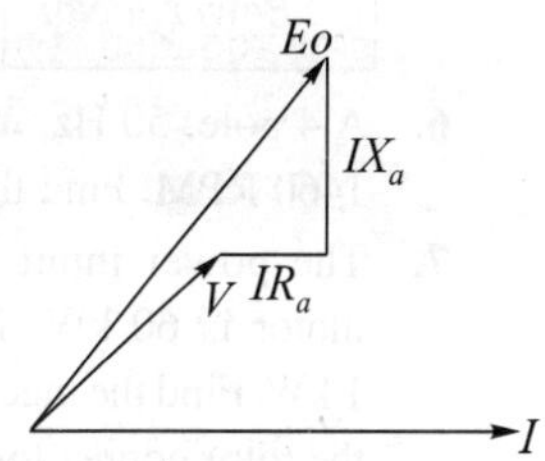

$IR_a = 618 \times 0.1 = 61.8$ V

$IX_a = 618 \times 0.66 = 408$ V

Terminal voltage/phase $= 11000/\sqrt{3} = 6350$ V/ph

$\phi = \cos^{-1}(0.85) = 31.8°$; $\sin \phi = 0.527$

From the diagram

$$E_0 = \sqrt{(V \cos \phi + IR_a)^2 + (V \sin \phi + IX_a)^2}$$

$$E_0 = \sqrt{(6350 \times 0.85 + 61.8)^2 + (6350 \times 0.52 + 408)^2} = 6625 \text{ volts}$$

Then Line voltage $E_1 = \sqrt{3}\, E_{ph} = \sqrt{3} \times 6625 = 11480$ Volts $= 11.48$ kV

$$\%\, R = \frac{E_0 - V}{V} \times 100 = \frac{6.625 \times 10^3 - 6.35 \times 10^3}{6.35 \times 10^3} \times 100 = 4\%.$$

PROBLEMS

1. The resistance and leakage reactance of a transformer are 0.15 Ω and 0.7 Ω. Primary voltage is 440 V and primary current is 50 A at a power factor of 0.8 lagging. Find the primary induced emf.

2. A 220/440 V, transformer has primary resistance and reactance each of 0.5 Ω and secondary resistance and reactance each of 1.2 Ω. Find the secondary terminal voltage when supplying a load current of 15 A at power factors of 0.8 lag. and 0.85 lead.

3. A 11000/220 V, 50 KVA transformer has a primary resistance of 0.55 Ω and a secondary resistance of 0.023 Ω. If the transformer is designed for a maximum efficiency at (2/3)rd load, find the efficiency when the transformer delivers full load at 0.8 p.f lag.

4. Determine the core area, number of turns and the position of the tapping points for a 500 KVA, 50 Hz, single phase, 6600/5000 V auto-transformer, assuming the emf/turn as 8 V for a maximum flux density of 1.3 Wb/m^2.

5. A 20 KVA transformer is designed for a maximum efficiency of 0.98 at (2/3)rd full load, unity power factor. Find the all-day efficiency if the load coming on the transformer over a day is as below:

No. of hours	10	08	04	02
Load in kW	03	15	12	—
Power factor	0.6	0.8	0.85	—

6. A 4 pole, 50 Hz, induction motor is running at 1460 RPM. Find the slip and the slip-speed.

7. The power input to a three phase induction motor is 60 kW. The stator losses total up to 1 kW. Find the mechanical power developed and the rotor copper losses per phase if the motor is running at 3% slip.

8. The power input to a three phase, 50 Hz induction motor is 41 kW. The stator losses are 1 kW. Friction and windage losses are 2 kW. The speed of the motor is 960 RPM. Determine (*i*) slip (*ii*) BHP and (*iii*) the rotor copper loss of the motor.

9. The rotor emf of a three phase, 440 V, 4-pole, 50 Hz induction motor makes 84 complete cycles per minute when the shaft torque is 203.5 Nm. Calculate HP of the motor.

10. The power input to a three phase, 6-pole, 50 Hz, 970 rpm induction motor is 42 kW. The stator losses are 1.2 kW and the friction and windage losses are 1.8 kW. Find (*i*) slip (*ii*) rotor output (*iii*) the rotor copper loss and (*iv*) the efficiency.

11. A 50 Hz, 8-pole induction motor has a full load slip of 4%. The rotor resistance is 0.001 Ω per phase and stand still reactance is 0.005 Ω per phase. Find the ratio of the maximum to the full load torque and the speed at which the maximum torque occurs.

12. An induction motor has a rotor resistance of 0.02 Ω and a standstill reactance is 0.1 Ω. Determine the value of total resistance of the starter at the rotor circuit for obtaining the maximum torque at start.

13. A 6 pole alternator is driven at 1200 RPM. Determine the frequency of generated emf. If this alternator supplies power to a 10 pole induction motor, find its speed when the slip is 3%.

14. A *Y*-connected, three phase, 4 pole, 50 Hz, alternator has a single layer winding in 24 slots. There are 50 turns in each coil and flux per pole is 0.05 Wb. Find the open circuit line voltage.

15. A 6 pole, *Y*-connected, three phase, 50 Hz alternator has 12 slots/pole and 4 conductors/slot. The winding is (5/6)th full pitched. Determine the line emf, if a flux of 25 m Wb is sinusoidally distributed.

16. A three phase, *Y*-connected alternator on open circuit is required to generate a line voltage of 3.6 kV, 50 Hz, when driven at 500 RPM. The stator has 35 slots/pole/phase and 10 conductors/slot. Assuming all conductors per phase to be in series and coils to be full pitched, calculate (*i*) number of poles (*ii*) flux/pole.

17. A three phase, *Y*-connected, 50 Hz, 8-pole generator has 72 slots and 10 conductors/slot. The flux/pole is 24.8 mWb, sinusoidally distributed and the coils are full pitched. Find the speed and line emf.

18. A 400 V, 50 KVA, 50 Hz, 3 phase, *Y*-connected armatures has a resistance of 0.1 Ω per phase. An excitation of 2.5 A produces on open circuit, an emf of 130 V. The same excitation produces, current of 90 A on short circuit. Determine the full load regulation of the alternator for a power factor of 0.8 lagging.

19. The input to a 11 kV, *Y*-connected synchronous motor is 50 A. The effective synchronous reactance and the resistance per phase are 0.9 and 0.95 Ω respectively. Calculate the power supplied to the motor and the induced emf for power factors of 0.8 lag and 0.8 lead.

20. A 60 KVA, 220 V, 50Hz, single phase alternator has an effective armature resistance if 0.015 ohm and an armature leakage reactance of 0.06 ohm. Find the voltage induced in the armature when the alternator is delivering rated current at a load power factor of (*a*) unity (*b*) 0.7 Lag (*c*) 0.7 leading.

21. Calculate the rms value of the induced emf per phase of a 10 pole, 3 phase, 50 Hz alternator with 2 slots per pole per phase and 4 conductors per slot in two layers. The coil span is 150 . the flux per pole has a fundamental component of 0.12 Wb and a 20% third harmonic component. (Harmonic emf = $E_s = 4.44\, K_{c3}\, K_{d3}\, f_3\, \phi_3\, T$ and $K_{c3} = \cos 3\alpha/2 = 0.707$ ($\alpha = 30$)

$$K_d = \frac{\sin mn\beta/2}{m \sin \beta/2} \quad n = \text{order of harmonic} = 3$$

and $\phi_3 = \frac{1}{3} \times 20\%$ of fundamental.

8 CHAPTER

Domestic Wiring

The domestic service mains terminate at the energy meter. In turn, from the energy meter to different parts of the building. The supply mains are drawn through several distribution boards located suitably in various parts of the building. Connection to the other circuits/branches are made from these distribution boards. Thus during repairs, only that circuit affected may be disconnected without hampering the other circuitry.

For protecting the cable and wires in a circuit against damage from an excessive current, *fuse* is used which heats up to melting point and breaks the circuit. Tin, lead, zinc, antimony, copper, aluminum, etc. can be used for fuse wire.

8.1 ELECTRICAL WIRING

The four best conductors available for the transmission of electricity are: silver, copper, aluminum and iron. Due to their heavy cost, silver and copper are not used. Although the electrical conductivity of aluminium is inferior to that of copper, it is mostly used for all purpose like overhead lines, underground cables and house wiring cables.

There are several wiring systems in use. Each system of wiring has its own particular advantage. No one system is suited for all installations. Great care must therefore, be taken in the selection of the wiring system, depending on working voltages, atmosphere, class of building and size of installation. The system of wiring can be *tree system* or *distribution system*. For domestic installations, the following systems of wiring are used:

Cleat wiring, Cab Tier Sheathed (CTS) System, Tough Rubber Sheathed (TRS) wiring system, Wooden casing and capping, Lead-sheathed wiring, Conduit wiring—open conduit and concealed conduit systems, etc.

Of these, conduit wiring has a very long life and provides a very good mechanical protection. It is costlier and requires a highly skilled labour. Hence, nowadays, CTS wiring is preferred, which is economical and provides good protection from dampness. Cleat wiring is very cheap but lasts short. The above mentioned wiring systems are briefed below:

- *Clear system*: Porcelain cleats spaced at regular intervals are used to support the insulated conductors (VIR wires) as in Fig. 8.1. This system of wiring is economical and skilled labour is not required. However, since the conductors are not totally concealed, they are susceptible for mechanical damages and require maintenance.

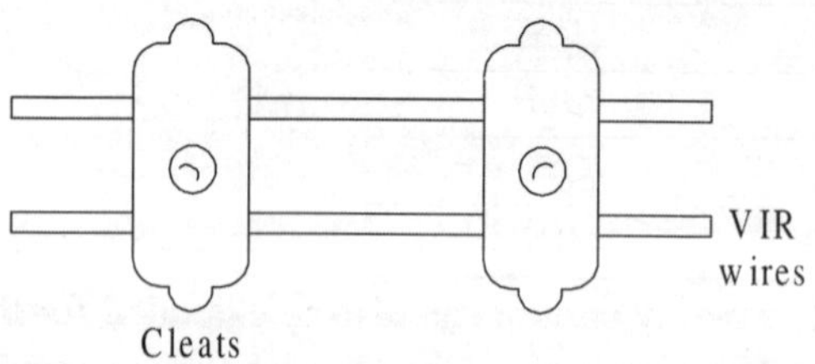

Fig. 8.1 *Cleat wiring*

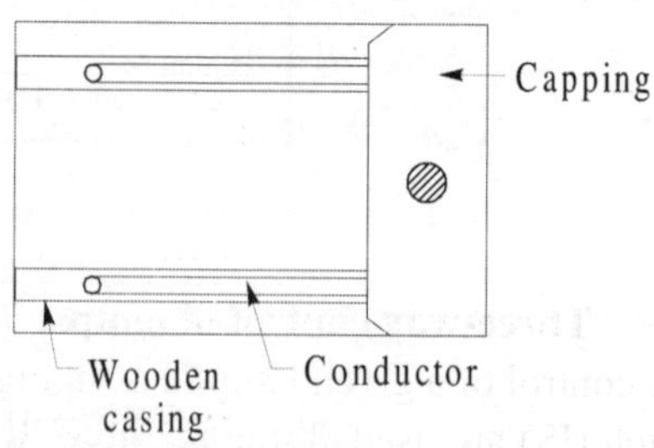

Fig. 8.2 *Casing and Capping*

- *Wooden casing and capping*: Insulated wires are run in the grooves cut in wood and covered as shown in Fig. 8.2. Screws on the cappings makes a firm bondage between the casing and cappings. This system is economical and the insulated wires are not exposed to mechanical damage. However, wood is susceptible for damage by ants besides the obvious possibility of fire risk.
- *The CTS system*: This system is very widely used. Here, the insulated conductors are totally covered by a thick coating of tough rubber similar to the CAB tyre. The wiring is done on wooden battens which are fixed to the walls or ceilings by wooden guttas and chips. The details are as in Fig. 8.3. This system has no fire risk, and since the wires are not exposed there is no possibility of mechanical damage. However, the system is quite costly.

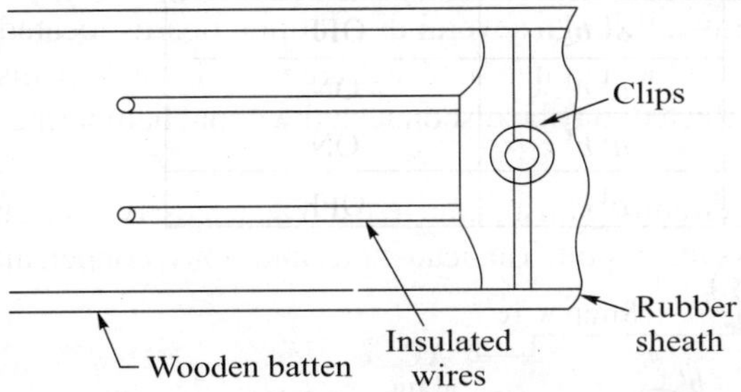

Fig. 8.3 *CTS wiring*

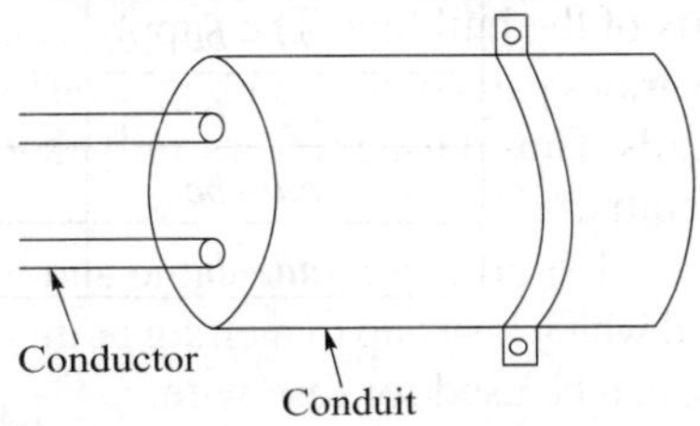

Fig. 8.4 *Conduit wiring*

- *Conduit system:* Steel or Galvanized iron pipes were used as conduit pipes. However, these are being replaced by the PVC-pipes nowadays. Due to the flexibility being offered by the PVC pipes, the system is also known as *Flexible Conduit System*. The details of the conduit system are as shown below in Fig. 8.4. The two types of conduits in use are: Open type and *Concealed type*. In the open conduits, the pipes are run on the walls and ceilings and in the concealed type, pipes are concealed inside the wall or ceilings and as such are not visible.
- *Lead covered system*: This is similar to the previous one except that instead of the rubber sheath, lead sheath is used. The system involves no life hazard and there is no mechanical damage to conductors. However, the system is quite costly.

8.2 LAMP CONTROL

Two-way control of lamps: Of the different lamp circuits used in practice, the staircase wiring is usually done by two-way control. The lamp circuit is controlled by two 2-way switches. Each switch will have 3 terminals as shown in Fig. 8.5. The wires used between the switches are called as strap wires. Table 8.1 gives the switching sequence of the switches for different positions of the lamp.

Table 8.1 Switching sequence (2-way control)

Position of switch		*Lamp status*
S_1	S_2	
$a\ b$	$a^1\ b^1$	ON
$a\ c$	$a^1\ b^1$	OFF
$a\ b$	$a^1\ c^1$	OFF
$a\ c$	$a^1\ c^1$	ON

Three-way control of lamps: The principle of two-way control can also be extended for three way control of a given lamp *L*, as in Fig. 8.6. Here, two 2-way switches S_1 and S_2 and one intermediate switch (IS) are used. Table 8.2 gives the switching sequence of the switches for different positions of the lamp. The principle can thus be extended for multipoint control of a single lamp, if required.

Table 8.2 Switching sequence (3-way control)

Position of switch			*Lamp status*
IS	S_1	S_2	
ab – cd	*ab*	$a^1 b^1$	ON
ab – cd	*ab*	$a^1 c^1$	OFF
ab – cd	*ac*	$a^1 b^1$	OFF
ab – cd	*ac*	$a^1 c^1$	ON
ad – bc	*ab*	$a^1 b^1$	OFF
ad – bc	*ab*	$a^1 c^1$	ON
ad – bc	*ab*	$a^1 b^1$	ON
ad – bc	*ab*	$a^1 c^1$	OFF

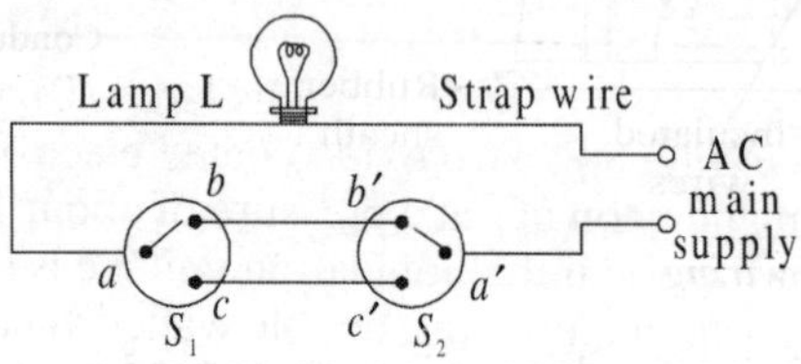

Fig. 8.5 *Two way control of lamp*

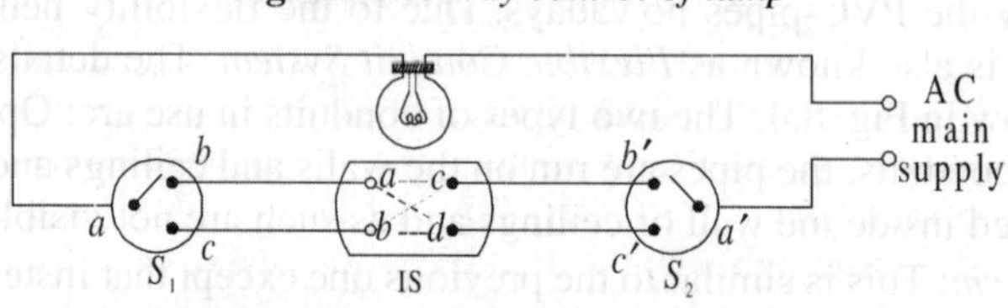

Fig. 8.6 *Two way control of lamp*

8.3 FLUORESCENT LAMP

Fluorescent lamp is essentially a gas discharge tube. A voltage is applied between two electrodes of a tube containing gas. Once the voltage exceeds the critical voltage, ionization voltage, gas is ionized and the ionized gas emits radiation, partly in the visible range and partly in the ultraviolet or infrared range. It is known that certain minerals absorb ultraviolet light and re-radiate in the visible region. One of the main sources of ultraviolet radiation is an electric discharge through mercury vapour at low pressure.

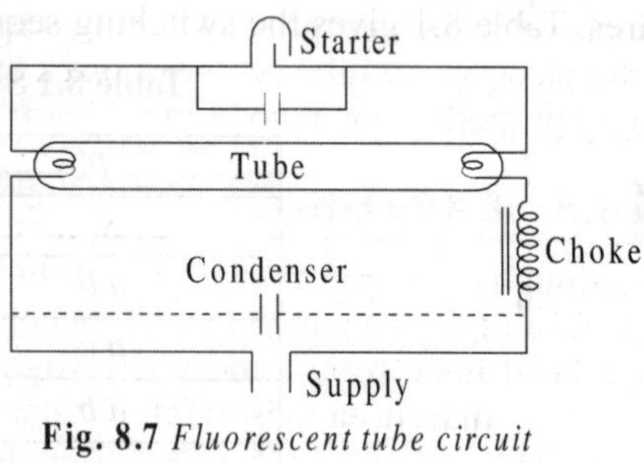

Fig. 8.7 *Fluorescent tube circuit*

Construction: Fig. 8.7 shows a fluorescent lamp circuit which has the basic parts such as the tube, choke and starter. Due to low pressure, the lamp is in the form of a long tube, the inside of which is coated with phosphor to convert ultraviolet light into visible light. Phosphor coatings produce the required colour, for instance:

Cadmium tungstate-blue, zinc silicate-Green, Cadmium borate pink and so on. The tube contains a small amount of mercury and argon gas at a pressure of 2.5 mm of Hg. When the temperature increases, the mercury vaporizes and thus takes over the conduction of current. At each end of the tube, the electrodes are of spiral form made of tungsten and coated with an electron emitting material. The choke is connected in series with the tube filament which provides a voltage impulse for starting the lamp and acts as a *ballast* during running. The filament is connected to a *starter* which is a small cathode glow lamp with metal strips electrodes.

Working: The working of a Fluorescent lamp is as follows: The electrodes are open, when the starter is cold. When connected to supply, full voltage is impressed on the starter. A glow discharge is set up in the starter which warms the electrodes and causes the bimetal strip to bend and touch the electrodes. The circuit gets closed and current flows though the filaments, thereby causing emission of free electrons. At the same time, voltage at starter falls to zero and the bimetal strip cools down. The starter electrodes then open and interrupt the circuit current. Its effect is to induce high voltage surge of about 1000 volts in choke. This high voltage produces an arc between lamp electrodes and the lamp lights up immediately. Then starting switch contacts are left open. The current flow through the circuit is now only through the tube and choke. Resistance of the tube being less, the current flow is through the high inductance choke resulting in a poor power factor (of the order of 0.5). A condenser is connected across the supply as shown to improve the power factor.

8.4 SODIUM VAPOUR LAMP

These lamps are of low luminosity and hence their length is large. To get the required length, it is made in the form of a U-tube as shown in Fig. 8.8. Two oxide coated electrodes are sealed into the ends. The inner tube contains a little sodium and neon gas at a pressure of about 10 mm of Hg. A small amount of Argon is also placed in the tube so that the initial ionization voltage is reduced. The electrodes are made of oxide coated tungsten. The U-tube is enclosed in a double walled vacuum flask to keep the temperature within working range.

Working: Earlier to lamp being on, sodium is in solid form (up to about 60°C), deposited on the sides of the tube walls. When the power is on, it operates as a low pressure neon lamp with pink color. When the lamp gets warmed (temperature more than 200°C), sodium is vaporized and it radiates yellow light. Thus, after 10 to 15 minutes, the lamp starts emitting full light. The maximum efficiency is at 220°C.

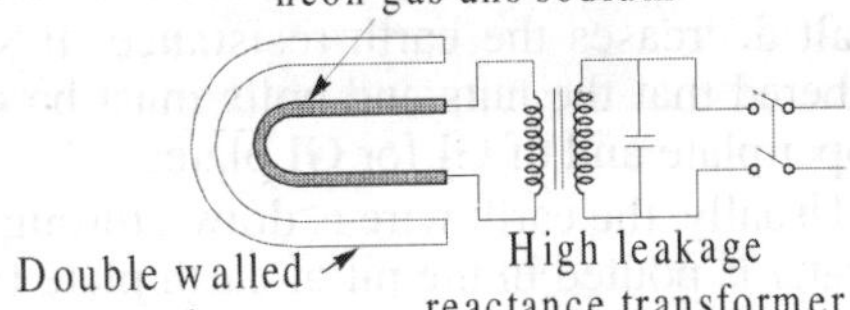

Fig. 8.8 *Sodium vapour lamp*

To start the discharge, a striking voltage of 380 V is required for a 40 Watt lamp and 450 V for 100 W lamp. These voltages are obtained from a high reactance transformer or auto-transformer. At no load, the voltage is very high which falls down as the lamp starts giving light. As such, the regulation of transformer is poor.

These lamps are usually used for *street lighting*. A capacitor is connected across the supply to improve the power factor. The life of this lamp ends when the filament burns out or the cathode fails to emit electrons or tube becomes black due to sodium vapour action. The sodium vapour lamp should be hung properly so that sodium will not blacken the inside walls of the tube.

8.5 EARTHING

Earthing is required to save human life from danger of shock or death. Earthing effectively blows out the fuse of any apparatus which becomes leaky. It protects large buildings and all machines fed from overhead lines from atmospheric lightning by taking all voltage of lightning through the lightning arrestors. Indeed, earth is an infinite source and a sink. Since the neutral of every alternator and transformer is earthed, earthing helps to maintain the line voltage constant. A good earthing is one which gives very low resistance to the flow of heavy current of a given circuit.

The earth's potential is always taken as zero for all practical purposes. The electrical appliances or machines when connected with earth attain zero potential and are said to be earthed. A wire coming from the ground 2.5 to 3 meters deep from an electrode is called *earthing*. Double earth is used for a 3-phase machine and equipment. This gives minimum resistance to the flow of whole current of that apparatus in case of short circuit, leakage, etc. When double earth is used, there is an advantage of redundancy. Earthing can be done in different ways: plate earthing, pipe earthing, etc. The earth resistance for copper wire is 1 ohm and for G.I. wire, it should not be more than 3 ohm. Earth resistance can be measured by a megger. The earth resistance should be kept as low as possible, so that the total current can easily pass through the earth wire. This resistance increases during summer days. It can, then could be reduced by pouring water, increasing the plate area, increasing the depth, or by keeping the electrodes in parallel.

8.5.1 Plate Earthing

For good earthing in electric substations, plate earthing is used. Here, the looping earth wire is bolted effectively with the earth plate, made up of copper of size (60 × 60 × 0.318) cm and embedded 3 meters in ground. Copper plates are found to be most effective earth electrodes and are not affected by the soil moisture, they do not get rusted. But, on account of its high material cost, galvonized iron (GI) plates are preferred and used for normal works.

In case, the soil resistivity is high, the plate should be placed vertically in ground at a higher depth. A schematic diagram of plate earthing is shown in Fig. 8.9.

The plate is kept with its face vertical and is so arranged that it is embedded in an alternate layer of coke and salt for a minimum thickness of about 15 cm. Thc coke salt decreases the earth resistance. It should be remembered that the nuts and bolts must be of copper for copper plate and of GI for GI plates.

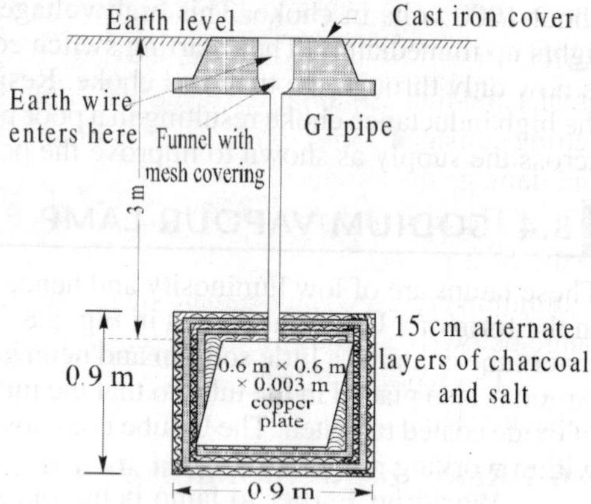

Fig. 8.9 *Plate earthing*

Usually, the earth wire is drawn through a 01 pipe fitted with a funnel on the top through which salty water is pouted in the pit of earth plate from time to time, especially in summer season when the soil moisture will decrease to a large extent which will increase the earth resistance.

The conductivity and hence the earthing efficiency increases with the increase of plate area and depth of embedding. The only disadvantage is that discontinuity of earth wire with plate below the earth cannot be observed physically and hence may lead to wrong decisions which may result in heavy loss in the event of a fault of a circuit.

8.5.2 Pipe Earthing

Here, a 2 meter long GI pipe of 38 mm diameter is buried vertically in ground to work as earth electrode. The depth depends on the soil conditions and there is no standard for this. The earth wires are fastened to the top section of the pipe with nuts and bolts. The pit area around the GI pipes is filled with salt and coal mixture for improving the soil conditions and efficiency of the earthing system. The schematized diagram of pipe earthing is shown in Fig. 8.10. The contact surface area of GI pipe with soil is more in

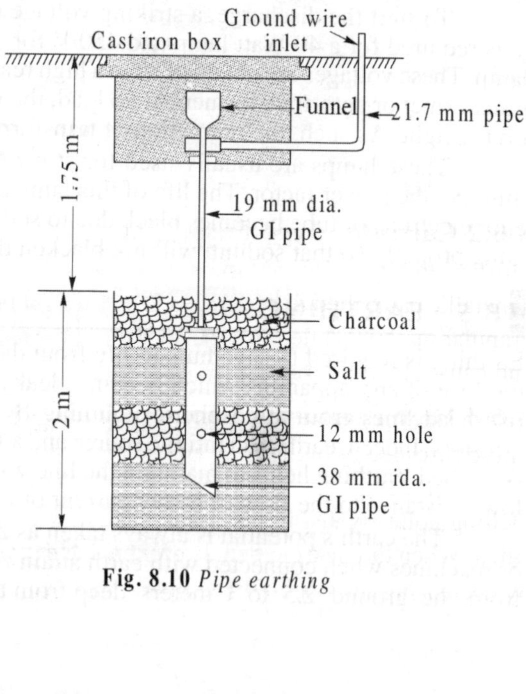

Fig. 8.10 *Pipe earthing*

comparison to the plate because of its circular cross section and hence can take up heavy leakage currents for the same electrode size. Also, since the earth wire connection with the GI pipe is above the ground level, checks can be made for carrying out continuity tests as and when desired, which is very difficult in the case of plate earthing.

8.6 FUSES

A fuse is a wire or a strip of short length of material having low melting point and is connected in an electric circuit to protect the equipment. The fuse is placed in between the supply and the equipment which to be protected connected in series electrically. Whenever an abnormal condition occurs then the current drawn by the equipment exceeds the rated current and thus the fuse gets heated and melts or breaks and thus isolating the electrical equipment from the supply, thus protecting the equipment from getting damaged. It also protects the cables and wires which otherwise get heated and burnt the insulation and damage the conductors.

The fuse materials should have low resistance, high conductivity and free from oxidation. Silver is the best material for fuse but because of its scarcity and costly metal, tin, zinc, lead, copper and aluminium are used as fuse materials. The alloy of Tin and Lead are used for low range of currents of range below 10A, and for higher range of currents copper and its alloys are used.

The types of fuses available are Rewirable or Kit-Kat type, Cartridge type and High Rupturing Capacity (HRC) fuse.

8.6.1 Rewirable or Kit-Kat Fuse

Rewirable or Kit–Kat Fuse consists of a metal fuse element connected between two metal contacts which separated and supported by the insulation base. A porcelain fuse carrier holding the fuse element can be inserted into the base without opening the main switch. Removal and replacement of fuse wire is done in this carrier without having any contact with the live part. This is as shown in Fig. 8.11 below:

Fig. 8.11 *Kit–Kat fuses or Rewirable Fuses*

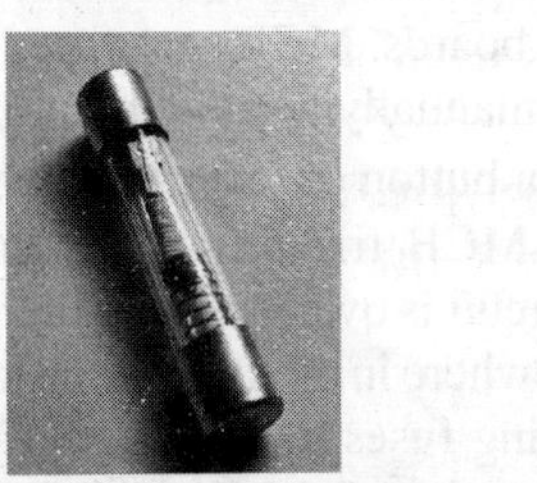

Fig. 8.12 *Cartridge fuses of lower rating*

8.6.2 Cartridge Type Fuse

This is a totally enclosed type of fuse unit and consists of an insulating container with ends sealed with a metallic cap called the cartridge. The fuse container encloses a fuse element and filled with powder or granular material called filler. Under the abnormal conditions, the fuse gets heated to a high temperature and causes to vapourise.

8.6.3 High Rupturing Capacity (HRC) Fuse

These fuses are of high rating and so they are used in high voltage installations. It consists of a ceramic tube with metal caps and fixing tags. The fuse element is a silver strip of special shape with a low melting point riveted in the center. The fuse element is completely surrounded by chemically purified silica. When the fuse element is broken due to overload the silica prevents the formation of arc and there by decreasing the rise in the temperature of the fuse and its surroundings.

8.7 ELECTRIC SHOCKS

The electric shocks are caused when we touch the metal parts of the equipment, or machine frame when the phase wire is in contact with the metal parts of the equipment or machine. The effect of electric shock will be severe if the current is in the range of 100mA and above. It is not only the leakage current but also other factors like supply voltage and resistance of body which adds in giving the shock. The leakage current is given as I = E/R. Where E is the supply voltage and R is the resistance of the body. The resistance of the body may be different from person to person and also depends on the wetness of the equipment. If the body of the machine is wet or when the hand is wet the shock will be severe.

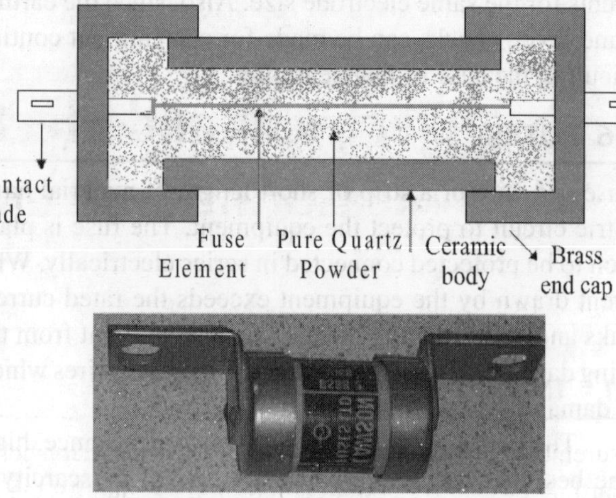

Fig. 8.13 *HRC fuse*

The low frequency of the current may result in very severe shocks than the high frequency currents. The path taken by the current through the body, survival is possible, if the path of leakage current is not found through chest or heart but it may result in severe burns on the parts of the body depending upon the value of current.

8.8 MINIATURE CIRCUIT BREAKER (MCB)

Miniature Circuit Breaker (MCB) is a relatively small circuit breaker fitted in consumer units and small distribution boards. MCBs are fitted in consumer units in place of fuses. They have the advantage that they can be manually reset without having to replace wire as in the case of a traditional fuse. The MCBs have either a button or lever that can be flicked to reset it.

The MCB tripping is an indication that, either the circuit is overloaded or there may be short circuit somewhere in the system. To identify a faulty circuit causing fuses to blow or MCB to reset can be a tricky process. Initially try to remember what appliances were switched on or what happened at the time the fault occurred.

Fig. 8.14 *MCB for single phase circuits*

Over loading is a relatively easy problem to solve, it is caused by using too many appliances on one circuit exceeding the power rating of the circuit, causing the fuse to blow or MCB to trip. The solution is, never use all the appliances, at the same time or change the rating of the circuit breaker along with the wiring system.

If the circuit is not being overloaded the next step is to inspect all the outlets, lights, flexes and appliances using the blower circuit. Look for the damage that could have caused a short circuit and repair it.

Electrical and Electronic Measuring Instruments

9

CHAPTER

9.1 INTRODUCTION

Measurement of a quantity is the result of a comparison between the unknown quantity and its predefined standard. A measuring system is required to quantify the parameters involved and establish clear rules about their relative values. Early systems of measurements were based on imprecise units, while the modern measurement systems are based on accurately defined units. Many standard measuring units have been established at different levels of measurements. The significance of electrical measurements and measuring instruments is evident from the rapid developments in the field of electrical engineering owing to the developments in their measuring devices. Lord Kelvin once said, *when you can measure what you are speaking about and express them in numbers, you know something about it and when you cannot measure it or when you cannot express it in numbers, your knowledge is of a meager and unsatisfactory kind. It may be the beginning of knowledge, but you have scarcely in your thought advanced to the stage of science.*

The measurement is meaningful only if the standards are accurately defined, reliable and commonly accepted, the methods used are well proven and the circuit conditions are little affected by the introduction of the measuring systems. The parameter under measurement is referred as *measurand* and it is always measured in terms of its numeric value. The process of measurement through a meter is referred as *instrumentation.* Electrical measuring instruments are the most common devices used not only for the measurement of electrical quantities, but also for all other quantities, which could be transformed into an electrical signal. The usual quantities to be measured are current, voltage, power, energy, frequency, power factor, etc. The various circuit parameters also need to be measured such as resistance, inductance, capacitance, etc. An umpteen number and varieties of measuring instruments have been developed for measurement purposes. In other words, measurement and instrumentation are based on different methods depending upon the characteristic features of the quantity being measured.

9.2 MEASURING INSTRUMENTS

9.2.1 Requirements of Instruments

A measuring instrument should possess some of the following important characteristic features:

- It should have a very high instrument *efficiency* which is the ratio of the quantity being measured to the power utilized by the instrument at full scale.

- It should have a high sensitivity which is the ratio of the magnitude of the output signal to the magnitude of the quantity being measured. The inverse of this ratio is the Inverse Sensitivity or Deflection Factor.
- The output of the instrument should be linearly proportional to the input. In such cases, the scale will be uniform and hence easier to calibrate.
- It should have a very low *threshold* which is the minimum value of below which the change in output cannot be detected by the instrument.
- It should have lowest *dead time* which is the minimum time required for the instrument to respond to a change in the quantity being measured.
- It should virtually have no *dead zone* where dead zone is the largest change of the input quantity for which there is no output of the instrument. Dead zone is caused due to friction, hyterisis, backlash, etc.
- It should have perfect reproducibility (precision) which is specified in terms of the scale readings over a given period of time. This is different from repeatability which is defined as the variation of scale readings and is random in nature.
- It should not have any *drift*. For an instrument, perfect reproducibility means that the instrument has no drift. This means that for a given input, the measured values are constant and do not vary with time.
- It should have minimum *noise*. Noise is any signal that does not convey any useful information. Noise is due to extraneous disturbances caused by many sources such as stray fields, shocks and thermal stresses.
- It should be modifiable and properly priced.

9.2.2 Classification

The measuring instruments can be used for measurement of various electrical, electronic and mechanical parameters in a variety of ways. Thus they are classified as discussed below:

Analog and Digital instruments: Display wise the instruments can be analog or digital. With the advancement in digital techniques, the analog signals are usually converted into digital signals (by ADC) and are displayed with a digital panel meter. Printouts can also be obtained for recording. Even the analog signals may be recorded by using a self-balancing type potentiometric strip chart recorder. How-ever, the digital display recording has the advantage that human reading and operational errors are comparatively reduced. Analog ammeters and voltmeters are similar in their operating principles. Their action, in general, depends on a deflecting torque produced. In ammeters, this torque is due to the current to be measured or a definit fraction of it and in voltmeter, the torque is due to a current proportional to the voltage under measurement. Thus, all the ammeter and voltmeters are current measuring devices. The ammeters are put in series with and voltmeters are connected across the measuring circuit.

Absolute and Secondary instruments: Based on the need for calibration instruments can be absolute or secondary instruments. An absolute instrument can directly be used for the measurement without any calibration. Measured value is known in terms of the constant of the instrument and deflection. *Raleigh current balance meter, Tangent galvanometers* are of such type. A secondary measuring instruments needs calibration before being used. The calibration is done in comparison with a suitable absolute instrument or with another secondary instrument which is already calibrated. *Energymeters, Ammeters, Voltmeters* are of such type. The secondary instruments are further divided into *indicating instruments*, *recording instruments* and *integrating instruments.*

- The indicating or deflecting instruments are those which indicate the value of the measured. They consist of a pointer moving over a calibrated scale. Ammeters, Volumeters are a few examples of this category.
- Recording instruments measure the quantity as a record of the value of the measurand with reference to time. A strip-chart recorder is an example of this category.
- Integrating instrument sum up the value of the measurand over a selected period of time. AH meters, KWH meters are a few examples of this category.

9.2.3 Operating Torques

The following are the three torques which are essential for the smooth and effective working of instruments:

Deflecting or operating torque, T_d : This is produced by utilizing one or more effects of electric current, as listed in Table 9.1. This torque is responsible for movement of the pointer along a scale. Invariably, in all the secondary instruments, a pointer will have to deflect due to the torque produced by the measured value on a calibrated scale. It is clear therefore that the torque produced shall depend on the magnitude of the measurand.

Retarding or controlling torque T_c: This is obtained either by a spring or by gravity control method. This torque, also called, controlling or restoring torque, ensures that there is an equilibrium between the deflecting and restoring torque, at which the pointer shows the required value of the measurand. There has to bean opposition for the movement of the pointer so that it quickly indicates a position against a controlling torque. Controlling torque is produced either by the spring control or by gravity control which are shown schematically in Fig. 9.1.

Table 9.1. Instruments based on effects of electric current

Instruments	*Effects of electricity utilized*
Moving Iron Instruments	Magnetic effect
Moving Coil Instruments	Electromagnetic effect
kWh Meter	Induction effect
Dynamometer Watt meter	Electrodynamic effect
Hot wire Instruments	Thermal effect

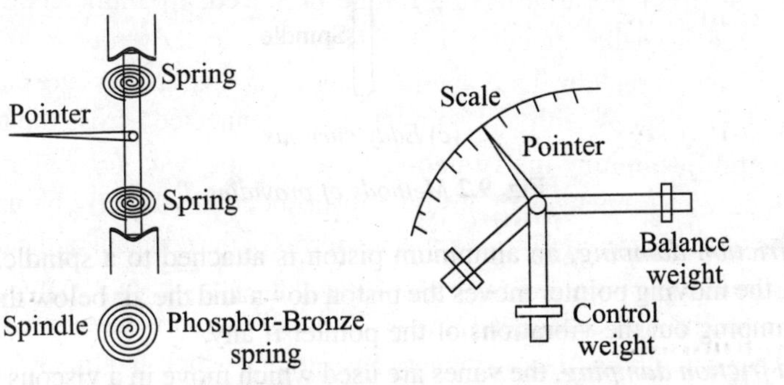

Fig. 9.1 *Methods of providing T_c : (a) Spring control (b) Gravity control*

- In the *spring control* method, a phosphor bronze spring is attached to the spindle and placed at the base of the pointer. When the pointer moves under the influence of the deflecting torque the spring tension builds up and hence the controlling torque increases until it equals the deflecting torque corresponding to the position of the value under measurement.
- In the *gravity control* method weights are attached vertically below the spindle. When the spindle is in equilibrium, pointer is at zero. The deflecting torque moves the pointer up, weights move clockwise, but gravity pulls them back. This torque-gravity pull opposes the deflecting torque, and when the two torques are equal, the pointer points the value being measured. However, in this method the equipment has to be in vertical position.

Damping torque, T_D: At equilibrium, the pointer indicates a steady state, stable value. However, due to the inertia of the moving system, the pointer may overshoot in either direction and as such it may start vibrating. It is thus required to have a torque, *damping torque,* to ensure a steady reading. This is required to bring the moving system to rest quickly by damping out the oscillations of the pointer. This is provided by air friction, fluid friction or eddy currents, which are shown schematically in Fig 9.2.

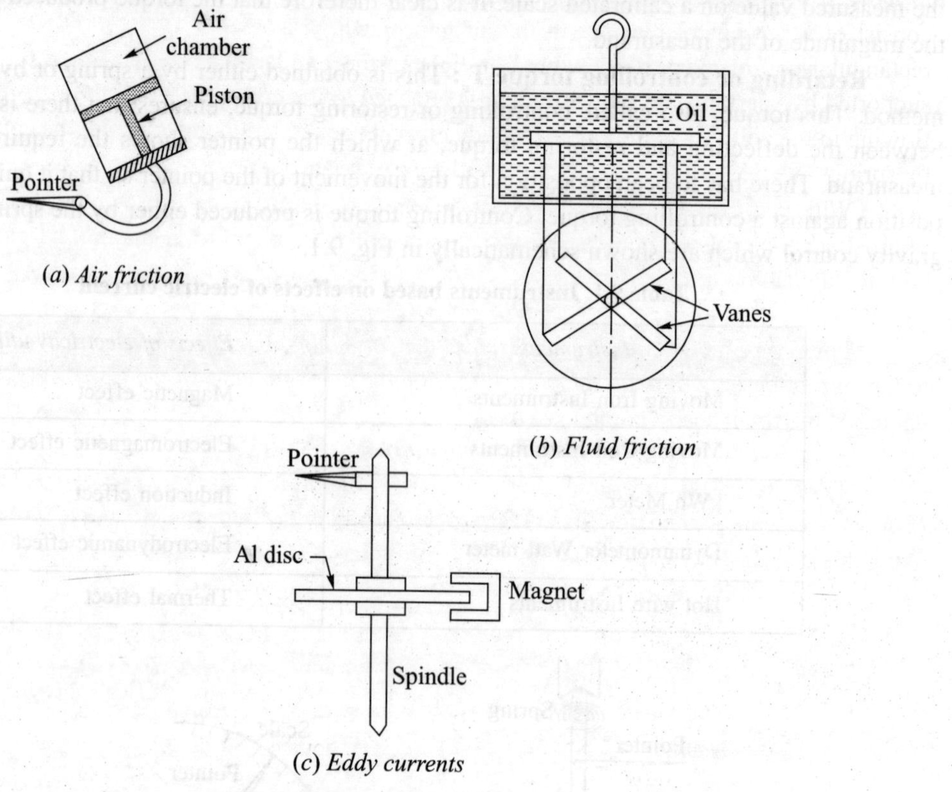

Fig. 9.2 *Methods of providing T_d*

- In air *friction damping*, an aluminum piston is attached to a spindle. Due to the deflecting torque, the moving pointer moves the piston down and the air below the piston is compressed, thus damping out the vibrations of the pointer if any.
- In *fluid friction damping*, the vanes are used which move in a viscous fluid, when the spindle rotates. This results in a torque which opposes the motion of the spindle and thus damping out the vibrations of the pointer if any.

- In *eddy current damping*, the eddy currents induced in an aluminum disc generate a torque along with the flux producing the eddy current. This is in such a direction as to oppose the movement of the pointer.

9.2.4 Moving Coil Instruments

Moving coil instrument (MC): The moving coil instruments can be of *permanent magnet type* (PMMC) or *dynamometer type*. The permanent magnet, polarized instruments are used for the measurement of DC voltage/current while the dynamometer type instruments are used for the measurement of power in both DC and AC circuits.

The operation of PMMC instrument is based on the principle that: *when a current carrying conductor is placed in a magnetic field, it is acted upon by a force, which tends to move it to one side, out of the field.* These instruments consist of a permanent magnet, in the air gap of which a rectangular coil of many turns wound on light former is placed as shown in the Fig. 9.3. The coil is supported by bearings and a light pointer is attached to the coil. Deflecting torque is due to the current flowing in the coil. The damping is by eddy currents generated in the core and the controlling torque is by springs. These springs also function as the current leads.

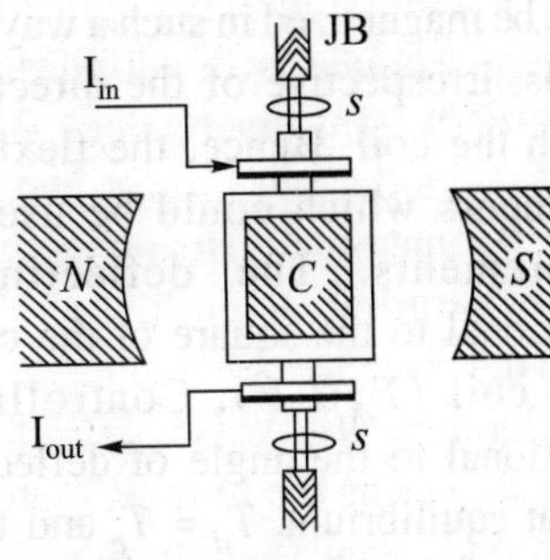

Fig. 9.3 *PMMC instrument*

With B as Flux density (Wb/m^2), l, the length or depth of coil (m), b, breadth of coil (m), A, area of cross section (= $bl\ m^2$), N, the number of turns of the coil, and I as the current passing through the coil, the deflecting torque is given by:

$$T_d = NBI\,l\,b\ = (B\,A\,N)\,I\ \text{Nm} \qquad ...(9.1)$$

For a constant flux density field (due to the permanent magnet) the deflecting torque is proportional to the current passing through the coil, $T_d\,\theta\,I$ and the controlling torque is proportional to the deflection angle. At the final steady pointer position,

$$T_d = T_c, \text{ so that } I \propto \theta \qquad ...(9.2)$$

Thus, in PMMC instruments, as the deflecting angle is directly proportional to the measurand (I or V), the scale is uniform. Such instruments are mainly used for DC works alone. The method of using this instrument as an ammeter or as a voltmeter is as per the scheme shown in Fig. 9.4.

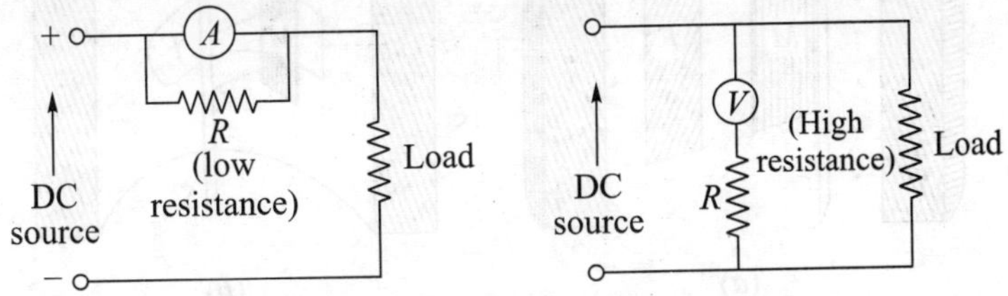

Fig. 9.4 *PMMC ammeter and voltmeter*

9.2.5 Moving Iron Instruments

The moving iron (MI) instruments are of either *attraction type or repulsion type.* In either case, the required magnetic field is produced by the MMF of a current carrying coil and they can be used as an ammeter or as voltmeter. They have the advantage that they may be used on both AC and DC.

Attraction type MI instruments: The basic principal of working of an attraction type instrument is as shown in Fig. 9.5. The operation depends on the attraction, of a single piece of soft iron, into a magnetic field. If a pointer is fixed to the spindle carrying the disc, then the current through the coil causes deflection. More the current through the field, more is the deflection. The iron disc will always be magnetized in such a way that it is pulled inwards, irrespective of the direction of current through the coil. Hence, the flexibility of these instruments which could be used for AC/DC measurements. The deflecting torque is proportional to the square of the current flowing in the coil ($T_d \alpha I^2$). Controlling torque is proportional to the angle of deflection ($T_c \alpha \theta$). Thus, at equilibrium, $T_d = T_c$ and thus deflection angle $\theta \alpha I^2$ (or V^2). Hence the scale is non-uniform or uneven. The damping is provided by air friction damping and control is by gravity control.

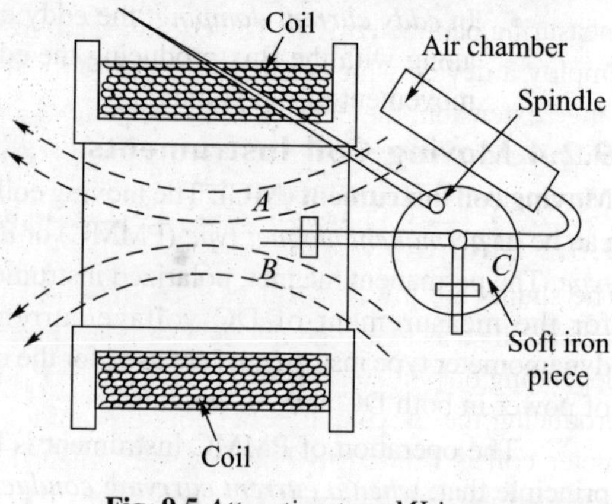

Fig. 9.5 *Attraction type MI instruments*

Repulsion type MI instruments: In the repulsion type MI instrument, there are two vanes, one fixed and the other movable. These are similarly magnetized when the current flows through the coil and hence there is a force of repulsion between the vanes, causing the movement of the movable vane and thus indicating the measurand. Two designs that are commonly used here are Radial vane type and co-axial vane type as shown in Fig. 9.6. The radial vane type has radial strips of iron and the coaxial van type has both fixed and moving vanes as sections of co-axial cylinders. The fixed vane is attached to the coil and the movable vane to the spindle of instrument. Clearly, whatever may be the direction of current in the coil of the instrument, the vanes are so magnetized that there is always a force of attraction/ repulsion between the vanes. MI instruments are thus useful on both DC and AC. The working of these instruments is affected by stray magnetic fields, and changes in frequency and temperature.

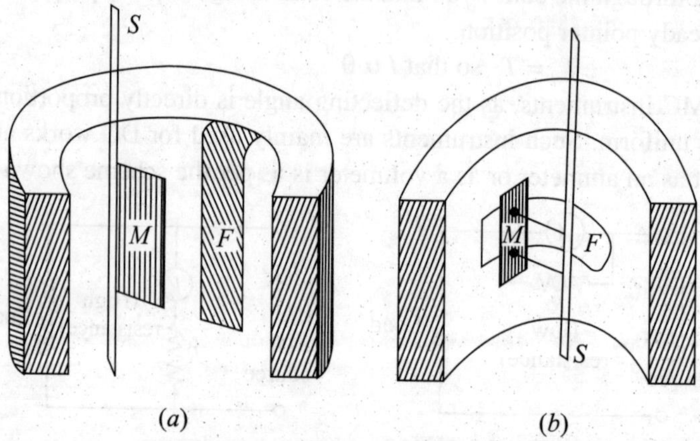

Fig. 9.6 *Repulsion type MI instruments (a) Radial vane type (b) Co-axial vane type [M: Moving vane, F: Fixed vane, S: Spindle]*

9.3 RANGE EXTENSION OF METERS

The range is the maximum value of the measured that can be measured by a given meter. The range of voltmeters, ammeters, etc., is limited by the current carrying capacity of the control springs, high measuring parameters, etc. Thus, for measurement of large current and voltage values, it is necessary to employ a device which reduces the current and voltage of the instrument by a known proportion. For range extension, the devices used are: *shunts and current transformers* (for ammeters) and *multipliers* and *potential transformers* (for voltmeters). Shunt and multipliers can be used for both AC and DC instruments, while the instrument transformers can be used only for AC instruments.

9.3.1 Shunts

The shunts are low resistances used in ammeters for range extension. They are connected across the meter coil so as to extend the range as shown in Fig. 9.7. The shunt is made of Manganin or Constantan depending on whether it is used for DC or AC. With I_m as the current flow through the meter capable of producing the maximum deflection, precautions are to be taken to ensure that the current through the meter coil is limited to I_m. However, when the current to be measured is large, alternative path is provided *via*, the low resistance shunt, R_{sh}.

Finding R$_{sh}$: Voltage drop across the meter is $I_m R_m$, and voltage drop across the shunt is $I_{sh} R_{sh}$. And $I_{sh} = I - I_m$. Thus, with I as current to be measured, I_m as the current through the meter coil for full scale deflection (*fsd*) and m (= I/I_m) as the multiplying power of shunt,

$$I_m R_m = I_{sh} R_{sh} = (I - I_m) R_{sh} \text{ so that,}$$

$$R_{sh} = I_m R_m/(I - I_m) = R_m/(I/I_m - 1) = R_m/(m - 1) \qquad ...(9.3)$$

The current range of a DC multi-range ammeter can be further extended by using a number of shunts, selected by a selector switch.

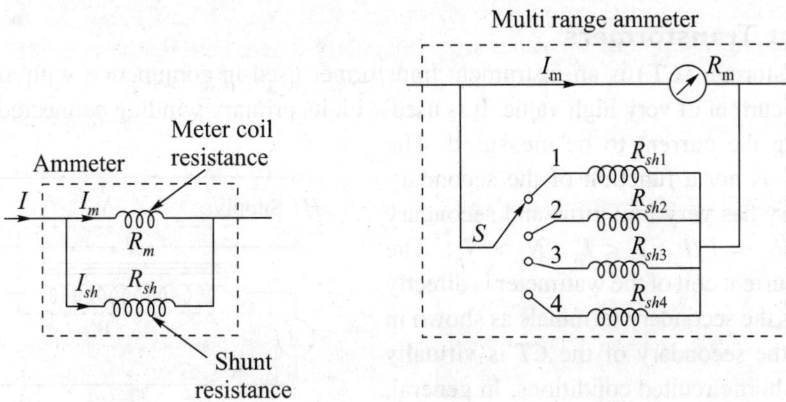

Fig. 9.7 *Shunts for (a) Ammeter (b) Multi-range ammeter*

9.3.2 Multipliers

The multipliers are high resistances used in voltmeters for range extension. They are connected in series with the meter coil as shown in Fig. 9.8. Manganin and constantan are preferred for multipliers.

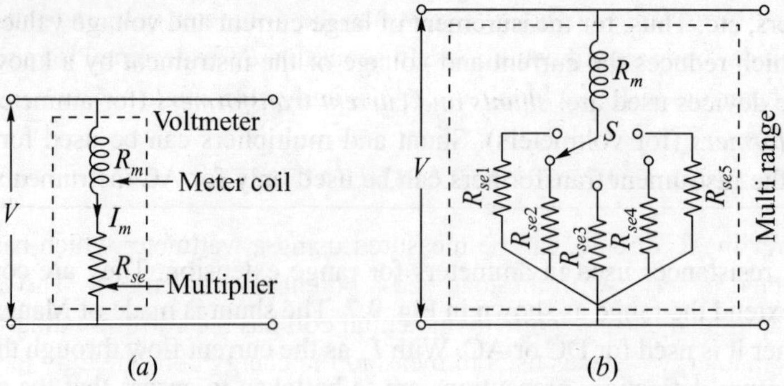

Fig. 9.8 *Multipliers for (a) Voltmeter (b) Multi-range voltmeter*

Finding R_{se}: With V_i as voltage to be measured, V_m as the voltage across the meter coil for full scale deflection and m (= V/V_m) as the multiplying power of the multiplier, we have

$$V = I_m R_m + I_m R_{se}$$

$$= I_m (R_m + R_{se})$$

$$R_{se} = (V - I_m R_m)/I_m$$

$$= (V/I_m) - R_m$$

$$= R_m(m - 1) \quad \text{...(9.4)}$$

9.3.3 Current Transformers

The current transformer (*CT*) is an instrument transformer used in conjunction with an ammeter for measurement of current of very high value. It is used with its primary winding connected in series with the line carrying the current to be measured. The primary current is not a function of the secondary load. The primary has very few turns and secondary many turns ($N_s/N_p = I_p/I_s$; $I_s < I_p$; $N_s > N_p$). The ammeter or the current coil of the wattmeter is directly connected across the secondary terminals as shown in Fig. 9.9. Thus, the secondary of the *CT* is virtually operated under short circuited conditions. In general, a *CT* is designed for a standard current of 5 A. Constructionally, it can be wound type of bar type. The errors in *CT* include *ratio errors* and *phase angle errors.*

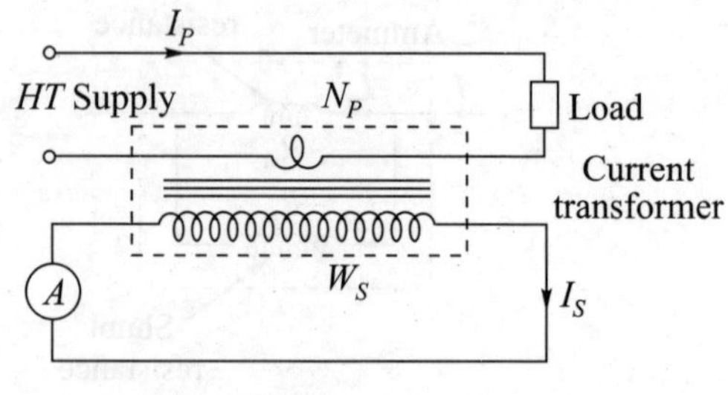

Fig. 9.9 *Current transformer*

9.3.4 Potential Transformers

The potential transformer (*PT*) is an instrument transformer used in conjuction with a voltmeter for measurement of voltage of very high value. It is used with its primary winding connected across the high voltage to be measured and a voltmeter connected across the secondary winding as shown in Fig. 9.10. *PTs* are used to operate voltmeter, the potential coil of wattmeters and relays from HV lines. The secondary winding of a *PT* consists of a very few turns and the primary

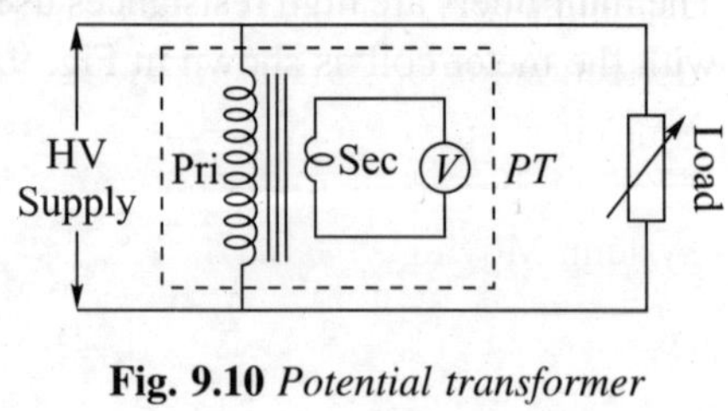

Fig. 9.10 *Potential transformer*

has large number of turns. The secondary circuit has the voltmeter only and thus secondary of a *PT* operates virtually under open circuit conditions. In general, a *PT* is designed for a standard load voltage of 100 to 200 V. The errors in *PT* include *ratio errors* and *phase angle errors.*

9.4 POWER AND ENERGY MEASUREMENTS

The electrical power in *AC* circuits can be measured using a wattmeter which basically consists of a current coil connected in series with the load and a potential coil across it. The current coil carries a current proportional to load current while the potential coil has the corresponding voltage across it. On similar principles, an energy meter is used to measure the energy consumed by the load on the circuit.

9.4.1 Dynamometer Type Wattmeter

The dynamometer type wattmeter is widely used to measure power consumption in an *AC* circuit. It consists of two fixed coils, F_1 and F_2 and a movable coil, M as shown in Fig. 9.11. In a wattmeter the fixed coil or the current coil (*CC*) caries the main current and the moving coil or pressure coil (*PC*) carries a current proportional to the voltage of the circuit. Torque is produced and hence the moving coil rotates due to the magnetic field produced by the current flow. Thus, the deflecting torque is proportional to both currents *i.e.,* $T_d \propto (I_1 I_2)$ since $I_2 \propto V$. As power in the circuit is VI_1, $T_d \propto VI_1$. Further, controlling torque is $T_c \propto \theta$ (deflection). At steady state $T_c = T_d$ and hence deflection indicates directly the power consumed. The damping is generally obtained by air friction damping. These meters are more expensive and the stray magnetic fields can affect their accuracy, unless properly shielded. When power measurement of a high voltage circuit is involved, suitable instrument transformers may be used.

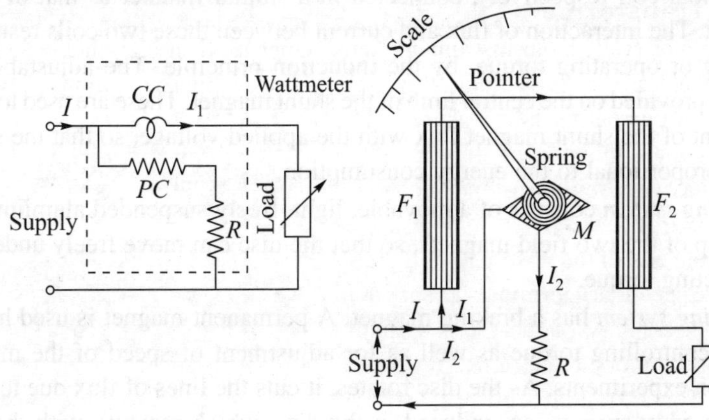

Fig. 9.11 *Dynamometer type wattmeter (a) Schematic diagram (b) Equivalent circuit*

9.4.2 Induction Type Energy Meter

The induction type energy meter works on the induction effect of electric current for production of the deflection torque. It is used to measure the energy consumption in a given circuit over a given period of time. It is an integrating type of instrument, recording always the integrated value of the measurand over the period of time considered. Constructionally, it consists of four basic systems : Deflecting system, Moving system, Braking system and Recording system, as schematically shown in Fig. 9.12.

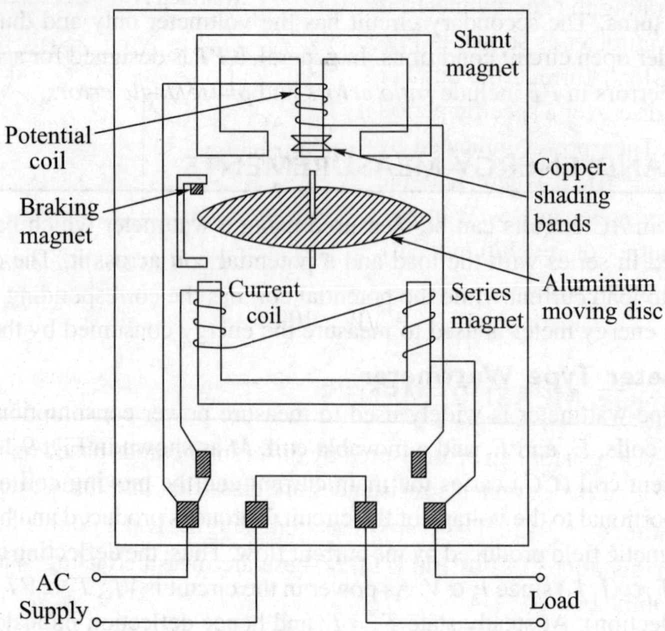

Fig. 9.12 *Single phase energy meter*

- The *deflecting system* consists of the series and shunt magnet arrangement, with current coil and potential coil respectively, connected in a similar manner as that of the dynamometer wattmeter. The interaction of flux and current between these two coils results in the required deflecting or operating torque, by the induction principle. The adjustable copper shading bands are provided on the central limb of the shunt magnet. These are used to obtain quadrature adjustment of the shunt magnet flux with the applied voltage, so that the speed will then be directly proportional to the energy consumption.
- The *moving system* consists of a movable, light, freely suspended aluminium disc, placed in the air gap of the two field magnets, so that the disc can move freely under the influence of the deflecting torque.
- The *braking system* has a braking magnet. A permanent magnet is used here to provide the required controlling torque as well as for adjustment of speed of the moving disc during calibration experiments. As the disc rotates, it cuts the lines of flux due to the brake magnet the hence eddy currents are induced in the disc, which reacting with the flux, produces a controlling torque. As such, the controlling torque depends on the speed of rotation of the disc. Thus the number of revolution of the disc over a period of time is a measure of energy, which is utilized by the circuit under consideration.
- The *recording or registering system* consists of a registering mechanism which records on a continuous basis the integrated value of the energy consumed by the load circuit. This record is proportional to the number of revolutions and hence the speed of he moving disc.

Calibration: In comparison with a wattmeter, the energy meter can be calibrated. Different load adjustments, lag adjustment, creep adjustment, etc., are carried out on the energy meters prior to calibration. For calibrating the energy meter, it is connected with a wattmeter as shown in Fig. 9.13. For a particular load current, the number of rotation (R) of the disc over a specific period of time (T) is noted. Then power indicated by the energy meter, $W_E = KR/T$, where K is the constant of the energy meter in Rev/Watt-sec. (generally given in terms of revolution/kWh). If W_l is the indicated reading, then

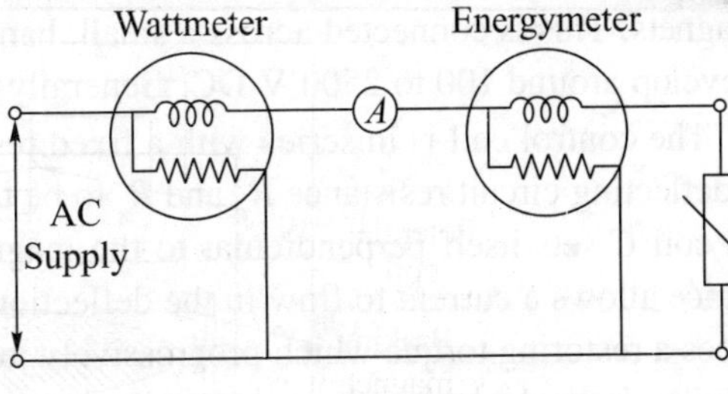

Fig. 9.13 *Calibration of energy meter*

$$\text{Error} = [(W_E - W_l)/W_E]\ 100\% \qquad ...(9.5)$$

9.5 RESISTANCE MEASUREMENTS

The resistance of a given resistor can be measured by different methods based on its range of numerical value. For convenience of measurements resistances are classified into three categories as under:

- **Low resistance (< 1 Ω):** These are measured using Kelvin's double bridge, *AV* method etc.
- **Medium resistance (1 Ω to 100 k Ω) :** These are measured using Wheatstone's bridge, *AV* method, Ohmmeter etc.
- **High resistance (> 100 k Ω) :** These are measured using *AV* method, loss of charge method, Megger etc.

The operating principle of the very commonly used instruments, ohmmeter and megger are discussed in detail below:

9.5.1 Ohmmeter

Ohmmeter is an instrument used to measure the given resistance. Fig. 9.14 shown a simple ohmmeter. It has coils C_1 and C_2 arranged with their axes mutually perpendicular and a magnetic needle fixed at the intersection axis. The coil C_1 has less number of turns and C_2 has large number of turns R_x is the resistance to be measured. A hand generator is connected at the source point.

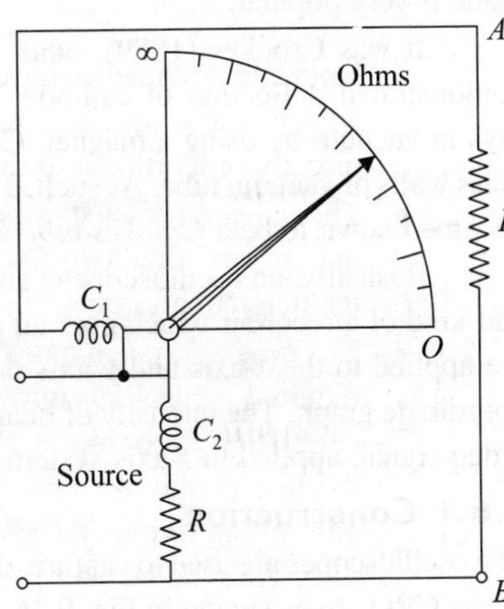

Fig. 9.14 *Ohmmeter*

- When R_x is very low, a large current flows through C_1 thereby setting up a strong magnetic field. Although C_2 has current in it, it is small and thus the resulting magnetic field is due to C_1 alone and thus a null reading is indicated.
- When R_x is very high, the current through C_1 is zero and the resultant flux may be regarded as that produced due to C_2 only. Thus, the needle shows infinity.

9.5.2 Megger

Ohmmeter principle is used in this instrument. It is one of the common modern portable equipment used for testing the insulation resistances. The moving system consists of the control and deflection coil, C and D, rigidly mounted at right angles to one another and they can rotate about an axis between the magnets. This is connected across a small, hand driven DC generator as shown in Fig. 9.15, which can develop around 100 to 2500 V DC. Generally it is of the order of 500 Volts.

The control coil is in series with a fixed resistance R_c and the deflecting coil is in series with a fixed deflecting circuit resistance R_d and R_x to be tested, as shown. If R_x is ∞, no current flows through *D* and coil *C* sets itself perpendicular to the magnetic axis, the pointer reading *infinity*. A lower test resistance allows a current to flow in the deflection coil and hence turns it clockwise. The control coil produces a restoring torque which progressively increases with the angular deflection, ($T_c \propto \theta$) and the equilibrium is reached when the two opposing torques are equal ($T_d = T_c$). The scale is directly calibrated in megaohms from zero to infinity using known standard values.

9.6 CATHODE RAY OSCILLOSCOPES (CRO)

From the history of electrical engineering it is clear that the development of all instrumentation has relied upon the ability of measuring instrument to capture and display data for the observer's convenience. Oscilloscope is the most versatile electronic measuring instrument available. The ability of the oscilloscope to display high speed phenomena for easy observation has made it very popular.

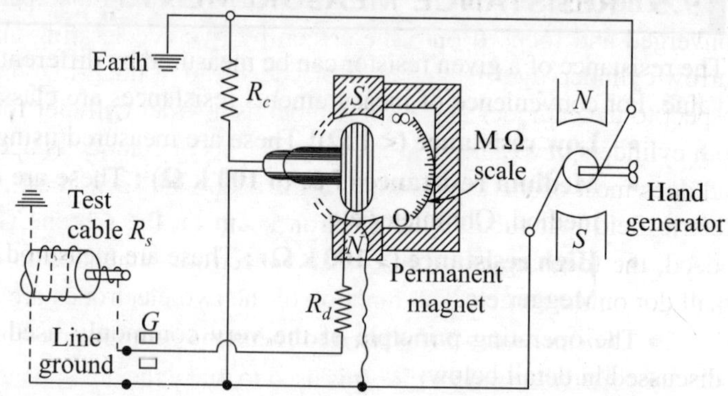

Fig. 9.15 *Megger—the insulation resistance tester [D : Deflection coil, C: Control coil, P : Pointer, G : Generator, G : Guard ring]*

It was Crookes (1879), who demonstrated deflection of cathode rays in vacuum by using a magnet. Cathode rays were shown capable of causing phosphorescence on glass walls of vacuum tube. As such, a cathode ray aimed at a Fluorescent target with dynamic deflection became known to be a *Crookes tube* which later became popular as a *Cathode Ray Tube* (CRT).

Basically, an oscilloscope is an electron beam voltmeter, which uses a beam instead of a pointer and kind of a recorder which uses an electron beam instead of a pen. One set each of electrical signals are applied to the *x*-axis and *y*-axis deflection system. Hence the cathode-ray beam tracks out the *x*-*y* coordinate graph. The intensity of beam may be controlled by an electrical signal, some times called the video signal, applied to *z*-axis system.

9.6.1 Construction

The oscilloscopes are used to capture, display and analyse an electrical signal. The constructional features of the CRO are as shown in Fig. 9.16. It consists of an *electron gun, horizontal* and *vertical deflection plates* and a *phosphor screen*.

The electron gun assembly: This consists of indirectly heated cathode with heater, control grid, first and second anodes. Control gird is cylindrical with a small aperture in line with the cathode. The negative bias applied to the grid controls the beam current and thus the control grid provides the *intensity control*.

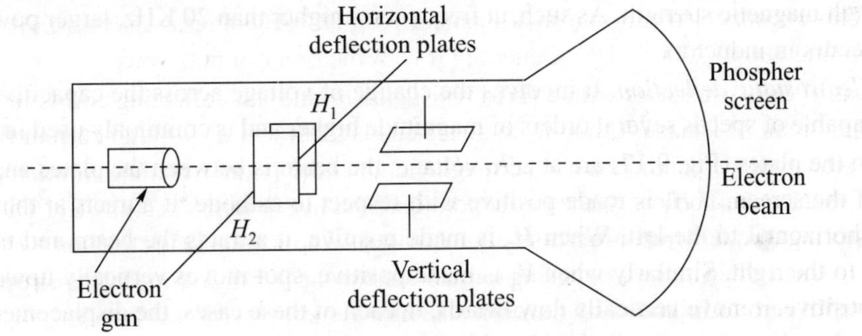

Fig. 9.16 *Cathode ray oscilloscope*

The focus assembly: The beam emerging from the aperture is highly divergent and as such, is converged and focused onto the screen by two accelerating anodes as shown in Fig. 9.17. Another narrow cylinder, the first anode, is placed ahead of the grid cylinder which is kept highly positive with respect to the cathode. The second anode is a wider cylinder following the first. Along with the beam, both cylinders have a narrow aperture. The second anode is operated at a still higher positive potential and does most of the acceleration of the beam. As such, the first and the second cylinders produce an electric field that focuses the electron beam on the screen. This control is called the *focus control.* Indeed, the focusing of beam contains electrodes intended to ensure the beam pattern converge to a small dot on the screen. The function of the two electrodes are as under:

- *Focus control*: It is used to focus the beam into a smallest dot at the target.
- *Astigmatism control*: It is used to make the dot appear equidistant both from the screen centre and perimeter.

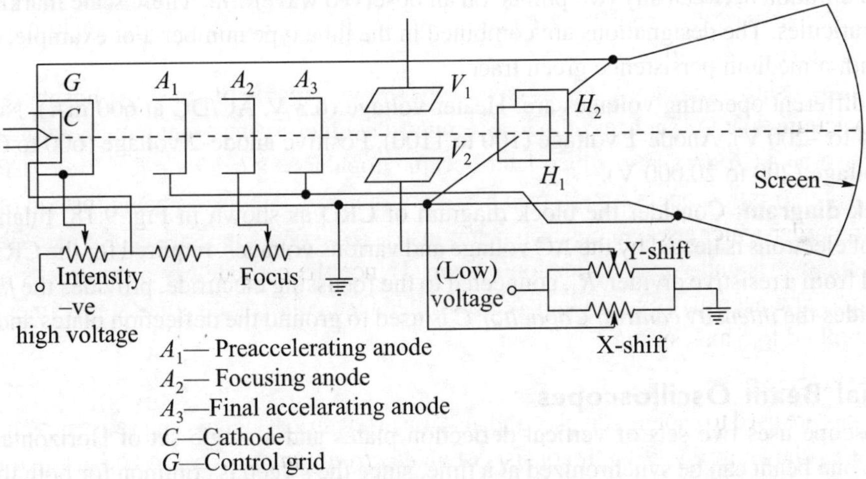

Fig. 9.17 *Control of the oscilloscope*

The deflection mechanism: The horizontal and the vertical plates constitute the beam-deflection region. The following two types of deflections are used:

- *Magnetic deflection*: It is accompanied by changing the magnetic field pattern, and is done by changing the current through the inductors. At high frequencies, inductors with few turns are necessary to obtain fast changes. However, larger currents are required to bring out a high magnetic strength. As such, at frequencies higher than 20 KHz, larger power dissipation occurs in inductors.

- *Electrostatic deflection*: It involves the change of voltage across the capacitive plates and is capable of speeds several orders of magnitude higher and is commonly used in oscilloscopes.

When the plates (Fig. 9.17) are at zero voltage, the beam is between the plates and the spot is at the centre of the screen. If H_1 is made positive with respect to cathode, it attracts at the beam and the spot moves horizontal to the left. When H_2 is made positive, it attracts the beam and the spot moves horizontally to the right. Similarly when V_1 is made positive, spot moves vertically upwards and when V_2 is made positive, it move vertically downwards, in each of these cases, the displacement of the beam is proportional to the voltage applied to the plates.

CRT and phosphor screen: The display part of the CRO is the cathode ray tube, the front portion of which, the Face plate, is the picture screen. This is usually a flat surface with an area of 100 cm^2. The material coated on the target is capable of converting electrical energy into light energy. When the electron beam bombards the screen, *fluorescence* is observed. Later even when the beam is removed, a *phosphorescence* remains for some time. Indeed, in order not to loose the phosphorescence it is required to refresh the phosphor. Depending on the time of persistence, phosphors are classified as: *short-persistence* (excitation level less than 1 m sec and long-persistence (excitation level less than 1 minute or more).

Phosphors by trade names *P*1 (yellow, green), *P*2 (green), *P*3 (green) are available in the short persistence range and *P*19 (orange), *P*26 (orange), *P*33 (orange) etc., are available for long persistence. It is worth noting that fast varying waveforms require short persistence phosphor, and vice-versa.

Scale marking are made on or near the CRT screen to help user analyse the waveform. The number of scale divisions multiplied by the appropriate switch settings gives the amplitude difference and the time duration between any two points on an observed waveform. These scale markings are also known as graticules. The designations are combined in the tube type number. For example, the 5*GP*1 is a 5" tube with a medium persistence green trace.

The different operating voltages are: Heater voltage (6.3 V, AC/DC at 600 mA), Negative grid voltage (–14 to –200 V), Anode-1 voltage (100 to 1100), Positive anode-2 voltage (600 to 6000 V) and Anode-3 voltage (200 to 20,000 V).

Block diagram: Consider the block diagram of CRO as shown in Fig. 9.18. Filament for the generation of electrons is heated by the AC voltage and various voltages, required for the CRT operation, are obtained from a resistive divider. R_3, connected to the focussing electrode, provides the *focus control* and R_5 provides the *intensity control. Capacitor C* is used to ground the deflection plates and the second anode.

9.6.2 Dual Beam Oscilloscopes

This oscilloscope uses two sets of vertical deflection plates and a single set of Horizontal deflection plates. Only one beam can be synchronized at a time, since the sweep is common for both the inputs. In order to lock both beams to the CRT screen, the signals must have the same frequency or must be related harmonically. In case of dual trace oscilloscope, the single electron beam is split into two by an electronic switch. Two signals are displayed simultaneously. Signals pass through identical vertical channels or vertical amplifiers.

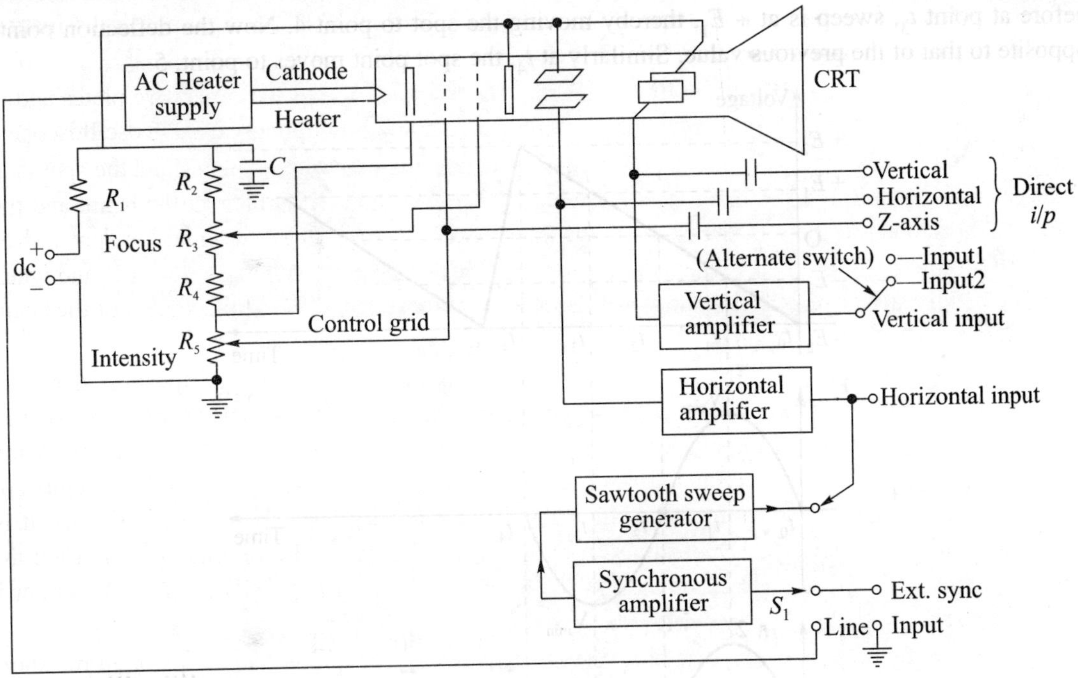

Fig. 9.18 *Block diagram of CRO*

A mode control switch enables the oscilloscope to operate in two modes. When the switch is in the *alternate* position, the electronic switch feeds each signal alternately to the vertical amplifier. This electronic switch alternately connects the main vertical amplifier to channels A and B and adds a different DC component to each signal. This DC component directs the beam alternatively to the upper or lower half of the screen.

9.6.3 Time Base

With the signal to be displayed as the y input and with a variation of x input, x-y coordinates are located. Speed at which the signal moves on the target screen, depends on the x input which varies linearly with time. Such a sweep circuit combined with display gating functions is termed *time base*. This may vary from 10 to 5 seconds per division, with a better time accuracy and linearity. A saw tooth wave form applied to the horizontal deflection plates will move the beam back and forth across the CRT screen.

- The DC voltage may be measured directly on a calibrated screen from the length of the straight line trace, it produces. This trace conveys nothing when an AC voltage waveform is applied. What is expected is a graph of the voltage traced on the screen by the AC spot. To obtain an x-y display, a signal voltage applied to the y plates moves the spot vertically to positions corresponding to the instantaneous values of the signal. Simultaneously the spot is moved horizontally by a sweep voltage applied to the horizontal plates. This effect produces a trace on the screen.

Consider the timing diagram of the waveform of sweep and the signal trace as shown in Fig. 9.19. At t_0, sweep voltage is $-E_2$. Sweep puts the point on the screen at point 1. While, at t_1 the amplitude of the signal has increased, sweep has increased to $-E_1$ ($> -E_2$) and hence spot moves to point 2. At t_2, the sweep is at zero and as such, there is no horizontal deflection and the spot is at the centre point, 3. As before at point t_3, sweep is at $+ E_1$, thereby moving the spot to point 4. Now the deflection point is opposite to that of the previous value. Similarly at t_4, the spot point moves to point, 5.

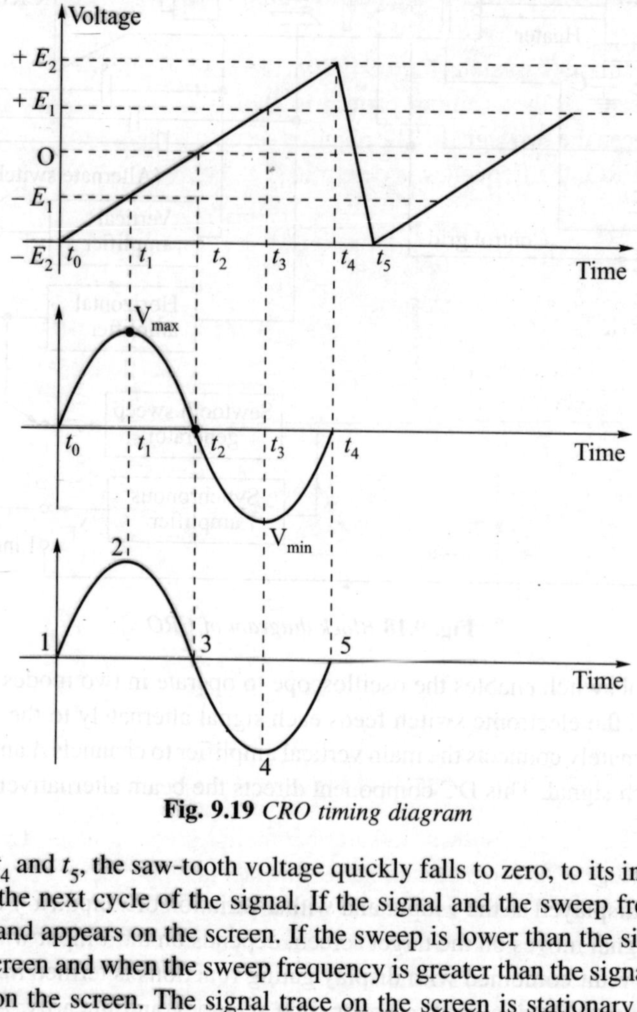

Fig. 9.19 *CRO timing diagram*

Now between t_4 and t_5, the saw-tooth voltage quickly falls to zero, to its initial value of $- E_2$ and is thus ready to trace the next cycle of the signal. If the signal and the sweep frequencies are equal, a single cycle is traced and appears on the screen. If the sweep is lower than the single, several traces of signal appear on the screen and when the sweep frequency is greater than the signal frequency, a portion of the signal is seen on the screen. The signal trace on the screen is stationary only when the signal frequency is equal to or an integral multiple of the sweep frequency. This frequency range of sweep varies very widely in the oscilloscope.

9.6.4 Applications

The CRO is most useful for diode testing, measurement of AC/DC voltages, and the corresponding Frequency, Period and Phase.

Measurement of DC voltage: When DC voltage is the input, the deflection of the beam is brought about by adjusting the vertical attenuator expressed in *V*/div, where div is the number of divisions deflected.

Measurement of AC voltage: When AC voltage is the input, the deflection of the beam on either side of the *zero* reference is observed so that, the peak to peak voltage of the voltage, $V_{\text{peak to peak}}$ = (Volts/div. × No. of divisions). For instance, if Volts/div. is unity and if the deflection of the beam is at +2 and –2, then $V_{p\text{–}p} = 4 \times 1 = 4$ Volts.

Measurement of frequency and period: Essentially, at least one complete cycle of the waveform is displayed on the scree. The period, T is equal to [(time / div.) × No. of div.], and its reciprocal is the frequency.

Phase measurement (Lissajous figures): With the x and y inputs of the oscilloscope fed externally (without internal sweep, y), the resulting pattern is known as the *Lissajous* figures. This shows the phase difference between the two signals. The required set up is as shown in Fig. 9.20. Once the Lissajous pattern is got on the CRO, the frequency is determined as below:

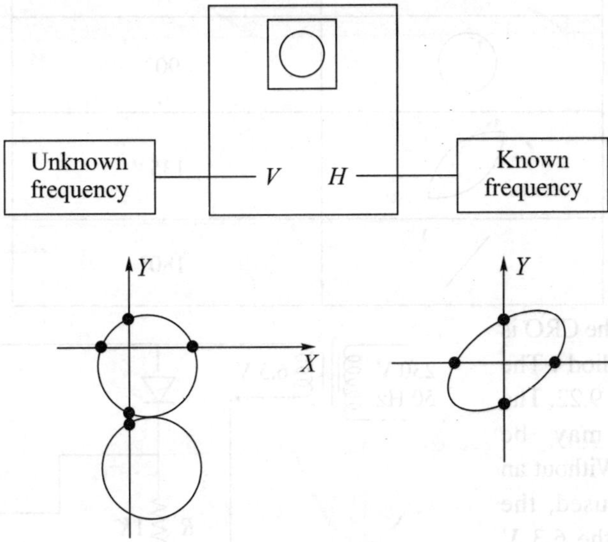

Fig. 9.20 *Lissajous diagram*

Draw the two axes, x-y as shown. Ensure that the intersection in the Lissajous Figure does not involve the x-y axis [Fig. 9.20(c)]. The number of intersections on the x-y axis are noted. Then, with f_1 as the frequency fed to the y input and f_2 as the frequency fed to the x input, f_1/f_2 gives the ratio of number of x intersection of that of y intersections. For instance, $f_1/f_2 = 2/2 = 1$ [Fig. 9.20 (b)] and $f_1/f_2 = 2/4 = 1/2$ [Fig. 9.20(c)]. If f_1 and f_2 are known, the other frequencies can be computed.

Measurement of phase difference: In addition, phase difference between signals can also be determined by using the Lissajous Figures as. Figure 9.21 indicates the Lissajous pattern when the two inputs are sinusoids.

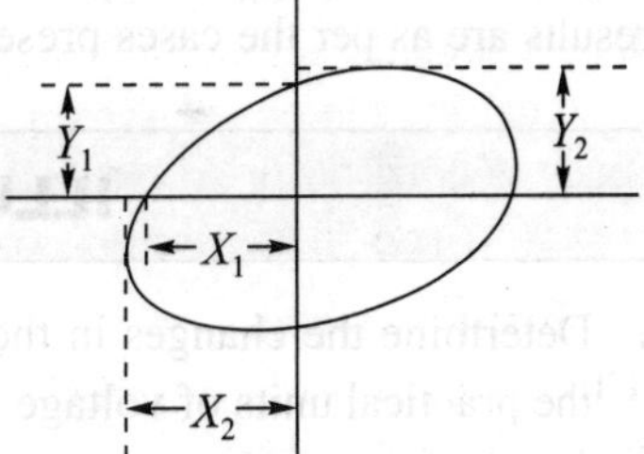

Fig. 9.21 *Measurement of phase difference*

With the intercepts y_1, x_1, y_2 and x_2 as in Fig. 9.21, the phase difference, θ between the two signals is such that

$$\sin \theta = y_1/y_2$$
$$= x_1/x_2$$

The patterns for two sine waves of same frequency with various phase differences are as summarized in the Table 9.2.

Table 9.2. Phase angle for various standard Lissajous patterns

Pattern	*Phase difference*
	0°
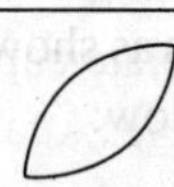	45°
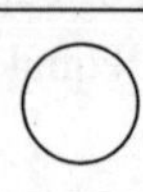	90°
	135°
	180°

Diode testing: The CRO is also used for testing a diod : The setup is as shown in Fig. 9.22. The *V-I* characteristics may be observed on the CRO. Without an internal sweep being used, the setup is connected to the 6.3 V supply. This provides an horizontal trace which is proportional to the applied voltage. The vertical trace is provided by the voltage developed across resistor, *R*. The test results are as per the cases presented in Fig. 9.23.

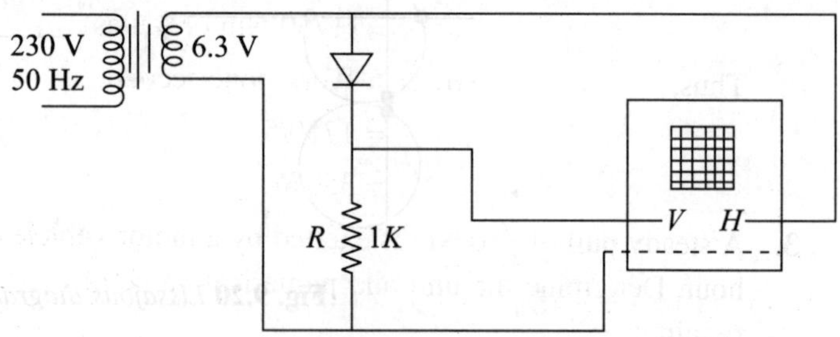

Fig. 9.22 *Diode testing using CRO*

ILLUSTRATIVE EXAMPLES

1. Determine the changes in the size of units of resistance-*R*, inductance-*L* and capacitance-*C*, if the practical units of voltage and current were each made thousand times as large as they are, at present.

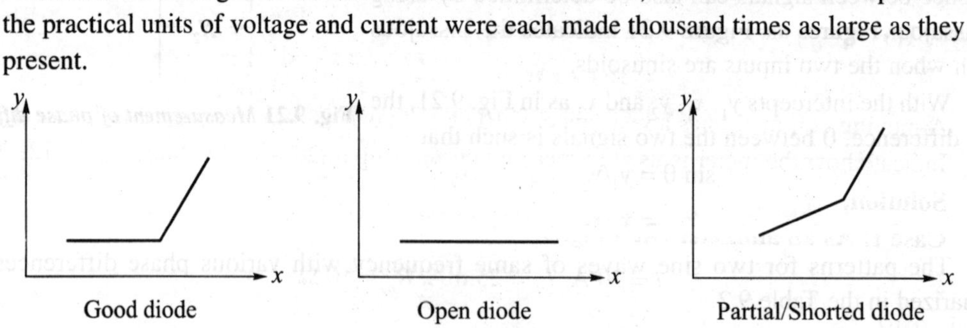

Fig. 9.23 *Diode testing results*

Solution: Consider the expression for resistance give by $R = V/I$. Since both the units of voltage and current are increased by equal proportions, the value and hence the unit of resistance, R remains the same.

Consider the expression for the self induced EMF, e_L in an inductive coil given by $e_L = L\, di/dt$. Thus L = (EMF) (time)/current. Since both the units of voltage and current are increased by equal proportions, the unit of inductance, L also remains the same.

Consider the expression for charge stored in a parallel plate capacitor, Q given by $Q = CV$. Since Q = (current) (time), we have C = (current) (time)/voltage. Again, since both the units of voltage and current are increased by equal proportions, the unit of capacitance, C remains the same.

Thus the magnifying values of voltage and current in equal proportions, do not result in the alteration of the unit values of R, L and C.

2. A body is moved in the direction of the force at an uniform velocity through a distance of 25 meters in 5 seconds when a force a force of 70 Newtons is applied. Calculate the unit and value of power required.

Solution:

Work done = force × distance

= (70 N) (25 m)

= (1750 Nm or joules)

Thus, Power = Work done/second

= 1750/5

= 350 W.

3. A steady pull of 750 Nm is exerted by a motor vehicle on a trailer, when its speed is 80 km per hour. Determine the unit and numerical value of the work done in 30 minutes and the power required.

Solution:

Distance moved = (80/60) (30)

= 40000 meters

Work done = force × distance

= 750 × 40,000

= 30000 kWs or Mega joules.

Power = work done in kWh/Time in Hrs.

= (30,000/3600) / (30/60)

= 16.67 kW.

4. A moving coil meter has a resistance of 10 Ω and takes 25 mA to produce full scale deflection. Indicate how the meter is used to measure currents up to 20 A and voltages up to 120 V.

Solution:

Case 1: As an ammeter (Ref. Fig. 9.7):

$$I = 20\text{ A},\ I_m = 25\text{ mA},\ R_m = 10\ \Omega$$

and $R_{sh} = R_m/[(I/I_m) - 1] = 12.52\ \text{M}\Omega$

Case 2: As a voltmeter (Ref. Fig. 9.8):

$$V = 120\ \text{V},\ I_m = 25\ \text{mA},\ R_m = 10\ \Omega$$

and $R_{se} = (V/I_m) - R_m = 4.79\ \text{k}\Omega$

5. A moving coil instrument takes 50 µA for *fsd*. Its coil resistance is 100 Ω. Find the value of the series resistance needed if it is to be used as a 0 to 75/150/300 volts voltmeter. Also find the sensitivity of the meter.

Solution: [Ref. Fig. 9.8 (*b*)]

$$R_{se1} = (V_1/I_m) - 1 = 75/(50 \times 10^{-6}) - 1$$
$$= 1.4999\ \text{M}\Omega$$
$$R_{se2} = (V_2/I_m) - 1 = 150/(50 \times 10^{-6}) - 1$$
$$= 2.999\ \text{M}\Omega$$
$$R_{se3} = (V_3/I_m) - 1 = 300/(50 \times 10^{-6}) - 1$$
$$= 5.4999\ \text{M}\Omega$$

Sensitivity of the meter $= [R_{total}/V]\ \Omega/\text{volt}$

$$= [75/(50 \times 10^{-6})]/75 = 20\ \text{k}\Omega/\text{volt}.$$

PROBLEMS

1. The resistance of a galvanometer is 720 Ω. Find the resistance of the shunts so that 1/10th and 1/1000th of total current passes through the galvanometer.
2. A moving coil instrument takes 25 mA to give *fsd*, the potential difference required being 85 mV. Indicate how it can be adopted for use as a millivoltmeter reading 0 to 100 mV and a milliammeter reading 0 to 50 mA.
3. A moving coil instrument takes 15 mA to produce *fsd*, the potential difference across its terminals being 75 mV. Indicate how the instrument can be used as a voltmeter reading 0 to 100 V and an ammeter reading 0 to 50 A.
4. A moving iron voltmeter takes a current of 0.1 A to produce *fsd* on a 220 volt DC supply. The coil inductance is 1.0 H. This meter is connected across a 220 V, 50 Hz source. Find the reading on the meter.
5. An induction type single phase energy meter has a constant of 1000 rev/kWh. A heater of 2 kW is connected to this meter for the measurement of energy over a time period 2 hours. If the meter makes 3000 revolutions during the period, find the % error of the meter if any.

10 CHAPTER

Semiconductor Devices

10.1 INTRODUCTION

In this chapter, the behaviour of semiconductor devices such as the diode, the Zener and Tunnel diodes, the transistor and the silicon controlled rectifier are discussed.

The diode does not exhibit bilateral characteristics *i.e.*, it conducts in one direction only. It is used in a variety of circuits for a variety of uses, the most important of which, perhaps, is a.c. to d.c. conversion. Zener and Tunnel diodes are special types of diodes. The former is used for voltage regulation while the latter may be used to generate high frequency square waves.

The Transistor is a device which is capable of signal amplification. It may be used for voltage, current or power amplification. A unijunction transistor is a special kind of transistor which may be used for generating ramp or pulse waveforms.

The silicon controlled rectifier (SCR) is used extensively for power control. It is capable of controlling the flow of megawatts of power at the expense of a few milliwatts. In fact, this device has opened up a new branch of engineering called power electronics.

10.2 ATOMIC STRUCTURE

All matter can be reduced to elements which are made up of a number of molecules; these in turn may be subdivided into atoms. An atom is the smallest particle of matter which can enter into chemical combination. As the atoms of the various elements differ in nature, the study of the atomic structure yields information about the intrinsic nature of the element. Based on experimental work, several atomic structures have been proposed of which Bohr's model is the simplest and gives one sufficient insight to an understanding of the atomic properties.

10.2.1 Bohr's Atomic Model

According to Bohr, the atomic structure is similar to that of our solar system. Most of the mass of the atom is concentrated in a small region at the centre of it, called the nucleus. The nucleus has a diameter of $\cong 10^{-2}$ cm and is surrounded by one or more negatively charged particles of negligible mass known as electrons. The electrons revolve around the nucleus in elliptical orbits and are distributed within a radius of about 10^{-8} cm. The nucleus is comprised of protons and neutrons. A proton is a particle which bears a positive charge equal in magnitude to that carried by the electron; its mass, is however, 1835 times as great. The neutron is a neutral particle which has the same mass as the proton. The mass number of an atom is equal to the sum of the number of protons and neutrons in that atom. The atom, on the whole, is electrically neutral.

The number of electrons revolving around the nucleus in a specified orbit is given by $2n^2$ where n is the orbit number. The first orbit, $n = 1$, is closest to the nucleus.

When the orbits are filled to capacity with electrons in accordance with the above rule, the orbits are said to be tightly coupled. If there should be electron vacancies in an orbit, the electrons are said to be coupled loosely. The electrons in the outermost orbit of an atom are known as valence electrons.

The orbiting electrons posses kinetic as well as potential energy. The energy associated with an electron increases with its distance from the nucleus *i.e.*, an electron in the second orbit possesses greater energy than an electron in the first orbit. The electrical properties of a material are governed by the number of electrons in the outermost orbit or shell. The number of electrons in the outermost orbit is known as the valency of the metal.

10.2.2 Atomic Structure of Sodium

Figure 10.1 shows the atomic structure of Sodium. It has only one electron in its outermost shell ($n = 3$) which is loosely coupled to the nucleus. A small amount of external energy can dislodge this electron and make it available for movement through the material. Such materials are known as *conductors*. Usually they have less than four electrons in the outermost orbit.

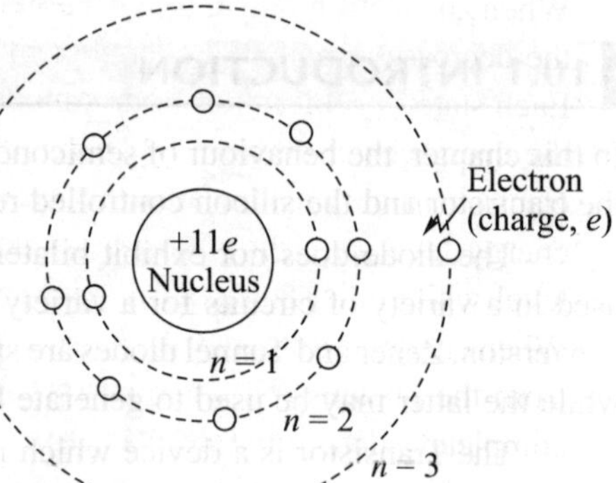

Fig. 10.1 *Atomic structure of sodium*

10.2.3 Atomic Structure of Neon

From Fig. 10.2 it is seen that the outermost orbit ($n = 2$) is fully occupied. It is quite difficult to dislodge these tightly coupled electrons from their orbit. This class of material is known as an *insulator*. The number of electrons in the outermost orbit is usually more than four.

10.3 THE ELECTRON

The electron is the basis of electronics and all electronic devices. The mass of an electron is only $0.9106 \cdot 10^{-27}$ g and it carries a negative charge of $1.6 \cdot 10^{-19}$ C. Under the action of suitable external forces, electrons part from their atoms by escaping from higher orbits; the atom, having lost an electron, is no longer neutral. It now bears a net positive charge and is known as an ion.

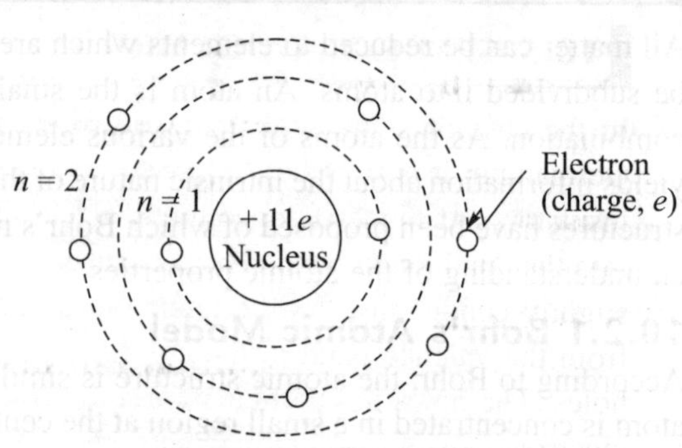

Fig. 10.2 *Atomic structure of neon*

Generally speaking, that branch of science dealing with the flow of electrons in vacuum, gases and in semiconductors is known as electronics. One may wonder why the electron plays such an important role in modern technology? Indeed, its discovery was followed by that of protons, neutrons, photons, mesons and hyperons—a whole family of the so called elementary particles. Yet we have a subject of study known as electronics and none named after the other particles. This is not simply due to the fact that the electron was discovered first but rather due to certain qualities possessed by it.

A neutron is electrically neutral and is 1840 times heavier than the electron. Because of its electrical neutrality it is quite indifferent to the applied electric field and cannot be controlled by it. On the other hand, an electron is charged negatively and it tends to be attracted by a positive potential. By varying this potential, it is possible to control the flow of electrons.

The proton, of course, has a positive charge but is 1840 times as heavy as the electron. The heavy proton can not compete with the agile electrons.

Electrons posses insignificant mass and inertia and the application of an external force can cause it to accelerate easily along controlled paths.

10.4 ENERGY BAND THEORY OF CRYSTALS

When an electron falls through a potential of one volt its kinetic energy increases by an amount equal to the decrease in potential energy or by $qV = 1.6 \cdot 10^{-9}$ Joules. This energy is known as an electron volt. Each state or orbit in the Bohr's model is associated with a unique value of energy. Figure 10.3 shows the energy level diagram for the Hydrogen atom. The negative signs signify that work is done by the electron in moving towards the nucleus. The lowest energy level (n = 1) is known as normal or ground level while other states are known as excited levels. When energy is imparted to an electron, it moves away from the nucleus. The amount of energy required to completely detach an electron from the influence of the nucleus is known as the *ionization potential*. For Hydrogen atom this is equal to 13.6 eV.

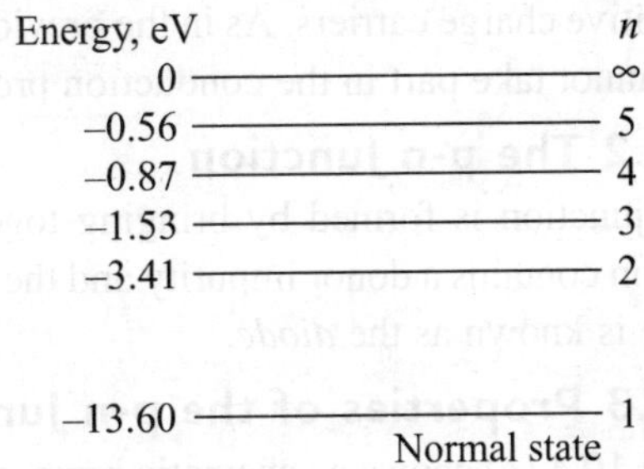

Fig. 10.3 *Energy bands in hydrogen atom*

As explained in Chapter 1, when many atoms are brought together to form a solid, the energy levels, which are sharply defined for a single atom, broaden into energy bands. The conduction and the valence bands result which are separated by the forbidden energy gap.

10.5 SEMICONDUCTORS

In the case of semiconductors, the forbidden energy gap is of the order of one electron volt. For Germanium it is 0.785 eV while for Silicon it is 1.21 eV at 0°K. At 0°K these materials behave like insulators. At higher temperatures, electrons in the valence band acquire sufficient energy and move into the conduction band. These electrons are free to move around and therefore the material becomes slightly conducting. As the temperature increases, the conductivity increases. When electrons move from the valence band to the conduction band, they create vacancies in the valence band known as holes. The holes too participate in the flow of current and are comparable in effectiveness to the free electron. A semiconducting material of the type described above is known as an *intrinsic* (*pure*) *semiconductor*.

When certain impurities are added to a semiconductor, it results in energy states in the forbidden energy gap located slightly below the lower level of the conduction band. Because of this feature, sufficient thermal energy is imparted, at room temperature, to the electrons in the newly created state to elevate them into the conduction region. Such semiconductors are known as *extrinsic semiconductors*.

10.5.1 n- and p-type Extrinsic Semiconductors

The conductivity of Silicon may be increased by the addition of proper impurities. Silicon has a valency of four. If a pentavalent element* such as Arsenic is added to it in small quantities, the four outermost orbit electrons of Silicon and the four outermost orbit electrons of Arsenic form tight bonds. Since the outermost orbit of Arsenic contains five electrons, one electron is left over. Thus each impurity atom donates one electron to the Silicon atom. Arsenic, in this instance, is known as a donor material. With the addition of a small amount of thermal energy the extra electron becomes a free electron and can partake in the conduction process. This type of semiconductor is called *n* type because of the presence of negative charge carriers in an electrically neutral crystal. The net positive charges created are immobile and do not contribute to the conduction of current.

If a small quantity of a trivalent** element such as Indium is added to Silicon, only three electrons are available to combine and form tight bonds. If a fourth electron is borrowed from a neighbouring Silicon atom, the remaining bond can be completed. This, however, creates a hole and gives rise to the possibility of current conduction by positive charges. Indium, in this instance is known as an acceptor atom because it accepts an electron. The resulting semiconductor is called *p* type—signifying the presence of positive charge carriers. As in the previous case, the resulting net negative charge created is immobile and cannot take part in the conduction process.

10.5.2 The p-n Junction

A *pn* junction is formed by bringing together *p* and *n* type semiconductor crystals. One side of the junction contains a donor impurity and the other side contains an acceptor impurity. This single junction device is known as the *diode*.

10.5.3 Properties of the p-n Junction

Figure 10.4 (*a*) shows a schematic representation of both *n* and *p* type semiconducting materials.

Suppose a *pn* junction is formed as shown in Fig. 10.4 (*b*). Due to the high concentration of holes in the *p* material and electrons in the *n* material, there is a tendency, at the junction, for the free electrons to move over the *p* material and the holes to the *n* material. This process is called *diffusion*. Due to diffusion, positive and negative charges build up on the *n* and *p* sides of the junction. As a result further diffusion is prevented from taking place—the positive charge on the *n* side repels holes and the negative charge on the *p* side repels the free electrons. A barrier may therefore be considered to be set up which prevents further movement of charge carriers.

Owing to the distribution of charges as described above, work has to be done to transport a unit positive charge across the junction from the *p* to the *n* side. In other words, a potential difference exists across the junction as depicted in Fig. 10.4 (*b*). This potential is of the order of 0.3 V for a Germanium *pn* junction. As the mobile carriers have been depleted in the vicinity of the junction, it is also known as a *depletion layer*.

A *pn* junction is said to be forward biased when the external voltage applied across the junction acts in a direction to reduce the potential barrier [Fig. 10.4 (*c*)]. It is clear that in order to achieve this effect the *p* type material should be connected to a positive potential and the *n* type material to a negative potential. The result is a net flow of charge carriers across the junction.

---

*an element which has a valency of 5.

**an element with a valency of 3.

On the other hand, if the external voltage applied to the junction is in such a direction as to increase the potential barrier, Fig. 10.4 (*d*), reverse biasing results. The resulting current flow is practically zero. It is thus that the *pn* junction behaves like a switch. The switch is closed when the junction is forward biased and open when it is reverse biased.

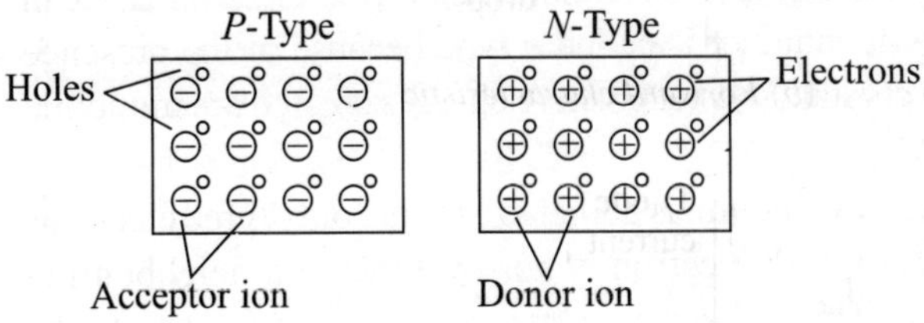

(*a*) *Schematic of p and n type materials*

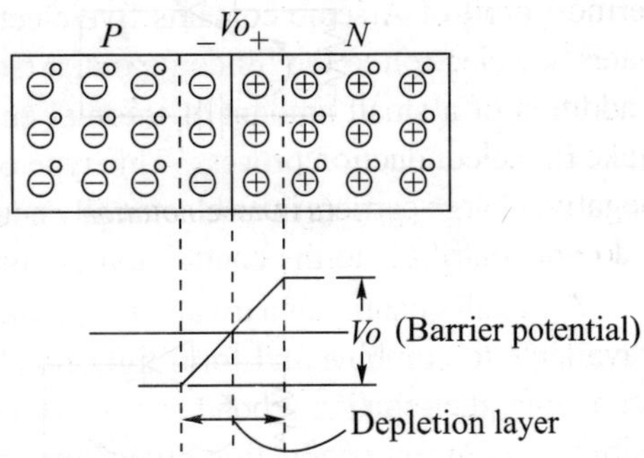

(*b*) *p-n junction, showing depletion layers*

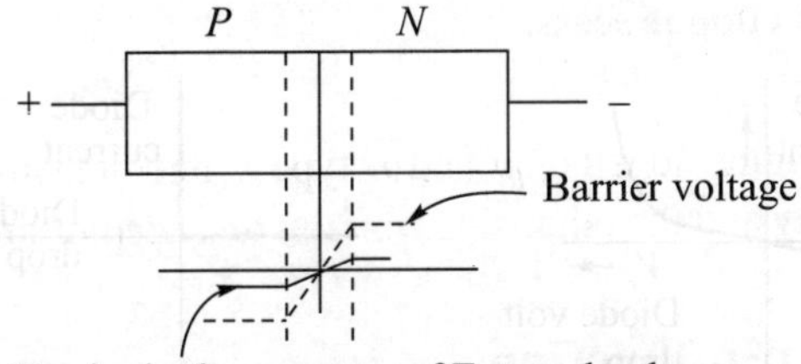

(*c*) *Forward biased junction*

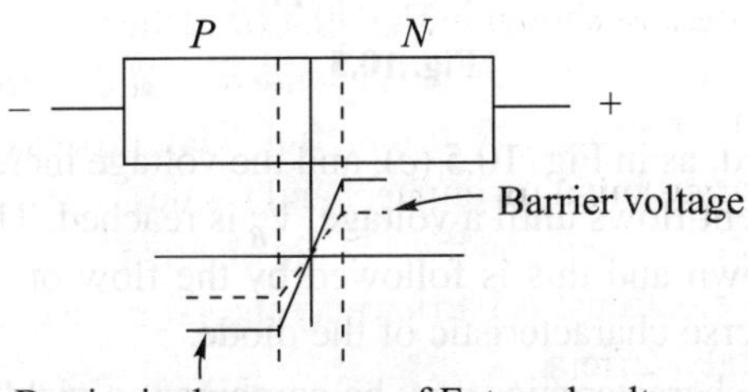

(*d*) *Reverse biased junction*

Fig. 10.4

10.6 DIODE CHARACTERISTICS

The symbolic notation of a diode is shown in Fig. 10.5 (*a*). An adjustable dc supply is connected across it so as to forward bias the diode. For small applied voltages the current flow and the voltage drop across the diode are both small. As the voltage is increased, at a certain point, the current increases sharply as shown in Fig. 10.5 (*b*). The corresponding value of diode voltage, V_r, is known as the *knee voltage*. As the current is increased further, the voltage does not increase by much. In fact the diode internal forward drop may be considered to stay constant at the voltage V_r beyond the knee point. For

Silicon diodes, V_r = 0.7 V while for Germanium diodes V_r = 0.3 V. The graph of Fig. 10.5 (*b*) is the forward characteristic of the diode.

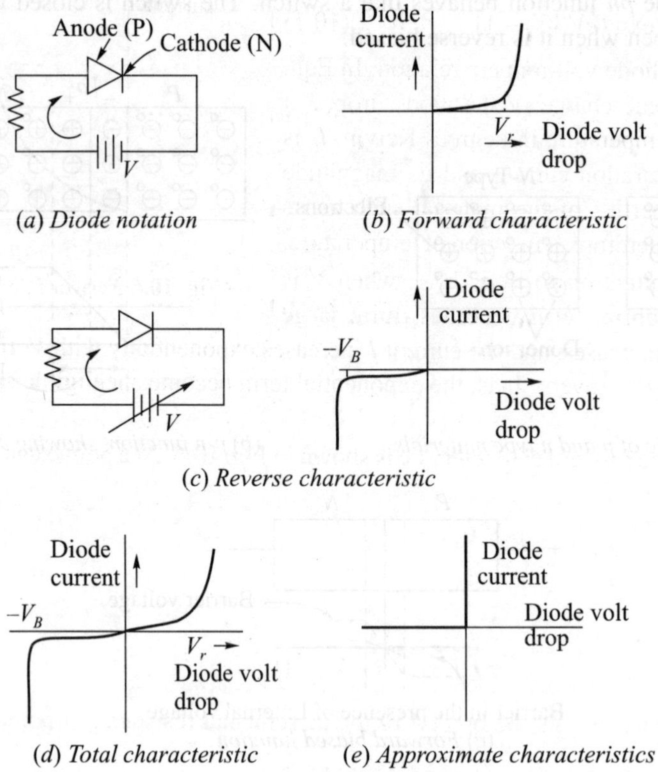

(*a*) *Diode notation* (*b*) *Forward characteristic*

(*c*) *Reverse characteristic*

(*d*) *Total characteristic* (*e*) *Approximate characteristics*

Fig. 10.5

If the dc supply is reversed, as in Fig. 10.5 (*c*), and the voltage increased starting from zero volts it is found that only a small current flows until a voltage, V_B is reached. This is the *breakdown point*; at this voltage the diode breaks down and this is followed by the flow of a large current. The graph of Fig. 10.5(*c*) is known as the reverse characteristic of the diode.

The forward and reverse characteristics may be combined to yield the total diode characteristic depicted in Fig. 10.5 (*d*). Since V_r is much smaller than V_B, the total characteristic may be approximated as shown in Fig. 10.5 (*e*). This, in fact, is the volt-amp characteristic of the ideal diode. If the applied voltage is equal to or greater than zero volts, the diode does not offer any resistance to current flow. On the other hand, if it is reverse biased, the diode does not permit any current flow. The diode may therefore be looked upon as a voltage controlled switch. This property of the diode finds use in a variety of applications one of the most important being rectification of ac signals *i.e.*, conversion of ac into dc.

10.7 DIODE FORWARD RESISTANCE

Although the forward resistance of a diode is low (ideally zero), it is necessary to take it into account, in certain instances, as in rectifier analysis. This resistance is comprised of two parts—the ohmic resistance of the diode material and contacts and the resistance offered by the junction of the diode. This is indicated in Fig. 10.6.

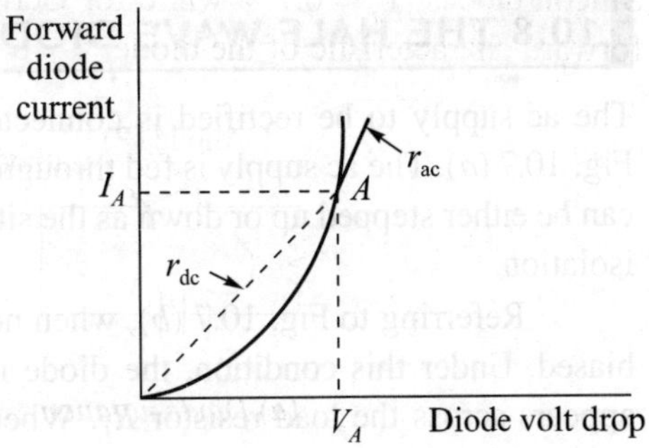

Fig. 10.6 *Forward characteristic of a diode*

The expression for current flow through the diode is given by

$$I = I_0 \,[\exp\,(eV/kT) - 1] \qquad ....(10.1)$$

and is known as the diode volt-ampere relation. In Eqn. 10.1, e is the electronic charge, V the diode drop, k a constant and T the temperature in degrees Kelvin. I_0 is the small reverse saturation current and its magnitude depends on the properties of the material such as its conductivity and is, therefore, a function of temperature.

Turning our attention to Eqn. 10.1, when V is positive, the exponential term becomes quite large compared to 1, as V increases, and the current I increases exponentially with V. If V is negative, and of sufficient magnitude *i.e.*, reverse bias, the exponential term becomes negligible and the reverse current I_0 results.

A portion of the forward characteristic is shown in Fig. 10.6. At a point such as A, the dc resistance is

$$r_{dc} = \frac{V_A}{I_A}$$

$$= \frac{V_A}{I_0[\exp\,(eV/kT) - 1]} \qquad ...(10.2)$$

The ac resistance around the point A or the incremental resistance at point A is

$$r_{ac} = \left(\frac{dV}{dI}\right)_A$$

and $$\frac{1}{r_{ac}} = I_0 \frac{e}{kT} \exp eV/kT$$

$$= \frac{e}{kT}(I + I_0) \qquad ...(10.3)$$

At a temperature of 20°C, $\frac{kT}{e} = 25$ mV

and $$r_{ac} = \frac{0.025}{(I + I_0)}$$

$$\cong \frac{0.25}{I} \text{ ohms} \qquad ...(10.4)$$

Equation 10.4 expresses the resistance offered to small variations in current flow at point A.

10.8 THE HALF WAVE DIODE RECTIFIER

The ac supply to be rectified is connected in series with the diode and the load resistance R_L as in Fig. 10.7 (*a*). The ac supply is fed through a transformer. This serves a dual purpose. First, the ac supply can be either stepped up or down as the situation warrants. Secondly, the transformer provides electrical isolation.

Referring to Fig. 10.7 (*b*), when node *A* is positive with respect to node *B*, the diode is forward biased. Under this condition, the diode may be considered as a closed switch and the input voltage appears across the load resistor R_L. When node *A* goes negative with respect to node *B*, the diode is reverse biased and behaves like an open switch. Hence the voltage across the load resistor is zero. This pattern repeats itself and the output voltage waveform, across R_L, is as shown in Fig. 10.7 (*c*); it is seen that the waveform is unidirectional. Its average value, is the dc output voltage $V_o \cdot V_o = I_{av} R_L$, where

$$I_{av} = \frac{1}{2\pi} \int_0^{2\pi} i \, d\theta$$

$$= \frac{1}{2\pi} \int_0^{\pi} \frac{V_m \sin \theta \cdot d_\theta}{R_L}$$

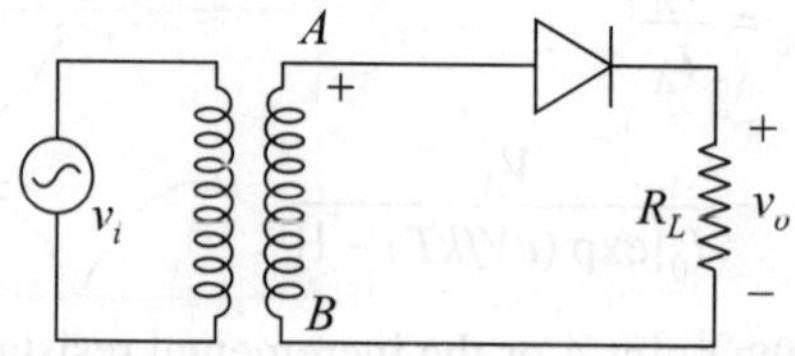

(*a*) *A diode Half wave rectifier*

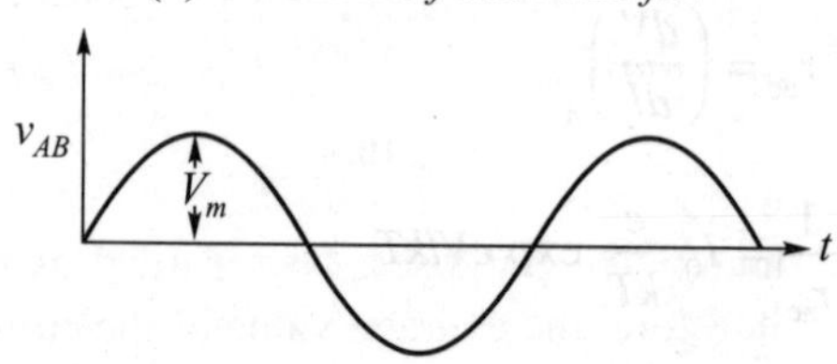

(*b*) *Voltage across the secondary of the transformer*

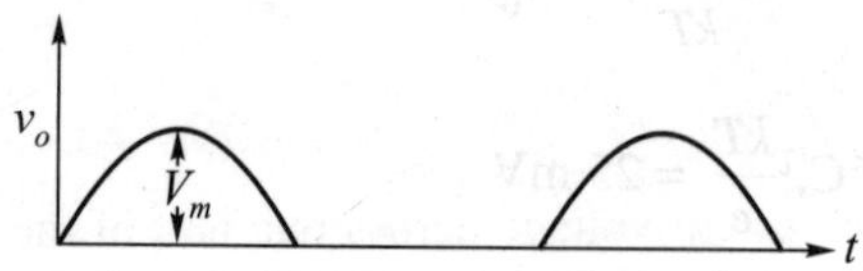

(*c*) *Output voltage waveform*

Fig. 10.7

Here $V_m \sin \theta$ is the applied voltage and $\theta = wt$.

Thus $$I_{av} = \frac{I_m}{\pi} \text{ and} \quad ...(10.5)$$

$$V_o = \frac{V_m}{\pi}$$

The dc power output is

$$P_o = \left(\frac{I_m}{\pi}\right)^2 R_L \qquad ...(10.6)$$

10.9 THE FULL WAVE DIODE RECTIFIER

Two diodes D_1 and D_2 are shown in Fig. 10.8. This circuit uses a transformer which has a center tapped secondary winding. The characteristic of this transformer is that the instantaneous polarity of node *A* is always opposite (180° out of phase) to that of node *B*. The center tap, node *C*, is at ground potential. Therefore, when node *A* is positive with respect to node *C*, D_1 is forward biased and behaves like a closed switch. The voltage appearing across R_L is thus identical to that across nodes *A* and *C*. During the other half cycle, that is, when node *B* goes positive with respect to node *C*, D_2 conducts. Hence, the voltage appearing across R_L is identical to that across nodes *B* and *C*. The output voltage does not change sign and is unidirectional.

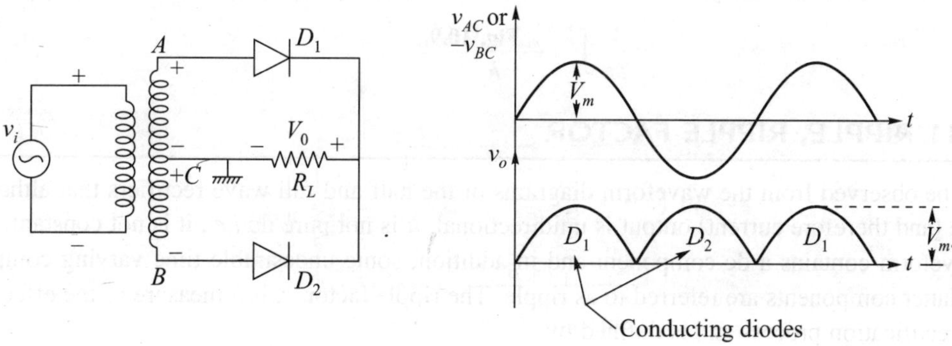

(*a*) *Full wave rectifier using two diodes* (*b*) *Output from a full wave rectifier*

Fig. 10.8

This circuit can, for computational purposes, be regarded as two half wave circuits each of which work for one half cycle. Therefore, the average value of the current through the load resistor R_L is $\frac{2I_m}{\pi}$ and

$$V_0 = \frac{2V_m}{\pi} \qquad ...(10.7)$$

where V_m is the maximum value of the voltage across one half of the secondary winding. When diode D_1 conducts the maximum voltage at the cathode end of D_2 is equal to V_m. At this instant the voltage at the anode end of D_2 is $-V_m$. Hence this diode should be capable of withstanding a voltage of $2V_m$ volts applied in the reverse direction. This voltage is known as the *peak inverse voltage* (PIV).

10.10 FULL WAVE BRIDGE RECTIFIER

The need for the centre tapped transformer is eliminated in this set up which is shown in Fig. 10.9 (*a*). When node *A* is positive, diodes D_1 and D_2 are both forward biased and the voltage across R_L is the same as that across nodes *A* and *B*. During the negative half cycle, *B* goes positive. Now diodes D_3 and D_4 conduct and once again the voltage across the load resistor is the same as that across nodes *B* and *A*.

CHAPTER 10

From Fig. 10.9 (*b*) it is seen that the output voltage across R_L is unidirectional. Unlike the previous case (with a center tapped transformer), the PIV appearing across each diode is only V_m, where V_m is the maximum value of the secondary transformer voltage in Fig. 10.9 (*a*). This is so because two diodes are in series during both the conducting and nonconducting periods.

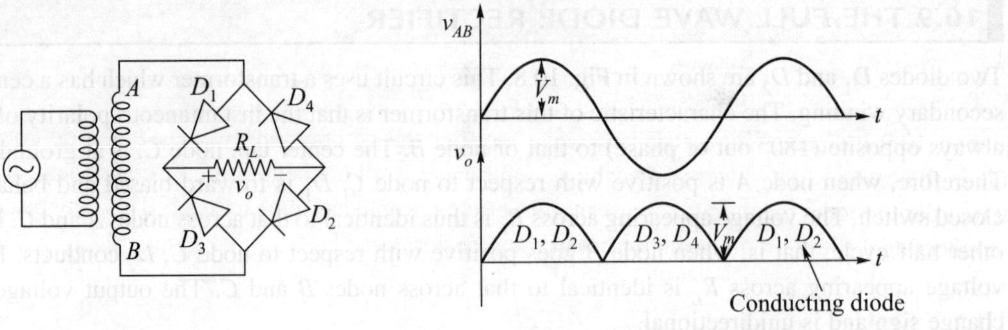

(*a*) *Bridge rectifier* (*b*) *Output from a bridge rectifier*

Fig. 10.9

10.11 RIPPLE, RIPPLE FACTOR

It may be observed from the waveform diagrams of the half and full wave rectifiers that although the voltage (and therefore current) output is unidirectional, it is not pure dc *i.e.*, it is not constant. That is, the waveform contains a dc component and in addition, some undesirable time varying components. These latter components are referred to as ripple. The ripple factor, *r*, is a measure of the effectiveness of the rectification process and is defined by

$$r = \frac{V_{ac}}{V_o} = \frac{\text{rms value of ac components}}{\text{average value of output}}$$

Considering the output to comprise of V_{dc} and a time varying V_{ac}, the rms value of the output V_{RMS} is given by

$$V_{RMS}^2 = \frac{1}{T}\int_0^T [V_o + V_{ac}]^2\, dt$$

where *T* is the time period of the output waveform. Therefore,

$$V_{RMS}^2 = \frac{1}{T}\int_0^T [V_0^2 + V_{ac}^2 + 2V_{dc}\, V_{ac}]\, dt$$

$$= V_0^2\,\frac{T}{T} + V_{ac}^2 + 0$$

The last term yields zero upon integration because alternating term, V_{ac}, is not squared. Thus,

$$V_{RMS}^2 = V_0^2 + V_{ac}^2$$

and the ripple factor

$$r = \frac{V_{ac}}{V_0} = \left\{\left(\frac{V_{RMS}}{V_0}\right)^2 - 1\right\}^{1/2} \qquad ...(10.8)$$

It can be proved that, for the half wave rectifier $V_{\text{RMS}} = \frac{V_m}{2}$; for the full wave rectifier $V_{\text{RMS}} = \frac{V_m}{\sqrt{2}}$. Using Eqns. 10.5, 10.7, and 10.8, one obtains

and
$$\left.\begin{aligned} r_{\text{half wave}} &= 1.21 \\ r_{\text{full wave}} &= 0.48 \end{aligned}\right\} \quad \text{...(10.9)}$$

Equation 10.9 indicates that in the half wave rectifier the ac component exceeds the dc component while in the case of full wave rectifier the ac component is 48 per cent of the dc component. It is clear that in order to render the output voltage more useful the ripple has to be reduced. This may be achieved by connecting a filter circuit at the output of the rectifier.

10.12 SHUNT CAPACITOR FILTER

A suitable capacitor C is connected across the load resistor R_L of the half wave rectifying circuit as in Fig. 10.10 (*a*) to achieve filtering action. The inertial action of the capacitor enables the smoothening of the pulsating output voltage. The action of the filter may be understood upon study of the waveforms in Fig. 10.10 (*b*). During the positive half cycle, the diode conducts thereby charging the capacitor to the peak value of the supply voltage V_m*. When the ac input voltage falls to a value less than V_m, the diode is reverse biased and therefore ceases to conduct. However, the capacitor now discharges with a time constant R_LC which is usually adjusted to be >> than half a period of the ac waveform. Due to the long time constant of discharge, the output voltage is maintained at a fairly constant value during the negative half cycle of the input. During the next positive cycle the diode is forward biased when the input ac voltage exceeds the capacitor voltage. The diode conducts and the capacitor voltage increases and follows the ac input voltage until it is charged to a voltage of V_m. From the figure it is clear that if R_LC is sufficiently large, the charge lost by the capacitor during the negative half cycle will be small, therefore the ripple will be small.

The diode current flows in the form of pulses as shown in Fig. 10.10(*b*). In practice a small resistor is connected in series with the diode to limit the amplitude of the current pulse. This resistor is sometimes referred to as surge limiting resistor.

It is easily seen that the maximum PIV in the circuit of Fig. 10.8 is $2V_m$. It may be shown that the ripple factor, r, is given by

$$r = \frac{1}{4\sqrt{3}\, R_L\, Cf} \quad \text{...(10.10)}$$

where R_L = load resistor value in ohms
C = capacitance in Farads
f = supply frequency

*This is true if the charging time constant of the capacitor is much smaller than one quarter of a period of the ac waveform—which is usually the case.

As expected, if $R_L C \to \infty$, $r \to 0$.

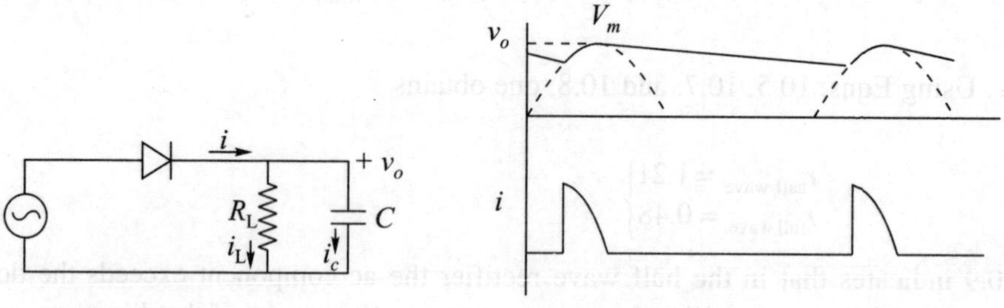

(a) *Shunt capacitance filter* (b) *Output from a shunt capacitor filter*

Fig. 10.10

10.13 VOLTAGE REGULATION

When a filter is connected at the output of a rectifier, the ripple content is greatly reduced. However, the average value of the output voltage or the dc output changes as the value of the load resistor changes and also as the input voltage changes. The change in the dc output voltage from a no load to a full load condition, under constant ac input voltage, expressed as a percentage of the full load value, is known as voltage regulation.

$$i.e., \ \% \text{ Regulation} = \frac{V_{\text{no load}} - V_{\text{full load}}}{V_{\text{full load}}} \times 100 \qquad \text{...(10.11)}$$

In a regulated power supply the regulation should be as low as possible (ideally zero). This achieved by connecting regulators or regulating circuits at the output of the rectifier/filter combination.

10.14 ZENER DIODE

A zener diode is a silicon diode with a very sharp breakdown characteristic *i.e.*, once the applied voltage under reverse bias conditions equals the breakdown voltage, the current increases very rapidly and the diode voltage stays essentially constant. This region is referred to as the zener region. Such a characteristic is obtained by addition of suitable quantities of an impurity material to Silicon. In contrast with a junction diode, a zener diode can, without burning out, dissipate a certain amount of power in the breakdown region. For example, if the reverse breakdown voltage of a zener diode is 50 V and the maximum power it can dissipate in the zener region is 500 mW, it implies that the maximum permissible reverse current is 10 mA.

When a zener diode is operated in the breakdown region it may be regarded as a constant voltage source. Fig. 10.11 shows the symbol used to represent a zener diode. Its volt-ampere characteristic and an equivalent circuit valid in the breakdown region are also shown. The breakdown voltage is known as the *zener voltage*.

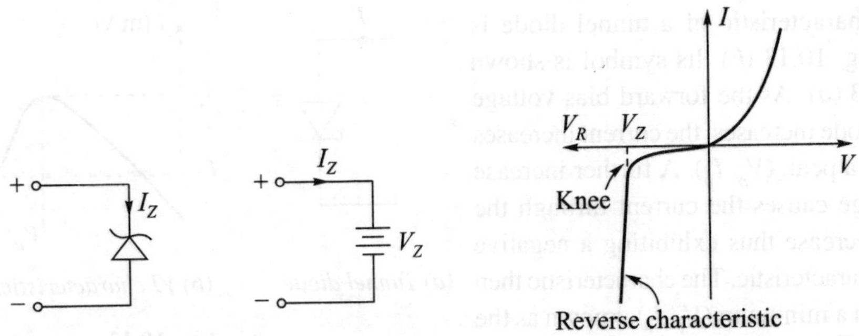

(a) *Zener diode symbol* (b) *Equivalent circuit on breakdown region* (c) *VI characteristics of zener diode*

Fig. 10.11

10.15 ZENER DIODE VOLTAGE REGULATOR

A zener diode may be used as a voltage regulator to enable the dc output voltage of a filtered supply to be independent of the input voltage fluctuations. Referring to Fig. 10.12 the input voltage V is considered to vary in the range 100–120 volts. Since this is in excess of V_Z, the zener voltage, the diode works in the breakdown region and may therefore be replaced by a battery of voltage V_Z, as shown. When $V = 100$ V the voltage drop across the 5 kΩ resistor is 40 V. Under this condition the current I is $= 40 \cdot 10^{-3}/5 = 8$ mA and the load current is $60 \cdot 10^{-3}/10 = 6$ mA. Applying KCL at node A, $I_Z = 2$ mA. On the other hand when $V = 120$ volts, the voltages drop across the 5 kΩ resistor is 60 V; $I = 12$ mA. The load current is still 6 mA as V_Z is constant but $I_Z = 6$ mA. Thus, the output voltage is constant and independent of input voltage fluctuations. As the input voltage increases, the zener current increases. The zener diode current rating determines the upper bound of the input voltage fluctuation.

10.16 THE TUNNEL DIODE

The depletion layer in a junction diode is relatively wide. If the degree of doping is increased greatly, the junction becomes thin—of the order of 100 Angstroms.* The volt-ampere characteristic such *pn* junctions are very different from that of ordinary junction diodes. The departure in the characteristics is attributed to quantum mechanical tunnelling of charge carriers across the narrow junction. This means that many carriers tunnel through the junction with velocity of light even though they do not possess sufficient energy to overcome the potential barrier. Thus, even if the applied voltage is less than 0.3 V, in the case of a forward biased Germanium diode, large currents may flow. This phenomenon was first observed and studied by Esaki in 1958. The diode is therefore known as an *Esaki* or *tunnel diode*.

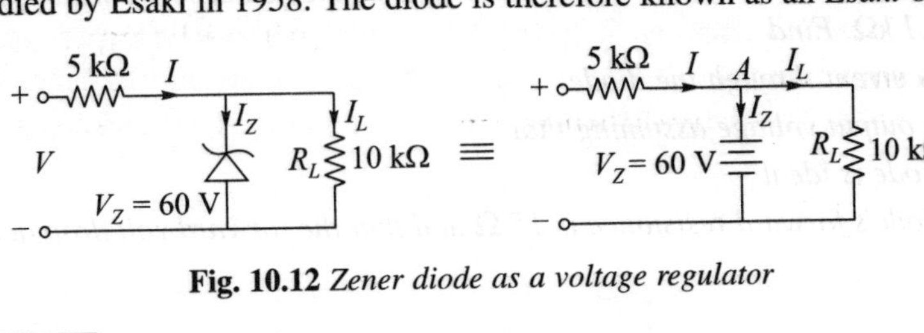

Fig. 10.12 *Zener diode as a voltage regulator*

*One angstrom = 10^{-10} m.

CHAPTER 10

A typical characteristic of a tunnel diode is shown in Fig. 10.13 (*b*). Its symbol is shown in Fig. 10.13 (*a*). As the forward bias voltage across the diode increases, the current increases and reaches a peak (V_p, I_p). A further increase in the voltage causes the current through the device to decrease thus exhibiting a negative resistance characteristic. The characteristic then goes through a minimum (V_v, I_v), known as the valley point. When the diode voltage exceeds the valley point voltage the diode current once again increases in an exponential manner as in a conventional diode. With reverse voltages, there is no breakdown effect as with conventional diodes.

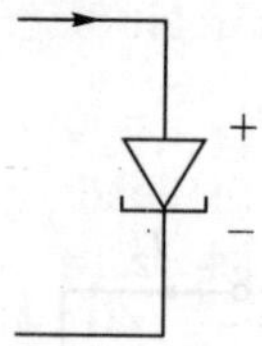

(*a*) *Tunnel diode*

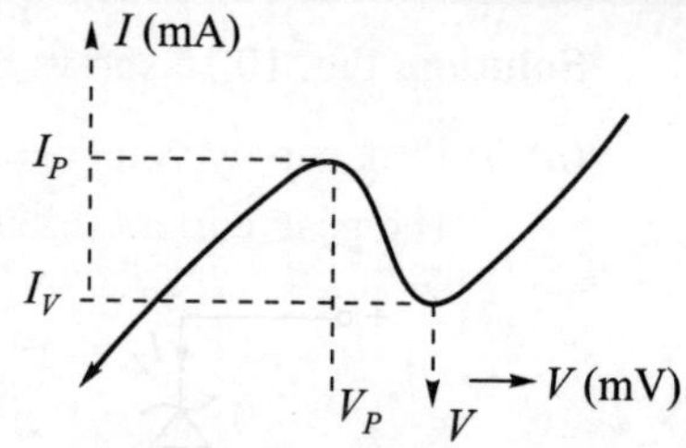

(*b*) *VI characteristics of Tunnel diode*

Fig. 10.13

Tunnel doides may be used for the generation of high frequency (10 GHz) square waves. In such circuits the negative resistance of the diode is used to cancel the positive resistance in a tuned circuit. It is the presence of positive resistance that is responsible for losses and causes the oscillations in a tuned circuit to decay.

10.17 THE SCHOTTKY DIODE

This is a metal-semiconductor junction diode *i.e.*, one side of the junction is metallic while the other side comprises of a *n* type extrinsic Silicon semiconducting material as shown in the sketch in Fig. 10.14. The metal region possesses large numbers of electrons in the conduction band and the *n* type semiconducting region is doped lightly.

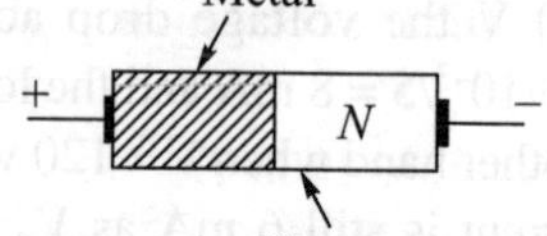

(*a*) *Schottky diode*

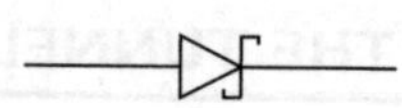

(*b*) *Diode notation*

Fig. 10.14

Under conditions of forward bias, high energy electrons are injected into the metal region. These charge carriers are called "hot carriers" as they crossover with large amounts of energy. The current flow in a Schottky diode is solely due to electrons; this device is therefore known as a *unipolar diode*. In ordinary junction diodes the conduction is due to electrons and holes. Such devices are termed as *bipolar*.

Due to the absence of holes in the Schottky diode, there is no depletion layer; this device is therefore fast acting and is used for the rectification of very high frequency signals (> 300 MHz).

Example 10.1. *An ac voltage of rms value 110 V is connected in series with a junction diode and a load resistor of 1.1 kΩ. Find*

(*i*) *the peak current through the diode*

(*ii*) *the peak output voltage assuming that*

(*a*) *the diode is ideal*

(*b*) *the diode's forward resistance is 15 Ω and that the forward volt drop across it is = 0.7 V.*

Solution. Fig. 10.15 shows the circuit diagram.

(*a*) (*i*) Peak supply voltage = $110\sqrt{2}$ = 155.5 V

The peak current through the load

$$= \frac{155.5}{1.1\ \text{k}\Omega} = 0.141\text{A}$$

(*ii*) the peak output voltage is 155.5 V

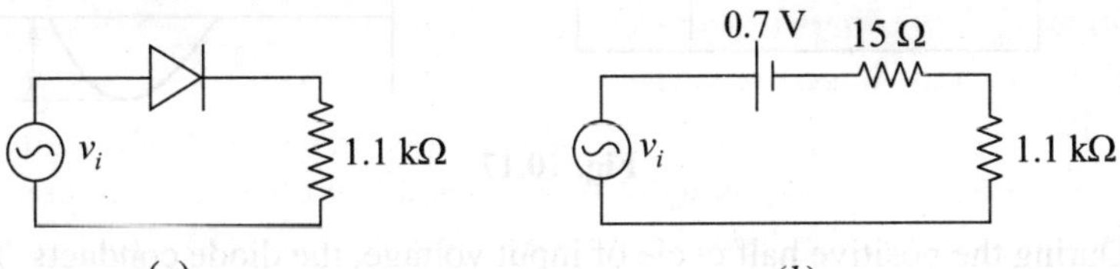

(*a*) (*b*)

Fig. 10.15

(*b*) (*i*) In this instance the equivalent circuit of Fig. 10.15 (*b*) applies and the peak current is

$$\frac{(155.5 - 0.7)}{1.1\ \text{k}\Omega + 15\ \Omega} = 0.1388\ \text{A}$$

(*ii*) the corresponding peak voltage output is

$$= (0.1388)\ (1.1\ \text{k}\Omega) = 152.68\ \text{V}$$

Example 10.2. *The input to the diode circuit shown in Fig. 10.16 is a sine voltage waveform with a peak value of 100 V. Sketch* v_o *assuming that the diode is ideal.*

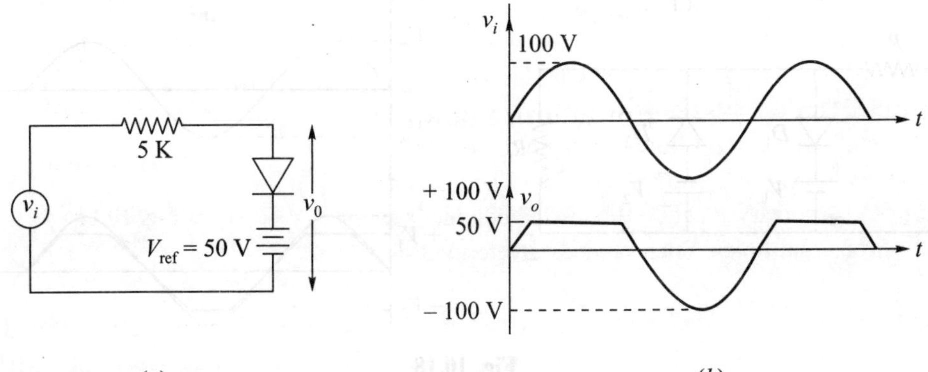

(*a*) (*b*)

Fig. 10.16

Solution. During the positive half cycle the diode behaves like a closed switch if it is forward biased *i.e.*, the supply voltage value exceeds 50 V. When v_i > 50 V, current flows; the diode drop is zero volts and the output is held at 50 V. The remaining 50 V is dropped across the 5 kΩ resistor.

During the negative half cycle the diode is reverse biased and behaves like an open switch. The output voltage v_o therefore follows the input voltage. The input and output waveforms are shown in Fig. 10.16 (*b*).

Example 10.3. *A 100 volt peak to peak ac voltage is applied to the circuit of Fig. 10.17. Sketch the output voltage assuming the diode to be ideal.*

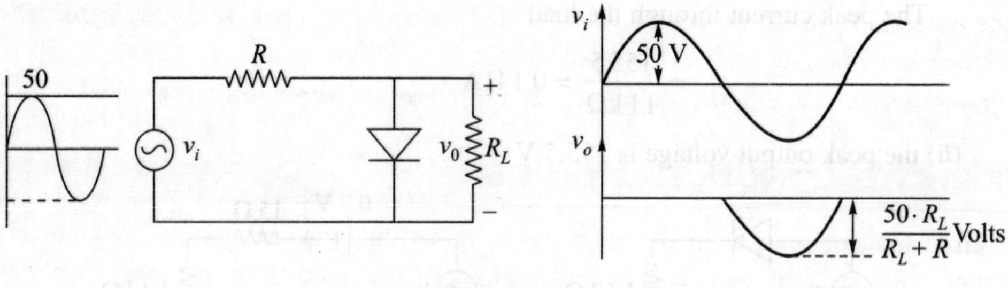

Fig. 10.17

Solution. During the positive half cycle of input voltage, the diode conducts. The voltage across it is therefore zero volts which is the output voltage.

During the negative half cycle the diode is reverse biased and behaves like an open switch. The circuit, now, acts as a voltage divider and the output voltage is

$$= \frac{R_L}{R_L + R} v_i.$$

The circuit therefore removes or clips the positive going portions of the input waveform and is known as a positive clipper.

Example 10.4. *A 100 V peak to peak ac voltage is applied to the two way clipper shown in Fig. 10.18. Sketch the output waveform, assuming ideal diodes.*

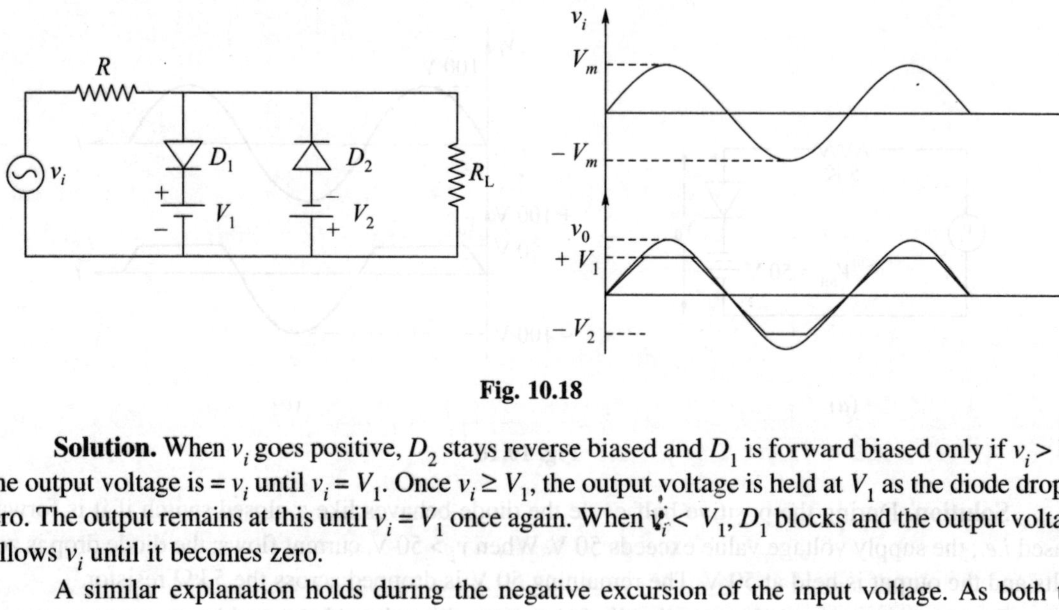

Fig. 10.18

Solution. When v_i goes positive, D_2 stays reverse biased and D_1 is forward biased only if $v_i > V_1$. The output voltage is = v_i until $v_i = V_1$. Once $v_i \geq V_1$, the output voltage is held at V_1 as the diode drop is zero. The output remains at this until $v_i = V_1$ once again. When $v_i < V_1$, D_1 blocks and the output voltage follows v_i until it becomes zero.

A similar explanation holds during the negative excursion of the input voltage. As both the positive and negative portions of the input waveform are clipped, this circuit is known as a two way clipper.

An interesting extension of the above example is as below:

Figure 10.19 shows the circuit (called a series clipper). During its positive excursion, if the input signal, v_i, is < V_1 neither diode conducts and the output voltage is zero volts. When the input signal magnitude exceeds V_1 diode D_1 conducts the output follows the input. A similar explanation holds during the negative going portion of the input signal.

It may be seen that although the input contains noise the output is a clean signal.

10.18 PHOTO CONDUCTIVE DIODES

Intrinsic semiconductors may be made to conduct by imparting light energy on to the *pn* junction. As a consequence, the electrons gain energy and partake in the conduction process. The response of Germanium, in photoconduction, is shown in Fig. 10.20. Both small and large area junctions are manufactured; the latter are used to convert solar energy into electricity and also find application in satellites. Silicon photo diodes have a conversion efficiency (light energy to electrical energy) of 15% while Gallium Arsenide diodes have slightly lower efficiencies, of the order 11%.

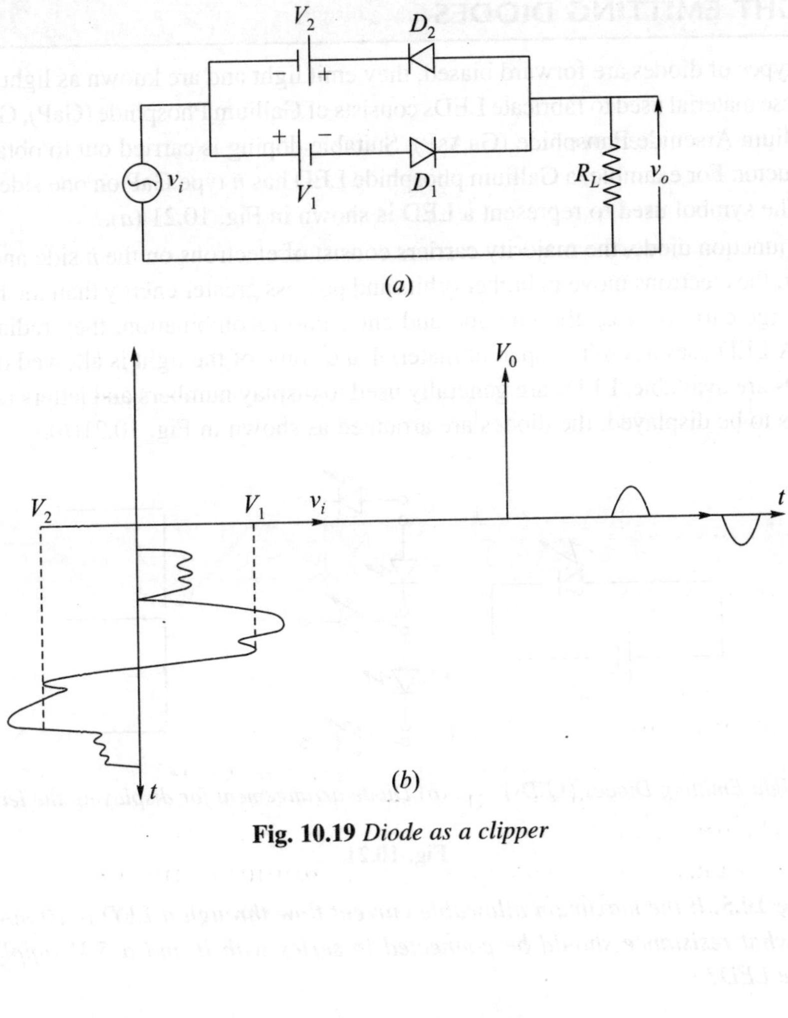

Fig. 10.19 *Diode as a clipper*

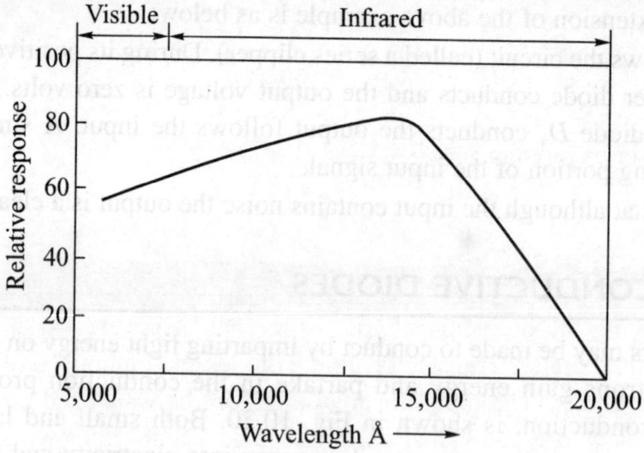

Fig. 10.20 *Response of Germanium in photoconduction*

10.19 LIGHT EMITTING DIODES

When certain types of diodes are forward biased, they emit light and are known as light emitting diodes (LEDs). The base material used to fabricate LEDs consists of Gallium Phosphide (GaP), Gallium Arsenide (GaAs) or Gallium Arsenide Phosphide (GaAsP). Suitable doping is carried out to obtain a *p* type or *n* type semiconductor. For example, a Gallium phosphide LED has *n* type GaP on one side and *p* type GaP on the other. The symbol used to represent a LED is shown in Fig. 10.21 (*a*).

As in a junction diode, the majority carriers consist of electrons on the *n* side and holes on the *p* sides. However, the electrons move in higher orbits and possess greater energy than the holes. Therefore when these charge carriers cross the junction and enter into recombination, they radiate energy in he form of light. A LED uses a semitransparent material and some of the light is allowed out. Red, yellow and green LEDs are available. LEDs are generally used to display numbers and letters (alphanumerics). If the letter *E* is to be displayed, the diodes are arranged as shown in Fig. 10.21(*b*).

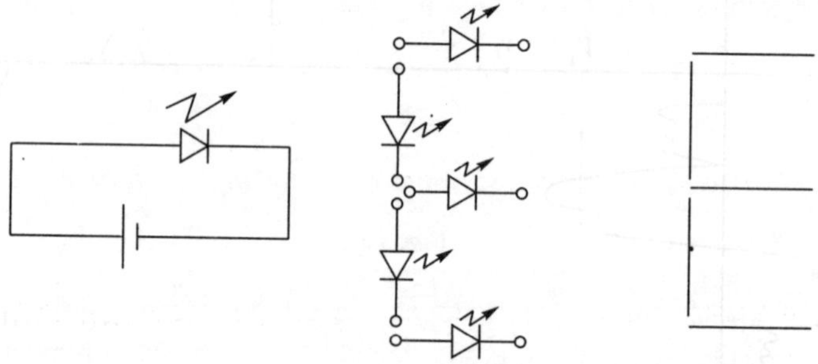

(*a*) *Light Emitting Diodes (LEDs)* (*b*) *Diode arrangement for displaying the letter E*

Fig. 10.21

Example 10.5. *If the maximum allowable current flow through a LED is 10 mA and the diode drop is 1.5 V, what resistance should be connected in series with it and a 5 V supply? What is the resistance of the LED?*

Solution. The resistance of the LED is $= \dfrac{1.5}{10 \text{ mA}} = 150\ \Omega$

The required series resistance $= \dfrac{5 - 1.5}{10 \text{ mA}} = 350\ \Omega.$

10.20 TRANSISTORS

The principle underlying the operation of transistors was discovered in 1948 at the Bell Telephone laboratories in the United States. Transistors, unlike diodes, are comprised of two *pn* junctions forming either a *pnp* or *npn* structure. The transistor may therefore be visualized as consisting of two back to back diodes spaced closely together. Transistors are capable of amplifying weak (low amplitude) electrical signals. They possess sufficient mechanical strength and have practically unlimited life.

10.21 PNP AND NPN TRANSISTORS

A *pnp* transistor is fabricated by sandwiching an *n* type material between two pieces of a *p* type material. As may be noted from Fig. 10.22, the larger *p* region is known as the collector while the other *p* region is the emitter. The middle region constitutes the base. Likewise, a *npn* transistor is fabricated by sandwiching a *p* type material between two pieces of *n* type material.

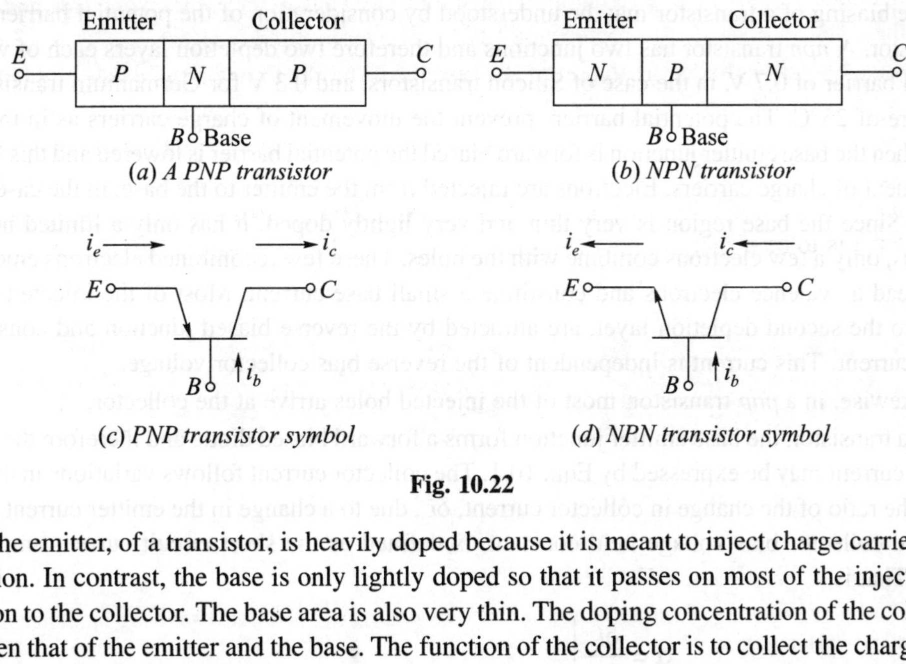

Fig. 10.22

The emitter, of a transistor, is heavily doped because it is meant to inject charge carriers into the base region. In contrast, the base is only lightly doped so that it passes on most of the injected charge carriers on to the collector. The base area is also very thin. The doping concentration of the collector lies in between that of the emitter and the base. The function of the collector is to collect the charges emitter by the emitter. The collector area is the largest of the three regions as it has to dissipate more heat than either the base or the emitter.

It is clear Fig. 10.22 that the transistor has two junctions, one between the base and emitter and the other between the base and the collector. The transistor, as mentioned before, may therefore be visualized as consisting of two diodes connected back to back—the base-emitter and base-collector diodes. These are referred to as the emitter and collector diodes.

Figure 10.22 also shows the symbol used to represent both types of transistors. The direction of the arrow points in the direction of conventional current flow. In a *pnp* transistor, current flows from emitter to base whereas in a *npn* transistor, it flows from base to emitter. The conventional directions of emitter, base, and collector currents, i_e, i_b and i_c are shown in the same figure.

10.22 BIASING A TRANSISTOR

Since the emitter is meant to emit charge carriers, the emitter base junction should be forward biased. Since these carriers are meant to be collected by the collector, this junction should be reverse biased. The biasing connections are as shown in Fig. 10.23.

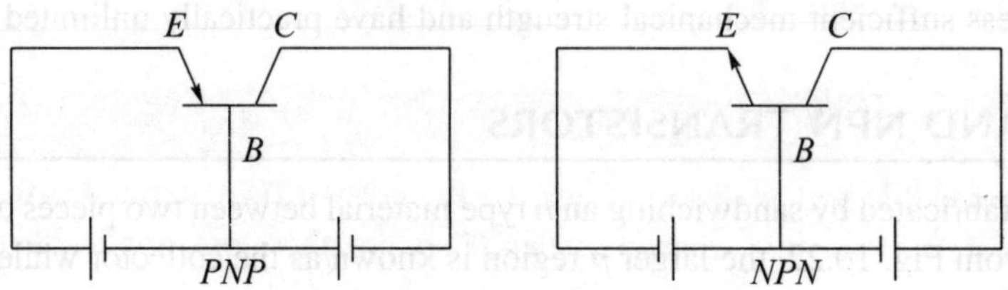

Fig. 10.23 *Biasing a transistor*

The biasing of a transistor may be understood by consideration of the potential barriers present in a transistor. A *npn* transistor has two junctions and therefore two depletion layers each of which has a potential barrier of 0.7 V, in the case of Silicon transistors, and 0.3 V for Germanium transistors, at a temperature of 25°C. The potential barriers prevent the movement of charge carriers as in the case of diodes. When the base emitter junction is forward biased the potential barrier is lowered and this facilitates the movement of charge carriers. Electrons are injected from the emitter to the base, in the case of a *npn* transistor. Since the base region is very thin and very lightly doped, it has only a limited number of holes. Thus, only a few electrons combine with the holes. These few recombined electrons emerge from the base lead as valence electrons and constitute a small base current. Most of the injected electrons diffuse into the second depletion layer, are attracted by the reverse biased junction and constitute the collector current. This current is independent of the reverse bias collector voltage.

Likewise, in a *pnp* transistor, most of the injected holes arrive at the collector.

In a transistor, the base emitter junction forms a forward biased diode and therefore the variation of emitter current may be expressed by Eqn. 10.1. The collector current follows variations in the emitter current. The ratio of the change in collector current, δi_c, due to a change in the emitter current, δi_e, with the applied collector bias voltage held constant, is defined as the short circuit current amplification factor, α. That is,

$$\alpha = \left.\frac{\delta i_c}{\delta i_b}\right|_{V_{CB}\ \text{constant}} \qquad \text{...(10.12)}$$

α lies in the range 0.95–0.99. A second amplification factor known as the collector to base short circuit current amplification factor, h_{fe}, is defined as

$$h_{fe} = \left.\frac{\delta i_c}{\delta i_b}\right|_{V_{CE\text{constant}}} \quad \text{...(10.13)}$$

From Kirchoff's current law,

$$i_e = i_c + i_b \quad \text{....(10.14)}$$

From Eqn. 10.14,

$$\delta i_b = \delta i_e - \delta i_c \quad \text{...(10.15)}$$

Using Eqn. 10.12 in Eqn. 10.15,

$$\delta i_b = (1 - \alpha)\delta i_e \quad \text{...(10.16)}$$

Since, $h_{fe} = \dfrac{\delta i_c}{\delta i_b} = \dfrac{\delta i_c}{\delta i_e}\dfrac{\delta i_e}{\delta i_b}$, it follows that

$$h_{fe} = \frac{\alpha}{1-\alpha} \quad \text{...(10.17)}$$

It should be noted that both α and h_{fe} (Eqns. 10.12 and 10.13) are defined as the slope, at a point, on the i_c, versus i_e, and the i_c versus i_b characteristics. They are, therefore, applicable to signals of small amplitude, commonly known as small ac signals.

10.23 TRANSISTOR CHARACTERISTICS

Of the three terminals of a transistor, one is always common to both input and output. Depending on the terminal that is common, a transistor may be operated in any of three configurations *i.e.*, common base, common emitter and common collector.

10.23.1 The Common Base Circuit

Figure 10.24 (*a*) shows the circuit that may be used to obtain the volt-amp characteristics of the configuration.

If V_{CC} is held constant and V_{BB} increased from zero volts; the emitter current, I_E, increases with V_{BE}. This increase is slow at first, as shown in Fig. 10.24 (*b*). Once V_{BE} exceeds a few tenths of a volt, the emitter current increases significantly with further increases in the abasement voltage.

If V_{CC} is increased, to say 10 V from 1 V, the characteristic, changes only slightly as may be seen from the same figure. It is clear that the emitter base portion of the transistor behaves like a forward biased semiconductor diode.

As far as the collector current is concerned, it is almost equal to the emitter current as may be seen from Fig. 10.24 (*c*). Even if the collector base junction voltage is increased, by increasing V_{CC}, the collector current I_C, remains constant if I_E is held constant *i.e.*, V_{BB} is constant. This situation prevails until the collector base voltage equals the breakdown voltage of this junction upon which the collector current increases significantly, as shown in Figure 10.24 (*d*). However, transistors are never operated in this mode.

In the common base configuration α is almost unity but less than it. Also, I_C, the collector current is independent of V_{CB} and therefore this configuration may be employed when a constant current source is needed.

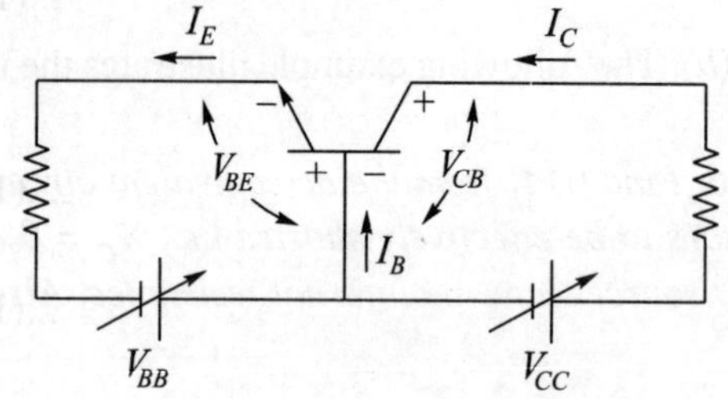

(a) *Transistor in common base (CB) configuration*

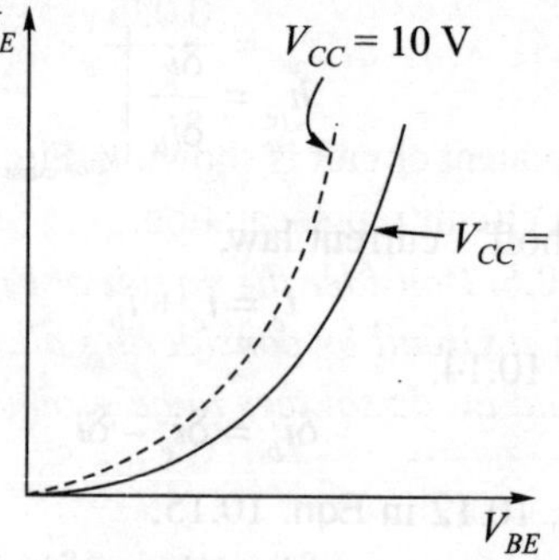

(b) *Input characteristic of transistor in CB mode*

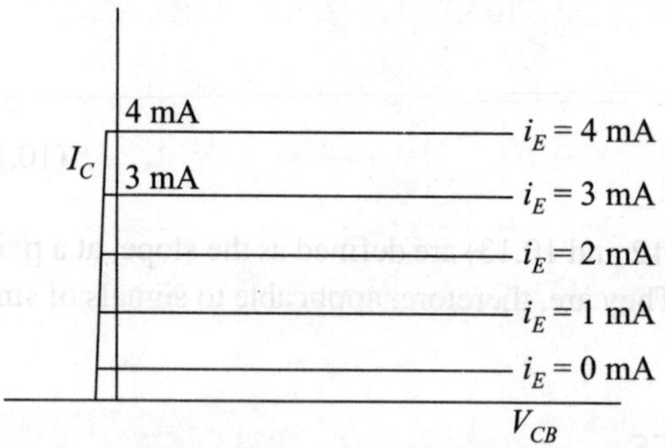

(c) *Output characteristic in CB mode*

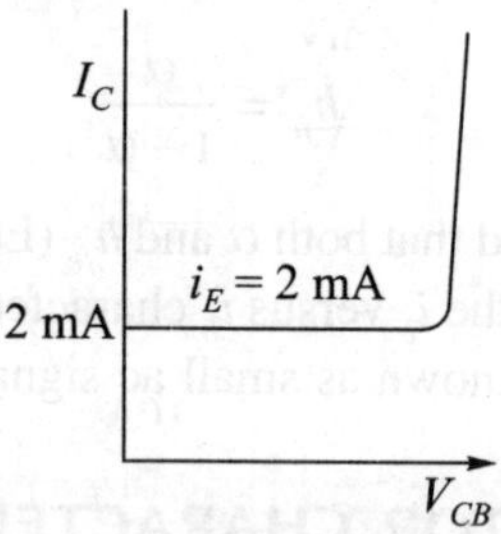

(d) *Variation of I_C vs V_{CB} characteristic*

Fig. 10.24

From the above it should be clear that the base emitter and base collector junctions may be modelled by a diode and a current source respectively as in Fig. 10.25 (*a*). Amplification of ac signals is accomplished by applying it at the input (*i.e.*, base emitter circuit) in the presence of bias voltages. The ac signal amplitude is usually so small so that the net voltage applied in the base emitter circuit oscillates with small amplitude around a dc level of V_{BB}. Small variations also occur in the magnitudes of I_E and V_{BE} around their dc levels. The base emitter diode may, for small signal ac analysis, therefore be replaced by a resistor in accordance with Eqn. 10.4.

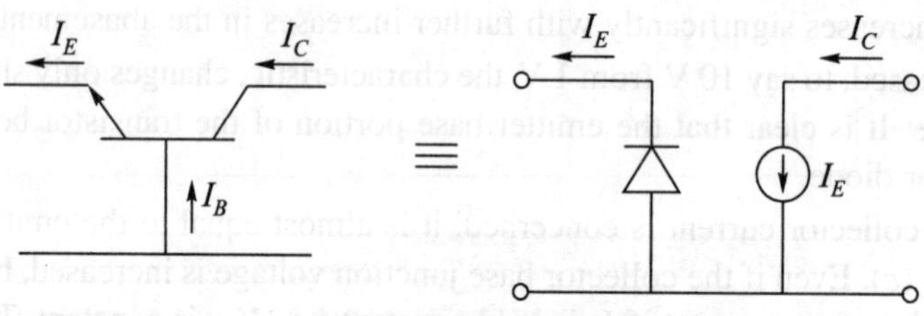

(a) *Transistor equivalent circuit*

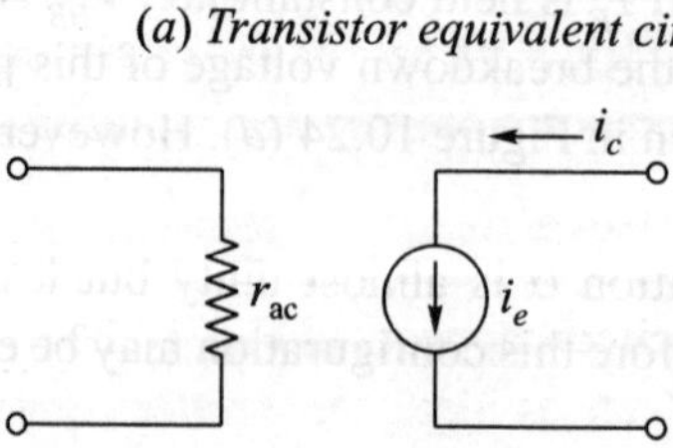

(b) *AC equivalent circuit*

Fig. 10.25

$$r_{ac} = \frac{0.025}{I_E} \qquad \text{...(10.18)}$$

The ac equivalent circuit is shown in Fig. 10.25 (*b*). The following example illustrates the use of such an equivalent circuit representation.

Example 10.6. *Consider the circuit of Fig. 10.26. Find (i) I_E from the dc equivalent circuit and (ii) the ac equivalent circuit by considering all capacitors to be effectively shorted i.e., $X_C = 0$ at the signal frequency and all dc sources to be grounded i.e., sources have no internal resistance. Also find the output voltage.*

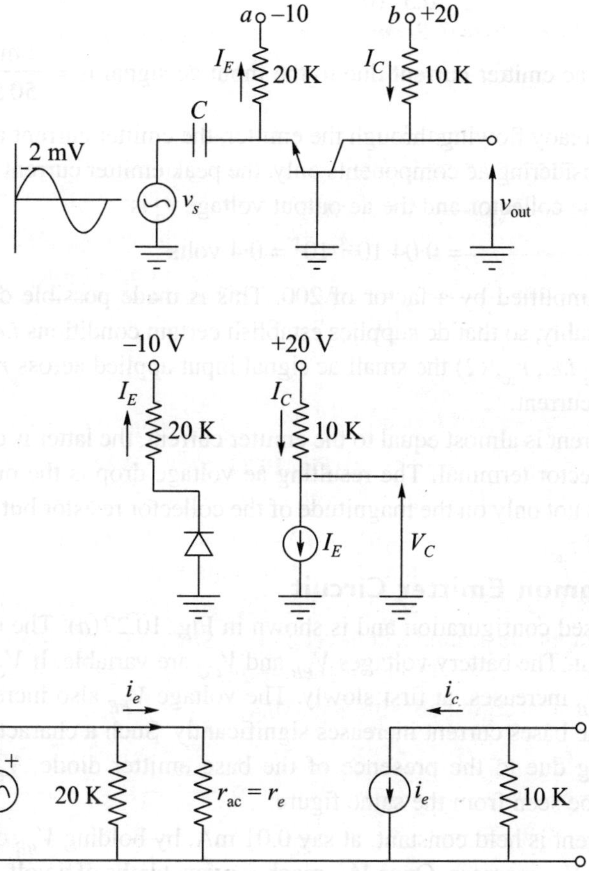

Fig. 10.26

Solution. In Fig. 10.26, –10 and +20 volt batteries are connected between nodes *a* and ground and *b* and ground respectively, *i.e.*, node *a* and *b* are held at a negative and positive potential respectively. To simplify the circuit drawing, the batteries are omitted and replaced with a node and an indication of the voltage applied.

(*i*) In the dc case, one need not be concerned with the capacitor *C* and the input ac signal (the capacitor blocks dc). The dc equivalent circuit appears in Fig. 10.26 (*b*). The base emitter junction is a forward biased diode. Considering the diode as ideal, the emitter current, I_E is

$$= \frac{10}{20 \cdot 10^3} = 0.5 \text{ mA}$$

(*ii*) The ac equivalent circuit is shown in Fig. 10.26 (*c*). Note that the 20 kΩ resistor is effectively in parallel with the signal source as the capacitor has been replaced with a short. From Eqn. 10.18,

$$r_{ac} = \frac{0.025}{I_E}$$

$$= \frac{0.025}{0.5 \cdot 10^{-3}} = 50\ \Omega$$

The peak value of the ac emitter current due to the input ac signal is $= \frac{2 \text{ mV}}{50\ \Omega} = 0.04$ mA. Since a dc current of 0.5 mA is already flowing through the emitter, the emitter current now varies within limits of 0.54 and 0.46 mA. Considering ac components only, the peak emitter current of 0.04 mA flows through the 10 kΩ resistor at the collector and the ac output voltage v_o is

$$= 0{\cdot}04{\cdot}10^{-3}\ 10^4 = 0{\cdot}4 \text{ volts}$$

The input voltage is amplified by a factor of 200. This is made possible due to the fact that (1) the transistor is biased suitably, so that dc supplies establish certain conditions *i.e.*, I_E, $I_C \cong I_E$ and establish a certain value of r_{diode} *i.e.*, r_{ac}, (2) the small ac signal input applied across r_{ac} causes a small variation in the flow of emitter current.

Since the collector current is almost equal to the emitter current, the latter is considered to flow through the resistor at the collector terminal. The resulting ac voltage drop is the output voltage. The voltage gain therefore depends not only on the magnitude of the collector resistor but also on the prevailing bias condition *i.e.*, value of r_{ac}.

10.23.2 The Common Emitter Circuit

This is most widely used configuration and is shown in Fig. 10.27(*a*). The emitter is common to both the output and the input. The battery voltages V_{BB} and V_{CC} are variable. If V_{CC} is held constant and V_{BB} increased from zero, I_B increases, at first slowly. The voltage V_{BE} also increases. Once V_{BE} exceeds a few tenths of a volt the bases current increases significantly. Such a characteristic, Fig. 10.27(*b*), may be regarded as arising due to the presence of the base emitter diode. V_{CC} has little effect on the characteristic as may be seen from the same figure.

If the base current is held constant, at say 0.01 mA, by holding V_{BB} constant and V_{CC} increased from zero, both I_C and V_{CE} increase. Once V_{CE} reaches a few tenths of a volt, the base collector junction becomes reverse biased and I_C attains its maximum value. I_C remains at this value in spite of further increases in V_{CE}. It is found that $I_C \cong 1$mA *i.e.*, $I_C >> I_B$. Similarly curves are obtained for other values of I_B as shown in Fig. 10.27(*c*). If the voltage V_{CC} is increased further a point is reached when V_{CE} exceeds the breakdown voltage of the base collector junction and I_C rises dramatically as shown in Fig. 10.27(*d*). From Fig. 10.27(*c*) it is seen that the collector current is 100 times as large as the base current. This is because practically all the charge carriers emitted by the emitter reach the collector while only a few of the charges reach the base terminal.

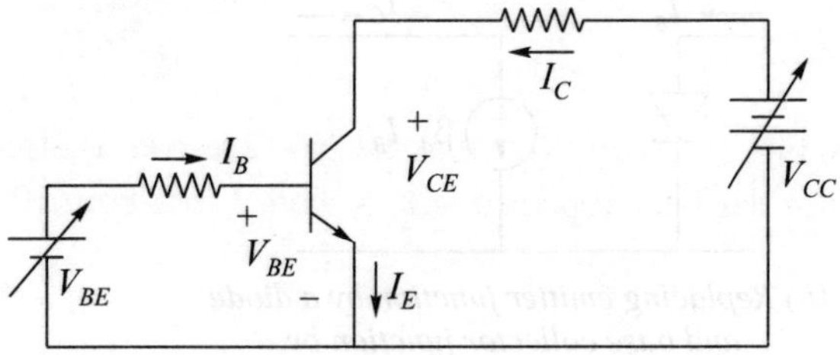

(*a*) *Transistor in Common Emitter (CE) configuration*

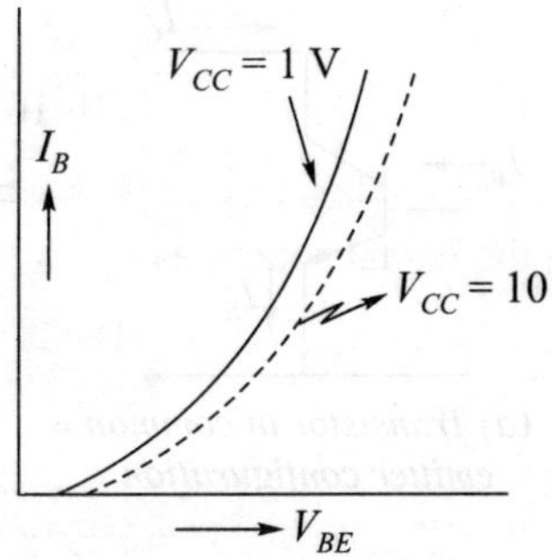

(*b*) *Input characteristic of transistor in CE mode*

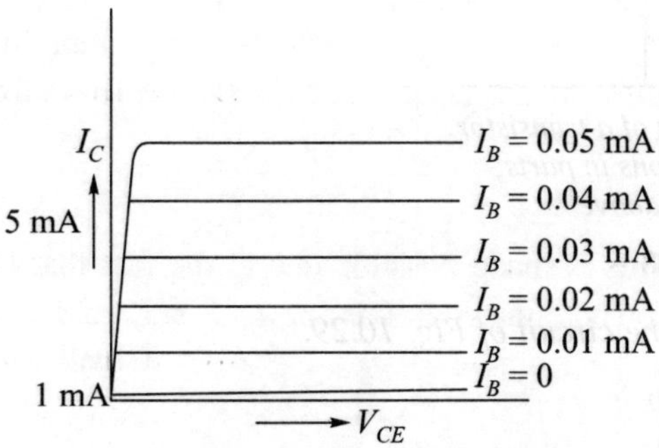

(*c*) *Output characteristic in CE mode*

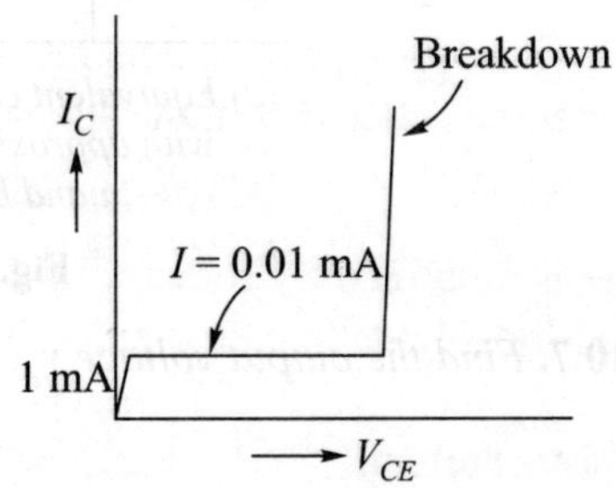

(*d*) *Variation of I_C vs V_{CE} characteristic*

Fig. 10.27

Thus we may write

$$\frac{I_C}{I_B} = \beta_{dc}$$

or $$I_C = \beta_{dc} I_B \qquad ...(10.19)$$

In Fig. 10.27(*c*) we may, therefore, label the *y*-axis as $\beta_{dc} I_B$ instead of I_C. $\beta_{dc} I_B$ is the dc current gain.

From the above discussion it is clear that the base emitter junction may be replaced by a forward biased diode and the base collector junction by a constant current source, $\beta_{dc} I_B$, as shown in Fig. 10.28.

Turning back to the small signal ac equivalent circuit, the diode modelling the base emitter junction may be replaced by r_{ac} (Eqn. 10.4) where,

$$r_{ac} = \frac{0.025}{I_B}$$

$$= \frac{0.025}{I_C}\beta_{dc} = \frac{0.025}{I_E}\beta_{dc}$$

$$= \beta_{dc} r'_e \qquad ...(10.20)$$

CHAPTER 10

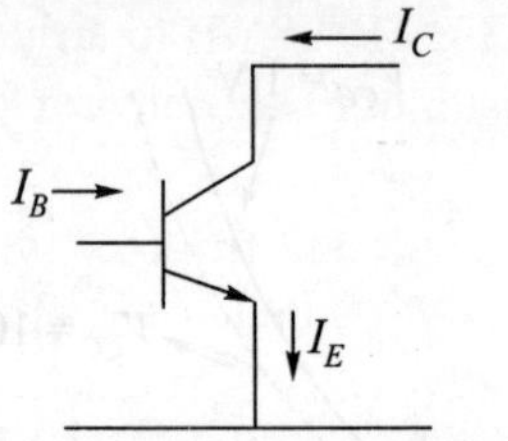

(a) *Transistor in common emitter configuration*

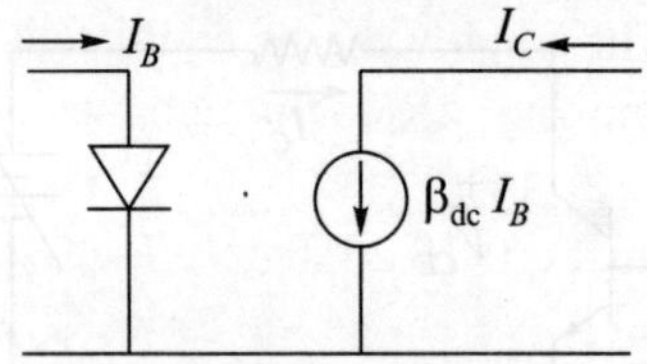

(b) *Replacing emitter junction by a diode and base collector junction by a constant current source*

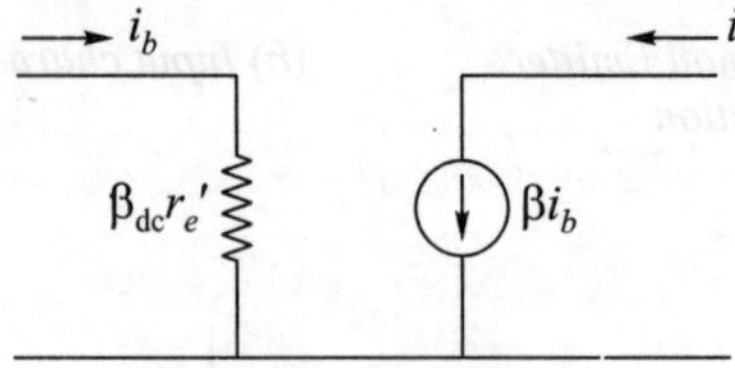

(c) *Equivalent circuit of a transistor with approximations in parts a and band above*

Fig. 10.28

Example 10.7. *Find the output voltage v_o for the circuit of Fig. 10.29.*

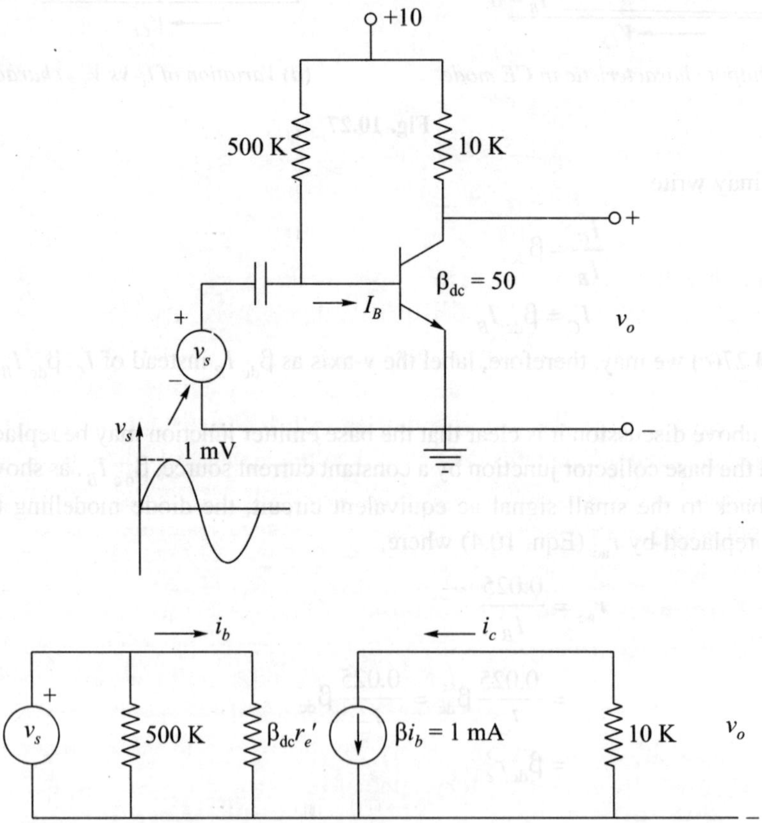

Fig. 10.29

Solution. We will employ the ac equivalent circuit of Fig. 10.28 (*b*) to arrive at the solution. Once i_b is found, i_c is known. i_c flows through the collector resistor of 10 kΩ and provides the output. In order to find i_b we need to find r'_e and β_{dc}.

r'_e is found from Eqn. 10.20. The bias base current I_B is found from knowledge of the bias voltage V_{BB} (+10V) and by assuming the forward biased base emitter diode to be ideal.

$$I_B = \frac{10}{500 \text{ k}\Omega} = 20 \ \mu\text{A}$$

Now,

$$I_C = \beta_{dc} I_B$$
$$= 50 \ (20 \ \mu\text{A})$$
$$= 1 \text{ mA} = I_E$$

and

$$r'_e = \frac{0.025}{10^{-3}} = 25 \ \Omega$$

so that

$$r_{ac} = \beta_{dc} r'_e$$
$$\cong 50 \ (25) = 1250 \ \Omega$$

Application of the ac input voltage causes an ac base current with maximum value $\frac{v_s}{r_{ac}}$ *i.e.*,

$i_b = \frac{10^{-3}}{1250} = 0.8 \ \mu\text{A}$. Note that the base current now varies between the limits of 20.8 and 19.2 μA.

Considering the ac component only, since $i_c = \beta i_b$,

$$i_c = 0.50(0.8)$$

Note that in the above step we should have used β instead of β_{dc}.

$$i_c = 40 \ \mu\text{A}$$

The ac output voltage, across the 10 kΩ resistor is $(4.0 \cdot 10^{-6})\ (10^4)$ or 0.4 V, thus providing a voltage gain of 400.

Once again this is made possible by proper biasing of the transistor *i.e.*, the dc supply establishes a certain I_B and I_C. The operating point, on the I_B versus I_C characteristic, is such that a large β results. In other words, the slope is large and corresponding to a small change in the value of I_B, a large change in I_C results. When the small ac signal is applied at the input it causes variations in base current which appear as large variations in collector current. This current flows through the collector resistor and provides the output voltage. Note that, once again, we are considering small signals which justifies the use of β, the small signal amplification factor.

10.23.3 The Common Collector Circuit

The circuit diagram of this configuration is shown in Fig. 10.30 (*a*); the ac equivalent circuit appears in Fig. 10.30 (*b*) which is similar to that of the common emitter configuration. Once again, the base emitter junction may be modelled as a forward biased diode and the base collector junction by a constant current source. Figure 10.30 (*a*) shows the necessary voltage supplies to ensure proper bias *i.e.*, operating condition. Proper bias results in a satisfactory value of β.

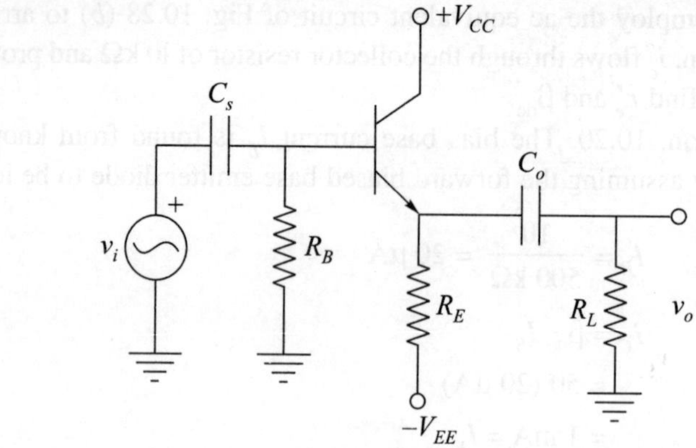

(a) *Transistor in common collector (CC) configuration*

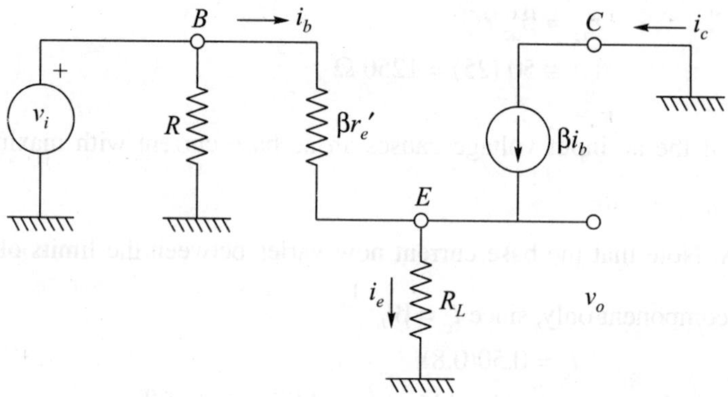

(b) *AC equivalent circuit*

Fig. 10.30

Referring to the ac equivalent circuit (the capacitors are replaced by short circuits at the signal frequency under consideration).

$v_o = i_e r_L$ where r_L is the parallel combination of R_E and R_L.

Since $$i_e \cong i_c$$

$$v_o \cong i_c r_L$$

$$= \beta i_B r_L$$

By applying of KVL in the input loop,

$$v_i = i_B \beta r_e' + i_e r_L$$

$$\cong i_B \beta r_e' + i_B \beta r_L$$

and $$v_i = \beta i_B (r_e' + r_L) \quad ...(10.21)$$

The voltage gain is $\dfrac{v_o}{v_i} \cong \dfrac{\beta i_B r_L}{\beta i_B (r_e' + r_L)}$

$$= \frac{r_L}{r_e' + r_L} \qquad ...(10.22)$$

Since $\dfrac{r_e'}{r_L} << 1$, the gain

$$\frac{v_o}{v_i} \cong 1 \qquad ...(10.23)$$

The input resistance r_{in} is $\dfrac{v_i}{i_B}$

The definition is valid at the base of the transistor. From Eqn. 10.21,

$$r_{in} = \beta\,(r_e' + r_L) = \beta\, r_L \qquad ...(10.24)$$

because $r_e' << r_L$.

Since β is large the input resistance is high. It can be shown that the output resistance of this configuration is $= r_e'$ and is therefore low.

This amplifier is therefore suited to function as a buffer between a source with high internal resistance and low resistance load. Connection of the load directly to the source is not recommended as the output voltage will be vastly decreased.

Example 10.8. *For the circuit of Fig. 10.31, find (a) the voltage gain (b) the input resistance looking into the base and (c) the input resistance of the circuit at the point of connection of the input signal. Assume β = 50.*

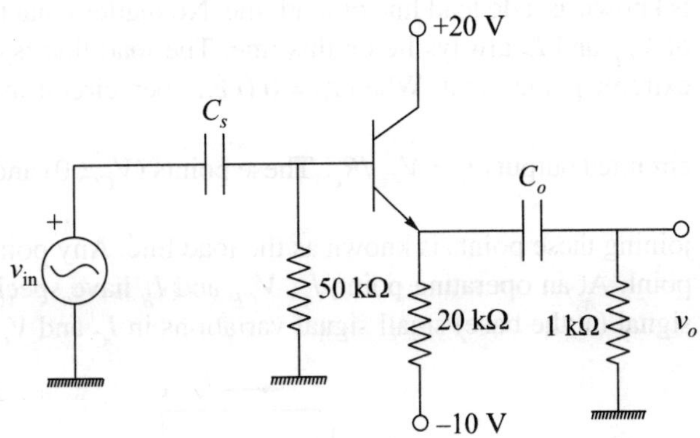

Fig. 10.31

Solution.

(*a*) In order to find the gain we need r_e'. To determine r_e' we need to find I_E. From the circuit diagram,

$$I_E = \frac{10}{20 \cdot 10^3} = 0.5 \text{ mA}$$

and
$$r_e' = \frac{0.025}{5 \cdot 10^{-4}} = 50 \text{ ohms}$$

The effective load resistor, considering the capacitor to be a short circuit, is the parallel combination of the 20 kΩ and 1 kΩ resistors, *i.e.*, r_L = 20 kΩ//1 kΩ = 952 Ω.

The voltage gain, from Eqn. 10.22, is

$$= \frac{1}{1+\frac{50}{952}} = 0.95$$

(*b*) The input resistance, looking into the base, is

$$= \beta\,(r'_e + r_L)$$
$$= 50\,(0.5 + 0.952)$$
$$= 50.1 \text{ k}\Omega$$

(*c*) The required input resistance is the parallel combination of the value found in part (*b*) and the 50 kΩ resistor.

i.e., 50 kΩ//50.1 kΩ

$$= 25.02 \text{ k}\Omega.$$

10.24 LOAD LINE

The common emitter circuit and its output characteristics are shown in Fig. 10.32. By application of KVL to loop AXYA one obtains that

$$V_{CC} = I_C R_C + V_{CE}$$

or
$$V_{CE} = V_{CC} - I_C R_C \qquad \text{...(10.25)}$$

This is the equation of a straight line. When drawn on the I_C versus V_{CE} output characteristics, it is known as a dc load line or load line. No matter what the value of R_C may be, the corresponding values of V_{CE} and I_C always lie on this line. The load line is easily drawn by locating the coordinates of two extreme points on it. When $I_C = 0$ (*i.e.*, open circuit in loop AXYA), $V_{CE} = V_{CC}$; if $V_{CE} = 0$ (*i.e.*, short circuited output) $I_C = V_{CC}/R_C$. These points (V_{CC}, 0) and $\left(0, \frac{V_{CC}}{R_C}\right)$ are marked in Fig. 10.32(*b*). The line joining these points is known as the load line. Any point on the load line is known as an operating or *Q* point. At an operating point, I_C, V_{CE} and I_B have specific values. Due to the application of a small ac signal (at the base) small signal variations in I_C and V_{CE} take place about the operating point.

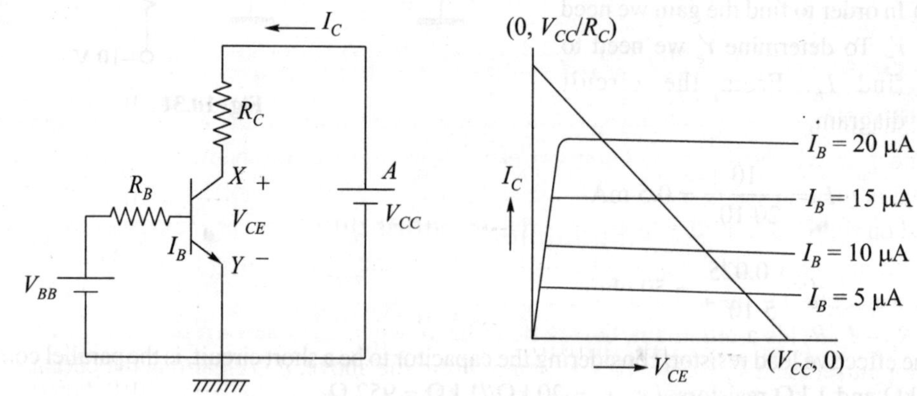

(a) Transistor in common emitter configuration (b) Output characteristics and load line

Fig. 10.32

Example 10.9. *Consider the circuit of Fig. 10.33. Draw the load line and find the operating point corresponding to a base current of 30 μA. Assume β_{dc} = 30.*

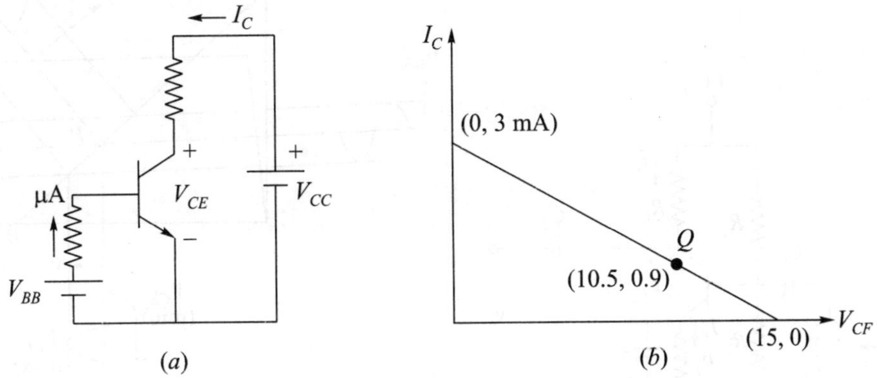

Fig. 10.33

Solution.

From $V_{CC} = I_C R_C + V_{CE}$

When $V_{CE} = 0$, $I_C = V_{CC}/R_C = 15/5\ \text{k}\Omega = 3$ mA

When $I_C = 0$, $V_{CE} = 15$ V

These two points enable one to draw the load line. To determine the operating point, the collector current should be found corresponding to a base current of 30 μA.

Since $I_C = \beta_{dc}\, I_B$,

$$I_C = 30 \cdot 30$$

$$= 900\ \mu\text{A or } 0.9\ \text{mA}$$

Since $V_{CE} = V_{CC} - I_C R_C$, we obtain

$$V_{CE} = 15 - (0.9 \cdot 10^{-3})\,(5 \cdot 10^{-3})$$

$$= 15 - 4.5 = 10.5\ \text{V}$$

The operating point (V_{CE}, I_C) is therefore (10.5 V, 0.9 mA). This corresponds to a base current of 30 μA.

10.25 GRAPHICAL AC ANALYSES USING THE LOAD LINE

Consider the common emitter circuit and its characteristics shown in Fig. 10.34. As pointed out, once the load line is drawn, the operating point, corresponding to a base current, may be determined. Suppose an ac signal is input at the base, which causes a base current variation of ±5 μA. These variations are superposed on the 10 μA of dc which flows due to the bias conditions. The corresponding variation in collector current may be obtained graphically as shown in the figure. It may be noted that when the base current is a maximum, the collector current is also a maximum. Therefore V_{CE} which is equal to $[V_{CC} - I_C R_C - I_C R_E]$ is a minimum. On the other hand, when the base current is at its maximum, so is the collector current and V_{CE} is now a maximum. From the above, it is clear that the output is in phase opposition to the input (*i.e.*, 180° phase shift).

CHAPTER 10

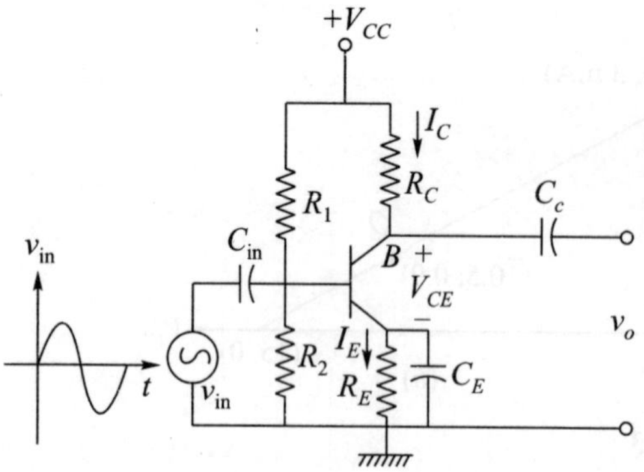

(*a*) *Transistor in CE configuration*

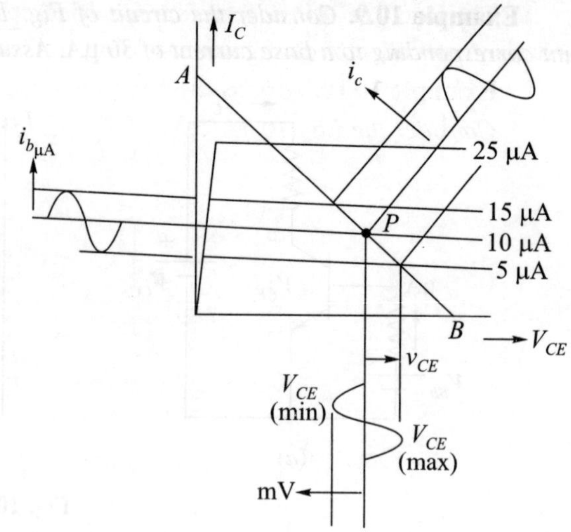

(*b*) *Graphical ac analysis using load line*

Fig. 10.34

Also, as point out earlier, small changes in the signal value at the base cause large changes in the output voltage value. This amplification property arises solely due to the characteristics of the biased transistor.

The choice of the operating point on the load line can affect the shape of the output signal. Suppose, the operating point is shifted to point *B* [Fig. 10.34 (*b*)]. It is easily seen that the bottom half of the output signal gets clipped. Likewise, if the operating point coincides with *A*, the top half of the output signal will be clipped. In order to avoid signal distortion, the location of the operating point should be fixed appropriately by proper choice of the values of resistors, R_1, R_2 and R_E *i.e.*, proper biasing.

The amplifier of Fig. 10.34 (*a*) is known as a *RC* coupled amplifier because resistors and capacitors are used to couple the signal to the amplifier and the output to the load. The input capacitor C_{in} is used to isolate the input ac signal from the dc bias voltage. C_{in} is 10 μF. C_E(≈100 μF) is used to provide a low reactance path to ac signals. In its absence, the ac signal current flows through R_E and produces a voltage drop which subtracts from the output and therefore reduces amplification.

C_C (≈10 μF) couples the output of the amplifier to the next stage or load. C_C isolates dc signals in one stage from the next while allowing coupling of ac signals.

In order to obtain the load line we apply KVL to the loop comprising of V_{CC}, R_C, V_{CE} and R_E, and obtain

$$V_{CE} = V_{CC} - I_C(R_C) - I_E R_E$$

$$\cong V_{CC} - I_C(R_C + R_E)$$

Since $\quad I_C \cong I_E.$

When $\quad V_{CE} = 0, I_C = \dfrac{V_{CC}}{R_C + R_E}$

and when $\quad I_C = 0, V_{CE} = V_{CC}$

The load line, *AB*, is therefore specified. It is possible to draw load lines for the common base and common collector configurations using similar techniques.

Example 10.10. *Various aspects mentioned above are brought out from the example below. Consider the Fig. 10.34 (c).*

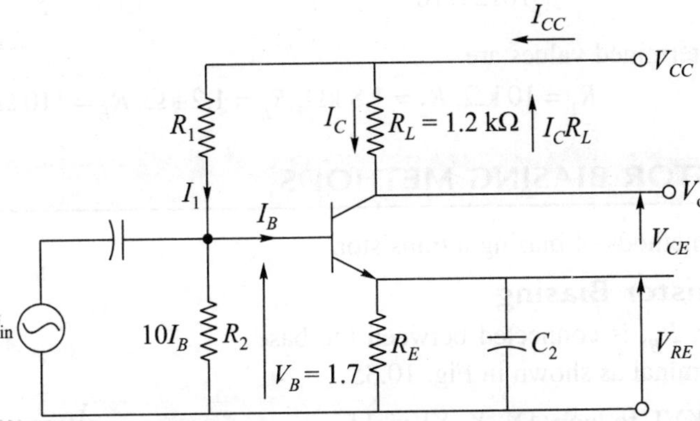

Fig. 10.34 (*c*) *Common emitter circuit*

Solution. From the Fig. 10.34 (*a*) and (*b*) we have roled that the signal amplification depends on the operators point *P*. The best operating point is as close to the centre position of the load line.

From Fig. 10.34 (*c*), we role (by Kirchoff's law)

$$V_B = V_{CC} \cdot \frac{R_2}{R_1 + R_2}$$

Also for $R_L = 1.2$ kΩ

$$I_C = \frac{V_{CC} - V_{BE}}{R_L} = \frac{12 - 1}{1200} = 9.2 \text{ mA}$$

$$I_B = \frac{I_C}{\beta} = \frac{9.2}{100} = 92 \text{ mA}$$

As such, R_1 and R_2 are chosen to give a base current of 92 mA. Current flowing through the potential divider circuit has to be large compared to the actual base current I_B. Thus,

$$10R_2 I_B = V_{BE} + V_{RE} \quad \text{and} \quad R_2 = 1.8 \text{ k}\Omega$$

It is also assumed that the current flow through R_2 is 10 times the current flow through the base at 1012 μA (≃1 mA).

At junction *A*, without input signal at V_{in}.

$$I_1 = I_B + 10I_B$$

and

$$I_1 R_1 = V_{CC} - (V_{RE} + V_{BE})$$

and thus

$$R_1 = \frac{V_{CC} - (V_{RE} + V_{BE})}{I_1}$$

Voltage across $R_1 = V_{CC} - 1.7$ V

(V_{RE} + 0.7 for silicon transition)

$$= \frac{10 \cdot 3}{1012 \times 10^{-6}} = \mathbf{10.2\ k\Omega}$$

As such, the determined values are

$$R_1 = 10\ \text{k}\Omega,\ R_2 = 1.8\ \text{k}\Omega,\ R_L = 1.2\ \text{k}\Omega,\ R_E = 110\ \Omega.$$

10.26 TRANSISTOR BIASING METHODS

We will discuss three methods of biasing a transistor.

10.26.1 Base Resistor Biasing

A high valued resistor, R_B, is connected between the base and the V_{CC} battery terminal as shown in Fig. 10.35.

Application of KVL to loop $AX_1\ X_2\ YA$ yields

$$V_{CC} = I_B R_B + V_{BE} \quad \text{...(10.26)}$$

where V_{BE} is the internal base to emitter voltage drop. It is the forward volt drop associated with the base to emitter diode. From Eqn. 10.26,

$$R_B = \frac{V_{CC} - V_{BE}}{I_B} \quad \text{...(10.27)}$$

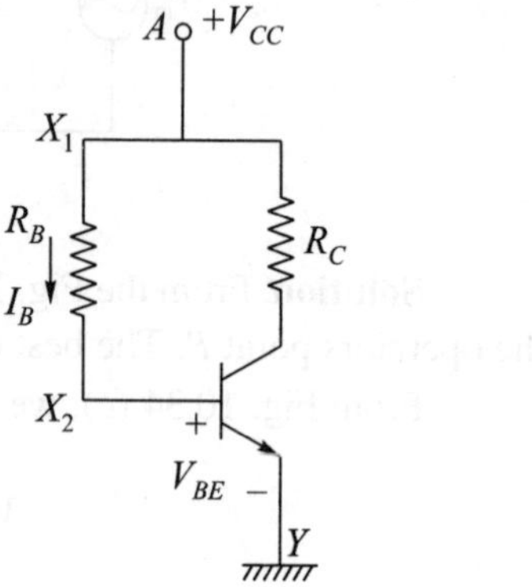

Fig. 10.35 *Base resistor biasing*

and the collector current I_C is given by

$$I_C = I_B \beta_{dc} \quad \text{...(10.28)}$$

If V_{CC} and I_B are known, R_B is found. The value of V_{BE} may be obtained from the manufacturer's data sheets.

In fact $V_{BE} << V_{CC}$ ...(10.29)

Therefore Eqn. 10.27 reduces to

$$R_B = \frac{V_{CC}}{I_B} \quad \text{...(10.30)}$$

The advantage of this method of biasing is that only a single resistor, R_B, is required. The disadvantage is that should the transistor be replaced with another with a different value of β_{dc}, the bias conditions and therefore the operating point changes.

Example 10.11. *Determine the operating point for the circuit of Fig. 10.36. If β_{dc} changes to a value of 50, find the new operating point.*

Solution. Using Eqn. 10.26, I_B will be determined. I_C is then obtained from Eqn. 10.28 and V_{CE} from Eqn. 10.25. Thus the operating point (V_{CE}, I_C) is determined. The solution proceeds as follows

$$I_B = \frac{V_{CC} - V_{BE}}{R_B}$$

$$\cong \frac{V_{CC}}{R_B} = 10/500 \text{ k}\Omega$$

$$= 20 \ \mu\text{A}$$

Now, $\quad I_C = \beta_{dc} I_B$

$$= 100 \cdot 20 \cdot 10^{-6} = 2 \text{ mA}$$

Since $\quad V_{CE} = V_C C - I_C R_C$

$$= 10 - 2 \cdot 10^{-3} \cdot 2 \cdot 10^3 = 6 \text{ V}$$

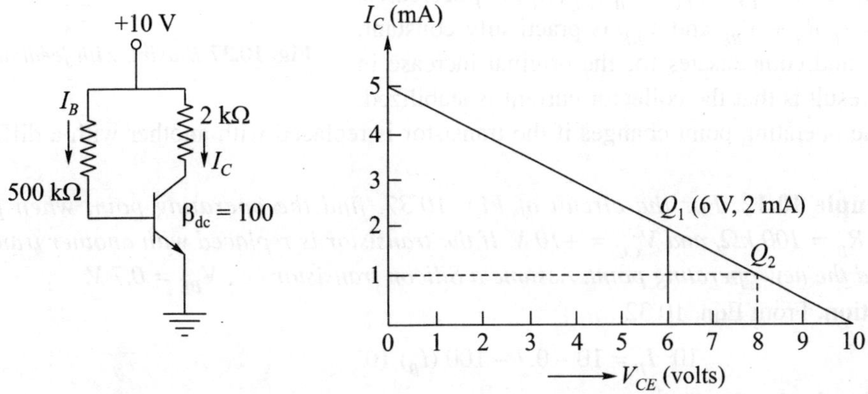

(a) *Circuit for Ex. 10.11* (b) *Q-point for problem in Ex. 10.11*

Fig. 10.36

The operating point bears the coordinates (6 V, 2 mA). This is identified by the point Q_1, in Fig. 10.38 (*b*). Q_1 is situated on the load line which joins the points (0.5 mA) and (10 V, 0) situated on the two axes.

When β_{dc} changes to a value of 50, the load line is not affected but the position of the operating point changes.

Following similar calculations it may be found that the coordinates of the new operating point are (8 V, 1 mA). This point is identified by Q_2 in the figure.

10.26.2 Biasing with Feedback Resistor

This simple method is illustrated in Fig. 10.37. A resistor R_B is connected between the collector terminal and the base.

Application of KVL in loop AXTYA yields

$$V_{CC} - I_C R_C - I_B R_C - I_B R_B - V_{BE} = 0$$

Rearranging,

$$R_B = \frac{V_{CC} - C_{BE} - I_C R_C - I_B R_C}{I_B}$$

Since $\quad I_C = \beta_{dc} I_B,$

$$R_B = \frac{V_{CC} - V_{BE} - (\beta_{dc} + 1)I_B R_C}{I_B} \quad ...(10.31)$$

Since $\beta_{dc} >> 1$,

$$R_B = \frac{V_{CC} - V_{BE} - \beta_{dc} I_B R_C}{I_B} \quad ...(10.32)$$

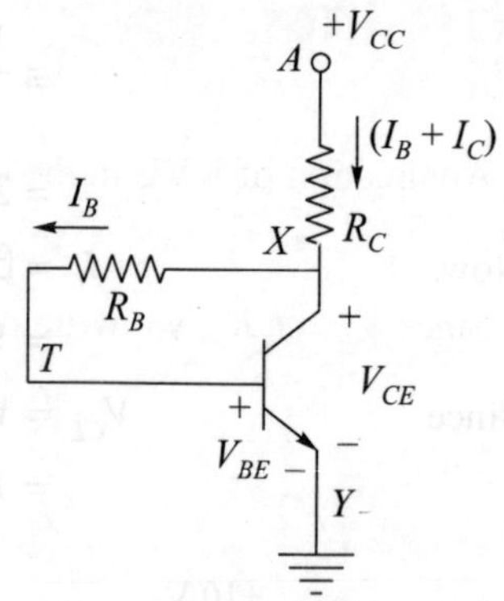

Fig. 10.37 *Biasing with feedback resistor*

As the transistor temperature increases, β_{dc} increases and so does I_C. Since $V_{CE} = V_{CC} - (I_B + I_C) R_C$, V_{CE} decreases. Since $V_{CE} = I_B R_B + V_{BE}$ and V_{BE} is practically constant, I_B decreases and compensates for the original increase in I_C. The net result is that the collector current is stabilized. However, the operating point changes if the transistor is replaced with another with a different value of β_{dc}.

Example 10.12. *For the circuit of Fig. 10.37, find the operating point when $\beta_{dc} = 100$, $R_C = 1\ k\Omega$, $R_B = 100\ k\Omega$, and $V_{CC} = +10\ V$. If the transistor is replaced with another transistor with $\beta_{dc} = 50$, find the new operating point. Assume a Silicon transistor i.e., $V_{BE} = 0.7\ V$.*

Solution. From Eqn. 10.32

$$10^5 I_B = 10 - 0.7 - 100\ (I_B)\ 10^3$$

Solving for I_B, one obtains

$$I_B = 0.046 \text{ mA}$$

The collector current $I_C = \beta_{dc} I_B = 4.6$ mA

Now,

$$V_{CE} = V_{CC} - (I_B + I_C)R_C$$

$$\cong V_{CC} - I_C R_C$$

$$= 10 - 4.6 \times 10^{-3}.10^3 = 5.4 \text{ V.}$$

The coordinates of the operating point are

(5.4 V, 4.6 mA)

If $\beta_{dc} = 50$, following the above procedure, it can be shown that the coordinates of the new operating point are (6.9 V, 3.1 mA). Note that both these points lie on the load line which joins the points (10 V, 0 mA) and (0 V, 10 mA).

10.26.3 Voltage Divider Bias Network

Two resistors R_1 and R_2, Fig. 10.38, are connected to form a voltage divider. The voltage across R_2 is connected to the base of the transistor.

If the base current, I_B, is small compared to I_1, the current flowing through R_1 is the same as that flowing through R_2. Thus,

$$I_1 = \frac{V_{CC}}{R_1 + R_2} \quad ...(10.33)$$

and the voltage applied to the base

$$V_B = I_1 R_2 = \frac{V_{CC} R_2}{R_1 + R_2} \qquad ...(10.34)$$

Application of KVL in the bottom loop yields

$$V_B = V_{BE} + V_E$$

Since $V_E = I_E R_E$, we write that

$$V_B = V_{BE} + I_E R_E$$

or
$$I_E = \frac{V_B - V_{BE}}{R_E} \qquad ...(10.35)$$

Since $I_C \cong I_E$

$$I_C \cong \frac{V_B - V_{BE}}{R_E} \qquad ...(10.36)$$

also, application of KVL yields

$$V_{CC} = I_C R_C + V_{CE} + I_E R_E$$
$$\cong I_C R_C + V_{CE} + I_C R_E$$
$$= I_C (R_C + R_E) + V_{CE}$$

Therefore
$$V_{CE} = V_{CC} - I_C (R_C + R_E) \qquad ...(10.37)$$

It is worth noting that β_{dc} does not enter into any of the above expressions. The biasing and the resulting operating point is independent of the value of β_{dc}. This is a desirable feature and consequently this method is widely used.

Example 10.13. *In the circuit of Fig. 10.38, $R_C = 1\ k\Omega$, $R_E = 2\ k\Omega$, $R_1 = 10\ k\Omega$, $R_2 = 5\ k\Omega$ and $V_{CC} = 10$ V. Find the coordinates of the extremities of the load line and the Q point. Assume Silicon transistor.*

Solution. From Eqn. 10.37, when $I_C = 0$

$$V_{CE} = V_{CC} = 10 \text{ V}$$

and when $V_{CE} = 0$,

$$I_C = \frac{V_{CC}}{R_E + R_C} = \frac{10}{3} \cdot 10^{-3} = 3.33 \text{ mA}$$

This enables us to locate the extreme points on the load line and the load line itself.

From Eqn. 10.34, $V_B = \frac{10}{3}$ V and from Eqn. 10.36,

$I_C = \dfrac{\frac{10}{3} - V_{BE}}{2 \cdot 10^3}$. Assuming $V_{BE} = 0.7$ V, (Silicon transistor),

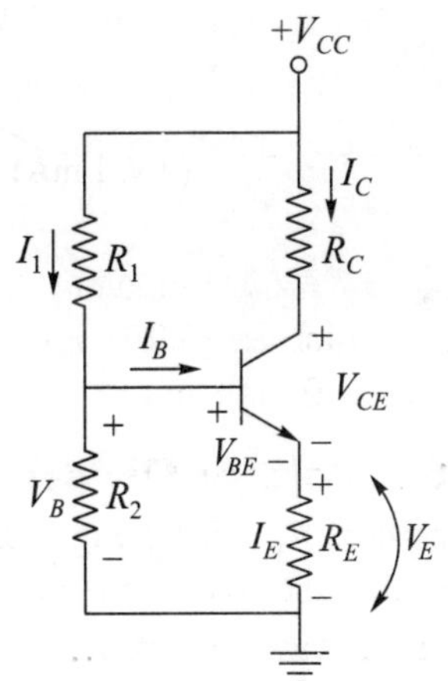

Fig. 10.38 *Voltage divider bias network*

$$I_C = 1.316 \text{ mA}$$
$$\cong I_E$$

and from Eqn. 10.37,

$$V_{CE} = 10 - 1.316 \cdot 10^{-3} (3 \cdot 10^3)$$
$$= 6.055 \text{ V}.$$

The operating point is (6.055 V, 1.316 mA).

10.27 THE TRANSISTOR SWITCH

In digital circuits, it is necessary to use switches so that the output level jumps from a low to a high value *i.e.* a zero to a one. The output level is 'one' when the switch is open and is 'zero' when the switch is closed. For example, with switch S closed in Fig. 10.39 (*a*), the output, tapped off node x is at ground potential. When switch S is opened, node x acquires the potential of V_{CC}. Instead of using a mechanical switch, which is slow and introduces contact problems, one uses an electrical switch which consists of a transistor operating in the common emitter configuration, Fig. 10.39 (*b*). The corresponding load line is drawn on the $I_C - V_{CE}$ characteristics in Fig. 10.39 (*c*).

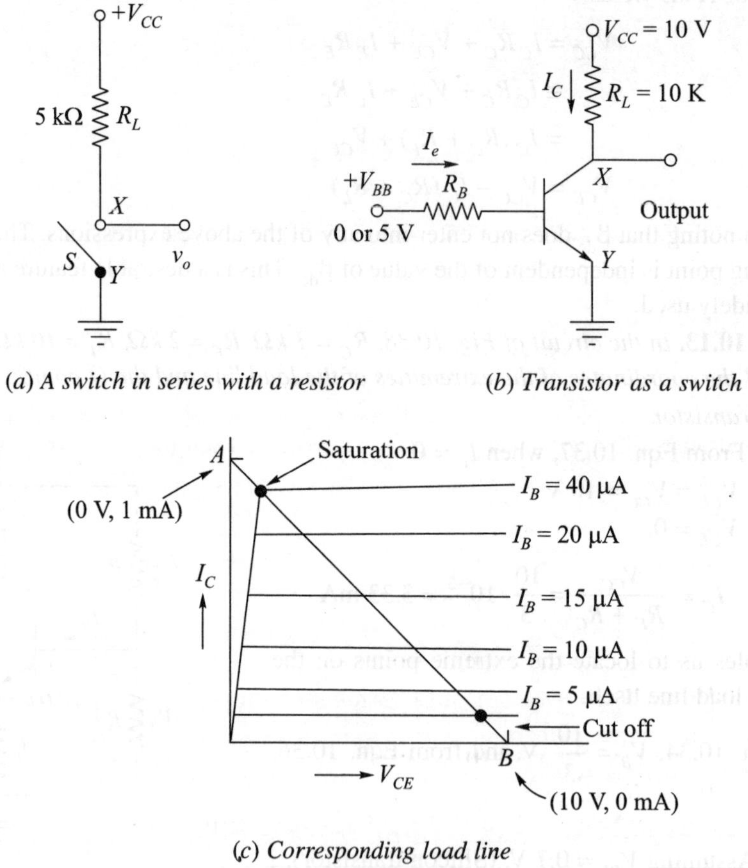

(*a*) *A switch in series with a resistor* (*b*) *Transistor as a switch*

(*c*) *Corresponding load line*

Fig. 10.39

Since the bias voltages and conditions are defined the position of the corresponding operating point is fixed. If the base voltage, V_{BB}, is increased, I_B increases; I_C increases while V_{CE} decreases; the operating point moves up along the load line. The load line intersects the I_C axis at the 1 mA point. This is the transistor saturation point as I_C is a maximum. Ideally $V_{CE} = 0$ here. In reality V_{CE} is very small and $I_{C(\text{sat})}$ is slightly less than 1 mA. When operated in this manner, at the saturation point, $V_{CE} \approx 0$ and the output tapped off node *x* in Fig. 10.39 (*b*) is therefore zero. We may therefore consider the transistor as a closed switch between the collector and emitter terminals, *i.e.*, nodes *X* and *Y* in Fig. 10.39. The converse happens if the base voltage is decreased. Now I_B and I_C decrease while V_{CE} increases and the operating point moves down along the load line. The load line intersects the V_{CE} axis at 10 V [Fig. 10.39 (*c*)]. This is known as the transistor cut off point because both I_C and I_B are ideally zero here. In reality a small I_C does flow at cut off and $V_{CE} \approx 10$ V. When operated at the cut off point, $V_{CE} \approx 10$ V $= V_{CC}$ and $I_C \approx 0$. We may therefore consider the transistor as an open switch between the collector and emitter terminals. The transistor therefore behaves like a switch between its collector and emitter terminals. The condition of this switch (open or closed) depends on the magnitude of the base current I_B. If $V_{BB} = 0$, $I_B = 0$, the transistor operating point is moved to cut off and the switch is open. In order to enable the switch to close we must ensure that the operating point moves over to the saturation point by allowing sufficient base current to flow. The required base current to switch the transistor "ON" may be found as follows for the circuit of Fig. 10.39 (*b*).

Since $$I_{C(\text{sat})} = \frac{V_{CC}}{R_L}$$

$= 1$ mA, the corresponding base current,

$$I_B = \frac{I_{C(\text{sat})}}{\beta_{dc}} = \frac{10^{-3}}{50} = 0.02 \text{ mA}$$

Assuming a β_{dc} of 50.

We have to choose R_B so that

$$I_B = \frac{V_{BB} - V_{BE}}{R_B} \geq 0.02 \text{ mA}$$

For Silicon transistors, the forward drop, V_{BE} is ≈ 0.7 V. Therefore,

$$\frac{V_{BB} - 0.7}{R_B} \geq 0.02 \text{ mA}$$

or $$R_B \leq \left(\frac{V_{BB} - 0.7}{2 \cdot 10^{-5}}\right) \text{ ohms} \qquad ...(10.38)$$

Since $V_{BB} = 5$ V, $R_B \leq 215$ kΩ

It is clear that when $V_{BB} = 0$ the output V_{CE} is high (*i.e.*, 10 V). When V_{BB} is high (5 V), the output V_{CE} is low (≈ 0 V). The output is therefore the inverted version of the input. The transistor switch is therefore also known as an *inverter*.

10.28 COMPARISON OF AMPLIFIER CONFIGURATIONS

Table 10.1 summarizes the features of the three configurations. Generally speaking, it is desirable for an amplifier to exhibit high input resistance (impedance) and low output resistance. Also is must be borne in mind that amplification (current, voltage, or power) is achieved at the expense of the power supplies. The law of conservation of energy is not violated.

Table 10.1: Comparison of the three amplifier configurations

Feature	*Common base*	*Common emitter*	*Common collector*
Voltage gain	≈10	≈500	<1
Current gain	<1	≈300	≈100
Power gain	High	Very High	High
Input impedance	Low (≈100 Ω)	Higher (≈10^3 Ω)	Very High (≈5·10^5 Ω)
Output impedance	Very High (≈5·10^5 Ω)	High (≈5.10^4 Ω)	Low (≈10^3 Ω)

10.29 THE UNIJUNCTION TRANSISTOR

The unijunction transistor, UJT, has only one *pn* junction. It comprises of one emitter and two bases. The emitter which is a *p* type material is doped heavily and contains a large number of holes; the base region is only slightly doped. The resistance between the two bases is of the order of 5–10 kΩ. In Fig. 10.40, R_1 and R_2, are the internal resistances between the emitter and base 1 and the emitter and base 2 respectively. The emitter and the *n* type base form a diode. When the UJT is biased, R_1 and R_2 form a voltage divider and the voltage across R_1 is

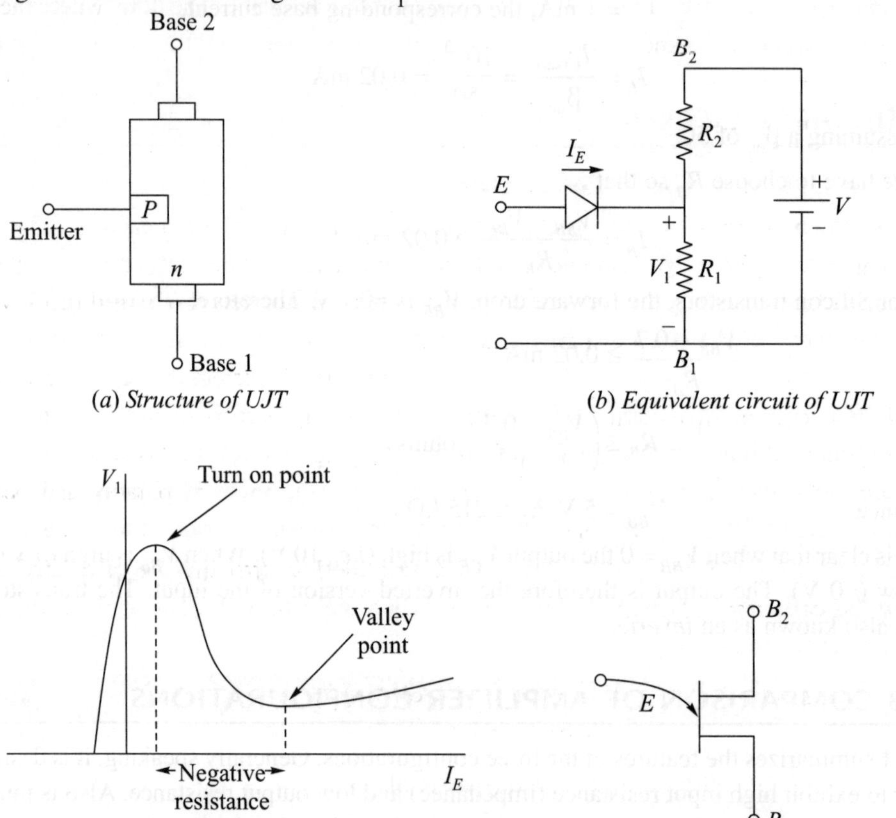

(*a*) *Structure of UJT* (*b*) *Equivalent circuit of UJT* (*c*) *VI characteristic of UJT* (*d*) *Symbol of UJT*

Fig. 10.40

$$V_1 = \frac{VR_1}{R_1 + R_2} = \frac{R_1 V}{R_{BB}} \quad ...(10.39)$$

where $R_{BB} = R_1 R_2$ is the resistance between the two bases. The ratio $\frac{R_1}{R_{BB}}$ is known as η, the *intrinsic stand off ratio* and varies from 0.5 to 0.8. Equation 10.39 may be written as

$$V_1 = \eta V \quad ...(10.40)$$

From Fig. 10.40 (*b*), it is clear that unless the input voltage at the emitter exceeds ηV, the emitter diode will be reverse biased. This assumes that the diode is ideal; otherwise the input voltage should exceed the sum of ηV and the forward volt drop of the diode. Once the junction is forward biased, initially, I_E increases with V_1. With increasing input voltage an enormous amount of holes are injected into the base 1 region of the UJT because of the heavily doped *p* type emitter. This increases the conductivity between the emitter and base 1 and R_1 is drastically reduced. Therefore V_1 decreases while I_E increases. This behaviour is opposite to that expected from consideration of Ohm's law. The region of the *V–I* characteristic where such behaviour is exhibited is known as a negative resistance region. V_1 reaches a minimum value and the voltage and current corresponding to this point are known as the *valley* voltage and current respectively. Beyond the valley point, the device saturates and V_1 does not increase by much as I_E increases, Figure 10.40 (*c*) shows the characteristic. The point where the negative resistance region commences is known as the *turn on* point. The symbol for UJT is shown in Fig. 10.40 (*d*).

10.30 UJT APPLICATIONS

10.30.1 The UJT Saw Tooth Generator

The circuit is shown in Fig. 10.41. When V_{CC} is applied, the capacitor C commences its charge up and its voltage begins to increase. No sooner the capacitor voltage reaches the turn on value, operation of the device takes place in the negative resistance region. The capacitor gets discharged quickly; the UJT turns off at the valley voltage point and the capacitor commences its charge up again. The operation of the circuit continues in cyclical fashion and a saw tooth output results across the capacitor. Resistors R_3 and R_2 limit base current flow during UJT operation. The rising portion of the capacitor voltage is actually an exponential function. It appears linear if the charging time constant is small. Also shown in Fig. 10.41 are the voltage pulses across R_2 and R_3. These are opposite in polarity and occur when current flows through the respective resistors *i.e.*, during the discharge period of the capacitor.

The time period and hence, frequency of the saw tooth output may be calculated as below. Assume that the capacitor C is initially uncharged. When the supply, V_{CC}, is applied, the capacitor voltage v_C rises exponentially to

$$v_C = V\,[1 - \exp(-t/R_1C)] \quad ...(10.41)$$

when $v_C = \eta V_{CC}$, the following equality holds.

$$\eta V_{CC} = V\,[1 - \exp(-t/R_1C)]$$

and $$T = R_1 C \log_e \frac{1}{(1-\eta)}$$

$$= 2.3\, R_1 C \log_{10} \frac{1}{1-\eta}$$

The frequency of oscillation, f is

$$f = \frac{1}{T} = \frac{1}{2.3\, R_1 C \log_{10} \frac{1}{(1-\eta)}} \quad ...(10.42)$$

The frequency of the oscillation is determined by the time taken for v_C to attain the value ηV_{CC} since the discharge occurs rapidly.

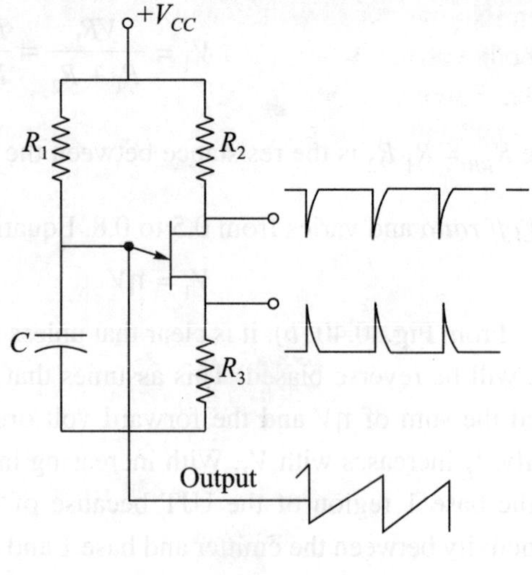

Fig. 10.41 *UJT as a saw tooth generator*

10.30.2 UJT Overvoltage Indicator

Figure 10.42 shows the circuit. If $v_{in} < \eta V$, the device and lamp L are both off. Once $v_{in} > \eta V$, the capacitor discharges rapidly through the lamp which lights thereby indicating the occurrence of an overvoltage.

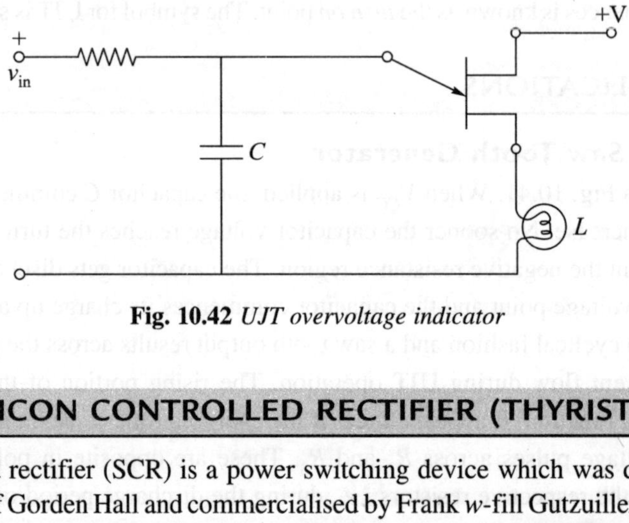

Fig. 10.42 *UJT overvoltage indicator*

10.31 THE SILICON CONTROLLED RECTIFIER (THYRISTOR)

The silicon controlled rectifier (SCR) is a power switching device which was developed during 1957 under the leadership of Gorden Hall and commercialised by Frank w-fill Gutzuiller. As the characteristics of this device are similar to that of a Thyratron, it is also known as a Thyristor. Essentially, the SCR operates like an electrical switch; the switch can be turned on by application of a suitable control signal. The SCR is capable of controlling the flow of large amounts of power at the expense of a small control power. Indeed, SCR is a general electric trade name for a thyristor.

10.31.1 Principle of Operation of a SCR

The SCR is a three terminal, four layer device and has an anode, a cathode and a gate as shown in Fig. 10.43 (*a*). The symbol used to represent a SCR is shown in Fig. 10.43 (*b*). With reference to Fig. 10.43 (*c*), when no gate voltage is applied, junction J_2 is reverse biased while junctions J_1 and J_3 are forward biased. The situation is similar to that which exists in an *npn* transistor with the base circuit open. No current flows through the load R_L and the SCR is said to be cut off. If the applied anode-cathode voltage is increased beyond a certain voltage, called the breakover voltage, junction J_2 breaks down. Following this, the SCR conducts heavily and current flow occurs through R_L. The SCR is said to be "ON" and this is possible because the remaining two junctions J_1 and J_3 are forward biased.

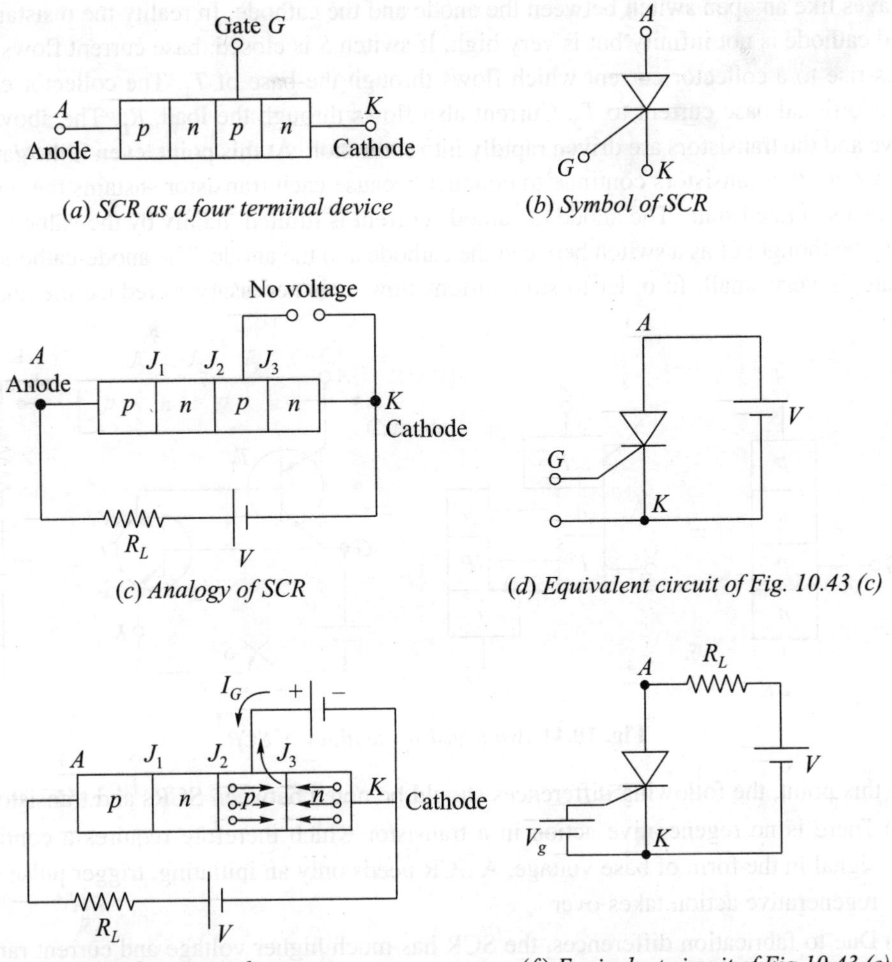

(a) *SCR as a four terminal device* (b) *Symbol of SCR*

(c) *Analogy of SCR* (d) *Equivalent circuit of Fig. 10.43 (c)*

(e) *Inducing anode current* (f) *Equivalent circuit of Fig.10.43 (e)*

Fig. 10.43

When the gate is made positive with respect to the cathode, as in Fig. 10.43 (*e*), junction J_3 is forward biased while J_2 is reverse biased. Movement of electrons and holes takes place across J_3 from the *n* to the *p* type material and from the *p* to the *n* type material. Electrons from junction J_3 are attracted towards J_2 and a gate current flows. Once gate current flows, the anode current increases; the increased current makes more electrons available at J_2. This process continues and in a short time the junction J_2 breaks down and the SCR goes into conduction. Once the SCR is "ON", the gate looses control. Even if the gate voltage is removed, the current flow through R_L does not decrease. In order to stop the flow of current the anode to cathode voltage should be reduced to zero.

Figures 10.43 (*d*) and (*f*) show the circuit equivalents of Figs. 10.43 (*c*) and (*e*) respectively.

10.31.2 Two Transistor Equivalent Circuit of a SCR

The SCR may be visualized as a combination of a *pnp* and an *npn* transistor as shown in Fig. 10.44. With the applied voltage V less than the breakover voltage and $V_g = 0$, *i.e.* switch S open, the bias voltage for transistor T_2 is absent. The current flow through R_L is, therefore, also absent. In this state the SCR behaves like an open switch between the anode and the cathode. In reality the resistance between anode and cathode is not infinity but is very high. If switch S is closed, base current flows through T_2. This gives rise to a collector current which flows through the base of T_1. The collector current of T_1 provides additional base current to T_2. Current also flows through the load, R_L. The above process is cumulative and the transistors are driven rapidly into saturation. At this point, even if the gate voltage is reduced to zero, the transistors continue to conduct because each transistor sustains the conduction of the order in a saturated state. The anode to cathode current is limited mainly by the value of R_L and the device may be thought of as a switch between the cathode and the anode. The anode-cathode resistance, in this state, is very small. In order to stop current flow, it is necessary to reduce the anode-cathode voltage to

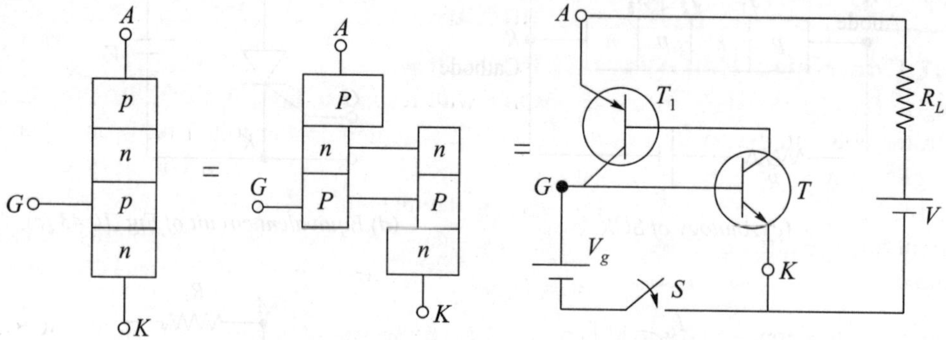

Fig. 10.44 *Two transistor analogy of SCR*

At this point, the following differences should be noted between SCRs and transistors,

(*i*) There is no regenerative action in a transistor which therefore requires a continuous gate signal in the form of base voltage. A SCR needs only an initiating, trigger pulse after which regenerative action takes over.

(*ii*) Due to fabrication differences, the SCR has much higher voltage and current ratings than a similarly sized transistor. In fact, SCRs rated at 10 kV, 500 A (5 MW power handling capacity) are available.

(*iii*) The transistor is usually required to operate in the active region (between cut off and saturation) whereas a SCR is used as a switching device. The power losses in a transistor are higher than those in a SCR.

10.31.3 SCR Volt Amp Characteristics

Figure 10.45 shows the variations of anode-cathode volt drop with anode current for various values of gate signal. With zero gate voltage, as the anode voltage is increased, a point is reached such as B in Fig. 10.45 when the junction J_2 [Fig. 10.43 (*c*)] breaks down. The SCR will turn on and the voltage across it is reduced to a low value (point C, Fig. 10.45). From this point onwards further current increases are accompanied by a small increase in the voltage.

In the presence of a gate voltage, the junction J_2 breaks down at a lower voltage as illustrated in Fig. 10.45. Thus, gate current controls the voltage at which the SCR turns on and behaves like a closed switch. Normally the SCR is operated only in the presence of gate voltage so that control of SCR 'turn ON' is retained.

If the voltage applied to the anode-cathode terminal is reversed and increased, breakdown results when the applied voltage equals the reverse breakdown voltage corresponding to point D in Fig. 10.45. The SCR now conducts in the reverse direction.

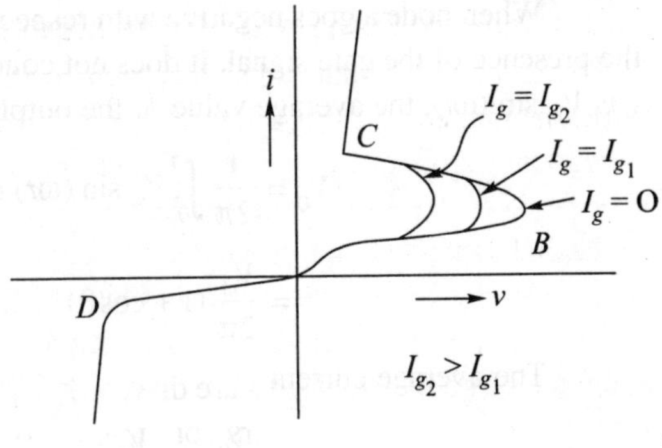

Fig. 10.45 *Volt-amp characteristic of SCR*

10.32 SCR APPLICATIONS

10.32.1 Controlled Half Wave SCR Rectifier

Referring to Fig. 10.46, when node *a* is positive with respect to node *b*, the SCR is forward biased. However, the point on the positive cycle at which it goes into conduction or turns on depends on the value of gate current. The greater the gate current, the lesser is the forward voltage at which the SCR can be turned on. This is accomplished by varying the magnitude of resistor *r*. Suppose that sufficient gate current flows to turn on the SCR when the instantaneous value of the applied voltage equals V_1. Let this value correspond to an angle $\omega t_1 = \theta$. Until $v = V_1$, the SCR is 'OFF'. The SCR turns 'ON' at $t_1 = \dfrac{\theta}{\omega}$ and supplies power to the load until the zero crossing of applied voltage *i.e.*, the SCR conducts during the time $\dfrac{\theta}{\omega} \le t \le \dfrac{\pi}{\omega}$. The angle θ, $0 \le \theta \le 180°$, is known as the *firing angle*.

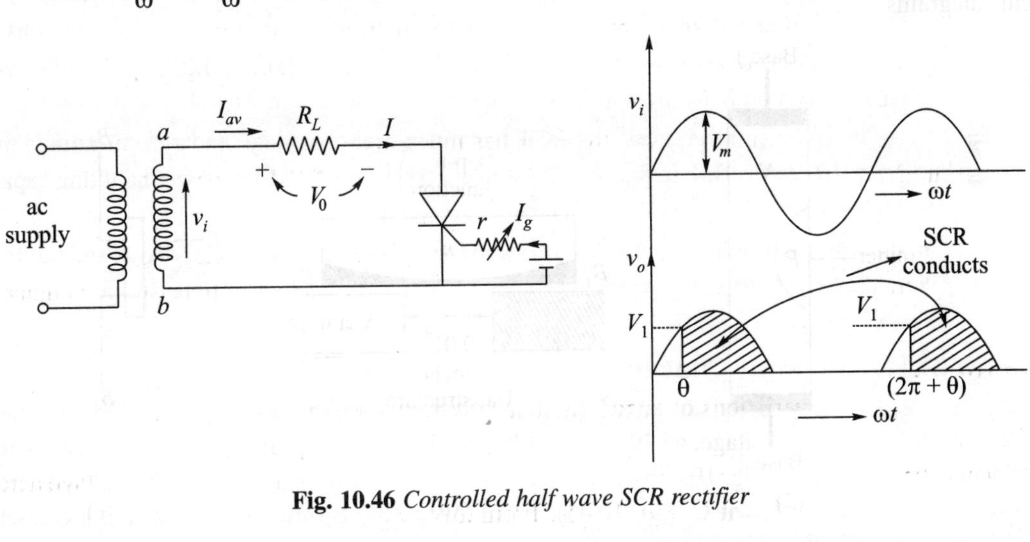

Fig. 10.46 *Controlled half wave SCR rectifier*

CHAPTER 10

When node a goes negative with respect to node b, the SCR is reverse biased. Therefore, even in the presence of the gate signal, it does not conduct. This process repeats itself. If the applied ac voltage v is $V_m \sin(\omega t)$, the average value of the output voltage, across R_L is

$$V_0 = \frac{1}{2\pi}\int_{\theta}^{\pi} V_m \sin(\omega t)\, d(\omega t)$$

$$= \frac{V_m}{2\pi}(1+\cos\theta) \qquad ...(10.43)$$

The average current

$$I_{av} = \frac{V_0}{R_L} = \frac{V_m}{2\pi R_L}(1+\cos\theta) \qquad ...(10.44)$$

Note that if $\theta = 0$, $I_{av} = \frac{V_m}{\pi R_L}$. This is the result we obtained for the half-wave rectifier, Eqn. 10.5.

If $\theta = \pi$, $\quad I_{av} = 0$

and if $\theta = \pi/2$, $\quad I_{av} = \frac{V_m}{2\pi R_L} \qquad ...(10.45)$

From Eqn. 10.43 and 10.45, it should be clear that the greater the magnitude of the firing angle, the lesser the value of the average current.

10.32.1.1 Triggering of SCRs

There are several methods of triggering SCRs. Some of them are discussed here.

(*a*) **Uni Junction Transistor for Triggering SCRs.** The basic structure of a unijunction transistor (UJT) is shown in Fig. 10.47 (*a*) and (*b*). It indicates that into the *N*-type semiconductor material, *P* type material has been diffused. Contacts are then made to the device as shown; these are referred to as the emitter, base 1 and base 2 respectively. Figure (*c*) shows the schematic symbol used to denote a UJT in circuit diagrams.

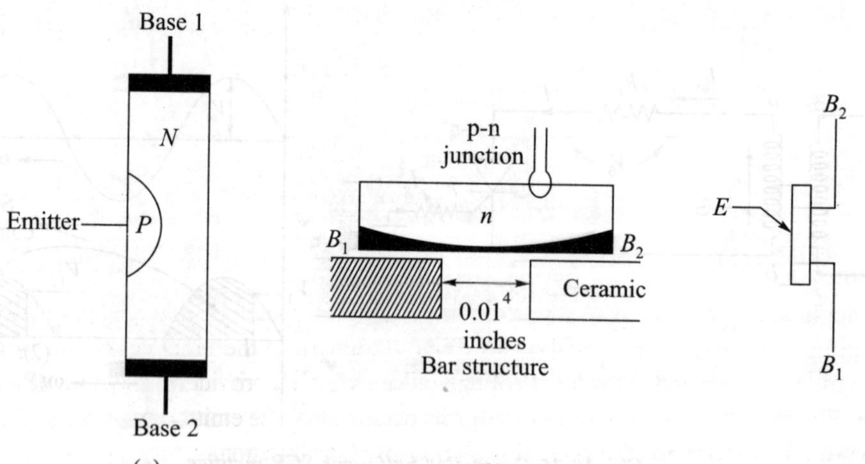

Fig. 10.47 *Unijunction transistor*

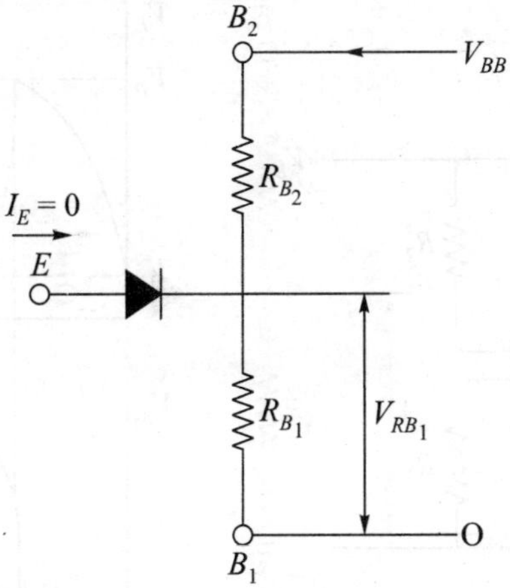

Fig. 10.48 *Equivalent circuit of unijunction transistor*

As the emitter voltage is increased, the current is very small—just a few micro amps. When the peak point is reached, the current rises rapidly, until at the valley point the device runs into saturation. At this point R_{B_1} is at its lowest value, which is known as the saturation resistance.

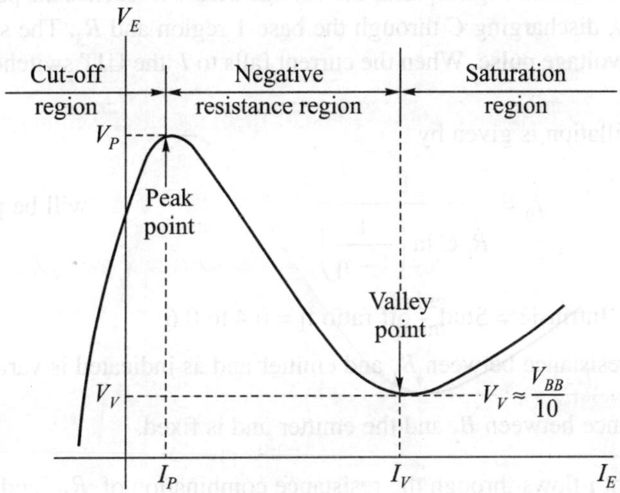

Fig. 10.49 *Characteristics of UJT*

UJT Oscillator

The simplest application of a UJT is as a relaxation oscillator. Capacitor is charged gradually and then discharged rapidly. The basic circuit is shown in Fig. 10.50 (*a*). In the practical circuit of figure (*b*), R_3 limits the emitter current and provides a voltage pulse, while R_2 provides a measure of temperature compensation. Figure 10.50 (*c*) shows the waveforms occurring at the emitter and base 1; the first is an approximation to a saw tooth and the second is a pulse of short duration.

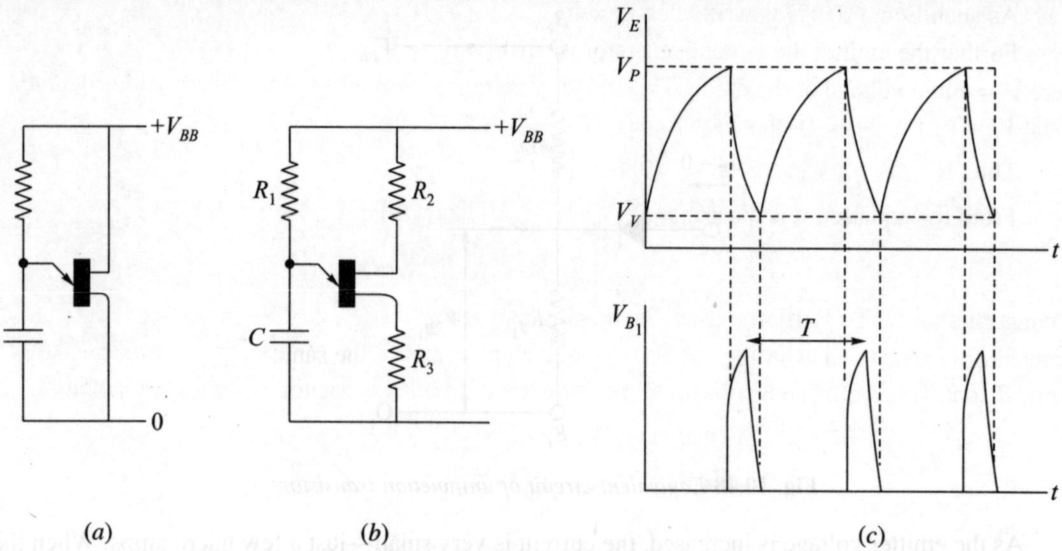

Fig. 10.50 *Relaxation oscillator*

The capacitor C charges through R_1 until the voltage across it reaches the peak point. The emitter current then rises rapidly, discharging C through the base 1 region and R_3. The sudden rise of current through R_3 produces the voltage pulse. When the current falls to I_v the UJT switches off and the cycle is repeated.

Frequency of oscillation is given by

$$f_0 = \frac{1}{R_1 C \ln\left(\frac{1}{1-\eta}\right)} \quad \text{(will be proved subsequently)}$$

Intrinsic = Stud – off ratio η = 0.4 to 0.6

Thus R_{B_1} is the resistance between B_1 and emitter and as indicated is variable.

R_{B_2} is the resistance between B_2 and the emitter and is fixed.

If $I_E = 0$, a current i flows through the resistance combination of R_{B_1} and R_{B_2}.

$$i = \frac{V_{BB}}{R_{B_1} + R_{B_2}} \quad \text{...(10.46)}$$

$$V_{RB_1} = V_1 = \left(\frac{R_{B_1}}{R_{B_1} + R_{B_2}}\right) V_{BB} \quad \text{...(10.47)}$$

The ratio $\left(\frac{R_{B_1}}{R_{B_1} + R_{B_2}}\right)$ is known as the Intrinsic Ratio and is denoted as η

As such Eqn. (10.47) is written as $V_1 = \eta V_{BB}$ ...(10.48)

Further the emitter diode conducts only when $V_E = V_r + V_1$ ...(10.49)

where V_r = cut in voltage of the diode. This value of voltage is termed as peak voltage and is denoted as V_p and $V_p = V_r + V_1$ (Refer Fig. 10.49)

Thus $V_p = V_r + \eta V_{BB}$ ...(10.50)

From the equation it is clear that if $V_E < V_p$, UJT is OFF

$V_E > V_p$, UJT is ON

To construct an UJT Oscillator (Say Oscillating at 1 kHz)

A capacitor is connected as in Fig. 10.50 (*a*), equivalent circuit of the same is shown in Fig. 10.50 (*b*). During T_s charging of the capacitor takes place (as UJT is OFF), capacitor charges exponentially.

$$v_s = V_f - (V_f - V_{in})\, e^{-t/RC}$$

$$= V_{BB} - (V_{BB} - V_{in})\, e^{-t/RC}$$

At $t = T_s;\ V_S = V_p$

Hence $$V_p = V_{BB} - (V_{BB} - V_r)\, e^{-T_s/RC}$$

Thus $$e^{-t/RC} = \left(\frac{V_{BB} - V}{V_{BB} + V_V}\right) \qquad (\text{at } t = T_s)$$

Thus $$\frac{T_s}{RC} = \log e\left(\frac{V_{BB} - V_v}{V_{BB} - V_p}\right)$$

Hence $$T_s = RC \log_e\left(\frac{V_{BB} - V_v}{V_{BB} + V_p}\right)$$

Hence $$f = \left(\frac{1}{T_s + T_1}\right) \cong \frac{1}{T_s} \qquad (\text{As } T_s >> T_1)$$

Then $$f = \frac{1}{RC \log e\left(\dfrac{1}{1 - V_p/V_{BB}}\right)} = \frac{1}{RC \log e\left(\dfrac{1}{1-\eta}\right)}$$

Either V_E or V_{B_1} may be used for triggering SCRs. (Preferably V_{B_1})

If for *Ex.* *f* required is 1 kHz, $t = 1/f = 1$ m sec.

$$V_{BB} - V_p = 10 - 7.25 = 2.75 \text{ V}$$

and $$V_{BB} - V_v = 10 - 1 = 9 \text{ V}$$

Thus $$C = \left(\frac{0.001}{10^4 \ln (9/2.75)}\right) \cong 84 \text{ nF}$$

CHAPTER 10

Generally $R_2 = 470\ \Omega$ (some times not required)

$$R_3 >> R_{BB}\ ;\quad R_3 \cong 47\ \Omega$$

$$R_3 < R_{BB}$$

10.32.1.2 Power Control using Thyristor

Phase control is the most common form of thyristor power control. The thyristor is held in the OFF condition—that is, all current flow in the circuit is blocked by the thyristor. Then the thyristor is triggered into an 'ON' condition by the control circuitry.

Half wave power control may be done using one thyristor and triggering it suitably. Also full wave AC power control, is achieved by connecting two SCRs in inverse parallel.

Figure 10.51 illustrates voltage waveform. Delay angle is the time during which the thyristor blocks the line voltage. The conduction angle is the time during which the thyristor is on. It is important to note that the circuit current is determined by the load and power source. For simplification, assume the load is resistive; that is, both the voltage and current waveforms are identical.

The figure also indicates the various methods of triggering SCRs.

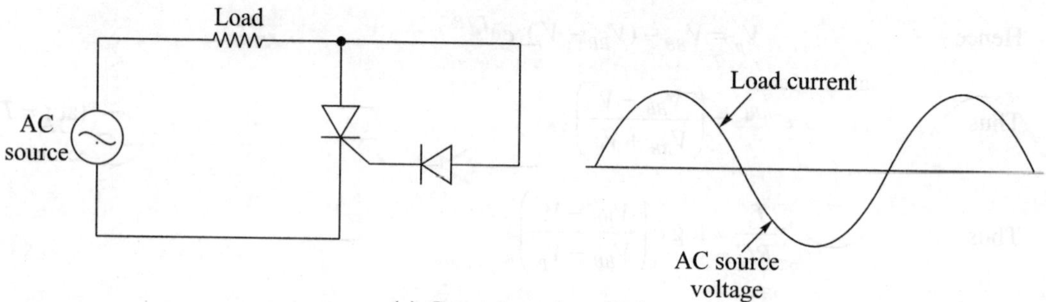

(a) Gate trigger in a diode

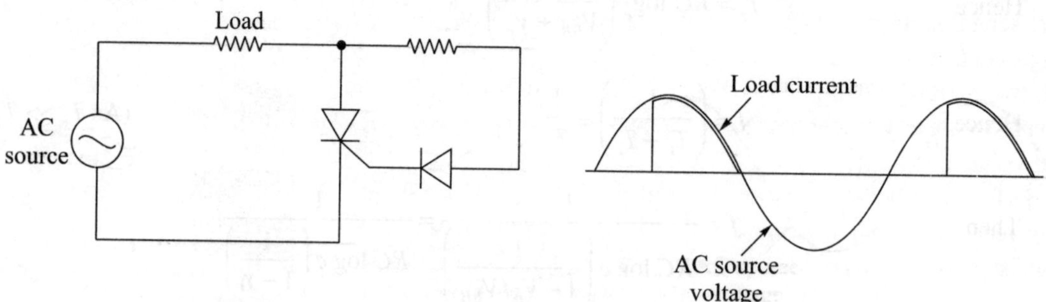

(b) Gate trigger in a diode with a current limiting resistor

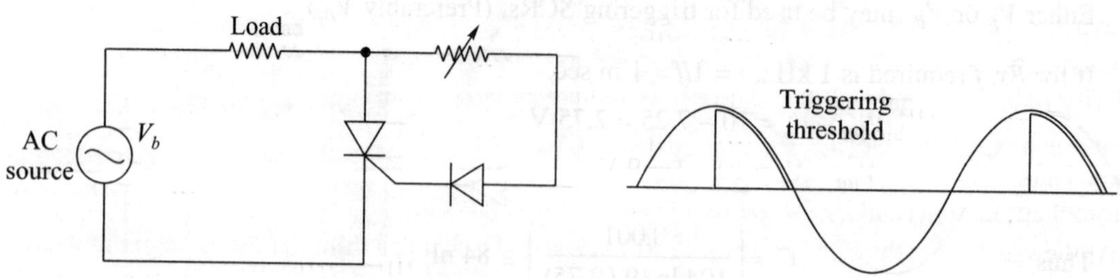

(c) Gate trigger—variable resistantor

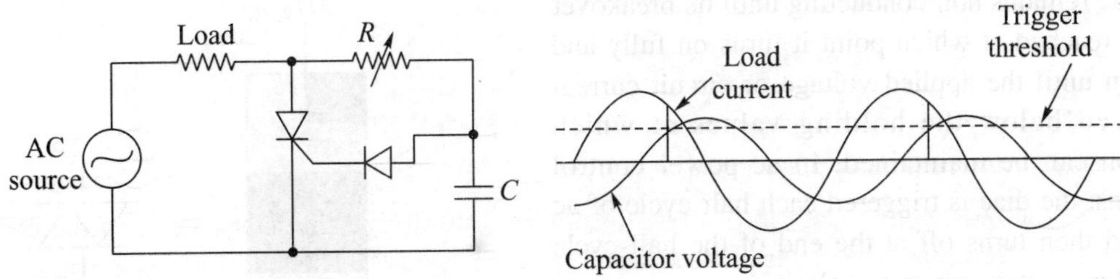

(d) Triggering angle varied through the R and C combination

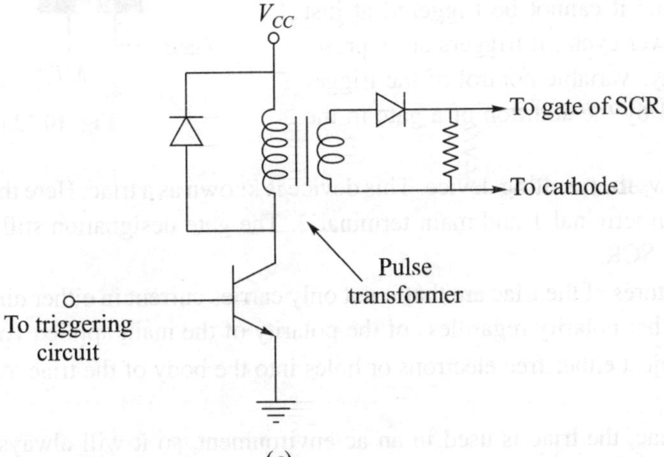

(e)

Fig. 10.51 *Various methods of triggering SCR for power control*

10.32.1.3 The Diac and Triac

We have seen that SCR require a dc voltage of the correct polarity for working. In continuation, when ac power control is required (phase control) two SCRs are required to be connected back to back. It would be better if we have a single device which operates for both polarities of input voltage. It would be nice if we could have some sort of SCR that works for either polarity, so it can be used with an applied ac voltage. We may recall that four layer devices essentially means connecting two transistors back to back in a single silicon crystal. Can we extend this concept and connect two SCRs back to back?

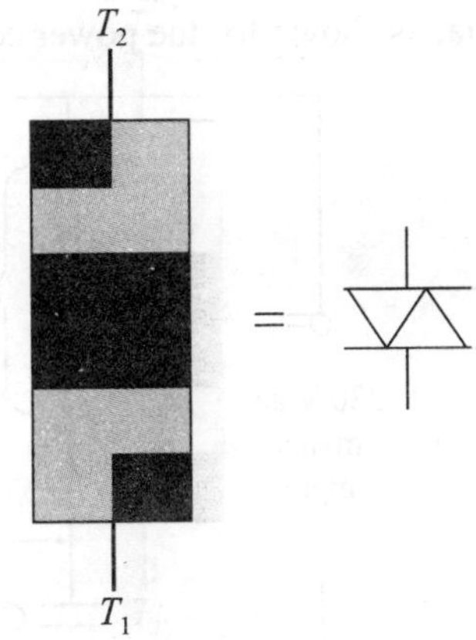

Fig. 10.52 *(a) Diac*

Figure 10.52 shows the resulting five-layer device which is known as a diac. The connections are named terminal 1 (T_1) and terminal 2 (T_2). Each terminal can serve as either anode or cathode according to the polarity of the applied voltage. The same applied polarity also determines which of the end junctions is active, and which one is bypassed. Thus if T_1 is positive with respect to T_2, T_1's *N*-type region is ignored (electrons are pulled away from that junction) and its *P*-type region serves as the anode.

At the same time, the relative negative voltage at T_2 pulls holes from the *P*-type region towards the terminal (removing them from the next junction), but tends to push electrons from its *N*-type region across that junction into the *P*-type region, thus making them available for conduction.

Diac remains non-conducting until its breakover voltage is reached at which point it turns on fully and remains on until the applied voltage or circuit current are reduced below the holding values at which conduction can be maintained. In ac power control applications, the diac is triggered each half cycle of ac power, and then turns off at the end of the half-cycle when the line voltage reverses polarity.

The drawback of the diac is the same as it was for the four-layer diode; it cannot be triggered at just any point in the ac power cycle; it triggers at its preset break over voltage only. Variable control of the trigger point may be achieved by the addition of a gate to the diac.

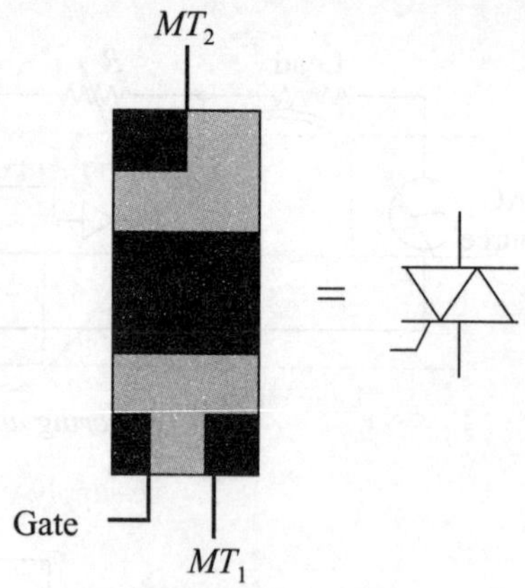

Fig. 10.52 *(b) Triac*

The figure shows the resulting device. This device is known as a triac. Here the main connections are simply named main terminal 1 and main terminal 2. The gate designation still applies and is still used as it was with the SCR.

The useful features of the triac are that it not only carries current in either direction, but the gate trigger pulse can be either polarity regardless of the polarity of the main applied voltage.

The gate can inject either free electrons or holes into the body of the triac to trigger conduction either way.

As with the diac, the triac is used in an ac environment, so it will always turn off when the applied voltage reaches zero at the end of the current half-cycle. If we apply a turn-on pulse at some controllable point after the start of each half-cycle, we can directly control what percentage of that half-cycle gets applied to the load, which is typically connected in series with MT_2. This makes the triac an ideal candidate for light dimmer controls and motor speed controls. A typical application of a diac and triac is shown for the power control of the load as shown in Fig.10.53.

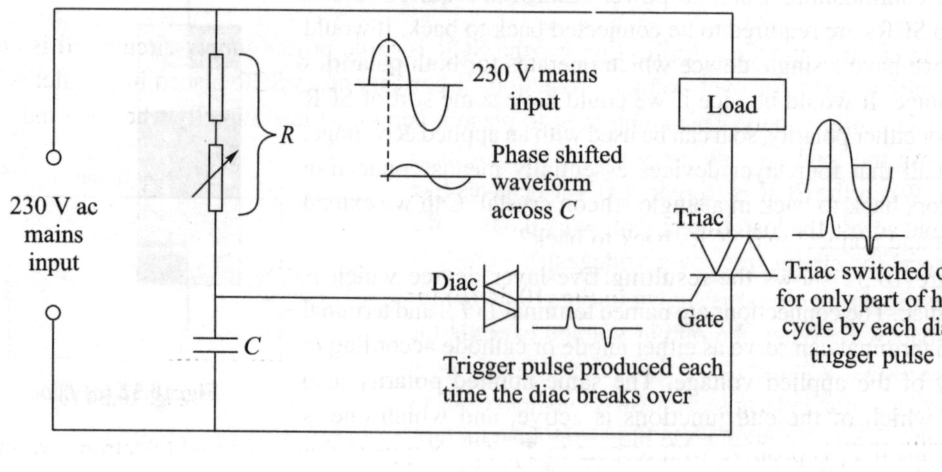

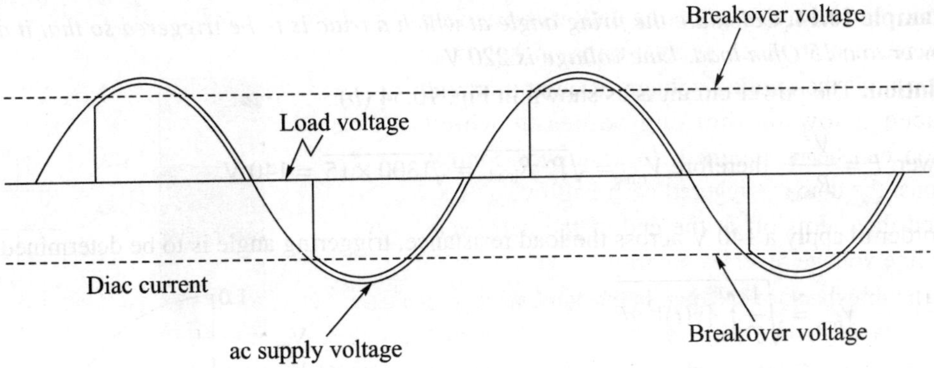

Fig. 10.53 *Simple ac power circuit*

The capacitor is charged through R with a time constant RC. No sooner the capacitor charges to a value of the break-over voltage of the Diac, a pulse is produced as shown in the figure and this pulse triggers the Triac, thereby connecting the load to the supply. Once the voltage across the Triac reverses, it goes off and again in the other portion of the input power the above process repeats.

Another application of SCR is given below:

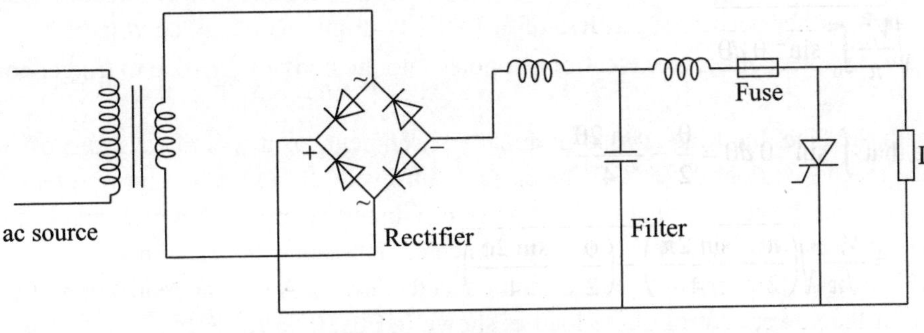

Fig. 10.54 *(a)*

An interesting practical application for the SCR is in dc power supply circuit and is called a 'Crowbar' circuit used for over-voltage protection. It consists of an SCR placed in parallel with the output of a dc power supply. This being used to place it across the load directly whenever the voltage placed across the load crosses the set limit over-voltage protection. When the SCR is triggered ON it behaves like Crow-bar put across the load (thereby blowing the fuse and hence protects the circuit from over-voltages).

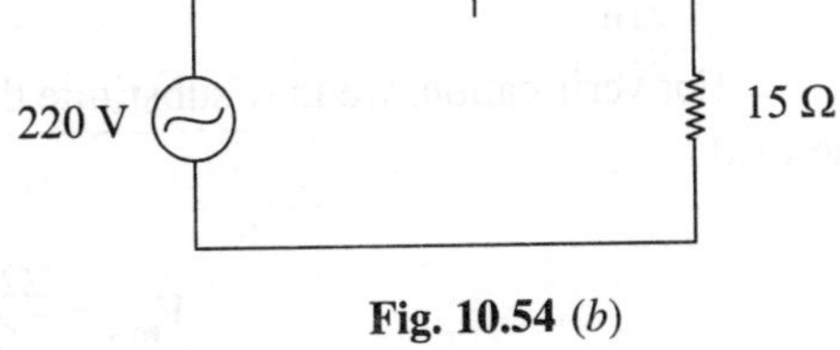

Fig. 10.54 *(b)*

The triggering circuit is shown in Fig. 10.54 (*b*) for the Crow-bar SCR. When the output voltage exceeds the zener break down voltage (set voltage for protection), it charges the capacitor and triggers the SCR and hence places a short circuit across the output and blows the fuse thereby protecting the circuit.

Example 10.14. *Calculate the firing angle at which a triac is to be triggered so that it delivers 1.3 kW power to a 15 Ohm load. Line voltage is 220 V.*

Solution. The power circuit is as shown in Fig.10.54 (*b*).

$$\text{Power, } P = \frac{V_{\text{rms}}^2}{R_{\text{load}}} \text{ therefore } V_{\text{rms}} = \sqrt{P \cdot R_{\text{load}}} = \sqrt{1300 \times 15} = 140 \text{ V}$$

In order to apply a 140 V across the load resistance, triggering angle is to be determined.

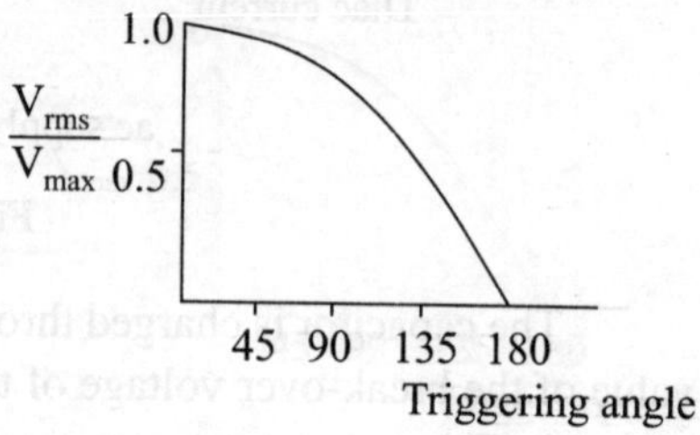

$$V_{\text{rms}} = \sqrt{\frac{1}{T}\int_0^T [v(t)]^2 \, dt}$$

$$v(t) = 0 \text{ ...... } 0 \le \theta \le \phi$$

$$v(t) = V_m \sin\theta \text{ ..... } \phi \le \theta \le \pi$$

Substituting, we get

$$V_{\text{rms}} = \sqrt{\frac{1}{\pi}\left[\int_0^{\phi} [0]^2 \, d\theta + \int_{\phi}^{\pi} (V_m \sin\theta)^2 \, d\theta\right]}$$

$$= \sqrt{\frac{V_m^2}{\pi}\int_{\phi}^{\pi} \sin^2\theta \, d\theta}$$

We note that $\int \sin^2\theta \, d\theta = \frac{\theta}{2} - \frac{\sin 2\theta}{4}$

$$\text{Thus } V_{\text{rms}} = \frac{V_m}{\sqrt{\pi}}\sqrt{\left(\frac{\pi}{2} - \frac{\sin 2\pi}{4}\right) - \left(\frac{\phi}{2} - \frac{\sin 2\phi}{4}\right)}$$

$$= \frac{V_m}{\sqrt{\pi}}\sqrt{\left(\frac{\pi - \phi}{2}\right) + \left(\frac{\sin 2\phi}{4}\right)}$$

Indeed, graph of rms value V_s firing angle graph are drawn and this facilitate the determination of the firing angle for obtaining the firing angle to impress a certain rms voltage across the load.

From the graph we note that $\phi = 98°$ (for a value of $\phi \; \frac{140}{220} = \frac{7}{11} = 0.63$ a normalised factor)

For verification, we may substitute this value in the equation for V_{rms} and find out V_{rms} applied to the load.

$$V_{\text{rms}} = \frac{220}{\sqrt{\pi}}\sqrt{\left(\frac{\pi - 1.71}{2}\right) + \left(\frac{\sin 196}{4}\right)} = 141 \text{ V}$$

which is the value that we obtain previously.

10.32.2 Controlled Fullwave SCR Rectifier

Figure 10.55(*a*) shows the circuit diagram. Each of the SCRs conduct for a maximum of one half cycle, *i.e.,* SCR-1 is forward biased when node *A* is positive with respect to node *B*. In Fig. 10.55, the gate current is adjusted to a value so that SCR-l turns on at the instant of time corresponding to $\omega t_1 = \theta$. When SCR-1 is on, SCR-2 is reverse biased and therefore does not conduct even though triggered. SCR-2 conducts at an identical firing angle (made possible by adjusting its gate current). The output waveform is shown hatched in Fig. 10.55 (*b*).

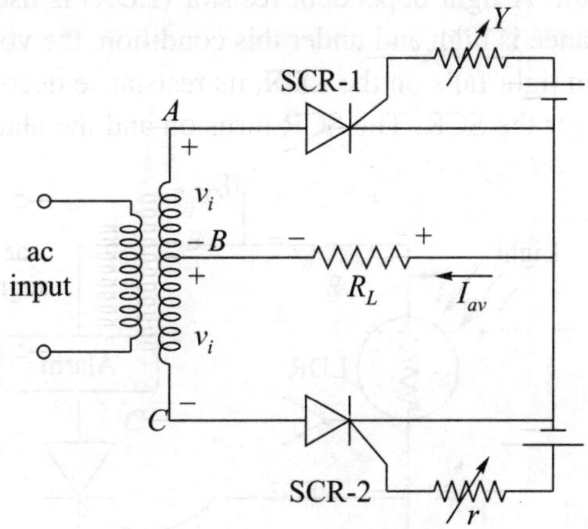

(*a*) *Controlled full wave SCR rectifier*

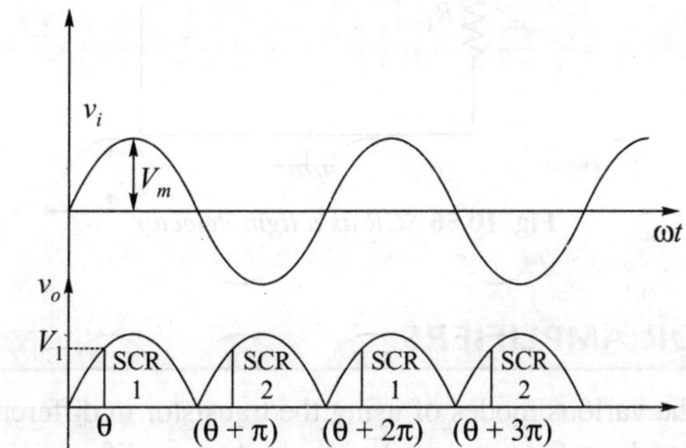

(*b*) *Output waveform*

Fig. 10.55

If $v = V_m \sin(\omega t)$ is the ac output of each half of the center tapped transformer, the average value of the voltage developed across R_L is

$$= V_0$$

$$= \frac{1}{\pi}\int_{\theta}^{\pi} V_m \sin(\omega t)\, d(\omega t)$$

$$= \frac{V_m}{\pi}(1 + \cos\theta) \qquad ...(10.51)$$

CHAPTER 10

and $$I_{av} = \frac{V_0}{R_L}$$

$$= \frac{V_m}{\pi R_L}(1+\cos\theta) \quad ...(10.52)$$

10.32.3 SCR Light Detector

Figure 10.48 shows the circuit. A light dependent resistor (LDR) is used. In the absence of any light falling on the LDR, its resistance is high and under this condition, the voltage available across R_1 is too low to trigger the SCR. When tight falls on the LDR, its resistance decreases and the voltage available across R_1 is sufficient to trigger the SCR. The SCR turns on and the alarm sounds.

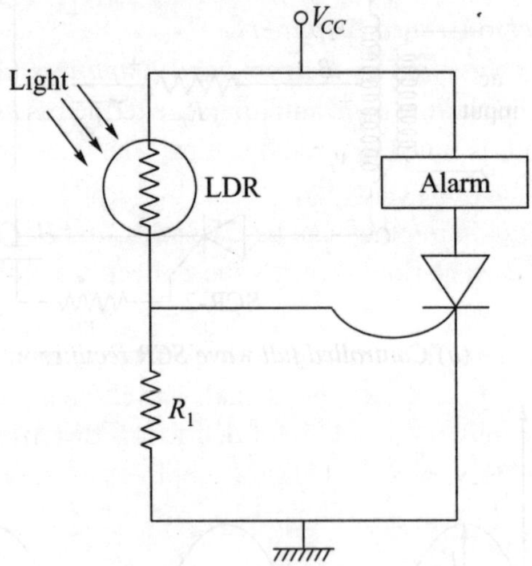

Fig. 10.56 *SCR as a light detector*

10.33 TRANSISTOR AMPLIFIERS

In the previous sections, the various modes of using the transistor in different configurations has been presented. Quite often, a number of stages may be required to amplify a signal power-wise so that it is suitable for the operation of another device. A typical example is the pick up from a microphone and finally the signal operating a loud speaker. In this section, the working of various types of power amplifiers classified on the basis of frequency and modes of operation are explained.

10.33.1 Classification of Amplifiers

Based on the *configuration*, the amplifiers can be *Common Base, Common Emitter* or *Common Collector* Amplifiers.

Based on the *function performed*, they can be *voltage amplifiers* or *power amplifiers*. The purpose of an voltage amplifier is to boost the signal level whereas in a power amplifier, it is to boost the power level.

Depending on the *number of stages of amplification*, the amplifiers they can be *single stage* or *multistage amplifier.*

Based on the *range of frequencies* at which the amplifiers are used, they can be:

- *Audio Amplifiers*: Used for amplifying signals in the frequency range 20 Hz to 20 kHz.
- *Video Amplifiers*: Used for amplifying video signals of frequencies above 20 kHz and below a few MHz. or
- *Radio Frequency Amplifiers*: Used for amplifying signals of frequencies above a few kHz up to several hundred MHz. In AM radios, the frequency ranges from 455–1605 kHz, where as in FM radios it ranges from 88–108 MHz.

In terms of the *signal level*, amplifiers can be *Small-signal amplifiers* (peak to peak changes in collector current is <10% of the quiescent current) or *Large-signal amplifiers* (a peak to peak signal uses most of the load line).

According to *type of the coupling*, amplifiers can be *DC amplifiers*, *RC Coupled Amplifiers*, *Transformer Coupled Amplifiers* or *Tuned Amplifiers*.

Amplifiers can also be classified as *Narrow band Amplifiers* (450–560 kHz) and *Wide band amplifiers* (DC to several MHz). Narrow band amplifiers are termed as *tuned RF Amplifiers* as the load, which is a resonant tank circuit, is tuned to a radio station. The wide band amplifiers have a resistive load. Class *C* amplifiers fall under this category.

Based on the *mode of operation*, they can be *Class A, Class B, Class C* or *Class AB amplifiers.* This is largely based on the current flow through the collector circuit throughout the input signal conditions.

- *Class A Amplifiers*: Here, the output is the replica of the input signal as the collector current flows throughout the cycle of the input signal. The efficiency of an ideal Class *A* amplifier is 25%. The class *A* amplifier enjoys high fidelity, low distortion but suffers from low output power and low efficiency. A typical class *A* amplifier is as shown in Fig. 10.57.

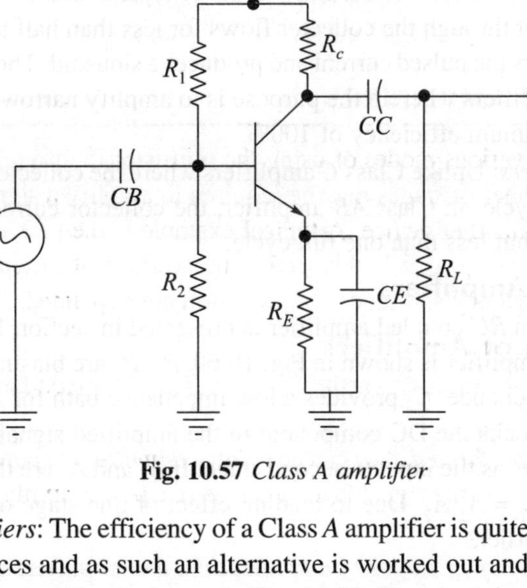

Fig. 10.57 *Class A amplifier*

- *Class B Amplifiers*: The efficiency of a Class *A* amplifier is quite low and cannot be acceptable in many instances and as such an alternative is worked out and this is a Class *B* amplifier. A typical Class *B* amplifier is shown in Fig. 10.58. Each transistor is used once in a half-cycle and is cut-off during the other half-cycle. This, obviously, introduces distortion. As such, another transistor is used which conducts during the other half-cycle. This ensures that there is no signal distortion, During the positive half-cycle of the input signal, v_1 is applied to the base of T_1(T_2 is turned off as its base is at a negative voltage). T_1 conducts and produces a negative voltage across the loud speaker transformer. The amplifier introduces a phase shift of 180° and hence the polarity of the signal reverses. During the negative half of the input signal, all signals are reversed and a positive voltage is developed across she loud speaker. The loud speaker thus receives a complete cycle of the amplified signal. In the absence of any input signal, both transistors are off and thus the current drain through the collector is avoided. The maximum efficiency is 78.5%. The disadvantage is obviously the use of a coupling transformer which is bulky and expensive. However, in the newer designs, the use of transformer is avoided.

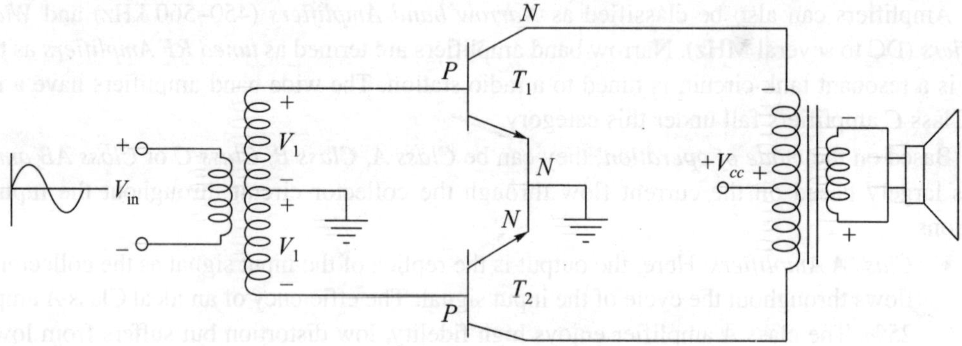

Fig. 10.58 *Class B amplifier*

- *Class C Amplifier*: Unlike Class *B* amplifiers where a transformer was a necessity, in Class *C* amplifier, a resonant circuit is used as a load. A typical Class *C* amplifier is shown in Fig. 10.59. The current through the collector flows for less than half a cycle. However, a filter at the collector, filters the pulsed current and produces a sinusoid. The amplifier finds application in turned *RF* amplifiers wherein the purpose is to amplify narrow band signals. It is possible to achieve a maximum efficiency of 100%.
- *Class AB Amplifiers*: Unlike Class *C* amplifiers where the collector current flows for a period less than half a cycle, in Class *AB* amplifier, the collector current flows for a period more than half a cycle but less than one full cycle.

10.33.2 RC Coupled Amplifiers

The basic configuration of an *RC* coupled amplifier is presented in section 10.25. The circuit of a two-stage *RC* Coupled voltage amplifier is shown in Fig. 10.60. R_1, R_2 are biasing resistors. R_e also helps in fixing the bias. Emitter capacitance, C_e provides a low impedance path for AC signals and blocks DC. Coupling capacitance, C_e blocks the DC component in the amplified signal of the first stage. The AC output of the first stage serves as the input to second stage. If A_1 and A_2 are the gains of two stages, then theoretically overall gain, $A_T = A_1 A_2$. Due to loading effect of one stage on the other, overall gain is lower than that suggested earlier.

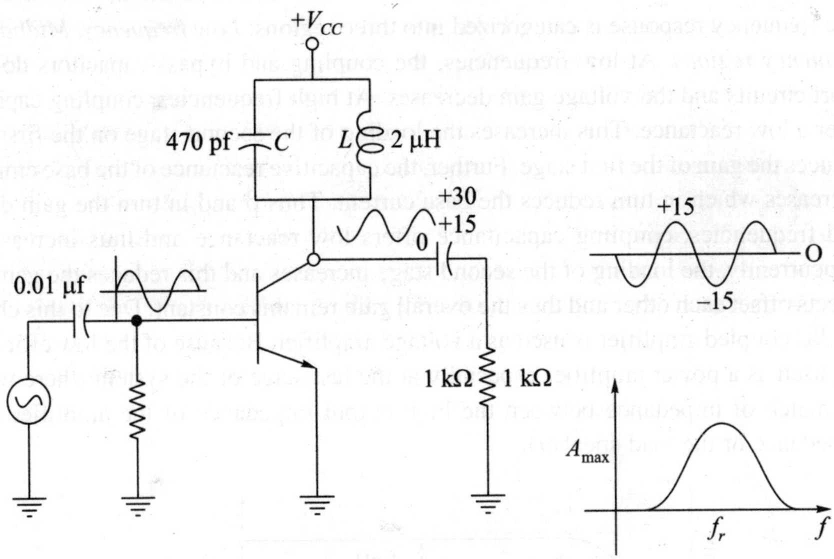

Fig. 10.59 *Class C tuned amplifier*

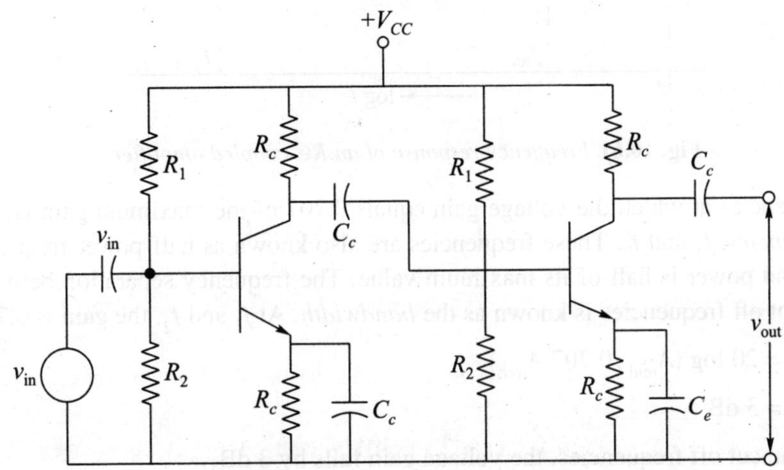

Fig. 10.60 *Two stage RC coupled amplifier*

Frequency response of the Amplifier: The frequency response of an amplifier is a graph of its gain vs frequency. It is quite important to know the frequency response of an amplifier. The power gain of an amplifier, $A = P_o / P_i$ and the power gain expressed in dB, and defined as the logarithm of ratio of power output to power input is:

$$A_{dB} = 10 \log A \text{ where } A = P_o/P_i$$

$$= 10 \log (V_0/V_1)^2 \text{ (As } P = V^2/R)$$

$$= 20 \log (V_0/V_1)$$

$$= 20 \log A_v \qquad ...(10.53)$$

A typical frequency response characteristic is shown in Fig. 10.61. Some of the important details of the frequency response are as follows:

- The frequency response is categorized into three regions: *Low frequency, Midband* and *High frequency regions.* At low frequencies, the coupling and bypass capacitors do not act like short circuits and the voltage gain decreases. At high frequencies, coupling capacitance will offer a low reactance. This increases the loading of the second stage on the first and as such reduces the gain of the first stage. Further, the capacitive reactance of the base emitter junction decreases which in tum reduces the base current. Thus β and in turn the gain decreases. At mid-frequencies, coupling capacitance offers low reactance and thus increases the gain. Concurrently, the loading of the second stage increases and this reduces the gain. These two effects offset each other and thus the overall gain remains constant. Due to this characteristic, the *RC* coupled amplifier is used as a voltage amplifier. Because of the low efficiency, this is not used as a power amplifier especially at the last stage of the system (there will also be a mismatch of impedance between the high output impedance of the amplifier and the low impedance of the load speaker).

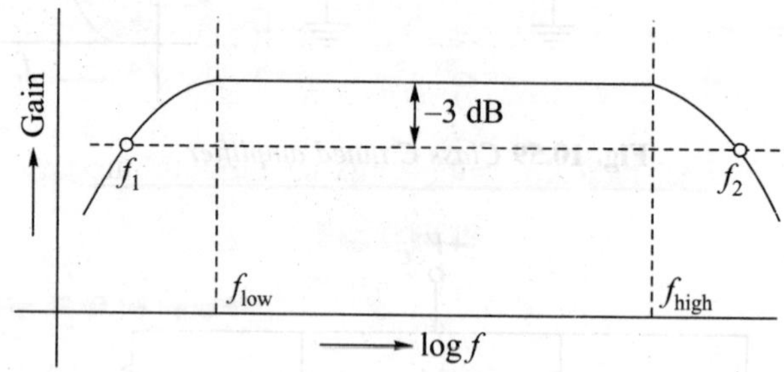

Fig. 10.61 *Frequency response of an RC coupled amplifier*

- Frequencies at which the voltage gain equals 0.707 of the maximum gain are called *cut off frequencies*, f_1 and f_2. These frequencies are also known as half-power frequencies because the load power is half of its maximum value. The frequency separation between the above two cut off frequencies is known as the *bandwidth.* At f_1 and f_2, the gain is 0.707 A_{mid}.

$$= 20 \log (A_{mid} / 0.707\, A_{mid})$$

$$= 3 \text{ dB} \qquad ...(10.54)$$

Thus at the cut off frequencies, the voltage gain falls by 3 dB.

Types of Feedback Amplifiers

1. Depending on the quantity to be amplified (current/voltage), amplifiers may be classified into four classes. Feedback topologies in each case are given as follows:

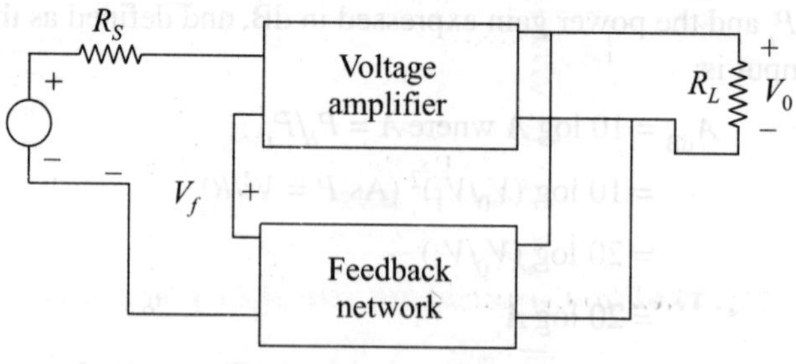

Fig. 10.62 *(a) Series shunt feedback*

- Voltage amplifiers are used when the input impedance is required to be high, output impedance is required to be low.
- The circuit is known as voltage mixing and voltage sampling topology. Also known as series-shunt feedback.

2. The topology below indicates the sampling of the output in series and the feedback is in shunt. This mode is called current mixing current samplers known as shunt-series feedback.

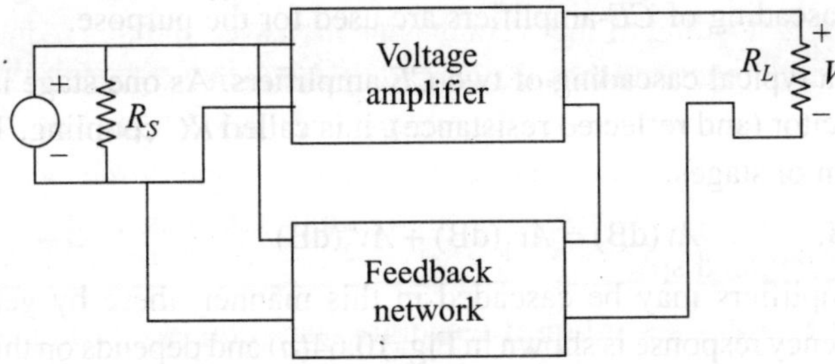

Fig. 10.62 (*b*) *Shunt-series feedback*

3. Topology in Fig. 10.63 (*c*) indicates voltage mixing current sampling

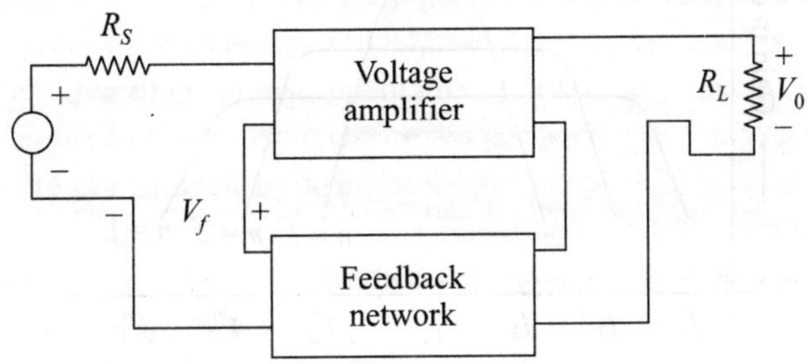

Fig. 10.62 (*c*) *Voltage mixing and current sampling circuit*

Transconductance amplifiers are amplifiers in which the input signal is a voltage and the output signal is a current.

Voltage mixing current sampling topology is used.

Also called Series-Series feedback.

4. Topology below indicates current mixing voltage sampling.

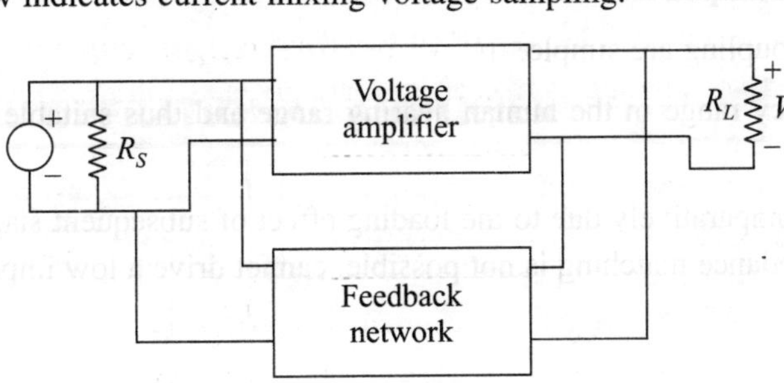

Fig. 10.62 (*d*) *Current mixing, voltage sampling feedback*

CHAPTER 10

- Transresistance amplifiers the input is current signal output is the voltage signal.
- The presence of the parallel connection at both input and output makes the feedback topology known as shunt-shunt feedback.

Common Emitter Transistor Configuration has already been considered in the previous section for the amplification of the given signal. As, *CE* mode has both current and voltage amplification it is generally used for the amplification/strengthening the signal. In fact, when the amplification of the signal is not sufficient, cascading of *CE*-amplifiers are used for the purpose.

Fig. 10.63 shows a typical cascading of two *CE* amplifiers. As one stage is coupled to the other stage by means of a capacitor (and reflected resistance), it is called *RC* coupling. The overall gain is the product of individual gain of stages.

In terms of the dB, $Av(\text{dB}) = Av_1(\text{dB}) + Av_2(\text{dB})$

An number of amplifiers may be cascaded in this manner, there by getting a high value of Av(dB). The overall frequency response is shown in Fig. 10.64(*a*) and depends on the number of stages(n).

Loading as also the gain of amplifier is explained previously with reference to Fig. 10.64.

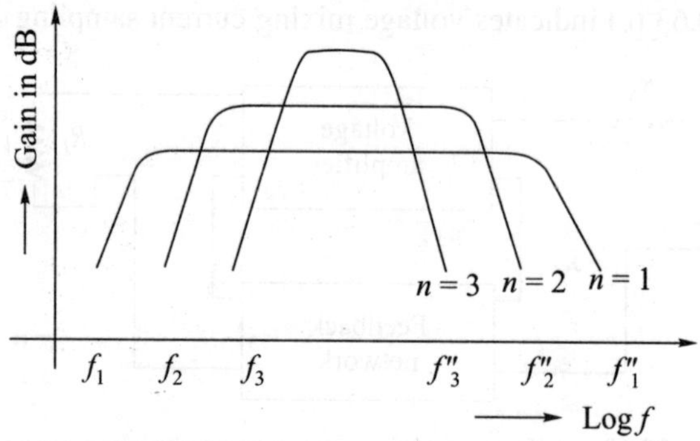

Fig. 10.63 (*a*) *Effect of cascading on bandwidth*

Figure shows the gain frequency curve of a multistage amplifier. As may be observed the bandwidth ($BW = f_2 - f_1$) of the overall system depends on the number of stages(n) of cascading. Larger the number of cascading, lesser is the bandwidth with high gain.

Features of RC coupled amplifiers

1. Biasing and coupling are simple.
2. Good frequency range in the human hearing range and thus suitable in the public address systems.
3. Lower gain comparatively due to the loading effect of subsequent stages on the proceeding stages as impedance matching is not possible, cannot drive a low impedance load directly.

10.33.3 Feedback Amplifiers

It is observed from the base resistor biasing given in Fig. 10.35 that the position of the operating point varies when a different transistor is used (β changes). Indeed, an attempt to stabilize the Q point was the *Emitter feedback* bias shown in Fig. 10.64. As I_C increases, V_E increases, causing V_B to increase, thereby reducing I_B. This opposes the original increase in I_C. This is called the *Feedback* because the change in emitter voltage is fed back to the base circuit. As it opposes the original change in the collector current, it is called *negative feedback*.

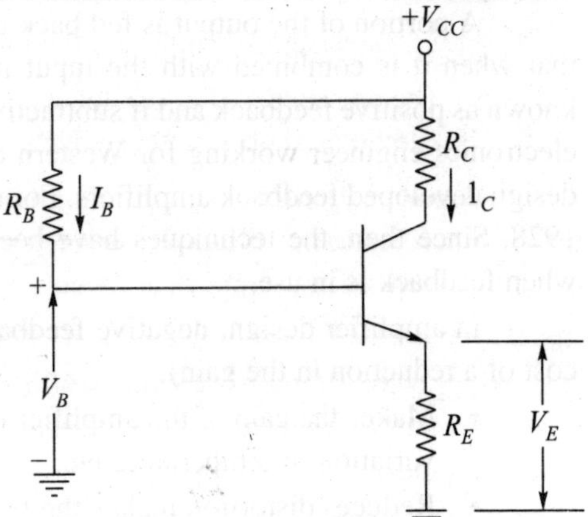

Fig. 10.64 *Emitter feedback biasing*

Fig. 10.65 shows a two stage RC coupled feedback amplifier. Feedback is to the resistor, r_e of the first stage.

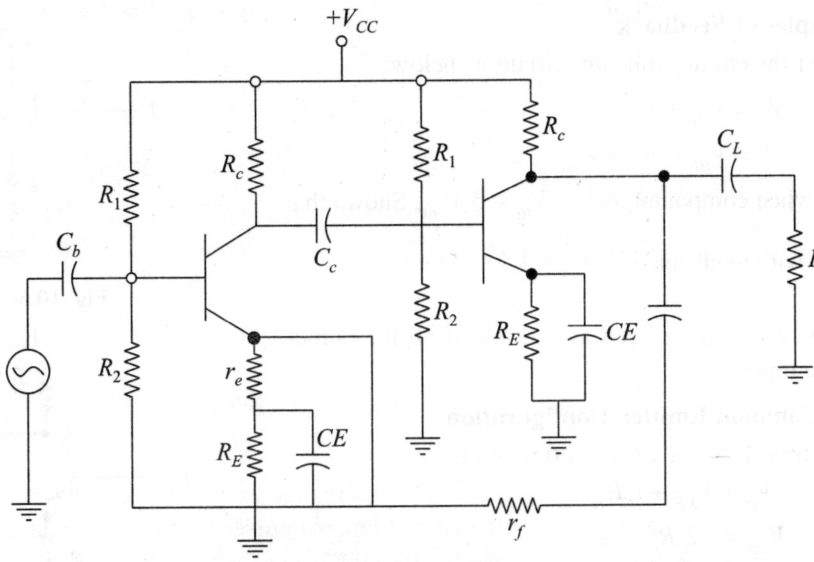

Fig. 10.65 *Two stage feedback amplifier*

A resistance, r_f is connected to the emitter of the first transistor. Due to the voltage divider circuit formed by r_e, and r_f the AC voltage between the emitter and ground is

$$V_e = [V_{out}/(r_f + r_e)]\, r_e \qquad ...(10.55)$$

If the output voltage increases for some reason, then V_e increases. This decreases V_{be} of the first stage thereby decreasing V_c and thus V_{out}. On the other hand, if output decreases, V_{be} and V_c increase and hence V_{out} increases. Clearly, any change in the output when suitably fed back opposes this change thereby maintaining the output at a fairly constant value.

On the other hand, if the feed back voltage applied to the input circuit aids the input signal, being in phase with it, a *positive feedback* occurs and thus increases the gain of the amplifier. These are called *positive feedback amplifiers*. The chapter on *oscillators* considers this aspect in detail.

A portion of the output is fed back and mixes with the input. Indeed, the feedback may be such that when it is combined with the input may be additive or subtractive. If additive the feedback is known as positive feedback and if subtractive feedback is known as negative feedback. Harold Black an electronics engineer working for Western electric company, while searching for a suitable method of design developed feedback amplifiers. For use in Telephone repeaters feedback amplifiers were used in 1928. Since then, the techniques have been in wide use. The diagram below indicates the instances when feedback is in use.

In amplifier design, negative feedback is applied to affect one or more of the following (at the cost of a reduction in the gain):

- Makes the gain of the amplifier less sensitive to the variations of circuit components such as variation of temperature etc.
- Reduces distortion makes the frequency response curve a flat one. This allows us to design desired frequency response characteristics.
- Reduces the effect of noise-either internal or due to interference.
- Controls the input and output impedance depending upon the topology of feedback.

Typical Examples of Feedback

Consider the emitter follower circuit as below:

$$V_{in} = V_{BE} + V_{out}$$

$$V = V_{BE} = V_{in} - V_{out}$$

Which when compound to $V = V_{in} - \beta\, V_{out}$. Shows that

$\beta = 1$, the gain with feedback is $A \dfrac{1}{\beta} = 1$

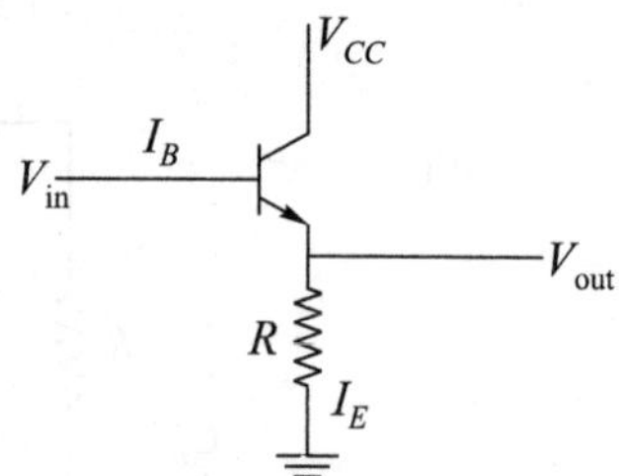

Fig. 10.66 (*a*)

The gain of 1 can be seen as a result of all the output feedback to the input.

Feedback in Common Emitter Configuration

Fig. 10.66 (*b*) shows a *CE* configuration

$$V_{in} = V_{BE} + I_E R_E$$

$$V_{out} = -I_C R_C$$

Then, $\quad V_{BE} = V_{in} + \dfrac{\beta + 1}{\beta\, R_C} R_E\, V_{out}$

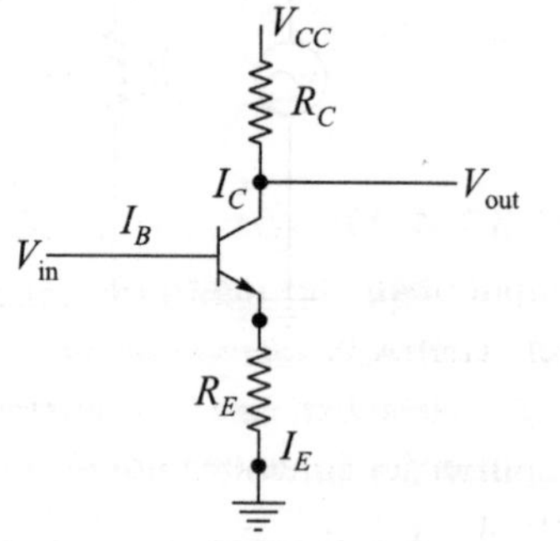

Fig. 10.66 (*b*) *shows a CE configuration.*

Amplification of –ve feedback with a value of β

$$A \approx \frac{1}{\beta} = \frac{-\beta R_C}{(\beta+1)\, R_E}$$

Which when compared to the form

$$V' = V_{in} - \beta V_{out}$$

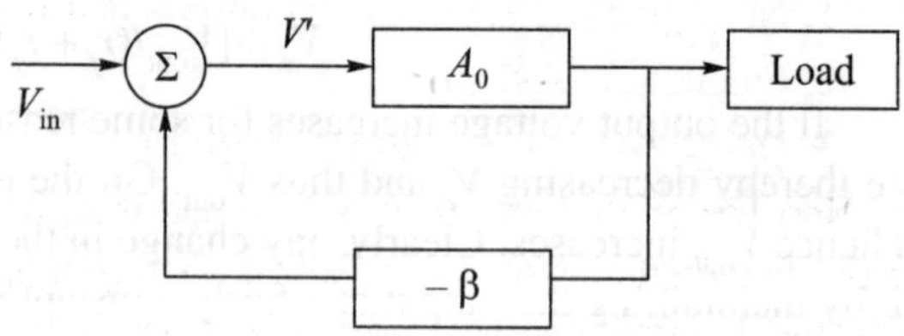

Fig.10.66 (*c*) *Concept of feedback;Feedback network* – β; *Forward gain* A_0

Gives $\beta = \frac{-\beta+1}{\beta R_C} R_E$ which corresponds to the voltage gain obtain by other methods $A_f \approx \frac{-R_C}{R_E}$.

All the above advantages are of the cost of gain. Positive feedback results in oscillations. This is taken up under 'oscillators'. The general feedback structure is as below.

Part of the output signal is taken back to the input with a negative sign.

$$V' = V_{in} - \beta V_{out}$$

$$V_{out} = A_0 V$$

Substitute $\quad V_{out} = A_0 (V_{in} - \beta V_{out})$

$$= V_{out} [1 + A_0\beta] = A_0 V_{in}$$

Then $\quad V_{out} = \frac{A_0}{1 + A_0\beta} V_{in}$

$$\text{Gain} = \frac{V_{out}}{V_{in}} = \frac{A_0}{1 + A_0\beta} \approx \frac{1}{\beta} \qquad (\text{if } A_0\beta >> 1)$$

Which when compared to the form

$$V' = V_{in} - \beta V_{out}$$

Given $\quad \beta = \frac{-\beta+1}{\beta R_C} R_E$

which corresponds to the voltage gain (approx) obtained by other methods

$$A_f \simeq \frac{R_C}{R_E}$$

10.33.4 Distortion in Amplifiers

Output of an ideal amplifier is an amplified version of the input. As the output is a replica of the input, there cannot be any distortion.

However, due to nonlinear characteristics of the device, used for amplification, the output of an amplifier for some conditions will not be the true replica of the input. Such an output is called distorted output.

There are three types of distortions encountered in Amplifiers. They are:

1. None-linear distortion (Amplitude distortion)
2. Frequency distortion
3. Delay distortion (phase distortion).

Non-linear distortion: It is assumed that the transistor is perfectly a linear device. That is the dynamic characteristics of a transistor is a straight line over the operating range. However, in practical circuits, the dynamic characteristics is not perfectly linear. Due to this factor, output waveform differs from the input signal. Such a distortion is known as 'non-linear' or 'amplitude distortion'. This causes the new frequency components to be introduced in to the output (generally called Harmonics), which is not present in the input signal.

Typically a sine wave at the input may result in rounded off peak's at the output resulting in distortion. This introduces frequency components not present in the input, and is referred to as non linear or amplitude distortion.

Frequency distortion: This type of distortion exists when the signal component's of different frequencies are amplified differently. This distortion is due to internal capacitance and coupling capacitance of the circuit.

A plot of gain *v.s* frequency of an amplifier is called as the frequency response of an amplifier. If this plot is not a horizontal straight line over the range of frequencies under consideration. The circuit is said to exhibit frequency distortion over this range.

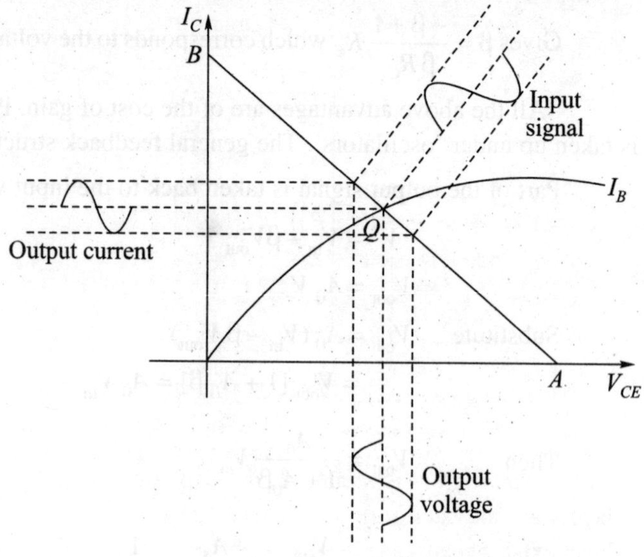

Fig. 10.67 *Transistor characteristics*

Delay distortion: It is a phase shift distortion. It results due to unequal phase shifts of signal's of different frequencies. Fig. 10.57 shows the *CE* transistor characteristics. *Q* is the operating characteristics. Input and output signal's are plotted. *AB* is the load line.

As may be observed from the I_C vs V_{CE} characteristics of the *CE* configuration amplifier, there is phase inversion of 180° between the input and output.

10.34 FIELD EFFECT TRANSISTORS

For the working of a transistor, the necessary charge carriers are *electrons* and *holes*. Thus it is a bipolar device. The Field Effect Transistor (FET) has only one kind of a charge carrier and it is an *unipolar* device. It may be recalled that vacuum tubes also have only electrons as carriers. FEE has similar characteristics to that of vacuum tube pentode. Due to their high input impedance, FETs are preferred over transistors in certain applications. As there are no minority carriers in FET, no stored charge need be removed before the device is switched off and as such it is faster than the transistor. Depending on the fabrication technology, there are two kinds of FETs: junction field effect transistor (JFET) and metal oxide semiconductor field effect transistor (MOSFET).

10.34.1 Principle of JFET

An FET comprises of drain, source and gate with a *n*-type semiconductor diffused with two layers of *p*-type as shown in Fig. 10.68. The two *p*-regions are connected internally with one output terminal. This constitutes the *n*-channel FET.

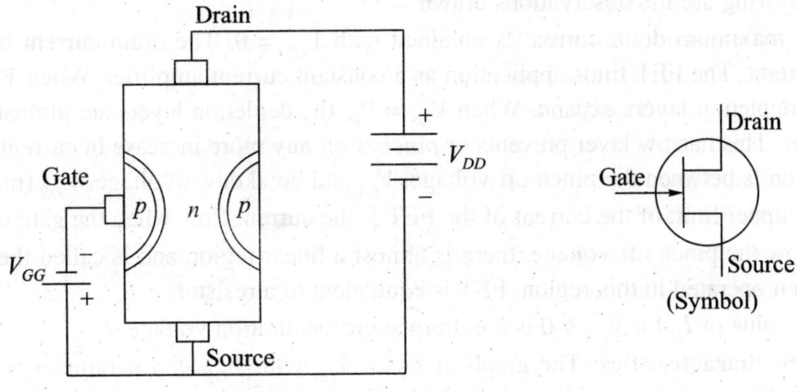

Fig. 10.68 *Biasing of n-channel FET*

Field effect is related to the depletion layers around each *p*-region. These depletion layer exists because free electrons diffuse from the *n*-region into *p*-region. The recombination of free electrons and holes creates the depletion layer. The gate-source junction is reverse-biased and hence $I_G \cong 0$. This amounts to the very high input impedance. Also, as may be seen, when the gate-source bias is made more and more negative, depletion region increases and thus the drain source current decreases. The working of a *p*-channel FET is complementary to that of the *n*-channel FET.

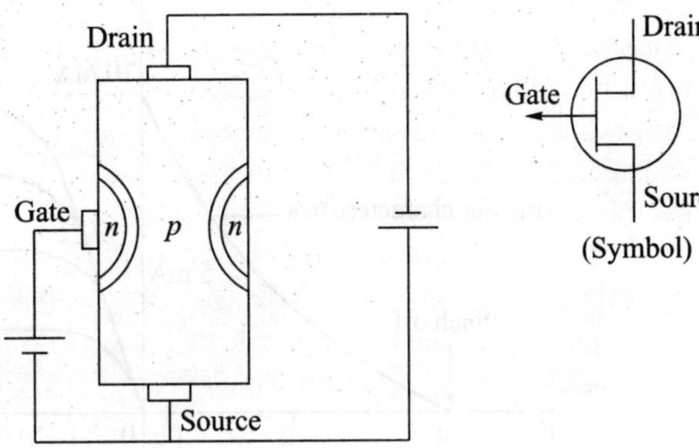

Fig. 10.69 *Biasing of p-channel FET*

A typical *p*-channel FEE with the symbolic representation is in Fig. 10.69.

Output characteristics: The graph of I_D *vs.* V_{DS} with V_{GS} as a parameter as shown in Fig. 10.70, is known as the *drain* characteristics or output *characteristics*.

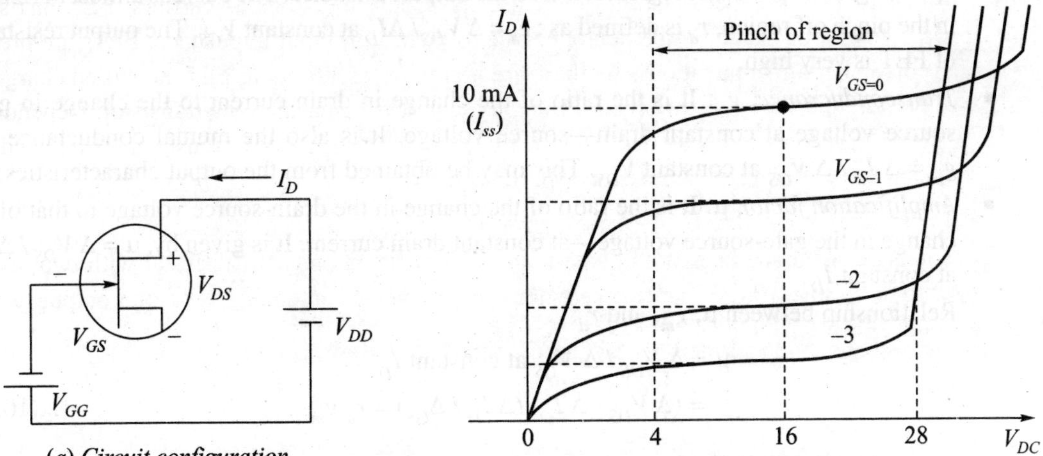

(*a*) *Circuit configuration*

(*b*) *Drain curves*

Fig. 10.70 *Output characteristics of EET*

The following are the observations drawn:

- The maximum drain current is obtained with $V_{GS} = 0$. The drain current becomes almost constant. The FET finds application as a constant current amplifier. When V_{DS} is increased, the depletion layers expand, When $V_{DS} = V_P$, the depletion layers are almost touching each other. This narrow layer prevents or *pinches off* any more increase in current V_P. The active region is between the pinch off voltage, V_{PA} and breakdown voltage, V_{DS} (max).
- The upper limit of the current of the FET is the current flow when the gate is shorted, I_{DSS}.
- Below the pinch off voltage, there is almost a linear region and is called the ohmic-region. When operated in this region, FET is equivalent to a resistor.
- The value of I_D for $V_{GS} = 0$ is the drain-source saturation voltage, I_{DSS}.

Transfer characteristics: The graph of I_D *vs.* V_{GS} with V_{DS} as a parameter as shown in Fig. 10.71, transfer characteristics.

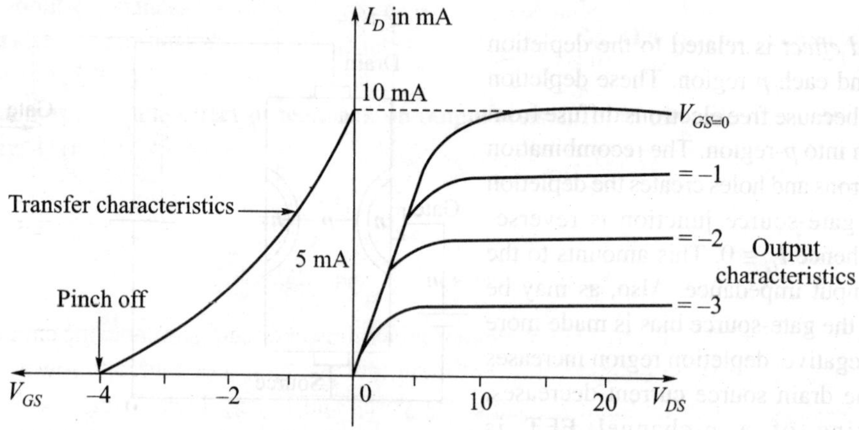

Fig. 10.71 *Transfer characteristics of FET*

The parameters required for defining the transfer characteristics of FET are:

- *Drain resistance, r_d*: It is the AC resistance between the drain and source, when the FET is operating in the pinch-off region. It is also the output resistance, The curve is almost horizontal in the pinch off region, r_d is defined as : $r_d = \Delta V_{DS} / \Delta I_D$ at constant V_{GS}. The output resistance of FET is very high.
- *Transconducrance, g_m*: It is the ratio of the change in drain current to the change in gate-source voltage at constant drain—source voltage. It is also the mutual conductance and $g_m = \Delta I_D / \Delta V_{GS}$ at constant V_{DS}. This may be obtained from the output characteristics.
- *Amplification factor, μ*: It is the ratio of the change in the drain-source voltage to that of the change in the gate-source voltage—at constant drain current. It is given by, $\mu = \Delta V_{DS} / \Delta I_{GS}$ at constant I_D.

  Relationship between μ, g_m, and r_d.

$$\mu = \Delta V_{DS} / \Delta V_{GS} \text{ at constant } I_D$$

$$= (\Delta V_{DS} / \Delta I_D)(\Delta I_D / \Delta_{GS}) = r_d\, g_m \qquad ...(10.56)$$

10.34.2 FET-Amplifiers

Common source amplifier: This is similar to a common emitter transistor amplifier as shown in Fig. 10.72. Since the coupling and bypass capacitors are shorted, the signal is directly coupled to the gate. Since the source is bypassed to the ground, applied AC input appears between the gate and the source. This generates the current in the drain resistance and produces the required voltage which is an amplified and inverted version of the gate signal.

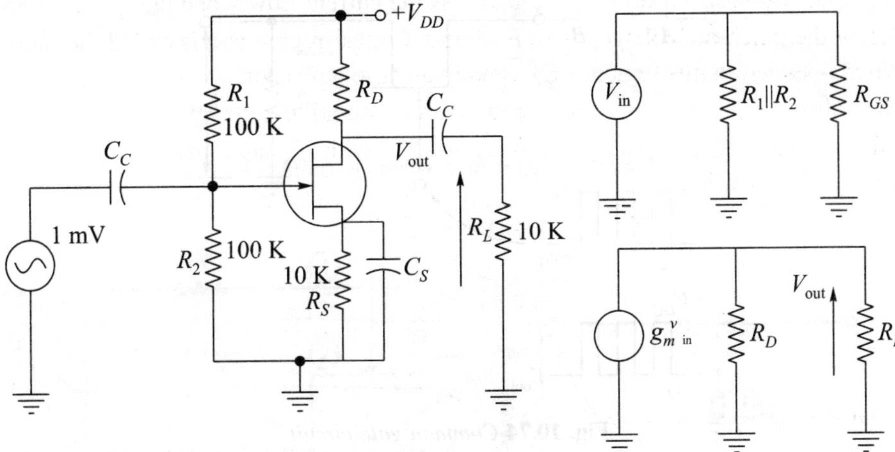

Fig. 10.72 *Common source amplifier*

Source follower: The Fig. 10.73 indicates a source follower circuit (similar to the emitter follower of transistor circuits). As in an emitter follower circuit, voltage gain of a source follower is less than unity. The advantage is that the input resistance increases and is very high. With $r_s = R_s \parallel R_L$, it is possible to derive that the voltage gain is $g_m r_s / (1 + g_m r_s)$.

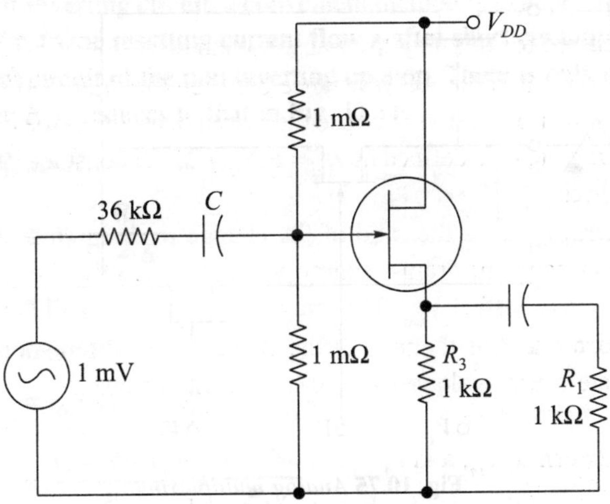

Fig. 10.73 *Source follower*

Common gate circuit: The Fig. 10.74 indicates a common gate circuit used for getting an output of chopped waveform of the input as shown. The gate voltage is a continuous square wave that continuously switches the FET on and off. Input is a continuous square wave and the output is its sampled version.

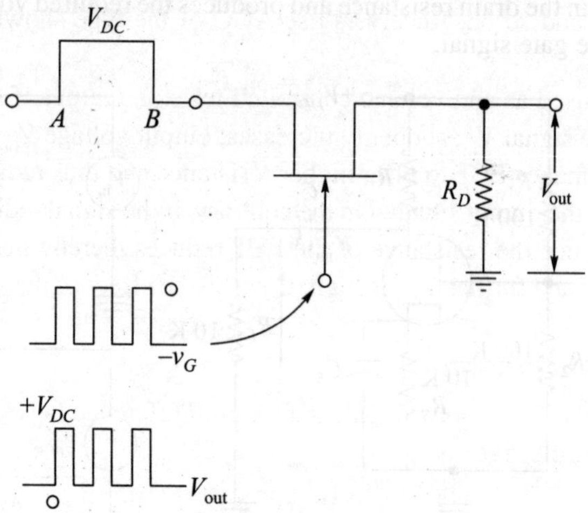

Fig. 10.74 *Common gate circuit*

10.34.3 Applications

Analog multiplexing: One of the interesting applications of FET is in multiplexing, *many into one*. One of the inputs will be connected to the output at a time depending on the gate input. For Ex. (Ref. Fig. 10.75) when V_1 is high, V_2 and V_3 are low, sine wave appears across R_D and so on.

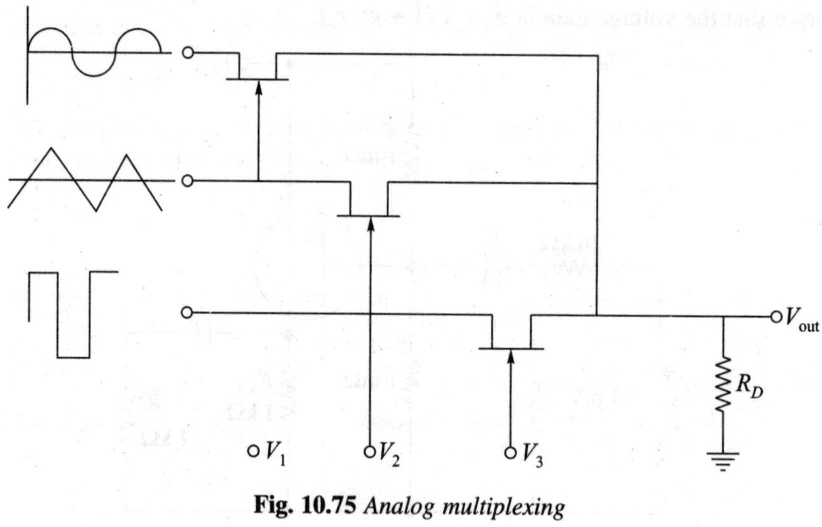

Fig. 10.75 *Analog multiplexing*

Automatic gain control: All broadcasting stations are not of the same strength. When certain volume is fixed for a weak station, at times the audio might be comfortable to the ears. However, with a strong station (without changing the volume control), the sound becomes high and would be uncomfortable. Hence is the need for volume control. Also, the volume may change due to the signal fading-weather conditions and so on. Receivers use AGC of the type shown in Fig. 10.76 to prevent this.

Indeed, the FET is used as and voltage controlled resistor. Output of the negative peak detector is the V_{GS} to the FET. If the signal V_{in}, suddenly increases, output voltage V_{out} increases thus increasing V_{GS} (more negative). This makes FET to offer higher resistance and thus reduces the input signal to the amplifier thereby reducing the output signal. On the contrary, if the signal reduces, V_{out} reduces and thus V_{GS} is less negative and hence the resistance of the FET reduces thereby making V_{in}, appearing at the amplifier to become higher and further V_{out} is high. Clearly, the effect of the sudden change in the input signal is offset by FET.

10.34.4 Principle of MOSFET

As with JFET, MOSFET also has a source, gate and drain. Difference between JFET and MOSFET is that, in case of MOSFET the gate is insulated from the channel. Hence, the gate current is even smaller than in FET, and is called *Insulated Gate Field Effect Transistor* (IGFET). Further, MOSFET may be broadly divided into two categories: *depletion mode* and *enhancement mode*. More commonly used type is the enhancement mode type. This mode is used in discrete circuits for power and digital switching in integrated circuits.

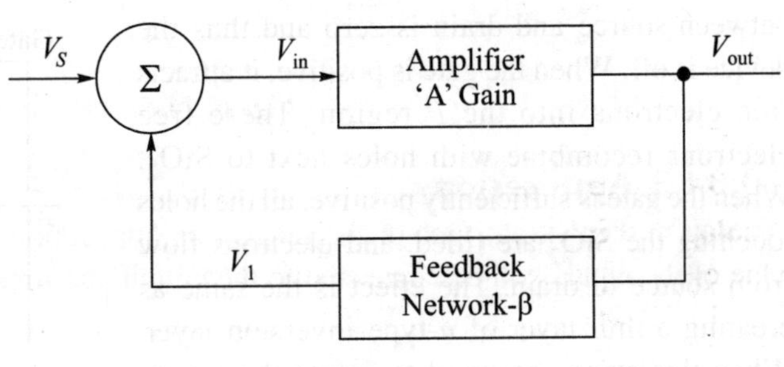

Fig. 10.76 *Automatic gain control (AGC)*

Depletion-mode MOSFET: A thin layer of silicon dioxide is deposited as shown in the Fig. 10.77. This is an insulator. The gate is insulated from the channel, very little current can flow even if the voltage is positive.

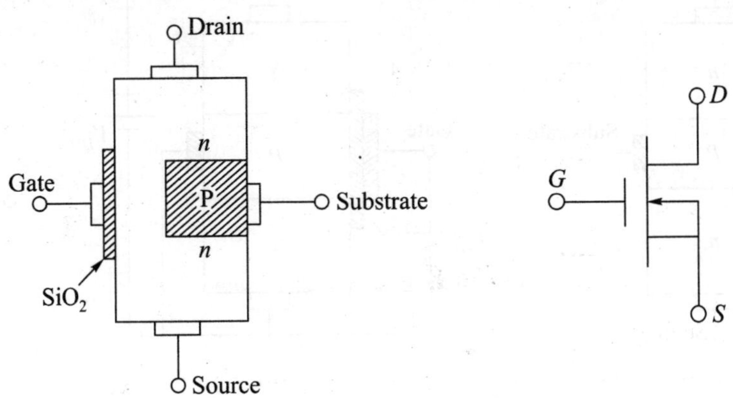

Fig. 10.77 *Depletion layer MOSFET*

Fig. 10.78 shows the biasing of the depletion-mode MOSFET. The *p*-region is called the substrate. If an electron has to flow from source to drain it has to pass though the narrow channel between the gate and the *p* substrate.

Electron flow is from source to drain. These electrons will have to pass through the narrow channel of the *p* substrate. The channel width is controlled by the gate voltage (as with FET). When the gate is sufficiently negative in magnitude, there is a cut off in the drain-source current. As such, the working of a depletion mode MOSFET is similar to that of FET. Due to the reason that the gate is insulated, it is also possible that the gate-source voltage could also be positive. In such an event, the positive gate voltage increases the number of free electrons flowing through the channel. More positive this voltage is, more is the conduction from source to drain.

Enhancement-mode MOSFET (E-MOSFET): Compared to the depletion mode MOSFET, in the E-MOSFET, the substrate has extended till the SiO_2 and there is no channel. The biasing of the E-MOSFET is as shown in Fig. 10.79. It indicates that when $V_{GS} = 0$, current flow between source and drain is zero and thus the device is off. When the gate is positive, it attracts free electrons into the *P* region. These free electrons recombine with holes next to SiO_2. When the gate is sufficiently positive, all the holes touching the SiO_2 are filled, and electrons flow from source to drain. The effect is the same as creating a thin layer of *n*-type inversion layer. When this exists, required to create the *n*-type inversion layer and this voltage is called the *threshold* voltage, V_{GS}(th). The typical value of this voltage ranges from 1 to 3 volts.

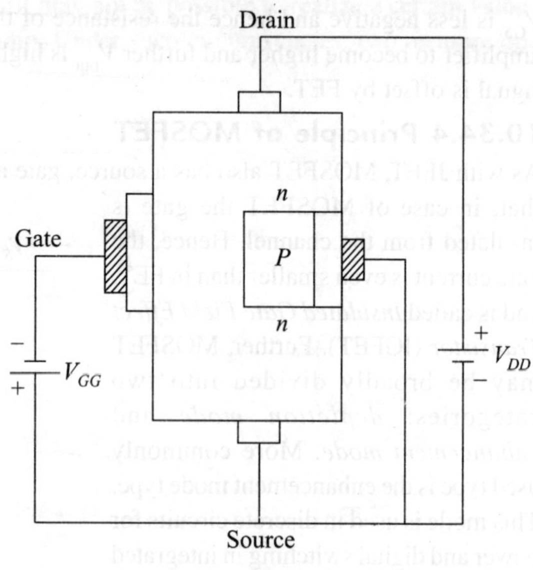

Fig. 10.78 *Biasing of depletion layer MOSFET*

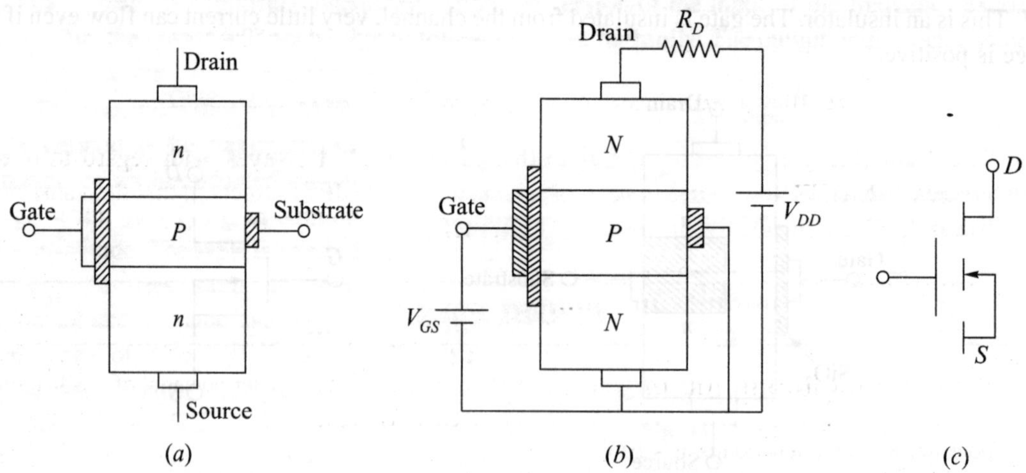

Fig. 10.79 *E-MOSFET biasing and symbolic representation*

A very important difference between the JFET and E-MOSFET is that the former depends for its working on the depletion layer where as the latter depends on the threshold voltage (with 0 gate voltage JFET is ON while E-MOSFET is OFF).

Operating characteristics: The Drain characteristics of an N-channel deplation mode MOSFET and E-MOSFET are shown in Fig. 10.80.

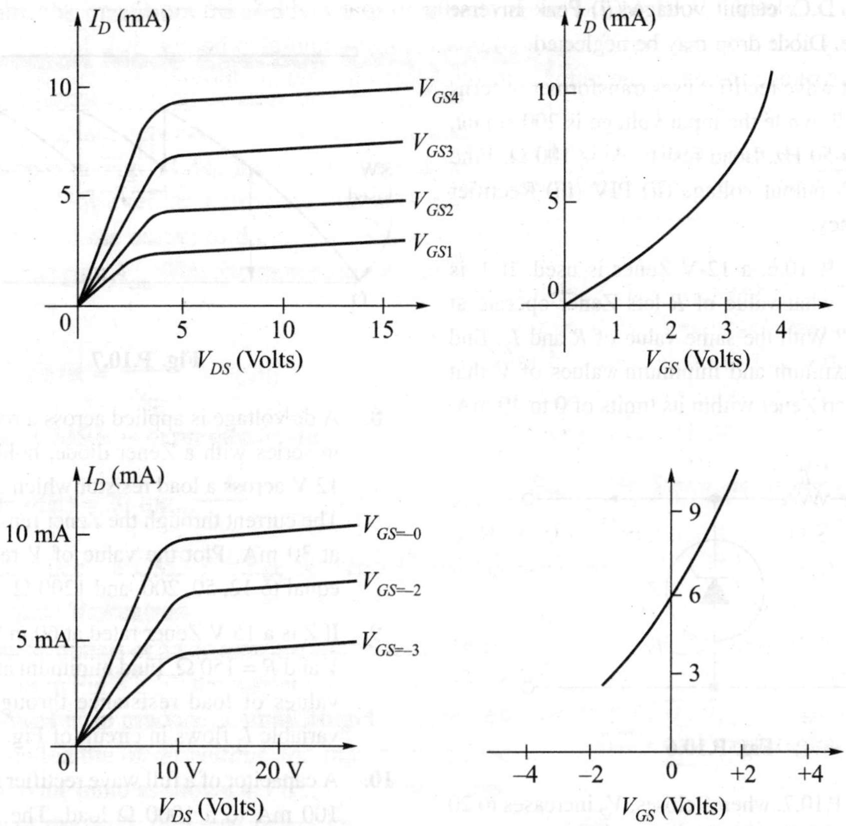

Fig. 10.80 *Characteristics of the N-channel depletion mode MOSFET*

The drain characteristics are similar to that of the JFET. However, with regard to transfer characteristics, E-MOSFET is comparable to the characteristics of JFET except in that the value of V_{GS} is negative in JFET and is positive in case of E-MOSFET.

PROBLEMS

1. Barrier potential increases with temperature. Explain. If at 25°C, the barrier potential of a Silicon diode 0.7 V, find the barrier potential when the barrier potential is raised to 80°C. Also, calculate the barrier potential when the junction is at – 20°C.
2. If the saturation current of a Silicon diode in 2.5 na (nano ampere) at 25°C, find the saturation current at 100°C.

3. Breakdown voltage of a diode is 100 Volts. If the maximum power dissipation is 0.5 watt, find the approximate value of breakdown current that burns diode.
4. A half wave rectifier uses transformer of turns ratio 2:1. If the primary voltage is 200 sin 314*t*, find (*i*) D.C. output voltage (*ii*) Peak Inverse Voltage. Diode drop may be neglected.
5. An half wave rectifier uses transformer of turns ratio 1:2, while the input voltage is 200 sin ω*t*, and *f* = 50 Hz, Load resistance is 100 Ω. Find (*i*) D.C. output voltage (*ii*) PIV (*iii*) Rectifier efficiency.
6. In Fig. P. 10.6, a 12-V Zener is used. If *V* is 22.5 V, what value of *R* lets Zener operate at 25 mA? With the same value of *R* and I_Z, find the maximum and minimum values of *V* that will keep Zener within its limits of 0 to 40 mA.

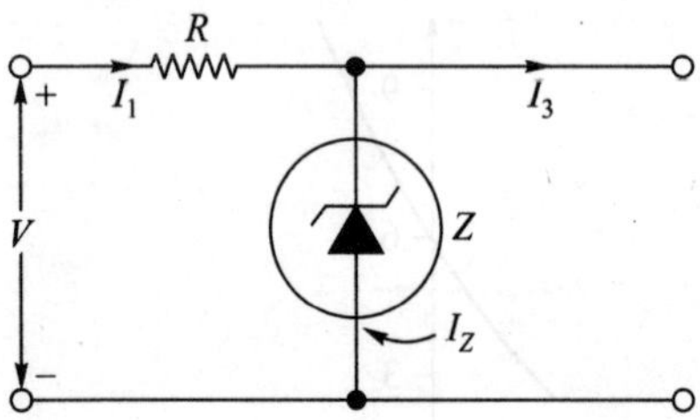

Fig. P.10.6

7. In Fig. P.10.7. when *S* closes, V_Z increases to 20 V so that Zener diode *Z* conducts; instantly the Zener current discharges the capacitor to 15 V. When V_Z drops below 15 V, the Zener current stops; so V_Z again increases, firing *Z* again at 20 V. (*a*) Find the length of time *T*. (*b*) Find the frequency of the pulses at the output.

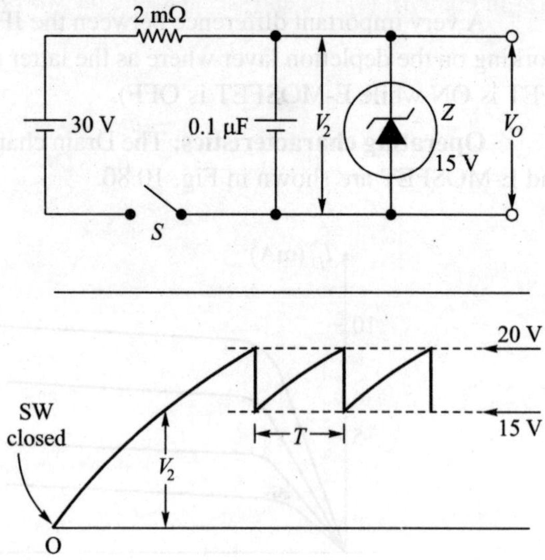

Fig. P.10.7

8. A dc voltage is applied across a resistor or *R* Ω in series with a Zener diode, holding constant 12 V across a load resistor which also has *R* Ω. The current through the Zener remains constant at 30 mA. Plot the value of *V* required for *R* equal to 12, 50, 200, and 1200 Ω.
9. If *Z* is a 15 V Zener rated at 60 mA. Let *V* = 27 *V* and *R* = 150 Ω. Find minimum and maximum values of load resistance through which the variable I_3 flows in circuit of Fig. P.10.6.
10. A capacitor of a full wave rectifier has to supply 100 mA to a 1000 Ω load. The ripple factor should be 0.005, What should be the transformer voltage? Find also the size of the capacitor to be used.

11. In Fig. P.10.11, find and sketch the output waveforms.

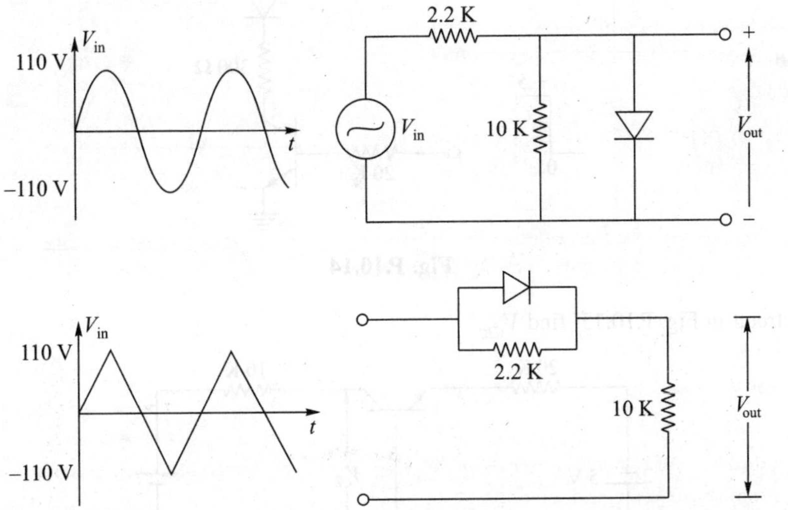

Fig. P.10.11

12. For the Fig. P.10.12 sketch the output waveform v_o.

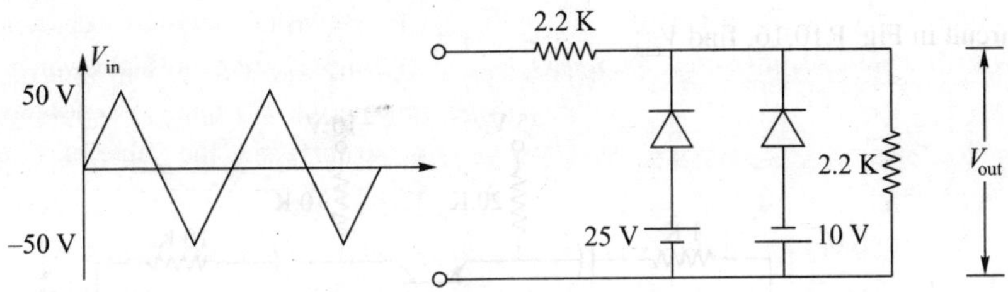

Fig. P.10.12

13. For the circuit shown in Fig. P.10.13, sketch the output waveform across the diode. Coupling capacitor reactance may be taken as zero.

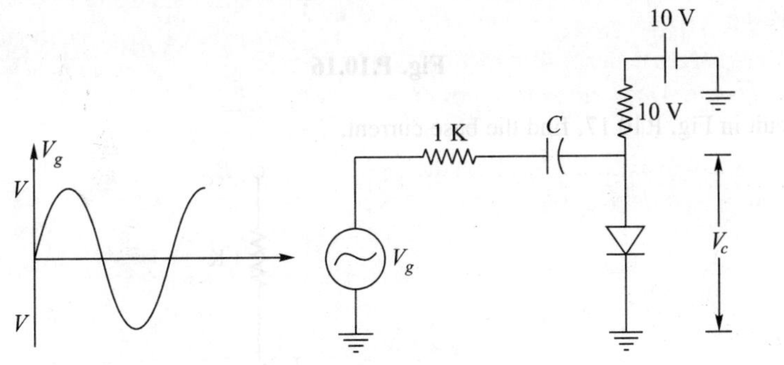

Fig. P.10.13

14. The LED of Fig. P.10.14 has 1.5 V across it and 10 mA through it. Find its resistance. If the transistor has a V_{CE} (sat) of 0.6 V, find the value of I_C (sat).

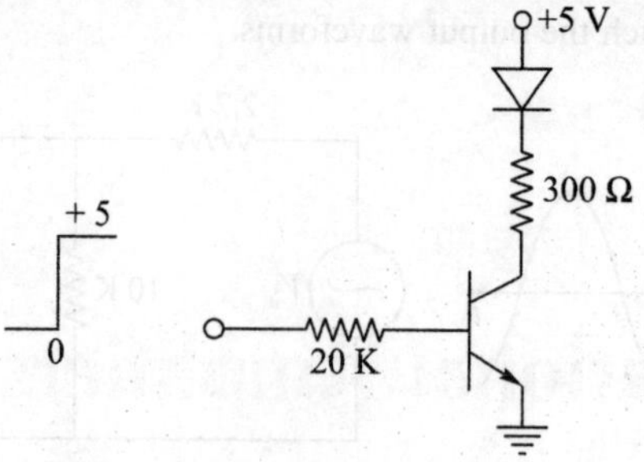

Fig. P.10.14

15. For the circuit in Fig. P.10.15, find V_{CB}.

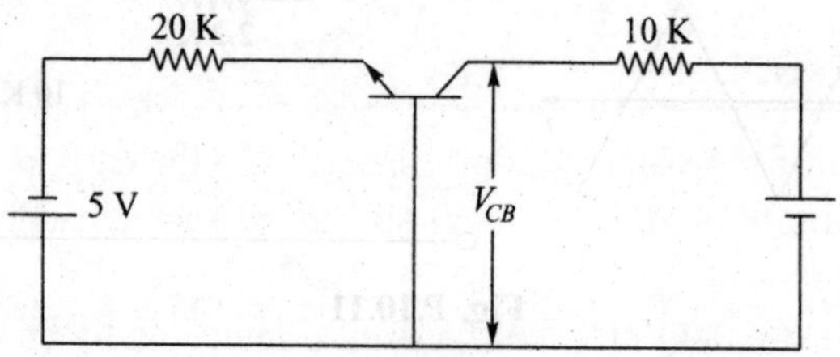

Fig. P.10.15

16. For the circuit in Fig. P.10.16, find V_{out}.

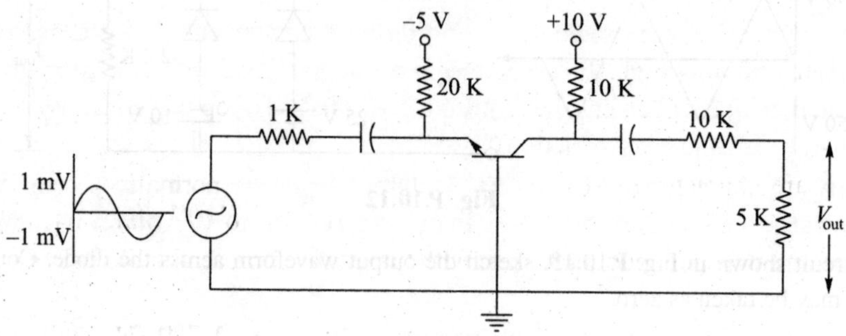

Fig. P.10.16

17. For the circuit in Fig. P.10.17, find the base current.

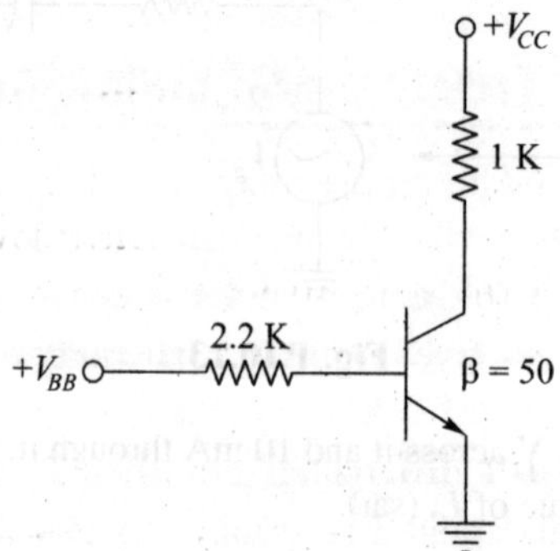

Fig. P.10.17

11 CHAPTER
Operational Amplifiers

11.1 INTRODUCTION

The term operational amplifier (op amp) has originated from the early use of this type of amplifier in analog computers to perform basic mathematical operations such as addition, subtraction, integration, differentiation and scaling.

The op amp is an extremely efficient, versatile device and techniques for using it are easily acquired. As a consequence, it is one of the most popular electronic devices in use today. Its applications are not limited to those involving mathematical operations; it may be used for ac to dc conversion, ac/dc amplification, signal conditioning, in instrumentation and in many special system designs. Indeed, the use of the op amp is limited only by the ingenuity of the user.

Early op amps were constructed by using discrete components (transistors and resistors) and consequently their cost was high. In 1965, the first integrated circuit version (many transistors and resistors fabricated on one silicon chip) was introduced. The use of op amps increased considerably and was accompanied by drastic cost reductions.

Op amps are characterized by special features which are normally absent in other types of amplifiers. Typically, the input impedance of an op amp is $\approx 10^7$ to 10^{12} ohms, its output impedance is $\approx$ 10 to 50 ohms and the open loop gain (gain with no feedback present in the circuit) is of the order of 10^4 to 10^6.

There are a host of op amps available commercially—the μA 709, 741, 749 etc.; all of them do not have identical characteristics.

In this chapter we will study the basic features of op amps, their principle of operation and some of their applications.

11.2 THE IDEAL OPERATIONAL AMPLIFIER

Figure 11.1 (*a*) shows the symbol used for representing an op amp. Nodes 1 and 2 are the input terminals, and node 3 is the output terminal. Since the op amp is an active device, it requires a dc power supply for its operation. As shown in Fig. 11.1 (*b*), a positive and a negative supply V^+ and V^- are connected to terminals 4 and 5. In addition to these five terminals, there may be others which extend the usefulness of the operational amplifier.

The op amp is also known as a differential amplifier. This implies that the op amp senses the difference between the input signals applied at terminals 1 and 2, and amplifies the difference by an amount A. The output v_0 is therefore given by

$$v_0 = A(v_2 - v_1) \qquad ...(11.1)$$

where v_1 and v_2 are the input signals and the constant A is known as the open loop gain since no feedback loop exists, in Fig. 11.1, connecting the output terminal to input terminals.

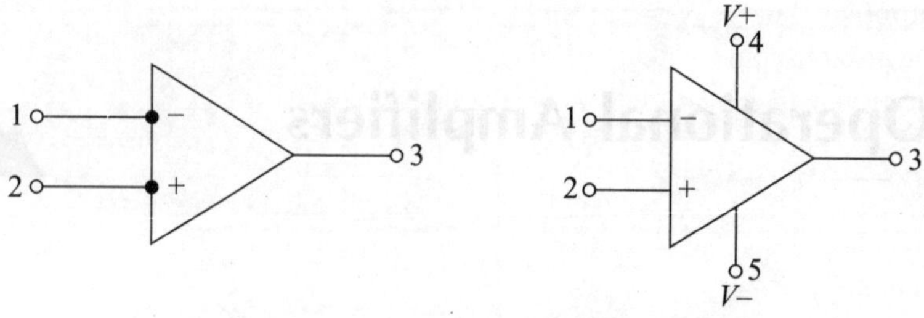

(*a*) *Op amp symbol* (*b*) *Op amp with power supply terminals*

Fig. 11.1

The design of an op amp circuit and an understanding of its operation are greatly simplified by use of the following four ideal op amp properties.

(*i*) The ideal op amp does not draw any current from voltage sources connected to its input terminals. This implies that the input impedance of an op amp is infinity ohms.

(*ii*) The voltage at the output terminal is independent of the current drawn from it. In other words, the output impedance is zero.

(*iii*) The ideal op amp will amplify signals of any frequency with equal gain. This means that the ideal op amp has infinite bandwidth.

(*iv*) The open loop gain of an ideal op amp is very large *i.e.*, infinity.

Figure 11.2 shows two input signals v_1 and v_2 connected to an op amp. By application of the ideal op amp properties, we conclude that no current enters the op amp at terminals 1 and 2. The output v_0 is given by Eqn. 11.1 and is indicated in Fig. 11.2. It should be noted that in the expression for the output, v_0, the signal input at terminal 1 appears with a negative sign attached to it. On the other hand, the input signal at terminal 2 appears in Eqn. 11.1 without alteration in its sign. Terminal 1 is therefore called the *inverting* terminal while terminal 2 is known as the *non-inverting* terminal. Because of this, negative and positive signs appear at terminals 1 and 2 respectively.

11.3 SATURABLE PROPERTY OF AN OP AMP; THE COMPARATOR

Consider the circuit of Fig. 11.2. The output, $A(v_2 - v_1)$, reduces to either Av_2 or $-Av_1$ depending on whether v_1 or v_2 is zero. Although A is ideally infinite, the output of an op amp does not vary from $+\infty$ to $-\infty$; rather, it is limited by the power supply voltage magnitudes. If the supply voltages are ±15 V, the output is limited to approximately ±10 V. Once the output reaches this level, it does not increases any further even if the input voltages are increased. The amplifier is then considered to be saturated.

It appears that a circuit of the type shown in Fig. 11.2 is of little or no practical value since the saturation condition, for all practical op amps, will be reached for rather low amplitude signal levels at the input. This is partially true. Almost all op amp circuits employ feedback as will be discussed in the next section. However, the basic circuit of Fig. 11.2 does find an important practical application in its use as a comparator.

In a comparator circuit, a variable voltage v_2 may be fed to the non-inverting terminal and constant voltage V_{REF} fed to the inverting terminal. Let us suppose that $V_{REF} = 5$ V, $A = 20{,}000$ and let the power supply voltage be ±15 V. Output Saturation will be attained at +10 V when $v_2 - v_1 \approx \frac{v_0}{A} = 0.5$ mV. Since $v_1 = V_{REF}$ is fixed, it implies that v_2 has to exceed it by 500 μV for the ap amp to saturate. Likewise V_{REF} has to be greater than v_2 by 500 μV for the output to saturate at – 10 V. Practically, the variable v_2 is compared to V_{REF} and the op amp output indicates when $v_2 \gtrless V_{REF}$; the circuit is therefore known as a comparator. Since the reference voltage is connected to the inverting terminals, the comparator is identified as a non inverting comparator. If the reference voltage is zero, the circuit functions as a zero crossing comparator or detector.

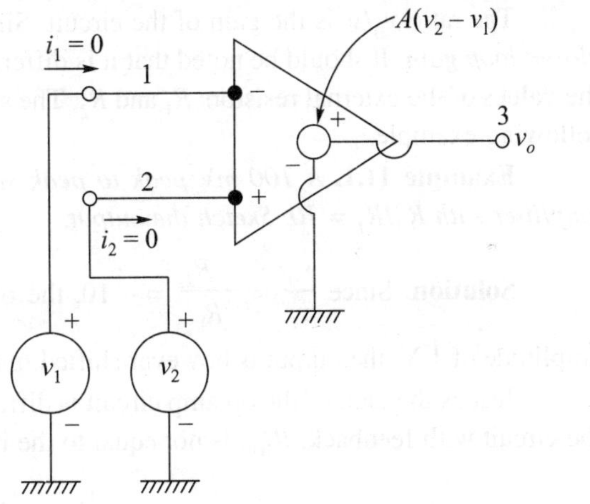

Fig. 11.2 *Input signals v_1, v_2 connected to an op amp*

11.4 THE INVERTING OP AMP CIRCUIT

Unlike the comparator, the op amp inverter circuit employs feedback *i.e.,* a portion of the output is fed back into the input. Since the feedback is applied at the inverting terminal, it is referred to as negative feedback. Consider the circuit of Fig. 11.3. R_2 is the feedback resistor. The input is connected to the op amp via the input resistor R_1. Using ideal op amp properties, since $A = \infty$,

Eqn. 11.2 yields

$$v_2 - v_1 = \frac{v_0}{A} = 0$$

Since terminal 2 is at ground potential, it follows that a virtual short circuit exists between terminals 2 and 1 *i.e.,* $v_1 = 0$ volts. This should not be confused with an actual short circuit which demands that terminals 1 and 2 be joined together physically.

Applying KCL at terminal 1

$$\frac{v_i - v_1}{R_1} = \frac{v_1 - v_0}{R_2}$$

Since $v_1 = 0$, the above reduces to

$$\frac{v_i}{R_1} = \frac{-v_0}{R_2}$$

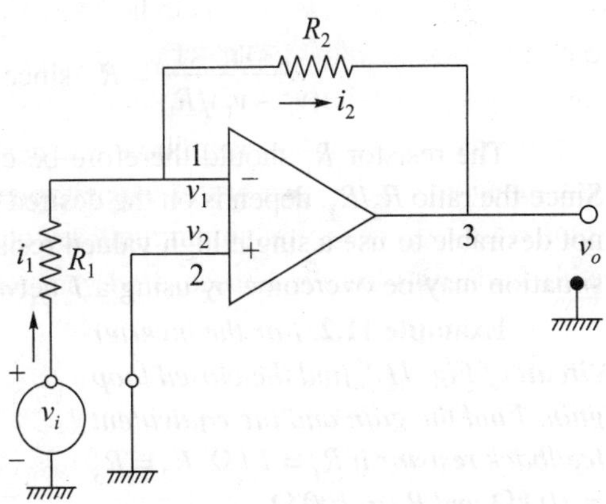

Fig. 11.3 *Op amp comparator*

or
$$\frac{v_0}{v_i} = \frac{-R_2}{R_1} \quad \text{...(11.2)}$$

CHAPTER 11

The ratio v_0/v_i is the gain of the circuit. Since a feedback loop exists, the gain is known as the *closed loop gain*. It should be noted that it is different from A, the open loop gain, and depends only on the values of the external resistors R_1 and R_2. The significance of the negative sign is highlighted by the following example.

Example 11.1. *A 100 mV peak to peak sine waveform of voltage is applied to an inverting amplifier with $R_2/R_1 = 10$. Sketch the output.*

Solution. Since $\frac{v_0}{v_i} = \frac{-R_2}{R_1} = -10$, the output is also a sine waveform with a peak to peak amplitude of 1 V; the output is however shifted in phase w.r.t. the input by 180° as shown in Fig. 11.4.

Just as the gain of the op amp circuit is different from the open loop gain, the input resistance of the circuit with feedback, R_{ifb}, is not equal to the input resistance, R_i, of the op amp.

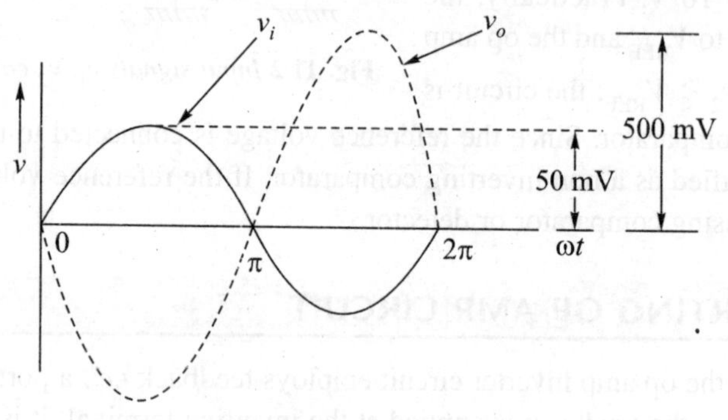

Fig. 11.4 *Fig. for Ex. 11.1*

$$R_{ifb} = \frac{v_i}{i_1}$$

$$\frac{v_i}{(v_i - v_1)/R_1} = R_1, \text{ since } v_1 = 0.$$

The resistor R_1 should therefore be chosen so that the circuit does not load the input source. Since the ratio R_2/R_1, depends on the desired gain, it is possible that R_2 may be impractically high. It is not desirable to use a single high valued resistor because of the poor tolerance associated with it. This situation may be overcome by using a *T* network in the feedback loop as in the following example.

Example 11.2. *For the inverter circuit of Fig. 11.5 find the closed loop gain. Find the gain and the equivalent feedback resistor if $R_1 = 1$ kΩ, $R_2 = R_3 = 10$ kΩ and $R_4 = 100$ Ω.*

Solution. The circuit of Fig. 11.5 is equivalent to that in Fig. 11.6 since node 1 is virtually at ground potential.

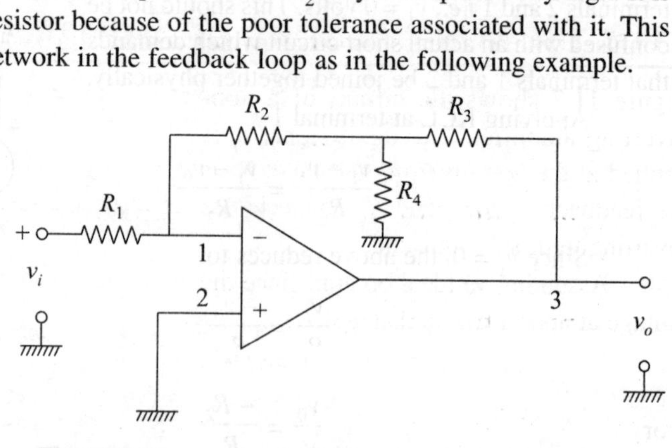

Fig. 11.5 *Op amp circuit with T network in feedback loop*

The equivalent feedback resistor,

$$R_f, \text{ is} = \frac{v_0}{i_{sc}}$$

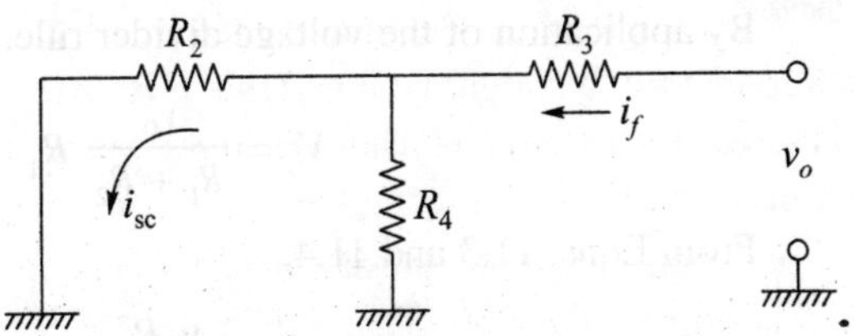

Fig. 11.6 *Equivalent circuit of circuit in Fig. 11.5*

Also, $$i_f = \frac{v_0}{R_3 + \dfrac{R_2 R_4}{R_2 + R_4}}$$

Using the current divider rule,

$$i_{sc} = i_f \frac{R_4}{R_2 + R_4} = \frac{v_0 R_4}{R_2 R_3 + R_3 R_4 + R_2 R_4}$$

Therefore, $$R_f = \frac{v_0}{i_{sc}}$$

$$= \frac{R_2 R_3 + R_3 R_4 + R_2 R_4}{R_4} = \left(R_3 + R_2 + \frac{R_2 R_3}{R_4}\right)$$

The gain, $$\frac{v_0}{v_i} = \frac{-R_f}{R_1} = -\left(\frac{R_3 + R_2 + \dfrac{R_2 R_3}{R_4}}{R_1}\right)$$

Substituting numerical values,

$$R_f = 1020 \text{ k}\Omega$$

and $$\frac{v_0}{v_i} = -1020.$$

It should be clear from this example that it is possible to realize a high value of equivalent feedback resistor and, therefore, high gain by use of low value feedback resistors connected in *T* formation.

The output resistance, in the presence of feedback, will be dealt with in a later section.

11.5 THE NON-INVERTING OP AMP CIRCUIT

CHAPTER 11

Figure 11.7 shows the circuit of a non-inverting amplifier. The input signal v_i is applied at the non-inverting terminal. R_2 is the feedback resistor and R_1 connects the inverting terminal to ground.

Assuming an ideal op amp since the voltage at node 1 tracks that at node 2,

$$v_1 = v_i \qquad \text{...(11.3)}$$

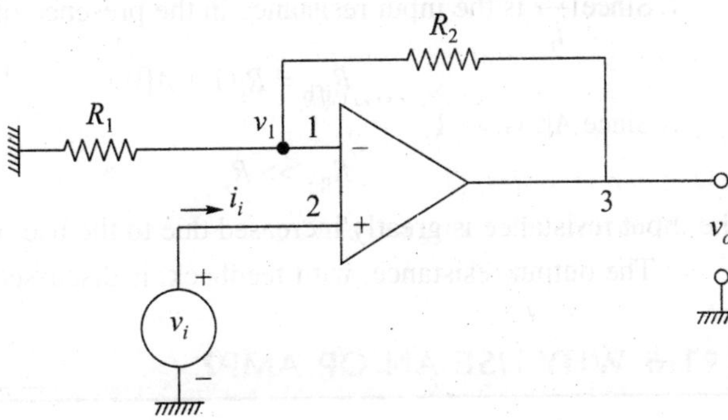

Fig. 11.7 *Op amp as a non-inverting amplifier*

By application of the voltage divider rule,

$$V_1 = \frac{v_0}{R_1 + R_2} R_1 \qquad ...(11.4)$$

From Eqns. 11.3 and 11.4,

$$v_i = \frac{v_0 R_1}{R_1 + R_2}$$

or

$$\frac{v_0}{v_i} = \left(1 + \frac{R_2}{R_1}\right) \qquad ...(11.5)$$

It is worthwhile to compare this last expression, the gain of the non-inverting amplifier, with that in Eqn. 11.2.

The input resistance of the non-inverting op amp circuit, R_{ifb}, is different from that of the op amp itself, R_i.

In order to find an expression for R_{ifb}, we depart from the ideal op amp assumptions and therefore a voltage v_d exists between the input terminals of the op amp. If i_i is the current entering the non-inverting terminal,

$$v_d = i_i R_i \qquad ...(11.6)$$

Also $\quad v_d = v_i - v_1$

or $\quad v_i = v_d + v_1$

From Eqn. 11.4 $\quad v_i = v_d + \beta v_0$ where

$$\beta = \frac{R_1}{R_1 + R_2}$$

and using Eqn. 11.1, we obtain

$$v_i = v_d(1 + A\beta) \qquad ...(11.7)$$

Using Eqn. 11.6 in Eqn. 11.7,

$$\frac{v_i}{i_i} = R_i(1 + A\beta)$$

Since $\frac{v_i}{i_i}$ is the input resistance in the presence of feedback, R_{ifb},

$$R_{ifb} = R_i(1 + A\beta) \qquad ...(11.8)$$

Since $A\beta$ is >> 1,

$$R_{ibf} >> R_i$$

The input resistance is greatly increased due to the use of negative feedback.

The output resistance, with feedback, is discussed in section 11.7.

11.6 WHY USE AN OP AMP?

Suppose two signals v_1 and v_2 are to be summed using resistors R_1 and R_2 in the circuit of Fig. 11.8. The output is tapped across R_0, and R_L is the load resistor.

Application of KCL at junction A yields

$$\frac{v_1 - v_0}{R_1} + \frac{v_2 - v_0}{R_2} = \frac{v_0}{R_0} + \frac{v_0}{R_L}$$

Representing the parallel combination of R_0 and R_L by R_p, we obtain

$$v_0\left[\frac{1}{R_p} + \frac{1}{R_1} + \frac{1}{R_2}\right] = \frac{v_1}{R_1} + \frac{v_2}{R_2}$$

The output voltage v_0 is given by the expression

$$v_0 = \frac{v_1\left[\frac{R_p}{R_1}\right] + v_2\left[\frac{R_p}{R_2}\right]}{\left[1 + \frac{R_p}{R_1} + \frac{R_p}{R_2}\right]}$$

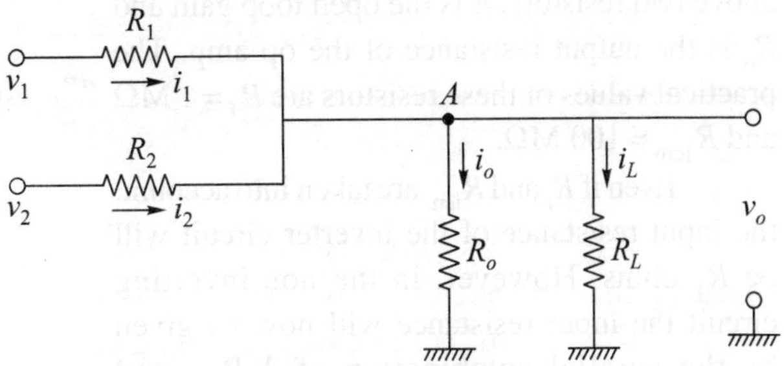

Fig. 11.8 *Summing two inputs using an op amp*

from which it is seen that v_0 depends on R_L. If it is desired to make v_0 independent of R_L, it is necessary to choose $R_0 << R_L$. This will result in a large signal attenuation which is undesirable.

To overcome this difficulty, an amplifier with some gain must be used. However, the use of a conventional amplifier (such as RC coupled) introduces other problems. With a RC coupled amplifier one needs an infinite value of coupling capacitance if dc signals are to be amplified. Also, its value depends on the frequency or frequency components of the signal. With transformer coupling, dc signals can not be amplified. Direct coupling may be employed using difference amplifiers. However, since the gain of a single stage is limited, many stages have to be used. Moreover the design of such a circuit requires advanced knowledge of circuit design.

Alternatively, we may use an operational amplifier—a specialized amplifier. As pointed out earlier, its used is easily mastered. We have already noted that the closed loop gain of the op amp depends only on circuit components external to it and is independent of the open loop gain, A, of the amplifier. The op amp is thus a well suited device whose use effectively circumvents problems which are present if a conventional amplifier is used.

11.7 OP AMP CHARACTERISTICS

In contrast with the properties of an ideal op amp, a practical op amp possesses finite values of input resistance, gain, bandwidth and output resistance. These and other characteristics of op amps and op amp circuits are examined in this section.

11.7.1 Input and Output Resistances

The equivalent circuit of an op amp is shown in Fig. 11.9. Looking into terminals 1 and 2 one sees the resistance R_i, the input resistance of the op amp. When these two terminals are tied together the resistance from this common point to ground is R_{icm}—known as the common mode input resistance. Symmetry with respect to the terminals 1 and 2 is maintained in the equivalent circuit by connection of resistors of value $2R_{icm}$ from each of these terminals to ground. The equivalent resistor R_{icm} is the parallel combination of the above two resistors. A is the open loop gain and R_0 is the output resistance of the op amp. The practical values of these resistors are $R_i = 1\ M\Omega$ and $R_{icm} = 100\ M\Omega$.

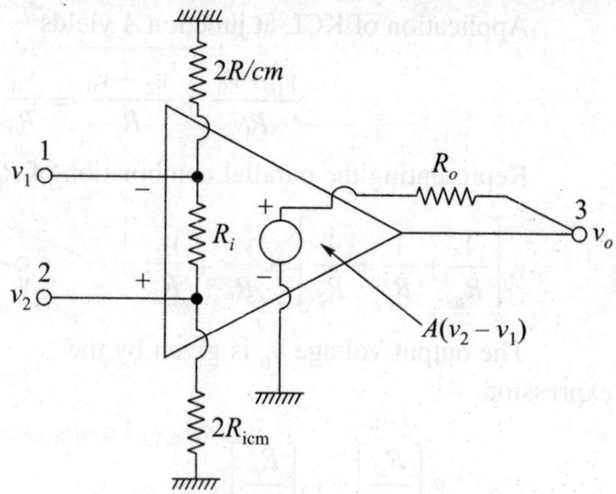

Fig. 11.9 *Op amp equivalent circuit*

Even if R_i and R_{icm} are taken into account, the input resistance of the inverter circuit will be R_1 ohms. However, in the non-inverting circuit the input resistance will now be given by the parallel combination of $2R_{icm}$ and $R_i(1 + A\beta)$ (Eqn. 11.8).

To demonstrate the effect of feedback on output resistance, in the case of the inverting circuit, consider Fig. 11.10 (*a*), we have

$$i_2^* = \frac{v_1 - v_0}{R_2}$$

$$v_0^* = A(v_2 - v_1) = -Av_1,$$

$$i_2 = \frac{\frac{v_0}{A} - v_0}{R_2}$$

$$= \frac{-v_0[1 + A]}{AR_2} = \frac{-v_0}{R_2A/(1 + A)} \qquad ...(11.9)$$

Equation 11.9 shows that as far as the output is concerned the effect of feedback, at the output, is equivalent to the presence of a resistor $\frac{R_2A}{(1 + A)}$ ohms connected between the output and ground. This is shown in Fig. 11.10 (*b*) from which it is apparent that the output resistance is the parallel combination of R_0 and $R_2A/(1 + A)$.

$$R_{ofb} = \frac{R_0R_2A/(1 + A)}{R_0 + R_2A/(1 + A)}$$

$$= \frac{AR_0R_2}{AR_2 + R_0(1 + A)}$$

If $A >> 1$ and $R_2 >> R_0$

$$R_{ofb} \cong R_0 \qquad ...(11.10)$$

*Note that we have discarded op amp assumptions as $A \neq \infty$ and $v_1 \neq 0$.

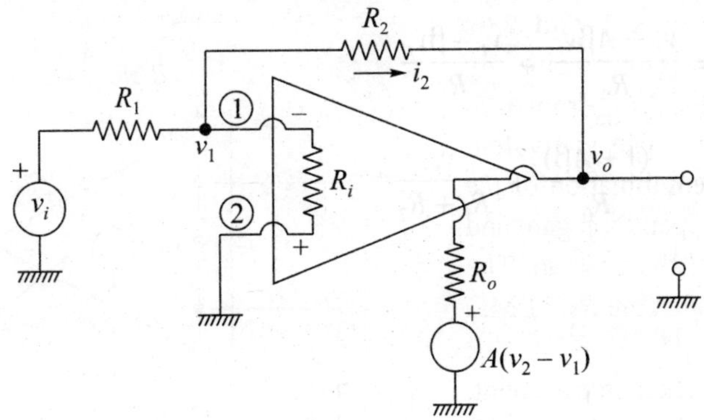

(a) *Effect of feedback on output resistance*

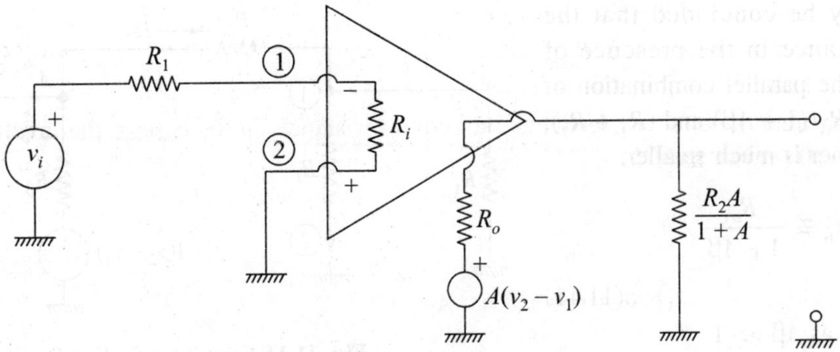

(b) *Equivalent circuit of Fig. 11.10 (a)*

Fig. 11.10

Turning to the non-inverting circuit, a convenient method is to apply a test source v_t at the output and measure the ratio of v_t to the resulting current flow i_t after short circuiting all independent voltage sources* in the equivalent circuit of the non inverting op amp. There is only one such source, the input v_i. The circuit for finding $R_{of\,b}$ reduces to that in Fig. 11.11.

Since $\quad R_i >> R_1$,

$$v_1 \cong v_t \frac{R_1}{R_1 + R_2}$$

$$= \beta v_t$$

Applying KCL at node *A*

$$i_t = i_0 + i_2$$

$$= \frac{v_t - A(-v_1)}{R_0} + \frac{v_t - v_1}{R_2}$$

*That this is a valid procedure may be explained as follows. Suppose the op amp circuit is replaced by its Thevenin equivalent at the output *i.e.* v_{th} and R_{th}.R_{th} is the required output resistance. Now apply the test source v_t at the output after short circuiting v_{th}; $i_t = \frac{v_t}{R_{th}}$ and $\frac{v_t}{i_t} = R_{th}$. Note that dependent sources are not short circuited.

CHAPTER 11

$$= \frac{v_t + A\beta v_t}{R_0} + \frac{v_t - \beta v_t}{R_2}$$

$$= v_t \frac{(1 + A\beta)}{R_0} + \frac{v_t}{R_1 + R_2}$$

Since $\frac{1}{R_{\text{of b}}} + \frac{i_t}{v_t}$

$$= \left[\frac{1}{R_0/(1 + A\beta)} + \frac{1}{(R_1 + R_2)}\right]$$

It may be concluded that the output resistance in the presence of feedback is the parallel combination of the resistors $R_0/(1 + A\beta)$ and $(R_1 + R_2)$; since the former is much smaller,

$$R_{\text{of b}} \cong \frac{R_o}{1 + A\beta} \quad ...(11.11)$$

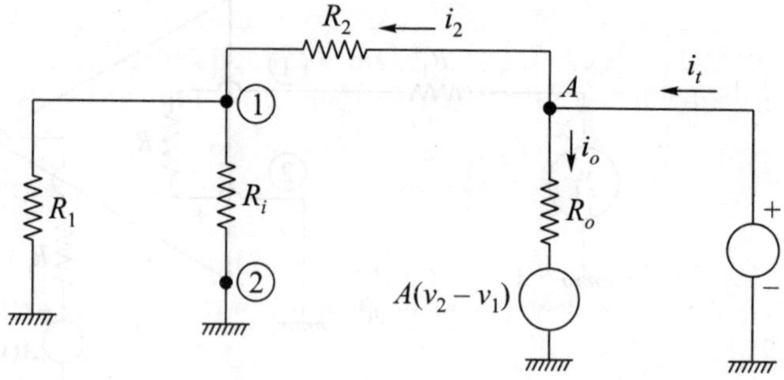

Fig. 11.11 *Circuit for finding $R_{\text{of b}}$*

In fact as $A\beta >> 1$

$$R_{\text{of b}} \cong \frac{R_o}{A\beta} \quad \text{and} \quad << R_o$$

The output resistance of the non-inverting circuit, in the presence of feedback, is much lesser than the output resistance of the op amp itself.

11.7.2 Bandwidth

The frequency response of an op amp is usually specified by the manufacturer and is typically like that shown in Fig. 11.12. The frequency f_1 is known as the internal break frequency and is determined by components of op amp circuity. It must be remembered that the gain, A, is that of the op amp itself determined without the presence of feedback and is known as the open loop gain. At a frequency f_1, the gain A is lower than its low frequency value by 3 dB.

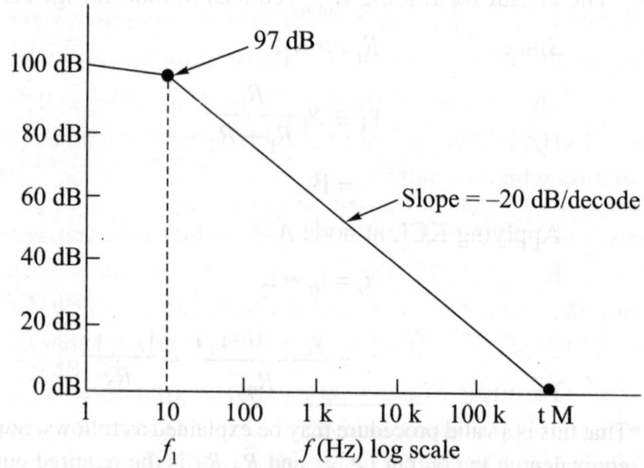

Fig. 11.12 *Frequency response of an op amp*

Consider the non-inverting circuit shown in Fig. 11.13. The expression for gain, Eqn. 11.5, was derived on the assumption that $A \to \infty$. For finite value of A, referring to Fig. 11.13, the differential voltage amplified by the op amp is $\left\{v_i - \frac{R_1}{R_2 + R_1} v_0\right\}$. If $\beta = \frac{R_1}{R_2 + R_1}$, the voltage amplified is $\{v_i - \beta v_o\}$. From Eqn. 11.1, since

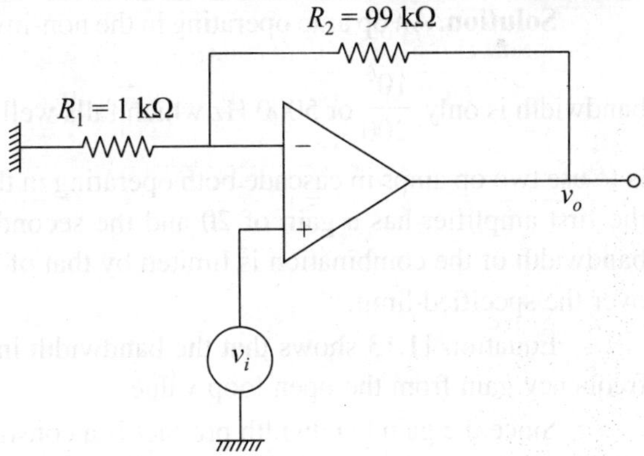

Fig. 11.13 *A non-inverting amplifier*

$$v_0 = A\{v_i - \beta v_0\}$$

$$v_0 = \frac{A}{1 + A\beta} v_i$$

and the gain, A_{fb}, with feedback is

$$\frac{v_0}{v_i} = \frac{A}{1 + A\beta} \qquad \text{...(11.12)}$$

If $A\beta >> 1$, Eqn. 11.12. reduces to Eqn. 11.5. From Fig. 11.13, $\beta = 10^{-2}$ and at low frequencies, from Fig. 11.12, $A = 10^5$; the product $A\beta \cong 1000 >> 1$ and the gain of the inverter circuit in the presence of feedback, A_{fb}, is $10^5/(1 + 1000) \approx 100$. If A were to stay constant as f increases, we can expect A_{fb} to remain at this value. As a matter of fact A varies with frequency. However, in the range $0 \le f \le f_1$, A does not decrease rapidly. At $f = f_1$, A is only 3 dB lower than its low frequency value, and from Eqn. 11.12, $A_{fb} = 70700/(1 + 707) = 99.86 \cong 100$. It is seen that A_{fb} is sensibly constant in the range $0 < f < f_1$.f_1 is known as the break frequency of the amplifier without feedback. For $f > f_1$, A decreases rapidly , $A\beta$ is no longer >> 1, and the gain A_{fb} decreases. At a certain frequency f_1', A_{fb} will drop to 3 dB below its low frequency value of 100; f_1' is known as the break frequency of the amplifier in the presence of feedback. It is easily checked, using Fig. 11.12 and Eqn. 11.12 that although A_{fb} falls with frequency the bandwidth of the circuit is greatly increased. The low frequency value of $A_{fb} \cong 100$. At a frequency f_1', $A_{fb} \cong 70.7$ and from Eqn. 11.12 $A = 241.3$. From Fig. 11.12, this corresponds to a frequency of ≈ 7 kHz.

This shows that the bandwidth of the circuit, with feedback, is greatly increased *i.e.*, from 10 Hz to ≈ 7 kHz. In fact, the gain bandwidth product of an amplifier is a constant as expressed by the following relation which is stated without proof.

$$f_1 A = f_1' A_{fb} \qquad \text{...(11.14)}$$

In Eqn. 11.13, A is the gain of the op amp at frequency f_1 and A_{fb} is the low frequency gain of the amplifier with feedback. For the inverter circuit under consideration $f_1 = 10$ Hz (From Fig. 11.12), $A = 70700$ *i.e.* (97 dB), and $A_{fb} = 100$. It follows that $f_1' = 7.07$ kHz.

Example 11.3. *An op amp has a gain bandwidth product of 10^6 Hz. Design a circuit which has a gain of 200 over a frequency range of 10 kHz. It is required that the circuit should have a large input resistance.*

CHAPTER 11

Solution. An op amp operating in the non-inverting mode may be used. If A_{fb} = 200 the obtainable bandwidth is only $\frac{10^6}{200}$ or 5000 Hz which falls well short of the specified figure of 10^4 Hz. The solution is to use two op amps in cascade both operating in the non-inverting mode as shown in Fig. 11.14. Here, the first amplifier has a gain of 20 and the second a gain of 10 yielding an overall gain of 200. The bandwidth of the combination is limited by that of the amplifier with A_{fb} = 20, *i.e.*, 5.10^4 which is well over the specified limit.

Equation 11.13 shows that the bandwidth increases by the same amount as the decrease in low frequency gain from the open loop value.

Since the gain bandwidth product is a constant,* it may not be possible to realize a certain value of gain for a specified bandwidth using only one op amp. Under such circumstances, two or more op amps should be used in cascade as in Example 11.3.

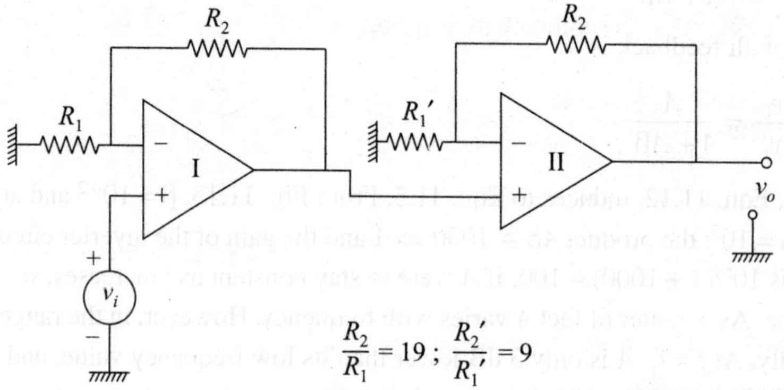

Fig. 11.14 *Circuit for Ex. 11.3*

11.7.3 Slew Rate

For all op amps and op amp circuits there exists a frequency below which the output, considering sinusoidal signals, is a faithful, undistorted, amplified version of the input. If the frequency exceeds a certain value, the output will not be able to follow the input faithfully. The output under such conditions is referred to as the *slew rate limited output*.

The maximum slew rate, MSR, may be defined as the maximum rate of change of an undistorted output voltage when supplying maximum output amplitude. The MSR is affected by many factors such as load capacitance and its value usually lies in the range of 1 to 100 volts per microsecond. Figure 11.15 shows a slew rate limited output waveform.

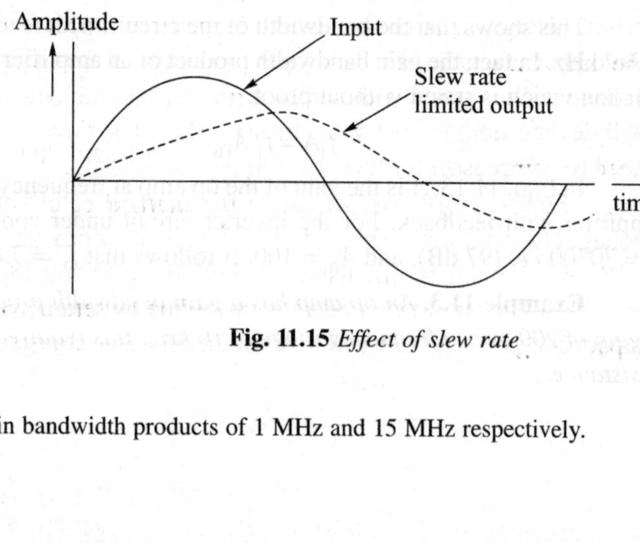

Fig. 11.15 *Effect of slew rate*

*The op amps μA741 and the LM118 have gain bandwidth products of 1 MHz and 15 MHz respectively.

The broken line output waveform corresponds to the case when the input frequency has a value corresponding to which the maximum slew rate is exceeded.

Let the output sinusoidal voltage be denoted by $v = V_m \sin(\omega t)$ where V_m is the maximum allowed output voltage. The derivative of the output has a magnitude of $|\omega V_m \cos(\omega t)|$ and the maximum value $\omega_m V_m$ is the maximum slew rate. For example if MSR = 1 V/μs and V_m = 10 volts, $\omega_m V_m = 2\pi f_m V_m = 10^6$ volts per sec. and $f_m = 10^6/20\,\pi \approx 15.9$ kHz. On the other hand, if the signal output has a maximum value of 8 volts, the maximum frequency, for undistorted output will be 19.875 kHz.

11.7.4 Common Mode Rejection Ratio (CMMR)

If the two input terminals of an op amp are tied together and a signal v_{cm} applied between this common point and ground, as shown in Fig. 11.16, the output should be $A(v_{cm} - v_{cm}) = 0$. However, in reality, the output is non zero and the ratio of the output to the input is known as the common mode gain A_{cm}. The common mode rejection ratio is defined by

$$\text{CMMR} = \frac{|A|}{|A_{cm}|}$$

Usually, CMRR is expressed in dB

$$\text{CMRR (dB)} = 20 \log_{10} \frac{|A|}{|A_{cm}|} \quad \text{...(11.14)}$$

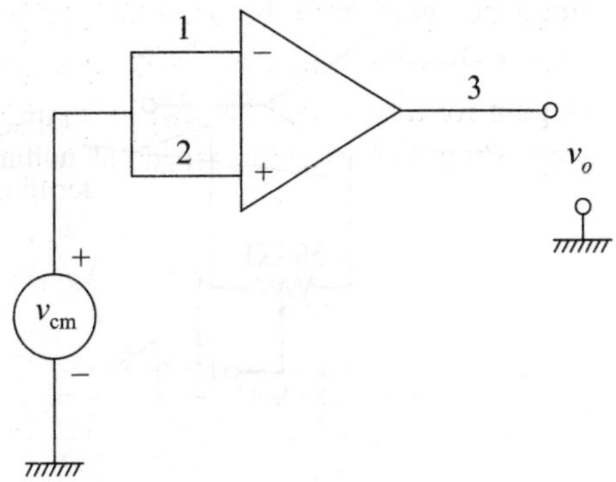

Fig. 11.16 *Illustrating common mode gain*

Typical values of CMMR range between 80 and 100 dB.

11.7.5 Offset Voltages

If the two input terminals of an op amp are connected together and grounded, as in Fig. 11.17; the output voltage is supposed to be zero. However, in practice, a small output voltage will exist. This is called the *offset voltage* and may be modelled by referring it to the input as shown in Fig. 11.17. The voltage V_{off} is usually of the order of a few millivolts.

From the model of Fig. 11.17 (*b*) it is evident that the offset, voltage, in an op amp closed loop circuit, appears at the output magnified by the closed loop gain. If the offset voltage is 4 mV and the closed loop gain in 100, the output will deviate from its true value by 400 mV. Thus, there is a need to compensate for this effect in precise work.

Figure 11.18 (*a*) illustrates the method of offset voltage compensation employed when the op amp is provided with two special terminals identified as offset nulling terminals. The nulling procedure is procedure by setting the input voltage to zero volts; the potentiometer is then adjusted

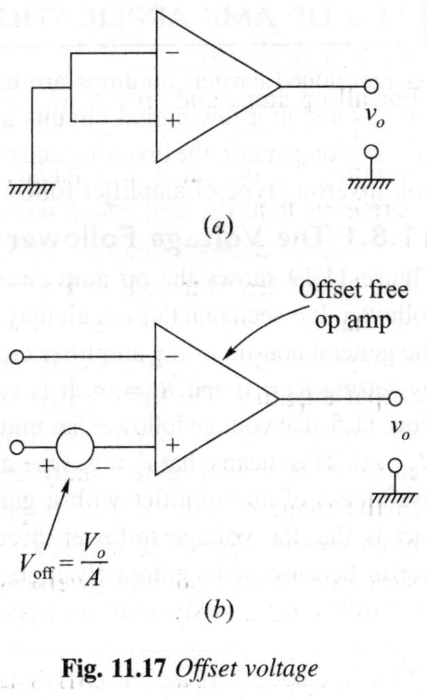

Fig. 11.17 *Offset voltage*

until the output is zero. In the case of op amp circuits with more than one input, all inputs should be set to zero before carrying out the nulling procedure.

The circuit of Fig. 11.18 may be used to compensate for offset errors when the op amp under use is not provided with offset nulling terminals; the nulling procedure is identical.

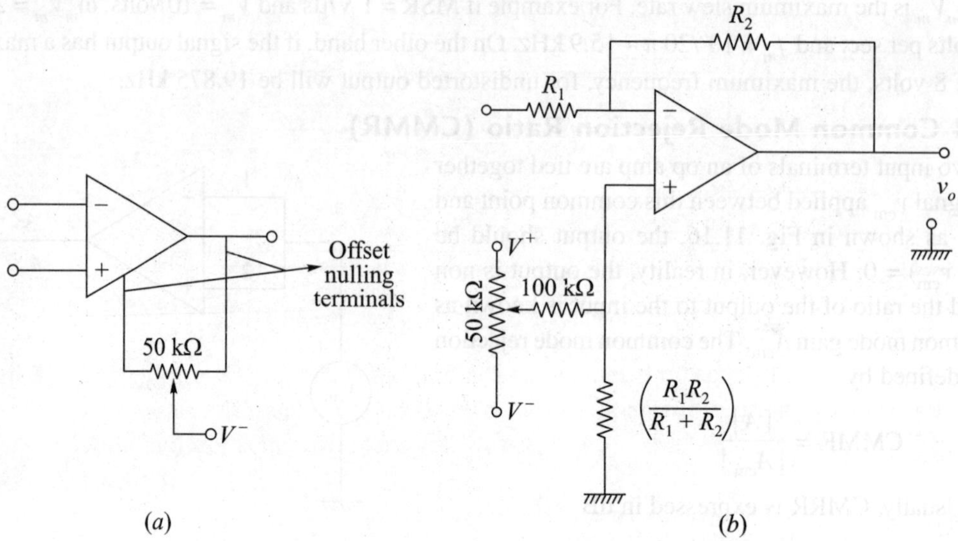

Fig. 11.18 *Cancellation of offset effect*

It should be mentioned that the offset effect is temperature dependent. Generally, this effect is of the order of 5 to 10μv/°C.

11.8 OP AMP APPLICATIONS

As mentioned earlier, op amps are used for a variety of purpose in linear and nonlinear electronics circuits and in a few digital circuits as well. We have already discussed three important applications, *i.e.*, the comparator, the inverting and non-inverting amplifier. In this section we first discuss an important non-inverting type of amplifier followed by a few other applications.

11.8.1 The Voltage Follower

Figure 11.19 shows the op amp circuit of a voltage follower. It is seen that this circuit may be derived from the general non-inverting amplifier circuit of Fig. 11.7 by setting $R_2 = 0$ and $R_1 = \infty$. It is easily seen, from Eqn. 11.5, that voltage follower has unity gain by letting $R_2 \to 0$. This means that $v_o = v_i$. One may question the usefulness of an amplifier with a gain of unity. The fact is that the voltage follower circuit is extremely useful because of its extremely high input resistance and low output resistance as may be seen from

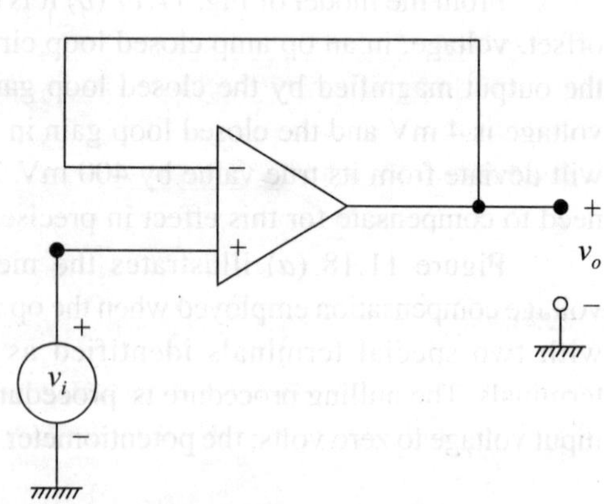

Fig. 11.19 *The voltage follower*

Eqns. 11.8 and 11.11 by inserting $\beta = 1$. This type of amplifier may therefore be used as a buffer to feed a low resistance load from a high resistance source.

11.8.2 Op Amp Summing and Subtracting Circuits

Consider the inverting circuit shown in Fig. 11.20. Two resistors, R_1 and R_2 are connected to the inverting terminal; the non-inverting terminal is connected to ground. Signals v_1 and v_2 are fed to the op amp via R_1 and R_2.

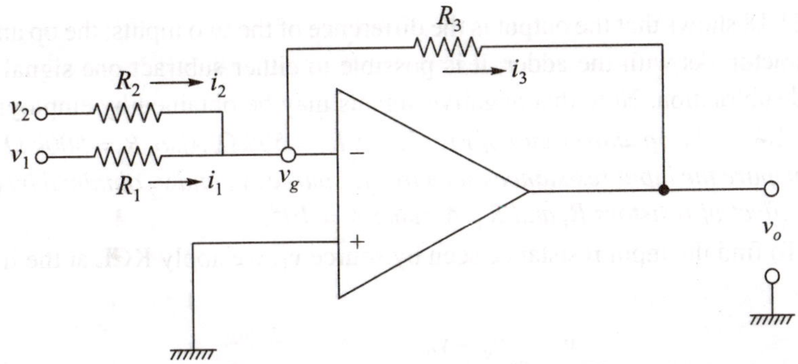

Fig. 11.20 *Inverting op amp*

Applying KCL at the junction of the three resistors, since no current enters the op amp (ideal assumption)

$$\frac{v_1 - v_g}{R_1} + \frac{v_2 - v_g}{R_2} = \frac{v_g - v_0}{R_3}$$

Further, since $v_g \approx 0$, the KCL expression may be written as

$$\frac{v_1}{R_1} + \frac{v_2}{R_2} = -\frac{v_0}{R_3}$$

If $R_1 = R_2 = R_i$ and $R_3 = R_f$, we obtain that

$$v_0 = \frac{-R_f}{R_i}(v_1 + v_2) \qquad ...(11.15)$$

Equation 11.15 indicates that the two input voltages v_1 and v_2 are summed by the circuit; the circuit is therefore known as an *adder*. In fact it is possible to sum any number of inputs using such a circuit. In order to sum n input voltages v_1, v_2, ..., v_n, one employs n input resistors R_1, R_2, ..., R_n through which the input signals are fed to the op amp. The expression yielding the output is

$$v_0 = -\frac{-R_3}{R_1}v_1 - \frac{-R_3}{R_2}v_2 \,....... - \frac{-R_3}{R_n}v_n \qquad ...(11.16)$$

If $R_1 = R_2 = ...\ R_n = R_i$ and $R_3 = R_f$, Eqn. 11.16 reduces to

$$v_0 = \frac{-R_f}{R_i}(v_1 + v_2 + \,......\ v_n) \qquad ...(11.17)$$

Equation 11.16 also indicates that it is possible to obtain a weighted sum of two or more input signals.

If the inputs to the op amp are v_1 and $-v_2$, the output is

$$v_0 = \frac{-R_f}{R_1}v_1 + \frac{R_f}{R_2}v_2$$

$$= R_f\left[\frac{v_2}{R_2} - \frac{v_1}{R_1}\right] \qquad ...(11.18)$$

Equation 11.18 shows that the output is the difference of the two inputs; the op amp may therefore be used as a subtractor. As with the adder, it is possible to either subtract one signal from another or obtain a weighted subtraction. Note that negative signals may be obtained by employing an inverter.

Example 11.4. *In the op amp circuit of Fig. 11.20, $R_1 = 50\,k\Omega$. Also, $R_i = 500k\,\Omega$ (input resistance of the op amp) Compare the input resistances seen by the sources v_1 and v_2 obtained by (i) including and (ii) excluding the effect of resistors R_i and R_3. Assume $A = 10^4$.*

Solution. To find the input resistance seen by source v_1, we apply KCL at the inverting terminal and obtain

$$i_1 = \frac{v_g}{R_i} + \frac{v_g - v_0}{R_3}$$

$$= \frac{v_g}{R_i} + \frac{v_g + Av_g}{R_3}$$

$$= v_g\left[\frac{1}{R_i} + \frac{1}{R_3/(1+A)}\right]$$

This shows that the input resistance, excluding resistor R_1, is the parallel combination of R_i and $R_3/(1 + A)$ because

$$v_g/i_1 = \left[\frac{1}{R_i} + \frac{1}{R_3/(1+A)}\right]^{-1}$$

The input resistance seen by source v_1 is

$$= \left[R_1 + \frac{R_iR_3}{R_3 + R_i(1+A)}\right]$$

Likewise, the input resistance seen by source v_2 is

$$= \left[R_2 + \frac{R_iR_3}{R_3 + R_i(1+A)}\right]$$

Inserting the given values, the input resistances seen by the two sources are 50.02 and 100.02 kΩ.

(*ii*) The values of the input resistances, excluding the effect of R_i and R_3 are 50 kΩ and 100 kΩ respectively. It is seen that these values are not too different from those obtained by inclusion of the effects of R_3 and R_i.

11.8.3 Op Amp Integrating and Differentiating Circuits

Figure 11.21 (*a*) shows the integrating circuit with capacitor C in the feedback loop. Invoking ideal op amp assumptions, since $v_g \approx 0$, application of KCL at that node yields

$$\frac{V_i}{R} = -C\frac{dv_0}{dt}$$

Solving for v_0,

$$v_0 = -\frac{1}{RC}\int_0^t v_i \, dt + v_0(0)$$

where v_0 (0) is the initial charge on the capacitor at $t = 0$ (constant of integration). From this expression it is clear that the output voltage is proportional to the integral of the input voltage. By use of appropriate circuits it is possible to set the initial condition to any desired value. Figure 11.21 (*b*) shows a differentiating circuit. Analysis of this circuit in an identical manner by application of KCL at the inverting node yields

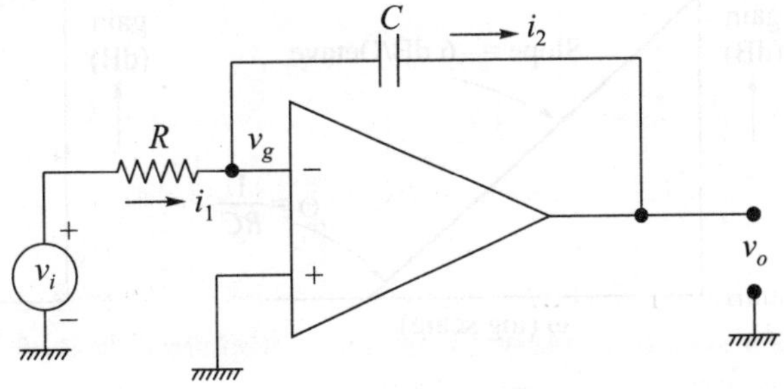

(*a*) *Op amp as an integrator*

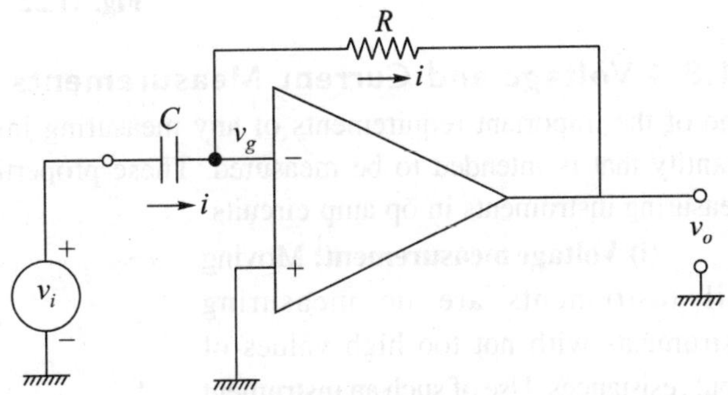

(*b*) *Op amp as a differentiator*

Fig. 11.21

$$C\frac{dv_i}{dt} = -\frac{v_0}{R}$$

Solving for v_0, $\quad v_0 = -RC\dfrac{dv_i}{dt}$

The output is proportional to the time derivative of the input. The frequency response of the integrating and differentiating circuits are shown in Fig. 11.22. Assuming sinusoidal signals, in both cases, the circuit gain is unity (zero dB) when $\omega = \dfrac{1}{RC}$. Also, if the frequency is doubled, the gain is halved for the integrating circuit and doubled for the differentiating circuit. Expressed in decibels the gain increased by $20 \log_{10}(1/2) \approx -6$ dB for each doubling of f in the former case and increases by $20 \log_{10}(2) \approx +6$ dB in the latter case. Since the gain of the integrating circuit decreases with increasing frequency, this circuit has an inherent noise suppressing property *i.e.* it has the property of discriminating against high frequency spurious signals which may appear at the input. The opposite is true with the differentiating circuit as the gain increases with frequency. Because of this feature, integrating circuits find more application in analog computers and other circuits.

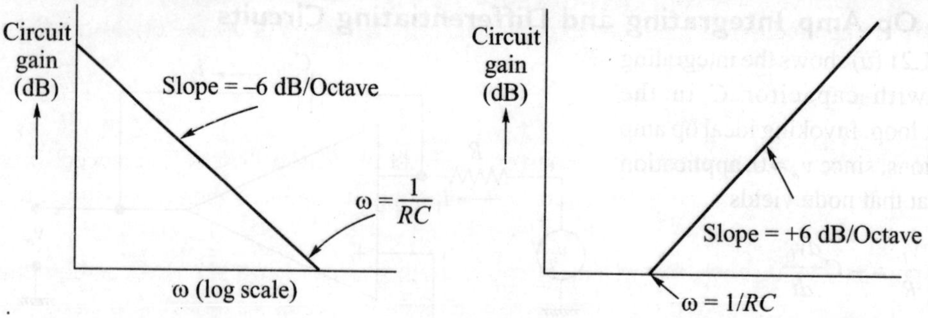

(a) *Frequency response of integrator* (b) *Frequency response of differentiator*

Fig. 11.22

11.8.4 Voltage and Current Measurements

One of the important requirements of any measuring instrument is that it should not affect the very quantity that is intended to be measured. These properties may be realized by incorporating analog measuring instruments in op amp circuits.

(i) Voltage measurement: Moving coil instruments are dc measuring instruments with not too high values of input resistances. Use of such an instrument in a circuit as shown in Fig. 11.23 (*a*) enables the combination to function as a high resistance voltmeter.

Invoking ideal op amp assumptions, the current flowing through the meter in Fig. 11.23 (*a*) is identical to that flowing through R_1. Since V_g follows V_i, $I_m = \frac{V_i}{R_1}$.

Note that I_m is independent of R_m, the meter resistance. Further, as the op amp is connected in the non-inverting mode, it exhibits a high input resistance and the effectiveness of the voltmeter as a measuring instrument is increased.

For example, consider a moving coil meter which shows full scale deflection when 10 V are applied across it. If the current through the meter under this condition is 2 mA, the input resistance of the basic instrument is 5000 ohms. Suppose it is desired to convert this instrument into a high resistance voltmeter, one would use the circuit of Fig. 11.23 (*a*). The input terminal of the voltmeter is now the non-inverting terminal of the op amp.

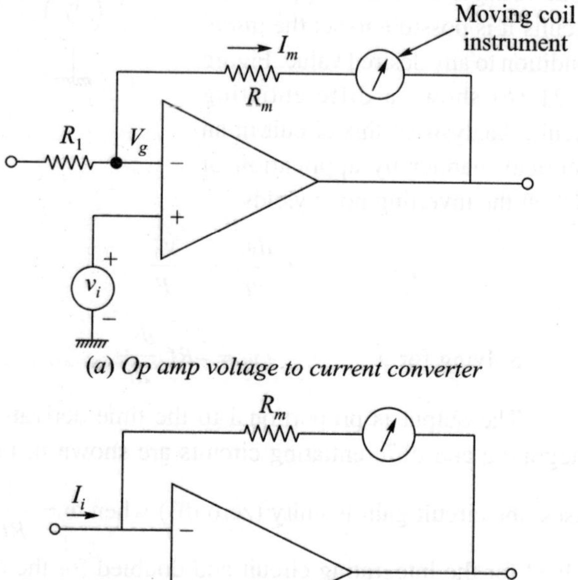

(*a*) *Op amp voltage to current converter*

(*b*) *Op amp current to voltage converter*

Fig. 11.23

When 10 V are applied to this input one expects full scale deflection of the meter; this implies that i_m = 2 mA. Therefore $R_1 = \dfrac{v_i}{i_m} = \dfrac{10}{2\,\text{mA}} = 5\ \text{k}\Omega$.

(ii) Current measurement: In the inverter circuit of section 11.4, R_1 is reduced to zero ohms thus making the input resistance of the circuit zero; the output voltage is then proportional to the input current *i.e.*, $v_0 = i_1 R_2$.

Figure 11.23 (*b*) shows the op amp circuit operating as described above. Generally, this current is used for the measurement of direct currents. Since an input current is converted to an output voltage, this circuit is also known as a current to voltage converter. On the other hand, the circuit of Fig. 11.23 (*a*) is known as a voltage to current converter. It should be noted that the circuit of Fig. 11.23 (*b*) should not be used to measure the current in a circuit in which the resistance is comparable to that of the meter movement.

11.8.5 Half Wave and Full Wave Rectifiers

In all the op amp circuits considered thus far, only linear elements have been included in the feedback loop. The insertion of a non-linear element, such as a diode, in this part of the circuit causes the op amp to function in a non-linear manner.

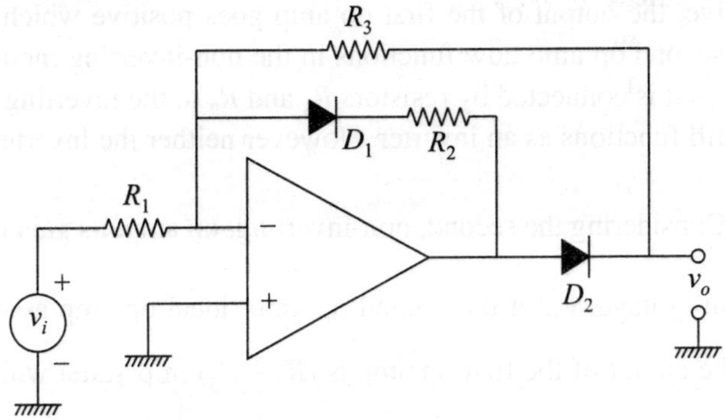

(*a*) *Op amp half wave rectifying circuit*

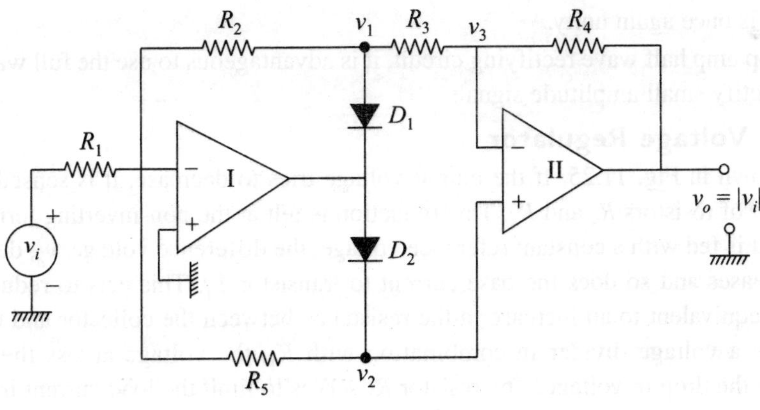

(*b*) *Op amp full wave rectifying circuit*

Fig. 11.24

Consider the circuit of Fig. 11.24 (*a*). The input signal v_i may be considered to be sinusoidal. If v_i goes negative, the output goes positive as the op amp is connected in the inverting mode; diode D_1 is turned off while diode D_2 is forward biased. The circuit therefore operates as a normal inverting amplifier and has a gain of R_3/R_1. If v_i goes positive, the output of the op amp goes negative turning D_2 off. Thus $v_0 = 0$ if $v_i > 0$ and the circuit functions as a half wave rectifier.

Compared with the conventional half wave rectifying circuit in Fig. 11.7 (*a*), this circuit has an advantage. In the former circuit, rectification is not possible unless the input voltage magnitude exceeds the threshold voltage of the diode *i.e.*, 0.7 V for Silicon diodes. Furthermore, the output voltage is lesser than the input by an amount equal to the diode voltage drop. This indicates that a conventional rectifier can not be used to rectify signals of magnitudes comparable to the diode threshold voltage. The op amp half wave rectifying circuit does not suffer from this disadvantage.

Op amps in combination with diodes may be used for full wave rectification as well as by using the circuit shown in Fig. 11.24 (*b*). Once again, considering sinusoidal signals, when v_i goes positive the output of the first op amp goes negative which forward biases diode D_1 and reverse biases D_2; $v_1 = -v_i$ constitutes the input to the inverting terminal of the second op amp whose non-inverting terminal is at virtual ground as it is connected to the inverting terminal of the first op amp through the resistor R_5. It is seen that both op amps function as inverters, each with unity gain if $R_1 = R_2 = R_3 = R_4 = R$. Therefore, $v_0 = v_i$. If v_i goes negative, the output of the first op amp goes positive which reverse biases D_1 and forward biases D_2. The second op amp now functions in the non-inverting mode its inverting terminal is now at virtual ground as it is connected by resistors R_3 and R_2 to the inverting terminal of the first op amp. The first op amp still functions as an inverter. However neither the inverter nor the non-inverting op amp, has unity gain. Considering the second, non-inverting, op amp, its gain is $\left(1 + \dfrac{R_4}{R_2 + R_3}\right) = 1.5$.

Since v_3 is equal to input voltage, v_2, of the second op amp (ideal op amp assumptions) the effective feedback resistance in the circuit of the first op amp is $(R_2 + R_3)$ in parallel with R_5 *i.e.* $\dfrac{2}{3}R$ assuming $R_5 = R$ as well. The gain of the inverting amplifier is therefore $\dfrac{-2}{3}\dfrac{R}{R} = \dfrac{-2}{3}$. The overall gain, when v_i goes negative, is once again unity.

Like the op amp half wave rectifying circuit, it is advantageous to use the full wave circuit when it is desired to rectify small amplitude signals.

11.8.6 Shunt Voltage Regulator

The circuit is shown in Fig. 11.25. If the output voltage tries to decrease, it is sensed by the voltage divider consisting of resistors R_3 and R_4. This reduction is felt at the non-inverting terminal. Since the inverting terminal is fed with a constant reference voltage, the difference voltage, v_d, decreases. The op amp output decreases and so does the base current to transistor T_1. This acts to reduce the collector current which is equivalent to an increase in the resistance between the collector and the emitter, r_{CE}. Since r_{CE} acts as a voltage divider in combination with R_1, the voltage across the load increases compensating for the drop in voltage. The resistor R_1 serves to limit the load current in case of a short circuit across the load.

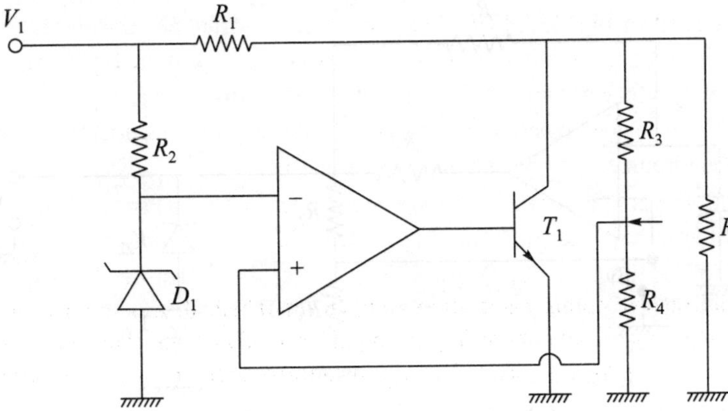

Fig. 11.25 *Shunt voltage regulator*

11.8.7 The Square Wave Generator

The circuit is shown in Fig. 11.26 and comprises of both positive and negative feedbacks *i.e.,* a portion of the output is fed back to both the non-inverting and inverting terminals of the op amp. The op amp compares these two inputs and therefore functions as a comparator in this circuit. Owing to the voltage regulating action of the back to back connected Zener diodes, the output remains at either $-V_{Z1}$ or $+V_{Z2}$. If the diodes are identical, $|V_{Z1}| = |V_{Z2}|$. The positive feedback factor, β, is derived from the voltage divider formed by resistors R_2 and R_3; $\beta = R_3/(R_2 + R_3)$ and is the fraction of the output which is fed back to the non-inverting terminal. The differential input into the op amp is therefore $(\beta v_0 - v_c)$. If the output is $+V_{Z2}$ the input to the op amp at the non-inverting terminal is $+\beta V_{Z2}$ and is fixed. The other input is voltage on the capacitor which attempts to charge up to $+V_{Z2}$ exponentially through R_f. However, when this voltage exceeds $+\beta V_{Z2}$ by a small amount of the op amp is driven into negative saturation and the output becomes $-V_{Z1}$. The non-inverting input to the op amp is now $-\beta V_{Z1}$ and capacitor C tries to charge up to $-V_{Z1}$ through R_f. When its voltage exceeds $|\beta V_{Z1}|$ by a small amount the op amp is driven to positive saturation and the output changes to $+V_{Z2}$. This process repeats itself and thus a rectangular wave is generated at the output. A square waveform results if $V_{Z1} = V_{Z2} = V_Z$. Let us suppose that the op amp functions as an ideal comparator. The output therefore changes sign when the charge on the capacitor reaches either $\pm\beta V_0$. Let us suppose that the output has just become $+V_Z$. At this time, $V_c = -\beta V_Z$. The driving voltage causing the capacitor to charge positively is $(V_Z + \beta V_Z)$ and the expression for capacitor voltage is given by

$$V_c = (V_Z + \beta V_Z)\{1 - \exp[-t/CR_f]\} - \beta V_Z \quad ...(11.19)$$

Let T be the time period of the output waveform. At $t = T/2$ the capacitor voltage becomes $+\beta V_Z$. Substituting these values in Eqn. 11.19 one obtains

$$+\beta V_Z = (V_Z + \beta V_Z) - e^{-\frac{T}{2R_f C}}(V_Z + \beta V_Z) - \beta V_Z$$

Solving for T from the last equation,

$$T = 2R_f C \ln\left[\frac{V_Z + \beta V_Z}{(1-\beta)V_Z}\right]$$

CHAPTER 11

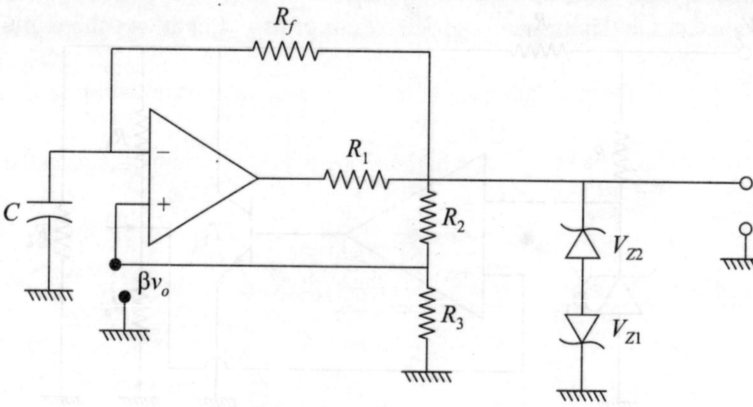

(a) *Op amp square wave generator*

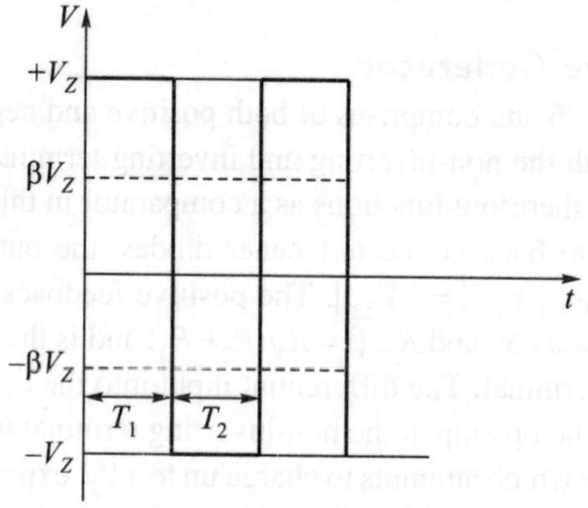

(b) *Output wave shape*

Fig. 11.26

$$= 2R_f C \ln\left[\frac{1+\beta}{1-\beta}\right] \qquad \text{...(11.20)}$$

Square waveforms in the frequency range 10 Hz to 10 kHz may be generated by using this circuit. The frequency is varied by varying R_f. The function of resistor R_1 is merely to limit the output current.

11.9 SIMULATION OF DIFFERENTIAL EQUATIONS

Op amp inverts, referred to sometimes as scale changers, op amp summers, and integrators may be connected suitably to solve a linear differential equation with constant coefficients by using a method known as the bootstrap method. Consider the differential equation

$$\frac{d^2y}{dt^2} + a\frac{dy}{dt} + by = c(t) \qquad \text{...(11.21)}$$

where a and b are constants and both y and c are functions of time. Let the specified initial conditions be $y(0) = 0$ and $\left[\frac{dy}{dt}\right]_{t=0} = -1$. The general method of solution of such an equation is as follows.

First, Eqn. 11.21 is rewritten with the highest order derivative appearing on the left hand side.

$$\frac{d^2y}{dt^2} = -a\frac{dy}{dt} - by + c(t) \qquad ...(11.22)$$

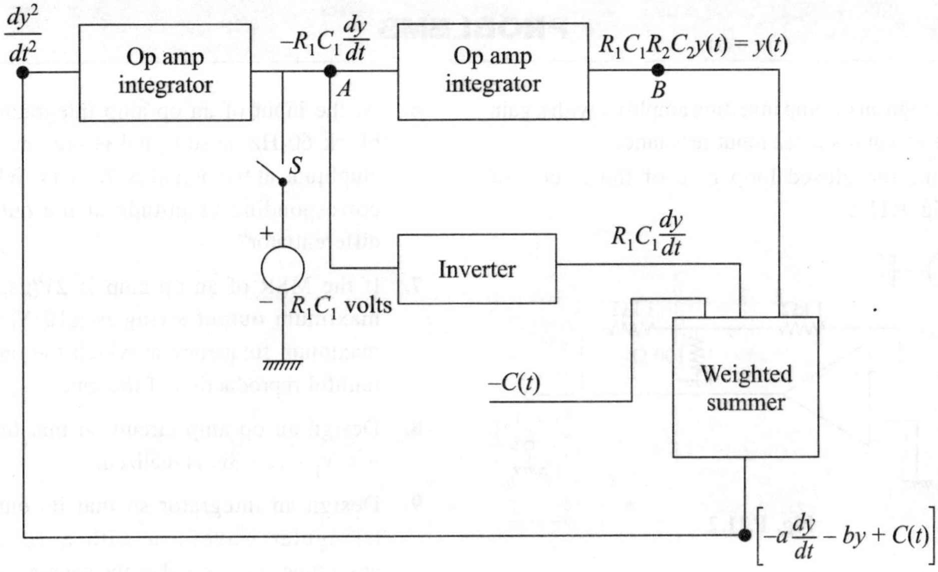

Fig. 11.27 *Simulation of differential equation*

Assuming $\frac{d^2y}{dt^2}$ to be known voltage signal, successive integration is performed by using op amp integrators, as in Fig. 11.27, to yield $-R_1C_1\frac{dy}{dt}$ and $-R_2C_2R_1C_1\,y(t)$ respectively. By choosing $R_2C_2 = \frac{1}{R_1C_1}$, the second integrator outputs the function $y(t)$. The rest of the circuit is generated to function $c(t) - by - a\frac{dy}{dt}$. Since this is equal to $\frac{d^2y}{dt^2}$, the output of the weighted summer is connected to the starting point; hence the name 'bootstrap method'. The solution, $y(t)$, may be observed using a recorder or an oscilloscope connected at node B. The initial condition $y(0) = 0$ is easily realized by ensuring that the capacitor in the second integrator is unchanged at $t = 0$. The output of the first integrator is $-R_1C_1\frac{dy}{dt}$. Since the initial condition $\frac{dy}{dt} = -1$ is specified therefore the initial voltage at node A is $-R_1C_1(-1) = +R_1C_1$. This is realized by connection of an appropriate voltage source at node which is removed to start the integration process, *i.e.*, switch s is broken at $t = 0$.

There is no unique way in which the solution may be realized. For example, we may write $R_1C_1 = R_2C_2 = 1(R_1 = 1\ \text{M}\Omega, C_1 = 1\ \mu\text{F})$ and introduce the factors a and b in the weighted summer.

The chief advantage of this method of solution or simulation lies in the fact that it is possible to observe the behaviour of $y(t)$, $\dot{y}(t)$ and $\ddot{y}(t)$ visually; the effect of parameters in the circuit such as damping etc. is readily demonstrated. A collection of op amps used to solve differential equations is known as an analog computer.

PROBLEMS

1. Design an op amp inverting amplifier with a gain of –50 and a 2 kΩ input resistance.
2. Find the closed loop gain of the circuit of Fig. P.11.2.

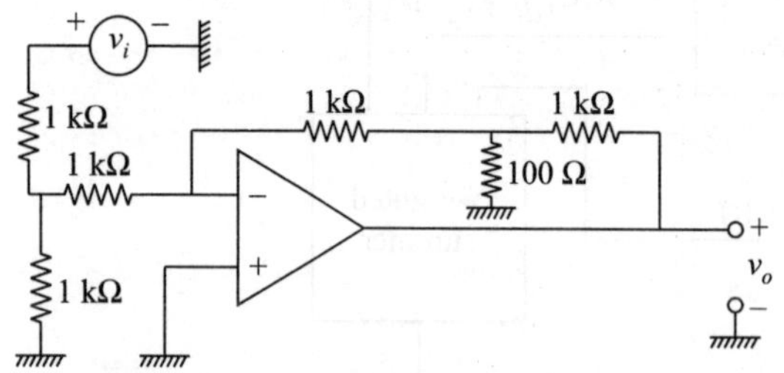

Fig. P.11.2

3. Using an input resistor of 1 MΩ, design op amp circuit, with a gain of –100, without using a feedback resistor exceeding 1 MΩ in value.
4. Design an op amp circuit so that the voltage function $v_0 = v_i - 5v'_i$ is realized.
5. Using ideal op amp assumptions find v_0 in Fig. P.11.5.

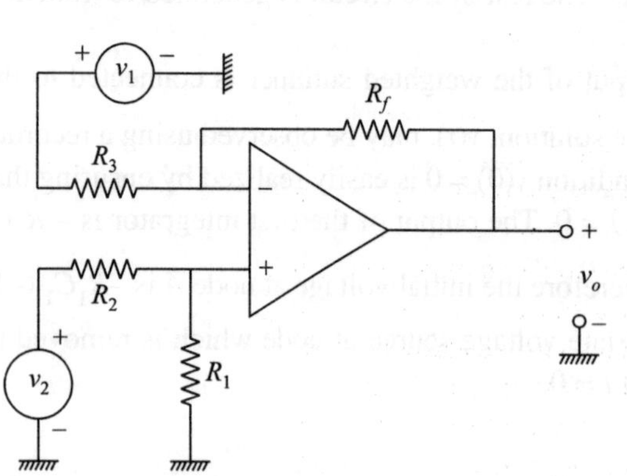

Fig. P.11.5

6. At the input of an op amp integrator a 2 mv pk-pk 60 Hz noise signal is present. Find the amplitude at the output is RC = 1s. What is the corresponding amplitude at the output of a differentiator?
7. If the MSR of an op amp is 2*V*/μs, and the maximum output swing is ±10 V, find the maximum frequency at which the output is a faithful reproduction of the input.
8. Design an op amp circuit so that the output $v_0 = v_1 + v_2 - 3v_3$ is realized.
9. Design an integrator so that its output is a triangular waveform with a 10 V pk-pk amplitude. The period of the square wave input is 10 ms with a pk-pk value of 10 V.
10. In Fig. P.11.10, $A = 500$, $R = 10^6\ \Omega$ and $i_g = 0$. Plot the output voltage, $V_0(t) = 0.5$ V (step) and $C = 10\ \mu$F.

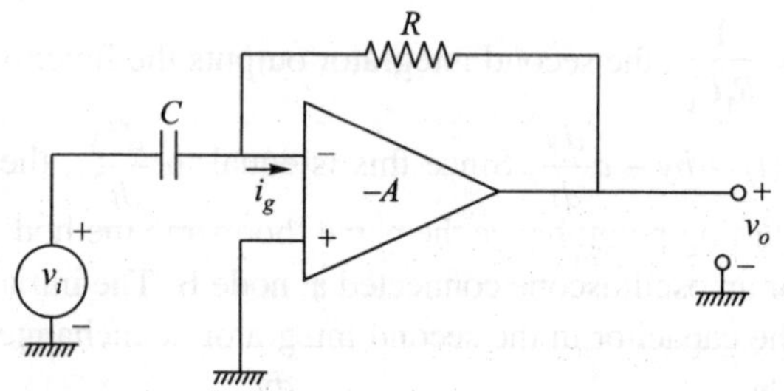

Fig. P.11.10

11. In Fig. P.11.11, $R = 10\ \text{k}\Omega$, $c = 0.5\ \mu\text{F}$ and $v_c(0) = -1$ volt. If $v_i = +1$ V (step), find v_0 at $t = 15$ ms.

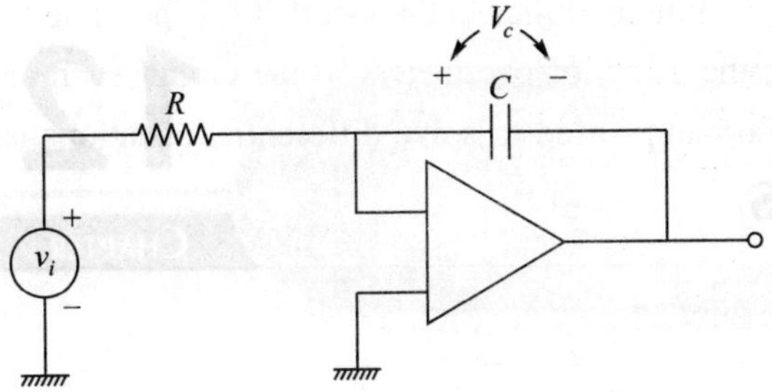

Fig. P.11.11

12. Given the differential equation

$$2\frac{d^3y}{dt^3} + \frac{1}{2}\frac{d^2y}{dt^2} + \frac{dy}{dt} + 2y = u_{-1}(t)$$

with $y(0) = 1/2$, $y'(0) = 3/2$ and $y'(0) = 1$, design a suitable circuit to simulate it. $u_{-1}(t)$ is a step function which is non zero for all time after $t = -1$ sec.

13. Generate the function of Fig. P.11.13 using op amp circuits.

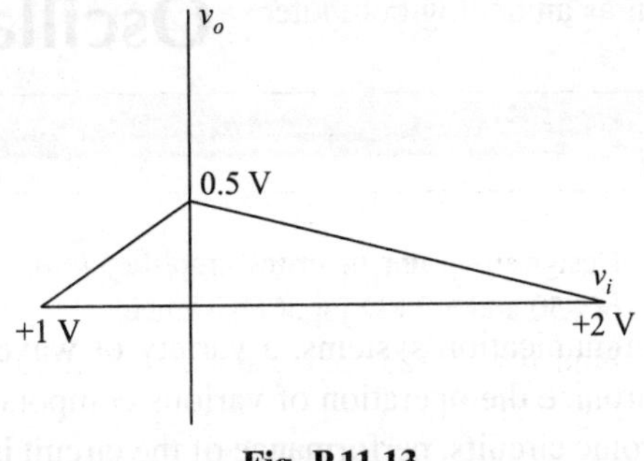

Fig. P.11.13

12 Oscillators

CHAPTER

In communication systems, a variety of waveforms are used as information carriers. In computers to synchronize the operation of various components, a common signal is used, clock. For testing various electronic circuits, performance of the circuit is studied for different types of input waveforms. As such, need arises to generate the various signals at different frequencies. In general, *oscillators* can be:

- *linear oscillators*—circuits generating sinusoidal signals. Ex. Wein Bridge oscillator, *RC* phase shift oscillator, Colpitts oscillator, Hartley oscillator, etc., and
- *relaxation oscillators*—circuits generating non-sinusoidal signals Ex. Multivibrators, Sweep generators, etc.

12.1 MECHANICAL OSCILLATOR

Consider a pendulum as shown in Fig. 12.1. It is made to oscillate by drawing the weight to position *A* and let go. The pendulum swings back and forth between the positions *A* and *C* through *B*, until the energy stored in the weight comes to zero. This is due to the transfer of energy from potential to kinetic energy.

Each swing will be shorter in length than the previous one due to the friction at *P* and air friction as clearly indicated by the oscillogram of Fig. 12.2. Ideally, if there were to be no losses or the losses were to be supplied externally, then the swings on either side would be equal and the amplitude variation would be a sinusoid as shown.

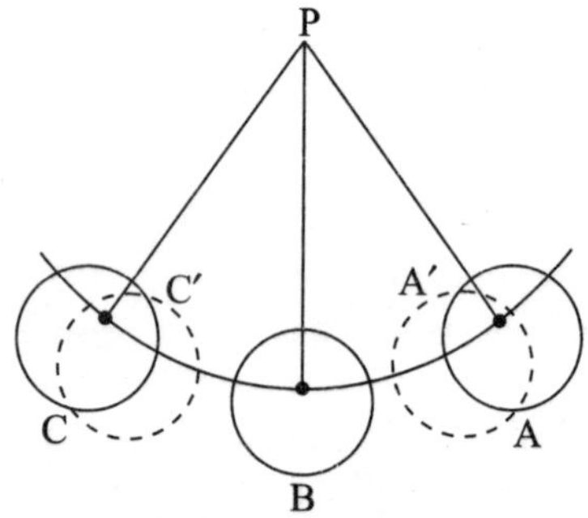

Fig. 12.1 *Mechanical pendulum*

As an equivalence, in electric circuits if a charged capacitor is connected across an inductor, called tank circuit, the various stages of the capacitance-inductance charge flow are as shown in Fig. 12.3. The capacitor charges in either direction as also the electromagnetic field. This process would have continued if the inductor and capacitor were to be ideal. However, due to the losses taking place, the oscillations finally die out. Thus the tank circuit generates damped electrical oscillations. Thus, there is an interchange of energy between capacitor and inductor and the energy in electrostatic field is converted into energy in electromagnetic field.

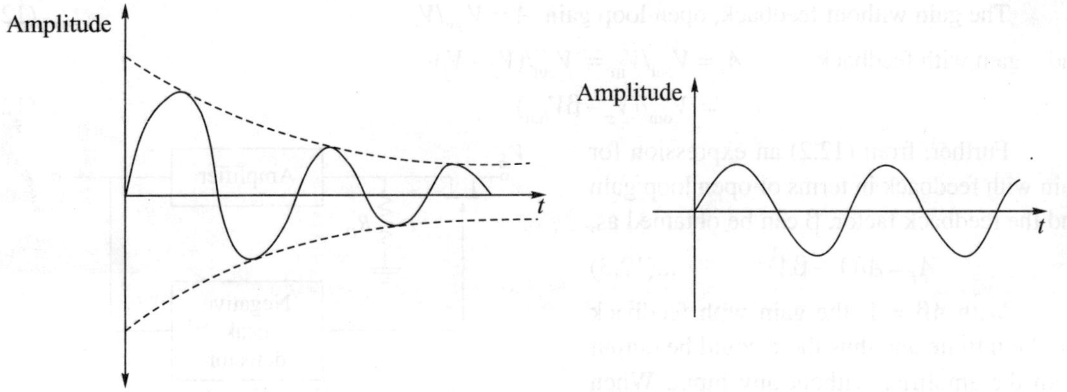

(a) *Damped oscillations* (b) *Undamped oscillations*

Fig. 12.2 *Amplitude variation of the oscillating pendulum*

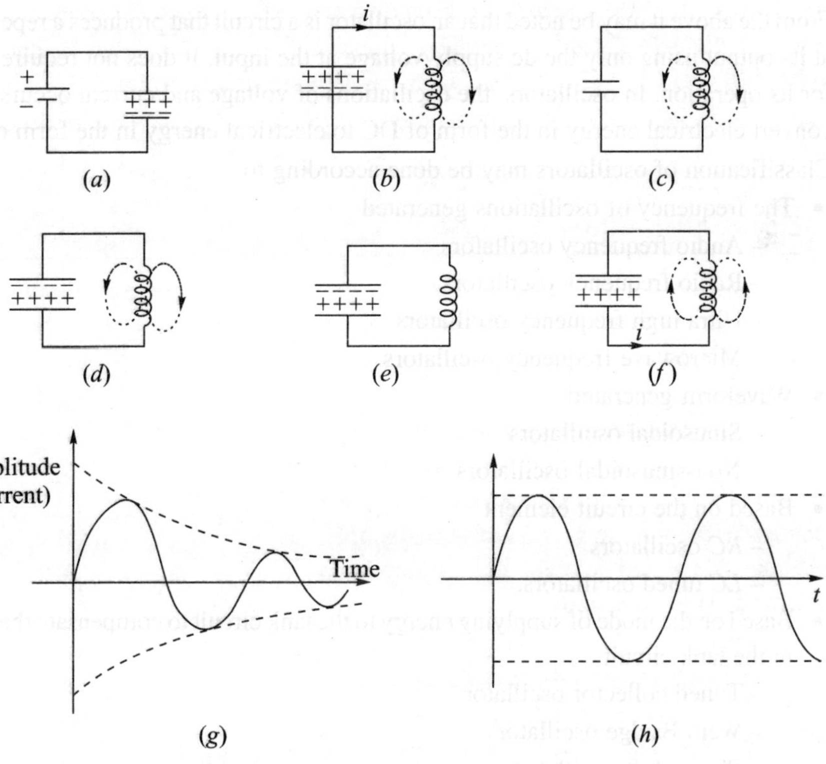

Fig. 12.3 *Various stages of the capacitance-inductance charge flow*

If the losses were compensated at a proper time, electrical oscillations of constant amplitude result in undamped oscillations. If the output of a transistor amplifier with positive feedback is fed back to a tank circuit as shown in Fig. 12.4, then it can supply the losses in the tank circuit and enable the tank circuit to generate sinusoidal oscillations.

The gain without feedback, open loop gain, $A = V_{out}/V_s$ ...(12.1)

and gain with feedback, $A_f = V_{out}/V_{in} = V_{out}/(V_s - V_f)$

$= V_{out}/(V_s - \beta V_{out})$ ...(12.2)

Further, from (12.2) an expression for gain with feedback in terms of open loop gain and the feedback factor, β can be obtained as,

$A_f = A/(1 - \beta A)$ ...(12.3)

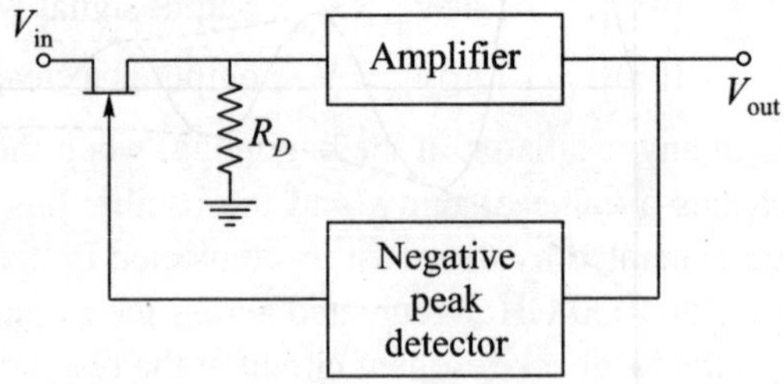

Fig. 12.4 *Feedback circuit of the oscillator*

With $A\beta = 1$, the gain with feedback will be infinite and thus there could be output from the amplifier without any input. When an amplifier with a positive feedback is used, no external input is required as the feedback itself is the input signal. When the feedback signal is large enough, with correct phase, then there will be an output although there is no external input.

(*a*) From the above it may be noted that an oscillator is a circuit that produces a repetitive waveform at its output using only the dc supply voltage at the input. It does not require an input signal for its operation. In oscillators, the oscillations of voltage and current occurs and oscillation convert electrical energy in the form of DC to electrical energy in the form of AC.

(*b*) Classification of oscillators may be done according to

- The frequency of oscillations generated
  - Audio frequency oscillators
  - Radio frequency oscillators
  - Ultra high frequency oscillators
  - Microwave frequency oscillators.
- Waveform generated
  - Sinusoidal oscillators
  - Non-sinusoidal oscillators.
- Based on the circuit element
  - *RC* oscillators
  - *LC* tuned oscillators.
- Based on the mode of supplying energy to the tank circuit to compensate the loses occurring in the tank circuit
  - Tuned collector oscillator
  - Wein Bridge oscillator
  - Phase shift oscillator
  - Hartley oscillator and Colpitts oscillator.

12.2 SINUSOIDAL OSCILLATOR

With reference to the basic amplifier block schematic of Fig. 12.4, if the combined phase shift of the signal while passing through the amplifier and also the feedback gain network is zero (or 360°), then the feedback signal, V_f is in phase with V_{in}. In the absence of the external input to the amplifier, the output of the feedback network, $A\beta V_{in}$ drives the amplifier. The output of the amplifier varies with $A\beta$ as under:

- If $A\beta < 1$; $A\beta V_{in} < V_{in}$; output signal will die out
- If $A\beta > 1$; $A\beta V_{in} > V_{in}$; output signal would build up
- If $A\beta = 1$; $A\beta V_{in} = V_{in}$; output is a steady wave ...(12.4)

In any oscillator, at the beginning, when the power is on, output voltage builds up, after which $A\beta$ reaches a value of unity, and the oscillations sustain. The initial voltage comes from the noise voltage generated by the resistors connected in the circuit. The thermal noise voltage (at frequency of the order of 1000 GHz) generated across the resistor is amplified. This amplified noise voltage passes through the feedback resonant circuit at the resonant frequency. The loop gain is greater than unity and the loop phase shift is zero. As such, oscillations build up only at the resonant frequency of the feedback circuit. This criteria is also known as *Barkhausen Criterion*. This criterion produces the required oscillations theoretically. However, when we consider the resonant circuit in the feedback path, the physical parameters of the components cannot be kept constant for a long time to come.

12.2.1 RC Phase Shift Oscillator

The basic structure of the phase shift oscillator is shown in Fig. 12.5. It consists of an amplifier with an *RC* feedback circuit. As a single *RC* is capable of producing a phase shift of less than 90°, three section *RC* circuits are designed to produce a total of 180° phase shift. If the value of the gain of the amplifier is sufficiently high, then oscillation is sustained.

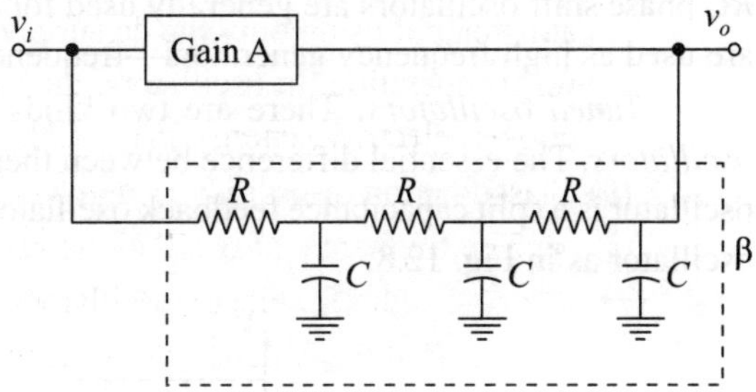

Fig. 12.5 *The RC phase shift oscillator*

It is possible to derive an expression for the frequency of oscillations in terms of circuit parameters to be given by

$$f = \frac{1}{2\pi RC\sqrt{6}} \quad ...(12.5)$$

Further, it can easily be shown that the minimum gain of the amplifier to produce sustained oscillations is 29.

A typical transistor *RC* phase-shift oscillator is as in Fig. 12.6. For this case, the (Eqn. 12.5) gets transformed to

$$K = R_C/R \quad \text{and} \quad f = \frac{1}{2\pi RC\sqrt{6+4K}} \quad ...(12.6)$$

The minimum h_{fe} required would be equal to (4K + 23 + 29/K). For an optimum value of K of 2.7, h_{fe} = 44.5. An OP-AMP RC phase-shift oscillator is shown in Fig. 12.7.

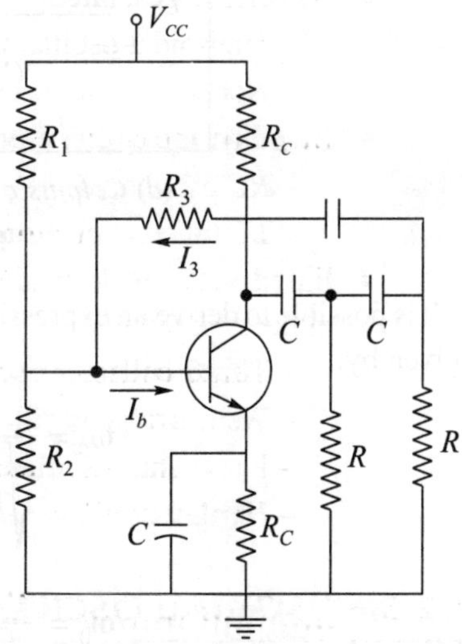

Fig. 12.6 *Transistorized RC phase shift oscillator*

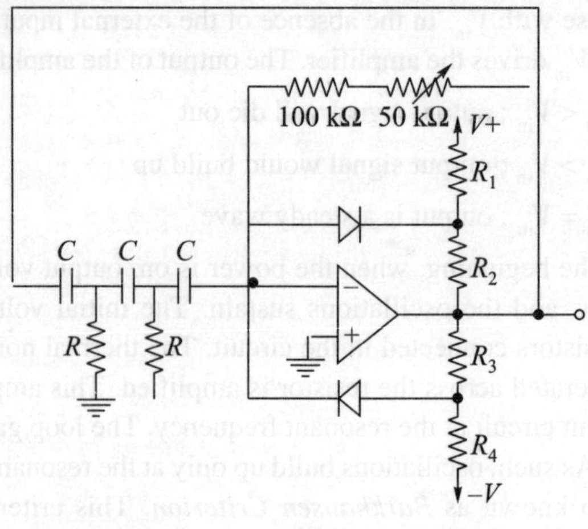

Fig. 12.7 *RC OP-AMP phase shift oscillator*

12.2.2 LC Oscillators

RC phase shift oscillators are generally used for the generation of low frequencies while *LC* oscillators are used as high frequency generators—frequency range being 100 KHz to 100 MHz.

Tuned oscillators: There are two kinds of oscillators in this category: *Colpitts* and *Hartley oscillators*. The essential difference between them is the mode of deriving the feedback signal. Colpitts oscillator is a split capacitance feedback oscillator while Hartley oscillator is a split inductance feedback oscillator as in Fig. 12.8.

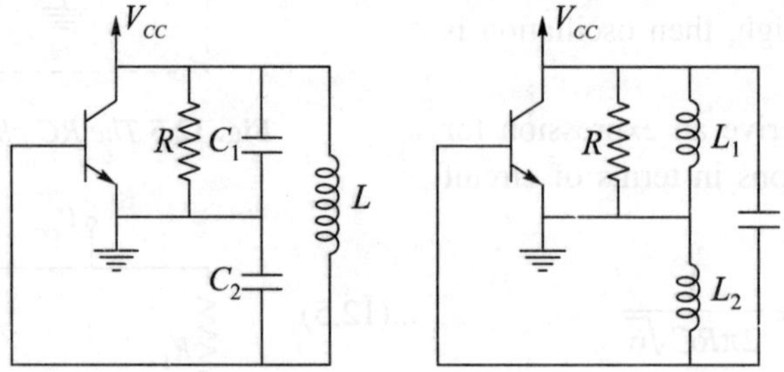

(a) Colpitts oscillator *(b) Hartley oscillator*

Fig. 12.8 *Tuned oscillators*

It is possible to derive an expression for the frequency of oscillations in terms of circuit parameters to be given by:

$$\omega_0 = \frac{1}{\sqrt{L\left(\frac{C_1 C_2}{C_1 + C_2}\right)}} \quad \text{(Colpitts oscillator)}$$

$$\omega_0 = \frac{1}{\sqrt{(L_1 + L_2)C}} \quad \text{(Hartley oscillator)}$$

The transistorized Colpitts and Hartley oscillators are shown in Fig. 12.9. The respective values of minimum amplifier gains are C_2/C_1 and L_2/L_1.

12.2.3 Crystal Oscilator

Crystal oscillator employs a quartz crystal in the feedback loop. In fact, when an ac at a certain frequency is applied across the crystal, it is observed that the crystal *vibrates* at the same frequency. The converse, when the crystal is made to vibrate mechanically, by subjecting it to compression, or mechanical strain, it is found to generate an ac voltage (oscillation). This phenomenon is called "Piezo-electric effect".

The circuit of a crystal oscillator is shown in Fig. 12.10 (*a*)

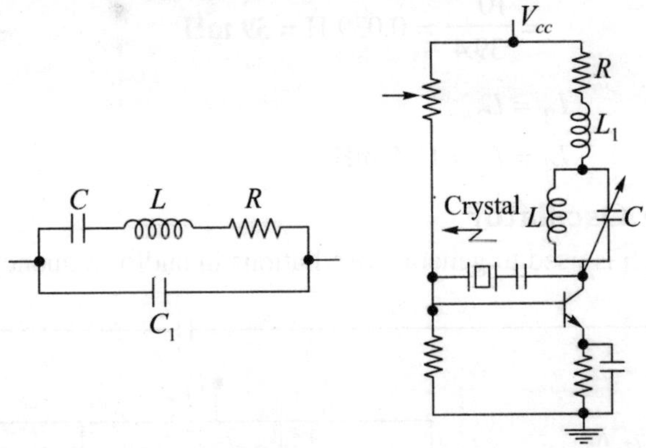

(*a*) *LC is tuned such that it is the natural frequency of the crystal*

(*b*) *The equivalent circuit of the crystal*

Fig. 12.9

The equivalent circuit of the crystal is shown in Fig. 12.10 (*b*) as a series—parallel *RC* circuit and can operate in either series or parallel resonance mode.

The series resonant frequency is given by $f_s = \dfrac{1}{2\pi\sqrt{LC}}$

The parallel resonant frequency is given by $f_p = \dfrac{1}{2\pi\sqrt{LC_{eq}}}$

Where $$C_{eq} = \frac{CC_1}{C + C_1}$$

One of the great advantage of crystal is that it exhibits high quality factor $\left(Q = \dfrac{\sqrt{L/C}}{R}\right)$ of several hundreds. Thus, the frequency stability is very good and is stable in oscillators employing crystal in the feedback loop.

Example 12.1. *Design the values of L_1, L_2 and C for a Hartley oscillator if the frequency of oscillation is 100 kHz.*

We know, $$f = \frac{1}{2\pi\sqrt{C(L_1 + L_2)}} \text{ Hz}$$

Select $$C = 0.1\ \mu\text{F}$$

$$f^2 = \frac{1}{4\pi^2(C(L_1 + L_2))}$$

Hence, $$(L_1 + L_2) = \frac{1}{4\pi^2 . C \cdot f^2}$$

$$= \frac{1}{4 \times \pi^2 \times 0.1 \times 10^{-6} \times (100 \times 10^3)^2}$$

$$= \frac{10^{-3}}{39.4} = 0.039 \text{ H} = \mathbf{39\ mH}$$

If $L_1 = L_2$

Then $L_1 = L_2 = 18.5$ mH.

12.2.4 Wein Bridge Oscillator

It is an *RC* oscillator which is used to generate oscillations in audio frequency range.

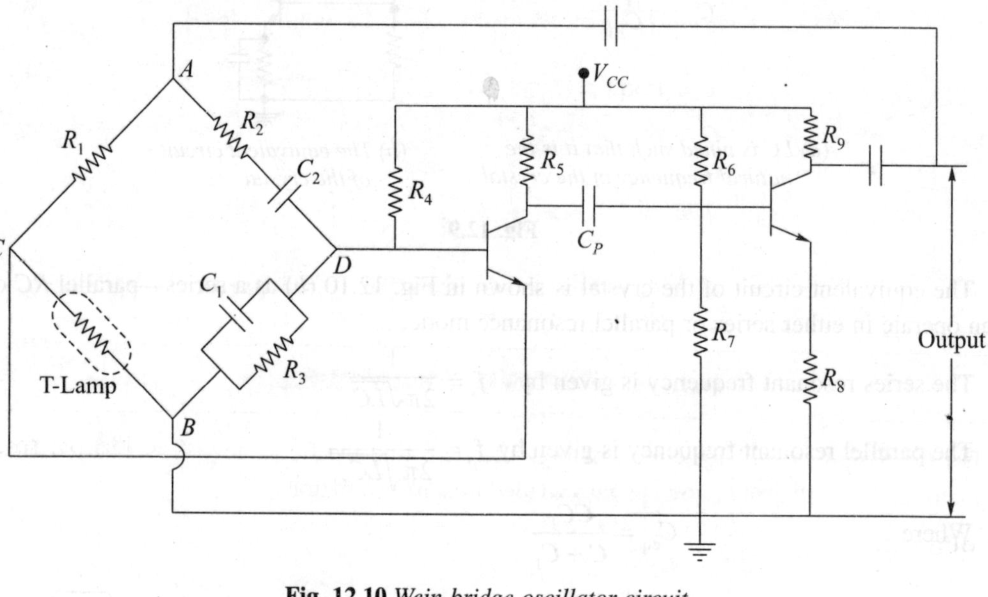

Fig. 12.10 *Wein bridge oscillator circuit*

R_1 and *T*-Lamp help to stabilize the amplitude of output voltage. The two transistors give a phase shift of 360°

$$f = \frac{1}{2\pi\sqrt{R_2 C_2 R_3 C_1}}$$

In general $R_2 = R_3 = R,\ C_2 = C_1 = C$

$$f = \frac{1}{2\pi\sqrt{R^2 C^2}} \quad i.e. \quad \frac{1}{2\pi RC}$$

Example 12.2. *In a Wein-bridge oscillator R = 1 kΩ and C = 0.1 μF, find the frequency of oscillations.*

$$R = 1\ \text{k}\Omega \quad C = 0.1\ \mu\text{F}$$

$$f = \frac{1}{2\pi RC}\ \text{Hz} = \frac{1}{2\pi \times 1 \times 10^3 \times 0.1 \times 10^{-6}}\ \text{Hz}$$

$$f = 1600\ \text{Hz}.$$

Example 12.3. *Find the values of L and C for a Colpitts oscillator whose frequency of oscillations is 40 kHz.*

$$f = 40\ \text{kHz}\ ;\ f = \frac{1}{2\pi\sqrt{LC}}$$

$$LC = \frac{1}{4\pi^2 f^2}$$

$$C = 1.583\ \text{nf}$$

Let $C_1 = C_2$

$$C = \frac{C_1C_2}{C_1 + C_2} = \frac{C_1}{2} = \frac{C_2}{2}$$

$$C_1 = C_2 = 2 \qquad C = 2\ (1.583\ \text{nf}) = 3.166\ \text{nf}.$$

ILLUSTRATIVE EXAMPLES

1. For the Colpitts oscillator circuit of Fig. 12.11(*a*), find the frequency of oscillation, feedback factor and the minimum voltage gain needed to start oscillations.

Solution.

$$\omega_0 = \frac{1}{\sqrt{L\left(\dfrac{C_1C_2}{C_1 + C_2}\right)}},\ \omega_0 = 2\pi f_o$$

$$f_o = 1.363\ \text{MHz}$$

Feedback factor, $\beta = C_1/C_2 = 0.1$

Minimum gain required, $(1/\beta) = 10$.

2. For the Hartley oscillator circuit of Fig. 12.11(*b*), find the frequency of oscillation, feedback factor and the minimum voltage gain needed to start oscillations.

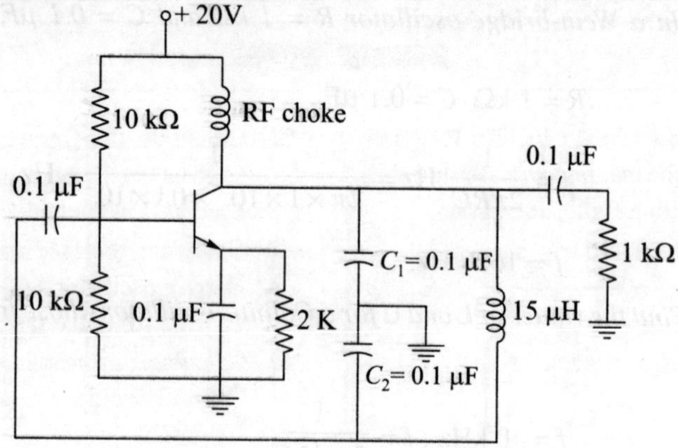

(*a*) *Colpitts oscillator*

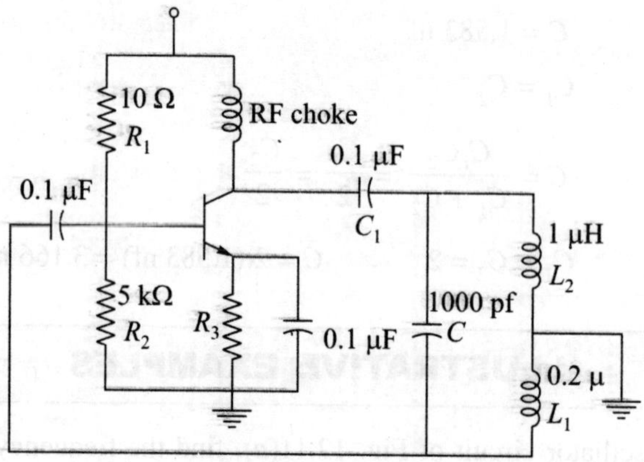

(*b*) *Hartley oscillator*

Fig. 12.11 *Transistorized LC oscillators*

Solution.

$$f_o = \frac{1}{2\pi\sqrt{LC}} \quad \text{where } L = L_1 + L_2$$

$$f_o = 145.3 \text{ kHz}$$

Feedback factor, $\beta = L_1/L_2 = 0.2$

Minimum gain required, $(1/\beta) = 5$.

PROBLEMS

1. For the *RC* network shown in Fig. P.1, find V_0/V_i and find out the maximum phase shift that can be obtained with a finite attenuation.

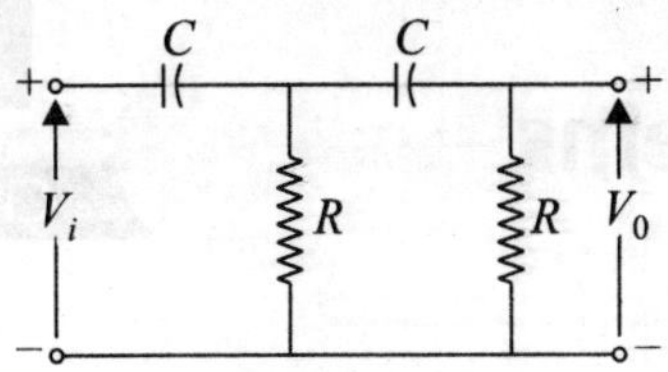

Fig. P.12.1

2. For the feedback circuit of an *RC*-phase shift oscillator shown in Fig. P.2, find (*i*) V_0/V_i (*ii*) input impedance (*iii*) frequency of oscillation and (*iv*) minimum voltage gain of the amplifier.

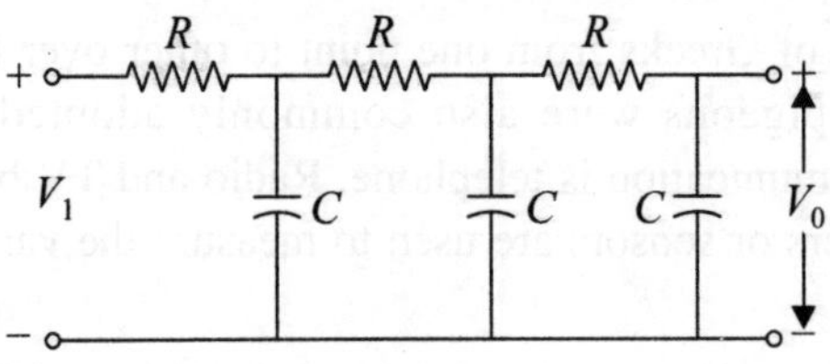

Fig. P.12.2

3. Calculate the frequency of oscillation of a Colpitts oscillator with $C_1 = C_2 = 750$ pF and $L = 5$ mH in the tank circuit.
4. Calculate the frequency of oscillation of a Hartley oscillator with $L_1 = L_2 = 20$ mH and $C = 100$ μF in the tank circuit.
5. Calculate the frequency of oscillations of a Colpitt's oscillator with $C_1 = C_2 = 400$ pF and $L = 1$ mH.
6. The tank circuit of a Hartley oscillator has an Inductance of $L_1 = L_2 = 150$ μH. The expected oscillations are at 75 kHz. Design the tank circuit.
7. Estimate the values of *R* and *C* for an output frequency of 100 Hz in a Wein-Bridge oscillator.

13 CHAPTER

Communication Systems

Word *communication* essentially refers to the transmission of information from one point to other. It is used in different contexts as, communication or contact, as between various sections of the armed forces, *liason*, sending telegrams through automatic exchanges. Thus communicate means to *make known*.

Simplest communication recorded since the days of Greeks from one point to other over long distance is through fire and smoke signals. Carrier pigeons were also commonly adopted for communication purposes. A very common mode of communication is telephone. Radio and TV bring information from different places. A variety of transducers or sensors are used to measure the various atmospheric conditions.

In fact, one of the easy solutions employed even today is to use a pair of wires to carry the electrical signals, information (called intelligence). Subsequently, owing to man's desire to go faster *Radar*, *Microwave Systems* and *Satellites* came up. Today, communication system encompasses *voice*, *text*, *picture* etc.

13.1 INTRODUCTION

The model of Fig. 13.1 can be used in a communication system which involves some basic signal processing operation in the transmission of information, irrespective of the mode and nature of transmission. In the process of communication, several equipment are to be used in an integrated manner. This set up as a whole is called the *communication system*.

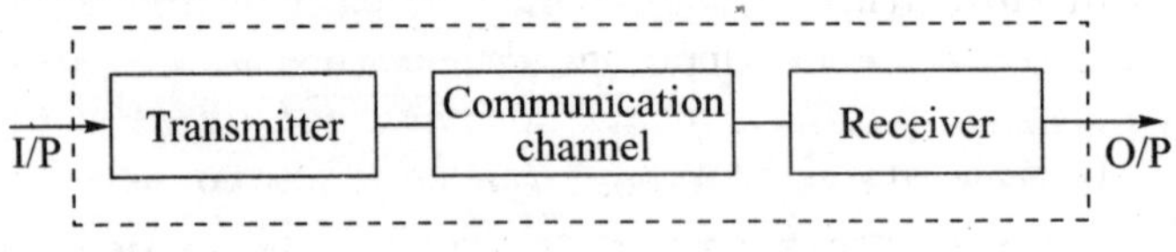

Fig. 13.1 *Communication system*

To use a communication system, input signal is invariably an electrical signal. If any physical parameters such as the information data is to be transmitted, and if the data produced is not an electrical signal, then an input transducer is to be used to convert the physical parameters into an electrical signal.

Indeed, at the receiving end, electrical signal will have to be converted into the original physical parameter suitably. This again is done by a transducer. The processes are as shown schematically in Fig. 13.2.

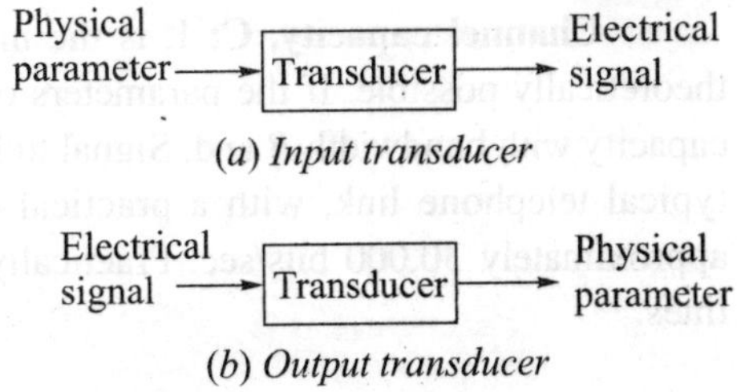

Fig. 13.2 *Signal conversion*

Electrical oscillations could be produced using oscillators and the output frequency may be altered by varying the circuit parameters. This frequency of the order of KHz or MHz is called the Radio Frequency waves. These are also termed as carrier waves, as they carry information at the time of transmission of data. Clearly, the communication system has the main components: *Transmitter*, *Communication Channel* and *Receiver*.

- *Transmitter*: It processes the input signal in a form suitable for transmission over the *communication channel*—wire or wireless media. This operation is called *modulation* and it is a process designed to match the properties of the signal to be transmitted to that of the channel—through the use of carrier wave. It is the systematic variation of some attributes of the carrier waveform such as the amplitude, phase or the frequency in accordance with a function of the input signal.
- *Communication channel*: It provides physical connection between the transmitter and the receiver. The channels are generally of two types: *point to point channels* (*Ex.* Telephone wire, Cables, Microwave links, etc.) and *broadcast channels* (*Ex.* Satellite in geostationary orbit wherein many receiving stations can get the information from the satellite).
- *Receiver:* It processes the signal and produces an *estimate* of the original message signal. This operation is called *demodulation*. The word *estimate* is used, as the receiver cannot recover the signals perfectly. In addition to the demodulation, the receiver also performs amplification and filtering.

Based on the type of modulation scheme and the nature of output of the information source, communication systems may be categorized as:

- *Analog communication systems* — designed to transmit analog signals using analog modulation methods.
- *Digital communications systems* — designed to transmit digital information using digital modulation schemes.
- *Hybrid systems* — use sampled and quantized values of an analog message signal for digital modulation schemes for transmitting.

Frequency bandwidth: It is generally defined as the range of frequencies that could be transmitted free of distortion over a channel. For example, the telephone line has a Bandwidth (BW) of 3 kHz. Due to this limitation, the signal may suffer *amplitude* and *phase distortion* as it travels over the channel. In addition, unpredictable electrical signals, referred to as noise, also corrupts the signal. Indeed, although some of the degrading effects of the channel can be removed or compensated for, effect of noise cannot be completely compensated. As such, removal of noise from the signal is the key to the design of the system. A basic method of improving the system performance corrupted by noise is to increase the signal power. This however cannot be done indefinitely. Thus at the receiving end, tolerable signal to noise ratio is to be taken into account which is quite an important parameter.

Channel capacity, C: It is the maximum rate at which nearly errorless data transmission is theoretically possible. If the parameters of the channel are known, C may be computed. The channel capacity with bandwidth B and, Signal to Noise Ratio, S/N is given by [$B \log_2 (1 + S/N)$] bits/sec. For a typical telephone link, with a practical bandwidth of 3 kHz and $(S/N) = 10^3$, channel capacity is approximately 30,000 bits/sec. Practically, a channel capacity of 9.6 kBPS is used on the telephone lines.

13.2 MODULATION

Due to the enormous amount of power required for transmission purposes and the large size antennas required, the information/intelligence such as voice frequency/audio signals cannot be transmitted over long distances. For example, for transmission at 15 kHz, height of the transmitting and receiving antenna is about 5000 meter. It is customary to modulate the high frequency (radio wave) information waveform by another waveform called the carrier waveform and transmit the resulting waveform. At the receiving end, the information signal is separated from the carrier (Demodulation). Further, the advantage of modulation is the possibility of transmission of various frequencies on the same channel. At the receiving end, the information signal is separated out from the carrier.

The antenna size for radiation purposes is of the order of $\lambda/4$, where λ is the wavelength. As the transmission signal is generally of voice frequency, the size of the antenna becomes large. As such, using high frequency and modulating the signal to be transmitted, the antenna size reduces. Further, if the frequency band is narrow, the design of the transmitter and receiver is simple. Hence, always the attempt is made to narrow the band of frequencies. For instance, consider the voice frequency from 300 Hz to 3000 Hz. If transmission is done at the message bandwidth, (Lowest/Highest) frequency ratio is (300/3000) = 1:10: On the other hand, if the modulation is done with a carrier of 500 kHz, we have the minimum and maximum frequency at (550 – 3) = 497 and (500 + 3) = 503 and hence as before the frequency ratio is (497/503). This narrow banding is desirable while designing the transmitter and receiver.

Broadly, it is possible to transmit the information such that the signal information is present either in the amplitude or in the phase of the carrier. These two modulation types are described as *Amplitude Modulation* and *Angle Modulation* respectively. These methods are used for simultaneously sending/transmitting the signals over a single channel (using different carriers for different data).

13.2.1 Amplitude Modulation

The signal to be transmitted requires a shift of the range of frequencies, and later a shift back to the original frequency range after reception, referred to as modulation. In *amplitude modulation* (AM), the amplitude of a sinusoidal carrier wave is varied in accordance with the information bearing signal. With A_c as carrier amplitude and f_c as carrier frequency, the sinusoidal carrier wave $c(t)$ is defined by:

$$c(t) = A_c \cos 2\pi f_c t \qquad \text{...(13.1)}$$

Now, amplitude modulation is defined as a process in which the A_c is varied with the message signal $m(t)$. With k_a as the amplitude sensitivity of the modulation, an AM wave is thus defined as,

$$s(t) = A_c [1 + k_a m_a(t)] \cos (2\pi f_c t) = A(t) \cos \omega_c t \qquad \text{...(13.2)}$$

Here, $A(t)$ denotes the envelope of the modulated wave. Two cases need to be considered: $| k_a m_a (t) | < 1 \ \forall \ t$. ($A$ is always positive) and $| k_a m_a(t) | > 1$ for some t.

The maximum absolute value of $k_a m_a(t)$ gives modulation index or depth of modulation as given by:

m_a = ratio of modulating signal amplitude to the carrier signal amplitude.

$$= A_m/A_c$$

$$= \frac{|A(t)|_{\max} - |A(t)|_{\min}}{|A(t)|_{\max} + |A(t)|_{\min}} \qquad \text{...(13.3)}$$

A typical amplitude modulation process is described in Fig. 13.3.

Based on the numerical value of m_a, the following three cases arise:

- $m_a > 1$, carrier is said to be *over-damped* and the envelope is distorted.
- $m_a < 1$, carrier is said to be *under-damped*.
- $m_a = 1$, carrier is said to be *critically/level* damped.

Spectrum of AM wave: The spectrum is a graphical representation of Amplitude *vs*. Frequency. Consider the equation for AM wave with,

$$m_a = k_c A_m,\ \omega_m = 2\pi f_m, \text{ and } \omega_c = 2\pi f_c,$$

$$s(t) = A_c\,[1 + m\cos(2\pi f_m t)]\cos(2\pi f_c t)$$

$$= A_c \cos\omega_c t + (m_a A_c/2)\cos(\omega_c + \omega_m)t + (m_a A_c/2)\cos(\omega_c - \omega_m)t \qquad \text{...(13.4)}$$

Three cases arise as under (Fig. 13.4).

- *carrier component:* $A_c \cos\omega_c t$.
- *upper side band (USB) component:* $(m_a A_c/2)\cos(\omega_c + \omega_m)t$.
- *lower side band (LSB) component:* $(m_a A_c/2)\cos(\omega_c - \omega_m)t$.

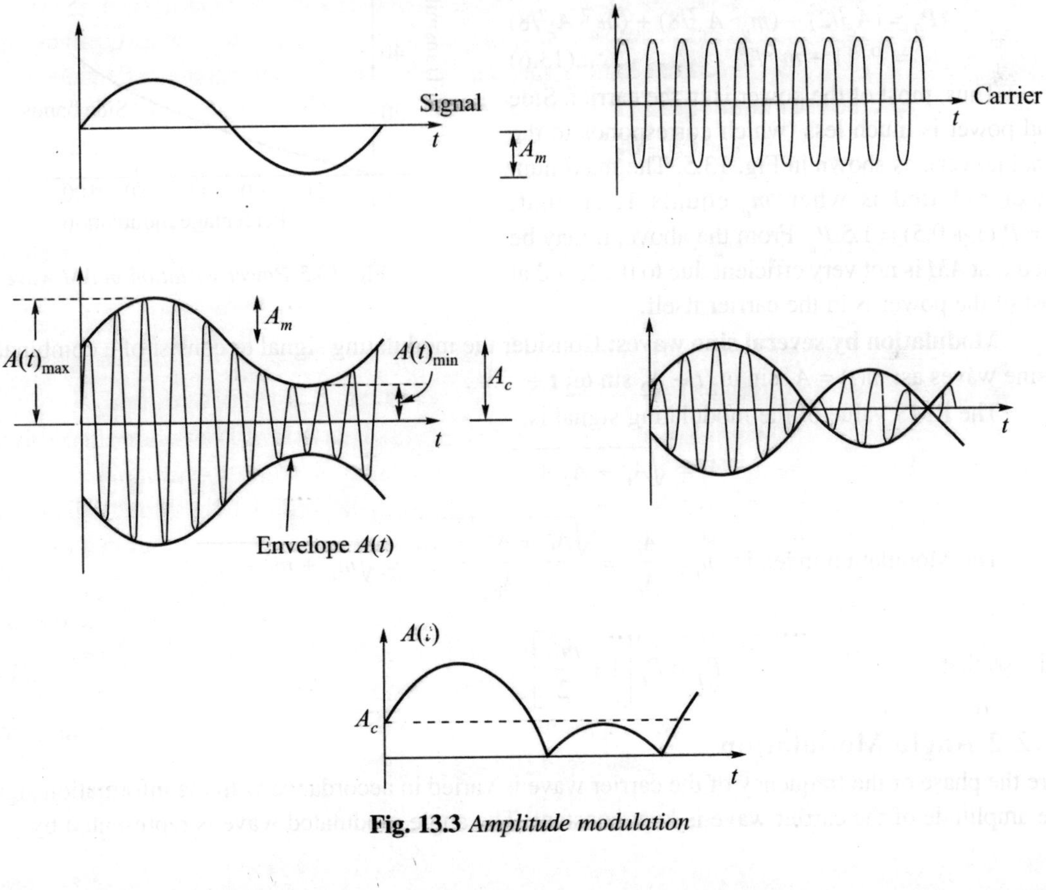

Fig. 13.3 *Amplitude modulation*

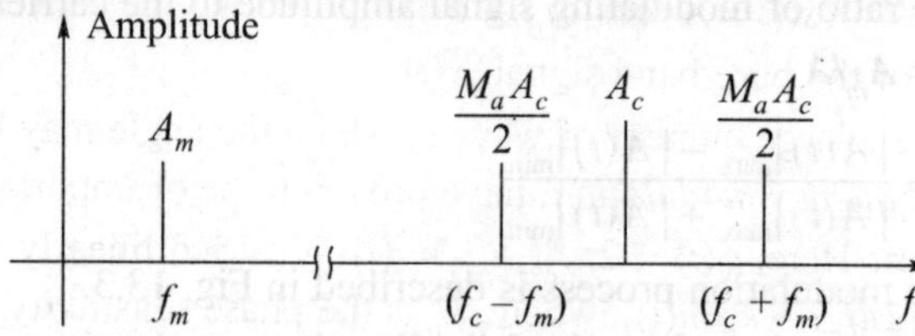

Fig. 13.4 *Frequency spectrum of AM wave*

The bandwidth equals $[(f_c + f_m) - (f_c - f_m)] = 2f_m$. This suggests that the frequency separation between the two carriers should be at least twice the frequency of the modulating signal. In practice, the AM wave, $s(t)$ wave, is a voltage or current wave.

Power in AM wave: The AM wave will have 3 power components: P_{carrier}, P_{LSB} and P_{USB}. The LSB and USB power components depend on the modulation depth. Thus, the total power radiated is given by

$$P_T = P_{\text{carrier}} + P_{\text{LSB}} + P_{\text{USB}}$$

The average power delivered, P_T, to a resistor R, say 1Ω is given by:

$$P_{\text{carrier}} = (A_c^2/2);$$

$$P_{\text{USB}} = P_{\text{LSB}} = m_a^2 A_c^2/8 \text{ so that}$$

$$P_T = (A_c^2/2) + (m_a^2 A_c^2/8) + (m_a^2 A_c^2/8)$$

$$= P_c [1 + m_a^2/2] \quad \text{...(13.6)}$$

Thus, most of the power is in the carrier. Side band power is much less (which corresponds to the signal power), as shown in Fig. 13.5. The maximum power radiated is when m_a equals 1, so that, $P_T = P_c(1 + 0.5) = 1.5\,P_c$. From the above, it may be noted that *AM* is not very efficient due to the fact that most of the power is in the carrier itself.

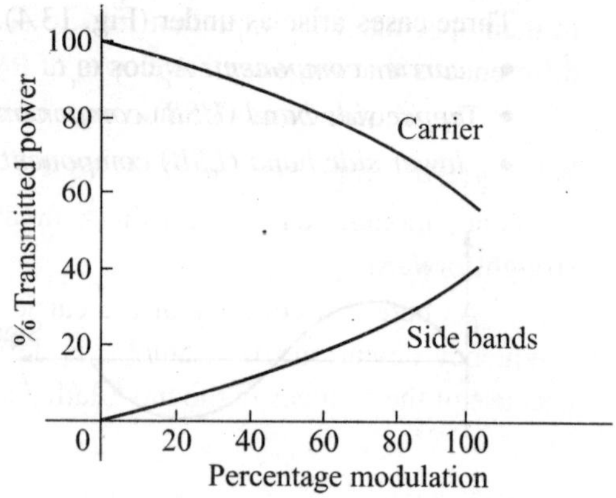

Fig. 13.5 *Power variation in AM wave*

Modulation by several sine waves: Consider the modulating signal to consist of a combination of sine waves as: $m(t) = A_1 \sin \omega_1 t + A_2 \sin \omega_2 t + \ldots\ldots$

The RMS value of the modulating signal is,

$$A_t = \sqrt{A_1^2 + A_2^2 + \ldots\ldots}$$

$$\text{The Modulation index is, } m_t = \frac{A_t}{A_c} = \frac{\sqrt{A_1^2 + A_2^2 + \ldots\ldots}}{A_c^2} = \sqrt{m_1^2 + m_1^2 + \ldots\ldots}$$

and so that,

$$P_T = P_c\left[1 + \frac{m_t^2}{2}\right] \quad \text{...(13.7)}$$

13.2.2 Angle Modulation

Here the phase or the frequency of the carrier wave is varied in accordance with the information signal. The amplitude of the carrier wave is kept constant. The angle modulated wave is represented by,

$$s(t) = A_c \cos[\omega_c t + \phi(t)] \quad ...(13.8)$$

where, $\phi(t)$ is a function of the base band signal, $x(t)$.

Although there are a large number of ways in which the angle may be varied, the two methods: *phase modulation* and *frequency modulation*, have proved to be of importance.

Phase modulation: Here, $\phi(t) = 2\pi f_c t + k_p m(t)$, is varied linearly with the information signal $m(t)$. Thus $s(t) = A_c \cos[2\pi f_c t + k_p m(t)]$, where, k_p is the phase sensitivity of the modulator.

Frequency modulation: Here, $f_i(t)$ is varied linearly with the message signal $m(t)$ as $f_i(t) = f_c + k_f m(t)$, where f_c is the frequency of un-modulated carrier, and k_f is the frequency sensitivity of modulator (*Hz/V*), so that, $\theta(t) = 2\pi f_c t + 2\pi k_f \int_0^t m(t)\,dt$.

Thus, in the time domain, frequency modulated wave is defined as,

$$s(t) = A_c \cos\left[2\pi f_c t + 2\pi k_f \int_0^t m(t)dt\right] \quad ...(13.9)$$

The consequence of allowing the angular argument to be independent of $m(t)$ is that the zero crossing of the Phase Modulation wave or Frequency Modulation wave no longer have a perfect regularity in their spacing. This important feature distinguishes both PM and FM from AM. Another interesting difference is that the wave envelopes of PM and FM are constant as compared to that of AM.

The frequency modulation may be regarded as phase modulation in which the modulating wave is $[\int_0^t m(t)\,dt]$ in phase of $m(t)$. Also, $s(t)$ is a nonlinear function of the modulating wave $m(t)$. Hence frequency modulation is a non-linear modulation process. Consequently the process is not simple and straightforward.

As before, frequency of the carrier in frequency modulation may be written as $(\omega_c + k_f m(t))$. Frequency deviation, $\Delta f = \Delta\omega/2\pi$, is defined as the extent by which the carrier frequency changes because of the changes in the modulating signal. Further, it is possible to show that phase angle is given by

$$\phi(t) = \omega_c t + \frac{k_f}{\omega_m} \sin \omega_m t$$ and the instantaneous voltage equation is

$$e_{FM}(t) = A_c \cos\left[\omega_c t + \frac{k_f}{\omega_m} \sin \omega_m t\right]$$

$$= A_c \cos[\omega_c t + \beta \sin \omega_m t] \quad ...(13.10)$$

where, the ratio of the frequency deviation to the frequency of the modulating signal, $\beta = \Delta f/f_m$ is called the modulation index. The modulation index is generally greater than unity. Unlike the amplitude modulation, where there were two side bands, frequency modulation has infinite side bands. Thus the bandwidth of frequency modulation is much higher. The transmission bandwidth of a frequency modulation wave generated by a modulating wave of frequency f_m is

$$B \cong 2\Delta f + 2f_m = 2\Delta f\,(1 + 1/\beta) \quad ...(13.11)$$

This is known as Carlson's Rule. The general frequency band used in frequency modulation ranges from 88 to 108 MHz. The details of FM generation are in Fig. 13.6.

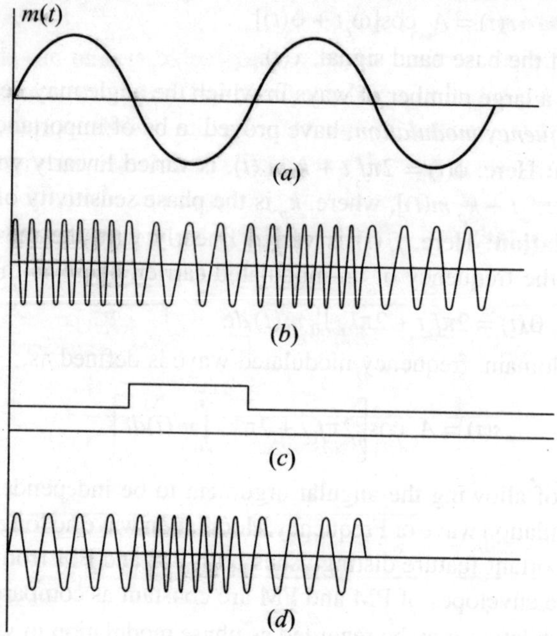

Fig. 13.6 *Details of frequency modulation (a and c): Information signal (b and d): Modulated signal*

13.2.3 Comparison of AM and FM

A comparison of the two modulation schemes: Amplitude modulation and Frequency modulation is as below:

- AM is the earlier method used for modulation purposes such as broadcasting at medium wave and short wave frequencies. The mode of propagation is by ground and sky waves. Thus AM is best suited for long distance transmission (>500 km).
- In AM, transmitted power is dependent on the modulation index while in FM, the power transmitted does not depend on it.
- Bandwidth of FM is larger than that of AM.
- As the carrier amplitude is constant in FM, it is more immune to noise signals compared to AM and as such, FM is used in places where high fidelity transmission is warranted.
- Equipment required for the FM transmission is more complex and expensive than that required in AM.

13.3 RADIO SYSTEMS

Radio *Telegraphy* and *Telephony* are the two basic methods of radio communication system. In radio telegraphy, intelligence or data is transmitted directly by the carrier waves at radio frequency without modulation. As such, these waves are called continuous wave carriers. In radio telephony, carrier wave is either amplitude modulated or frequency modulated and hence demodulation is required at the receiving end.

13.3.1 Radio Telegraphy

The transmitter and the receiver sections of radio telegraphic system are shown in Fig. 13.7. Only written messages may be transmitted using Morse Code—all letters are converted into a combinations of dashes and dots. A dot is represented by two cycles and a dash is represented by 5.5 cycles of the carrier wave. Desired RF waves are generated by the oscillator. If these waves are continuously interrupted according to Morse Code, the coded information may be transmitted over the carrier. Interruption may be done by means of power supply and a morse key.

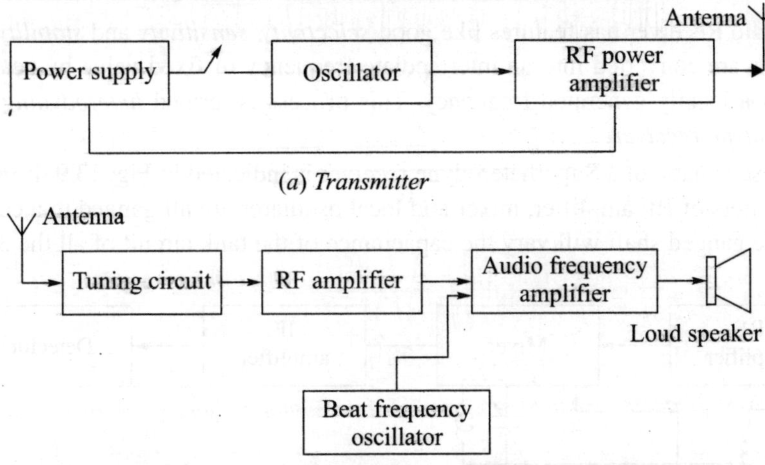

(*a*) *Transmitter*

(*b*) *Receiver*

Fig. 13.7 *Radio telegraphy*

This interrupted waveform after suitable amplification is transmitted via the antenna. The receiving antenna receives these continuous wave carrier signals after amplification and RF waves are converted into AF waveform. For this purpose, output of a beat frequency oscillator is added to the RF oscillations. Decoded AF signals, containing the intelligence, after further amplification are transmitted.

13.3.2 Radio Telephony

The transmitter and the receiver sections of radio telephonic system are shown in Fig. 13.8. Here the voice can be directly transmitted. The microphone converts voice to electrical signals. The electrical signals are amplified. RF waves are generated by the oscillator. The audio waveforms are put on the carrier in the Modulator. This carrier wave is put onto antenna, which transmits the modulated waves. The receiver will have a receiving antenna.

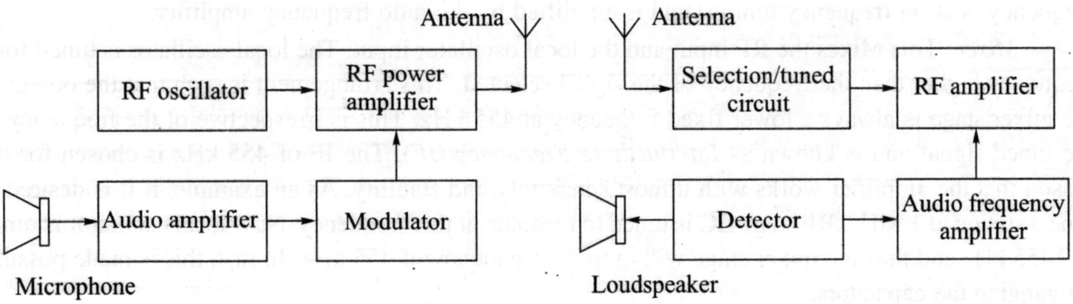

(*a*) *Transmitter* (*b*) *Raceiver*

Fig. 13.8 *Radio telephony*

The selection or tuning of the required frequency is done and this RF is amplified. The detector demodulates the RF signal and extracts the original AF modulating signal. The detector may be a crystal detector or a diode detector. When the RF carrier signal passes through the detector, the half cycles of the wave are suppressed. The filter separates the AF signals which after amplification drives a loud speaker and converts AF into sound waves.

13.4 SUPERHETERODYNE RECEIVER

This type of a Radio Receiver has features like good *selectivity, sensitivity* and *stability*. All incoming modulating signals are converted into an intermediate frequency of fixed value by beating the carrier frequency against a locally generated frequency. This process is termed *heterodyning* and hence the name *Superheterodyne receiver*.

The block schematic of a Superheterodyne receiver is indicated in Fig. 13.9. It may be seen that the variable capacitors of RF amplifier, mixer and local oscillator are all ganged to a common shaft so that rotation of the ganged shaft will vary the capacitance of the tank circuit of all the 3 blocks.

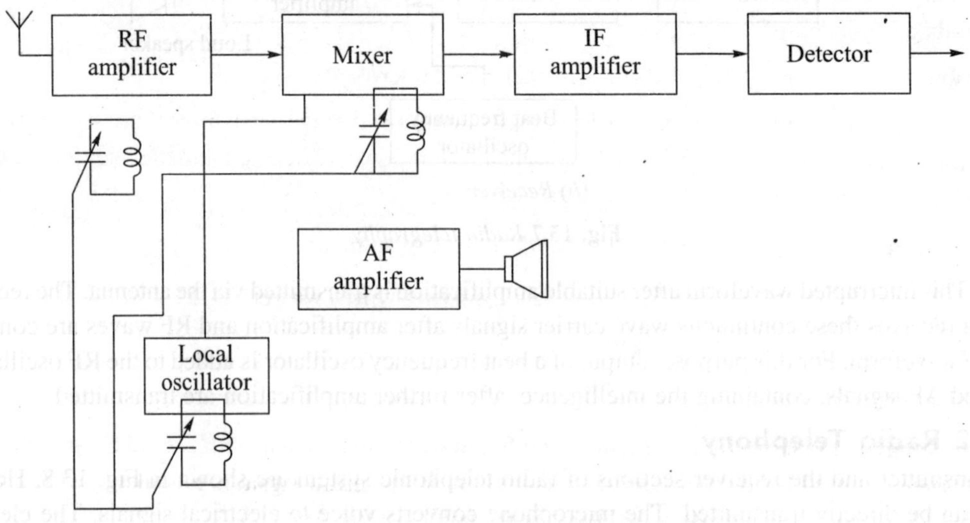

Fig. 13.9 *Block schematic of superheterodyne receiver*

RF amplifier: This stage functions like a filter and amplifier. Tuning allows only that wanted frequency (station frequency tuning) and is amplified by the ratio frequency amplifier.

Mixer: This Mixes the RF input and the local oscillator input. The local oscillator is tuned for a frequency higher than the frequency of the signal selected. This arrangement is such that the output of the mixer stage is always a lower fixed frequency at 455 kHz. This is irrespective of the frequency of the tuned signal and is known as *Intermediate Frequency (IF)*. The IF of 455 kHz is chosen for the reason that the amplifier works with utmost sensitivity and stability. As an example, if it is desired to tune a station at 1 MHz, RF stage LC is tuned to resonate at this frequency. Now local oscillator is tuned to 1455 kHz and thus the mixer stage will output a frequency of 455 kHz. In fact, this is made possible by ganging the capacitors.

IF Amplifier: The resulting 455 kHz signal is amplified by the IF amplifier and fed to the detector.

Detector: The functioning of the unit is essentially demodulation. This has diode detectors and filters in it. Diode suppresses all negative half cycles of the IF. The filters separate the audio signal from the IF carrier and AF signal is input to the AF amplifier. The output of AF amplifier drives the loud speaker.

ILLUSTRATIVE EXAMPLES

1. Maximum and minimum amplitudes of an AM modulated wave are 750 and 250 mV. Find the modulation depth.

Solution.

From the expression for modulation depth $m = (750 - 250)/(750 + 250) = 0.5$.

This means that the percentage of modulation is 50%.

2. Local AM transmitter broadcasts at a carrier power of 25 kW. Determine the radiated power at a modulation index of 0.6.

Solution. $P_T = P_C\,(1 + m_a^2/2) = 29.50$ kW

3. A local AM broadcasting station broadcasts with an average transmitted power of 10 kW. Modulation index is set at 0.5. Find the transmission power efficiency and the average power in the carrier component of the transmitted signal.

Solution. $P_T = P_C\,(1 + m_a^2/2) = 10$ kW so that,

$10 = P_C\,(1 + 0.52)/2$, solving which we get

$P_C = 8$ kW

Power efficiency is defined as $E = (P_T - P_C)/P_T = 20\%$

4. In a broadcast system, the maximum audio frequency transmitted is 5 kHz. Find the height of the antenna required for the purpose of transmission. If the audio signal is modulated with a signal of 10 MHz in the broadcast band. What is the height of the Antenna.

Solution. Height of the antenna needed for an effective radiation would be 1/2 of the wavelength and is given by

$$C = \lambda f$$

C = velocity of light in meters

λ = wavelength in meters

f = frequency in Hz

Then $$\frac{\lambda}{2} = \frac{C}{2f} = \frac{3 \times 10^8}{2 \times 5 \times 10^3} = 30 \text{ kms}$$

(without modulation)

$$= \frac{3 \times 10^8}{2 \times 10^6 \times 10} = 15 \text{ meters}$$

(with modulation modulating frequency = 10 MHz)

Hence the need for modulation.

PROBLEMS

1. For an AM, the amplitude of the modulating signal is 0.5 V and the carrier amplitude is 1 V. Find the modulation index.

2. A local AM broadcasting station broadcasts with an average transmitted power of 20 kW. Modulation index is set at 0.8. Find the saving in power if the power contained in the LSB alone is used.

14 CHAPTER

Digital Logic

14.1 INTRODUCTION

Computers have been extensively used for a variety of purposes in scientific, business and commercial applications since 1950's. Computers are essentially tools to solve problems quickly. These can also be used for playing games, drawing pictures, designing and so on. In general, computers may be classified into two main categories:

(*a*) Analog computer and (*b*) Digital computer.

An analog computer is one in which the signals are analogous to the system under study—example being the output signals from a strain gauge bridge, voltage output being analogous to the strain. Operations like addition, subtraction are carried out by using operational amplifiers (linear ICs).

A Digital computer is the one utilizing binary digits (0 and 1) for performing the mathematical operations.

Analog computers are mainly used for simulation studies whereas digital computers are used for solving a variety of problems (including simulation).

Digital computers use the binary number system for processing of data. This is due to the reliability of the electronic circuits when designed to operate for two state operation. Understanding of the number system and logic functions are the basic tools for the understanding of computers.

In the day-to-day transactions, we use decimal system in which digits 0, 1, 2, ..., 9 are used for forming any number. However, in the computer's use, binary system where only the numerical digits 0 and 1 (called binary digits or BITS) are used to form any number. These 1's and 0's are stored in logic circuits called registers (or stored in memory). The size of the register depends on the computer under consideration. 8 to 64-bit computers are in general use. The computer manipulates the 0 and 1 numbers for arriving at any result.

Data for working out a problem may be in the form of numbers, facts, etc. As the computer is capable of handling only binary numbers, these data, before it goes to the computer, is coded in the binary form. However, entering the data is generally done by using the decimal, octal or hexa decimal number systems (as it is quite difficult to enter data in binary number systems).

It is important that these number systems are understood especially with reference to the binary system and the decimal system.

14.2 DECIMAL SYSTEM

We use Decimal system in our day-to-day transactions. Decimal system has many advantages over the previous systems. To appreciate the importance of the decimal system, imagine the amount of difficulty involved in multiplying two Roman numbers (say IV × IX) and the ease with which the numbers are multiplied in the decimal system (4 × 9 = 36). It is easy to observe that Roman digit symbols have no positional values.

Indeed in Laplace's (famous mathematician) own words "It is India that gave us the ingenious method if expressing all numbers by means of 10 symbols, each symbol receiving a value of position as well as an absolute value, a profound and important idea which appears so simple to us now that we ignore the true merit".

However, the best number system for the computers is the binary system. As binary systems also follow the rules of the decimal system, the rules of the decimal system are first explained and these rules are then applied to the binary number system.

Decimal number system consists of 10 symbols (0 to 9), each symbol has a positional value as well as an absolute value as in the example below.

Example 14.1. *Explain the meaning of* $(5601)_{10}$

Solution.

$$5 \times 10^3 + 6 \times 10^2 + 0 \times 10^1 + 1 \times 10^0$$
$$= 5000 + 600 + 0 + 1 = 5601$$

The base or radix of the system is 10. This also means that there are 10 symbols in this system. In general, if the radix of a number is r, it will have r symbols and is written as $(a_n a_{n-1} a_{n-2} \ldots\ldots a_0 a_{-1} a_{-2} \ldots a_{-m})$ and its value would be $a_n r^n + a_{n-1} r^{n-1} + \ldots\ldots + a_0 r^0 + a_{-1} r^{-1} + a_{-2} r^{-2} + \ldots. + a_{-m} r^{-m}$, a_n, a_{n-1}, a_{-m} used must be one of the r symbols allotted in the system. a_n is called the most significant digit (MSD) and a_{-m} is called the least significant digit (LSD).

14.3 BINARY NUMBER SYSTEM

Binary number system has a radix 2. As such, only two symbols (0 and 1) are allowed. Each binary digit is known as a bit.

A number in the binary system is written as a string of 1s and 0s.

Example 14.2. *Convert the following binary numbers to decimal numbers:*

(a) 1101 *(b) 10001* *(c) 10101*

Solution.

(a) $(1101)_2 = (1 \times 2^3) + (1 \times 2^2) + (0 \times 2^1) + (1 \times 2^0)$
$= 8 + 4 + 0 + 1 = 13$

(b) $(10001)_2 = (1 \times 2^4) + (0 \times 2^3) + (0 \times 2^2)\ (0 \times 2^1) + (0 \times 2^0)$
$= 16 + 0 + 0 + 0 + 1 = 17$

(c) $(10101)_2 = (1 \times 2^4) + (0 \times 2^3) + (1 \times 2^2) + (0 \times 2^1) + (1 \times 2^0)$
$= 16 + 0 + 4 + 0 + 1 = 21$

Table 14.1: Decimal numbers from 0 to 9 and their binary equivalents

Decimal	*Binary equivalent*
0	$0 \ (0 \times 2^0)$
1	$1 \ (1 \times 2^0)$
2	$10 \ (1 \times 2^1 + 0 \times 2^0)$
3	$11 \ (1 \times 2^1 + 1 \times 2^0)$
4	$100 \ (1 \times 2^2 + 0 \times 2^1 + 0 \times 2^0)$
5	$101 \ (1 \times 2^2 + 0 \times 2^1 + 1 \times 2^0)$
6	$110 \ (1 \times 2^2 + 1 \times 2^1 + 0 \times 2^0)$
7	$111 \ (1 \times 2^2 + 1 \times 2^1 + 1 \times 2^0)$
8	$1000 \ (1 \times 2^3 + 0 \times 2^2 + 0 \times 2^1 + 0 \times 2^0)$
9	$1001 \ (1 \times 2^3 + 0 \times 2^2 + 0 \times 2^1 + 0 \times 2^0)$

14.3.1 Decimal to Binary Conversion

An easy way of converting a decimal number to a binary number is as below. The positional values are written as

..........2^5	2^4	2^3	2^2	2^1	2^0	
..........32	16	8	4	2	1	positional values

If, now, it is necessary to convert say $(39)_{10}$ to binary, add the positional values so that 39 is obtained. Those positional values that have been taken for counting will have values of 1. Those not required will have 0 value.

As such, decimal 39 would be

	32	16	8	4	2	1	positional value
$(39)_{10}$	1	0	0	1	1	1	value in binary
	(32	+ 0	+ 0	+ 4	+ 2	+ 1)	

However, as the decimal number to be converted grows in size, it is difficult to adopt the above procedure. In such a case the procedure as indicated below is used:

Example 14.3. *Convert $(39)_{10}$ to binary.*

Soution.

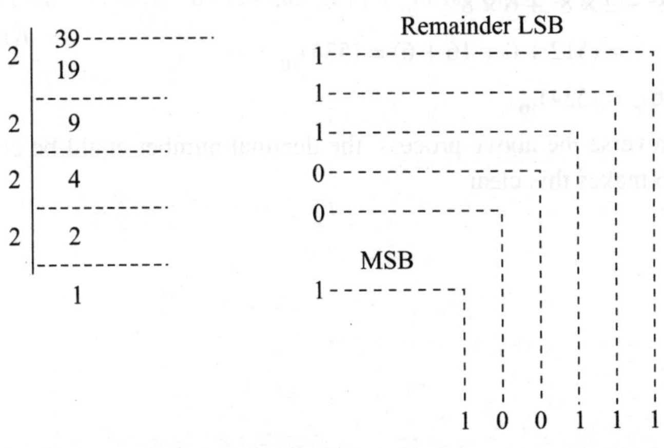

Thus $(39)_{10} = (100111)_2$

For converting a decimal fraction to binary, the procedure as indicated below is used.

Example 14.4. *Convert $(0.625)_{10}$ to binary.*

Solution.

			Integer value
0.625×2	=	1.250	1
0.250×2	=	0.500	0
0.500×2	=	1.000	1
$(0.625)_{10}$	=	$(0.101)_2$	1 0 1

14.4 OCTAL NUMBER SYSTEM

As the name suggests, the base is 8 in this system. In this system, there are 8 digits (0, 1, 2, 3, 4, 5, 6 and 7). While counting, numbers till 7 are encountered. However, on the next count, we return to 0 in the unit position (similar to 9 in decimal) and a carry is generated. As such, the resulting number is 10 (equivalent to decimal 9) and this process continues (till 17 and the next number would be 20) *i.e.*, each time a count greater than 7 is reached, a carry is generated.

In the octal system, the unit position or the least significant digit has a positional value of 8, the next digit has a positional value of 8^1 and so on:

$...8^4$	8^3	8^2	8^1	8^0
4006	512	64	8	1

This, as may be seen above, is exactly similar to the decimal system, the positional value being a power of 14.

14.4.1 Octal to Decimal Conversion

In order to convert any octal number to a decimal number, each digit is multiplied by its corresponding positional value. The following example makes the procedure clear.

Example 14.5. *Convert $(1026)_8$ to decimal.*

Solution.

$$1 \times 8^3 + 0 \times 8^2 + 2 \times 8^1 + 6 \times 8^0$$

$$= (512 + 0 + 16 + 6) = (534)_{10}$$

$$\therefore \quad (1026)_8 = (534)_{10}$$

If we were to reverse the above process, the decimal number could be converted into an octal number. Example 14.6 makes this clear.

Example 14.6. *Convert* $(534)_{10}$ *to octal.*

Solution.

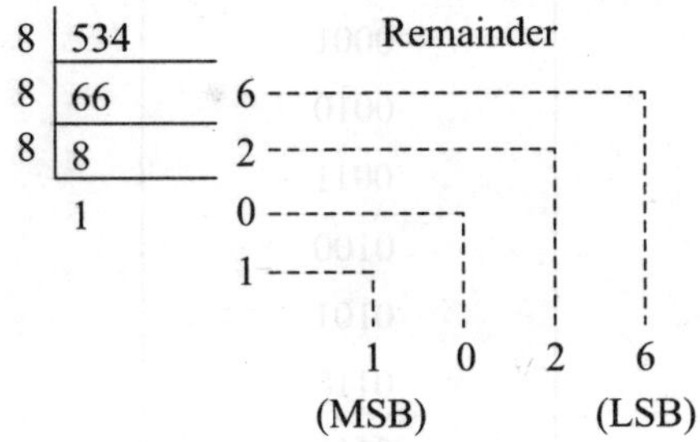

14.4.2 Binary to Octal Conversion

In the octal system, the radix 8 is a power of 2. It is possible to represent all the octal digits using three bits. That is, the octal numbers and their binary equivalents are as shown below:

Octal number	*Binary number*
0	000
1	001
2	010
3	011
4	100
5	101
6	110
7	111

In order to convert any binary number into an octal number, bits are separated into groups of 3 and the equivalent octal number is substituted. Separation into group of three begins from the LSB.

Example 14.7. *Convert* $(101111000001)_2$ *to octal.*

Solution.

101 111 000 001 (Groups of 3 bits are formed starting from LSB)

5 7 0 1 (Octal numbers are substituted for the above groups)

$\therefore$ $(101111000001)_2 = (5701)_8$

14.5 HEXADECIMAL NUMBER SYSTEM

This is another important number system widely used in microprocessors and computers. The radix in this system is 16 and as such, there are 16 basic symbols 0 through 9 and *A* through *F*. Also, by using 4 bits, it is possible to represent all the basic hexadecimal numbers. This is shown below:

Decimal number	*Binary number*	*Hexadecimal number*
0	0000	0
1	0001	1
2	0010	2
3	0011	3
4	0100	4
5	0101	5
6	0110	6
7	0111	7
8	1000	8
9	1001	9
10	1010	*A*
11	1011	*B*
12	1100	*C*
13	1101	*D*
14	1110	*E*
15	1111	*F*

14.5.1 Binary to Hexadecimal Conversion

When a binary number is given, it is possible to convert it into a hexadecimal number following the same procedure as was adopted in case of binary to octal conversions. However, it must be noted that in this case 4 bits are necessary to represent the hexadecimal number. Bits are arranged in groups of 4 starting from the LSB and an equivalent hexadecimal number is substituted.

Example 14.8. *Convert $(101111000001)_2$ to hexadecimal.*

Solution.

1011 1100 0001 (Groups of 4 bits are formed starting from the LSB)

B *C* 1 (Hexadecimal numbers are substituted for the above groups)

$\therefore \quad (101111000001)_2 = (B \quad C \quad 1)_{16}$

14.5.2 Hexadecimal to Decimal Conversion

Each hexadecimal digit is multiplied by the corresponding positional value [...$16^3, 16^2, 16^1, 16^0, 16^{-1}$...] and the resulting number is the equivalent decimal number.

Example 14.9. *Convert $(2BC3)_{16}$ to decimal.*

Solution.

$$2 \times 16^3 + B \times 16^2 + C \times 16^1 + 3 \times 16^0$$

$$= 2 \times 16^3 + 11 \times 16^2 + 12 \times 16^1 + 3 \times 16^0$$

$$= 8192 + 2816 + 192 + 3$$

$$= (11203)_{10}$$

If we were to reverse the above process, the decimal number could be converted to hexadecimal.

Example 14.10. *Convert* $(11203)_{10}$ *to hexadecimal.*

Solution.

		Remainder
16	11203	
16	700	3
16	43	C
	2	B
		2

2 B C 3

(MSB) (LSB)

$$(11203)_{10} = (2BC3)_{16}$$

14.6 BINARY ADDITION

In the decimal system when two numbers are added, if the sum is greater than 9, a carry is generated from the unit position to the 10s position and so on.

Similarly in the binary system, if the added value is greater than 1, a carry is generated. For various combinations of the augend and the addend, the table shows the carry and the sum.

a	*b*	*Sum*	*Carry*
0	0	0	0
0	1	1	0
1	0	1	0
1	1	0	1

Example 14.11. *Add the binary numbers*

1 1 0 1 and 1 1 1 1

1 1 1 1 carry generated.

Solution.

Augend	1 1 0 1
Addend	1 1 1 1
Sum	1 1 1 0 0

14.6.1 Addition in Other Number System

The above principle could be extended for the addition of two octal or hexadecimal numbers also. In the octal system, when two numbers are added if the sum is greater than 7 a carry is generated and in hexadecimal if the sum is greater than F (*i.e.,* decimal 15) then a carry is generated.

Example 14.12. *Add the octal numbers 350 and 762.*

Solution.

	350
	762
Sum	1332

(6 + 5 = 11 – 18 = 3 and a carry of 1)

(7 + 3 + 1 = 11 – 8 = 3 and a carry of 1)

Example 14.13. *Add the Hexadecimal numbers*

6 A B and 7 B C.

Solution. 6 A B

7 B C

Sum E 6 7

(B + C = 23 – 16 = 7 and a carry of 1)

(A + B + 1 = 22 – 16 = 6 and a carry of 1)

(6 + 7 + 1 = 14 = E)

14.7 BINARY SUBTRACTION

Rules for binary subtraction are similar to those of decimal subtraction. That is, if a larger quantity is to be subtracted from a smaller quantity, a borrow is taken from the next higher bit.

For various combinations of the minuend and the subtrahend, the table below shows the difference and the borrow:

a	*b*	*Difference*	*Borrow*
0	0	0	0
0	1	1	1
1	0	1	0
1	1	0	0

Example 14.14. *Subtract 110 from 1011.*

Solution.

	1	borrow
Minuend	1 0 1 1	
Subtrahend	1 1 0	
	0 1 0 1	

14.7.1 Subtraction in Other Number System

The above principle could be extended for the subtraction of two octals or hexadecimal numbers also. The following examples makes this clear:

Example 14.15. *Subtract $(257)_8$ from $(346)_8$.*

Solution.

Minuend	346
Subtrahend	257
	067

When the borrow is compensated 3 becomes 2, $(2-2)=0$ When a borrow is compensated 4 becomes 3, $5>3$ and thus a borrow from the next higher bit is taken (borrow = 8) and thus $[(3+8)-5]=6$ $7>6$ ∴ a borrow is taken from the next higher bit, borrow means 8 (as we are considering octal system) and thus $[(8+6)-7]=7$

Example 14.16. *Subtract* $(EF)_{16}$ *from* $(FE)_{16}$

Solution.

Minuend	*F*	*E*
Subtrahend	*E*	*F*
	0	*F*

When a borrow is compensated *F* becomes *E* and thus $E-E=0$

$F>E$ a borrow is taken from the next higher bit, borrow means 16 (Hexadecimal) and thus $[(16+E)-F]=F$

14.7.2 Complement Form of Subtraction in Decimal Numbers

In decimal system, there are two types of complements referred to as 10s complement and the 9s complement.

The 10s complement of any decimal number is formed by subtracting each digit of the number from 9 and then adding 1 to the least significant digit. Subtraction is then performed by simply adding the 10s complement of the subtrahend to the minuend and discarding the carry generated at the most significant digit. If no carry is generated, the resulting answer is negative and is in the complemented form. The true answer is the complement of the obtained result.

Example 14.17. *Perform the following using 10s complement method*

(*i*) *86 – 26* (*ii*) *26 – 86.*

Solution.

(*i*) Minuend 86

10s complement of subtrahend $26 = 99 - 26 + 1 = 74$

10s complement of Subtrahend 26 — 74 (add)

carry → 1 — 60

Carry discarded

∴ $86 - 26 = 60$

(*ii*) Minuend 26

10s complement of subtrahend $86 = 99 - 86 + 1 = 14$

10s complement of Subtrahend 86 — 14 (add)

40

No carry is generated and thus the answer 40 is in the complement form. Thus the answer is the 10s complement of 40 = –60 (as 99 – 40 + 1 = 60) with negative sign.

Similarly 9s complement subtraction also may be performed. 9s complement of a decimal number is formed by subtracting each digit of the number from 9. Now the 9s complement of the subtrahend is added to the minuend. Carry generated is added to the least significant digit. If no carry is generated, the answer is in the 9s complemented form.

Example 14.18. *Perform by 9s complement method*

(*i*) *86 – 26* (*ii*) *26 – 86.*

Solution.

(*i*) Minuend 86

9s complement of subtrahend 26 = 99 – 26 = 73

9s complement of Subtrahend 73 (add)

carry → 159 1 (add carry to LSB)

60

∴ 86 – 26 = 60

(*ii*) Minuend 26 9s complement of subtrahend 86 = 99 – 86 = 13

9s complement of subtrahend 13 (add)

39

No carry generated and thus the answer is in the 9s complement form with negative sign

As such, answer is 99 – 39 = – 60

14.7.3 Complement Form of Subtraction in Binary System

In the binary system, similar to the 10s and 9s complement, we have 2s and 1s complement representation.

2s complement of a binary number may be obtained by subtracting each bit of the number from 1, and then adding a 1 to the least significant bit. Subtracting each bit from 1 is as good as writing the given number by replacing 1 by 0 and 0 by 1 (this is called complementing the given number). Now, the 2s complement of the subtrahend is added to the minuend. If a final carry generated, it is discarded and the resulting number is the answer. However, if no carry is generated, the answer is in the 2s complement form.

Example 14.19.

(*i*) *Subtract 1001111 from 1010110 and*

(*ii*) *Subtract 1010110 from 11010 using 2s complement arithmetic.*

Solution.

(*i*) Minuend 1 0 1 0 1 1 0

2s complement of Subtrahend 0 1 1 0 0 0 1 $\overline{2}$ s of 1001111 is 110000 (replace 1s by 0s and 0s by 1s and add 1 to the LSB)

carry → 1 0 0 0 0 1 1 1

discard the carry generated. The answer is 111.

(*ii*) Minuend	1 1 0 1 0
2s complement of Subtrahend	0 1 0 1 0 1 0
	1 0 0 0 1 0 0

As no carry is generated, the answer is in the 2s complement form and the answer is $\overline{2s}$ of 1000100 = 0111100.

Similarly, 1s complement subtraction also can be done.

1s complement of a binary number is formed by replacing 1s by 0s and 0s by 1s. Now, the 1s complement of the subtrahend is added to the minuend. If an end carry is generated, the carry is added to the LSB. If no end carry is generated, the answer is in the 1s complement form.

Example 14.20.

(*i*) Subtract	1 0 0 1 1 1 1	from 1 0 1 0 1 1 0
and (*ii*) Subtract	1 0 1 0 1 1 0	from 1 1 0 1 0.

Solution. Using 1s complement arithmetic.

(*i*) Minuend	1 0 1 0 1 1 0	
1s complement of Subtrahend	0 1 1 0 0 0 0	
carry→	1 0 0 0 0 1 1 0	Add
	1	
Answer	0 0 0 0 1 1 1	

(*ii*) Minuend	1 1 0 1 0
1s complement of Subtrahend	0 1 0 1 0 0 1
	1 0 0 0 0 1 1

No end carry is generated and thus the answer is in the 1s complement form.

As such, answer is – 0 1 1 1 1 0 0

14.8 FRACTIONAL NUMBERS

If we write a number in decimal as say 12.75, we mean 75 is the fractional part and 12 is the whole number or integer. That is the whole number is separated from the fractional part by placing a decimal in between. Also, we understand the positional values as below:

$$1 \times 10^1 + 2 \times 10^0 + 7 \times 10^{-1} + 5 \times 10^{-2}$$

Similar to the above, we have the binary representation also, say the meaning of 110. 11 is

$$1 \times 2^2 + 1 \times 2^1 + 0 \times 2^0 + 1 \times 2^{-1} + 1 \times 2^{-2}$$

$$= 4 + 2 + 0 + 0.5 + 0.25$$

$$= (6.75)_{10}$$

Recall the methods we adopted to convert a binary number to an octal number and binary number to a hexadecimal number. Even if the binary number has a fractional part, same procedure of grouping the numbers into groups of 3 or groups of 4 is adopted (separately for the integer part and the fractional part).

Example 14.21. *Convert the following binary number to (i) Octal and (ii) Hexadecimal number 1 0 1 0 1 1 0 . 1 1 0 1 0 1.*

Solution.

(*i*) Octal:	0 0 1	0 1 0	1 1 0.	1 1 0	1 0 1
	1	2	6	6	5
(*ii*) Hexadecimal:	0 1 0 1	0 1 1 0.	1 1 0 1	0 1 0 0	
	5	6	*D*	4	

14.9 BINARY CODED DECIMAL NUMBERS

People communicating with the computer are normally well acquainted with decimal system. However, computer systems understand only binary numbers. As such, there is need to convert decimal system to binary system and vice-versa. Instead of converting, it is possible to code each decimal digit using binary digits. This is called the *Binary Coded Decimal* or BCD representation. Indeed, in all desk calculators, digital clocks, BCD representation is widely used.

There are 10 basic symbols in the decimal system. Maximum of 4 bits are required to represent all the numbers of the decimal system. This method of representing each of the decimal digit by 4 bits is known as encoding.

Example 14.22. *Convert (i)* $(15)_{10}$ *to BCD (ii)* $(56.75)_{10}$ *to BCD.*

Solution.

(*i*) $(1 \quad 5)_{10}$

$(0001 \quad 0101)_{BCD}$

[using 4 bits, BCD representation for 1 and 5 are written separately. As such, the resulting number 0001 0101 is the BCD equivalent of 15 decimal]

(*ii*) $(5 \quad 6 . 7 \quad 5)_{10}$

$(0101 \quad 0110 . 0111 \quad 0101)_{BCD}$

More Examples on Conversion of Numbers:

Example 14.22.1.

(*i*) Binary to Decimal Conversion

1. $(1010.11)_2 = 1 \times 2^3 + 0 \times 2^2 + 1 \times 2^1 + 0 \times 2^0 + 1 \times 2^{-1} + 1 \times 2^{-2}$

$= 8 + 0 + 2 + 0 + 0.5 + 0.25$

$= (10.75)_{10}$

2. $(0.11101)_2 = 1 \times 2^{-1} + 1 \times 2^{-2} + 1 \times 2^{-3} + 0 \times 2^{-4} + 1 \times 2^{-5}$

$= 0.5 + 0.25 + 0.125 + 0 + 0.03125$

$= (0.90625)_{10}$

(*ii*) Decimal to Binary Conversion

$(50.202)_{10} = (?)_2$

Divisor	Number	Remainder (Read ↑)
2	50	
2	25	0
2	12	1
2	6	0
2	3	0
	1	1
		1

Step	Carry (Read ↓)
0.202 × 2 = 0.404	0
0.404 × 2 = 0.808	0
0.808 × 2 = 1.616	1
0.616 × 2 = 1.232	1

$(50)_{10} = (110010)_2$

$(0.202)_{10} = (.0011)_2$

$(50.202)_{10} = (110010.0011)_2$

(*iii*) Binary to Octal Conversion

1. $(11101110101.10101100)_2 = (?)_8$

Grouping Direction ← . →

011	101	110	101	.	101	011	000
↑ Prefix '0'							↑ Postfix '0'
3	5	6	5	.	5	3	0

$(11101110101.10101100)_2 = (3565.530)_8$

2. $(.11110111011)_2 = (?)_8$

→

111	101	110	110
.7	5	6	6

$(.11110111011)_2 = (.7566)_8$

(*iv*) Octal to Binary Conversion

$(2551.333)_8 = (?)_2$

2	5	5	1	.	3	3	3
010	101	101	001	.	011	011	011

$(2551.333)_8 = (010101101001.011011011)_2$

(*v*) Binary to Hexadecimal

1. $(1011011101111111.0111111)_2 = (?)_{H \text{ or } 16}$

0101 1011 1011 1111 . 0111 1110

↑ Prefixed '0' (on the first group) ↑ Postfix '0' (on the last group)

5 *B* *B* *F* . 7 *E*

$(1011011101111111.0111111)_2 = (5BBF.7F)_H$

(*vi*) Hexadecimal to Binary Conversion

2. $(9BCA.BB)_{16} = (?)_2$

9	*B*	*C*	*A* . *B*	*B*
1001	1011	1100	1010 . 1011	1011

$(9BCA.BB)_{16} = (1001101111001010.10111011)_2$

(*vii*) Decimal to Octal Conversion

$(985.85)_{10} = (?)_8$

8	985	
8	123	1
8	15	3
	1	7

1731 (read upward)

$0.85 \times 8 = 8.90 \longrightarrow 6$
$0.80 \times 8 = 6.40 \longrightarrow 6$
$0.40 \times 8 = 3.20 \longrightarrow 3$
$0.20 \times 8 = 1.60 \longrightarrow 1$

6631 (read downward)

$(985.85)_{10} = (1731.6631)_8$

Thus $(985.85)_{10} = (1731.6631)_8$

14.10 BOOLEAN ALGEBRA

George Boole (1815–1864) developed an algebra known as Boolean algebra to evaluate the truth or falsity of a set of propositions either singly or joined together by the basic logical connections. This area of logic is also known as 'Calculus of propositions'. The use of symbols to represent propositions, connections truth and false conditions lead to the name 'Symbolic Logic'.

In 1938, Claude E. Shanon described the method of using Boolean algebra to represent two-state circuits (or Binary circuits). This principle is used in all switching networks (computers).

Essentially Boolean algebra uses three basic operations: AND function (similar to multiplication), OR function (similar to addition) and NOT function (similar to complementation or negation). Variables in this algebra are binary. That is, the variable can take only two values 1 or 0. This also may be thought of as true or false/yes or no.

14.10.1 Switching Circuits

Consider a lamp connected in series with two switches S_1 and S_2 as shown in Fig. 14.1 to a battery.

The lamp will light only when S_1 and S_2 are closed. For all other conditions, the lamp is off.

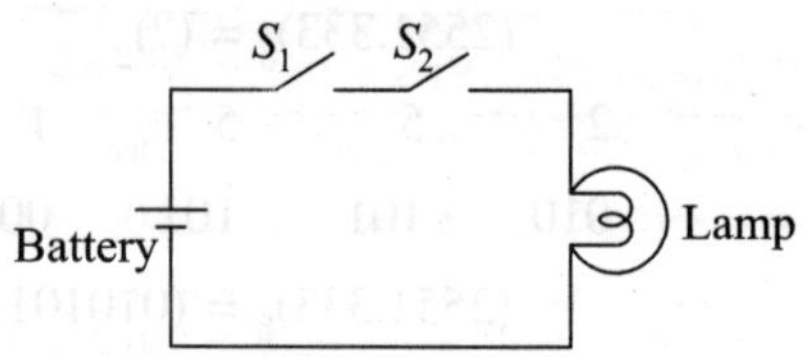

Fig. 14.1 *Lamp is ON when S_1 AND S_2 are closed*

Now consider the circuit as shown in Fig. 14.2 where switches S_3 and S_4 are connected in parallel and the combination being connected in series with the battery and the lamp.

From the figure it is clear that the Lamp is 'ON' (will light) for the following conditions:

(*i*) If S_4 is closed or

(*ii*) If S_3 is closed or

(*iii*) If both S_3 and S_4 are closed.

The above description of circuits makes the following clear:

(*i*) The switches have two positions — CLOSE or OPEN

(*ii*) The Lamp also has OFF or ON. For convenience, we use 0 or 1 to represent these values. Indeed, this 0 or 1 has no arithmetic significance but has only logical significance. These variables are called '*Boolean variables*'.

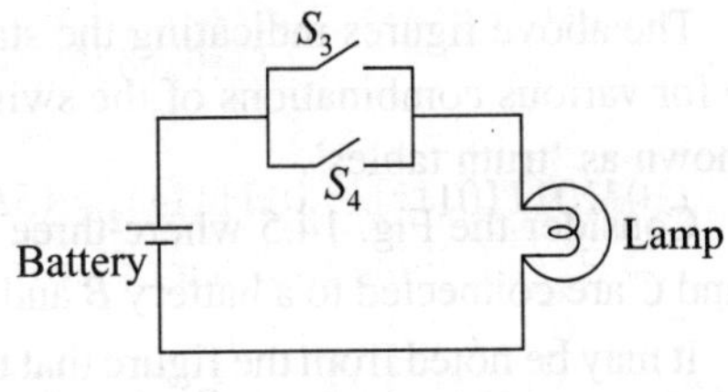

Fig. 14.2 *Lamp is ON when S_3 OR S_4 are closed.*

The working of the circuits of Figs. 14.1 and 14.2 may be represented as in the Fig. 14.3—This is also known as the '*truth table*'.

Switch S_1	*Switch S_2*	*Lamp*
OPEN	OPEN	OFF
OPEN	CLOSED	OFF
CLOSED	CLOSED	ON
CLOSED	OPEN	OFF

(*a*) Series connection of switches (Fig. 14.1)

Switch S_3	*Switch S_4*	*Lamp*
OPEN	OPEN	OFF
OPEN	CLOSED	ON
CLOSED	CLOSED	ON
CLOSED	OPEN	ON

(*b*) Parallel connection of switches (Fig. 14.2)

Fig. 14.3 *Truth table for operations in Figs. 14.1 and 14.2*

Instead of writing the tables as indicated above, symbols of 0 and 1 may be used for 'open/off' and 'closed/on' respectively. This is shown in Fig. 14.4.

S_1	S_2	*Output (L)*
0	0	0
0	1	0
1	1	1
1	0	0

(*a*)

S_3	S_4	*Output (L)*
0	0	0
0	1	1
1	1	1
1	0	1

(*b*)

Fig. 14.4 *Truth table for (a) Series connection (b) Parallel connection of switches*

From Fig. 14.4 (*a*), it may be noted that output (*L*) = S_1 AND S_2 or symbolically.

$$L = S_1 . S_2$$

From Fig. 14.4 (*b*), it may be noted that output (*L*) = S_3 OR S_4 or symbolically,

$$L = S_3 + S_4.$$

The above figures indicating the state of the Lamp for various combinations of the switch states are known as 'truth tables'.

Consider the Fig. 14.5 where three switches *A*, *B* and *C* are connected to a battery *B* and Lamp *L*.

It may be noted from the figure that the Lamp *L* is 'ON' for the following conditions:

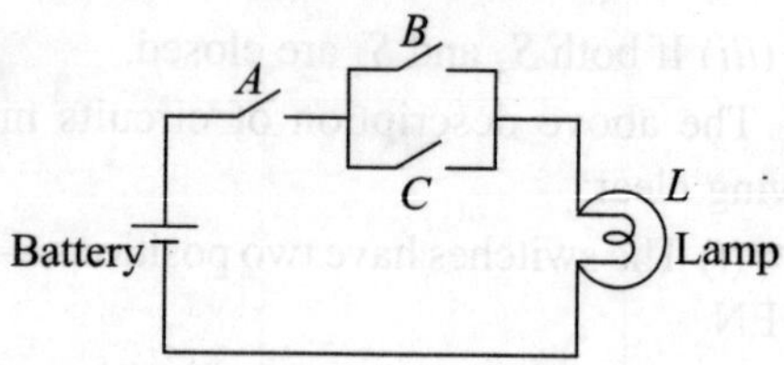

Fig. 14.5 *Switches A, B and C controlling Lamp L*

(*i*) '*A*' is closed and '*B*' is closed, '*C*' is open.

(*ii*) '*A*' is closed and '*C*' is closed, '*B*' is open.

(*iii*) '*A*' is closed and '*B*' and '*C*' are closed.

For the rest of the switch positions, Lamp is 'OFF' as:

(*i*) '*A*' is open and '*B*' is open, '*C*' is open

(*ii*) '*A*' is open and '*B*' is open, '*C*' is closed

(*iii*) '*A*' is open and '*B*' is closed, '*C*' is open

(*iv*) '*A*' is open and '*B*' is closed, '*B*' is closed

(*v*) '*A*' is closed and '*B*' is open, '*C*' is open.

The above statements may be written as 'Truth table' shown in Fig. 14.6 in which 0 represents 'open' or 'OFF' and 1 represents 'closed' or 'ON'.

A	*B*	*C*	*L*
0	0	0	0
0	0	1	0
0	1	0	0
0	1	1	0
1	0	0	0
1	0	1	1
1	1	0	1
1	1	1	1

Fig. 14.6 *Truth table for Fig. 14.5*

From the above, it is clear that '*L*' is ON for '*A*' ON AND '*B*' or '*C*'ON.

That is; $L = A \cdot (B + C)$

This is called the *Boolean* expression. Variables *A*, *B* and *C* are known as literals.

Negation of 'True' is 'False'.

That is negation of 1 is 0

and negation of 0 is 1

If *A* is a literal, negation or NOT of *A* is $\overline{A}$.

14.10.2 NAND Operation

AND the literals and then NOT it. This is known as NAND operation. Figure 14.7 shows a truth table for the NAND operation:

A	B	$A.B$ (AND)	$\overline{A \cdot B}$ (NAND)
0	0	0	1
0	1	0	1
1	0	0	1
1	1	1	0

Fig. 14.7 *Truth table for the NAND operation*

14.10.3 NOR Operation

OR the literals and then NOT it. This is known as NOR operation. Figure 14.6 shows the truth table for the NOR operation.

A	B	$A + B$ (OR)	$\overline{A + B}$ (NOR)
0	0	0	1
0	1	1	0
1	0	1	0
1	1	1	0

Fig. 14.8 *Truth table for the NOR operation*

14.10.4 Boolean Theorems

The following theorems depicted in Fig. 14.9 are important in the simplification of logical expressions. Logical variables (Boolean variables or literals) can, as we have seen before, take only two values '0' or '1'.

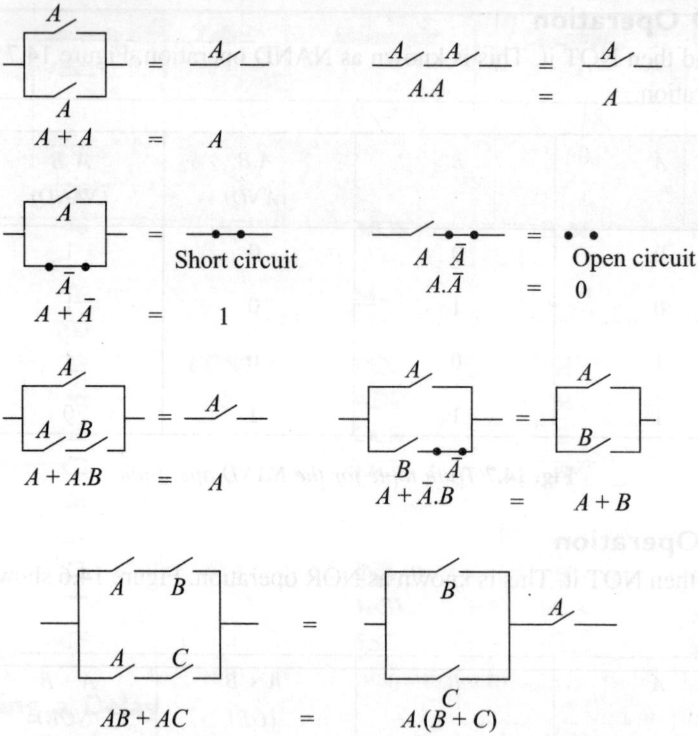

Fig. 14.9 *Combination of switches yielding various functions*

The above theorems may also be proved easily by the use of truth tables. This is shown in Fig. 14.10.

A	$\bar{A}$	$A + A$	$A.A$	$A + \bar{A}$	$A.\bar{A}$	$A + 1$	$A + 0$
0	1	0	0	1	0	1	0
1	0	1	1	1	0	1	1

Fig. 14.10 *Truth table for one literal*

From the above, it is clear that the following are valid:

$$A + A = A$$
$$A \cdot A = A$$
$$A + \bar{A} = 1$$
$$A \cdot \bar{A} = 0$$
$$A + 1 = 1$$
$$A + 0 = A$$

Figure 14.11 shows the truth table corresponding to certain relationships involving two variables *A* and *B*.

A	B	$A + A.B$	$A + B$	$A + \overline{A}.B$
0	0	0	0	0
0	1	0	1	1
1	0	1	1	1
1	1	1	1	1

Fig. 14.11 *Truth table for 2 literals*

From the above table, the following are valid:

$$A + A \,.\, B = A$$

$$A + \overline{A} \,.\, B = A + B$$

$$(A + \overline{A} \,.\, B) = (A + \overline{A}).(A + B) = A + B.$$

14.10.5 DeMorgan's Theorem

It may be of interest to know the original form of DeMorgan's theorem which he developed in the early 1800s.

The negative or contradictory of an alternative proposition is a conjunction in which the conjuncts are the contradictions of the corresponding alternates, and that the negative of a conjuctive is an alternative proposition in corresponding conjuncts'.

$$\overline{A + B} = \overline{A} \,.\, \overline{B}$$

and $$\overline{A \,.\, B} = \overline{A} + \overline{B}$$

Although, we have defined DeMorgan's theorem above for two variables, it is applicable for any number of variables as:

$$\overline{A + B + C + D} = \overline{A} \,.\, \overline{B} \,.\, \overline{C} \,.\, \overline{D}$$

$$\overline{A \,.\, B \,.\, C \,.\, D} = \overline{A} + \overline{B} + \overline{C} + \overline{D}$$

This theorem is proved by using truth table (Fig. 14.12)

A	B	$A + B$	$A + B$	$\overline{A} \,.\, \overline{B}$	$\overline{A \,.\, B}$	$\overline{A} + \overline{B}$
0	0	0	1	1	1	1
0	1	1	0	0	1	1
1	0	1	0	0	1	1
1	1	1	0	0	0	0

Fig. 14.12 *Truth table for proving DeMorgan's theorem*

Example 14.23. *Prove* $A\,.\,\overline{B} + B\,.\,C + \overline{C}\,.\,A = A + B\,.\,C$

Solution. As there are three variables, there are $2^3 = 8$ combinations. These 8 combinations may be written by writing the binary equivalents of decimal numbers 0 through 8.

Decimal No.	A	B	C	$\overline{B}$	$\overline{C}$	$A.\overline{B}$	$B.C$	$\overline{C}.A$	$\overline{C}A + A.\overline{B} + B.C$	$A + B.C$
0	0	0	0	1	1	0	0	0	0	0
1	0	0	1	1	0	0	0	0	0	0
2	0	1	0	0	1	0	0	0	0	0
3	0	1	1	0	0	0	1	0	1	1
4	1	0	0	1	1	1	0	1	1	1
5	1	0	1	1	0	1	0	0	1	1
6	1	1	0	0	1	0	0	1	1	1
7	1	1	1	0	0	0	1	0	1 ←equal→	1

Fig. 14.13 *Truth table*

It is clear from the truth table that

$$A\,.\,\overline{B} + B\,.\,C + \overline{C}\,.\,A = A + B\,.\,C$$

As the number of variables increases, verification of the Boolean expressions become tedious. Also, simplification of the Boolean expressions become almost impossible. As such, for this purpose a graphical method called 'KARNAUGH' map method is used. Even this method becomes quite involved when the variables are more. In such cases 'QUINE' — McCluskey's method of simplification is adopted. These methods are not discussed here as it is beyond the scope of this book.

14.10.6 Some Properties of Boolean Algebra

I. Commutative property

(*a*) $A + B = B + A$ (*b*) $A.B = B.A$

II. Associative property

(*a*) $A + (B + C) = (A + B) + C$ (*b*) $A(B.C) = (AB)C$

III. Distributive property

$$A\,(B + C) = AB + AC$$

IV. Duality property

The duality property states that, for any given Boolean relation, it is possible to derive an another Boolean relation by

(*a*) Changing '+' sign to an '.' sign (OR to AND)

(*b*) Changing '.' sign to '+' sign (AND to OR)

(*c*) If the expression consists 0's or 1's are replaced by 1's or 0's respectively.

Boolean relation	Dual Boolean Relation
$A + 0 = A$	$A \,.\, 1 = A$
$A + 1 = 1$	$A \,.\, 0 = 0$
$A + A = A$	$A \,.\, A = A$
$A + \overline{A} = 1$	$A \,.\, \overline{A} = 0$
$A + \overline{A}B = A + B$	$A(\overline{A} + B) = AB$
$(A + B)(A + C) = A + BC$	$AB + AC = A(B + C)$
$AB + \overline{A}C + BC = AB + \overline{A}C$	$(A + B)(\overline{A} + C)(B + C) = (A + B)(\overline{A} + C)$
$A + AB = A$	$A(A + B) = A$

V. Complement property

(*a*) $A \,.\, \overline{A} = 0$ (*b*) $A + \overline{A} = 1$

where $\overline{A}$ is the complement of A or A is complement of $\overline{A}$.

Similarly '0' is the complement of '1' or '1' is the complement of '0'.

VI. Idempotency property

(*a*) $A + A = A$ (*b*) $A \,.\, A = A$

is any variable added or multiplied with itself results the original variable in Boolean Algebra.

VII. Absorption property

(*a*) $A + AB = A$ (*b*) $A(A + B) = A$

Rules in Boolean algebra:

I. Representation of all Boolean variables by capital letters.

II. The complement of variable is represented by 'bar' over the letter ($\overline{A}$) or sometime represented by a prime symbol (A).

III. The logical AND function of two variables is represented by writing a 'dot' ($A \,.\, B$) between two letters or simply writing two letters (AB).

IV. The logical OR function of two variables is represented by writing '+' sign between two letter ($A + B$).

More Examples on Simplification of Boolean Expression:

1. $WXYZ + W\overline{X}YZ$

Solution. $= WYZ(X + \overline{X})$

$= WYZ.1$

$= WYZ$

2. $AB + ABC + ABD + ABE$

Solution. $= AB(1 + C + D + E)$

$= AB$ $[1 + A = 1]$

3. $XZ + Z(X + \overline{X}Y)$

Solution.

$$= XZ + XZ + \overline{X}YZ$$
$$= XZ + \overline{X}YZ$$
$$= Z(X + \overline{X}Y)$$
$$= Z(X + Y)$$
$$= XZ + YZ$$

4. Simplify the expression $AB + A\overline{C} + ABC(AB + C)$

Solution.

$$AB + \overline{AC} + A\overline{B}C(AB + C) = AB + \overline{AC} + A\overline{B}C.AB + A\overline{B}C.C$$
$$= AB + \overline{AC} + A\overline{B}C \qquad [C.C = C \text{ and } \overline{B}.B = 0]$$
$$= AB + \overline{A} + \overline{C} + A\overline{B}C$$
$$= AB + \overline{A} + \overline{C} + \overline{B}C \qquad [A + \overline{A}B = A + B]$$
$$= \overline{A} + AB + \overline{C} + C\overline{B}$$
$$= \overline{A} + B + \overline{C} + \overline{B}$$
$$= \overline{A} + \overline{C} + 1 \qquad [B + \overline{B} = 1]$$
$$= \overline{A} + 1$$
$$= 1$$

5. Simplify the given Boolean expression $y = \overline{A}\,\overline{B}\,\overline{C} + \overline{A}B\overline{C} + A\overline{B}\,\overline{C} + AB\overline{C}$

Solution.

$$y = \overline{A}\,\overline{B}\,\overline{C} + \overline{A}B\overline{C} + A\overline{B}\,\overline{C} + AB\overline{C}$$
$$= \overline{A}\,\overline{C}(B + \overline{B}) + A\overline{C}(B + \overline{B})$$
$$= \overline{A}\,\overline{C} + A\overline{C}$$
$$= \overline{C}(\overline{A} + A)$$
$$= \overline{C}$$

6. $XY + \overline{XZ} + X\overline{Y}Z(XY + Z)$

Solution.

$$= XY + \overline{XZ} + XY\overline{Y}Z + X\overline{Y}ZZ$$
$$= XY + \overline{XZ} + 0 + X\overline{Y}Z \qquad [X.\overline{X} = 0, X.X = X]$$
$$= XY + \overline{X} + \overline{Z} + X\overline{Y}Z$$
$$= X(Y + \overline{Y}Z) + \overline{X} + \overline{Z}$$
$$= X(Y + Z) + \overline{X} + \overline{Z}$$
$$= XY + XZ + \overline{X} + \overline{Z} \qquad [X + \overline{X}Y = X + Y]$$

$$= \overline{X} + Y + X + \overline{Z}$$

$$= 1 + Y + \overline{Z} \qquad [X + \overline{X} = 1]$$

$$= 1$$

7. Prove that $BCD + A\overline{C}\,\overline{D} + ABD = BCD + A\overline{C}\,\overline{D} + AB\overline{C}$

Solution.

$$BCD + A\overline{C}\,\overline{D} + ABD = BCD + A\overline{C}\,\overline{D} + (ABD)$$

$$= BCD + A\overline{C}\,\overline{D} + (ABD)(C + \overline{C})$$

$$= BCD + A\overline{C}\,\overline{D} + ABCD + AB\overline{C}D$$

$$= BCD\,(1 + A) + A\overline{C}\,(\overline{D} + DB)$$

$$= BCD + A\overline{C}\,(\overline{D} + B)$$

$$= BCD + A\overline{C}\,\overline{D} + AB\overline{C}$$

Hence L.H.S. = R.H.S.

14.11 LOGIC GATES

Logical operations AND, OR and NOT are said to be logically complete, that is, using these three types of operations, it is possible to realise any function. We now look into the possibilities of realising these logical functions by means of electronic circuits commonly called as *gates*.

14.11.1 AND Gates

Two diodes are connected to a resistor R which in turn is connected to a source of 10 volts as shown in Fig. 14.14.

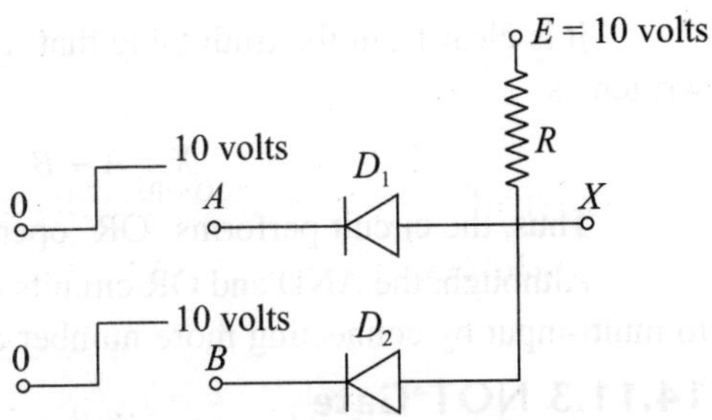

Fig. 14.14 *A two input AND gate*

At points A and B are applied the input voltage levels which are either 0 or 10 volts. X indicates the output point. Output as a function of the input will be considered now. When A and B are connected to ground (0 volt), D_1 and D_2 conduct, there by connecting point X to 0 volt. If A is at 10^2 volts, B at 0 volt, D_2 conducts (D_1 does not) thereby again connecting X to 0 potential. Similarly, when B is at 10 volts, A at 0 volt, D_1 conducts and again X is connected to 0 potential. However, when both A and B are at 10 volts, none of the diodes conduct and as such, points X remains at 10 volts (battery E = 10 volts). If now we consider 10 volts as 'Logical 1' and 0 volt as 'Logical 0', then the truth table may be drawn as in Fig. 14.15.

A	*B*	*X*
0	0	0
0	1	0
1	0	0
1	1	1

Fig. 14.15 *Truth table for the 'AND' function*

It is clear that $X = 1$ only when A and B both are equal to 1, which may be written as

$$X = A.B$$

Thus, the circuit performs the 'AND' operation.

14.11.2 OR Gate

Consider the arrangement shown in Fig. 14.16. We may consider the working of the circuit as we did previously. That is, when A and B are both at 0 volt, both diodes are reverse biased and thus X is at 0 volt. When A is at 10 volts and B is at 0 volt, D_1 conducts thereby connecting point X to 10 volts and so on, resulting in the truth table shown in Fig. 14.17.

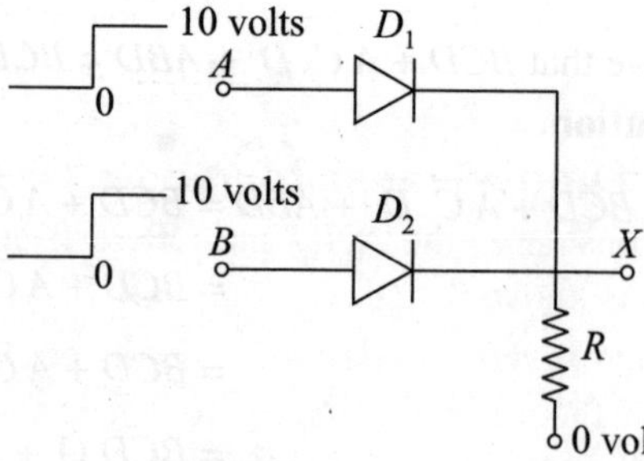

Fig. 14.16 *2-input OR gate*

A	B	X
0	0	0
0	1	1
1	0	1
1	1	1

Fig. 14.17 *Truth table for the OR function*

It is clear from the truth table that X is 1 if A is 1 or B is 1 or A and B are both 1. This may be written as

$$X = A + B$$

Thus, the circuit performs 'OR' operation.

Although, the AND and OR circuits explained above have only two inputs, these are extendable to multi-input by connecting more number of diodes.

14.11.3 NOT Gate

Consider a common emitter transistor circuit as in Fig. 14.18 base, being driven by a voltage source through a resistance R_B.

When the applied base voltage is at 0 potential, no base current flows and the transistor is off. Output X remains at the supply voltage of 10 volts. Now if A is at 10 volts, base current flows thereby collector current flows and thus the transistor goes to saturation (choosing suitable values of R_B and R_C). Hence X remains at 0 potential. The performance of the above circuit may be summarised as indicated in Fig. 14.19. As the output is the inverted version of the input (1 to 0 and 0 to 1), this circuit is also known as an *inverter*.

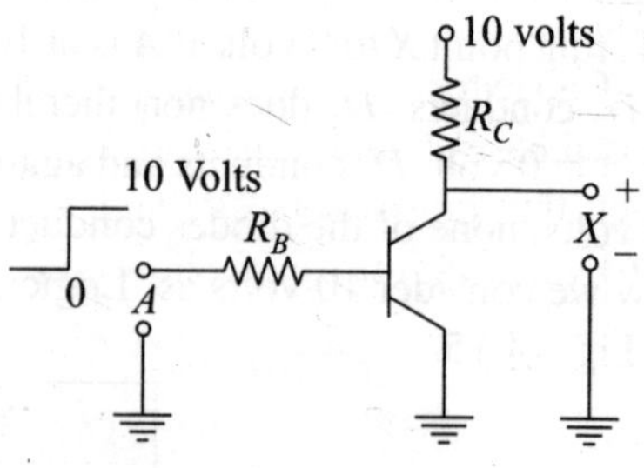

Fig. 14.18 *A NOT gate*

A	X
0	1
1	0

$X = \overline{A}$

Fig. 14.19 *Truth table for NOT gate (an inverter)*

14.11.4 Diode-Transistor Logic (DTL)

We have considered the AND and OR realisations using diodes in sections 14.10.1 and 14.10.2. This realisation is known as *Diode Logic* (DL).

When several diode logic circuits are cascaded, the input drive current to the circuit must be provided by the preceding stages. To ensure this resistor *R* in the circuit will have to be reduced. This is not generally possible unless different types of AND and OR gates are available. To avoid this situation (avoid loading effects) buffer amplifiers are used. This type of logical realisation is known as *Diode-Transistor Logic* (DTL).

Figure 14.20 shows the circuit diagram of this logic configuration. This is available even in the integrated circuit form.

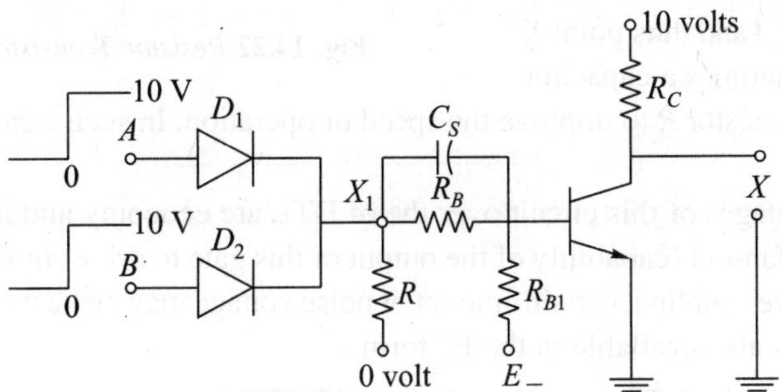

Fig. 14.20 *Diode-Transistor logic circuit*

D_1, D_2 and *R* form the DL-OR gate. Transistor basically forms a NOT gate. When *A* or *B* go high, Input base voltage to the NOT gate is high, this drives the transistor to saturation. Hence *X* remains at 0. Now when none of the inputs go high, input to the NOT gate is low, thereby driving the gate to cut off position.

Capacitor C_S in the base circuit aids the transistor to switch quickly without unduly increasing the stored base charge. Resistors *R*, R_B and R_{B1} are suitably adjusted so that when any one of the diodes conduct, the transistor is ON and when none of the diodes conduct, the transistor is OFF. Typically $E\_ = 10$ volts. Figure 14.21 shows the Truth table for this circuit operation.

A	B	X_1	X
0	0	0	1
0	1	1	0
1	0	1	0
1	1	1	0

Fig. 14.21 *Truth table for the circuit operation of Figure 14.20*

$$X_1 = A + B;\ X = \overline{X_1} = \overline{(A + B)}$$

This output refers to the NOR operation. As this logic gate is a combination of diodes and a transistor, this is known as *DTL logic*. This is available in the form of an integrated chip (a monolithic circuit so that we may not connect the discrete components). This operates at speeds of 2–20 MHz. Although produced in the form of an IC (Integrated circuit) chip, it is not economical.

14.11.5 Resistor-Transistor Logic (RTL)

When discrete components are used for the logic circuit, resistors are cheaper than diodes for use in AND, OR logic circuits.

The functioning of the circuit shown in Figure 14.22 is similar to that of Figure 14.20. When at least one of the inputs (*A* or *B*) goes high, the transistor is forward biased and goes to saturation thereby connecting point *X* to 0 potential. When both *A* and *B* are at 0 volt, the transistor is reverse biased (due to E_-) and thus point *X* is connected to E_+. Sometimes a capacitor is connected across the resistor *R* to improve the speed of operation. In such a case this gate is known as *RCTL circuit*.

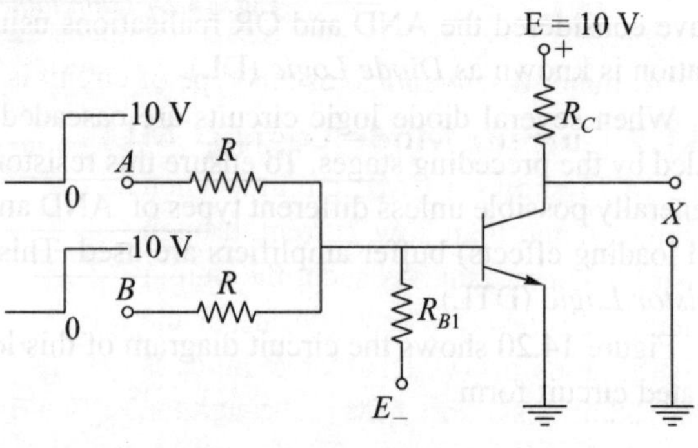

Fig. 14.22 *Resistor-Transistor logic circuit*

The major advantages of this circuit over the of DTL are economy and improved speed and the disadvantages are poor fan-out (capability of the output of this gate to drive similar gates) and less noise immunity (due to resistive coupling, certain amount of noise voltage may make the circuit to malfunction). However, this version is also available in the IC form.

14.11.6 Direct Coupled Transistor Logic (DCTL)

In this type of circuit, transistors acting as switches perform the logical operations. A DCTL circuit is shown in Fig. 14.23.

When both *A* and *B* are at 0 level, both transistors are not biased and thus will not conduct thereby connecting *X* to 10 volt (1 level). If only *A* is high (*B* at 0 level), the lower transistor can not conduct and thus *X* is connected to 1 level. Similarly if only *B* is at 1 level (*A* at 0 level) the upper transistor cannot conduct, thereby connecting *X* again to 1 level. However, when both *A* and *B* conduct, both transistors conduct thereby connecting *X* to 0 potential. Figure 14.24 shows the truth table. Clearly the circuit is a NAND gate.

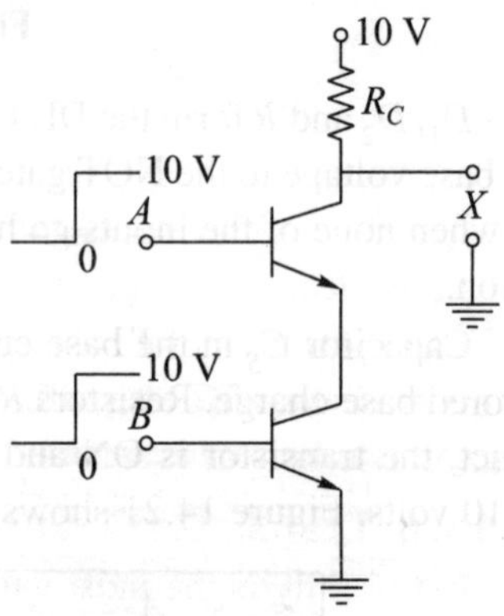

Fig. 14.23 *DCTL circuit*

A	B	X
0	0	1
1	0	1
0	1	1
1	1	0

$X = \overline{A.B}$

Fig. 14.24 *Truth table for Fig. 14.23*

A major disadvantage of this type of circuit is its poor noise immunity.

14.11.7 Current Mode Logic (CML)

Figure 14.25 shows a CML circuit. When both inputs A and B are low, current through transistor T is constant. As such, the output X remains at 0 level. When any one of the transistors goes on (when A or B input is present) additional current flows through the resistor R_e thereby cutting off the transistor T. Thus X is connected to 1 level. Figure 14.26 shows the Truth table.

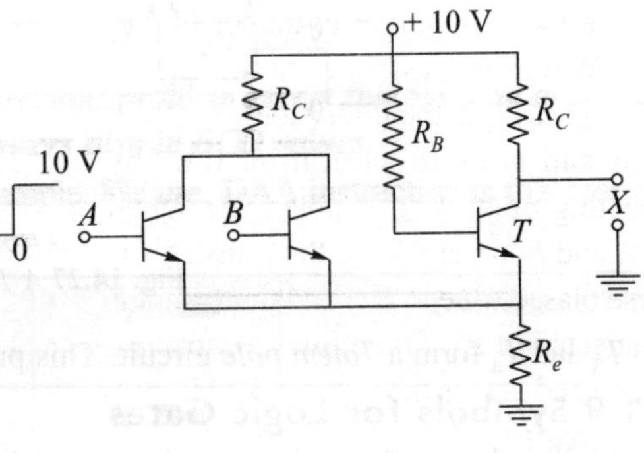

Fig. 14.25 *CML circuit*

A	B	X
0	0	0
1	0	1
0	1	1
1	1	1

$X = A + B$

Fig. 14.26 *Truth table for Figure 14.25*

It is clear from Fig. 14.26 that this circuit functions as an OR gate.

As the transistor T is biased, it works in the linear region and as such power requirements of such circuits are high. However, this type of circuit has good noise immunity and high speed. This type of circuit is also known as Emitter-coupled transistor logic (ECTL).

14.11.8 Transistor-Transistor Logic (TTL)

This TTL family is the most widely used in the industrial environment. The main difference between this circuit and others is that in this logic family common base configuration is used in place of the more usual common emitter configuration. A typical gate is shown in Fig. 14.27. This uses multiple emitter transistor. This circuit has similar characteristics as the DTL circuit. In addition TTL circuit is at least twice faster than DTL and also cheaper.

If both emitters of T_1 are high, both emitter base junctions are reverse biased. However, the collector-base junction is forward-biased and as such current flows through base of T_2, through R_1, thereby turning T_2 ON. T_2 turns ON T_3 and turns OFF T_4 thereby connecting X to the low level. As such if both A and B are high, output is low. Now if one of the inputs is low then base emitter junction of T_1 is forward biased thereby reverse biasing the collector-base junction. This reverse biases T_2 and as such turns ON T_4 and turns off T_3. This connects X to high level. As such when one of the inputs is low (or both low) output goes high. This corresponds to a logic function $X = \overline{A.B}$ (NAND).

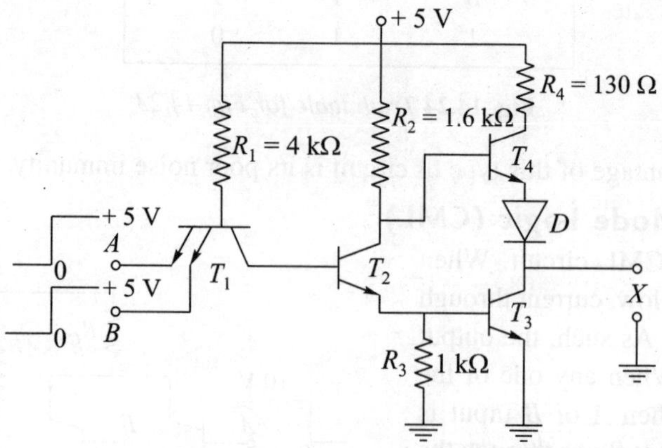

Fig. 14.27 *A TTL NAND gate*

T_3 and T_4 form a *Totem pole* circuit. This provides a low driving source impedance.

14.11.9 Symbols for Logic Gates

Figure 14.28 indicates the various symbols used for the three types of gates we have considered in the previous sections.

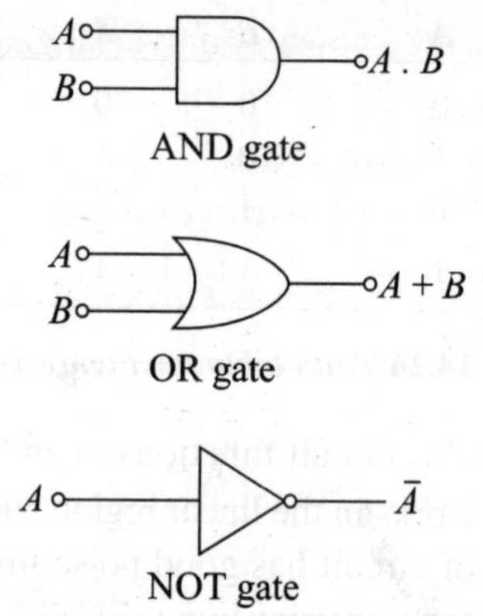

Fig. 14.28 (*a*) *Symbols for different logic gates*

Although the above AND or OR gates are shown with only two inputs, it is possible to have multiple inputs as well.

(*i*) NAND Gate

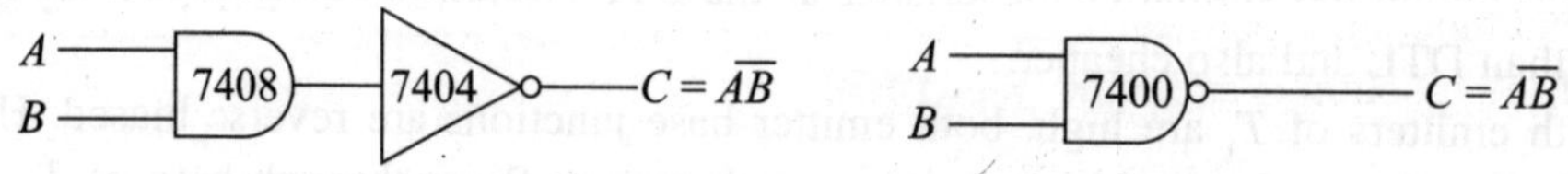

(*ii*) NOR Gate

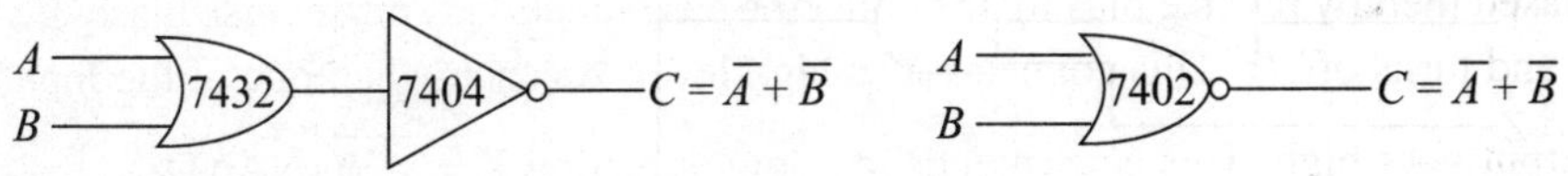

(*iii*) INVERTER Gate

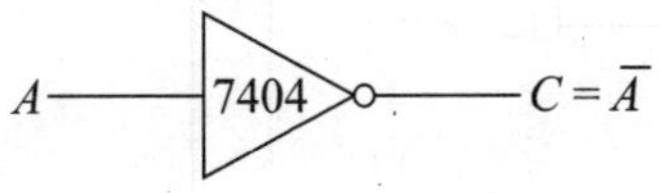

(*iv*) Exclusive OR Gate

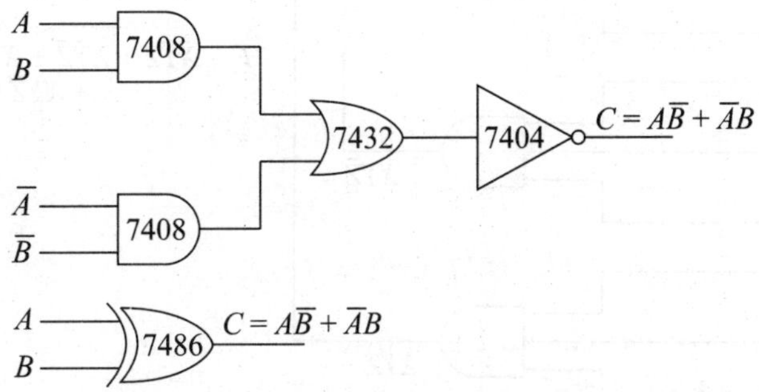

Fig. 14.28 (*b*)

Symbolically $A \oplus B$.

NAND gates is also NOR gates are known as universal gates—as any Boolean expression may be realised by using only NAND or any NOR gates. Figure 14.28 (*b*) Representations of gates.

The following example makes the point clear.

Example 14.24. *Realise the following Boolean expression using various gates.*

$$F = \overline{X}.\overline{Y}.Z + X.\overline{Y}.\overline{Z} + X.\overline{Y}.Z + X.Y.\overline{Z} + X.Y.Z$$

Solution. Very often while writing the Boolean expression for writing the AND functions, the dot is omitted.

We shall assume that only *X*, *Y* and *Z* variables are known ($\overline{X}$, $\overline{Y}$ and $\overline{Z}$ the complemented variables are also to be realised).

As may be observed from Fig. 14.14 three input AND gates and five input OR gate have been used.

Example 14.25. *Realise the Boolean expression*

$$F = A\overline{B} + \overline{A}B.$$

Solution. Output is one only when either *A* or *B* but not both are 1s *i.e.*, either *A* is 1 or *B* is 1 to make the output function 1. As such, the above expression is also known as an 'Exclusive-OR' function. Realisation of the function is as below (Fig. 14.30).

CHAPTER 14

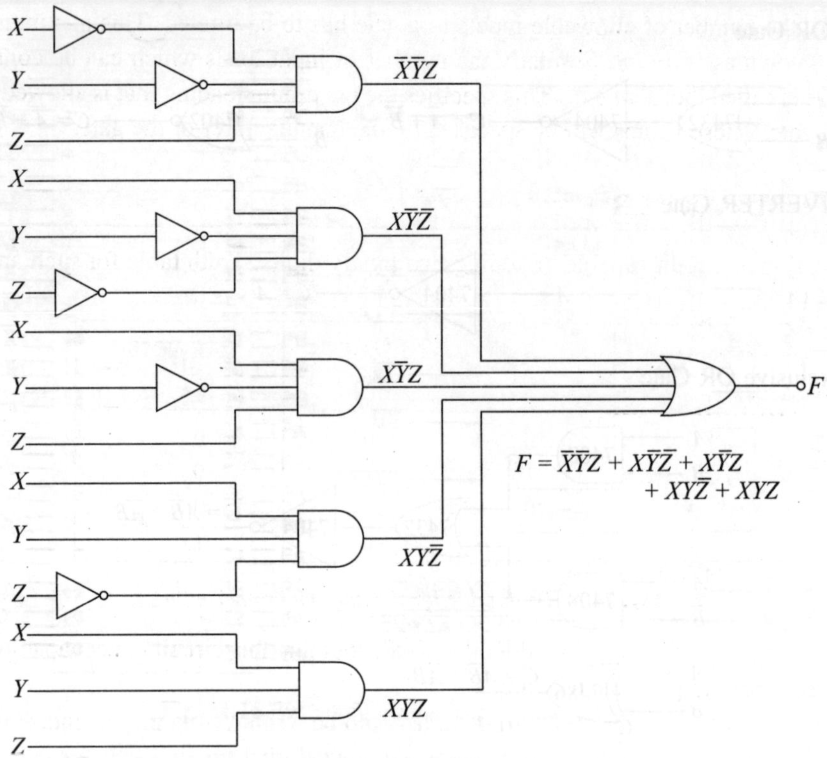

Fig. 14.29 *Realisation of Boolean expression*

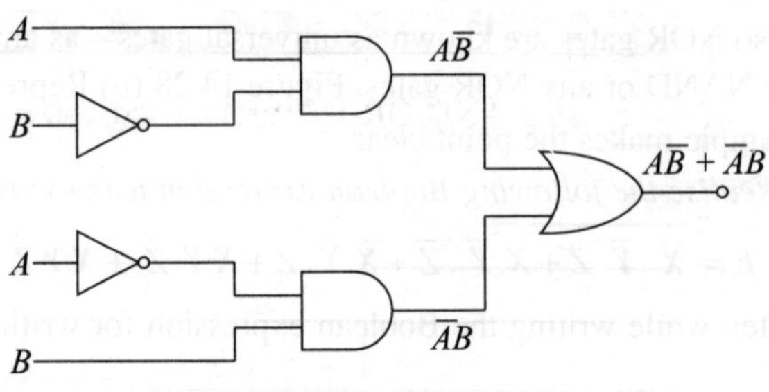

Fig. 14.30 *Realisation of an Exclusive-OR gate*

14.11.10 Fan in and Fan out Capabilities of Logic Gates

Theoretically it is possible to have any number of inputs provided we have ideal diodes. However, in practice, each diode will have finite forward and reverse resistances. Also, leakage current flows through the junction.

In any digital system, output of one gate is connected to the input of other gate forming loads (this may be seen from Fig. 14.30). As such, when the load current increases, the logic levels change. If this deviation is much, then the difference between the two logic levels may not be appreciable and the significance of logic levels 0 and 1 may be lost. Thus, in order to ensure a definite gap over wide range of temperature, the number of allowable inputs to a gate has to be limited. This maximum number of input gates is known as '*Fan in*'. Similarly the number of input loads which can be connected to the output of a gate is called the '*Fan out*'. This specifies the maximum loading that is allowed at the output terminals of a gate. These values will be specified by the manufacturer of the gate.

14.12 A HALF ADDER

Half adder is a digital circuit capable of adding two binary digits. Truth table for such an operation is shown in Fig. 14.31.

A	*B*	*SUM* (*S*)	*CARRY* (*C*)
0	0	0	0
0	1	1	0
1	0	1	0
1	1	0	1

Fig. 14.31 *Truth table for the half adder operation*

This circuit is known as an half adder due to the fact that this circuit is not capable of accepting a carry but is able only to generate the carry.

Boolean expression for the above truth table could be written (*A* is the augend, *B* is the addend, *S* is the sum and *C* is the carry). Observation of the table reveals that sum is 1, when *A* is 0 and *B* is 1 OR *A* is 1 and *B* is 0. Also carry is 1 when *A* and *B* are both 1.

That is $S = \overline{A}B + A\overline{B}$

and $C = AB$

Realisation of the half adder using AND-OR-INVERTER logic is as shown in Fig. 14.32.

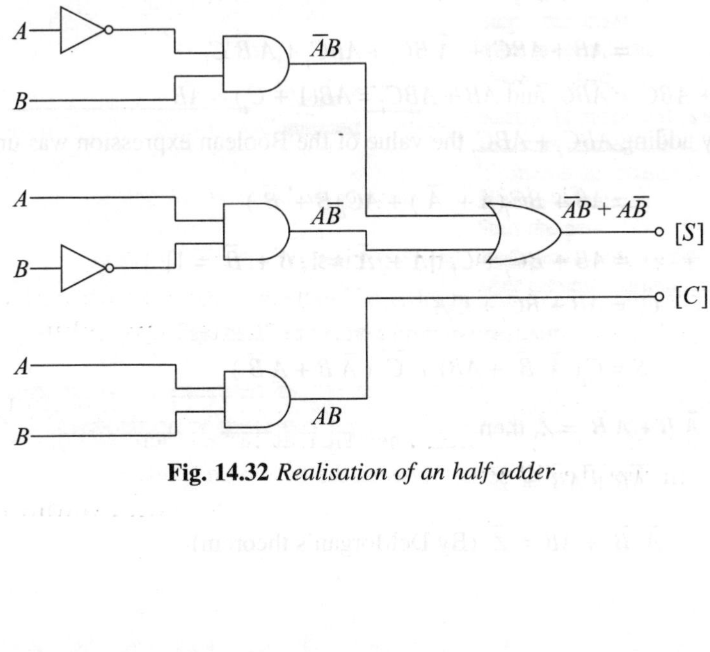

Fig. 14.32 *Realisation of an half adder*

14.13 A FULL ADDER

Full adder is a digital circuit capable of adding two binary numbers. This circuit is capable of generating the sum and carry besides being capable of accepting a carry. Figure 14.33 shows the truth table for a full adder. *A* is the augend, *B* is the addend, C_i is the carry input (generated by the preceding stage). *S* is the generated sum and C_0 is the generated carry (the carry input to the succeeding stage).

A	B	C_i	S	C_o
0	0	0	0	0
0	0	1	1	0
0	1	0	1	0
0	1	1	0	1
1	0	0	1	0
1	0	1	0	1
1	1	0	0	1
1	1	1	1	1

Fig. 14.33 *Truth table for full adder*

$$S = \bar{A}\,\bar{B}\,C_i + \bar{A}\,B\,\bar{C_i} + A\,\bar{B}\,\bar{C_i} + ABC_i$$

and
$$C_0 = \bar{A}\,BC_i + A\,\bar{B}\,C_i + AB\,\bar{C_i} + ABC_i$$

$$= \bar{A}\,BC_i + A\,\bar{B}\,C_i + AB(C_i + \bar{C_i})$$

$$= \bar{A}\,BC_i + A\,\bar{B}\,C_i + AB[C_i + \bar{C_i} = 1]$$

$$= AB + ABC_i + \bar{A}\,BC_i + ABC_i + A\,\bar{B}\,C_i$$

($ABC_i + ABC_i = ABC_i$ and $AB + ABC_i = AB(1 + C_i) = AB$

As such, by adding $ABC_i + ABC_i$ the value of the Boolean expression was unaltered)

$$= AB + BC_i(A + \bar{A}) + AC_i(B + \bar{B})$$

$$= AB + BC_i + C_iA[A + \bar{A} = 1, B + \bar{B} = 1]$$

As such, $$C_0 = AB + BC_i + C_iA$$

Again $$S = C_i(\bar{A}\,\bar{B} + AB) + \bar{C_i}\,(\bar{A}\,B + A\,\bar{B})$$

If we keep $\bar{A}\,B + A\,\bar{B} = Z$, then

$$\overline{AB + AB} = \bar{Z}$$

i.e., $$\bar{A}\,\bar{B} + AB = \bar{Z} \text{ (By DeMorgan's theorem)}$$

$$S = C_i \overline{Z} + \overline{C_i} Z \quad ...(i)$$

and
$$C_0 = AB + C_i(\overline{A}B + A\overline{B})$$
$$= AB + C_i Z \quad ...(ii)$$

with half adder as the basic building block, a full adder is realised as in Fig. 14.34.

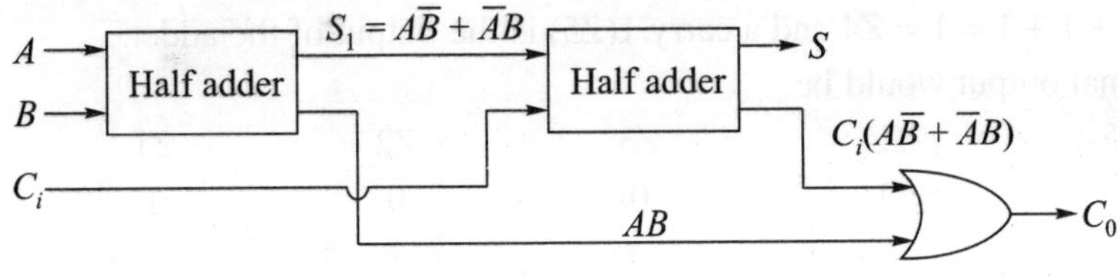

Fig. 14.34 *Realisation of full adder*

$$S = C_i \overline{S_1} + \overline{C_i}\, S_1$$

and
$$C_0 = AB + C_i(A\overline{B} + \overline{A}B).$$

14.14 A PARALLEL BINARY ADDER

Figure 14.35 shows the method of connecting full adders and half adders to add two binary numbers. If we assume that the binary numbers to be added are *X*4 *X*3 *X*2 *X*1 and *Y*4 *Y*3 *Y*2 *Y*1 the answer is *Z*4 *Z*3 *Z*2 *Z*1.

While we add the least significant bits, there is no carry to be handled and thus, only a half adder is used for this stage. For any other bit addition, there may be a carry from the preceeding stage and thus, full adders are used for these stages.

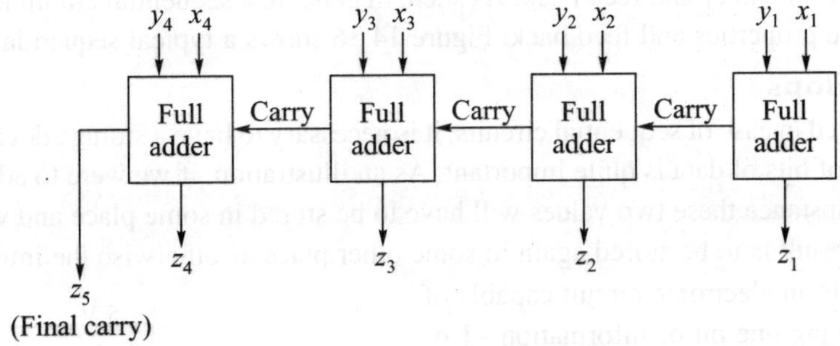

Fig. 14.35 *A parallel 4-bit binary adder*

To understand the working of the above circuit, let us consider adding two binary numbers 1011 and 1110:

$X4 \;\; X3 \;\; X2 \;\; X1 = 1\,0\,1\,1$

$Y4 \;\; Y3 \;\; Y2 \;\; Y1 = 1\,1\,1\,0$

(*i*) *X*1, *Y*1 *i.e.*, 1 and 0 are the inputs to the half adder.

$1 + 0 = 1 = Z1$ No carry is generated

(*ii*) 1(*X*2) and 1(*Y*2) are the inputs to the first full adder.

$$1 + 1 = 0 = Z2 \text{ and 1 carry is generated}$$

(*iii*) 0(*X*3) and 1(*Y*3) and carry 1 are the inputs to the second full adder.

$$0 + 1 + 1 = 0 = Z3 \text{ and a carry is generated.}$$

(*iv*) 1(*X*3) and 1(*Y*3) + 1(carry) are the inputs to the final full adder.

$$1 + 1 + 1 = 1 = Z4 \text{ and a carry } 1(Z5) \text{ is the output of the adder.}$$

As such final output would be

Z5	Z4	Z3	Z2	Z1
1	1	0	0	1

14.15 SEQUENTIAL LOGIC CIRCUITS

Output of logic circuits we have dealt with so far is a function of input. That is the output of the circuit depends only on the input to the circuit at that time. The logic circuits used to realise the Boolean expressions are known as *combinational circuits.* However, there exists another class of digital circuits known as sequential logic circuits where the output is not only a function of the present input, but also is a function of the past events. These circuits are incorporated in most digital systems as counters, sequence generators etc. As one of the requirements of the sequential circuit is to remember the past event. It should have memory and feed back. As such, in general, a sequential circuit is a combinational circuit with storage properties and feed back. Figure 14.36 shows a typical sequential circuit.

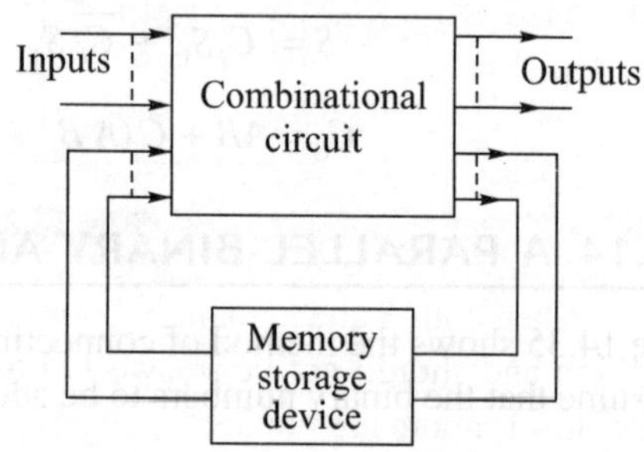

Fig. 14.36 *A sequenctial logic diagram*

14.15.1 Flip-Flops

As we have observed in case of sequential circuits, it is necessary to have a storage device. In computers, this remembering of bits of data is quite important. As an illustration. if we were to add two numbers *A* and *B*, in the first instance these two values will have to be stored in some place and when the addition is performed, the result is to be stored again in some other place as otherwise the information is lost.

A *flip-flop* is an electronic circuit capable of storing or memorising one bit of information –1 or 0. As such, a flip-flop can be in one of the two stable states (0 or 1) for even if it is not disturbed. The flip-flop can be made to change its state by 'Triggering'.

A simple flip-flop (also known as an *RS* latch) is shown in Fig. 14.37 where two transistors are connected back to back.

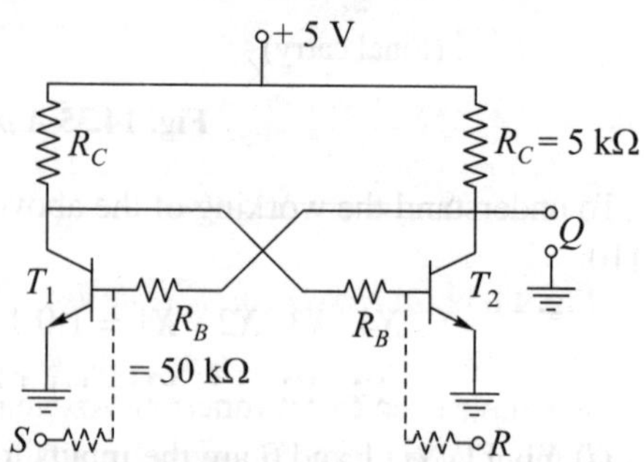

Fig. 14.37 *An RS latch*

If T_2 is in saturation, its collector is at 0 potential, which is the input to the base of T_1. That is, there is no base drive for T_1 and thus it is cut off and its collector is at 1 level. This inturn is the input to the base of T_2, which drives it to saturation. As such, T_1 is off and T_2 is ON. Hence $Q = 0$. Similarly if T_1 is in saturation, T_2 is off thereby making $Q = 1$.

Transition from one to the other state may be induced by having two more control inputs shown in dotted lines, called the *S* and *R* inputs. These inputs are either connected to 0 or to 1. A high *S* (set) input forces T_1 to go ON thereby making $Q = 1$ [High *S* will turn ON T_1 thereby its collector voltage falls to zero potential, this inturn is the input to the base of T_2. As there is no base drive, T_2 is off thereby *Q* goes to 1]. Now, if a high input is connected to *R*, it forces T_2 to go ON thereby making $Q = 0$. Now when $Q = 0$, even if a high input is connected to *R*, *Q* stays at 0 only. As such, the working of the circuit may be summarised in the form of a truth table shown in Fig. 14.38.

R	*S*	*Q*
0	*0*	*No change*
0	*1*	*1*
1	*0*	*0*
1	*1*	*Race condition*

Fig. 14.38 *Truth table for the RS latch*

When both *R* and *S* go high, both T_1 and T_2 transistors tend to go 'ON'. This creates an ambiguous condition and should not be allowed to occur. This is called the Race condition. On the other hand if both control inputs are connected to zero the state of the transistors previous to connecting the control inputs to zero would be maintained. Also, we have noted that when $Q = 1$ prior to giving a *S* input, even if *S* input is given there will be no change in *Q*. Similarly, when $Q = 0$, even if an *R* input is given, the state of the circuit will not change, that is, this circuit is capable of remembering the past state and dependingly it is capable of accepting the input (or latch the input) and change its state. If undisturbed, this circuit remains in its present state for any length of time and as such, this type of circuit is capable of remembering 1 bit of (0 or 1) information. If several bits of information are to be stored, several of these latches are to be connected appropriately.

The above function (or truth table) may be realised by connecting two NAND gates as shown in Fig. 14.39.

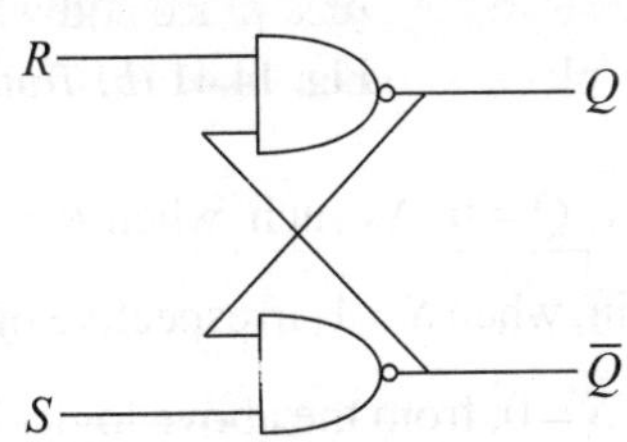

Fig. 14.39 *(a) NAND gates connected to form latch*

R	*S*	*Q*
0	*0*	*Race*
0	*1*	*1*
1	*0*	*0*
1	*1*	*No change*

Fig. 14.39 *(b) Truth table*

We have seen that a function $\overline{AB}$ may be realised by *AND*ing *A* and *B* and then *NOT*ing it. That is a two input AND gate followed by a NOT gate is required to realise the above function. These two gates together form a NAND gate, notation of that of a AND gate with a circle at the output point as shown in Fig. 14.39.

The working of the circuit may be analysed as below:

When R is low, irrespective of the other input ($\overline{Q}$), $Q = 0$. $\overline{Q} = 1$ when Q goes high both inputs to the other NAND gate are high (as $S = 1$) and as such, $\overline{Q} = \overline{1.1} = 0$.

Similarly when $S = 0$, irrespective of Q, output $\overline{Q}$ goes high ($\overline{Q} = \overline{0.Q} = 1$). As such, both inputs to the other NAND gate are high ($R = 1$) thereby taking Q to Zero ($Q = \overline{1.1} = 0$).

When both R and S inputs go low, irrespective of Q and $\overline{Q}$, both outputs (Q or $\overline{Q}$) tend to go high resulting in a Race condition.

When both R and S inputs go high, depending upon the previous output, the same status will be retained. This is in conformity with the truth table of Fig. 14.39 (*b*).

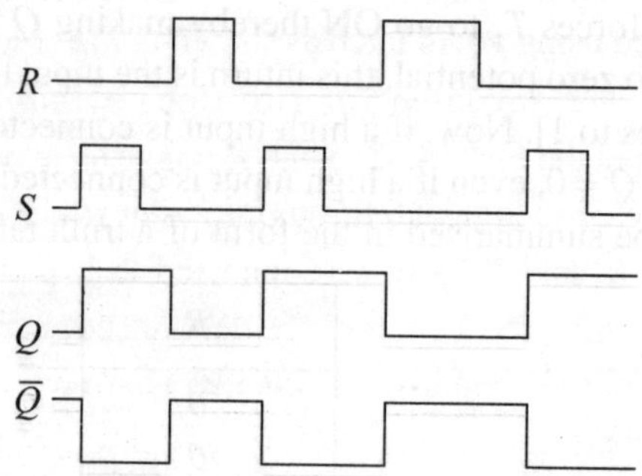

Fig. 14.40 *Waveforms of the RS latch*

The working may further be appreciated by the following waveforms of Fig. 14.40. We have seen that a function $\overline{A + B}$ may be realised by ORing A and B and then NOTing it. That is a two input OR gate followed by a NOT gate realises the above function (NOR function) and is known as the NOR gate. The standard notation is that of an OR gate with a circle at the output point as shown in Fig. 14.41.

It is also possible to construct the latch by using two NOR gates as shown in Fig. 14.41. Truth table indicates the behaviour of the circuit.

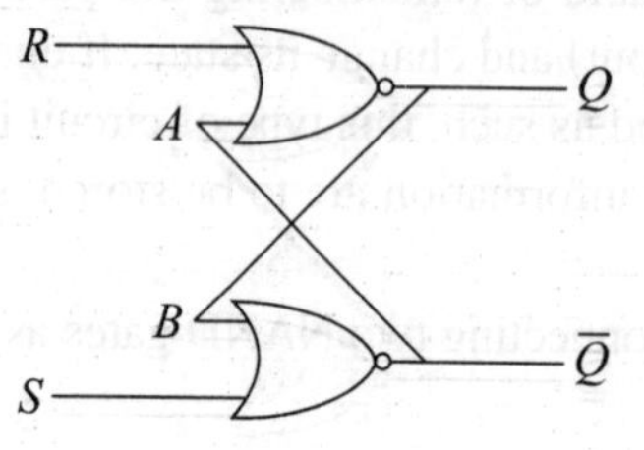

Fig. 14.41 *(a) RS latch using NOR gate*

R	*S*	*Q*
0	*0*	*No change*
0	*1*	*1*
1	*0*	*0*
1	*1*	*Race*

Fig. 14.41 *(b) Truth table*

Output $Q = \overline{R + A}$, that is if $R = 1$ or $A = 1$ or both = 1, $Q = 0$. As such, when $R = 1$, irrespective of A, $Q = 0$. Now output $\overline{Q} = \overline{S + B} = \overline{S + Q} = \overline{0 + 0} = 1$. Again, when $S = 1$, irrespective of B, $\overline{Q} = \overline{S + B} = \overline{1 + 0} = 0$ and $Q = \overline{R + A} = \overline{0 + 0} = 1$. When both $R = 0$ and $S = 0$, from the above logic, it may be seen that there is no change in the state of the latch as, if Q was 1 previously, we have $\overline{Q} = \overline{1 + 0} = 0$ and $Q = \overline{0 + 0} = 1$. As such the previous state of the flip-flop is maintained. If both $R = 1$ and $S = 1$, both Q and $\overline{Q}$ tend to go to zero, thereby resulting in a Race condition. These latches are generally used as *switch debouncers*.

When a mechanical switch is thrown from open to close, or close to open, contact bounce occurs and the contact makes and breaks for a fraction of a second (even in the best switch!) before setting in its new position. This could be avoided using an *RS* latch as shown in Fig. 14.42.

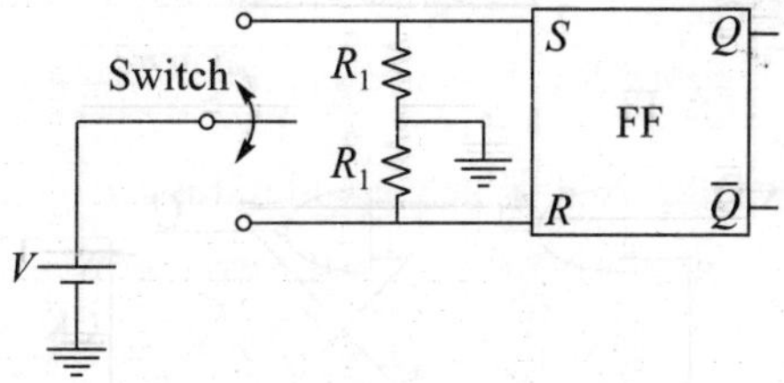

Fig. 14.42 *A switch debouncer*

The *RS* latch (or flip-flop) symbol is shown in the Fig. 14.42. *S* and *R* points have been connected to logical 0 through resistor R_1. These points (*S* and *R*) may be connected to logical 1 by throwing the switch (to be debounced) to any one of the positions. If the switch is at *R*, $Q = 0$ and if it is at *S*, $Q = 1$. Let use suppose that the switch makes contact with *S*, so that *Q* goes to 1. Now due to switch bouncing, *S* may go to zero, this condition is similar to $S = 0$, $R = 0$ (using NOR gate latch say). However, with this input condition, the previous state of the flip-flop continues (with $Q = 1$). Again the switch may bounce making $S = 1$. As *Q* is already at 1, this state continues. As such, we see that the switch bounce has not effect on the output of the flip-flop. The same phenomenon repeats when the switch is making contact with *R*. At the first contact, flip-flop changes its state to 0 and any number of later bounces has no effect on the working. This is illustrated in Fig. 14.43.

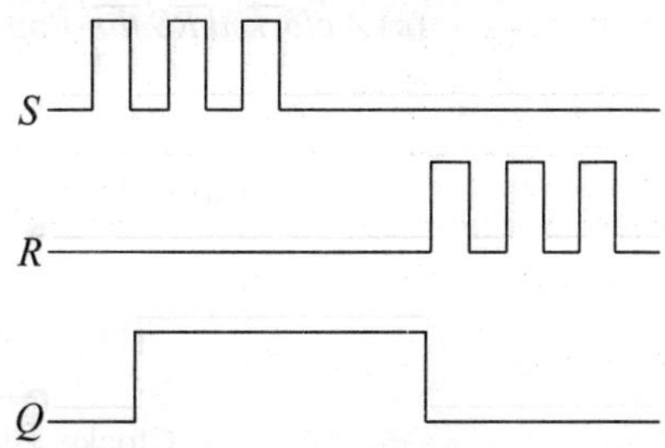

Fig. 14.43 *Timing diagram for the switch debouncer*

14.15.1.1 Clocked R-S Flip-Flop

When there are several flip-flops in the circuit, to coordinate the working of them, a square wave input (signal) called the *clock* is sent to all the flip-flops.

In this type of flip-flop, in order that the truth table mentioned before holds good, an additional input called clock need be considered. In the absence of the clock the flip-flop does not function at all. This type of flip-flop is known as *clocked R-S flip-flop*.

Figure 14.44 (*a*) shows the clocked *RS* flip-flop and the truth table for the working of this figure is shown in Fig. 14.44 (*b*). It is clear from the figure that if either *S* or *R* or both are present, unless the clock is also present, *A* and *B* both will be in 1 level which is the input to the basic latch. We have seen from Fig. 14.39 that it will not change the state of the latch, and as such *Q* does not change its state. When *S* is 1, *CLK* is 1, *A* is zero, irrespective of $\overline{Q}$ state, $Q = 0$. Any state = 1 and obviously $\overline{Q} = 0$. Similarly when $R = 1$, $CLK = 1$, $B = 0$ and irrespective of the state of Q, $\overline{Q} = 0$. (Any state) = 1 and obviously $Q = \overline{1.1} = 0$. When $S = 1$, $R = 1$, in the presence of the *CLK*, both *A* and *B* would be at 0 and hence *Q* and $\overline{Q}$ both tend to simultaneously go high, thereby establishing the race condition. Timing diagrams in Fig. 14.45 make the points clear.

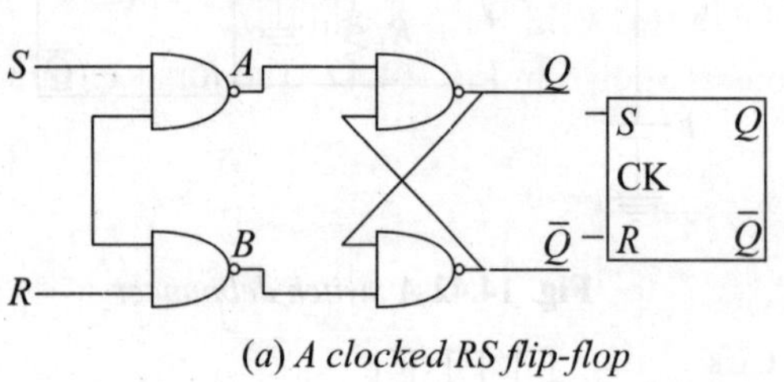

(a) *A clocked RS flip-flop*

R	*S*	*CLOCK*	*Q*
0	0	0	No change
0	1	0	No change
1	0	0	No change
1	1	0	No change
0	0	1	No change
0	1	1	1
1	0	1	0
1	1	1	Race

(b) *Truth table*

Fig. 14.44

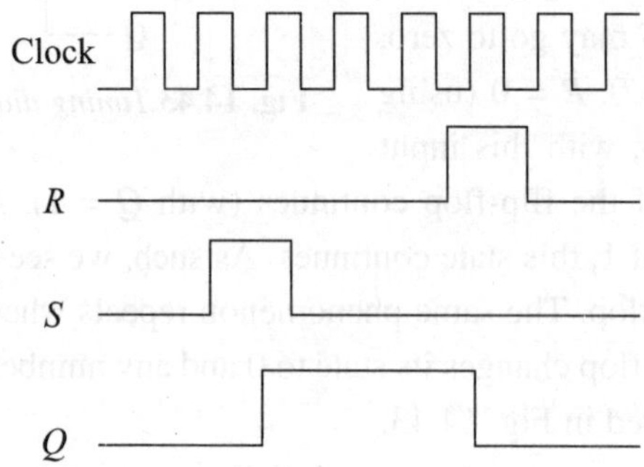

Fig. 14.45 *Timing diagram for the clocked RS flip-flop*

14.15.1.2 D Flip-Flop

We have seen before that the *RS* flip-flop attains the race condition for a specific sequence of inputs ($R = 0$, $S = 0$ for NAND gate *FF* and $R = 1$, $S = 1$ for NOR gate *FF*). This could be avoided by ensuring that *R* and *S* points always get completmentary inputs. This type of flip-flop is known as *D flip-flop.*

Figure 14.46 shows the circuit of the *D* flip-flop using two NAND gets (basic latch) along with a NOT gate. It is clear that under no circumstances *R* and *S* get the same input (either 0 or 1) due to the presence of the NOT gate. It may be seen that if $D = 1$, state of the flip-flop becomes 1. If $D = 0$, then the state of the flip-flop becomes 0. It appears as though such a flip-flop is not required at all as the output simply follows the input. However, a clocked *D* flip-flop shown in Fig. 14.46 (*c*) is of relevance here. It may be seen from the timing diagrams that the output does not change until a clock pulse is applied and this output stays till the next clock pulse is applied. That is, any input data may be delayed by one clock cycle using this circuit. It is clear from the figure that the output is identical to the input except that the output is shifted by one clock pulse. This is the reason why this flip-flop is called *Delay flip-flop.*

14.15.1.3 J-K Flip-Flop

We have seen in previous sections that $S = 1, R = 1$ or $S = 0, R = 0$ is not allowed depending on whether NOR or NAND gates are used for constructing the *RS* latch (to avoid Race condition).

A clocked *RS* flip-flop with certain modifications is shown in Fig. 14.47. The input terminals previously identified as *S* is shown as *J* and *R* as *K*.

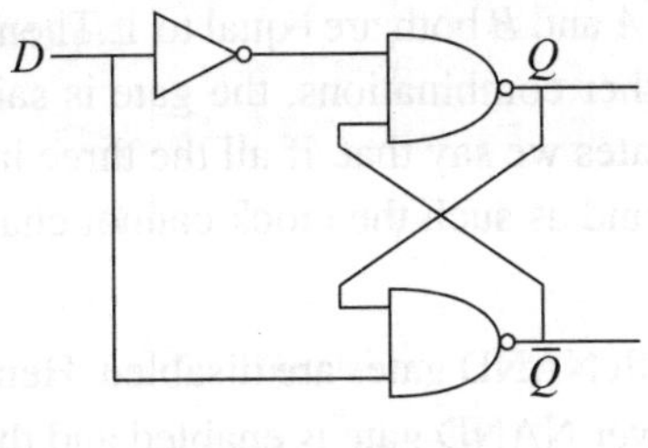

(*a*) *D flip-flop*

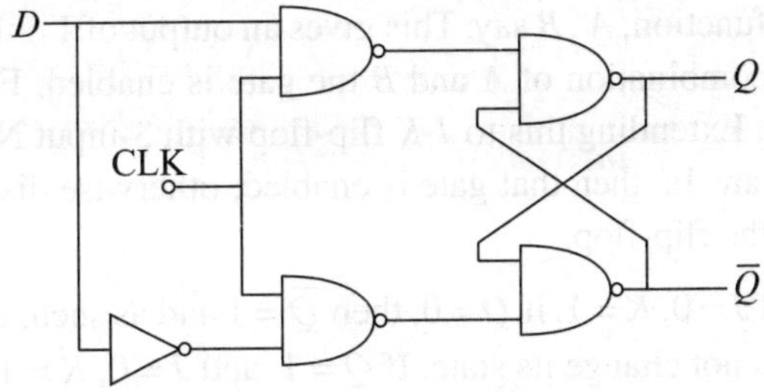

(*b*) *Clocked D flip-flop*

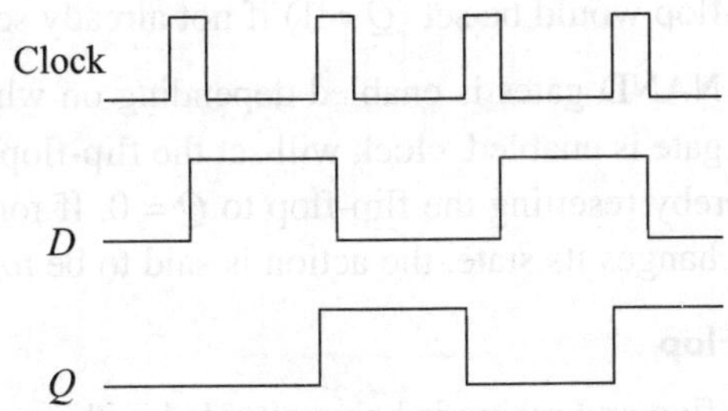

(*c*) *Timing diagram of the clocked D flip-flop*

Fig. 14.46

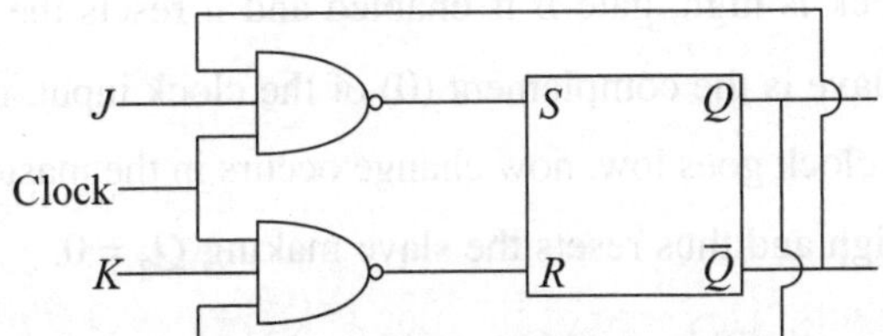

(*a*) *JK flip-flop*

J	K	Q
0	0	Q
0	1	0
1	0	1
1	1	$\overline{Q}$

(*b*) *Truth table of a JK FF*

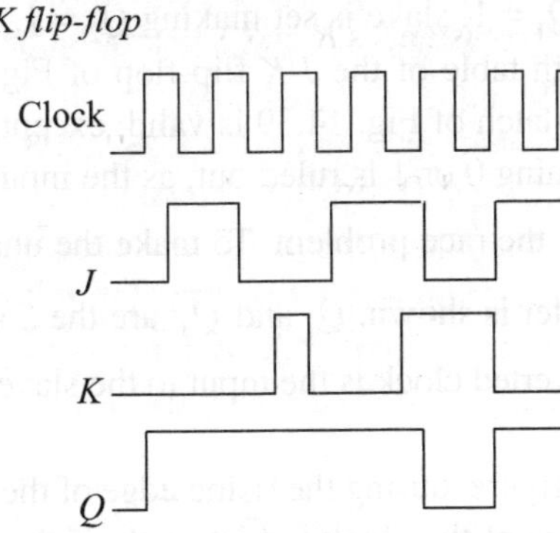

(*c*) *Timing diagram*

Fig. 14.47

In the clocked *RS* flip-flop (Figure 14.44), we have seen that the clock is steered by either *S* or *R*. However, in this case clock is steered not only by *S* and *R*, but also by the state of the flip-flop (as the output is one of the inputs to the 3-input Nand gates). Truth table and timing diagrams [Fig. 14.47 (*c*)] indicate the working of this circuit.

If $J = K = 0$, both NAND gates are disabled (when the output of the gate is 1 for the basic operation, then we say the gate is enabled for example, consider a 2-input NAND gate, the basic operation is AND function, $A . B$ say. This gives an output of 1 only when *A* and *B* both are equal to 1. Then we say for this combination of *A* and *B* the gate is enabled. For all other combinations, the gate is said to be disabled. Extending this to *J-K* flip-flop with 3-input NAND gates we say that, if all the three inputs to the gate are 1s, then that gate is enabled, otherwise disabled), and as such the clock cannot change the state of the flip-flop.

If $J = 0, K = 1$, if $Q = 0$, then $\overline{Q} = 1$ and as such, again both NAND gates are disabled. Hence flip-flop does not change its state. If $Q = 1$, and $J = 0, K = 1$, the lower NAND gate is enabled and the clock changes (steers) the state of the flip-flop.

Similarly if $J = 1, K = 0$, flip-flop would be set ($Q = 1$) if not already set.

If $J = K = 1$, then one of the NAND gates is enabled depending on whether Q is high or $\overline{Q}$ is high. If $Q = 0$ then the upper NAND gate is enabled, clock will set the flip-flop to $Q = 1$. If $Q = 1$, then the lower NAND gate is enabled thereby resetting the flip-flop to $Q = 0$. If for each clock input, as in this case, the output of the flip-flop changes its state, the action is said to be *toggling*.

14.15.1.4 J-K Master-Slave Flip-Flop

This is a modification of the *J-K* flip-flop and racing is being avoided in this case. This consists of two clocked *R-S* flip-flops one called the *Master* and the other called the *Slave* as shown in Fig. 14.48. Master is positively clocked and the Slave is being driven by the complement of the clock. The working of the circuit is as follows: If $Q_2 = 1$, $K = 1$, clock is high, gate *B* is enabled and it resets the master making $Q_1 = 0$ and $\overline{Q_1} = 1$. As the input to the slave is the complement (0) of the clock input, nothing happens during this instance. However, when the clock goes low, now change occurs in the master. But, the clock to the slave goes high. $\overline{Q_1}$ is already high and thus resets the slave making $Q_2 = 0$.

Similarly if $J = 1$, $Q_2 = 0$, $\overline{Q_2} = 1$, then gate *A* will be enabled, making $Q_1 = 1$ during clock = 1 when clock = 1 to the slave, due to $Q_1 = 1$, slave is set making $Q_2 = 1$.

For the Master operation, truth table of the *J-K* flip-flop of Fig. 14.47 holds good and for the slave operation, truth table of the *RS* latch of Fig. 14.39 is valid, except that the question of *S* and *R* of the slave input simultaneously becoming 0 or 1 is ruled out, as the input of this *FF* is from Master's Q and $\overline{Q}$ points, thereby circumventing the race problem. To make the understanding clear, in the timing diagram, the output Q_1 from the master is shown. Q_1 and $\overline{Q_1}$ are the *S* and *R* inputs to the slave which is also shown in the figure. As the inverted clock is the input to the slave, this also is shown. Finally the output of the slave Q_2 is also shown.

As may be observed from the figure, during the rising edge of the clock, the data is transferred to the master and during the trailing edge of the clock (which is the rising edge for the slave) the master information is transferred from master to the slave.

Two more points—preset and clear—are included into these flip-flops to increase their usefulness. In the normal use these points are connected to high. When the flip-flop is to be set before use, *PR* is made low. The symbolic notation for such a flip-flop is shown in Fig. 14.48 (*c*).

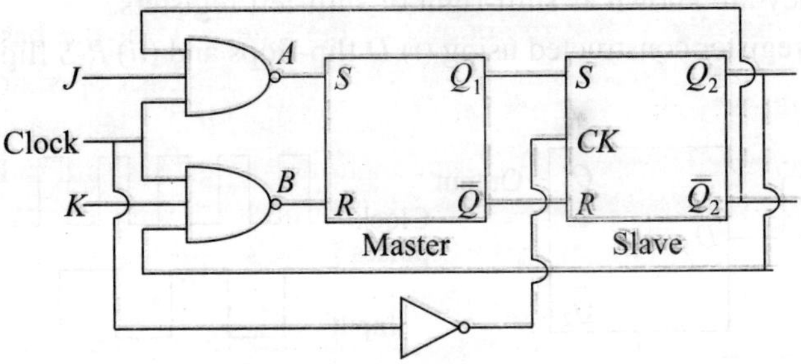

(*a*) *Master slave flip-flop*

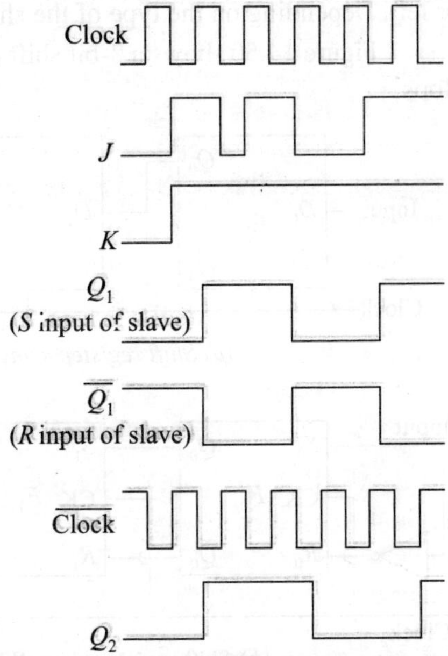

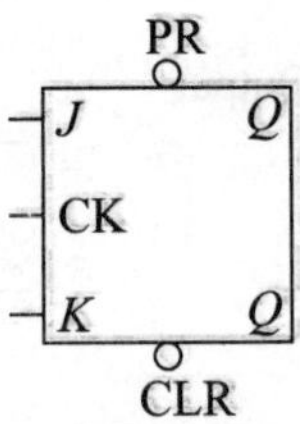

(*c*) *Symbolic representation*

(*b*) *Timing diagram*

Fig. 14.48 (*a*) *Master slave flip-flop* (*b*) *Timing diagram* (*c*) *Symbolic representation*

14.15.2 Registers

Register is a place where information can be written and read whenever required. Information is in the form of bits (0s and 1s). We have already seen that a flip-flop can store or register a binary digit. As such, a flip-flop is a single bit register. If it is necessary to store *N* bits, *N* flip-flops, are necessary and is to be connected to work as a single unit. This is generally known as a register. Figure 14.49 shows a 3-bit register. When clock is present, information $X_0\ X_1\ X_2$ is stored in the flip-flops $Q_0\ Q_1\ Q_2$.

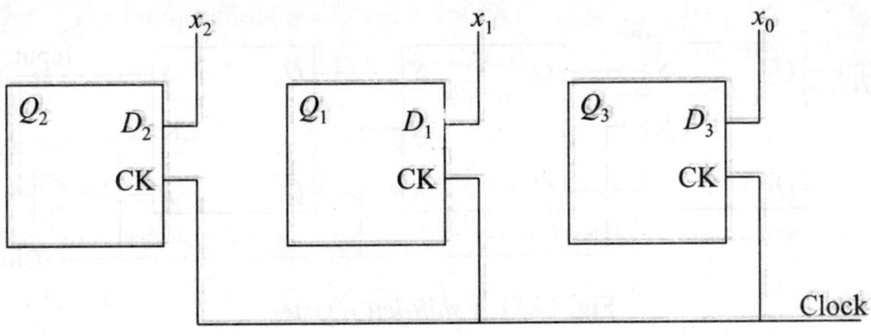

Fig. 14.49 *A three-bit shift register*

14.15.2.1 Shift Registers

On many occasions, it becomes necessary to shift the content of one flip-flop to the other. A chain of flip-flops permitting this type of shifting is known as a *shift register*. The shifting may be towards right or left. Depending on the type of the shift, they are known as shift-right or shift-left registers.

Figure 14.50 shows a 3-bit shift right register constructed using (*i*) *D* flip-flops and (*ii*) *R-S* flip-flops.

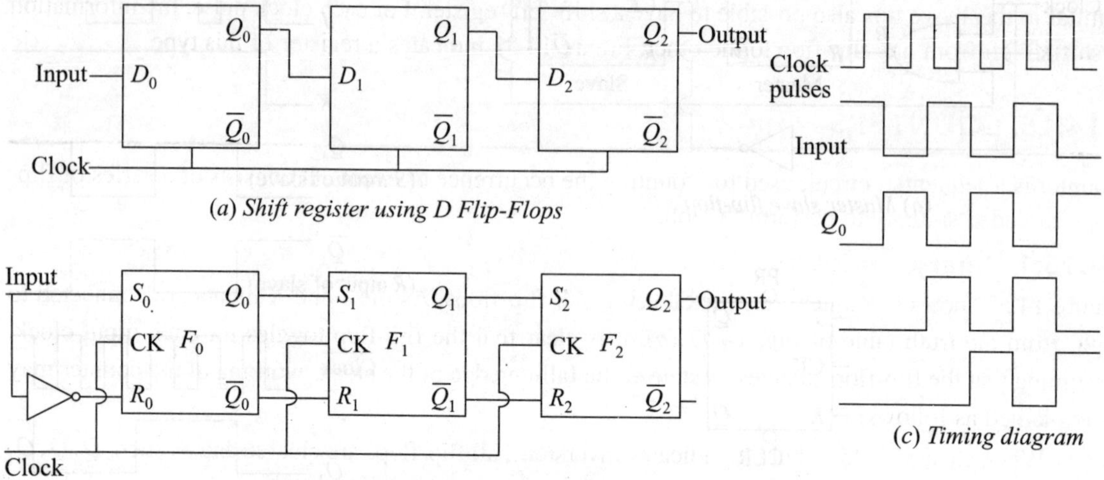

(*a*) *Shift register using D Flip-Flops*

(*b*) *Shift register using SR flip-flops*

(*c*) *Timing diagram*

Clock pulse	Q_0	Q_1	Q_2
1	1	0	0
2	0	1	0
3	0	0	1

(*d*) *State of flip-flops*

Fig. 14.50

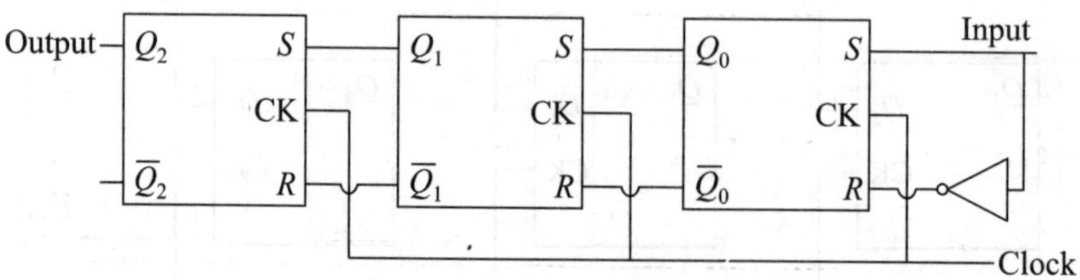

Fig. 14.51 *A shift-left register*

Clock is applied simultaneously to all the flip-flops. Input data is the input to the F_0 flip-flop. This content of F_0 is moved down to F_2 by the clock pulses and the output is taken from F_2 as shown.

In case of *D* flip-flops if D_0 contains 1 ($Q_0 = 1$) at each clock pulse, this information is shifted to the next succeeding flip-flops.

For the *RS-FF* registers, when $Q_0 = 1$, *S* input to $F_1 = 1$. At the resistance of the clock pulse, Q_1 goes to 1. Also when $\overline{Q_0} = 1$ at the instance of the clock, $\overline{Q_1}$ goes to 1.

Figure 14.50 (*c*) and (*d*) show the timing diagram and the various states of the flip-flops. As the flow of information is to the right, this is known as shift-right register.

14.15.2.2 Shift-Left Register

Similar to the above it is also possible to have a shift-left register. For each clock pulse, the information is shifted left from one flip-flop to the other. Figure 14.51 indicates a register of this type.

14.16 COUNTERS

Counter is a sequential circuit used for counting the occurrence of events. It consists of a series of flip-flops cascaded suitably to perform the job.

14.16.1 Binary Counters

Figure 14.52 shows a counter constructed using *J-K* flip-flops. As the *J* and *K* inputs are connected to high, from the truth table of Fig. 14.47 (*b*), it is clear that the flip-flop toggles for each input clock. Assuming that the flip-flop changes its state at the falling edge of the clock, working of the counter may be explained as follows:

When clear goes low (bubble indicates inversion), all flip-flops are cleared and as such, $Q_3\, Q_2\, Q_1\, Q_0$ would be 0000. When clear goes high, the counting is on. For each clock pulse input, F_0 toggles once per negative clock edge. F_1 receives one negative edge for each two clock pulse edge F_0 receives. This goes on. Table of Fig. 14.52 (*b*) lists the states of the flip-flops on a function of the number of applied clock pulses. This table also may be verified from the timing diagram shown in Fig. 14.52 (*c*).

We note from the table that the sequence of counting is exactly the same as the binary representation of the decimal number. Thus, a chain of flip-flops counts in the binary fashion. Hence flip-flop is also represented as binary.

A cascading of *n* flip-flops will count up to the number 2^n before it resets into its original state. As such, this is also known as a counter modulo 2^n or a ripple counter.

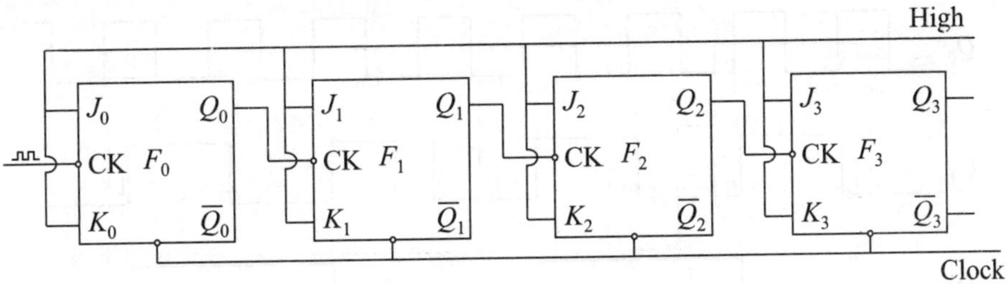

(*a*) *A four-bit binary counter*

Number of Clock pulses	*State of flip-flops*			
	F_3	F_2	F_1	F_0
0	0	0	0	0
1	0	0	0	1
2	0	0	1	0
3	0	0	1	1
4	0	1	0	0
5	0	1	0	1
6	0	1	1	0
7	0	1	1	1
8	1	0	0	0
9	1	0	0	1
10	1	0	1	0
11	1	0	1	1
12	1	1	0	0
13	1	1	0	1
14	1	1	1	0
15	1	1	1	1
16	0	0	0	0
17	0	0	0	1

(*b*)

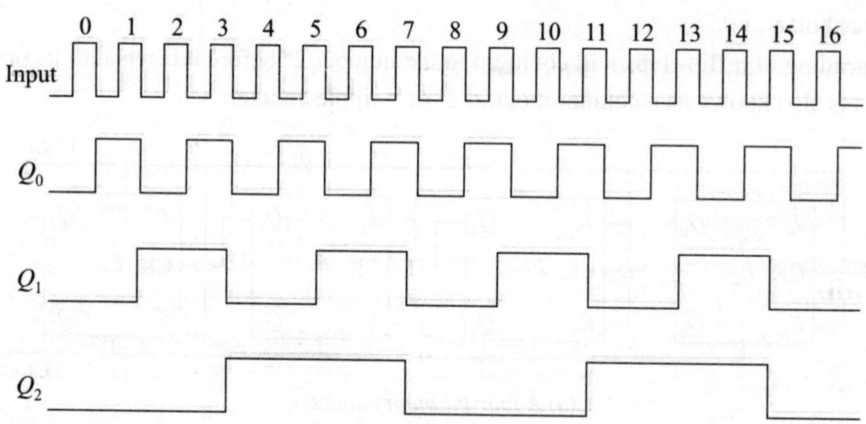

(*c*) *Timing diagram*

Fig. 14.52

14.16.2 Decimal Counter

This is a special case of the modulus counter and is supposed to count upto 10 pulses in the usual manner and then reset and start counting again.

In general, if we consider a mod—K counter where K is not a power of 2, then we use n flip-flops where n is the smallest number satisfying $2^n \geq K$. As such, for $K = 6$ or 7, $n = 3$. If we are considering a mod—10 counter, that is a decimal or decade counter $n = 4$ is to be chosen. It is also implicit that mod—K will have to skip $2^n - k$ states. The states that are to be omitted may be chosen by us.

As we have already seen, if the flip-flop is connected to operate in the toggling mode, it divides the input frequency (clock) by 2. As such, a flip-flop is regarded as a divide by 2 circuit. If the output of the first flip-flop is connected as the clock input to the second flip-flop, it becomes a divide by 4 circuit and so on. In general, a cascade of n flip-flops becomes a divide by 2^n circuit. As such, a counter may be regarded as a frequency division network. Using this principle, any frequency may be divided by an integer value.

Frequency counting also comes under this class. The input signal whose frequency is to be measured is converted into electrical pulses by means of a zero-cross detector and applied through an AND gate to a counter. We know that frequency is the number of counts (pulses) per second, if an AND gate is open for exactly 1 second (one input has a waveform which goes high for 1 second), number of pulses passing through this gate during this period [the other input to the AND gate] counted by a counter directly gives the frequency in Hz.

A practical method of realising this scheme is shown in Fig. 14.53. If we have a clock at 10^6 Hz and it we divide this by 10^6 resulting output is a 1 Hz clock. This toggles the JK flip-flop. Output of this flip-flop will give a waveform which is high for 1 second and low for the next 1 second. This is the input to an AND gate thereby allowing the other input to the AND gate to reach the counter for 1 second.

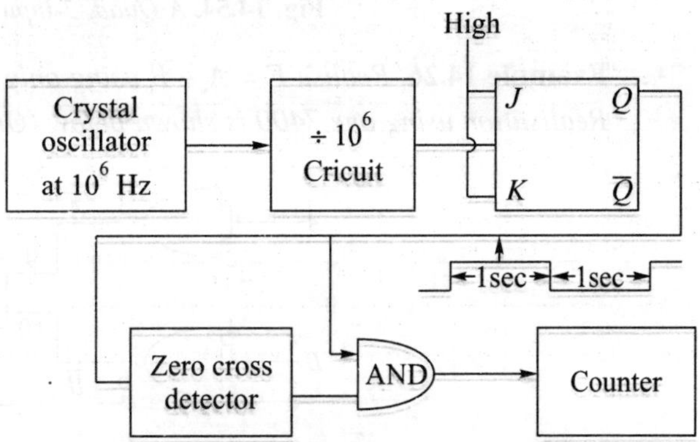

Fig. 14.53 *A frequency counter*

The count indicated by the counter gives the frequency of the waveform.

It is also possible to find the time elapsed between two events. One event sets a flip-flop. Output goes high which is the input to an AND gate, the other input to this gate being a clock of known frequency (say 1 MHz so that $T = 1$ micro sec.). Output of the AND gate being counted by a counter. Now the other event is made to reset the flip-flop, the output of the flip-flop goes zero, which makes the output to the AND gate to go to zero, thereby inhibiting the gate. Number of pulses counted by the counter are known as T is known. Thus time between the two events is directly known.

14.16.3 Integrated Circuits

Although we have explained so far the method of constructing the logic gates, flip-flops, registers and counters using the basic gates AND, OR and NOT gates for the proper understanding of the subject, generally no one now-a-days realises these in this fashion. All the devices such as AND, NAND, OR, NOR, flip-flops, shift registers, counters etc., are all available on a single silicon chip called the integrated circuit. Several pins have been brought out from the silicon chip and each pin is defined by the manufacturer of the chip (known as pin details). This greatly relieves the user from constructing the logic gates using discrete components.

As a typical example, consider an IC chip 7400. This is a Quad-2 input Nand gate. Pin connections are as shown in Fig. 14.54. Now the job of the user is only to connect V_{CC}, GND (maximum, minimum supply voltages under which the chip works satisfactorily, fan in an fan-out capabilities, etc., are all given by the chip manufacturers and in the form of data sheets), and suitable inputs to get proper outputs.

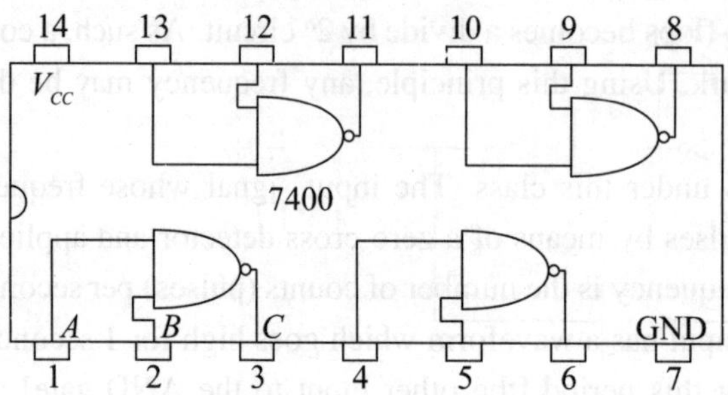

Input		Output
A	B	C
0	0	1
0	1	1
1	0	1
1	1	0

Truth table

Fig. 14.54. *A Quad, 2-input NAND gate IC chip*

Example 14.26. *Realise F = A + B using only NAND gates.*

Realisation using one 7400 is shown below (One gate is not used) in Fig. 14.55.

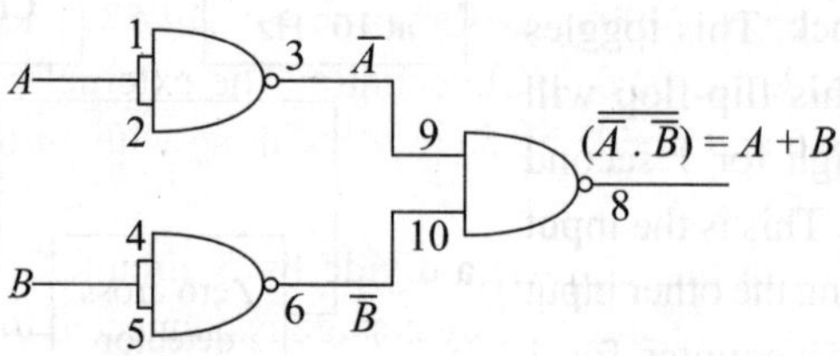

Fig. 14.55. *Realisation of OR gate using only NAND gates*

Solution. Apart from using the gates for realising the logic functions, there are other applications of the gates. One of the typical applications being the generation of square waves. Although gates of 7400 chip may be connected for the purpose, 7404 IC is used. This is an inverter chip having 6 gates as in Fig. 14.56. The logic symbol for an inverter as also the RTL scheme corresponding to it is shown in figure. As the name suggests, the function of an inverter is to change 0 to 1 and 1 to 0.

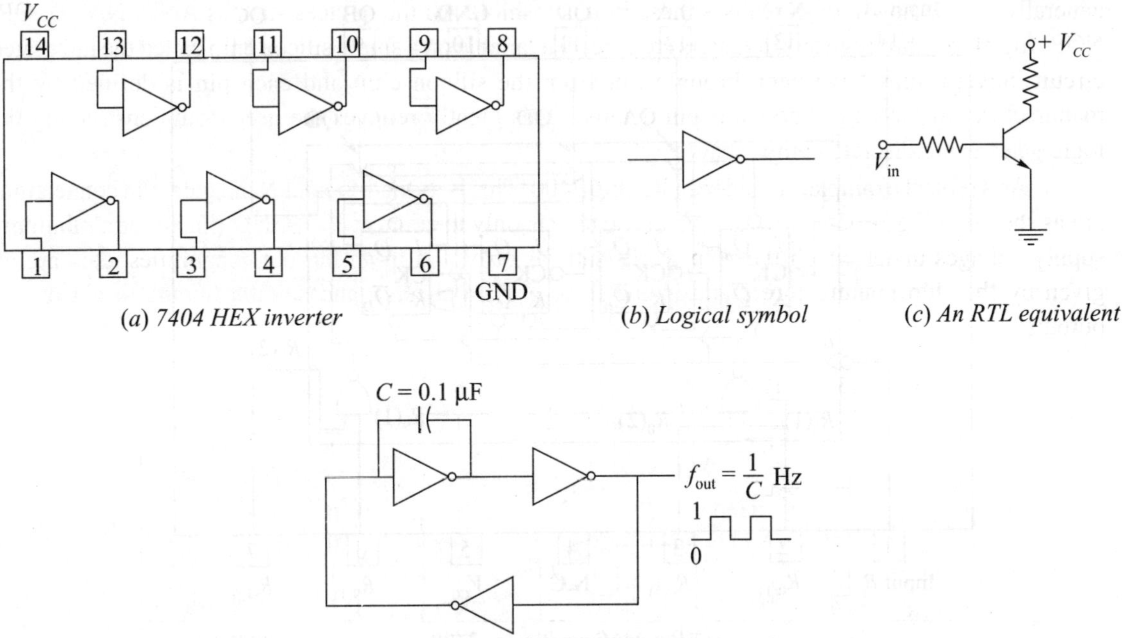

(a) *7404 HEX inverter* (b) *Logical symbol* (c) *An RTL equivalent*

(d) *An application*

Fig. 14.56

Example 14.27. *Realise a divide by 10, divide by 4, divide by 6 and divide by 8 circuit using the Decade counter 7490.*

Solution. The schematic of 7490 is as shown in Fig. 14.57. This TTL DIP chip is specifically designed to be used as a divide by 10 or BCD counter. The external connections required for divide by 10, divide by 4, divide by 6 and divide by 8 counters along with output waveforms are displayed in Fig. 14.58 (*a* to *h*).

There are two sections in this chip (*i*) a divide by 5 circuit (*ii*) a divide by 2 circuit. For the decade counter operation, output of the divide by 2 stage is connected to the input stage of divide by 5. BCD outputs are mentioned as *DCBA*.

Before closing this chapter, we shall see another IC which is an up/down counter-74190. We already know that counters count up to the mod-value and then start counting again from the 0 value. This is known as an *up-counter*. A down counter does the other way about. That is it can be presented with a number for each input pulse and counter decrements its output by 1 till its output reaches a zero value.

Pin details are shown in Fig. 14.59. This is an up/down BCD counter. It has an enable input which can start stop the counter. As at the enable input there is a bubble, it means that only when the low input is given, the counter is enabled. Also, when pin 5 goes low, counter starts counting up and when pin 5 is high, it counts down (shown a $\overline{\text{sup}}$/down). Pin 14 is the clock input.

A positive clock is required and at rising edges the counter works. Q_A is the least significant bit and Q_D is the most significant bit.

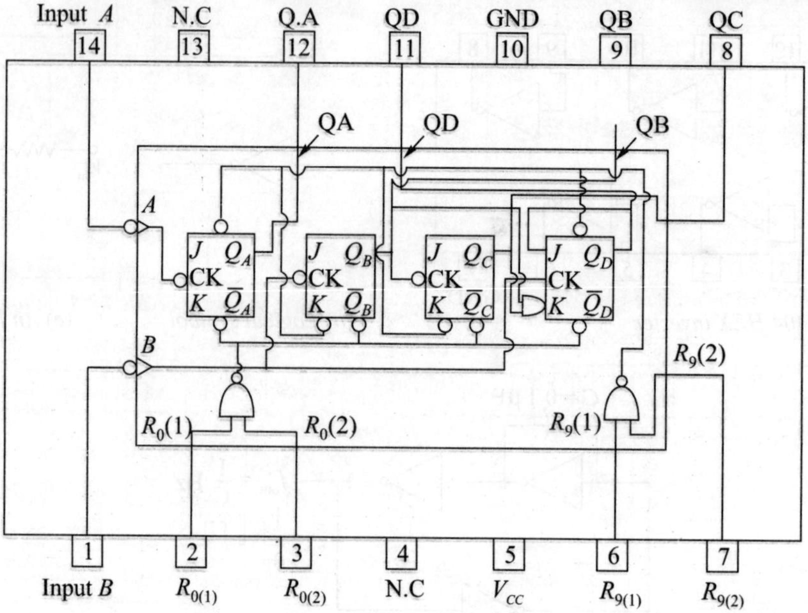

(a) Pin configuration of 7490

Count	Output			
	Q_D	Q_C	Q_B	Q_A
0	0	0	0	0
1	0	0	0	1
2	0	0	1	0
3	0	0	1	1
4	0	1	0	0
5	0	1	0	1
6	0	1	1	0
7	0	1	1	1
8	1	0	0	0
9	1	0	0	1

(b) Truth table

Reset/Set Inputs				Output			
$R_{0(1)}$	$R_{0(2)}$	$R_{9(1)}$	$R_{9(2)}$	Q_D	Q_C	Q_B	Q_A
H	H	L	X	L	L	L	L
H	H	X	L	L	L	L	L
X	X	H	H	H	L	L	H
L	X	L	X	Count			
X	L	X	L	Count			
L	X	X	L	Count			
H	L	L	X	Count			

(c) Mode selection-function table

Fig. 14.57

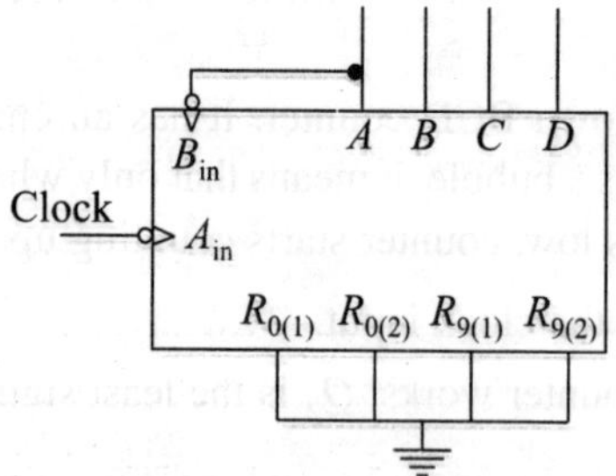

(a) 7490 as a decade counter

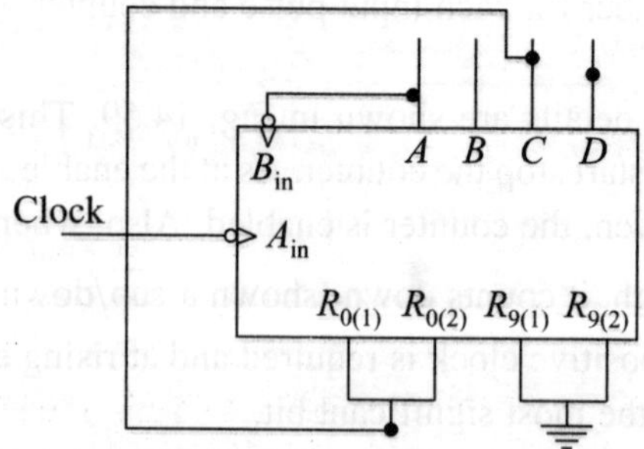

(b) 7490 as a divide by 4 counter

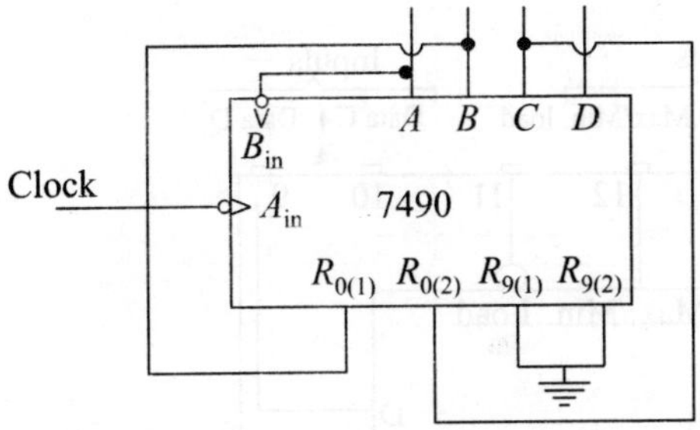

(c) *7490 as a divide by 6 counter*

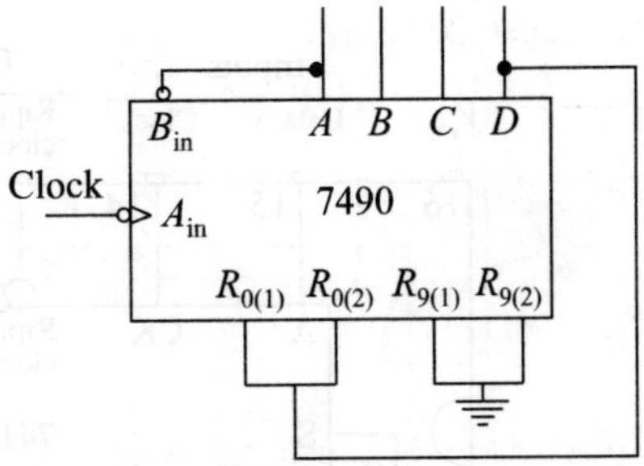

(d) *7490 as a divide by 8 counter*

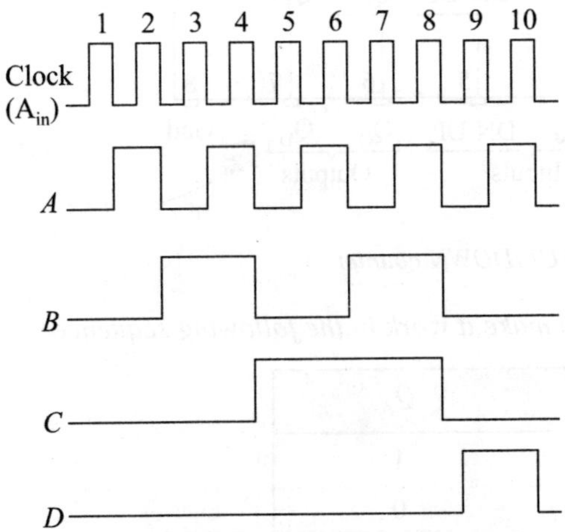

(e) *Output from a decade counter*

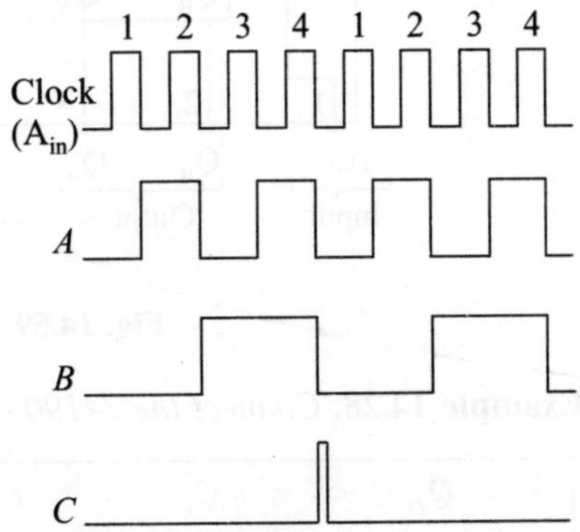

(f) *Output from a divide by 4 counter*

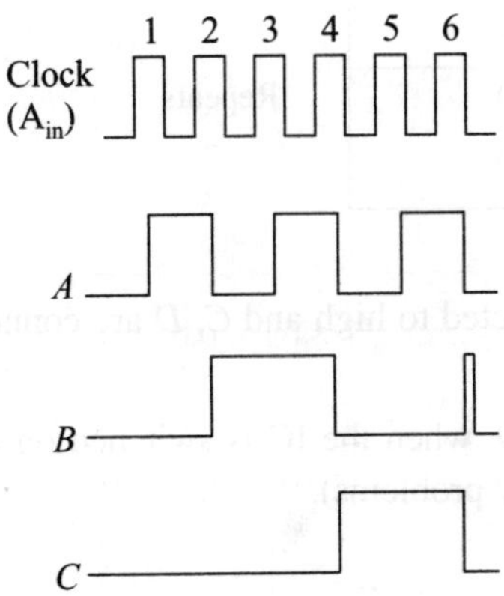

(g) *Output from a divide by 6 counter*

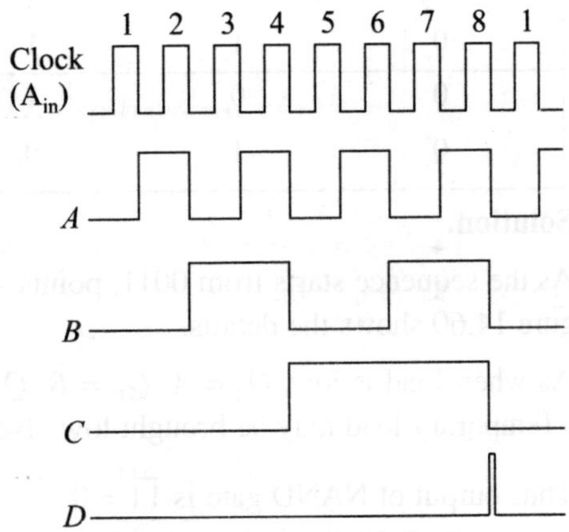

(h) *Output from a divide by 8 counter*

Fig. 14.58

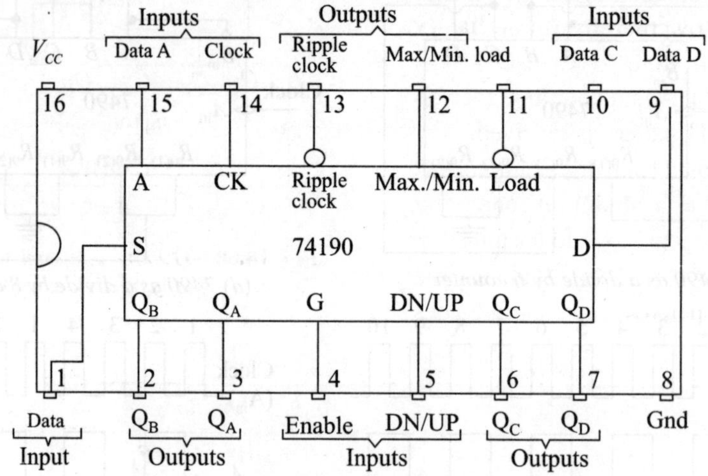

Fig. 14.59 *74190 UP/DOWN counter*

Example 14.28. *Connect the 74190 chip to make it work in the following sequence.*

Q_D	Q_C	Q_B	Q_A	
0	0	1	1	
0	1	0	0	
0	1	0	1	
0	1	1	0	
0	1	1	1	
0	0	1	1)	Repeats
0	1	0	0)	

Solution.

As the sequence starts from 0011, points *A*, *B* are connected to high and *C*, *D* are connected to low. Figure 14.60 shows the details.

As when load is low, $Q_A = A$, $Q_B = B$, $Q_C = C$, $Q_D = D$, when the IC is switched on $Q_A = 1$, $Q_B = 1$ (Temporary load may be brought low also in case of any problems).

Thus output of NAND gate is $\overline{1.1} = 0$

Thus the initial state of the outputs could be

$$Q_D Q_C Q_B Q_A = 0011$$

When a clock input is given, the output goes to 0100 (Now the NAND gate output is high and as such it starts counting).

then for the next clock pulse 0101
then for the next clock pulse 0110
then for the next clock pulse 0111

For this combination again the NAND gate output goes low thereby immediately bringing the output state to level 0011 (as DCBA state is 0011). Again counting goes on and resets when 0111 pattern is received.

As may be noted from this example, this counter can be used as a Modulo-*n* counter by a suitable logic connected to load terminal.

Table in Fig. 14.61 (*a*) indicates the status of flip-flop when decimal counting goes on.

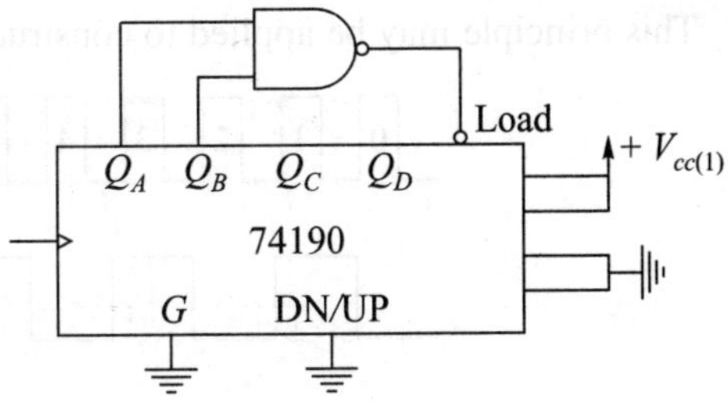

Fig. 14.60 *74190 as a counter with sequence 3, 4, 5, 6, 7, 3, 4, 5, 7 ...*

Number of clock pulses	State of flip-flops			
	F_3	F_2	F_1	F_0
0	0	0	0	0
1	0	0	0	1
2	0	0	1	0
3	0	0	1	1
4	0	1	0	0
5	0	1	0	1
6	0	1	1	0
7	0	1	1	1
8	1	0	0	0
9	1	0	0	1
10	1	0	1	0
	(0	0	0	0)
11	0	0	0	1

Fig. 14.61 (*a*) *State of flip-flops when counting is ON*

Figure 14.61 (*b*) shows the timing diagram required of a decade counter. Realisation of the same is shown in (*c*). As may be observed, when the 10th pulse occurs, all the four flip-flops will have to be reset and the counting will have to proceed as from the 0th pulse. With the occurrence of the 10th pulse $Q_3 = 1 = Q_1$. If we can AND these two inputs and reset Q_3 and Q_1 outputs (as already Q_0 and Q_2 outputs are at low), all the flip-flops will now be in the 0 state and the counting proceeds as before.

Counter can be cleared by a low clear or a low *B*. When CLR goes low, all the flip-flops are reset and the output of all flip-flops is 0000. When CLR goes high, counting starts as $\overline{Q_1 Q_3} = 1$ (initially). This output remains in this state till the state 1010 is encountered. No sooner this occurs, output *B* goes to 0. As such, output of *A* goes low and hence flip-flops are again reset. Thus counting restarts as before. As this scheme counts 10 pulses before it restarts counting (resets), it is known as a *decade counter*.

This principle may be applied to construct a counter of any base.

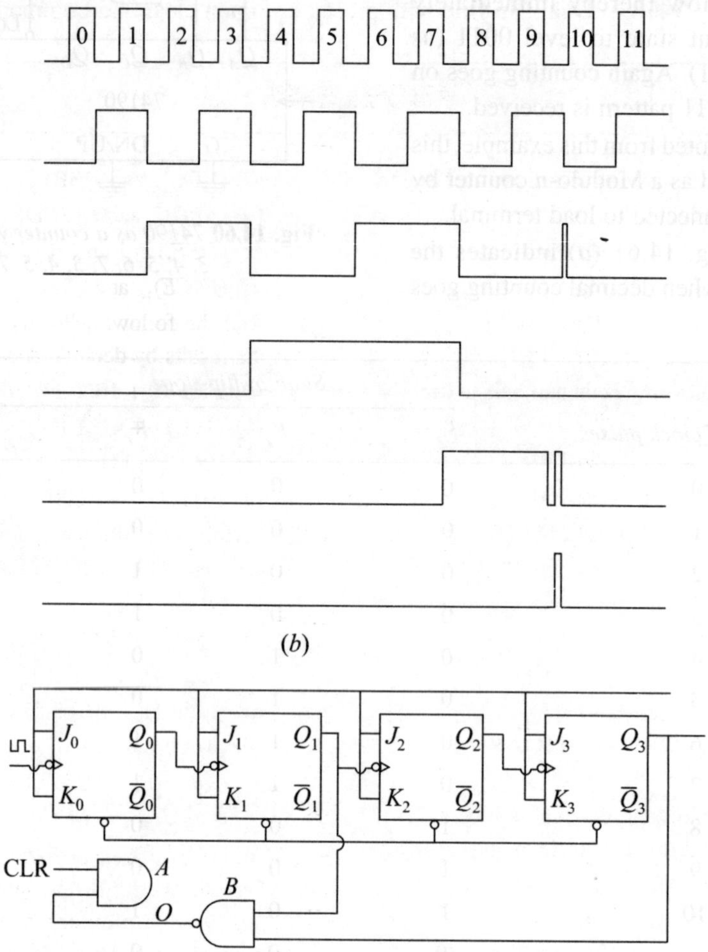

Fig. 14.61 *(b), (c) Timing diagram. Decade counter using JK flip-flops*

There are other types of counters in the IC version such as

7492 – Divide – by – 12 counter
7493 – 4-bit binary counter
74390 – Dual decade counter
74393 – Dual 4-bit counter
74191,193 – 4-bit binary up/down counter with load, clear etc.

Further, typically the following flip-flops in the IC version are available.

7474 – *D* flip-flop
7476 – *J-K* flip-flop
7470 – AND-gated *J-K* +ve edge triggered flip-flop with preset and clear
7472 – AND-gated *J-K* Master/Slave flip-flop with preset and clear.
7473 – Dual *J-K* flip-flop with clear
7475 – 4-bit bistable latch

7477 – 4-bit bistable latch

7478 – Dual flip-flop with preset, common clear and common clock etc.

PROBLEMS

1. Convert the following binary numbers to decimal numbers.
   (a) 1 1 0 (b) 1 0 1
   (c) 1 1 1 1 (d) 1 1 0 1
   (e) 1 0 1 0 1 (f) 1 1 0 0 1
   (g) 1 0 1 0 . 1 1 0 (h) 1 1 01 . 1 0 1
2. Convert the following octal numbers to decimal numbers.
   (a) 15 (b) 100
   (c) 66 (d) 760
   (e) 1170.4 (f) 1117.56
   (g) 125.65 (h) 364.35
3. Convert the following hexadecimal numbers to decimal numbers.
   (a) 18 (b) 26
   (c) 1A (d) *ID*
   (e) 21*F.FE* (f) 31*C.DE*
   (g) *FACE* (h) *CAD.CF*
4. Convert the following decimal numbers to (a) Binary (b) Octal (c) Hexadecimal and (d) BCD.
   (a) 2 (b) 15
   (c) 20 (d) 110
   (e) 650.55 (f) 700.125
   (g) 1110.25 (h) 1125.75
5. Convert the following binary numbers to equivalent (a) Octal (b) Hexadecimal and (c) Decimal.
   (a) 10010 (b) 110110
   (c) 11010.111 (d) 110101.10
   (e) 1111111101 (f) 101010101
   (g) 1000000.00001 (h) 1111111111.111111
6. Add the multiply the following numbers.
   (a) $(345)_8$ and $(567)_8$
   (b) $(107.2)_8$ and $(006.1)_8$
   (c) $(107.2)_8$ and $(006.1)_8$
   (d) $(636)_8$ and $(218)_8$
   (e) $(600.56)_8$ and $(300.46)_8$
   (f) $(12A)_{16}$ and $(13B)_{16}$
   (g) $(ABC)_{16}$ and $(ABCDE)_{16}$
   (h) $(DEF.12)_{16}$ and $(12EF.C)_{16}$
   (i) $(FACE)_{16}$ and $(BAD)_{16}$
7. Add the following binary numbers and check the results by decimal addition.
   (a) 1001.10 + 1000.11
   (b) 1111.11 + 1111.11
   (c) 101.01 + 1111.01
   (d) 101111.11 + 100011.10
8. Perform the following subtractions and check the answers by decimal subtraction.
   (a) $(76)_8 - (67)_8$
   (b) $(356)_8 - (267)_8$
   (c) $(456.04)_8 - (367.10)_8$.
   (d) $(1256.1)_8 - (0163.5)_8$
   (e) $(ABC)_{16} - (12C)_{16}$
   (f) $(ABCD)_{16} - (1CDE)_{16}$
   (g) $(4A9C)_{16} - (2BEF)_{16}$
   (h) $(FACE.E)_{16} - (1BDF.F)_{16}$
9. Perform the following subtractions by the 10s and 9s complement method. Convert the numbers to their equivalent binary numbers. Perform subtraction using 2s and 1s complement method.
   (a) $(345)_{10} - (298)_{10}$
   (b) $(298)_{10} - (345)_{10}$
   (c) $(5678)_{10} - (4999)_{10}$
   (d) $(3656)_{10} - (3784)_{10}$
10. Perform the following subtractions using 1s and 2s complement arithmetic and check the results by straight subtraction.
    (a) 111 – 010 (b) 1000 – 011
    (c) 011 – 1000 (d) 1111.01 – 1101.10
    (e) 1000 – 1000
11. Construct truth table for the following logical expressions.

(a) $Z = A\,\overline{B} + \overline{C}$ (b) $Z = A\,B + \overline{A}\,\overline{B}$

(c) $Z = A\,B + \overline{C}$

(d) $Z = (X + Y)\,(Y + Z)\,(XYZ)$

(e) $X = \overline{C}\,(\overline{B + D})$

(f) $Z = A\,\overline{B} + B\,\overline{C} + C\overline{A}$

(g) $Z = \overline{B}\;C + B\;\overline{C}$ (h) $A = BC\overline{D} + \overline{BC}\,D$

12. Write Boolean expressions for the following logic diagrams shown in Fig. P.14.12 (a, g).

X	Y	Z	F
0	0	0	1
0	0	1	1
0	1	0	1
0	1	1	1
1	0	0	0
1	0	1	0
1	1	0	0
1	1	1	1

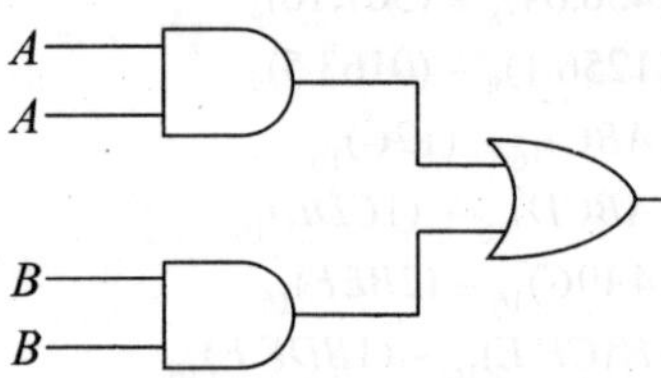

(a)

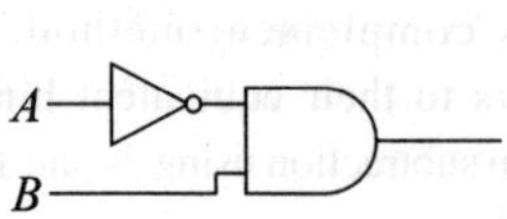

(b)

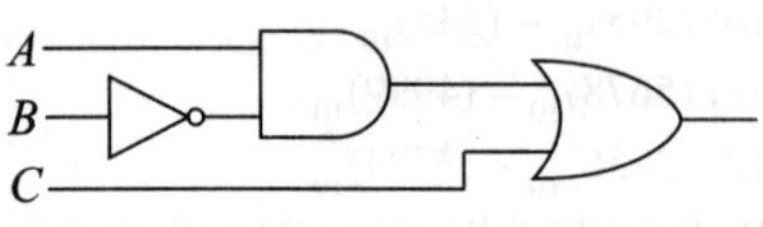

(c)

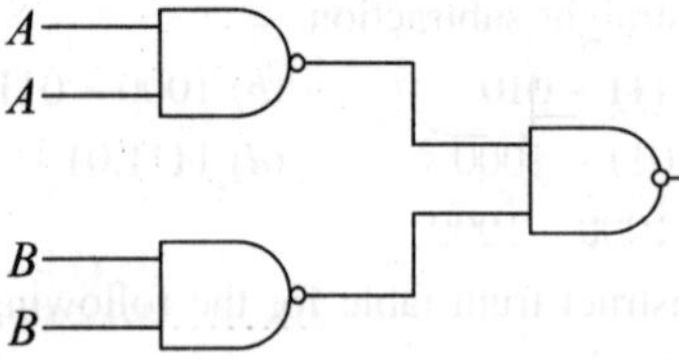

(d)

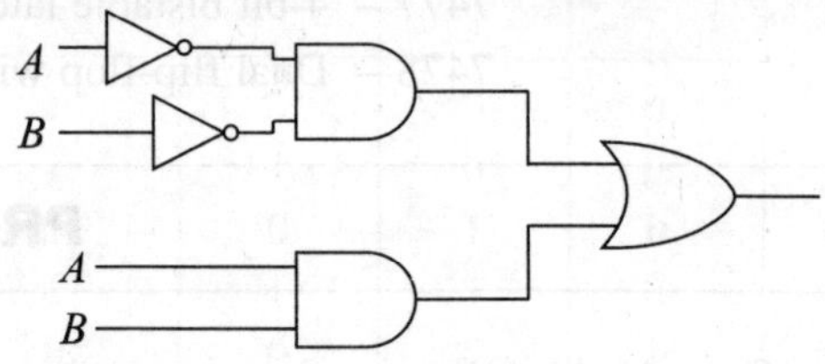

(e)

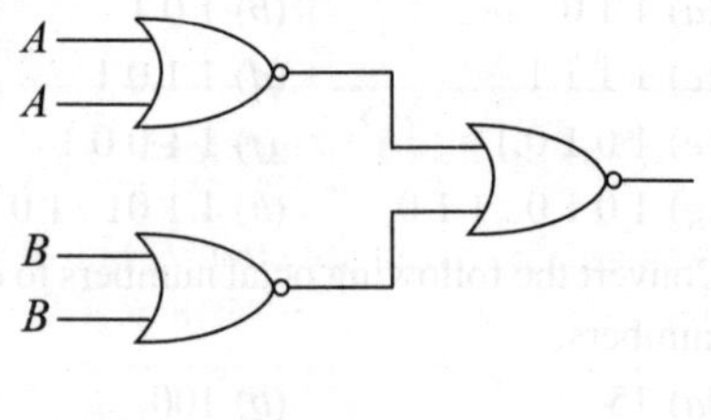

(f)

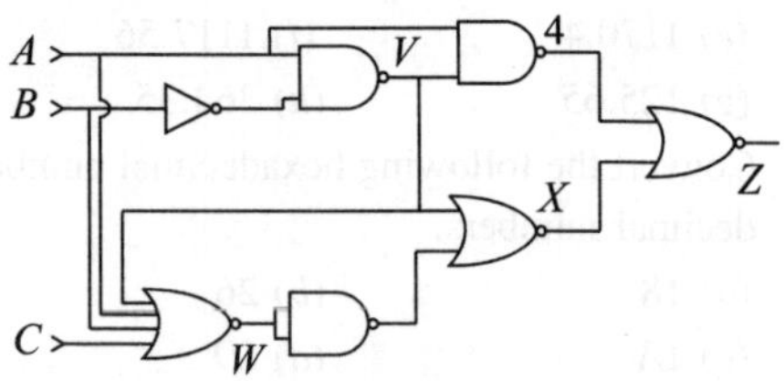

(g)

Fig. P.14.12

13. Draw the logic diagrams for the following Boolean expressions:

(a) $Z = \overline{\overline{XY} + \overline{YZ} + \overline{ZX}}$

(b) $Z = \overline{XY + YZ + ZX}$

(c) $Z = ABC + BCA + \overline{AB}$

(d) $Z = (X + Y)\,(Y + Z)\,(XYZ)$

14. Realise the function $Z = \overline{X}\,Y + X\overline{Y}$ using only NOR gates.

15. Realise the function $Z = \overline{XY} + XY$ using only NOR gates.

16. Using only NAND gates realise the function : $(X + Y)(\overline{Z} + \overline{Y})$

17. Using AND and OR gates realise the output function F given in the truth table of Fig. P.14.17.

X	Y	Z	F
0	0	0	1
0	0	1	1
0	1	0	1
0	1	1	1
1	0	0	0
1	0	1	0
1	1	0	0
1	1	1	1

Fig. P.14.17 *Truth table*

18. Realise the output function *D* and *B* given in the truth table of Fig. P.14.18.

X	Y	Z	D	B
0	0	0	0	0
0	0	1	1	1
0	1	0	1	1
0	1	1	0	1
1	0	0	1	0
1	0	1	0	0
1	1	0	0	0
1	1	1	1	1

Fig. P.14.18

19. Using the waveforms given below (Fig. P.14.19(*a*)), draw the waveform for the output of gate shown in Figs. P.14.19 (*b*) and (*c*).

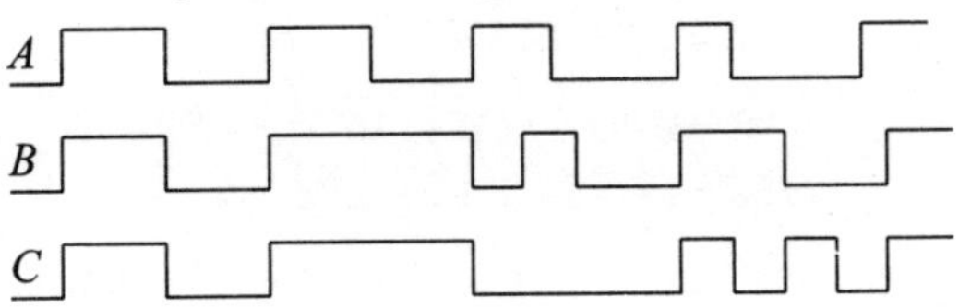

(*a*)

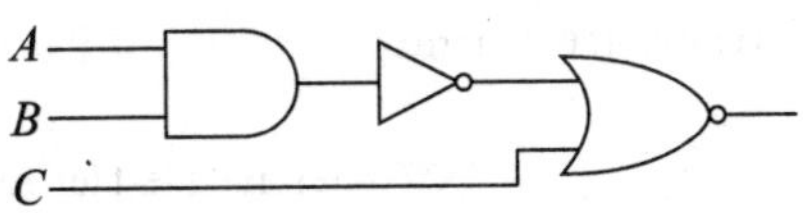

(*b*)

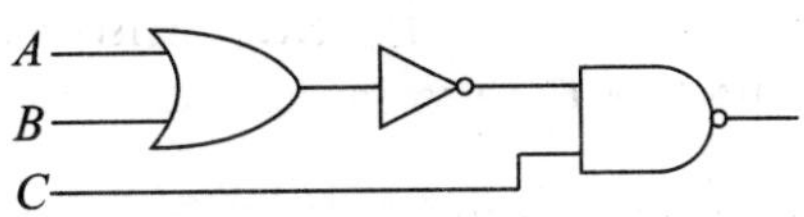

(*c*)

Fig. P.14.19

20. Draw the logic diagram for a gated *RS* flip-flop using NOR gates only. Write the truth table also.

21. What do you understand by racing as referred to flip-flops?

22. What disadvantage do you see in a Master-Slave *RS* flip-flop?

23. Construct a *J-K* flip-flop using NOR gates only. Draw the truth table.

24. Using the waveform of Fig. P.14.19 (*a*), draw the input and output waveforms for the diagram shown in Figs. P.14.24 (*a*) and P.14.24 (*b*).

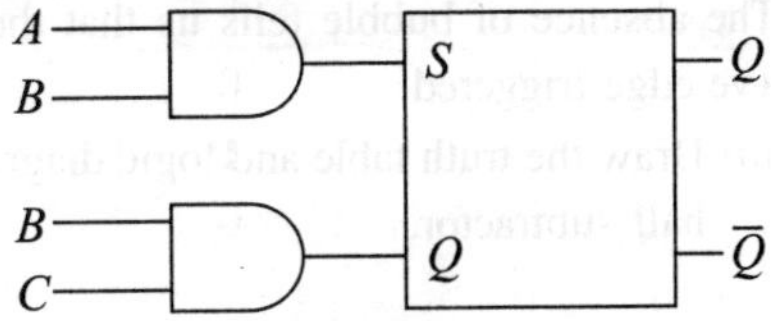

(*a*)

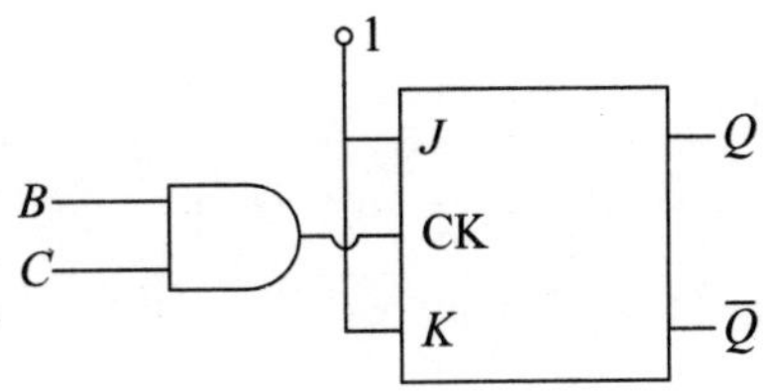

(*b*)

Fig. P.14.24 (*b*)

25. Using the waveform of Fig. P.14.19 (*a*), draw the input and output waveforms for the diagrams shown in Fig. P.14.25.

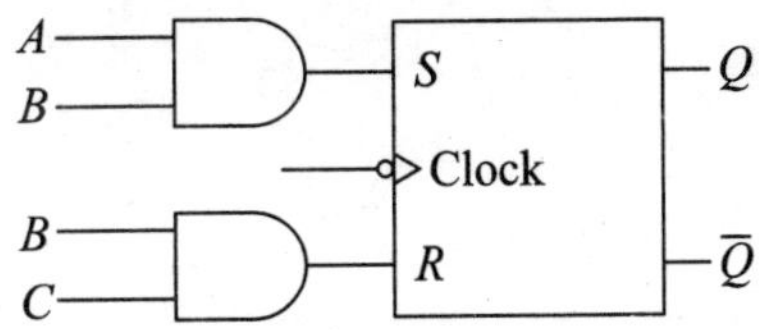

(*a*)

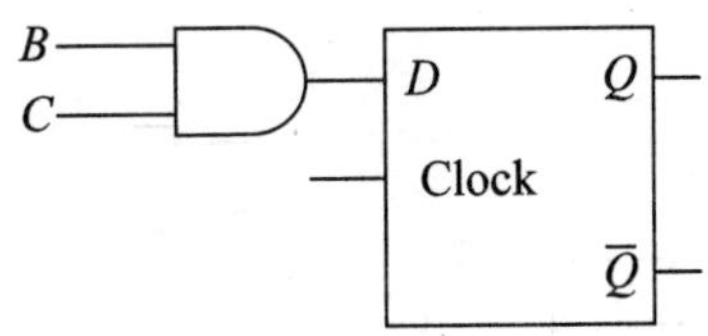

(*b*)

CHAPTER 14

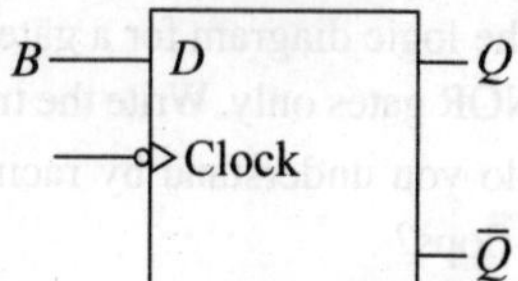

(*c*)

Fig. P.14.25

Note : > indicates the flip-flop is edge triggered. The presence of the bubble tells us that the *FF* is –ve edge triggered.

The absence of bubble tells us that the *FF* is +ve edge triggered.

26. (*a*) Draw the truth table and logic diagram of a half subtractor.

(*b*) Realise the above using only five NAND gates.

27. Draw the logic diagram of a shift-right register (3-bit) using *J-K* flip-flops.

28. Draw the truth table for a Mod-5 counter. Write the logic diagram (use any type of flip-flop).

29. Select an appropriate logical circuit that realises the expression $x^n = y^{n-1}$(x should have the value y had one clock period ago).

30. Design a frequency dividing network.

31. Design a 24 hour real-time clock using a 1 MHz (10^6 Hz) clock frequency. The clock is to give outputs of seconds, minutes and hours. (It should reset after 24 hours and start counting again).

Computer Concepts

15

CHAPTER

15.1 INTRODUCTION

Although computer development dates back to 17th century, computers have been put to use in real earnest since 1950s. During 1950s, digital computers were large in size and expensive. However, now due to the recent advancement in the technology, the general trend has changed. It is possible to develop and IC using LSI/VLSI technology which enables us to put millions of components active/passive on a square mm silicon wafer. These ICs have many possible applications. If an IC is to be developed for each of the applications separately, it becomes a costly affair. As such, a better idea is thought of *viz*. the use of an IC that can be programmed to tie the needs of many applications. Computer invariably use stored program concept. Input devices, output devices as also memories are required in any computer. Also a computer is supported to have the processing capabilities. In this chapter we will introduce the organizational details of a computer.

Microcomputers are used for a variety of purposes; a few examples are cited below:

- Instrumentation
- Communication systems
- Computer peripherals
- Test equipment
- Business equipment
- Industrial control
- Process control
- Signal processing
- Telephone switching
- Numerically controlled machines
- Gaming machines
- Counters
- CRT terminals
- Electronic cash register
- Consumer products

and the list goes on. Indeed, the number of applications is limited only by the designer's imagination!

A computer generally differs from the other electronic circuits as its operation is being controlled by a program, advantage being that the operation can be changed without rewiring the electronic circuit.

A microcomputer is built around a microprocessor. Microprocessor is a complex LSI (Large Scale Integration) device that has much of the processing capabilities of a large computer. Microprocessor contains the arithmetic and logic units, registers and counters that are required for the computer operation. To make a microcomputer, microprocessor is being augmented by other chips such as a ROM (Read Only Memory), RAM (Random Access Memory), input and output devices.

Microcomputers use the stored program concept. A set of instructions called a program resides in the memory of the computer directing the various units to perform specific tasks.

The word micro has been used with reference to the cost and also capabilities. The number of binary digits (bits) that can be processed at a time is known as *word length* of the computer. In general, a computer can do more work in a given time if the word length is more. Typically, the word length of a large computer is 32 to 64 bits whereas that of a microcomputer is 4 to 16 bits.

A large computer differs from a microcomputer in that it enables use of higher level languages (such as FORTRAN, BASIC, PL-1, PASCAL etc.,) for programming; (a set of instructions to be given to the computer). Also, the user need not really know the operation of the computer, as specially trained operators run the program on the computer and give the output to the users. It should be pointed out here that a general purpose computer is quite expensive.

On the other hand those who wish to use the microcomputer should be aware of the working of it. Unless the user knows the mode of the processor communicating with the memory, I/O devices and timings, it is seldom possible to write and execute programs. Also, programs are written using the assembly level language which is quite time consuming.

By 1969, integrated circuit technology had developed sufficiently and most of the required gates such as the arithmetic and logic circuits were available separately. About this time IC manufacturers integrated these chips and brought out a single chip called the microprocessor which had the capability of a complete computer.

INTEL in 1971, announced its first microprocessor (μP) having the capabilities to add, subtract, compare and perform AND and OR functions. It also could do the jobs as fetch, decode and execute operations. It was a 4-bit microprocessor capable of such operating on 4 bits of data at a time. This was 4004!

Later in 1973, INTEL announced an 8-bit μP, 8008 followed by better versions 8080 and 8085. Subsequently, a 16-bit μP was also announced – 8086.

There are, of course, other IC manufacturers in the market such as Motorola (6800), Fairchild (F 8), Zilog (Z 80), Texas Instruments (9900), Rockwell (PPS 4), Toshiba (TLCS 12), Signetics (2650) etc.

Recently, manufacturers have succeeded in placing ROMs, RAMs, I/O and clock on a single chip which is truly a microcomputer on a single chip! To extend the capabilities of this chip, more ROMs, RAMs can be added externally.

15.2 CONCEPTS OF A MICROCOMPUTER

Any computer is supposed to have:

- **An input device** by which external world users communicate with the computer.
- **An output device** using which the computer can communicate with the external world.
- **A CPU** which comprises of the control and the arithmetic and logic unit (performs computations on the input data, outputs the data on to the output device....).
- **Memory** to store the input results, store the intermediate values during computations, and the end results. This is called the data memory.

A set of instructions to direct the other units of the computer stored in the memory called the *program memory*. Fig. 15.1 shows the general concepts.

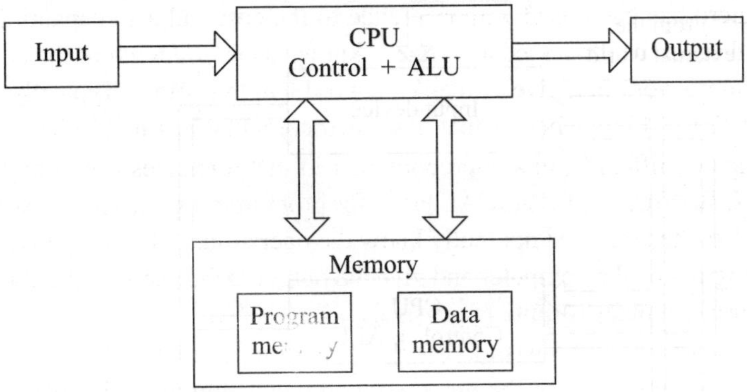

Fig. 15.1 *Functional components of a computer*

Devices are connected from one to the other by means of a group of conducting wires over which electrical signals are transmitted. Such a group of wires is called a **bus**. In any typical system, there are three distinct groups of buses—address bus, data bus and the control bus.

As the name suggests, over the **Address bus**, the microcomputer (μC) transmits the address of that device which it desires to access. Only the CPU can send the address and as such we say that address bus is **unidirectional**. If now the CPU wants to access a memory location 2100, this address is put on the address bus by the CPU. Although all memory locations get this address, only location 2100 responds.

Data bus is used to send and receive data to and from different devices and as such it is **bidirectional**.

Control bus may exercise control over the devices at the instance of the CPU or on the CPU at the instance of the devices. As such, control bus is **bidirectional**.

15.3 ARCHITECTURE OF A MICROCOMPUTER

The above mentioned bus and their control over functional parts of the computer is as shown in Fig. 15.2.

The width of the bus represents the number of signal wires constituting the bus. For example, in a 8-bit μP, data bus is 8-bit wide. Also, the processor is capable of processing 8-bits at a time. The width of the address bus gives us an indication of the local addressing capability of the μP. If we have a 16-bit address line, then the processor can address $2^{16} = 65536 = 64$ K bytes of memory (1 K = 1024 bits). An 8-bit μP will have a 16-bit address line.

15.4 STORED PROGRAM CONCEPT

The program concept is best understood by an example. Let us consider the example of inputting a letter *X* from an input device (may be a key board), storing this in the data memory and outputting this data on to an output device (may be a printer). Indeed, the input and output devices will have addresses (called port numbers). Fig. 15.3 shows the architecture of the computer as in Fig. 15.2.

In addition, address and contents in the program memory as also address of the data memory has been indicated. Contents of the program memory are generally in the ROM, and the data memory is a RAM. The sequence of operations is as below:

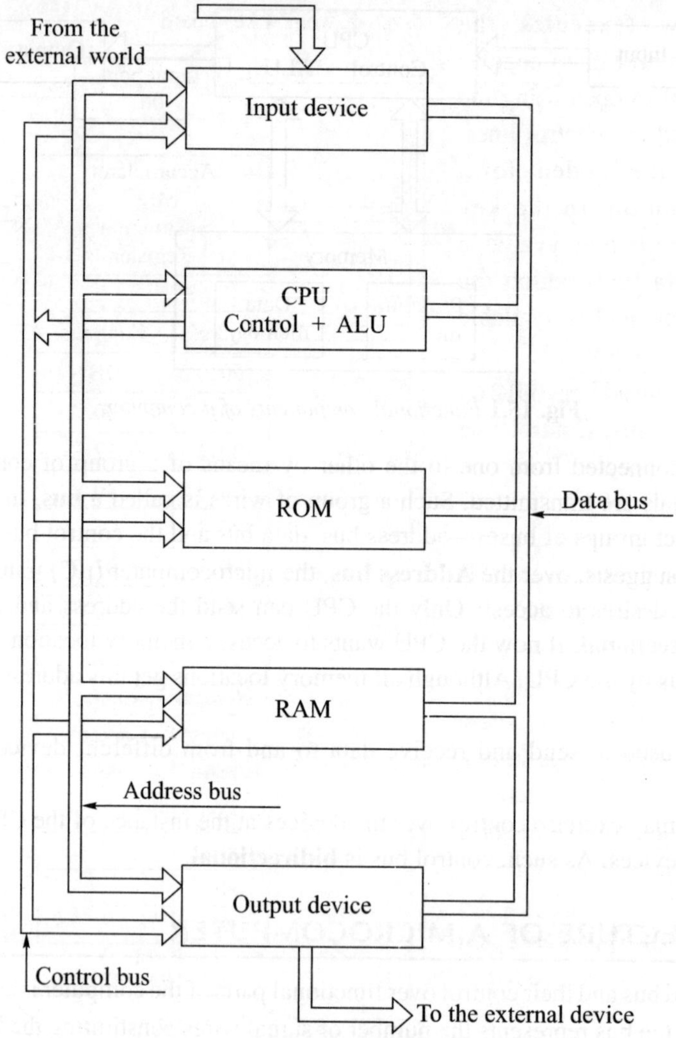

Fig. 15.2 *Architecture of a microcomputer*

* μPU sends out address 0010 on the address bus. Control line enables the program memory. Contents of location 0010 are available on the data lines. This being accepted by the μPU, is placed in a special register (memory location) called the Instruction Register. μPU now decodes this instruction as input data and knows that some more information is required before executing this statement as a whole. That is, it expects and answer input data from where? Thus, the μPU send address 0011 on the address lines again, and the control line enables the read input. The contents of 0011 *viz.*, 00 (address of the input port) are now available on the data lines. This is accepted by the μPU and placed in the instruction register. The entire instruction is now interpreted as input data from port 00.

* μPU now (executes the instruction and thus) enables the port 00 to open using the address and the control lines. Data in the coded form (corresponding to the key pressed-58) is now available on the data lines which the μPU accepts and is available at the accumulator.
* μPU sends out address 0012 on the address bus. Control line enables the program memory. Contents of 0012 *viz.*, 32 (meaning store data) are now available on the data lines. This data is accepted by the μPU and decodes the code as store data and it now expects the address of the location where the information is to be stored. Again 0013 address is sent by the μPU. Control line enables the program memory. Contents of 0013 are available on the data line (30). This is accepted by the μPU and is decoded as store data in memory location 0030. Now the μPU puts 0030 address on the address lines. Control line enables the write input of the data memory. Now the μPU puts the information stored in the accumulator (58) on the data lines being written into address 0030. μPU now places 0014 on the address lines and enables the read input of the program memory. Contents of 0014 *viz.*, *D*3 are placed on the data lines accepted by the μPU which interprets this as output data and expects some more data as output data. Hence 0015 address is placed by the μPU on the address lines, control line enables the program memory. Contents of 0015 *viz.*, (01 – address of output port) is accepted by the μPU and now is decoded as output data on to port 01. The μPU now activates port 01 using the address bus and the control lines. The μPU places the code for *X* (58 – contained in the accumulator) on to the printer.

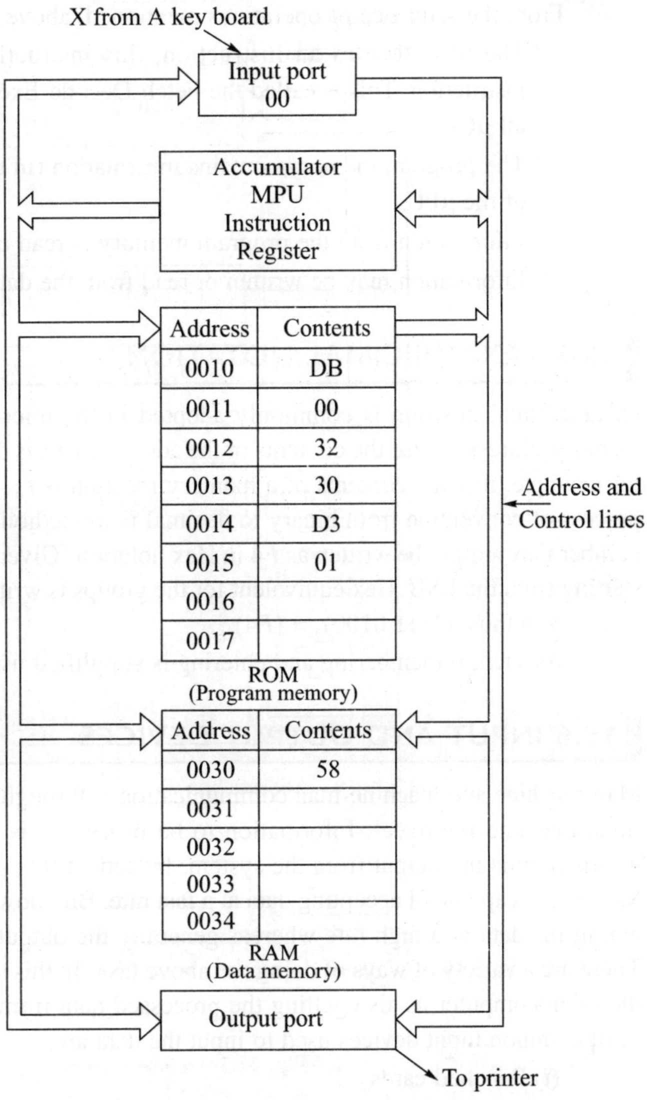

Fig. 15.3 *Architecture of a μC with program memory*

From the sequence of operations mentioned, above, the following points become obvious:

* The μPU fetches an instruction, this instruction is decoded and the μPU executes the instruction. This is called the Fetch-Decode-Execute sequence. The sequence is common to all μCs.
* The program memory contains information (in the coded form) which directs the functions of the μPU.
* Information from the program memory is read only (and not written).
* Information may be written or read from the data memory.

15.5 HEXA DECIMAL NOTATION

Hexa decimal notation is commonly adopted in the microcomputer systems for indicating both the memory address as also the contents of the address. This is due to the simplicity of the system. Consider, for example, that the contents of a memory location is (1111 0100) which is equivalent to (244). The process of conversion from binary to decimal is too tedious and time consuming. Whereas this binary number may simply be written as *F*4 in Hex notation (Given binary digits are grouped in terms of 4-bits starting from the LSB, Hex equivalent for the groups is written. In this case, $(0100)_2 = (4)_{16}$ and $(1111)_2 = (F)_{16}$ and thus, $(1111\ 0100)_2 = (F4)_{16}$.

As such, remembering and entering is simplified using the Hex notation.

15.6 INPUT AND OUTPUT DEVICES

Man-machine and machine-man communication is through the input and output devices also known as 'man-machine interface'. Information to be processed is the input to the system and the processed information is the output from the system. Indeed, at this stage there are many problems encountered. Machine is capable of accepting data at a fast rate. But, how to give data at this rate? Also, machine can output the data at a high rate whereas generally the output devices such as printers are slow devices. There are a variety of ways of doing the above task. In this section, various methods of inputting data to the microcomputer as also getting the processed data from the microcomputer will be discussed. The most common input devices used to input the data are:

(*i*) Punched cards
(*ii*) Punched paper tapes and.
(*iii*) Keyboards and CRT terminals.

Also the common output devices used to get the computed results are:

(*i*) Visual display units (VDUs or CRT Terminals)
(*ii*) Printers
(*iii*) Tape/Card punching machines.

15.6.1 Punched Cards

This is one of the widely and commonly used medium for entering data and obtaining data from the machine. A typical card is $7\frac{1}{3}''$ long, $3\frac{1}{4}''$ wide and 0.0067″ thick. Card has 12 rows and 80 columns so that holes could be punched in any one of the $12 \times 80 = 960$ positions. Information on a punched card is recorded using the 'Hollerith Code', an alpha-numeric code in which a single character is punched in each column of the card. Thus 80 characters may be represented on a card. A typical card is shown in

Fig. 15.4. The basic code is also shown in the same figure. As an example, the symbol 0 is coded by means of a punch in the 0th row; the symbol *A* is coded by punching a hole is the 12th row and the 1st

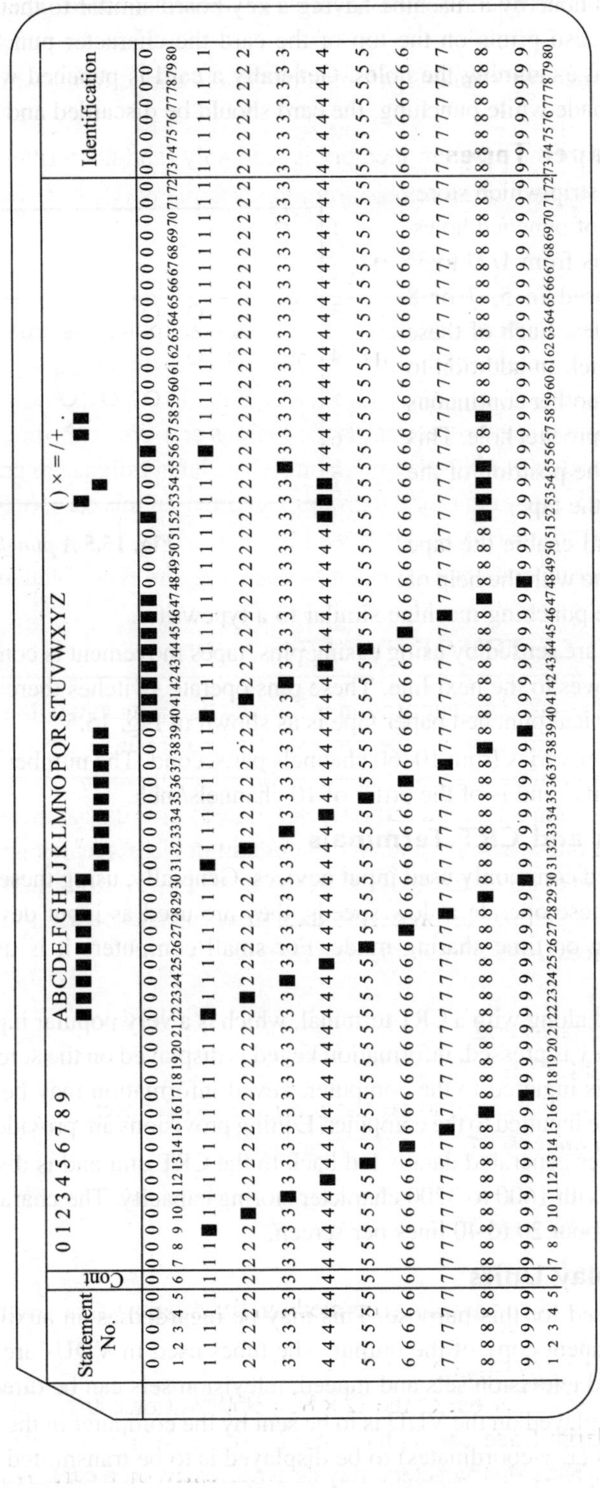

Fig. 15.4 *A Hollerith card*

row of the card (similarly $B = 12, 2$ (coordinates), $C = 12, 3$, $D = 12, 4$, $E = 12, 5$, $F = 12, 6$, $G = 12, 7$, $H = 12, 8$, $I = 12, 9$, $J = 11, 1$, $K = 11, 2$ $L = 11, 3$........).

Card punching is done by a machine having a key board similar to that of a normal typewriter. The punching machine also prints on the top of the card the character punched. This enables us to identify the card without examining the holes. Generally a card is punched with only one instruction and in case an error is made while punching, the card should be discarded and replaced by a new card.

15.6.2 Punched Paper Tapes

It is a continuous paper strip which stores information in the form of punched holes. Width of the tape various from 1/2" to 3" and information is stored in 5, 7 or 8 possible information holes. Each of these holes is known as channel. In addition to these channels, there is another continuous hole position called the sprocket hole. This is being used to locate the position of the information stored—of the tape.

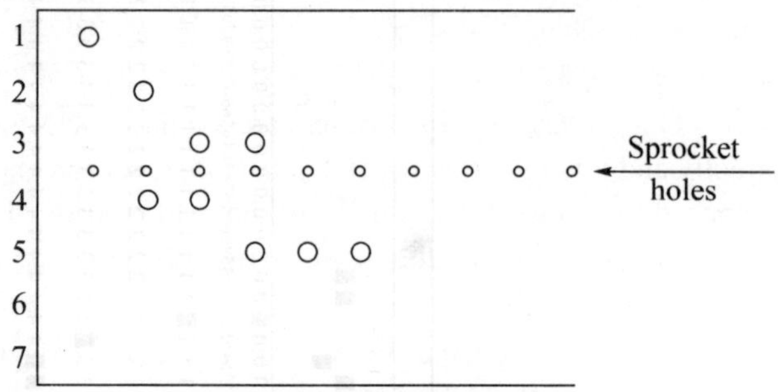

Fig. 15.5 *A punched paper tape*

Sprocket hole will enable the tape to advance to the next line with the help of a sprocket gear in a tape punching machine similar to a typewriter.

Generally, holes are sensed by using easing pins, tapes movement is continuous; stops while the coding is sensed and moves to the next line. These pins operate switches there by converting the holes into a binary code. A typical punched paper tape is as shown in Fig. 15.5.

Speed of the reader varies from 10–60 channels per second. The number of characters per inch is referred to as 'data density' and is of the order of 10 channels/inch.

15.6.3 Key Boards and CRT Terminals

Key boards are low speed commonly used input devices. Generally, using these 2 character/second can be inputted. Although these operate at low speeds, they are used as input devices to a fast computer when they are operating on time sharing mode. For small computers it is used as an on-line input device.

Key board is used along with a CRT terminal, which is a very popular input/output device. As an input device, when the key is pressed, information keyed is displayed on the screen of the CRT. As such, before any information is inputted to the computer, keyed information may be seen on the screen and after satisfaction it may be inputted to the computer. Editing provisions are provided for the CRT Terminal.

Also, the computer generated data is fed back to the CRT unit and is displayed. CRTs normally have a storage memory with 1600 to 3200 character storing capacity. The characters are arranged in 80 character per line with about 20 to 40 lines per screen.

15.6.4 Visual Display Units

A cathode-ray tube is used for this purpose. This may be regarded as an auxiliary output device as it does not deliver a permanent copy of the output. The tubes used in VDUs are the same type as those used in oscilloscopes and television sets and indeed, television sets can be directly used as VDUs.

The data to be displayed on the VDU is to be sent by the computer in the binary form. That is the coordinates of the points (x, y-coordinates) to be displayed is to be transmitted in the binary code. The circuitry in the VDU unit will convert this to analog voltage using *D/A* converters and this voltage is used to position the screen. Indeed, this takes lot of time as the computer need to send many points for displaying any character. Instead of wasting the precious computer time for doing such a job, the VDU itself has a built in memory and as such, receives data from the computer in the binary codes and stores the data in the VDU unit and generates the display from this stored data. Tubes capable of displaying data at the rate of over 100,000 words per minute are common.

15.6.5 Printers

Printers deliver permanent copies of the computed results. Computer makes all computations only in binary or in binary coded decimal form. It may be noted here that the process to be carried out while data is sent to the printer is the inverse of what was done when a key board was pressed.

On-line and off-line printers are available. On-line printers print data received by the computer directly and off-line printers print data from recorded magnetic tapes or discs. In both cases, printers are supposed to be fast as large data will have to be printed out.

Letter quality printers work on the principle of electronic typewriters and have speeds from 10 to 60 characters per second.

In Dot matrix printers a set of pins in a 9 × 7 solenoid actuated array are used to print characters. A character is printed by a proper selection of the 9 × 7 hammers driven against the paper; speeds of up to 330 characters per second are available.

Faster printers are constructed using raised characters distributed around a 'print wheel' which revolves constantly. When the character to be printed is in position, the print hammer strikes the ribbon against paper and thus against the raised character on the print wheel located behind the paper. This type of printer also requires memory and decode of its own. Speeds of 1250 lines per minute are available.

Speed of the above types of printers are limited due to the limitation in the mechanical speed of movement. However, several other types of printing such as Electromagnetic, Electrostatic, Thermal, Ink jet, Laser have been adopted to increase the speed of the operation.

15.6.6 Tapes and Punching Machines

As information to the computer may be inputted through tapes or cards, computer also can output the computed results in the same form. However, these punched tapes and cards must then be of interpreted ones. Indeed, magnetic/tape may also be used for this purpose. In this case, recording of data from the computer is much faster than even the fasterst printers. Finally, of course this (magnetic/tape) may be printed out using even a slow printer as the computer is not involved in this process.

15.7 MEMORY

It is apparent from the previous sections that both the program and the information to be processed are stored in the memory. When a program is to be executed, CPU reads instruction contained in the program one by one and executes it. There are many types of memory that could be used with the microcomputer systems. They range from floppy disks to semiconductors memories. However, although floppy disks may be used to store the program and the data, it is necessary that the program and the required data is to be either in the core memory or the semiconductor memory of the computer before execution starts. Thus core/semiconductor memories are known as *main memories* and floppy disks, magnetic tapes etc. are known as *auxiliary memories*.

We have noted in previous chapters that the basic memory device is a flip-flop. This can be realised by using magnetic cores or by semiconductors. A number of registers, in an order, each capable of storing a binary word is regarded as 'memory'. Indeed, one of the most active part in a computer is the 'memory'.

Core memory was extensively used for storing information. It may be worth nothing that in case of core memories, the control circuits are complex and require large space requiring more power, thereby creating more heat. For providing cooling facilities, core memories are to be centralized.

However, due to the rapid advances in IC technology, semiconductor memories, which are cheaper, faster, more compact requiring less space (requires 1/1000th of the space required by core memories of the same capacity) and less power are made possible. As such, they are slowly replacing core memories. In addition to the traditional uses, semiconductor memories are being used to hold the truth tables, look-up tables etc. exclusively depending on the type of the design. One of the main difference between the core memory and the semiconductor memory is that the core memory is non-volatile (stored data is not lost even when the power is off). However, semiconductor memory is volatile. Thus, whenever power is ON to restart the operation, reloading the contents to the memory is necessary. Although *Read* only memories may be used for the purpose of storing data, flexibility in cost especially when the program is under development and needs frequent changes warrents the use of mass storage devices such as the Floppy Disks. It is possible to have 64 K-bit of information on a silicon chip of size $1/4'' \times \frac{1}{4}''$. Obviously such a chip requires (64 K × 2) pins brought out (as a flip-flop outputs is 0 or 1—one pin for each flip-flop) and as it is necessary to access each flip-flop (one pin for each flip-flop). Bringing down these number of pins is not feasible. As such, this problem is circumvented by suitable binary codes which when impressed on the address lines of the semiconductor memory, is being decoded in the IC memory itself to represent a certain memory location in the IC and only the content of that location is made available at the output (on to the data lines) when the memory is read as such, in principle, the back structure of the 64 K memory is represented as shown in Fig. 15.6.

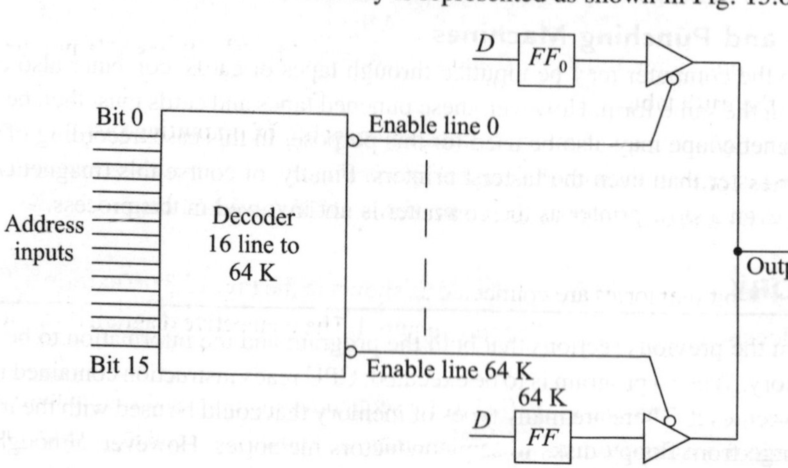

Fig. 15.6 *A block schematic of a 64 K memory*

The above principle is easily understood by considering a 3 to 8 decoder as shown in Fig. 15.7 the truth table for the same is shown in Fig. 15.7 (*b*). Depending on the bit values, *A* ... output would be activated, for example, if *ABC* = 001, output 1 would be activ...

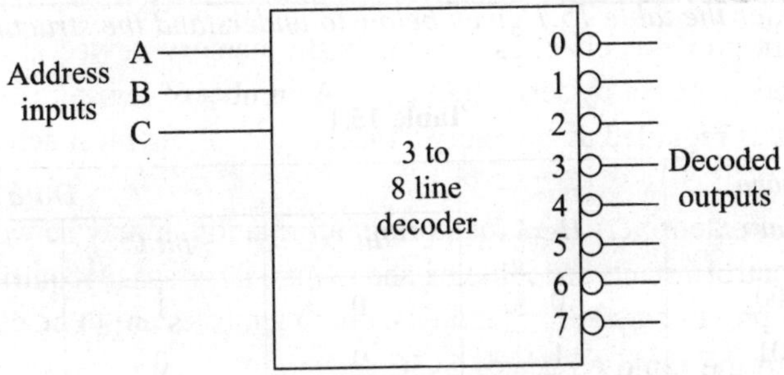

(a) *Block diagram of a 3 to 8 decoder*

Inputs CBA	Outputs selected
0 0 0	0
0 0 1	1
0 1 0	2
0 1 1	3
1 0 0	4
1 0 1	5
1 1 0	6
1 1 1	7

(b) *Truth table of the 3 to 8 decoder*

Fig. 15.7

As there are only three inputs *A*, *B* and *C* there could be $2^3 = 8$ possible unique combinations. This is shown in the truth table.

Although semiconductor memory is basically capable of outputting one bit of data, inorder to make the memories compatible with the control processing units (microprocessors) having 4 data lines and 8 data lines, 4-bit and 8-bit memories are available. 2716 is a VLSI chip with 2 K × 8-bit read only memory.

Two 256 × 4-bit memories are connected as shown in the Fig. 15.8 (*a*) to form a 256 × 6 memory. To address, 256 locations (2^8), address lines are required. The connective diagram is as shown in Fig. 15.8 (*b*).

This storage mode may be classified as (*i*) sequential memory and (*ii*) random access memory. Process of reading or writing from or into the memory is known as accessing the memory. Time taken for accessing any memory location is known as access time.

Example. *Consider the table 15.1 given below to understand the structure of a memory (RAM/ROM).*

Table 15.1

Decimal (Reg No)	*Column Binary*	*Hex*	*Data*			
			Bit D	*Bit C*	*Bit B*	*Bit A*
0	0000	0	0	1	0	0
1	0001	1	0	0	1	0
2	0010	2	0	0	0	0
3	0011	3	0	1	1	0
4	0100	4	1	0	0	1
5	0101	5	0	0	1	1
6	0110	6	0	0	0	1
7	0111	7	0	0	0	0
8	1000	8	1	0	0	0
9	1001	9	1	0	0	1
10	1010	*A*	1	1	1	1
11	1011	*B*	1	1	0	1
12	1100	*C*	1	0	0	1
13	1101	*D*	1	1	1	0
14	1110	*E*	1	0	0	1
15	1111	*F*	0	0	0	1

Let us now suppose that it is necessary that we would like to read the information from column No. 12, then the process involves

(*i*) Locating column 12

(*ii*) Reading the bits *D*, *C*, *B* and *A*.

Columns are known as addresses and bits *D*, *C*, *B*, *A* are known as contents. Locating the column is known as accessing the memory. Time required to access a memory location is known as the access time.

In case of sequential memories, access time depends on the location of the information. For example, in a cassette tape suppose a required song is at the end of the tape and if we are at the beginning of the tape, it is necessary to run the tape till the end of the tape when the song can be obtained. Thus, tape has to be moved from the beginning to the end and we say that the access time is long. On the other hand, if the required song is at the beginning of the tape, and if we are at the beginning of the tape, the song can be accessed fast, and thus the access time is small. These type of memories wherein the access time depends on the location (of data/information) are known as sequential memories.

However, in case of random access memories, irrespective of the memory location, access time is same and thus the name random access memory.

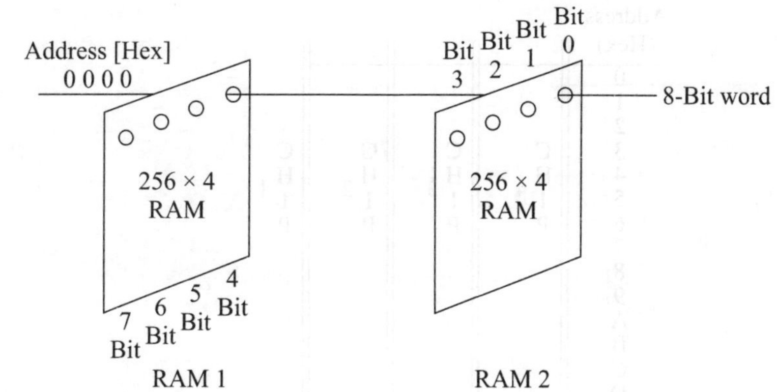

(*a*) *Two 4-bit memory chips connected to form an 8-bit memory chip*

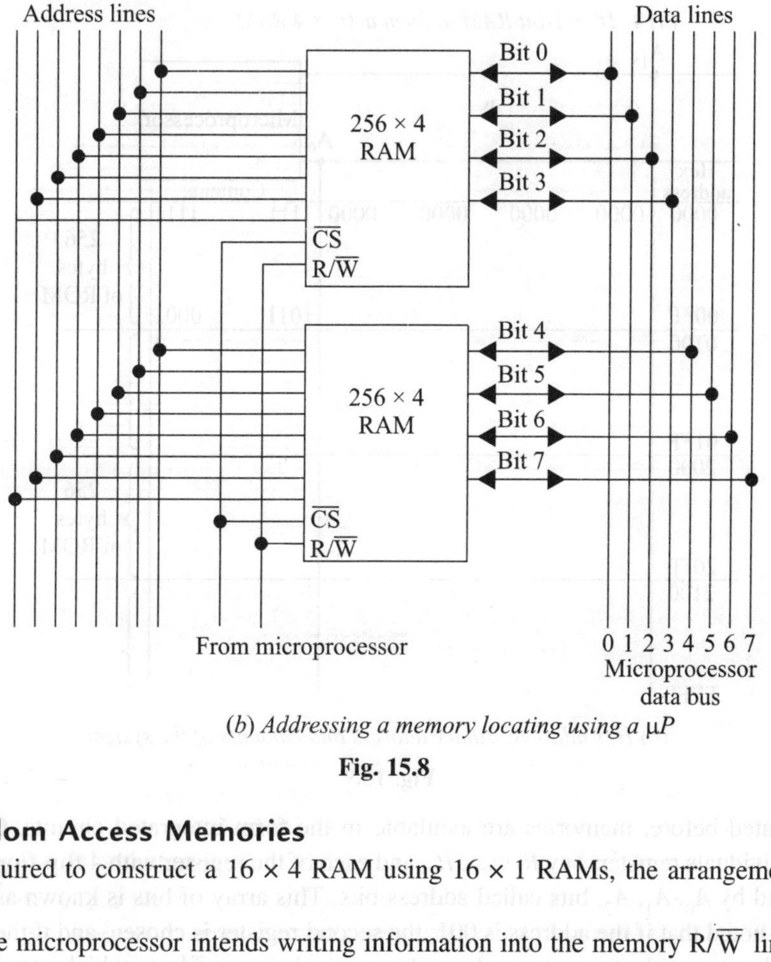

(*b*) *Addressing a memory locating using a μP*

Fig. 15.8

15.7.1 Random Access Memories

In case it is required to construct a 16 × 4 RAM using 16 × 1 RAMs, the arrangement is shown in Fig. 15.9.

When the microprocessor intends writing information into the memory R/$\overline{W}$ line, as shown in Fig. 15.8 (*b*), is made low and address to presented on the address lines. When Reading is to be done R/$\overline{W}$ line is made high. As the time required to access any location in the memory is same (or Read/Write memory) it is known as Random Access Memory (RAM). This memory is also known as volatile memory as the contents of the memory are wiped out when the power supply is off.

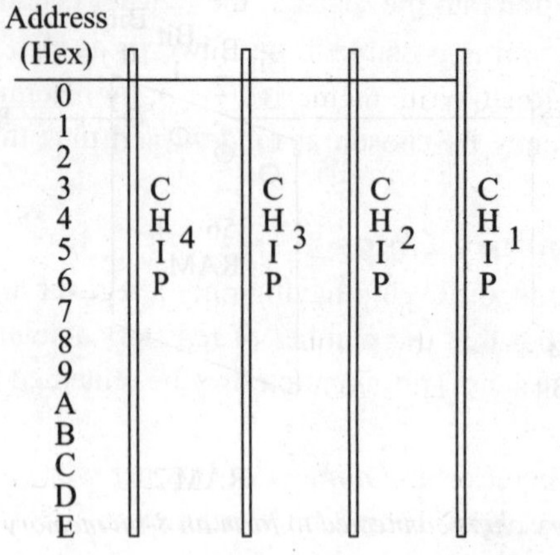

(a) 4, 16 × 1-bit RAM to form a 16 × 4 RAM

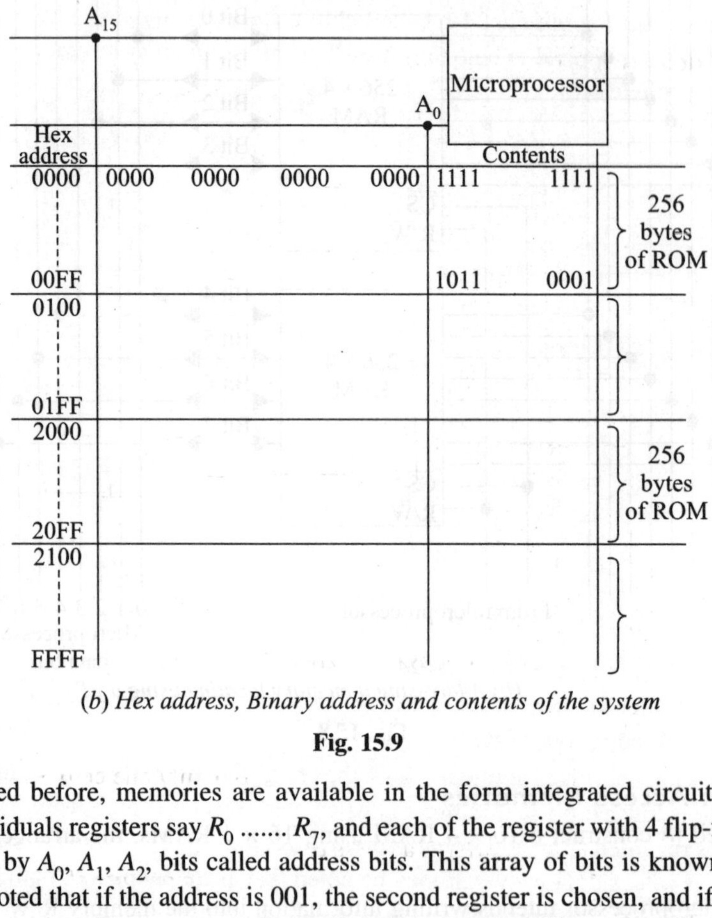

(b) Hex address, Binary address and contents of the system

Fig. 15.9

As indicated before, memories are available in the form integrated circuits. Consider a chip having eight individuals registers say R_0 .... R_7, and each of the register with 4 flip-flops. The registers may be identified by A_0, A_1, A_2, bits called address bits. This array of bits is known as *address*. From figure it may be noted that if the address is 001, the second register is chosen, and if the address is 111, 8th register is choosen and so on. As such, each register has an address which may be accessed by placing the address on the address lines.

Bits to be stored (written) into the addressed register are placed on the input terminals I_3, I_2, I_1, I_0. Now $\overline{WE}$ and $\overline{CS}$ are made low. This will ensure that inputs available on the output line I_0 .... I_3 will be written in to the register.

For retrieving information written into the register, the register is addressed, $\overline{WE} = 1$, $\overline{CS} = 0$.

In the memory we have chosen, it is possible to write words as also read words from it. These types of memories are regarded as a Read-Write memories. Also, by placing a suitable address on the address lines, any memory location may be chosen at random and thus this memory is known as a Random Access Memory (RAM).

15.7.2 Paralleling of the Memory Chips

In the previous example, we considered an IC chip having only a register and each register capable of storing only 4-bits. Now let us suppose that the number of registers available are inadequate and the number of bits per word also is insufficient. This situation may be remedied by the methods mentioned below:

Paralleling of chips: This increases the number of bits per word and is shown in Fig. 15.10. Two 4-bit/word chips have been connected to form 8-bit/word memory. However, the number of words remain same. The $\overline{CS}$ and $\overline{WE}$ terminals have been connected together so that both chips are selected together. Chip 1 stores least significant 4-bits and chip 2 stores the most significant 4-bits at the same address as single address is applied to both the chips. This procedure may be extended to form memories with more number of bits/word.

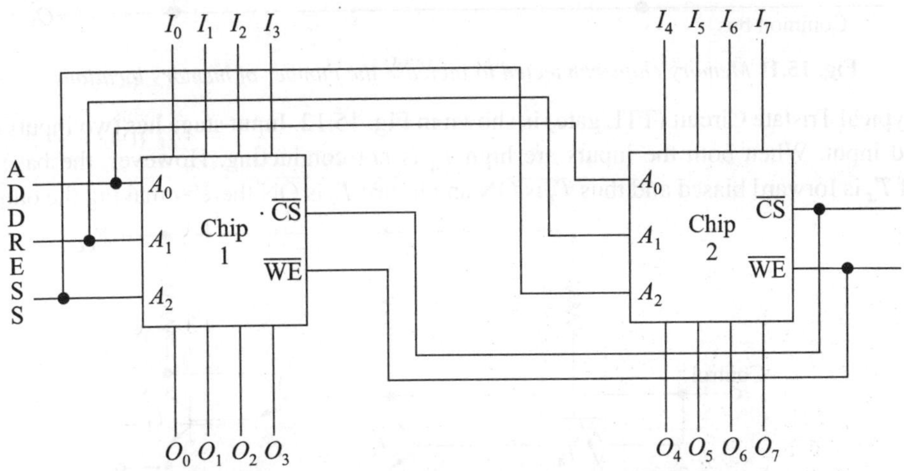

Fig. 15.10 *Memory chips connected to increase the word length*

Chips with organizations 256 × 1, 1024 × 1, 4096 × 1 are also available.

Two memory chips are connected as in Fig. 15.11 to increase the number of words keeping the number of bits/word fixed at four only.

As may be seen, address is applied to both the chips, But only one chip is made active at a time. When chip selector is low, chip 1 is selected and when chip selector is high, chip 2 is selected. As such, chip selector line is regarded as an additional address bit, called A_3. Thus when $A_3 = 0$, chip 1 is selected and $A_3 = 1$, chip 2 is selected. However, it may be noted that as the outputs of both chips are connected to the same line called the common bus (as the destination for both outputs may be same—a common bus is generally used), output of one chip will affect the output of the other directly causing 'Bus clash' (if Bit 00 = 0 of chip 1 and if Bit 00 = 1 of chip 2 there is a short circuit!). One way of avoiding this situation to disconnect the output from the common Bus (called Tristating the output) of the chip not selected. The common bus then can carry the output of the selected chip without interference from the other chip. Some chips are provided with Tristate outputs. If tristate outputs are not provided, external circuity should be added to make the outputs Tristate.

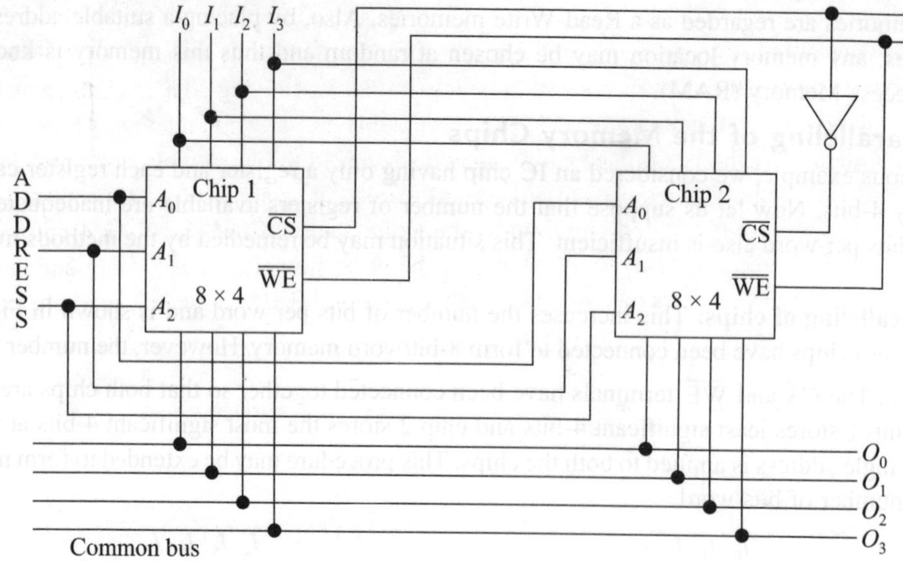

Fig. 15.11 *Memory chips connected to increase the number of memory locations*

A typical Tristate Circuit (TTL gate) is shown in Fig. 15.12. Input stage has two inputs called the control and input. When both the inputs are high T_4 is not conducting. However, the base collector junction of T_4 is forward biased and thus T_3 is ON and inturn T_2 is ON thereby making the output LOW.

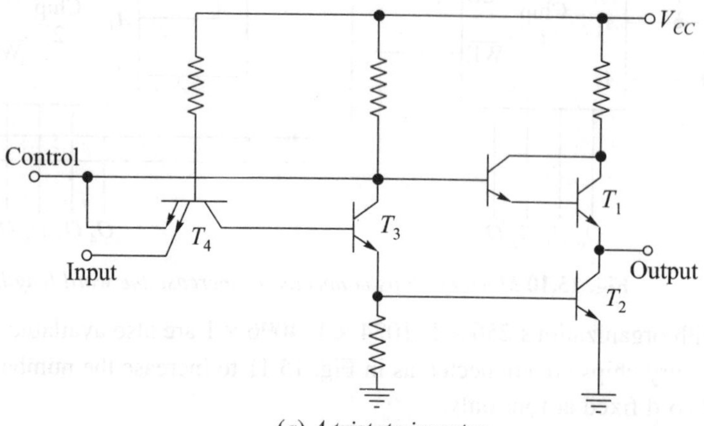

(a) *A tristate inverter*

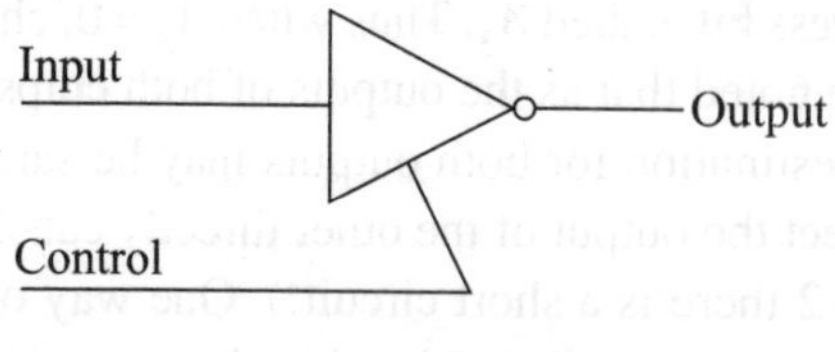

(b) *Symbolic diagram*

Input	Control	Output
0	0	
1	0	
0	1	1
1	1	0

(c) *Truth table*

Fig. 15.12

When control is High and input is Low, the base emitter junction of T_4 is biased and thus no current flows through the base of T_3. The Transistor T gets the required base drive and hence output is connected High.

When control is Low, irrespective of whether the input is 0 or 1, collector of T_3 is held Low, thereby neither T_1 or T_2 get the base drive and as such, output is 'floating'. This is known as the *High impedance state*. The symbolic diagram as also the Truth table are shown in the Figs. 15.12 (*b*) and (*c*).

The paralleling method explained earlier may be extended to more number of chips. Suppose a 32 word, 4-bit/word memory is required to address 32 words, 5 bits are required ($2^5 = 32$). As before, we have only 3 address bits applied common to the address bits of the chips. As 4 chips (of each 8 words) are required, the selection of the chip is to be done suitably using 2 more address bits A_3 and A_4. Now when we have 2 extra bits, we have 4 combinations, 00, 01, 11 and 10. As such, a decoding circuit (Fig. 15.13) is designed to do the job.

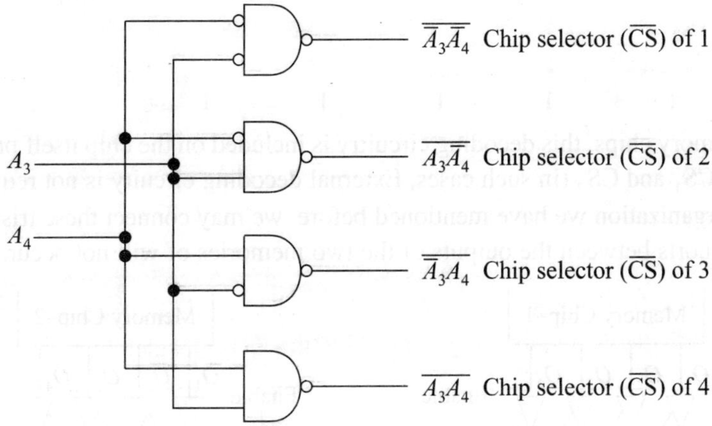

Fig. 15.13 *A decoder for chip selection*

Suitable outputs select the proper memories. For example, now the address bits are A_4, A_3, A_2, A_1, A_0 thereby making the address to vary as shown below:

A_4	A_3	A_2	A_1	A_0	
0	0	0	0	0	
0	0	0	0	1	
				.	
				.	chip 1
				.	
				.	
0	0	1	1	1	
0	1	0	0	0	
0	1	0	0	1	
				.	
				.	chip 2
				.	

0	1	1	1	1	
1	0	0	0	0	
1	0	0	0	1	
				⋮	chip 3
1	0	1	1	1	
1	1	0	0	0	
1	1	0	0	1	
				⋮	chip 4
1	1	1	1	1	

In many memory chips, this decoding circuitry is included on the chip itself providing A_3 and A_4 bits in the form of CS_1 and CS_2 (in such cases, External decoding circuity is not required).

In the bus organization we have mentioned before, we may connect these tristate switches as in Fig. 15.14 so that shorts between the outputs of the two memories of will not occur.

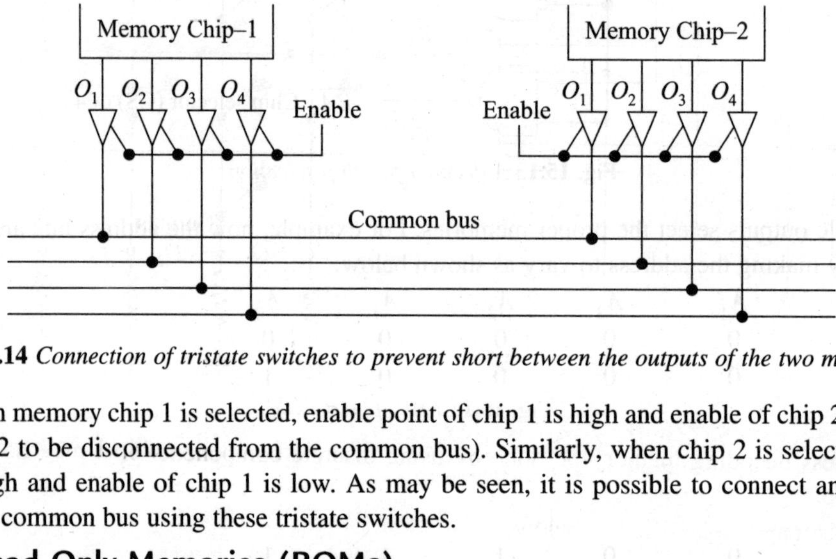

Fig. 15.14 *Connection of tristate switches to prevent short between the outputs of the two memories*

When memory chip 1 is selected, enable point of chip 1 is high and enable of chip 2 is low (This makes chip 2 to be disconnected from the common bus). Similarly, when chip 2 is selected enable of chip 2 is high and enable of chip 1 is low. As may be seen, it is possible to connect any number of devices to a common bus using these tristate switches.

15.7.3 Read Only Memories (ROMs)

Using the memory we have considered above, it is possible to Write information or Read information from the memory. However, in this section, we will discuss the kinds of memory which cannot be modified by a program. As such a ROM is a group registers which is required to store information which is not likely to be changed as often in a RAM.

It is worth nothing that the contents of the registers (Rows) cannot be changed when once we have introduced the diodes (of course by changing the diodes connected it is possible to do so!). It is only possible for us to read the memory and thus known as Read Only Memory (ROM).

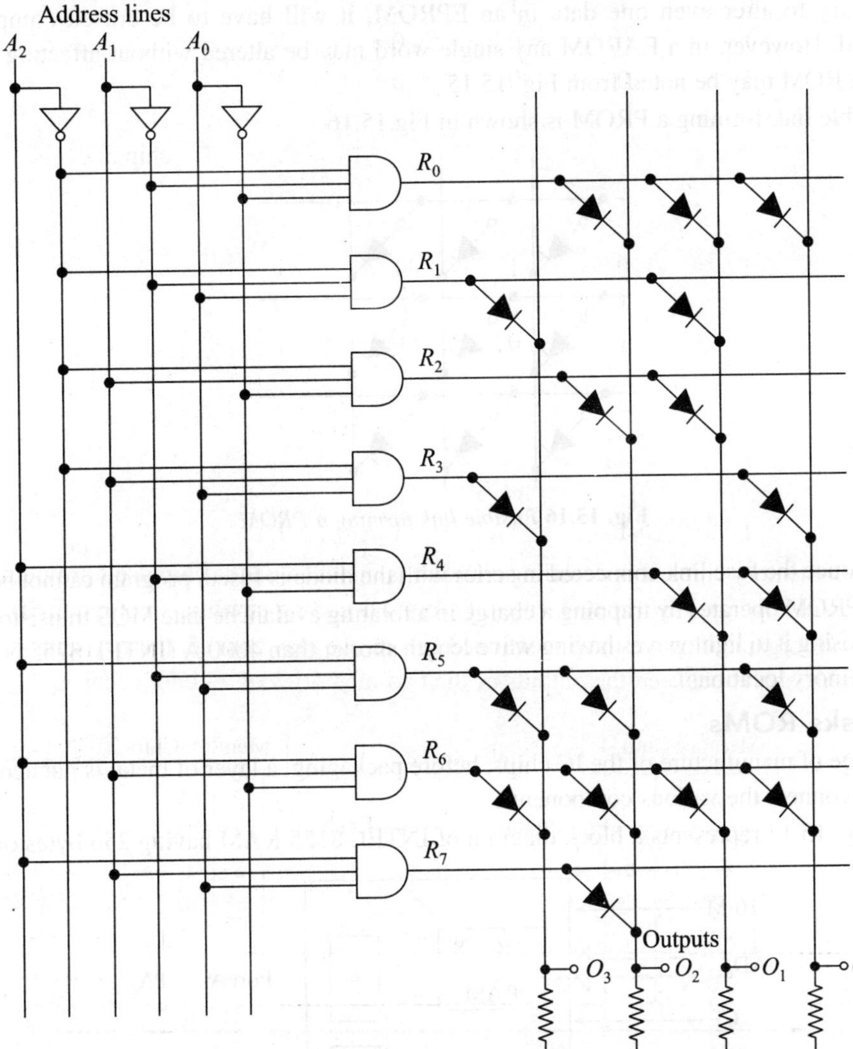

Fig. 15.15 *Principle of ROM*

Address decoding memory be done by using discrete components or it may be a part of the memory chip.

ROMs may be classified as below:

(*i*) Mask ROMs

(*ii*) PROMs

(*iii*) EPROMs

(*iv*) EAROMs.

There are two basic forms of PROM; the fusible link, which once programmed is permanent *i.e.*, it becomes a ROM. The ultraviolet erasable ROM (EPROM) can be erased by using an ultraviolet source. In such chips usually a glow window is provided in the chip.

In Electrically Alterable Read Only Memories (EAROM), data may be erased by applying a high voltage pulse to the programming pins. Advantages of the EAROM over that of EPROM is that when necessary to alter even one data in an EPROM, it will have to be erased completely and reprogrammed. However, in a EAROM any single word may be altered without affecting other data. Principle of a ROM may be noted from Fig. 15.15.

A fusible link forming a PROM is shown in Fig.15.16.

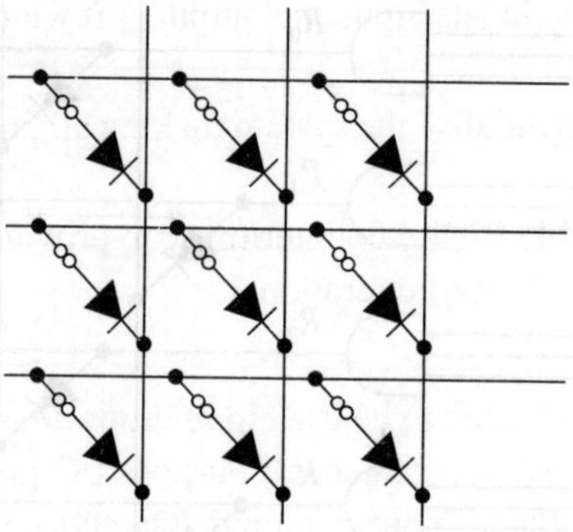

Fig. 15.16 *Fusible link forming a PROM*

When once the fuse link connected in series with the diode is fused, program cannot be changed.

The EPROM operates by trapping a charge in a folating avalanche gate MOS transistor. It can be erased by exposing it to light waves having wave length shorter than 4000 Å (INTEL 8755 is a EPROM of 2 K × 8 memory locations).

15.7.4 Masks ROMs

In the last stage of manufacture of the IC chips, before packaging, a layer of metal is put across the top of the chip to connect the various components.

The Fig. 15.17 represents a block diagram of INTEL 8155 RAM having 256 bytes of memory.

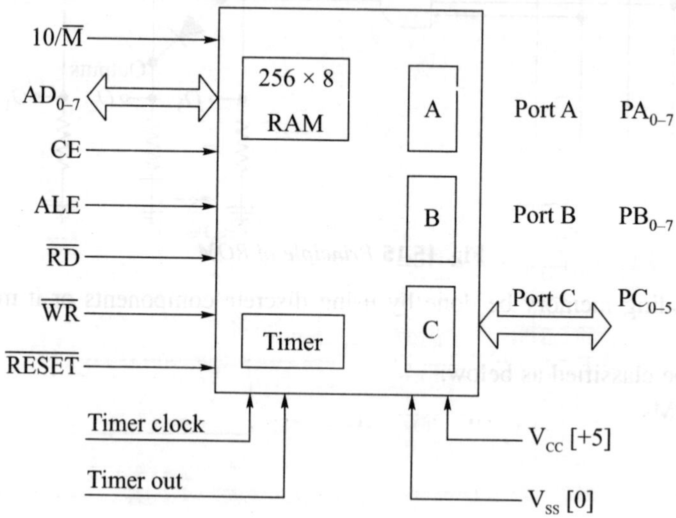

Fig. 15.17 *INTEL-8155 RAM*

There is a status register in the chip which can be programmed so that individual pins of port *A* (8-bits) and port *B* (8-bits) may function as output/input ports. This is known as each bit of ports programmable.

AD_{0-7} bus is used to address the memory as also the I/O ports, depending on IO/$\overline{M}$ line. If line goes high address is then to I/O ports, if this line goes low then the address is then to memory. Same address lines are also used for data transfer. If, say Information is to be written on to I/O then IO/$\overline{M}$ goes high, $\overline{WR}$ goes low. Similarly other operations may be carried out.

The 6th pin of port *C* can function as input and output port which also may be programmed using the command/status register.

A high on the reset pulse is to intialise the system making all ports inputs. CE is used for enabling the chip.

There is a 14-bit programmable Binary counter/timer to provide either a square wave or terminal count pulse for use in timing of any desired operation.

15.7.5 INTEL 8355 ROM

The INTEL 8355 is a ROM and an I/O chip to be used in microprocessor system. It is organized as 2048 words by 8-bits. The I/O portion consists of 2 general purpose I/O ports. Each I/O port has 8 lines and each line is individually programmable as input or output. The block diagram and the pin configuration of 8355 are shown in Fig. 10.21 (next chapter).

15.7.6 INTEL 8755 EPROM

This is a memory of 2048 × 8-bits, operation is similar to that of 8355 with additional characteristics that the memory can be erased and reprogrammed. Erasing may be carried out by exposing the chip to the ultraviolet light having wave length of 400 Å or shorter. The I/O portion consists of two general purpose I/O ports. Each I/O port has 8 lines, and each I/O port line is individually programmable as input or output. The block diagram and the pin configuration of 8755 are shown in Fig. 15.18.

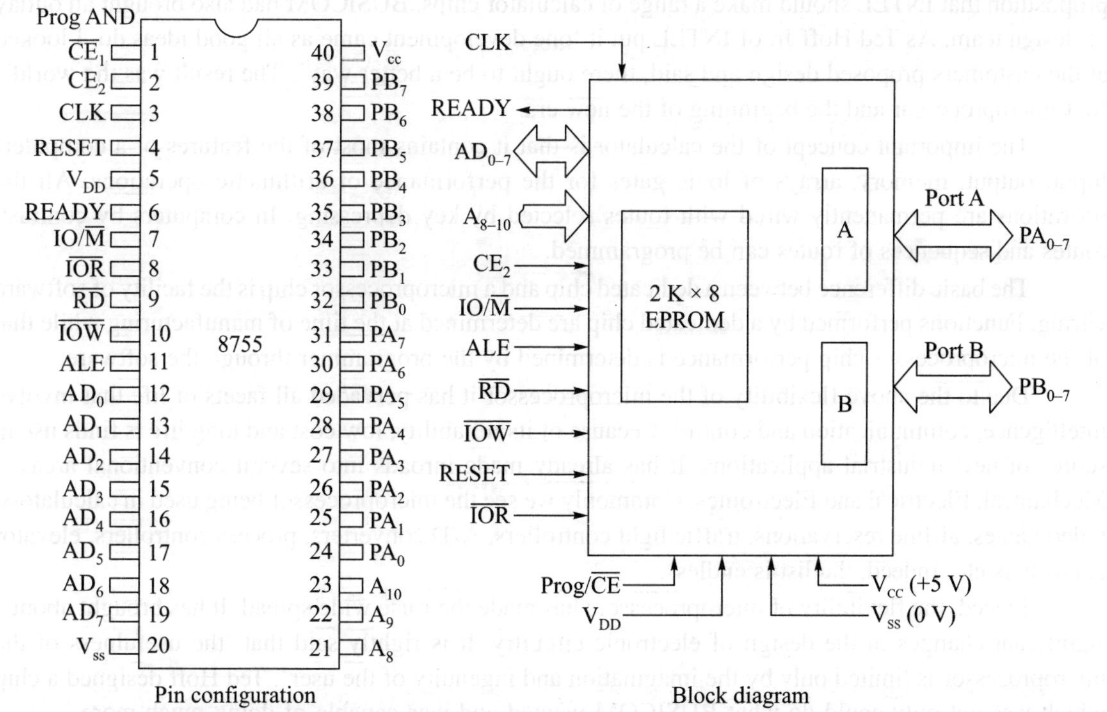

Fig. 15.18 *Pin configuration and block diagram of 8755 EPROM*

Microprocessor and Programming Applications

16

CHAPTER

16.1 INTRODUCTION

The two major contributions of the seventies were the invention of semiconductor memories and the single chip calculator. Although, many stake their claim regarding these inventions, it may be futile to try the identify the inventor. Although several companies *viz.*, Texas Instruments, National Semiconductor, Mostek and Fairchild were the pioneers, Fairchild company was particularly prominent.

In the year 1968, Robert Noyce, Gordan Moore and Andrew Grove left Fairchild to start a new firm, INTEL, for the purpose of making semiconductor memories. The then state-of-the-art was a single chip of 1024 bits of memory. INTEL's products were quite successful due to their good manufacturing techniques and technical support.

In the year 1969, a Japanese calculator company called BUSICOM approached INTEL with the proposition that INTEL should make a range of calculator chips. BUSICOM had also brought an outlay of design team. As Ted Hoff Jr. of INTEL put it 'one development came as all good ideas do. I looked at the customers proposed design and said, there ought to be a better way'. The result was the world's first microprocessor and the beginning of the new era.

The important concept of the calculator is that it contains most of the features of a computer-input, output, memory, arrays of logic gates for the performance of arithmetic operations. All the operations are permanently wired with routes selected by key depressing. In computers by contrast, routes and sequences of routes can be programmed.

The basic difference between a dedicated chip and a microprocessor chip is the facility of software wiring. Functions performed by a dedicated chip are determined at the time of manufacturing while that of the microprocessor chip performance is determined by the programmer through the software.

Due to the above flexibility of the microprocessor it has pervaded all facets of life that involve intelligence, communication and control. Because of its reliability, low cost and long life is finds use in scores of new industrial applications. It has already made inroads into several conventional areas—Mechanical, Electrical and Electronics. Commonly we see the microprocessor being used in calculators, video games, airline reservations, traffic light controllers, A/D converters, process controllers, elevator controllers etc. Indeed, the list is endless.

Indeed, the flexibility of microprocessors has made their use wide spread. It has brought about a significant changes in the design of electronic circuitry. It is rightly said that 'the usefulness of the microprocessor is limited only by the imagination and ingenuity of the user'. Ted Hoff designed a chip which was not only could do what BUSICOM wanted and was capable of doing much more .... !

He came out with the first world's programmable chip 4004 and announced it on 15th November, 1971. This was then called the 'microprogrammable computer on a chip'. The word 'microprocessor' did not come until 1972.

The 4004 was capable of processing 'words' of 4-bit length and contained a 4-bit parallel adder, sixteen, 4-bit registers, an accumulator and a push-down stack (on a single chip). 4004 along with ROM, RAM and shift register chips comprised the MCS-4 microcomputer system. It is interesting to note that the chip 4004 contained 2300 devices-a-density which was twice that of calculator chips of that time.

Although enough software was not supported by INTEL for the 4004 chip, being an entreprenurial firm, a device operating on 8-bit *viz.*, 8008 microprocessor was made public by INTEL in April, 1972.

Microprocessor considered as the standard first generation microprocessor was followed by 8080 the next year (1973).

To look back, the first computer was built in 1946, the ENIAC calculating machine used more than 18,000 vacuum tubes and occupied a very large space!

In 1960's transistors replaced vacuum tubes and ushered in the practical computing. Later, integrated circuits (example—an inverter circuit or a NAND circuit) were evolved. This technology of fabrication known as small scale integration (SSI) made computing faster and more reliable and compact. As the integrated circuit technology grew, medium scale integration (MSI) ICs like counters, adders etc., were used in fabricating the computer. In any conventional digital circuit, we have these SSI and MSI chips. Indeed, during the last two decades, semiconductor technology has gone through revolutionary changes thereby contributing to the growth of computer technology. As such, now we have the large scale integration (LSI) and very large scale integration (VLSI) chips using metal oxide semiconductor technology (MOS). On a single silicon chip, thousands of transistors are fabricated and connected suitably to perform the required task. This has brought the computer on a single chip, a reality thereby making use of less external connections and as such, making the system more reliable.

Following INTEL's introduction of the microprocessor, many companies have brought microprocessors into the market. List below shows some of the typical microprocessors and companies marketing them with some of their typical details.

Because of these wide variations, it is very hard to deal with all microprocessors. However, all processors will have some general features. Thus, as a representative of all these processors, Intels 8085 will be studied here. With the knowledge of 8085, the reader will not find it difficult to understand other microprocessors.

When learning about any microprocessor, it is necessary to study the following:

(*a*) Microprocessor architecture,

(*b*) Instruction set,

(*c*) Minimal system,

(*d*) Control signals and

(*e*) Pin functions.

Each of these would be studied in the coming sections with reference to 8080/8085.

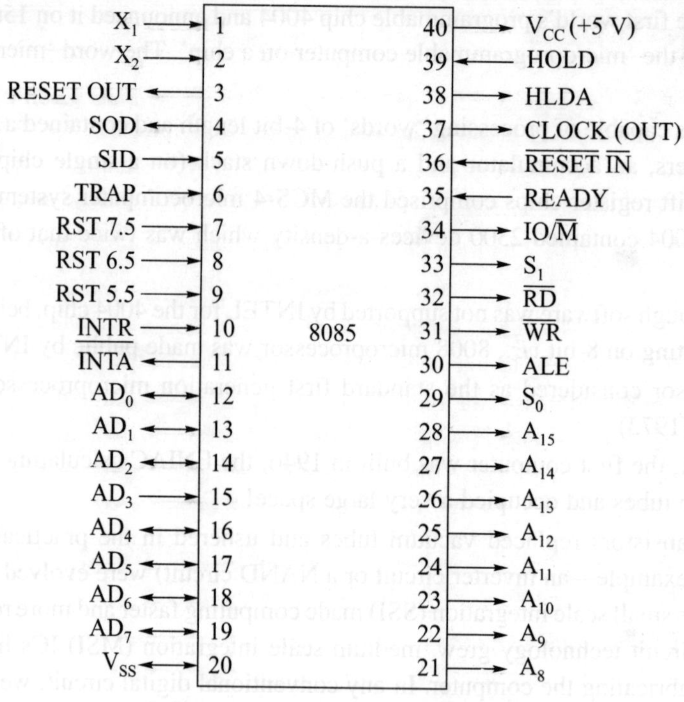

Fig. 16.1 *Pin diagram of 8085 µPU*

Table 16.1

Sl. No.	*Company*	*Name of Microprocessor*	*No. of data bit*	*No. of pins*	*No. of instructions*
1.	Fairchild	F8	8	40	70
2.	National Semiconductor	SC/MP	8	40	46
3.	INTEL	8080A	8	40	91
4.	Zilog	Z80	8	40	155
5.	Motorola	MC-6800	8	40	96
6.	Rockwell	PPS-8	8	42	105
7.	Signetics	2650	8	40	75
8.	Intensil	IM6100	12	40	63
9.	National Semiconductors	PACE	16	40	45
10.	General instruments	CPI 1600	16	40	66
11.	Texas instruments	TMS 9900	16	64	69
12.	Data General Corporation	Micronova	16	40	42
13.	INTEL	8085	8	40	95
14.	Zilog	Z-800	16	18	40
15.	INTEL	8086	16	40	93
16.	MOTOROLA	68000	16	64	61

16.2 8085 PIN DETAILS

Figure 16.1 shows the 8085 pin diagram. This is an 8-bit microprocessor housed on a 40-pin dual-in-line package (DIP). Manufacturers give the details of the pin descriptions. 8085 is an enhanced version of 8080. The instruction set of 8085 is similar to that of 8080. 8085 operates on a single power supply. It has a clock, system control and interrupt prioritization. In this sense, 8085 is a CPU on a single chip. This CPU is being augmented by memory and I/O chips to make a microcomputer system.

BUS: Address bus is 16-bit wide (A_{15}–A_8 [pins 21 to 28]) {upper byte} and AD_7–AD_0 [pins 12 to 19] {lower byte}. Indeed, AD_7–AD_0 functions as the lower byte of the address during some states and as the data bus (8-bit wide) during some other states. This is the reason for representing it as AD_0–AD_7 meaning thereby address-data lines. This mode of using the same pins for different purposes at different timings is known as *multiplexing*. Multiplexing is used as the number of pins that could be brought out is limited to 40. To indicate to the peripherals when data/address line is sending address and the instance when it is sent, ALE (pin 30)-address latch enable is used.

CLOCK: (Pins 1-2) A crystal need be connected across these two pins. The minimum frequency of the crystal is 6 MHz. The operating frequency is then 3 MHz.

RESET OUT and $\overline{\textbf{RESETIN}}$: (pin 3, pin 36) When pin 3 is high, the CPU is reset. This signal goes to peripheral chips, thereby resetting the peripheral chips also. When this line goes low, processing starts. When pin 36 is low, CPU resets the registers. It sends a high to pin 3. CPU remains reset until RESET IN goes high.

CLOCK OUT: (pin 37) CLK signal goes to peripheral chips and synchronises their timings.

SOD and SID: (pins 4 and 5) Serial output data line can be set to '1' or '0' through certain instructions in the program. It is possible to transmit serial data using this pin to serial output devices such as teletape, serial printer, CRT terminals etc. Serial input data (say from keyboard, teletape, CRT etc.), may be sensed by a program using this pin.

TRAP, RST 7.5, 6.5, 5.5, $\overline{\textbf{INTA}}$ and INTA: (pins 6-11) Interrupt is to draw the attention of the CPU to service a request, after attending this, the CPU can continue with the previous job. Interrupts are by priorities. Trap has the highest priority and RST 5.5 the least. INTR is a general purpose interrupt. This has lower priority than RST 5.5. Infact the INTR interrupt jumps to an address dictated by a special instruction received from a peripheral device when the MPU's interrupt acknowledge ($\overline{\textbf{INTA}}$) output is activated.

Vss and Vcc: (pins 20 and 40) Pin 20 is the system ground and pin 40 is supply point 5 V ± 5%.

IO/$\overline{\textbf{M}}$, S_0 and S_1: (pins 34, 29 and 33) These are control signals indicating the peripherals, the type of job the MPU is doing. The table below indicates the combination.

$\overline{\textbf{WR}}$ and $\overline{\textbf{RD}}$: (pins 31 and 32) These indicate whether a write or a read is done. A low $\overline{\textbf{WR}}$ means a write operation and a low $\overline{\textbf{RD}}$ means a read operation.

$IO/\overline{M}$	S_1	S_0	Status
0	0	1	Memory write
0	1	0	Memory read
1	0	1	I/O Write
1	1	0	I/O Read
0	1	1	OP Code fetch
1	1	1	Interrupt acknowledge
*	0	0	Halt
*	*x*	*x*	Hold
*	*x*	*x*	Reset
* = Tristate condition.			*x* = unspecified.

READY: (pin 35) When the printer is not yet ready to print the data this peripheral sends a low input to the 'Ready' pin indicating the μPU that the peripheral device is not yet ready to accept the data. This will make the μPU to ensure wait status. Eventually when the printer is ready, it sends a high ready signal indicating that MPU can compile the data transfer.

HLDA and HOLD: (pin 38 and 39) A high Hold is an indication to the CPU that some other device is in need of the address and data buses. Upon receiving the Hold high, CPU compiles the current data transfers on the buses. Now no read or write operation will be done by the CPU by making $IO/\overline{M}$, S_1 and S_0 tristated. Now HLDA goes high indicating the peripheral that the busses will be given to it in the clock cycle.

16.3 ARCHITECTURE

Figure 16.2 shows the architecture of 8085 microprocessor. The 8-bit internal data bus carries instructions and data between the CPU registers.

Accumulator (Acc) is an 8-bit register connected to the internal data bus as shown in figure. During any arithmetic or logic operations, one of the operands will be in the accumulator. After the operation, the result is also contained in the accumulator itself. For example, during subtraction, the minuend is in the accumulator. The other operand viz. subtrahend may be either in the memory or in any of the other registers. In such an event, memory or register contents are copied to the temporary register during one T state and added to the contents of the accumulator during the next T state. After the subtraction operation, the result is stored in the accumulator. It is the only register used to transfer data between the microprocessor and I/O devices.

As explained above, accumulator is rightly known as the center of all activities of the microprocessor.

In addition there are six (8-bit) general purpose registers B, C, D, E, H and L. These registers may be used either individually (as 8-bit registers) or in pairs (as 16-bit registers). When they are used in pairs only combinations BC, DE and HL are allowed.

Program counter (PC) is a 16-bit register which keeps track of the address of the instructions that are to be executed. Contents of program counter are updated automatically during execution.

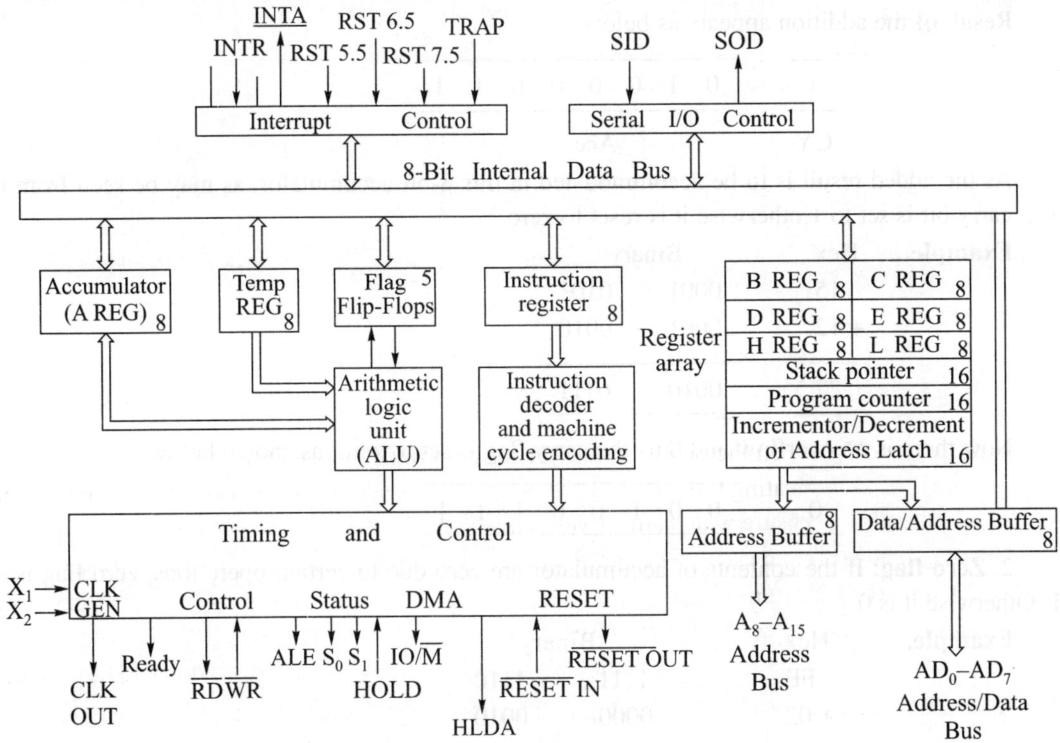

Fig. 16.2 *Functional block diagram of 8085 μPU*

A portion in the memory is generally reserved for storing some information which is to be used at a later point of time during execution. This portion of memory is usually known as a *stack*. The address of this location (16-bit wide) is pointed by a register called the *stack pointer*.

A set of flip-flops serve as condition flags. Depending on whether it is set/reset, the following conditions are indicated.

Contents of the flag register is in the format shown in Fig. 16.3.

D7	D6	D5	D4	D3	D2	D1	D0
S	Z		AC		P		CY

Fig. 16.3 *Flag configuration*

1. **Carry flag (CY):** Whenever there is an overflow of the accumulator due to an arithmetic operation the carry flag is set.

Example.	Hex	Binary	
	52	0101	0010
	+ F1	1111	0001
	143	1 0100	0011

Result of the addition appears as below:

1	0 1 0 0 0 0 1 1
CY	Acc

As the added result is to be accommodated in this 8-bit accumulator, as may be seen from the above, carry bit is set to 1 otherwise it is reset to zero.

Example.

Hex	Binary	
15	0001	0101
+ 12	0001	0010
27	0010	0111

Now there is no overflow and thus the carry flag is set to zero, as shown below.

0	0 0 1 0 0 1 1 1

2. **Zero flag:** If the contents of accumulator are zero due to certain operations, zero flag is set to 1. Otherwise it is 0.

Example.

Hex	Binary	
FE	1111	1110
+ 02	0000	0010
100	1 0000	0000

Now as accumulator contents are zero, the zero flag is set to 1. Indeed the carry flag is also set to '1' in this example as below:

1	1	0 0 0 0 0 0 0 0
Z	CY	Acc

3. **Auxiliary flag (AC):** If there is an overflow out of bit 3 of the accumulator similar to that of the overflow from bit 7, the AC flag is set.

Example.

Hex	Binary	
IF	0001	1111
+ 22	0010	0010
41	0100	0001

Contents of the acummulator and the flags are as below:

1	0 1 0 0 0 0 0 1

4. **Parity flag (P):** If the total number of 1s in the accumulator is odd, (after operations involving accumulator) parity bit is reset. If the total number of 1s in the accumulator is even, parity is even, parity bit is set to 1.

Example.	Hex	Binary
	04	0000 0100
	+ 24	0010 0100
	28	0010 1000

Accumulator has two numbers of 1s and hence parity bit is set to 1.

P	Acc
1	0 0 1 0 1 0 0 0

5. **Sign bit (S):** If an operation makes the 7th bit of the accumulator 1, the sign flag is set to '1'. Contents of the flag and accumulator are as below:

S	Acc
1	1 0 0 0 0 0 1 0

At this point, it is to be noted that flags are not affected after the execution of all instructions. For example,

we have MVI A, 00

which means that all bits of the accumulator become zero, but 'zero' flag is not affected. As such, to know which of the flags would be affected and after what operation, it is required to understand whether the accumulator is actively involved in the operation.

16.3.1 Address/Data Buffer

These are two 8-bit registers to which the content of stack pointer or program counter can be loaded. The external address bus and the address/data bus is driven by these buffers.

Whenever there is an OP code fetch, this is stored in the 8-bit instruction register. Contents of this register are available to the instruction decoder. The output of the decoder and the internal clock produce the machine cycle timings.

Timing and control section has a control sequence and an oscillator of synchronise all registers. The controller-sequencer has a ROM that stores all the micro routines needed for executing the instructions. When the instruction is fetched and decoded by the MPU, the starting address of the micro routine corresponding to the instruction is obtained and read out from the ROM. Suitable control signals are now sent to the buses.

The incrementer/decrementer can add 1 or subtract 1 from the contents of the stack pointer or program counter. Interrupt control, SID and SOD have been explained earlier.

16.4 INSTRUCTION FORMATS AND SET

No matter how sophisticated a computer is, it can do only what it is told to do. The inputs that cause the computer to perform specified actions are called instructions. A sequence of instructions each of which is recognised by computer and causes it to perform an operation is known as a *program*. Collection of

CHAPTER 16

instructions that the computer is capable of recognising is known as instruction set. Once stored and accessible to the CPU the sequence of instructions may be run any number of times to get the desired result. As we have already seen in the stored program concept, CPU receives data and instructions in the same form (one byte at a time). Difference being that the instruction is decoded in the instruction register and the data is sent to the registers or the ALU directly.

Although it is common to use single and two address instructions in microcomputers, there are other formats for instructions as well and are discussed below:

Any instruction is to contain the following information.

1. The operation to be performed.

   Example. If instructions are written as MVI

   ADD

   MOV

   It is necessary that the CPU should know the meaning of these so that it may generate the required timings for the execution of these instructions.

2. Operation to be performed on what data? This is known as the operand. The source of data is also to be given. There may be a single operand or two operands depending on the operation to be performed.

   Example. ADD instruction requires only one operand.

3. When once the operation is performed on the operands, results are to be stored in some locations.

4. When the above sequence is completed (executed), the next sequence is to start. As such, the next address of the instruction is to be specified.

   The format is as below:

Operation code	Address of Operand–1	Address of Operand–2	Address of Results	Address of Next Instruction

The number of bits required to handle this type of format would be quite high.

Example. If the OP code is 8 bits long, each of the address is 16 bits long (2^{16} = 64 k bytes of memory), each instruction format requires $8 + (16 \times 4) = 72$ bits long. Obviously, it is extremely difficult to handle so many number of bits in a microcomputer where the word length is 8 bits only.

In a microprocessor system where the memory size is of considerable importance, this format is not well suited. As such, several other methods have been devised for this purpose.

The first step in this direction is to ensure that the address of the next instruction to be executed is stored in a counter called the program counter PC. The CPU increments this counter after the instruction is executed and as such, the instruction is fetched automatically (Thus, to a certain extent the flexibility is lost as the instruction/data have to be stored in consecutive memory locations). This format is called the three-address instruction and the format is as shown below:

Operation Code	Address of Operand–1	Address of Operand–1	Address of Results

Even this type of instruction format requires a large memory. With 16-bit address as before, memory requirement for each instruction is $8 + (16 \times 3) = 56$ bits.

However, if the results may be stored in one of the operand addresses after the execution, then the address of results in the above format is not required thereby making the instruction format to look as below.

Operation Code	Address of Operand–1	Address of Results	Address of Operand–2

Further saving in memory may be made by using the accumulator as a combined source and destination location. The instruction format is as shown below:

Operation Code	Address of Operand

Example. ADD C, the meaning of this instruction is : Add the contents of the accumulator to the contents of the C register and store the results in the accumulator. From this, it may be noted that the original contents of the accumulator are being replaced by the result of addition. If the original contents of accumulator are to be saved, it is required to use other register memory.

16.4.1 Addressing Modes

Various methods of addressing are used for the following reasons:

– should be as fast as possible.

– should be as simple as possible.

– should be in a position to change the addresses without changing instructions.

– should provide easy access to large areas of memory.

Instructions can be 1, 2 or 3 bytes in length. As mentioned earlier, instructions (indicated by appropriate OP codes) are to operate on data/address (operands). These data/address may be located either in memory or in the internal registers of the CPU. In these cases there are four ways in which the location of these operands may be specified pertaining to the OP codes.

– Implied addressing

– Register addressing

– Immediate addressing

– Direct addressing

– Register indirect addressing.

16.4.1.1 Implied Addressing

Functions is implied by the instruction itself.

Example. CMA (Hex code – 2 F) means complement the accumulator

No flags are affected OP code ← Format

other examples being STC, RAR, RAL etc.

CHAPTER 16

16.4.1.2 Register Addressing

Operation and the operands source are specified.

Example. ADD C (Hex code - 81)
(mnemonic) (operand)

As we have already noted in the architecture of 8085, C register will be copied to the temporary register which is one of the inputs to the ALU. The other input to the ALU is form the accumulator. As such, the contents of the accumulator being added to the contents of the C register, result being stored in the accumulator. Z and CY flags are affected. Symbolically the above operation may be written as (A) ← (A) + (C)

[(*A*) means contents of the A register, (C) means contents of the C register etc.]

OP code	← Format

Other example are MOV A, B; CMP B; ADD B etc.

16.4.1.3 Immediate Addressing

Immediately following the OP code, data is specified.

Example. SUI 05 (Hex code is D6)
(mnemonic) (operand)

Operand 05 is the input to the temporary register. Now the inputs to the ALU being the contents of accumulator and 05. Symbolically, the operation is written as

(A) ⟵ (A) – 05 CY and Z flags are affected.

OP code	
Data	← Format

16.4.1.4 Direct Addressing

Following the OP code, the address of the operand in memory is mentioned.

Example. STA (Address) (Hex code 32)
(OP code)

Contents of the accumulator will be stored in the address.

```
MVI   A, FF
STA   2000
```

After the execution of first instruction, contents of the accumulator are FF. Location 2000 contains FF after the execution of the second instruction. Flags are not affected.

OP Code	
Lower byte address	← Format
Higher byte address	

Other examples are LDA 2040, JPM 2050, CALL 1020 etc.

16.4.1.5 Register Indirect Addressing

Only the OP code will be written. These instructions make memory reference using the contents of a register pair to point to the address of the operand.

Example.

	LXI	H, 2000
	MVI	A, 01
	ADD	M
	2040	03

Memory pointer (the H-L pair) is pointing to 2040 (location). Contents of 2040 are 03. Accumulator contains 01. As such, when ADD M is executed, 03 will be added to 01 and the result 04 is in the accumulator.

Symbolically (A) ← (A) + [(H) (L)]

Z and CY flags are affected

OP Code ← Format

Other examples are SUB M, MOV M, A, MOV M, B etc.

16.4.2 Instruction Set of 8080/8085

Microcomputers operate on the stored program concept. The program is stored in the program memory.

INTEL corporation groups the 8085 instructions functionally into the following categories:

- Data transfer group
- Arithmetic group
- Logic group
- Branch group
- Stack, I/O and machine control group.

Data transfer group instructions move data between registers or between memory and registers.

Arithmetic group instructions perform add, subtract, increment or decrement of data in registers or in memory.

Logical group instructions include AND, OR, Exclusive – OR, Compare, Rotate, Complement data in registers or in memory.

Branch group instructions contain conditional and unconditional jump instructions, subroutine CALL and return instructions.

Stack, I/O and machine control group includes I/O instructions, as well as instructions for maintaining the stack and internal control flags.

Meaning and abbreviations for maintaining the stack and internal control flags.

Meaning and abbreviations used in the following disciplines of the mnemonics is from INTEL User's Manual.

Various instructions (in the form of mnemonics) available are given by the supplier of the CPU. They also give the corresponding operation codes. As such, after writing the program using mnemonics, it is possible to hand code the program using the tables of the supplier.

The typical instruction set of 8085 is given in Table 16.1.

16.5 MINIMUM SYSTEM

When 8085 is augmented by two more chips *viz.* 8156 and 8355, we get the minimum system as shown in Fig. 16.4. We have already seen the pinout details as also the architecture of 8085. We now see the details of 8156 and 8355.

8156 is a (256 × 8) RAM. 8156 has also three I/O ports which can be programmed to act as input or output ports. Address/data of this could vary from

0000 0000 to 1111 1111

(only 8 lines are provided for address/data lines as it has $2^8 = 256$ memory locations to be addressed).

When ALE goes from high to low, address is latched to 8156. Chip enable CE is connected to A13 and thus, 8156 is enabled only when A13 is high.

8355 is a (2K × 8) ROM. 11 address lines are provided to this as the address-ability need be ($2^{11} = 2048$) 2K locations. This chip has two chip enable pins CE_1 and CE_2. CE_2 is connected to high (to a 5 V supply). $\overline{CE_1}$ is connected to A_{11}. Only when this line A11 goes low, ROM is enabled (complement to enabling RAM). While this address is being loaded to 8355, Ready pin of 8355 is low. When loading is over, Ready pin goes high.

ROM is enabled for the following addresses:

0000 0000 0000 0000
to 0000 0111 1111 1111 (0000 to 07FF)

RAM is enabled for the following addresses:

0000 1000 0000 0000
to 0000 1000 1111 1111 (0800 to 08FF)

Indeed, ROM address could have been

XXXX 0000 0000 0000
to XXXX 0111 1111 1111

Where 'X' indicates don't cares.

When don't cares are zeros, address is

0000 0000 0000 0000
to 0000 0111 1111 1111 (0000 to 07FF)

If A_{12} is high, then the ROM memory locations could be

0001 0000 0000 0000
to 0000 0111 1111 1111 (1000 to 17FF)

(this is known as the shadow)

Also A_{13} could be high, thereby yielding

0010 0000 0000 0000
to 0010 0111 1111 1111

Similar shadows could be got (15 shadows).

Similarly, RAM shadows also may be got

XXXX 1XXX 0000 0000
XXXX 1XXX 1111 1111

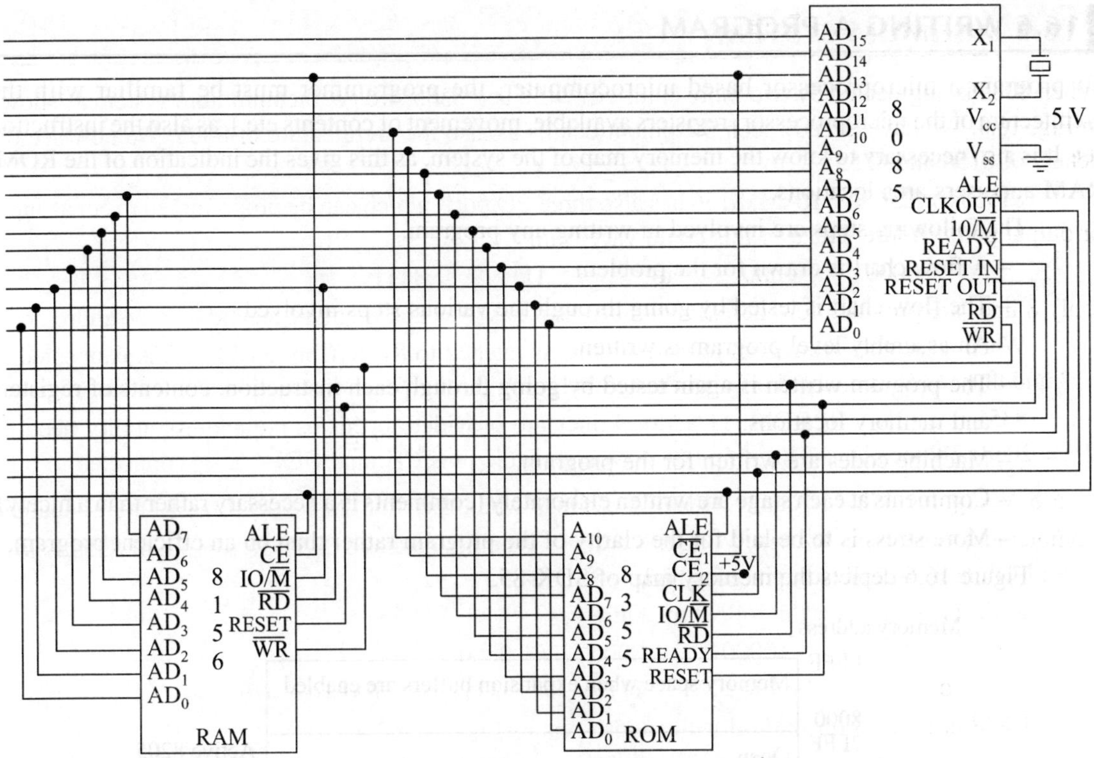

Fig. 16.4 *Minimal system*

This is equivalent to

0800 – 08FF

0900 – 09FF

0A00 – 0AFF

Generally the lowest ROM and RAM ranges are used and in this example it is

0000 – 07FF

and 0800 – 08FF

A typical memory map is shown in Fig. 16.5 where the ROM occupies the top most area. Next is the users and finally the stack.

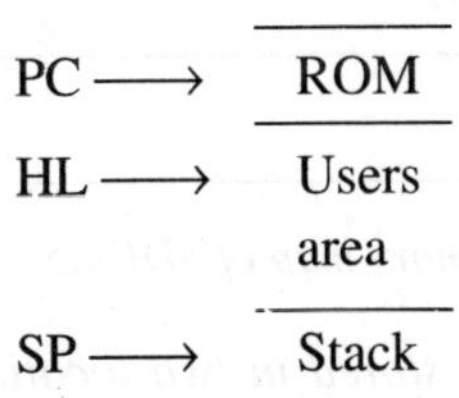

Fig. 16.5 *Memory map*

PC keeps track of the location of the next instruction to be executed and thus, PC will be pointed to ROM. Users area is accessible through the memory pointer (HL). Stack pointer is always pointing to the top of the stack.

CHAPTER 16

16.6 WRITING A PROGRAM

To program a microprocessor based microcomputer, the programmer must be familiar with the architecture of the microprocessor (registers available, movement of contents etc.), as also the instruction set. It is also necessary to know the memory map of the system, as this gives the indication of the ROM, RAM and users area locations.

The following steps are involved in writing any program.

- A flow chart is drawn for the problem.
- The flow chart is tested by going through the various steps involved.
- An assembly level program is written.
- The program written is again tested by going through each instruction, contents of registers and memory locations.
- Machine codes are written for the program.
- Comments at each stage are written elaborately (comments is a necessary rather than a nicety).
- More stress is to be laid for the clarity of the program rather than on an efficient program.

Figure 16.6 depicts the memory map of SDK-85.

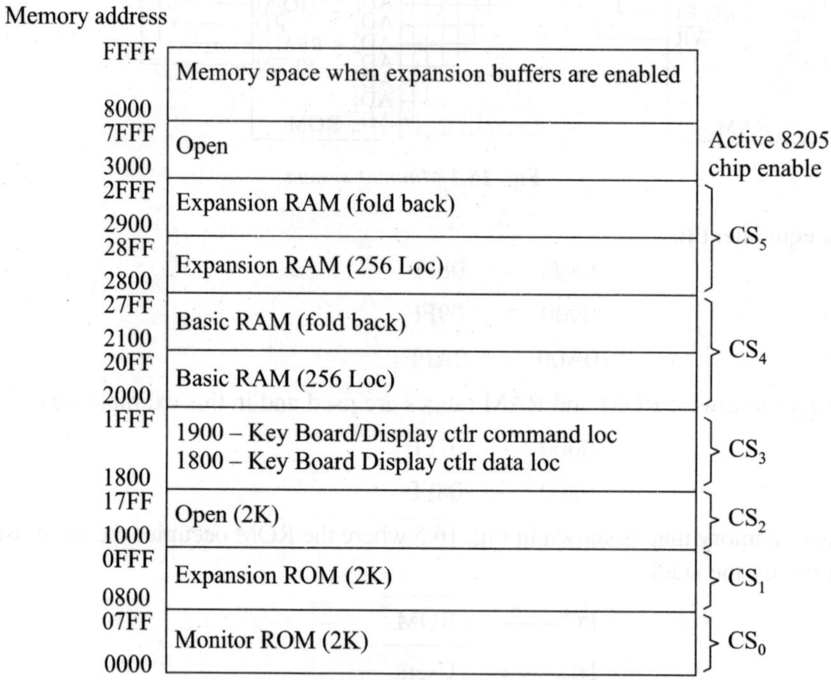

Fig. 16.6 *Memory map of SDK-85*

Example 16.1. *Let us add two numbers stored in two locations 2000 and 2001 and store the results in location 2002.*

Solution. A flow chart is written as shown in Fig. 16.7 (*a*).

Now we write the program as below:

Address (Hex)	*Contents (Hex)*	*Label*	*Mnemonic*	*Operand*	*Comments*
2010	21		LXI	H, 2000	Load HL pair with the address where the first data is present.
2011	00				
2012	20				
2013	76		MOV	A, M	As the centre of activity is 'A' register move the first data to A.
2014	23		INX	H	HL points to 2001
2015	86		ADD	M	(A) ⟵ (A) + (2001)
2016	23		INX	H	HL points to 2002
2017	77		MOV	M, A	Store accumulator contents in 2002 (answer)
2018	CF		RST	1	Return to monitor

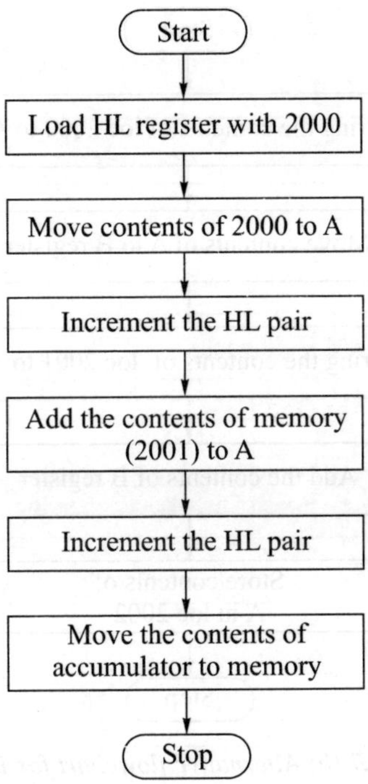

Fig. 16.7 (*a*) *Flowchart for Ex.16.1*

An alternative solution to the above program is shown in Fig. 16.7 (*b*). The corresponding program is also shown.

Address (Hex)	*Contents (Hex)*	*Label*	*Mnemonic*	*Operand*	*Comments*
2010	3A		LDA	2000	Load the 'A'
2011	00				register with
2012	20				contents of 2000
2013	47		MOV	B, A	Store the acc. contents in B
2014	23		LDA	2001	Load the 'A'
2015	01				register with
2016	20				contents of 2001
2017	80		ADD	B	(A) ⟵ (B) + (A)
2018	32		STA	2002	Store contents
2019	02				of 'A' register
201A	20				in 2002
201B	CF		RST	1	Return to monitor

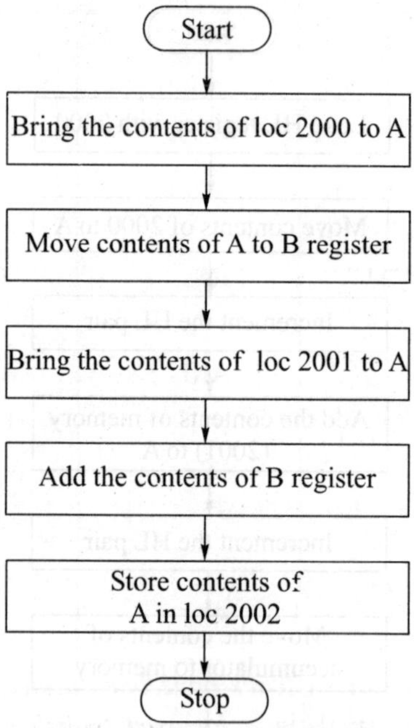

Fig. 16.7 (*b*) *Alternative flowchart for Ex.16.1*

Example 16.2. *A mechanical switch is attached to bit 0 of port 0.*

Write a program to wait for a switch closure. If the switch is closed let the control be returned to monitor (switch closed = 0, open = 1).

Figure 16.8 gives the flow chart. The program listing is also given below.

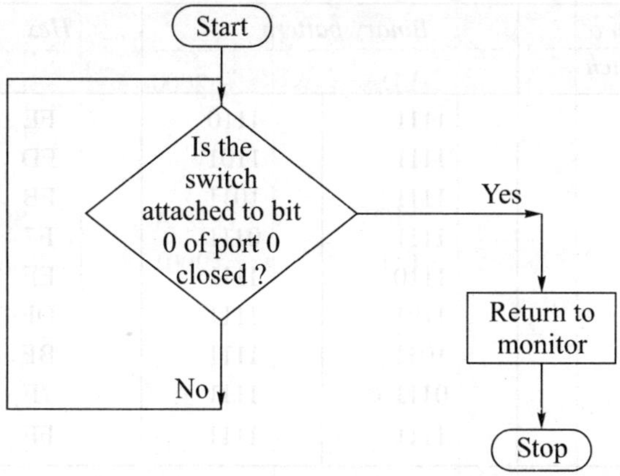

Fig. 16.8 *Flowchart for Ex. 16.2*

Address (Hex)	*Contents (Hex)*	*Label*	*Mnemonic*	*Operand*	*Comments*
2000	3E		MVI	A, 00	Clean ACC
2001	00				
2002	D3		OUT	02	Make all bits of
2003	02				port 00 to 8355
					as input port.
2004	DB	WAIT	IN	00	Get the state of
2005	00				the input switches
2006	E6		ANI	(01)	Isolate bit 1
2007	01			hex	
2008	C2		JNZ	WAIT	Is switch closed?
2009	04				
200A	20				No wait
200B	CF		RST	1	Return to monitor

Example 16.3. *Eight mechanical switches have been attached to the port 00. One switch is closed at a time. It is necessary to identify the switch closed. Switch attached to 0th bit is the 0th switch. Switch attached to 1st bit is the 1st switch etc.*

Binary patterns available at the input port for various switch closures are as given below:

Bit position of closed switch	*Binary pattern*		*Hex*
0	1111	1110	FE
1	1111	1101	FD
2	1111	1011	FB
3	1111	0111	F7
4	1110	1111	EF
5	1101	1111	DF
6	1011	1111	BF
7	0111	1111	7F
None	1111	1111	FF

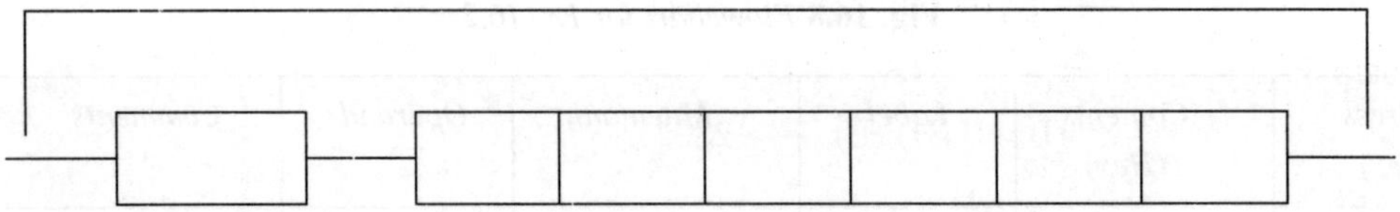

Let us suppose that switch at bit 1 is closed (switches are all debounced switches). The following sequence will give us the switch number as 1 which is stored in accumulator.

– Recognise whether any switch is closed at all.
– If closed, set a counter as = 0
– Shift the contents of accumulator right (b0 = CY)
– Text for the carry (if b0 = 1, when RAR is executed CY = 1 and thus switch at b0 is not closed). In this case carry = 1.
– Increment the counter (0 + 1 = 1). Again perform RAR. Now b0 = 0 (switch is closed) and thus CY = 0.
– Test for the carry. It is zero and thus control is transfered to the monitor.
– Contents of A = switch number = 1 in this case.

Example 16.4. *Add a series of numbers stored from location 2801 onwards. Length of series is stored in 2800. The sum is less than 256 so that his could be stored in a location.*

The relevant flow chart is shown in Fig. 16.9. The program listing is also given on next page.

We will examine the steps for a certain given data :

Say : (2800) = 03 : Length of series
(2801) = 04
(2802) = 05
(2803) = 07

Results : (2804) = 04 + 05 + 07 = (10) H

Step 1 : Length of count = 03 (B) = (03)

Step 2 SUM = 0 (A) = 00

Step 3:	(H) (L) ⟶ 2800	
	(H) (L) ⟵ (H) (L) + 1	(H) (L) ⟶ 2801
	(A) = (A) + (H) (L)	(A) = (A) + [(H) (L)] = 04
Step 4:	(B) = 02	(B) = 02
	If (B) = 0 STOP	
Step 5:	otherwise GO TO step 3	
	(H) (L) ⟶ 2802	
	(A) = (04) + (05) = 09	
Step 6:	(B) = 01	
Step 7:	(B = 0, GO TO step 3)	
	(H) (L) ⟶ 2803	
	(A) = 09 + 07 = (10) H	
Step 8:	(B) = 00	
	(B = 0 (H) (L) ⟶ 2804)	
	(H) (L) ⟵ (A)	

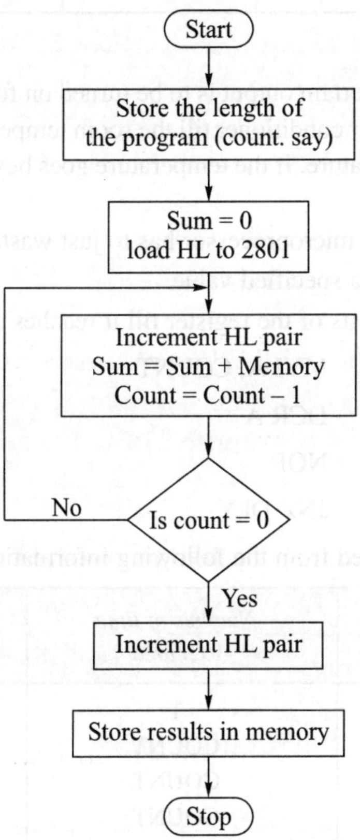

Fig. 16.9 *Flowchart for Ex. 16.4*

Address (Hex)	*Contents (Hex)*	*Label*	*Mnemonic*	*Operand*	*Comments*
2400	21		LXI	H, 2800	
2401	00				
2402	28				
2403	46		MOV	B, M	Length of array is stored in register B.
2404	3E		MVI	A, 00	
2405	00				
2406	23	CONT	INX	H	(H) (L) = (H) (L) + 1
2407	86		ADD	M	(A) = (A) + (H) (L)
2408	05		DCR	B	(B) = (B) – 1
2409	C2		JNZ	CONT	Is B = 0?
240A	06				
240B	24				
240C	23		INX	H	(H) (L) = (H) (L) + 1
240D	77		MOV	M, A	(H) (L) = (A)
240E	CF		RST	1	Return to monitor

16.6.1 Providing a Delay

In all the real time applications, a certain output is to be turned on for a specified time. For example, the processor may have to turn on an air conditioner till the room temperature is 22°C and then may have to turn it off. Keep sensing the temperature. If the temperature goes beyond 22°C it is to be turned on again and so on.

In all such applications, the microprocessor has to just waste time counting. This is done by

(*i*) Loading a register with a specified value.

(*ii*) Decrementing the contents of the register till it reaches zero value.

Example.

```
        MVI A, COUNT
        DCR A
DLY:    NOP
        JNZ DLY
```

The wasted time is calculated from the following information.

Instruction	*Number of time executed*	*Clock cycles per execution*
MVI	1	7
DCR	COUNT	4
NOP	COUNT	4
JNZ	COUNT	7 if no jump 10 if jump occurs

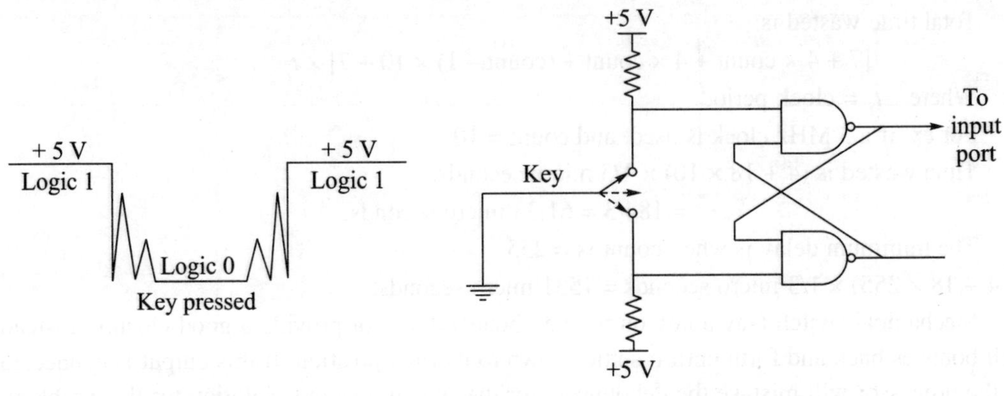

(a) Key bounce

(b) Key debouncing circuit using NAND gates

Fig. 16.10

Address (Hex)	Contents (Hex)	Label	Mnemonic	Operand	Comments
2400	3E		MVI	A, 00	
2401	00		OUT	02	All bits of port
2402	D3				00 of 8355 are
2403	02				input ports
2404	DB	WAIT	IN	00	Input ports get
2405	00				the input data
2406	FE		CPI	FF	
2407	FF				
2408	CA		JZ	WAIT	Any switch is
2409	04				closed? No wait
240A	24				
240B	06		MVI	B, FF	Delay program
240C	FF				
240D	05	DELAY	DCR	B	1.5 secs.
240E	00		NOP		
240F	C2	WAIT 1	JNZ	DELAY	
2410	0D				
2411	24				
2412	DB		IN	00	Get the data
2413	00				
2414	FE		CPI	FF	Are all switches
2415	FF				open?
2416	C2		JNZ	WAIT 1	NO, wait
2417	0F				
2418	24				
2419	CF		RST	1	Return to monitor

Total time wasted is:

$$[7 + 4 \times \text{count} + 4 \times \text{count} + (\text{count} - 1) \times 10 + 7] \times t_c$$

Where t_c = clock period.

For ex. if a 3 MHz clock is used, and count = 10

Time wasted is (4 + 18 × 10) × 1/3 micro seconds.

= 184/3 = 61.33 micro seconds.

The minimum delay is when count is = 255

i.e., (4 + 18 × 255) × 1/3 micro seconds = 1531 micro seconds.

Mechanical switch (say a key on the key board) does not provide a good closure. Instead, the switch bounces back and forth until it settles down to its final position. If this output is connected to a port, the processor will mistake the debouncers for the switch opening. Solution for this problem is of course to debounce a switch either making use of the NAND gate latch or by using a monostable circuit. Typical waveform when a switch bounces is shown in Fig. 16.10.

Instead of using the external hardware to debounce the switch, processor can be programmed to do this job and all that processor need to do is to wait till the switch has settled to its final value. Since the bounce is usually less than 1 milli seconds the following program will do the job.

Example 16.5. *A program to give the sine of a given angle is developed below. The principle is that of look up tables. This principle may be used for a variety of purposes.*

A flow chart for the purpose is shown in Fig. 16.11. Values of the sine of the angle in terms of 1 degree interval are solved in the memory in a sequential manner (This is called the look up table). Starting from 2401 values stored are from 1° to 89°, in steps of 1°. Contents of the table are in the BCD format.

- The address of the desired element is obtained by adding the starting address of the table to the element numbers.
- This address is used to obtain the element.

Let us verify the procedure by following the steps of the program when we would be required to find the sine of say 8°.

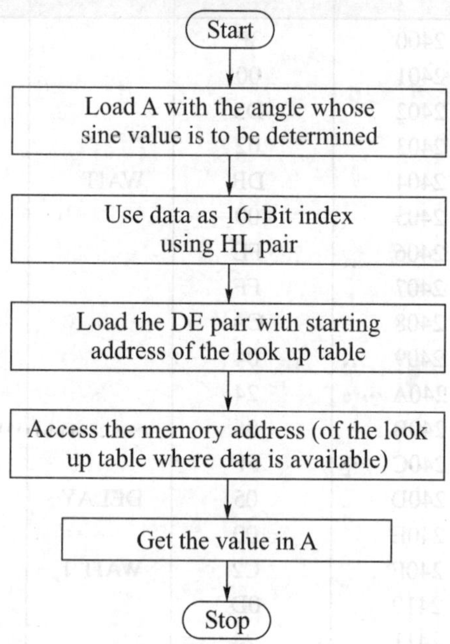

Fig. 16.11 *Flowchart for Ex. 16.5*

Step 1 : Input is at location (2040) A. This is moved to A(8)

Step 2 : (L) = 08

(H) = 00

Step 3 : (D) (E) 204F

Address (Hex)	*Contents (Hex)*	*Label*	*Mnemonic*	*Operand*	*Comments*
2000	3A		LDA	2040	Get data from 2040
2001	40				
2002	20				
2003	6F		MOV	L, A	Use data as a 16 bit pointer.
2004	26		MVI	H, 00	
2005	00				
2006	11		LXI	D, 204F	Load starting
2007	4F				address of look
2008	20				up table to DE pair
2009	19		DAD	D	Go to look up table
200A	7E		MOV	A, M	A has sine of angle
200B	CF		RST	1	Return to monitor

Look Up Table

Data Address	*Contents (BCD)*		
204F	0000	0000	Sine of 0°. (0.00)
2050	0000	0000	Sine of 1°. (0.02)
2051	0000	0011	Sine of 2°. (0.03)
2052	0000	0101	Sine of 3°. (0.05)
2053	0000	0111	Sine of 4°. (0.07)
2054	0000	1001	Sine of 5°. (0.09)
2055	0001	0000	Sine of 6°. (0.10)
2056	0001	0010	Sine of 7°. (0.12)
2057	0001	0100	Sine of 8°. (0.14)
20A8	1001	1001	Sine of 89°. (0.99)

Step 4: DAD D adds registers D and E to register H and L leaving the sum in registers H and L. the result if thus 0008 (H – L)

204F (D – E)

2057 (H – L)

Step 5: Now we move memory contents to the accumulator from the table. It is clear that contents of location 2057 contain the value sine of 8°. = (0.14)

Example 16.6. *This program places the contents of memory locations 2041 through 20F0 in a descending order. Length of array is stored in 2040.*

The required flow chart is shown in Fig. 16.12. The program listing is given on page 515.

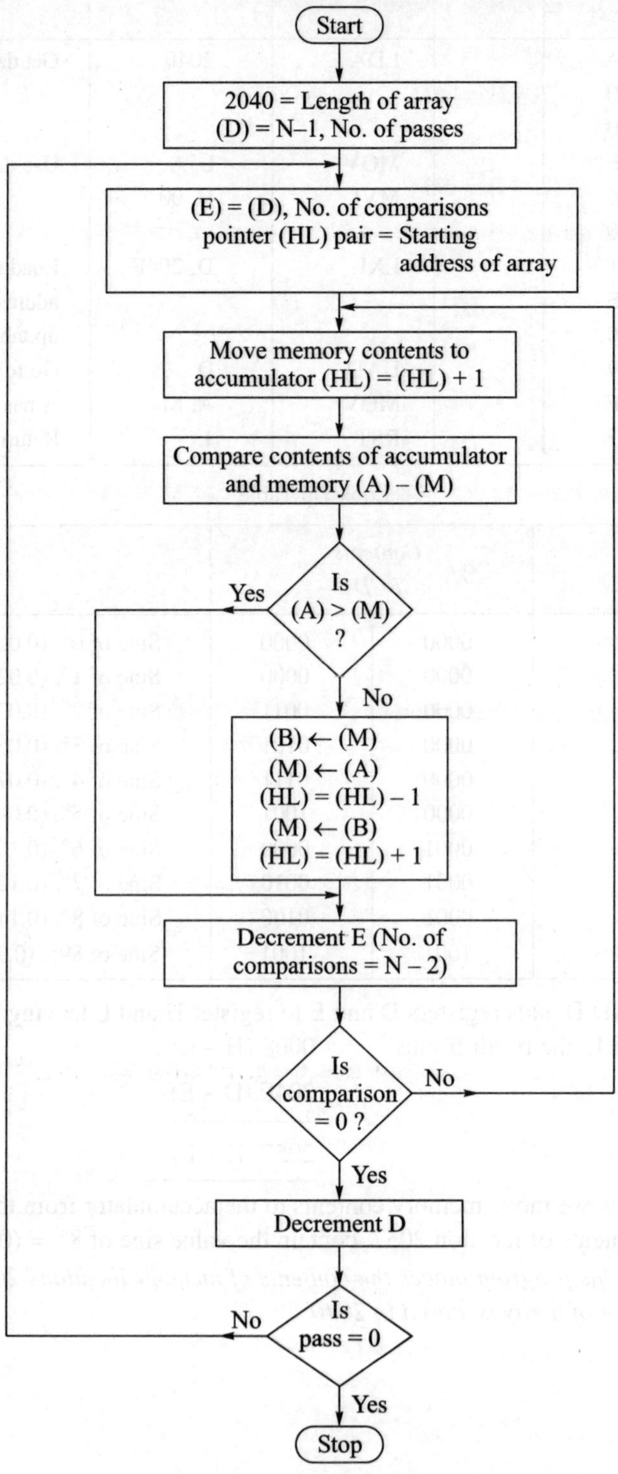

Fig. 16.12 *Flowchart for Ex. 16.6*

Data for this example is as below:

(2040) = length of array = 04
(2041) = 01
(2042) = 02
(2043) = 03
(2044) = 04

1. During the first pass the least number will be stored in 2044
   → comparison

	01	02	02	02
	02	01	03	03
PASS 1	03	03	01	04
	04	04	04	01

2. During the second pass the next least number of the array is stored in 2043.

	02	03	03
	03	02	04
PASS 2	04	04	02
	01	01	01

3. During this pass the next least number is stored in 2042.

	03	04
	04	03
PASS 3	02	02
	01	01

Answer. (2041) = 04
(2042) = 03
(2043) = 02
(2044) = 01 and thus the given array is arranged in the descending order.

Address (Hex)	*Contents (Hex)*	*Label*	*Mnemonic*	*Operand*	*Comments*
2000	21, 40, 20		LXI H	2040	Memory pointer points to the length of the array (N)
2003	56		MOV	D, M	Length of the array stored in register D.
2004	15		DCR	D	No. of passes = (N – 1).
2005	5A	L3	MOV	E, D	
2006	21, 41, 20		LXI H	2041	Memory pointer points to the beginning of the array.
2009	7E	L2	MOV	A, M	
200A	23		INX H		
200B	BE		CMP M		Compare the contents of memory with the acc. contents.
200C	D2, 14, 20		JNC: L1		If [A] > [M] go to label L 1 (no change in the contents of memory locations)
200F	46		MOV	B, M	Otherwise interchange the contents of memory locations
2010	77		MOV	M, A	
2011	2B		DCX	H	
2012	70		MOV	M, B	
2013	23		INX	H	
2014	1D	L1	DCR	E	
2015	C2, 09, 20		JNZ: L2		Are all comparisons over? if no, goto label L2. If yes make the next pass.
2018	15		DCR	D	
2019	C2, 05, 20		JNZ: L3		
201C	EF		RST 5		

Example 16.7. *The following program class memory locations 2050 through 2060. Typically the length of array is in location 2070.*

Figure 16.13 given on next page gives the flow chart. The program is listed below.

Address (Hex)	*Contents*	*Label*	*Mnemonic*	*Operand*	*Comments*
2400	AF		XRA	A	(A) = 0
2401	21		LXI	H, 2070	Memory printer
2042	70				points to 2070.
2043	20				
2044	46		MOV	B, M	B is used as a counter (length of array)
2405	21		LXI	H, 2050	Memory pointer
2406	50				points to 2050
2407	20				
2408	77	CONT	MOV	M, A	Contents of 2050 = 00
2409	05		DCR	B	
240A	23		INX	H	

240B	C2		JNZ	CONT	Is counter = 0?
240C	00				No count
240D	24				
240E	CF		RST	1	Return to monitor

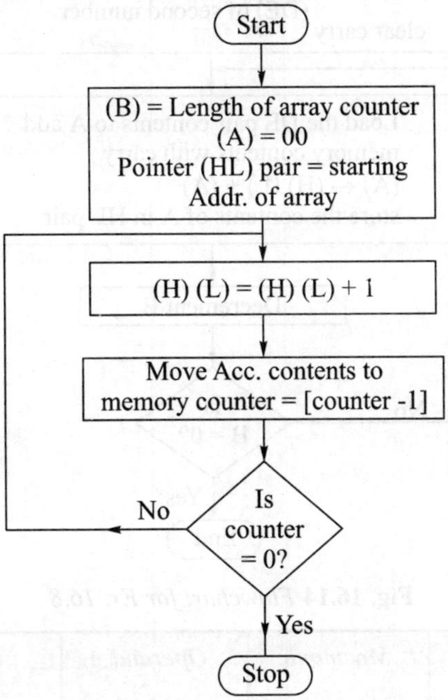

Fig. 16.13. *Flowchart for Ex. 16.7*

Example 16.8. *Addition of two numbers that are more than 8-bit long.*

Figure 16.14 given on next page gives the necessary flow chart. Program listing is also given on next page.

Data for example is as below:

Ist set of numbers (2040) = length of numbers = 04

(2041) = 01

(2042) = 04

(2043) = 05

(2044) = 08

2nd set of numbers

(2060) = 02

(2061) = 03

(2062) = 08

(2063) = 0A

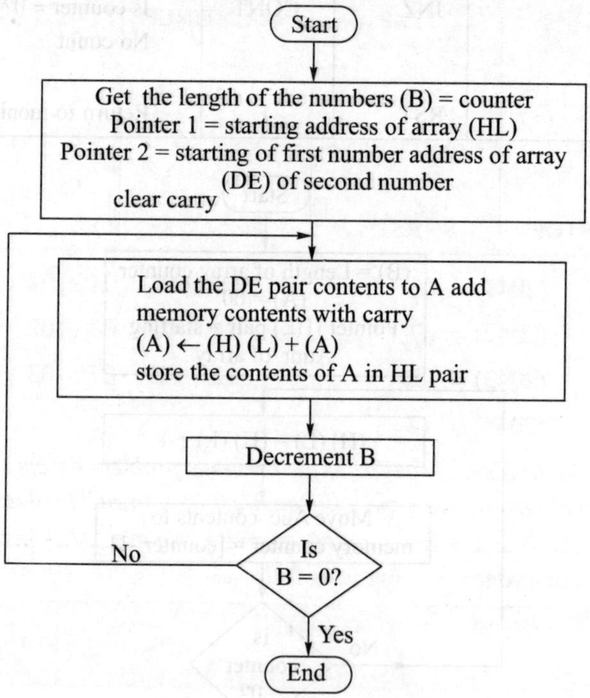

Fig. 16.14 *Flowchart for Ex. 16.8*

Address (Hex)	*Contents (Hex)*	*Label*	*Mnemonic*	*Operand*	*Comments*
2400			LXI	H, 2040	Length of numbers
2401					
2402					
2403			MOV	B, M	B = counter
2404			INX	H	
2405			LXI	D, 2060	
2406			ANA	A	Clear carry
2407					
2408					
2409		CONTINUE	LDA X	D	Bring the DE contents to A.
240A			ADC	M	Add memory contents to DE Register contents
240B			MOV	M, A	Store result in HL pair
240C			DCR	B	
240D					
240E			JNZ	CONT	Is count = 0? No count.
240F			JMP	STOP	
2410			INX	H	
2411			INX	D	

2412			JMP	CONTINUE	
2413					
2414					
2415					
2416					
2417					
2418		STOP	RST	1	

Answer. (2041) = 03   08 05 04 01

(2042) = 07   + 0A 08 03 02

(2043) = 0D   12 0D 07 03

(2044) = 12

Example 16.9. *This problem is similar to the previous problem except that the data available in locations are all BCD numbers and we expect the answers also in BCD values.*

Flow chart is similar to that of the previous example. We use, DAA instruction in this case after the ADC M instruction. The program listing is as follows.

Address (Hex)	*Contents (Hex)*	*Label*	*Mnemonic*	*Operand*	*Comments*
2400			LXI	H, 2040	
2401					
2402					
2403			MOV	B, M	
2404			INX	H	
2405			LXI	D, 2060	
2406					
2407					
2408					
2409		CONTINUE	LDA X	D	
240A			ADC	M	
240B			DAA		Decimal conversion
240C			MOV	M, A	
240D			DCR	B	
240E					
240F			JNZ	CONT	
2410					
2411					
2412					
2413			JMP	STOP	
2414		CONT	INX	H	
2415					
2416			INX	D	
2417			JMP	CONTINUE	
2418					
2419		STOP	RST	1	

Data for this example is

(2040) = 04 ⟶ Length of numbers.

(2041) = 10

(2042) = 15

(2043) = 12

(2044) = 18

(2060) = 20

(2061) = 15

(2062) = 18

(2063) = 23

(2041) = 30

(2042) = 30

(2043) = 30

(2044) = 41

18	12	15	10
23	18	15	20
41	30	30	30

16.7 8085 TIMINGS

All register transfers in 8085 occur with reference to a clock signal. Interval between two successive positive going transitions of the clock pulse is known as a state *i.e.*, a state lasts one period.

A machine cycle is the time required to transfer data to or from the memory.

An instruction cycle is the total time taken to fetch, decode and execute an instruction. A typical instruction cycle is shown in Fig. 16.15.

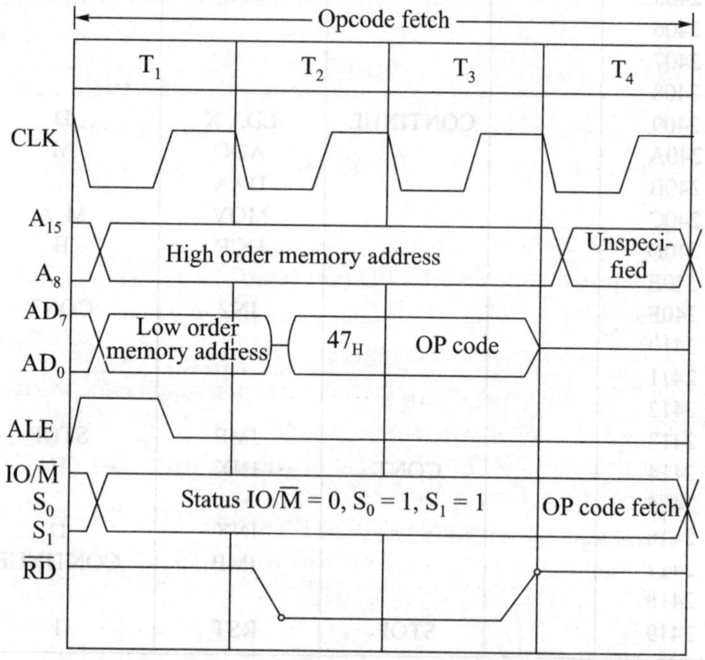

Fig. 16.15 *Timing diagram for execution of the instruction MOV B, A*

16.7.1 Fetch Operation

This operation causes the OP code of an instruction (one byte) to be brought to the CPU from the memory.

At the beginning of the first T state, the program counter contents are placed on the address bus. Memory responds during the next T state by placing its contents on the data bus. This data is accepted by the CPU in the next T state. This distinction of 3T states may not be so precise and this depends on a particular microprocessor. Indeed, the access time of the memory may be more than two clock cycles.

In such a case of microprocessor will have to wait for more than two clock cycles to compile the event. The microprocessor waits by introducing 'wait cycles'.

16.7.2 Decode and Execute

Decoding of the instruction follows the fetch cycle. If the OP code is only one byte long and the operand is in general purpose registers, then decoding and execution operations are performed.

During T_1, CPU sends on the address lines the address (16-bit) on A_8-A_{15} and AD_0-AD_7. (As the address or data bits may be at 1 or 0 levels, these signals are shown by two lines as indicated). In the T_2 state, we know that the contents of this address are put on the data lines. As such, ALE signal goes high during the positive transition of T_1 thereby latching the low byte address so that the complete address (low high) is available even after this clock state. When ALE is low AD_0-AD_7 will be used as the data lines.

The microprocessor sends a $IO/\overline{M}$ low at the beginning of T_1 state thereby indicating that memory operation states S_0, S_1 signals are high.

During T_2 state, $\overline{RD}$ goes low (read operation) thereby enabling memory. The data (OP code) is put on the data bus (dashed lines indicate the high impedance state). During T_3, this information is accepted by the CPU. $\overline{RD}$ is disabled during this cycle (when once the data is accepted). As this is the first machine cycle, the OP code is decoded during T_4 state. This completes the first machine cycle.

16.8 8156 RAM/I/O/TIMER

This is one of the three chips used in the minimum configuration. Figure 16.16 indicates the pin diagram and the architecture of this chip. The following are the features of the chip.

- It has 256 bytes of RAM.
- Two programmable 8-bit I/O ports (A&B).
- One programmable 6-bit I/O port (C).

One programmable 14-bit binary counter.

It has an 8-bit command register.

In the command register, bit 0 defines port A to be the input or

- output (0 = input, 1 = output).
- Bit 1 defines port B to be input or output.
- Bits 2 and 3 define port C to be input or output.

(00 = Input or ALT 1 11 = Output or ALT 2)

CHAPTER 16

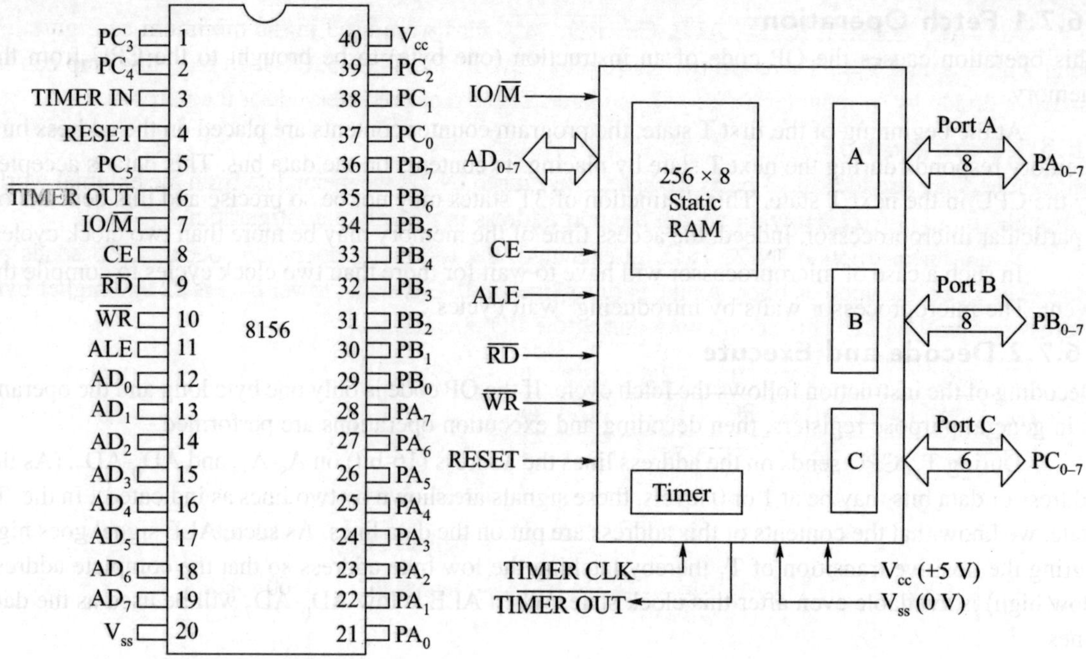

Fig. 16.16 *Pin configuration and architecture of 8156*

Figure 16.17 (*a, b*) shows the 8156 status and command register.

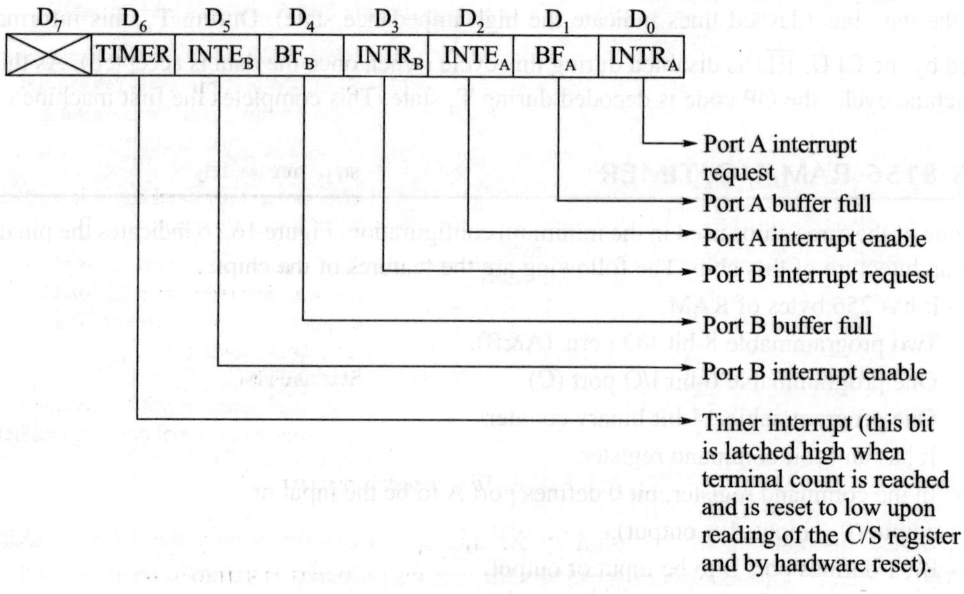

Fig. 16.17 (*a*) *8156 Status register*

From the Fig. 16.16, it may be noted that 22 pins are reserved for I/O ports (PA_0-PA_7-port 'A', PB_0-PB_7-port 'B', and PC_0-PC_5-port 'C').

AD_7-AD_0, RESET, IO/$\overline{M}$, ALE, CE, $\overline{RD}$, $\overline{WR}$ pins were used in the minimum configuration along with V_{SS} and V_{CC}. There are two more pins TIMER IN, TIMER OUT. In fact, this chip can be used as a divide by '*n*' counter as we will see later. These pins are reserved for the purpose.

16.8.1 Port Numbers

Port numbers are used for the 3-ports we have. If we write IN 22, we mean data from the external world is inputted on to port 22. How do we get the port address in minimum configuration?

When an instruction IN 22 is to be executed, the following operations occur: CPU sends an address of 22 on the address lines. As the address lines is 16 bits wide, lower byte is 22 and higher byte address also will be 22. This occurs only during the I/O operations.

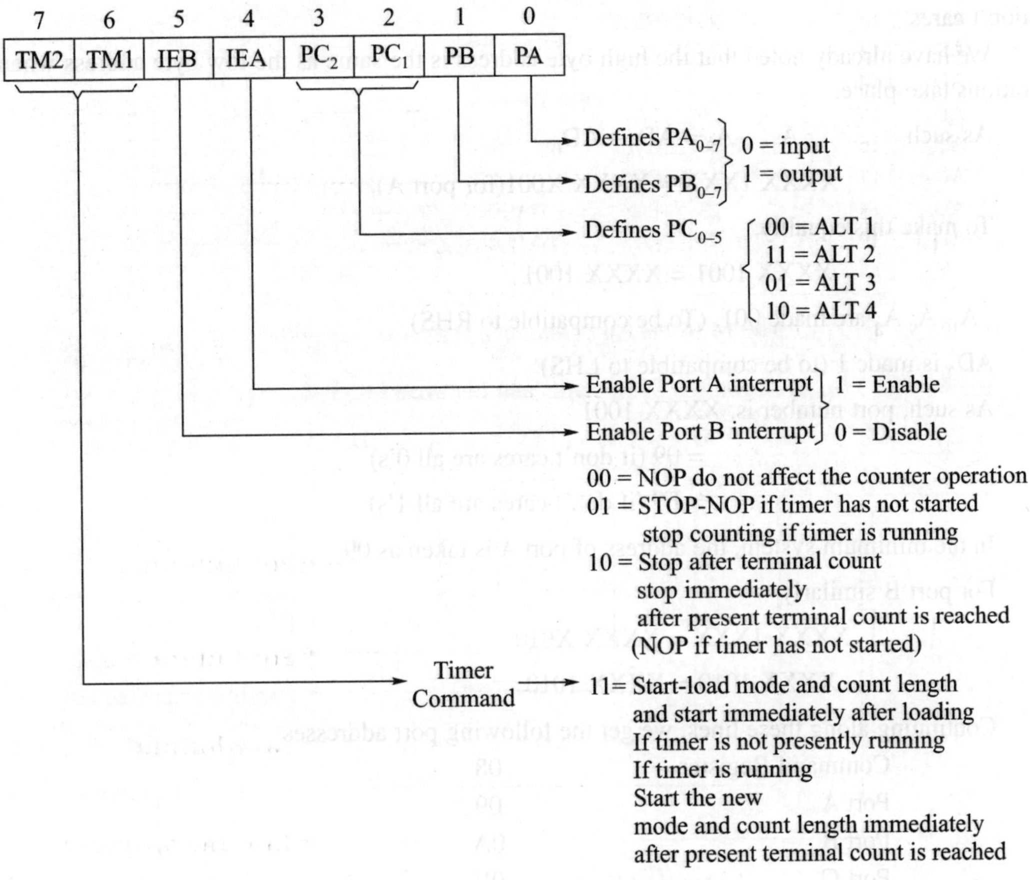

Fig. 16.17 (*b*) *8156 Command register*

IN/OUT instructions are executed by the microprocessor using only the 3-lower address bits (AD_0, AD_1 or AD_2). Combination of these bits for various purposes is summed up as follows.

AD_2	AD_1	AD_0	*Purpose*
0	0	0	Command and Status register
0	0	1	Port A
0	1	0	Port B
0	1	1	Port C
1	0	0	Lower 8 bits of timer
1	0	1	2 bits of timer mode and upper 6 of timer

From this it is clear that the address may lie between XXXX X000 and XXXX X101 where 'X's are don't cares.

We have already noted that the high byte address is the same as the low byte address when I/O operations take place.

As such $A_{15} - A_8 = AD_7 - AD_0$

XXXX 1XXX = XXXX X001(for port A)

To make this equality,

XXXX 1001 = XXXX 1001

i.e., $A_{10}\ A_9\ A_8$ are made 001. (To be compatible to RHS)

AD_3 is made 1 (to be compatible to LHS)

As such, port number is, XXXX 1001

= 09 (if don't cares are all 0's)

= F9 (if don't cares are all 1's)

In the minimum system, the address of port *A* is taken as 09.

For port B similarly

XXXX 1XXX = XXXX X010

i.e., XXXX 1010 = XXXX 1010

Continuing along these lines, we get the following port addresses

Command Register	08
Port A	09
Port B	0A
Port C	0B
Lower byte of timer count	0C
Timer mode and count (upper 6 bits)	0D

16.8.2 Configuration of the 8156 Ports

(*i*) All ports as inputs

SUB A: accumulator contains 0's

OUT 08: Output on command register thereby making all ports as input ports.

(*ii*) All ports as outputs

MVI A, 0F

OUT 08

(*iii*) Ports B and C as outputs and A as input port

MVI A, 07

OUT 08

16.8.3 Programs Using 8156

Example. The program below reads the switch (position) attached to port 09 (0th bit). Turns 'ON' an LED attached to port 0A (0th bit) if the switch is closed. Otherwise, LED is 'OFF'.

Procedure (*i*) Make port A as input port. Port B as output port sending a suitable command word to command register.

(*ii*) Get the input. Isolate the 0th bit see the status of this bit (if 0, switch is closed. If 1, the switch is open).

(*iii*) Output 0 on the 0th bit of port B if the switch at port A is closed (LED is ON). Otherwise output a 1 on the 0th bit (LED is OFF).

MVI A, 0000 0010

OUT 08 to make port A as input and port B as output port

MVI B, 1111 111

OUT 0A Output on port B this bit pattern so that LED is off.

1. Handshake Procedure : We have already noted that bits 2 and 3 (of the command register) define port C. If $B_3 = 0$, $B_2 = 1$ port A will be in handshaking (3 bits) together with 3-bit output. If $B_3 = 1$, $B_2 = 0$ ports A and B are available for handshaking mode. These are diagrammatically shown in Fig. 16.18.

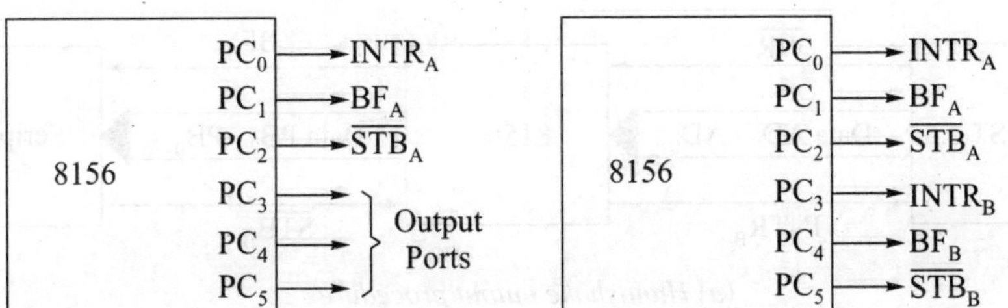

(*a*) *Handshaking and output* (*b*) *Handshaking for A and B*

Fig. 16.18

While operating in the handshaking mode, the status register shown in Fig. 16.17 (*a*) is used. Indeed, the status register can be read by IN 08. Now, the contents of the status register are available in the accumulator.

Generally, the I/O requirements are :

– The peripheral should be ready to receive data.

– Valid data then should be available to peripheral.

– Data should be received correctly.

From the above it is clear that the sender should know the status of the receiver (ready or busy) and also whether the data transfer is complete. On the other hand receiver must know whether new data is available.

There are two approaches to the above problem.

– A clock is used as a reference. All transfers take place with reference to the clock. Receivers must be ready at a time fixed by the clock so also the data and the transfer of information. That is both the transmitter and receiver must be synchronised with the clock. This is known as *synchronous transfer*. This approach has the advantage that no extra bits are necessary as all operations are fixed by the clock and as such, frequency of transfer could be higher. However, if the occurrence of the data is at irregular intervals, this approach cannot handle it effectively. For example, the pressing of a keyboard may occur very occasionally and at irregular intervals. In such cases the above approach is not used.

– In the second approach, the sender indicates to the receiver that valid data is available on the line. In turn, the receiver sends a READY for data signal as also a data accepted signal. These signals may be levels or pulses. Although no clock is required, extra bits are required which limit the rate of data transfer. Advantages being that no clock is required and the method is flexible.

Handshaking is used for implementing the asynchronous data transfer.

2. Handshake output procedure: Figure 16.19 (*a*) shows the procedure. CPU checks interrupt request (RST 6.5) if high, CPU performs an output operation by jumping into a service routine which includes OUT 0A instruction. This makes $\overline{WR}$ low. Now, accumulator contents are put on the data lines and INTR B goes low indicating that data has been received.

After the above process is completed, 8156 sends a BF_B high to the peripheral device. This transfers the data from 8156 to the peripheral. When the data is received, peripheral sends a low $\overline{STB_B}$ indicating that the data has been received. This process goes on till all the data is transferred to the peripheral.

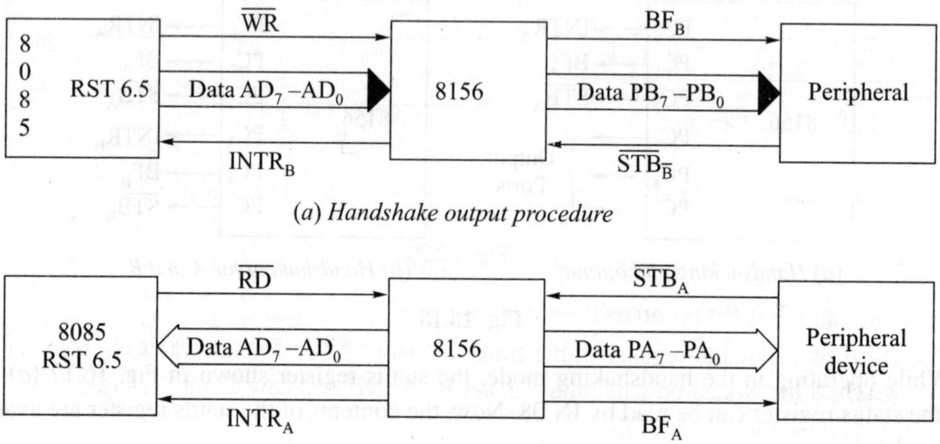

(*a*) *Handshake output procedure*

(*b*) *Handshake input procedure*

Fig. 16.19

3. Handshaking input procedure: Figure 16.19 (*b*) shows the procedure. The peripheral device places the data on the data lines ($PA_7 - PA_0$), sends a $\overline{STB}_A$ low informing 8156 that data is sent. 8156 acknowledges this by sending a BF_A high to the peripheral device.

After the above process is complete, 8156 sends a high INTR A to 8085. 8085 after recognising the interrupt, jumps to a service routine which includes IN 09. When this instruction is executed RD goes low, thereby enabling the CPU to read the data available on the data lines and is as such, available in the accumulator.

16.8.4 8156 Programmable Timer

Many applications of microprocessors are based on real-time. Such requirements are common in process and industrial control. Timing may be handled by (*i*) having delay routines (*ii*) programmable timers.

In the former method, delays of the required interval are generated by the microprocessor. As the processor need to generate the delay, all the while the microprocessor is engaged in this job and it cannot do any other job.

Whereas in the latter method the microprocessor has to determine how the timer operates, start the timer after completing its task (generating the required delay), inform the CPU by an interrupt. As such, in this method, the microprocessor may attend to any other work till it is interrupted.

8155 has a 14-bit timer that is presettable as indicated in Fig. 16.20 (*a*). The timer down counts the incoming TIMER IN pulses. The maximum number with which the counter may be loaded is 3FFF (0011 1111 1111 1111) (14 bits are one and last two bits are zeros). The timer operation is as below:

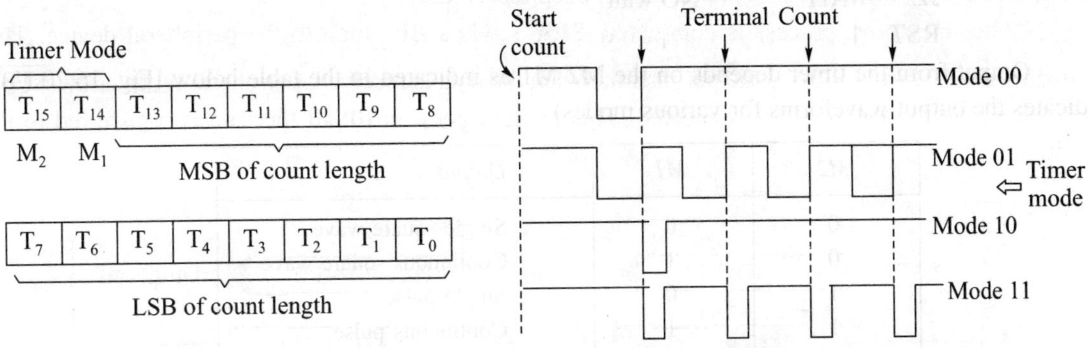

(*a*) *Timer bits of 8156* (*b*) *Timer modes*

Fig. 16.20

– Bit 6 and 7 of the command register are the timer command.

– Bit 6 of the status register is the timer interrupt bit and is set when the terminal count is reached and is cleared when the register is cleared or a new count is started.

Procedure for using the timer

– Load the counter registers with the desired number.
(ports 0C and ports 0D)

– Start the timer by setting 6 and 7 of the command register.

– Wait for bit 6 of the status register to go high.

Timer mode

T_{15}	T_{14}	T_{13}	T_{12}	T_{11}	T_{10}	T_9	T_8
M_2	M_1	MSB of count length					

T_7	T_6	T_5	T_4	T_3	T_2	T_1	T_0
LSB of count length							

Example.

```
XRA   A                 : Accumulator contents are 0's
OUT   0C                : Low order byte of timer loaded with 0's
MVI   A, 0011, 0000     : High order bits of timer loaded with 30.
OUT   0D
MVI   A, 1100, 0000     : 6th and 7th bits of command register made 1's to start timer.
WAIT: OUT 08
      IN   08
      ANI  0100, 0000   : Is terminal count reached?
      JZ   WAIT         : NO wait.
      RST  1
```

Output from the timer depends on the M2 M1 as indicated in the table below [Fig. 16.20 (*b*)] indicates the output waveforms for various modes):

M2	*M1*	*Output*
0	0	Single square wave
0	1	Continuous square wave
1	0	Single pulse
1	1	Continuous pulse

Fig. 16.21

Processor may effectively be used for other purposes during the timer counting down. Timer may be operated in the continuous mode and is made to interrupt the processor by connecting the TIMER OUT of 8155 to RST 7.5.

Example. Suppose we are required to get an output frequency from the timer at 200 Hz. What is the count to be loaded to the counter (timer is at 3.072 MHz)?

Now if X is the count length then,

$$\frac{3.072\times10^6}{X} = 2\times10^2 \qquad \text{thus } X = \frac{3.072\times10^6}{2\times10^2} = 15360$$

$$= 0011 \quad 1100 \quad 0000 \quad 0000$$

$$= (3\ C\ 0\ 0)\ \text{Hex}$$

Program below interrupts the processor at a frequency of 200 Hz and increments the memory location 082F at the instance of each interrupt.

```
LXI    SP, 080F                 : Initialize stack pointer
XRA    A
STA    082F
OUT    0C
MVI    A, 3C
OUT    0D
MVI    A, 1100, 0000,           : Start the timer
OUT    08
MVI    A, 0000, 1011 (RST 7.5)  : Unmask clock interrupt
       SIM
       EI
```

16.8.5 8355 ROM/I/O Port

This chip has a memory of 2K bytes of ROM and two general purpose 8-bit I/O ports. Figure 16.22 shows the pin details and architecture of 8355. A and B are the two ports. This is a 40 pin DIP chip. PA_0-PA_7 are the 8 pins for port A, PB_0–PB_7 pins for port B. 11 address lines are used for addressing the memory (AD_0–AD_7, A_8, A_9 and A_{10}). $\overline{CE_1}$ and CE_2 are the two chip enable pins to provide more flexibility to the designer. A low writes the contents of address-data bus into the selected port.

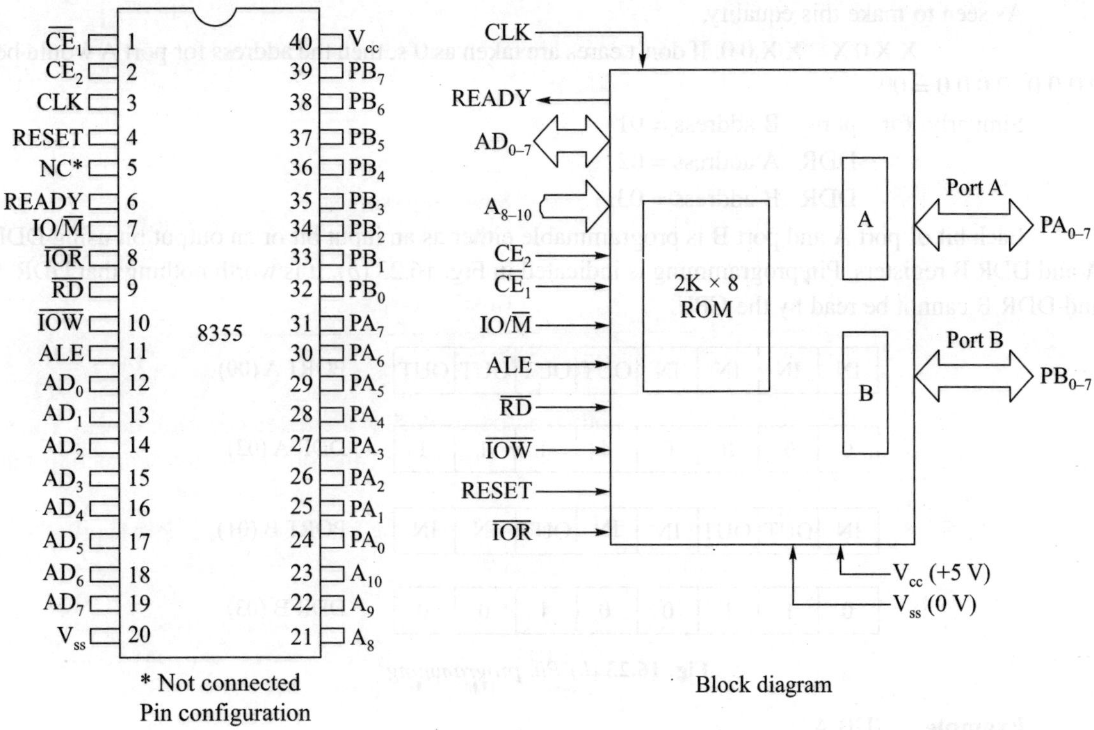

Fig. 16.22 *Pin configuration and block diagram of 8355*

For the two ports A and B, there are two registers called the *data direction registers* DDR A and DDR B. These registers determine whether pins of ports A and B are inputs or outputs.

Address bits of the register are as shown in Fig. 16.23 (*a*) below:

AD_1	AD_0	*Select*
0	0	PORT A
0	1	PORT B
1	0	DDR A
1	1	DDR B

Fig. 16.23 (*a*) *Address bits of the register*

If the chip select is connected to the 13th bit of the address line then the port addresses may be got as follows.

Port address may lie between

X X X X   X X 0 0

X X X X   X X 1 1

High byte address is to be the same as the low byte address. A_{13} is to be low.

As such, $A_{15} - A_8 = AD_7 - AD_0$

X X 0 X X X X X = X X X X X X 0 0 (for port A)

As seen to make this equality,

X X 0 X X X 0 0. If don't cares are taken as 0's, then the address for port A would be, 0 0 0 0 0 0 0 0 = 00

Similarly, for port B address = 01

DDR A address = 02

DDR B address = 03.

Each bit of port A and port B is programmable either as an input bit or an output bit using DDR A and DDR B registers. Pin programming is indicated in Fig. 16.23 (*b*). It is worth nothing that DDR A and DDR B cannot be read by the CPU.

IN	IN	IN	IN	OUT	OUT	OUT	OUT	PORT A (00)
0	0	0	0	1	1	1	1	DDR A (02)
IN	OUT	OUT	IN	IN	OUT	IN	IN	PORT B (01)
0	1	1	0	0	1	0	0	DDR B (03)

Fig. 16.23 (*b*) *Pin programming*

Example. SUB A

OUT 03; All bits of port B are input ports.

MVI A, 0001 1101

```
OUT 02;   Bits 0, 2, 3, 4 - Outputs) } of register A
          Bits 1, 5, 6, 7 - Inputs)  }
```

– Reset clears the DDR A making all ports as input ports.

The following example lights an LED attached to bit 1.

```
MVI     A, FF; All bits of port 1 are outputs
OUT     03
MVI     A,  1111  1110;  light LED 0.
OUT     01
RST     1
```

The following program turns on an LED for a certain time and turns it off for certain other period. This duty cycle is repeated.

```
          MVI  A, 1111   1111   : all bits of port A are outputs.
          OUT  02
REPEAT    MVI  A, 1111   1101   : lights the LED at bit 1.
          OUT  00
          MVI  A, FF
DELAY 1   NOP
          DCR  A                 } Delay loop produces a delay
          JNZ     DELAY 1        }
          MVI  A, 1111   1111 :  Turn's off the LED
DELAY 2   NOP
          DCR  A
          NOP
          JNZ     DELAY 2
          JMP     REPEAT
```

How to avoid shadows? How to expand minimum system?

When it is required to have more memory, more number of memory chips are to be added to the minimum system. When more memory is added there is always the danger of using shadow addresses. This can be avoided using the fully decoded scheme shown in Fig. 16.24.

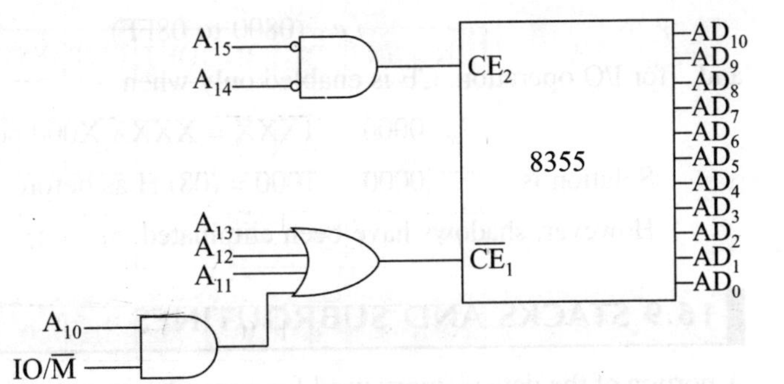

Fig. 16.24 *A method to avoid shadows*

As 10 lines are required to access the 2K memory, 11–15 bits are used for decoding purposes. From the Figure it may be noted that CE_2 is active if A_{15} and A_{14} are low.

Also CE_1 is assessed low if A_{10}, A_{11}, A_{12}, A_{13} are low (IO/$\overline{M}$ is low during memory operation and thus A_{10} has no effect).

$\therefore \quad A_{15}\, A_{14}\, A_{13}\, A_{12}\, A_{11} = 0\,0\,0\,0\,0$

Thus the range of the address could be

0000 0000 0000 0000

0000 0111 1111 1111 *i.e.*, 0000 to 07FF

As Don't cares have been eliminated, no shadows exist.

Now we will see the I/O shadows.

For the port A, $AD_0 = 0$, $AD_1 = 0$

$\therefore$ Address is 0000 00XX = XXXX XX00

$\therefore$ X's should be = 0.

or port A has an address of 00 unlike the previous case where shadow addresses used to exist. Similarly for the 8156 chip, the fully decoded circuit is as shown below.

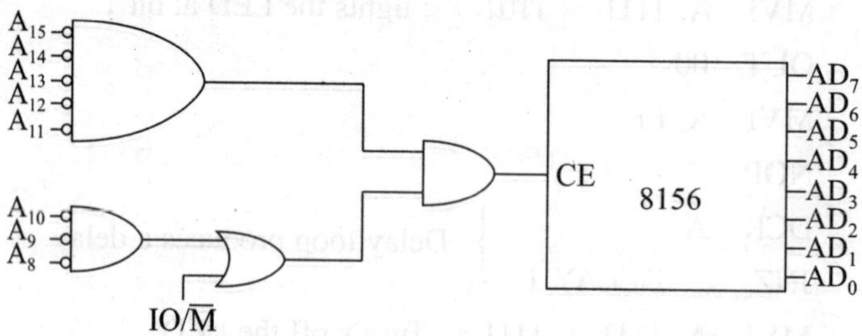

Fig. 16.25 *A fully decoded system for 8156*

CE is enabled only when $A_{15}\, A_{14}\, A_{13}\, A_{12}\, A_{11} = 00001$ and

$A_{10}\, A_9\, A_8 = 000.$

$\therefore$ Address range is 0000 1000 0000 0000

to 0000 1000 1111 1111

i.e., (0800 to 08FF)

and for I/O operation, CE is enabled only when

0000 1XXX = XXXX X000 port A

Solution is 0000 1000 = (08) H as before.

However, shadows have been eliminated.

16.9 STACKS AND SUBROUTINES

A portion of the data memory used for a specific purpose is known as stack. Stack (which can exist any where in the memory) is used to save some data vital to operation of the processor such as the return addresses. To the top of the stack, new data could be added (lowest address) or from the top of the stack data can be retrieved (called last in first out stacks—LIFOS). Adding a data onto a top of stack is known as the PUSH operation and retrieving the data from top of the stack is known as POP operation.

In some stacks, all the contents actually move when a PUSH or POP operation is done. This type of operation is as shown in Fig. 16.26.

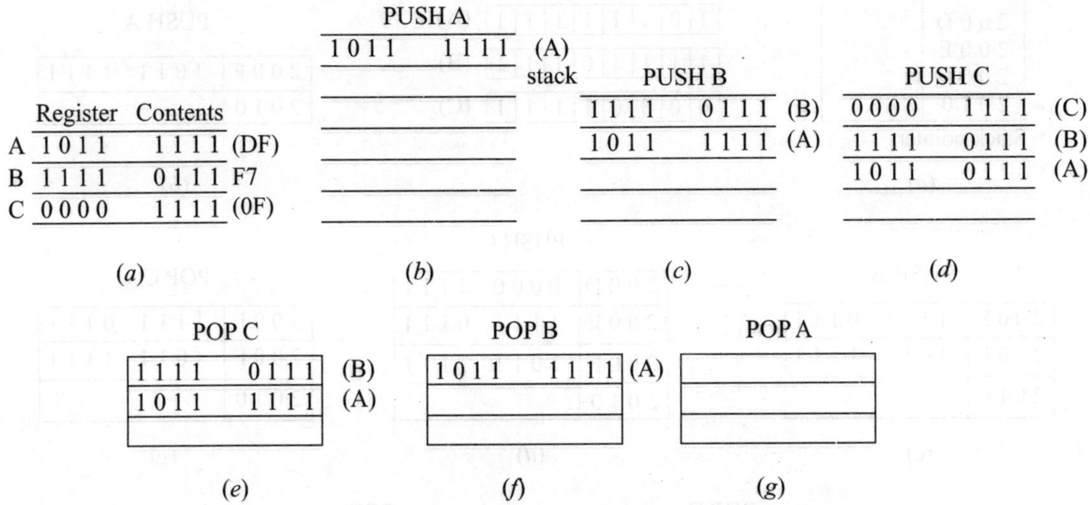

Fig. 16.26 *Stack operation*

Fig. 16.26 (*a*) above shows the contents of registers A, B, C. When it is required to store the contents of these registers in the stack (memory location), PUSH operations are used. When PUSH A operation is executed on the top of the stack, contents of the A register are being stored. Now when PUSH B operation is done, contents of A is pushed down and top of the stack now contains the contents of the B register. Similarly when PUSH C operation is done, contents of both locations where A and B have been stored are pushed down and again the top of the stack contains the contents of C.

When it is necessary to retrieve the A, B and C contents, POP operations are carried out which is just the opposite of the PUSH operation. However, it is to be noted that the top of the stack now contains the contents of C register and thus POP C is to be used. When this operation is executed, contents of B and A move up by one location each so that now the top of the stack contains the contents of the *B* register and thus POP B and subsequently POP A is to be used.

It is worth noting that contents of C was the one which was pushed on to the stack last but it was the information which was returned first. Thus these type of stacks are known as last in first out stacks (LIFOS).

However, in the 8085 processor the contents do not move. There is a 16-bit pointer called the stack pointer containing the top address of the stack. This stack grows from higher to lower memory locations. Whenever an interrupt occurs, processor stores the contents of the CPU registers temporarily on the stack, services the interrupt, retrieves the contents of the registers it had stored on the stack and continues with its original task.

Similarly, when a special program called a *subroutine* which may be used many times in the main program counter contents is saved on the stack. Subroutine is executed and the control returns to the main program by retrieving the program counter contents.

Figure 16.27 (*a*) shows that the stack pointer is pointing to the address 2010. When three PUSH operations are carried out contents of registers A, B, C in the stacks look as in Fig. 16.27 (*d*).

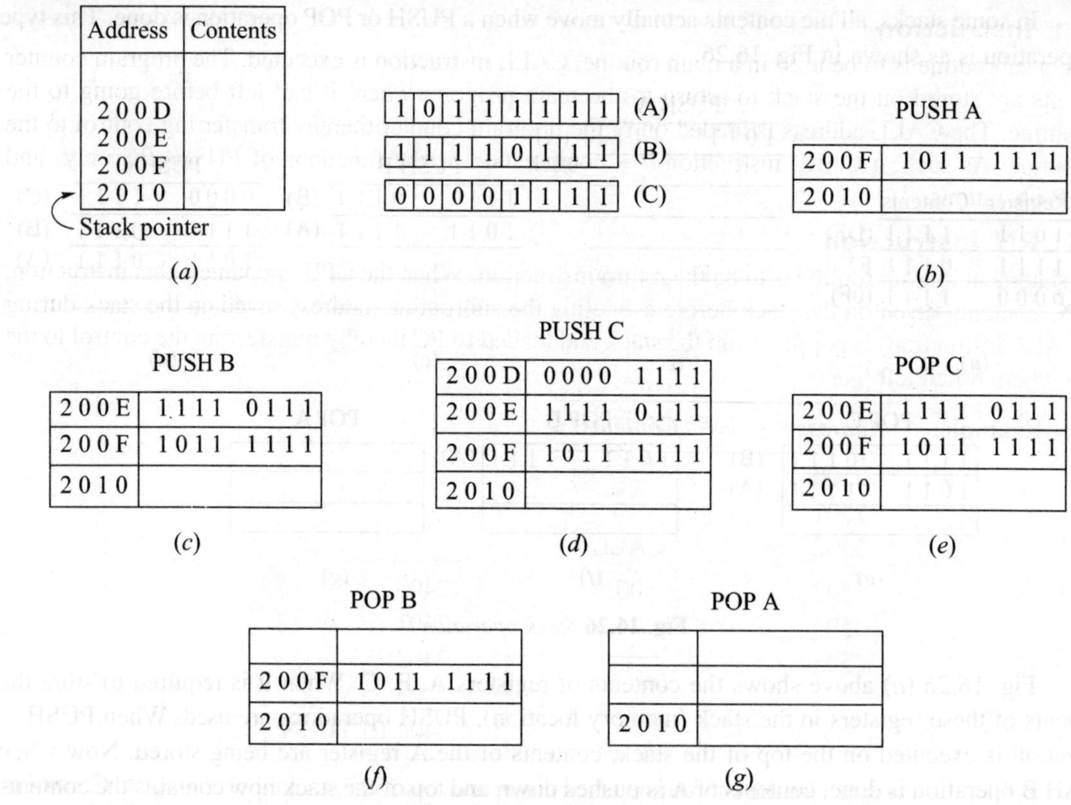

Fig. 16.27 *(a), (b), (c) and (d) Stack operation*

As may be noted, stack pointer is pointing to address 200D. When POP operations are carried out, Fig. 16.27 (*e*) show the stack pointer as also the contents in those addresses.

It could also be seen that the contents are not disturbed, but the stack pointer contains the proper address of the location. Also, if the contents are ordinarily stored in a register in any other memory location, the previous data (in the register/memory location) is lost. As such, before writing information at a memory location or register, it is necessary to store this information somewhere else and then use the location again (example: If (B) = 4A, and if we want to write on to B some other information say A4, it is necessary to store the present contents of B some where, say in C register by a statement as—MOV C, B; then MVI B, A4). Where as in a stack this operation of saving the data is automatic due to the presence of the stack pointer (when push operations are used). Initialisation of the state may be done by LXI SP address, or SPHL instructions.

SUBROUTINES

If in any program, a set of instructions are to be executed a number of times, instead of writing these instructions so many times, it is written only once in the form of a separate program called the 'subroutine' and is called by the main program each time this subroutine is required. A problem arises here that once the main program calls the subroutine and once the subroutine is executed, the control from the main program *i.e.*, before the control from the main program is transferred to the subroutine, the return address is to be stored some where. This saving is done using the 'stack'. When a CALL instruction is executed, this is done automatically.

CALL Instruction

When a subroutine is to be used in a main routine, CALL instruction is executed. The program counter contents are stored on the stack to return to the main program where it had left before going to the subroutine. The CALL address is loaded on to the program counter thereby transferring control to the subroutine. As such, a CALL instruction is a combination of the functions of PUSH (PC only) and JUMP operations.

RETURN Instruction

Last statement in a subroutine is to be the return instruction. When the CPU encounters this instruction, the PC contents saved on the stack before executing the subroutine (address saved on the stack during the CALL instruction) is popped from the stack and loaded to PC thereby transferring the control to the point where it had left.

Example.

Address	*Contents*	
2500		
2501		
2502	CALL	
2503	00	2400
2504	24	2401
2505		2402
		2403
		2404 RETURN

Before the execution of the subroutine takes place, address 2505 is saved on the stack. Control is transferred them to 2400. At 2404, a return statement will make the CPU to load the PC (from the stack) with 2505 there by enabling the program execution to continue from where it had left.

Registers used in the main program could also be used in the subroutine by saving registers on the stack and on return the contents of registers may be retrieved using instructions as PUSH PSW, PUSH H, POP H, POP PSW etc.

RST instruction is a special kind of CALL instruction, where the control is transferred to predecided locations specified by the designer. As such, CALL address indeed not be given at all. There are 8 RSTs which are all instructions, also known as software RSTs (This being in addition to the four hardware interrupts). Generally the vector location (address) of various RSTs is as below:

Restart	*Vector locations*
RST 0	0000
RST 1	0008
RST 2	0010
RST 3	0018
RST 4	0020
RST 5	0028
TRAP	0024
RST 5.5	002C
RST 6	0030
RST 6.5	0034
RST 7	0038
RST 7.5	003C

When an RST instruction is given, PC is saved (on the stack) and the control is transferred to the corresponding vector location.

Address (Hex)	*Contents (Hex)*	*Label*	*Mnemonic*	*Operand*	*Comments*
2500	31		LXI	SP, 20C2	Initialise the user stack pointer
2501	C2				
2502	20				
2503	3F		MVI	A, FF	
2504	FF				
2505	D3		OUT	02	
2506	02				
2507	3E	START	MVI	A, 00	
2508	00				
2509	D3		OUT	00	
250A	00				
250B	CD		CALL	DELAY	
250C	00				
250D	24				
250E	3E		MVI	A, FF	
250F	FF				
2510	D3		OUT	00	
2511	00				
2512	CD		CALL	DELAY	
2513	00				
2514	24				
2616	C3		JMP	START	
2517	07				
2518	25				
(DELAY)					
2400	06		MVI	B, FF	Subroutine delay
2401	FF				
2402	05	WAIT	DCR	B	
2403	C2		JNZ	WAIT	
2404	02				
2405	24				
2406	C9		RET		

Example. This example uses the concept of a subroutine in the main program to make the above points clear.

This program lights an LED connected to port 00 for a period of say T_1. It turns off the LED for the same period (T_2). This duty cycle is to be continuously repeated. A program for this purpose is as below.

As may be seen from the above program, a portion of the program MVI B, FF: DCR B : JNZ LOOP ; appears twice (repeated). Such a situation of using the same program repeatedly may occur on several occasions. Instead of repeating the program, this program that is used repeatedly is written as a subroutine. Whenever the main program wants to use it, it CALLs the subroutine.

Several subroutines (built in programs) would be available to the user (supplied by the manufacturers/supplier of the processor kits). The address of subroutines would be given along with monitor listing (in the memory map). For example,

- RDKBD (read key board)
- UPDDT (display routine)
- DELAY (to produce the required delay)

16.10 INTERRUPTS

A method of drawing the attention of the CPU by an external event only when required is known as *interrupt*. Unless interrupted, CPU will be doing its usual task. For example, a microprocessor based system is controlling a large induction motor. One of the tasks of the microprocessor is to make sure that the temperature of the machine does not exceed the safe limit. If the temperature exceeds the safety limit, then the microprocessor should immediately cut off the power supply to the motor. Ideally, the microprocessor is interrupted thereby making the processor to attend to the problem before the induction motor windings burn out.

As such, an interrupt signal causes the CPU to

- Finish executing the current instruction
- Suspend normal operation
- Jump to a special location where a group of instructions are written which will be executed by the CPU
- Return to the main program to the place where it had left.
- Faster response (Ready or other bits will not be tested by the CPU in the even of the interrupt)
- Processor may be employed more usefully (in the above example of the induction motor, the processor need not keep track of the temperature of the motor, the processor need not keep track of the temperature of the motor. There is an external circuit (a comparative) which informs the CPU when the safe temperature has been attained. As such, processor may be doing some job assigned to it in the normal course. Interrupt will draw the attention only when required. Typical characteristics of the interrupt system are:
  - Priorities are identified
  - Sources are identified.

A system in which each source must be executed is called a polling interrupt system. A system in which the CPU automatically directs control to the proper service routine is called vector interrupt system.

- Provision for enabling and disabling the interrupts. As we have seen from the pin out diagram and later from the architecture of 8085, interrupt inputs.
- **INTR** causes the CPU to fetch an instruction from a special external source. This is the least priority interrupt.

CHAPTER 16

– **TRAP** is of highest priority. It cannot be disabled. An interrupt at this pin causes the CPU to save the PC on the stack and jump to the location 0024.

– **RST 7.5** causes the CPU to save contents of the PC in the stack and jump to location 0034 - can be disabled.

– **RST 5.5** is the lowest priority interrupt; causes the CPU to save the contents of the PC in the stack and jump to location 002C can be disabled.

– The interrupts may be enabled or disabled by outputting suitable bits on to the interrupt mask register. In fact, there are two registers one can only be Read and one can only be Read and one can only be Written.

(*i*) Read only register (by RIM instruction)

D_7							D_0
SID	I7.5	I6.5	I5.5	IE	M7.5	M6.5	M5.5

Pending Interrupts (I7.5, I6.5, I5.5); Interrupt Enable Flag (IE); Interrupt Masks (M7.5, M6.5, M5.5)

– Interrupt masks—set if interrupts are disabled on the RST 5.5, RST 6.5 and RST 7.5 lines.

Mask bit 1—disable the interrupt.

Mask bit 0—enable the interrupt.

– Interrupt enable flag—1 interrupts are enabled.

– Pending interrupts bits—set if interrupts occurred on RST 7.5, 6.5 or 5.5 but were not recognised (because they were overridden).

Vectored Interrupt Key

This key available on the keyboard is connected to RST 7.5. Monitor does not supply a service routine for this key. When this key is pressed, control is transferred to 20CE of the RAM area. It is necessary we write a service routine elsewhere by writing a jump instruction at 20CE.

Example. This program below loads one entry from port 01 when vector key is depressed.

Address (Hex)	*Contents (Hex)*	*Label*	*Mnemonic*	*Operand*	*Comments*
2010			LXI	SP, 20C2	
2011					
2012					
2013			LXI	H, 2090	
2014					
2015					
2016			XRA	A	
2017			OUT	03	Make port B an input port
2018					
2019			MVI	A, 0B	RST 7.5 bit cleared
201A					
201B					
201C			SIM		

201D			EI		
201E			HLT	1	HLT may be cleared
201F			RST	2030	only by an interrupt.
20CE			JMP	01	
2030			IN		
2031					
2032				M.A	
2033			MOV		
2034			EI		
			RET		

PROBLEMS

1. Write a program which loads registers A, B, C and D with the same constant (say 3A). Try to optimise the program in such a way that the smallest number of program bytes are used.
2. Two bytes of data are stored in locations X and Y. Write a program to interchange the data in the locations using indirect addressing.
3. Write a program to add N binary numbers, considering the possible overflow.
4. Write a program to add N BCD numbers considering the possible overflow.
5. Try writing a program which can simulate DAA instruction (assume the DAA instruction is not directly available).
6. Write a program to find the number of 1's in a given byte of data.
7. Following a procedure similar to the above, write a program to count the number of 0's in a given byte. Try writing this program by not using RRc.
8. Write a program to multiply two binary numbers.
9. Write a program to perform division of two binary numbers.
10. Write a program to find the largest of N numbers and to display the number in the data field.

REFERENCES

1. Millman and Halkias : *Integrated Electronics*, McGraw-Hill, International Edition, 1971.
2. Chirlian, P.M.: *Basic Network Theory*, McGraw-Hill, International Edition.
3. Chirlian, P.M. : *Analysis and Design of Electronic Circuits*, McGraw-Hill, International Edition.
4. Van Valken Berg, M.E. : *Network Analysis*, PHI Pvt. Ltd., 1982.
5. Siskind, C.S. : *Electrical Circuits*, McGraw-Hill Edition, 1956.
6. Korn, G.A., and Korn T.M. : *Electronic Analog and Hybrid Computers*, McGraw-Hill Book Company, New York, 1964.
7. Graeme, J.G. and Tobey T.E.: *Operational Amplifiers, Design and Applications*, McGraw-Hill Book Company, New York, 1971.
8. Peatman, J.B. : *The Design of Digital Systems*, McGraw-Hill Book Company, New York, 1971.
9. Kohavi, Zvi : *Switching and Finite Automata Theory*, TMH Edition, 1978.
10. Morris Mano, M. : *Digital Logic and Computer Design*, PHI, 5th Edition, 1990.
11. Ramesh S. Gaonkar : *Microprocessors Architecture, Programming Applications with 8085/8085 A*, Wiley Eastern Edition, 1986.
12. Malvino Albert, P. : *Digital Computer Electronics*, TMH Edition, 1983.
13. Miller, Robert L. and John R. Miller (Edited): *Designing with TTL ICS*, McGraw-Hill, International edition 1986.
14. Leventhal, L.A.: *8080A-8085 ALP*, Mc Graw-Hill, International Edition, Computer Science, Edition, 1986.
15. *"The IC Catalog for Design : Engineers*, TI Inc., 1971.
16. Jacobowitz, Henry : *Basic Electronics*, Made simple books, Doubleday & Co. Inc., USA, 4th Edition, 1960.
17. Cotton, H. : *Electrical Technology*, Pitman Asia, 7th Edition, 1985.
18. Smith, Ralph, J. : *Electronics Circuits and Devices*, 2nd Edition, 1985.
19. Kerchner and Korkoran : *Alternating Current Circuits*, 3rd Edition, 1960.